250 Best Jobs™ Through Apprenticeships

Part of JIST's Best Jobs™ Series

Michael Farr and Laurence Shatkin, Ph.D.

Also in JIST's Best Jobs™ Series

- *Best Jobs for the 21st Century*
- *300 Best Jobs Without a Four-Year Degree*
- *200 Best Jobs for College Graduates*
- *50 Best Jobs for Your Personality*

JIST Works
America's Career Publisher

250 Best Jobs Through Apprenticeships

© 2005 by JIST Publishing

Published by JIST Works, an imprint of JIST Publishing, Inc.
8902 Otis Avenue
Indianapolis, IN 46216-1033

Phone: 1-800-648-JIST   Fax: 1-800-JIST-FAX   E-mail: info@jist.com   Web site: www.jist.com

Some Other Books by the Authors

Michael Farr

Seven Steps to Getting a Job Fast
The Quick Resume & Cover Letter Book
Getting the Job You Really Want
The Very Quick Job Search

Laurence Shatkin

Quick Guide to College Majors and Careers
Quick Guide to Career Training in Two Years or Less

Quantity discounts are available for JIST products. Please call 1-800-648-JIST or visit www.jist.com for a free catalog and more information.

Visit www.jist.com for information on JIST, free job search information, book excerpts, and ordering information on our many products. For free information on 14,000 job titles, visit www.careeroink.com.

Acquisitions Editor: Susan Pines
Development Editor: Stephanie Koutek
Cover and Interior Designer: Aleata Howard

Interior Layout: Carolyn J. Newland
Proofreaders: David Faust, Jeanne Clark
Indexer: Jeanne Clark

Printed in Canada

09 08 07 06 05   9 8 7 6 5 4 3 2 1

Library of Congress Cataloging-in-Publication Data

Farr, Michael.
  250 best jobs through apprenticeships / Michael Farr and Laurence Shatkin.
      p. cm. -- (JIST's best jobs series)
  Includes index.
  ISBN 1-59357-173-9 (alk. paper)
  1. Apprenticeship programs--United States. 2. Vocational guidance--United
States. 3. Occupations--United States. I. Title: Two hundred and fifty
best jobs through apprenticeships. II. Shatkin, Laurence. III. Title.
  HD4885.U5F37 2004
  331.25'922'0973--dc22
                                                    2004030439

We have been careful to provide accurate information throughout this book, but it is possible that errors and omissions have been introduced. Please consider this in making any career plans or other important decisions. Trust your own judgment above all else and in all things.

Trademarks: All brand names and product names used in this book are trade names, service marks, trademarks, or registered trademarks of their respective owners.

ISBN 1-59357-173-9

This Is a Big Book, But It Is Very Easy to Use

For your whole life, you've been hearing people tell you that education is the key to a good career. But the best-kept secret about careers is that most job skills are learned on the job. Still, young people face a chicken-and-egg problem: How do you get the job where you can learn the skills if you don't have the skills that qualify you for the job? A lot of young people solve this problem by getting a college degree that serves as a ticket to get them into the job.

But wouldn't it be marvelous if there were another formal career entry route besides college—an entry route that consisted mostly of on-the-job training, with only as much book learning mixed in as needed? Good news: This entry route already exists, and it's called apprenticeship. But so many people think apprenticeship is old-fashioned or it's only for "grease monkeys" and construction trades.

This book is designed to open your eyes. It will alert you to the many career possibilities that are open to you through apprenticeships. In fact, more than 800 apprenticeships are registered with the U.S. Department of Labor, and they are linked to over 300 occupations.

Because there are so many apprenticeable jobs to choose from, this book is also designed to narrow your thinking. The easy-to-browse lists of the best apprenticeable jobs will help you focus on the career opportunities that combine high rewards (good income, many job openings) with other features that matter to you, such as your interests.

Of course, a list goes only so far. To make a good career choice, you need to dig down into the details of what a job is like—what the tasks are, what skills are required, what the work environment is like, and so forth. This book provides a wealth of information on apprenticeable jobs, based on the most current data available from the U.S. Department of Labor and the Census Bureau.

After you've opened your eyes, narrowed your thinking, and dug into the details about an apprenticeable job, you may be ready to make your career move. So this book also tells you how to find out about apprenticeship programs in your area and how to become informed about the actual requirements of the programs that you find.

You may face a lot of competition to get into the apprenticeship program that appeals most to you. But in some industries and in some parts of the U.S., apprenticeships are begging for qualified applicants. Maybe a rewarding career is waiting for you to take the initiative—and the best part of all is that you will be paid to be an apprentice.

So get started in this book and learn about a route to career entry that doesn't require you to shell out tens of thousands of dollars in tuition or endure grueling basic training in a distant boot camp.

(continued)

(continued)

Credits and Acknowledgments: While the authors created this book, it is based on the work of many others. The occupational information is based on data obtained from the U.S. Department of Labor and the U.S. Census Bureau. These sources provide the most authoritative occupational information available. The job titles and their related descriptions are from the O*NET database, which was developed by researchers and developers under the direction of the U.S. Department of Labor. They, in turn, were assisted by thousands of employers who provided details on the nature of work in the many thousands of job samplings used in the database's development. We used the most recent version of the O*NET database, release 6. We appreciate and thank the staff of the U.S. Department of Labor for their efforts and expertise in providing such a rich source of data.

Table of Contents

Summary of Major Sections

Introduction. A short overview to help you better understand and use the book. *Starts on page 1.*

Part I: Overview of Apprenticeships. Part I is an overview of apprenticeship—what it is, where the opportunities are, what the requirements are, what the pros and cons are, and where to find out more. This section may clear up some misunderstandings you have about apprenticeship, and it will help you appreciate what apprenticeship has to offer you. *Starts on page 11.*

Part II: Master List of Nationally Registered Apprenticeships. This part lists all 876 apprenticeships that are currently registered with the U.S. Department of Labor. The apprenticeships are grouped according to interest fields, so you can easily find those in industries that appeal to you. *Starts on page 21.*

Part III: The Best Jobs Lists: Jobs You Can Enter Through Apprenticeship. The 35 lists in Part III show you the best apprenticeable jobs in terms of high salaries, fast growth, and plentiful job openings. You can also see which jobs are best when these factors are combined. Further lists classify the jobs according to their interest fields and several other features, such as jobs with the highest percentage of women and of men. Although there are a lot of lists, they are easy to understand because they have clear titles and are organized into groupings of related lists. *Starts on page 53.*

Part IV: Descriptions of the 250 Best Apprenticeable Jobs. This part provides a brief information-packed description of each of the 250 apprenticeable jobs that met our criteria for high pay, fast growth, or many openings. Each description contains information on earnings, projected growth, years of apprenticeship required, job duties, skills, related job titles, related knowledge and courses, and many other details. The descriptions are in alphabetical order. This structure makes it easy to look up a job that you've identified from Part II or Part III and that you want to learn more about. *Starts on page 121.*

Part V: Appendixes. This part contains four appendixes. Appendix A describes the parts of an apprenticeship standards document and explains its contents. Appendix B contains excerpts from apprenticeship standards documents. Appendix C lists contact information for state apprenticeship offices, and Appendix D explains the various skills listed in the job descriptions in Part IV. *Starts on page 487.*

Detailed Table of Contents

Introduction

Apprenticeship: "The Other Four-Year Degree"

Apprenticeship is a system of job training in which trainees become highly skilled workers through a combination of worksite learning and classroom learning. It is sometimes called "the other four-year degree" because it often takes four years and it results in a nationally recognized credential that can open the door to income and job security that may be as good as or better than what college graduates enjoy.

Where the Information Came From

The information we used in creating this book came mostly from databases created by the U.S. Department of Labor:

- We started with the jobs included in the Department of Labor's Registered Apprenticeship Information System (RAIS) database.

- We linked these jobs to occupations in the Department of Labor's O*NET (Occupational Information Network) database, which is now the primary source of detailed information on occupations. The Labor Department updates the O*NET on a regular basis, and we used the most recent one available—O*NET release 6.

- Because we wanted to include earnings, growth, number of openings, and other data not in the O*NET, we cross-referenced information on earnings developed by the U.S. Bureau of Labor Statistics (BLS). This information on earnings is the most reliable data we could obtain. For data on earnings, projected growth, and number of openings, the BLS uses a slightly different set of job titles than the O*NET uses. We were able to link the BLS data to many of the O*NET job titles in this book and tie growth and earnings information to the job titles in this book.

- To get figures on the percentage of women in occupations, we cross-referenced data from Census 2000.

1

Of course, information in a database format can be boring and even confusing, so we did many things to help make the data useful and present it to you in a form that is easy to understand.

How the Best Apprenticeable Jobs in This Book Were Selected

Here is the procedure we followed to select the 250 jobs we included in this book:

1. We began by obtaining from the U.S. Department of Labor the most up-to-date list of the apprenticeships registered with them. This list totaled 876.

2. The U.S. Department of Labor also provided a crosswalk that matches these apprenticeships to jobs in their O*NET database. Often more than one apprenticeship matched up with a single O*NET job. For example, there are apprenticeships for nine kinds of electricians. Thus, the number of apprenticeable jobs came to only 378.

3. The Department of Labor also provided a listing of the educational and/or training requirements for all the O*NET jobs. We eliminated all jobs that normally require a college degree. For example, even though there are registered apprenticeship programs for Meteorologist and Television Director, these careers normally require at least a bachelor's degree, so we eliminated these occupations. This left 325 apprenticeable jobs.

4. Next, we linked 324 of these jobs to Labor Department data: annual earnings, projected growth through 2012, and number of job openings projected per year. (One of the 325 occupations, Artillery and Missile Crew Members, had to be dropped because this data was not available.)

5. Using this data, we created three lists that ranked these 324 jobs on annual earnings, projected growth, and number of job openings projected per year. Each of these lists was then sorted from highest to lowest, and the jobs were assigned a number score from 324 (highest pay, for example) to 1 (lowest pay, for example).

6. We then added the number scores for each job from all three lists and created a new list that presented all 324 jobs in order from highest to lowest total score for all three measures.

7. To emphasize jobs that tend to pay more, are likely to grow more rapidly, and have more job openings, we selected the 250 job titles with the highest total scores from our final list. These jobs are the focus of this book.

For example, Police Patrol Officers has the highest combined score for earnings, growth, and number of job openings, so Police Patrol Officers is listed first in our 250 Best Apprenticeable Jobs list even though it is not the best-paying job (which is Municipal Fire Fighting and Prevention Supervisors), the fastest-growing job (which is Medical Assistants), or the job with the most openings (which is Janitors and Cleaners, Except Maids and Housekeeping Cleaners).

Understand the Limits of the Data in This Book

In this book we use the most reliable and up-to-date earnings, projected growth, number of openings, and other information available. The data came from the U.S. Department of Labor source known as Occupation and Employment Statistics. As you look at the data, keep in mind that the figures are estimates. They give you a general idea about the number of workers employed, annual earnings, rate of job growth, and annual job openings.

Understand that a problem with such data is that it is true only on the average. Just as there is no precisely average person, there is no such thing as a statistically average example of a particular job. We say this because data, while helpful, can also be misleading.

Take, for example, the yearly earnings information in this book. This is highly reliable data obtained from a very large U.S. working population sample by the Bureau of Labor Statistics. It tells us the average annual pay received as of May 2003 by people in various job titles (actually, it is the median annual pay, which means that half earned more and half less).

This sounds great, except that half of all people in that occupation earned less than that amount. For example, people who are new to the occupation or with only a few years of work experience often earn much less than the average amount. People who live in rural areas or who work for smaller employers typically earn less than those who do similar work in cities (where the cost of living is higher) or for bigger employers. People in certain areas of the country earn less than those in others.

What's especially relevant to this book is the fact that people who are working in trades for which they have completed an apprenticeship, especially those who are union members, tend to earn considerably more than workers who have learned informally or are not unionized. For example, in 2003 union members working in the private sector earned 21 percent more than nonunion workers. In the construction industry, the difference was 52 percent! Of course, not all former apprentices are union members, but someone who has completed an apprenticeship can expect to command a higher wage in that trade (especially at the beginning of a career) than someone whose skills are not documented. Keep this in mind when you look at the wage figures in this book.

Also keep in mind that the figures for job growth and number of openings are projections by labor economists—their best guesses about what we can expect between now and 2012. They are not guarantees. A major economic downturn, war, or technological breakthrough could change the actual outcome.

So, in reviewing the information in this book, please understand the limitations of data. You need to use common sense in career decision-making as in most other things in life. We hope that, using that approach, you find the information helpful and interesting.

How This Book Is Organized

The information about apprenticeships in this book moves from the general to the highly specific.

Part I. Overview of Apprenticeships

Part I is an overview of apprenticeship—what it is, where the opportunities are, what the requirements are, what the pros and cons are, and where to find out more. This section may clear up some misunderstandings you have about apprenticeship, and it will help you appreciate what apprenticeship has to offer you.

Part II. Master List of Nationally Registered Apprenticeships

Part II lists all 876 apprenticeships that currently are registered with the U.S. Department of Labor. You may be surprised at some of the titles that appear here. For each apprenticeship, you can see how many years it takes and what career it is related to. The apprenticeships are grouped according to interest fields, so you can easily find those that belong to industries that appeal to you.

Part III. The Best Jobs Lists: Jobs You Can Enter Through Apprenticeship

For many people, the 35 lists in Part III are the most interesting section of the book. Here you can see which apprenticeable jobs are best in terms of high salaries, fast growth, and plentiful job openings. You can also see which jobs are best when these factors are combined, and that list is broken out further according to the interest fields and several other features of the jobs. Look in the Table of Contents for a complete list of lists. Although there are a lot of lists, they are not difficult to understand because they have clear titles and are organized into groupings of related lists.

People who prefer to think about careers in terms of personality types will want to browse the lists that show the best jobs for the Artistic, Conventional, Enterprising, Realistic, and Social personality types. On the other hand, some people think first in terms of interest fields, and these people will prefer the lists that show the best jobs using the interest categories of the *Guide for Occupational Exploration*, a major source of career information.

We suggest that you use the lists that make the most sense for you. Following are the names of each group of lists along with short comments on each group. You will find additional information in a brief introduction provided at the beginning of each group of lists in Part III.

Best Jobs Overall: Apprenticeable Jobs with the Highest Pay, Fastest Growth, and Most Openings

This group has four lists, and they are the ones that most people want to see first. The first list presents all 250 apprenticeable jobs that are included in this book in order of their total scores for earnings, growth, and number of job openings. These jobs are used in the more-specialized lists that follow and in the descriptions in Part IV. Three more lists in this group present the 100 best-paying apprenticeable jobs, the 100 fastest-growing apprenticeable jobs, and the 100 apprenticeable jobs with the most openings.

Best Apprenticeable Jobs Based on Personality Types

This group provides lists of apprenticeable jobs for five of six personality types, based on a system that is used in a variety of popular career exploration inventories. The lists present the jobs in order of their total combined scores for earnings, growth, and number of openings. We explain the personality types in the introduction to these lists. (Of the usual six personality types, one is not linked to any apprenticeable jobs, so there are only five lists here.)

Best Apprenticeable Jobs Based on Interests

There are 13 lists in this group, and they contain all of the apprenticeable jobs from our 250 best jobs that fall within 13 of 14 major areas of interest. The number of jobs varies by list, and the lists are organized from highest to lowest total combined score for earnings, growth, and number of openings. (One of the 14 interest areas is not linked to any apprenticeable jobs, so there are only 13 lists here.)

Best Apprenticeable Jobs Based on Number of Years Required

Apprenticeships generally vary in duration from one to five years. Each of the seven lists in this group presents jobs for which it takes a specific amount of time to complete the related apprenticeship. The number of jobs varies by list. Within each list, the jobs are ordered from highest to lowest total combined score for earnings, growth, and number of openings.

Apprenticeable Jobs with the Highest Percentage of Women and Men

This group includes four lists that extract from the 250 best jobs only those that have a workforce with 70 percent or more women or men. One pair of lists orders these jobs by the percentage of women or men; the other pair orders the corresponding jobs by their total combined score for earnings, growth, and number of openings.

Most Popular Apprenticeships

This group contains a list of the 25 most popular apprenticeships and a list of the 24 jobs linked to these apprenticeships, ordered by their total combined score for earnings, growth, and number of openings.

Part IV. Descriptions of the 250 Best Apprenticeable Jobs

This part of the book provides a brief but information-packed description of each of the 250 best apprenticeable jobs that met our criteria for this book. The descriptions are presented in alphabetical order. This structure makes it easy to look up a job that you've identified in a list from Part II or Part III that you want to learn more about.

We used the most current information from a variety of government sources to create the descriptions. Although we've tried to make the descriptions easy to understand, the sample job description that follows—and the explanation of each of its parts—may help you better understand and use the descriptions.

Job Title →

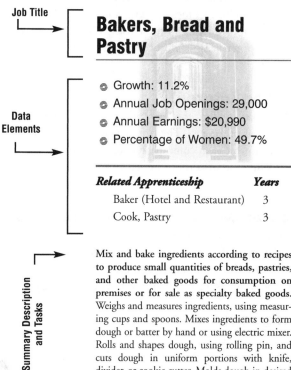

Bakers, Bread and Pastry

- Growth: 11.2%
- Annual Job Openings: 29,000
- Annual Earnings: $20,990
- Percentage of Women: 49.7%

Data Elements →

Related Apprenticeship	Years
Baker (Hotel and Restaurant)	3
Cook, Pastry	3

Summary Description and Tasks →

Mix and bake ingredients according to recipes to produce small quantities of breads, pastries, and other baked goods for consumption on premises or for sale as specialty baked goods. Weighs and measures ingredients, using measuring cups and spoons. Mixes ingredients to form dough or batter by hand or using electric mixer. Rolls and shapes dough, using rolling pin, and cuts dough in uniform portions with knife, divider, or cookie cutter. Molds dough in desired shapes, places dough in greased or floured pans, and trims overlapping edges with knife. Mixes and cooks pie filling, pours filling into pie shells, and tops filling with meringue or cream. Checks production schedule to determine variety and quantity of goods to bake. Spreads or sprinkles toppings on loaves or specialties and places dough in oven, using long-handled paddle (peel). Covers filling with top crust, places pies in oven, and adjusts drafts or thermostatic controls to regulate oven temperatures. Mixes ingredients to make icings; decorates cakes and pastries; and blends colors for icings, shaped ornaments, and statuaries. Cuts, peels, and prepares fruit for pie fillings. **SKILLS**—None met the criteria. ← **Skills**

GOE—Interest Area: 11. Recreation, Travel, and Other Personal Services. **Work Group:** 11.05 Food and Beverage Services. **Other Apprenticeable Jobs in This Work Group:** Bartenders; Butchers and Meat Cutters; Chefs and Head Cooks; Cooks, Fast Food; Cooks, Institution and Cafeteria; Cooks, Restaurant. **PERSONALITY TYPE:** Realistic. Realistic occupations frequently involve work activities that include practical, hands-on problems and solutions. They often deal with plants, animals, and real-world materials like wood, tools, and machinery. Many of the occupations require working outside and do not involve a lot of paperwork or working closely with others. ← **GOE** / **Personality Type**

RELATED KNOWLEDGE/COURSES—Food Production: Knowledge of techniques and equipment for planting, growing, and harvesting food products (both plant and animal) for consumption, including storage/handling techniques. **Production and Processing:** Knowledge of raw materials, production processes, quality control, costs, and other techniques for maximizing the effective manufacture and distribution of goods. **Sales and Marketing:** Knowledge of principles and methods for showing, promoting, and selling products or services. This includes marketing strategy and tactics, product demonstration, sales techniques, and sales control systems. ← **Related Knowledge/Courses**

WORK ENVIRONMENT—Standing; indoors; minor burns, cuts, bites, or stings; spend time making repetitive motions; very hot or cold. ← **Work Environment**

Here are some details on each of the major parts of the job descriptions you will find in Part IV:

- ◉ Job Title—This is the job title for the job as defined by the U.S. Department of Labor and used in its O*NET database. (If you are wondering why this is the title of a job, not an apprenticeship, see the explanation in the following section, "Why We Describe Apprenticeable Jobs, Not Apprenticeships.")

- ◉ Data Elements—This information comes from various U.S. Department of Labor and Census Bureau databases, as explained elsewhere in this Introduction.

- ◉ Summary Description and Tasks—The bold sentences provide a summary description of the occupation. It is followed by a listing of tasks that are generally performed by people who work in this job. We followed the listing of tasks in the O*NET database, except that where necessary we edited the tasks to keep them from exceeding 2,200 characters.

- ◉ Skills—The government provides data on many skills; we decided to list only those that were most important for each job rather than list pages of unhelpful details. For each job, we identified any skill with a rating that was higher than the average rating for that skill for all jobs. If there were more than eight, we included only those eight with the highest ratings, and we present them from highest to lowest score (that is, in terms of by how much its score exceeds the average score). We include up to 10 skills if scores were tied for eighth place. You can find definitions of the skills in Appendix D.

- ◉ GOE—This information cross-references the *Guide for Occupational Exploration* (or the *GOE*), a system that organizes jobs based on interests and is used in a variety of career information systems. We use the new third edition of the *Guide for Occupational Exploration,* as published by JIST. The description includes the major interest area the job fits into, its more specific Work Group, and a list of related apprenticeable job titles that are in this same GOE Work Group. This listing will help you identify other apprenticeable jobs that relate to similar interests or require similar skills. You can find more information on the *GOE* and its interest areas in the introduction to the lists of jobs based on interests in Part III.

- ◉ Personality Type—This part gives the name of the personality type that most closely matches each job, as well as a brief definition of this personality type. You can find more information on the personality types in Part III.

- ◉ Related Knowledge/Courses—This entry can help you understand the most important knowledge areas that are required for an apprenticeable job and the types of subjects you will likely study in the related coursework that is part of the apprenticeship. We used information in the O*NET database for this entry. We went through a process similar to the one we used for Skills (earlier in this list) to determine which entries were most important for each job. In this case, however, we listed at least two knowledge areas for each job, even if the ratings for those knowledge areas were lower than the average for all jobs.

◎ Work Environment—Often, what makes one job more appealing than another is the physical context of the work: whether you'll be mostly sitting or doing strenuous lifting, whether you'll be indoors at a pleasant temperature or baking in heat, and so forth. We used the O*NET ratings for Physical Work Context and applied a process similar to the one for Skills as described earlier.

◎ Further information—Some descriptions contain contact information for unions or other organizations.

Why We Describe Apprenticeable Jobs, Not Apprenticeships

When you look over the "best apprenticeable jobs" lists in this book or read the descriptions of jobs, keep in mind that these are lists and descriptions of *occupations* that you can enter through apprenticeship—they are not lists and descriptions of *apprenticeships*. Why did we do this?

First of all, because apprenticeships are usually sponsored and administered at the local level, nationally applicable statistics about them generally do not exist. It is impossible to create a useful list of best apprenticeships without good statistics for organizing the list. For example, nobody can tell you how many electrician apprenticeships there are throughout the United States, what the apprentice electricians are earning, how fast the programs are growing, or how many openings there are each year. On the other hand, we can readily obtain such figures for the *occupation* of Electricians and see how it stacks up against other jobs.

For this same reason—variations between one locally sponsored apprenticeship and another—it would be impossible for us to describe your locally available apprenticeships accurately. The work tasks you learn and the subjects you study in night classes may or may not be guided by national standards. (For examples of national standards, see Appendix B.)

Finally, it helps to remember that apprenticeship is only the front door to an occupation. It lasts only a few years, but the career it leads to may keep you employed for many years. Therefore, it would be a mistake for you to focus primarily on what lies immediately ahead. Take the long view. Consider what the jobs have to offer, and when you have found one that looks promising, investigate your local apprenticeship opportunities to decide whether you want to use this entry route to prepare for that goal.

There is one exception in this book to our focus on jobs rather than on apprenticeships: that is the list of the "Most Popular Apprenticeships" in Part III. But even here we take care to point out the limitations of the available data, which is derived from only 31 states.

How to Use This Book

This is a book that you can dive right into:

- **If you are uncertain about exactly what apprenticeship is,** you'll want to read Part I, which is an overview of this method of training. You'll learn about the typical requirements of an apprenticeship and the pluses and minuses of starting a career this way.

- **If you like lists and want an easy way to compare jobs,** turn to Part III. Here you can browse the apprenticeable jobs with the best pay, the fastest growth, and the most job openings. You can see these best jobs broken down in various ways, such as by interest field. The list in Part II, which includes every registered apprenticeship, will give you an idea of the variety of careers you can enter through this route.

- **For detailed information about apprenticeable jobs,** turn to Part IV and read the profiles of the jobs. We include 250 apprenticeable jobs and itemize their major tasks, their top skills, the main features of their work environment, and other factors you won't learn from the lists in Part III.

On the other hand, if you like to do things in a methodical way, you may want to read the sections in order:

- Part I will give you useful background on what apprenticeship is. This will help you decide whether this is the way you might want to start your career.

- The complete listing of registered apprenticeships in Part II will give you a sense of how varied the opportunities are.

- As you browse the lists of best jobs in Part III, you can take notes on the jobs that have the greatest appeal for you.

- Then you can look up the descriptions of these jobs in Part IV and narrow down your list. Ask yourself, Do the work tasks interest me? Does the work environment discourage me?

- When you have a short list of jobs you might like to apprentice for, you can consult Appendix C to identify the state office where you can learn about apprenticeship opportunities in your area.

- If you obtain the national apprenticeship standards for a program in your area, Appendix A can help you understand how to read the document—what to look for and what to look out for.

PART I

Overview of Apprenticeships

This part provides general information about apprenticeships: what they are, how they're funded, which industries use them, their entry and completion requirements, pros and cons, and how to find and evaluate an apprenticeship program.

What Is an Apprenticeship?

Apprenticeship is a form of job training that has been in use for centuries. The stonemasons who built the pyramids of Egypt learned their skills through an apprenticeship. So did the medieval scribes who copied the Bible by hand; the shipwrights who assembled the Niña, the Pinta, and the Santa María; the midwives who delivered the 20 children of Johann Sebastian Bach; and the gunsmiths who supplied Napoleon's army with firepower.

But apprenticeship is not a relic of another era. It has stayed up to date with changes in the economy and in technology. Nowadays apprentices may learn jobs like Internetworking Technician, Sound Mixer, or Photogrammetric Technician. Apprenticeship is an essential part of our modern economy, and more than one-third of a million Americans are presently registered as apprentices.

Even some of the terms used to describe apprenticeship have changed. In olden times, a person who completed an apprenticeship and became a fully qualified worker was called a "journeyman." The French word *journée* means the span of a day, so a journeyman was someone who could charge a fee for a day's work. Nowadays the term "journeyman" is still sometimes used, but it is being replaced by "journey worker" or "journeyperson." (In this book we use "journey worker.") Apprenticeship is definitely not all-male. In Part III you can find a list of the apprenticeable jobs with the greatest proportion of women workers.

Worksite learning has always been at the core of apprenticeship. Apprentices are supervised and taught by experienced workers who can pass on skills, work habits, strategies for problem solving, and obscure lore that often cannot be learned anywhere else. To learn all this, apprentices need to do more than just watch experienced workers or act as "helpers."

They perform real work tasks at higher and higher levels of skill, and they are rotated through all aspects of the job so that they learn the full range of skills.

Because modern jobs involve technology and take place in a complex business world, modern apprentices have to learn theory as well as practical skills. They need to master concepts that cannot be taught well at the worksite—for example, technical math, principles of mechanics, electronic circuits, business law, or human anatomy. So apprenticeships now include a component of classroom learning. These classes usually meet after working hours and may be held at a community college or a vocational school, by correspondence, or even on the Web.

Most forms of learning cost money, and college tuition is getting more expensive at an alarming rate. But apprentices earn while they learn. A survey of apprentices in 21 states found their average wage was $12.25 per hour, for an average annual income of $24,509. Apprentices start out at a rate of pay that is often only half the hourly rate of a journey worker, but as they gain work experience they get regular increases in pay. Of course, these increases depend on satisfactory performance at the worksite and in classes. During the last phase of the apprenticeship, they typically earn 90 percent of a journey worker's hourly rate. (When you see salary figures elsewhere in this book, keep in mind that these are based on the earnings of *everyone* working in the occupation—the apprentices, the journey workers, and the workers who entered through some route other than apprenticeship. Thus these figures are likely to be lower than the average journey worker's pay.)

How Are Apprenticeships Administered and Funded?

Small employers may create informal apprenticeships, but the kinds of apprenticeships discussed in this book are formal apprenticeships that are registered with the state and, most often, with the U.S. Department of Labor. (For a listing of state offices that register apprenticeships, see Appendix C.) These registered apprenticeships are created and funded by apprenticeship committees, which may be formed by employers, employer associations, labor unions, or some combination of these parties (or by a branch of the military that offers apprenticeship as part of military training). To be registered, the apprenticeships must meet certain standards for safety, fairness, and training. When an apprentice completes the program, the committee issues a certificate that confers journey worker status and that usually is recognized anywhere in the U.S.

What Industries Use Apprenticeships?

Apprenticeships have been created in a wide range of industries, and each year about four new apprenticeships are registered with the U.S. Department of Labor. The following diagram shows the number of people in apprenticeships within certain major industry groups in 2003. The diagram is based on figures from 31 states and does not represent the entire nation exactly, but it is probably a rough approximation of the actual breakdown. Although the construction industry clearly dominates, remember that the whole pie represents over one-third of a million people, so even the small slices represent a large number of apprentices. Furthermore, apprenticeship is growing as an entry route for other industries.

Figure 1: Percentage of people in apprenticeships by industry group, 2003.

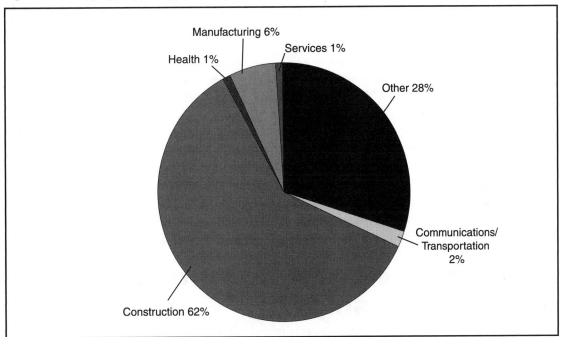

Here are some examples, from a variety of industry sectors, of apprenticeable jobs that are described in Part IV of this book. (Those industries that are starred have been targeted as special areas of growth under the President's High Growth Job Training Initiative; they are expected to fuel the U.S. economy in the years ahead and to need a good supply of trained workers.)

- **Automotive***: Automotive Body and Related Repairers; Automotive Master Mechanics; Automotive Specialty Technicians
- **Biotechnology***: Health Technologists and Technicians, All Other
- **Construction***: Electricians; Floor Layers, Except Carpet, Wood, and Hard Tiles; Plasterers and Stucco Masons
- **Energy***: Gaugers; Rotary Drill Operators, Oil and Gas; Petroleum Refinery and Control Panel Operators
- **Financial Services***: Tellers
- **Geospatial***: Mapping Technicians; Surveying Technicians

⊚ **Health Care***: Dental Assistants; Medical Secretaries; Pharmacy Technicians; Surgical Technologists

⊚ **Hospitality***: Bartenders; Chefs and Head Cooks; Hotel, Motel, and Resort Desk Clerks

⊚ **Information Technology/Networking***: Computer Operators; Computer Specialists, All Other; Data Processing Equipment Repairers

⊚ **Manufacturing***: Food Batchmakers; Mechanical Inspectors; Model Makers, Metal and Plastic; Numerical Control Machine Tool Operators and Tenders, Metal and Plastic; Production Inspectors, Testers, Graders, Sorters, Samplers, Weighers

⊚ **Military:** Avionics Technicians

⊚ **Public Sector:** Construction and Building Inspectors; Government Property Inspectors and Investigators; Municipal Fire Fighters; Postal Service Clerks

⊚ **Public Utilities:** Electrical Power-Line Installers and Repairers; Power Generating Plant Operators, Except Auxiliary Equipment Operators; Water and Liquid Waste Treatment Plant and System Operators

⊚ **Service and Retail Industries***: First-Line Supervisors/Managers of Retail Sales Workers; Food Service Managers; Private Detectives and Investigators

⊚ **Telecommunications:** Broadcast Technicians; Communication Equipment Mechanics, Installers, and Repairers; Station Installers and Repairers, Telephone

⊚ **Transportation***: Truck Drivers, Heavy; Motor Vehicle Inspectors

What Are the Entry Requirements of Apprenticeships?

Requirements vary, but they are usually related to the demands of the job.

Age. Usually the minimum age for entry is 18. In some cases it may be as low as 16, but not if the job is at all hazardous. There rarely is a maximum age. The average age of new apprentices is probably somewhere in the upper 20s.

Education. Usually a high school diploma or G.E.D. is required. Sometimes you need to have specific classes on your transcript, or having taken these classes may improve your chances of being accepted. These classes may be closely related to work tasks, such as blueprint reading or metal shop, or they may be fundamental subjects, such as algebra, that you need to know to succeed in the classes required by the apprenticeship. In highly technical fields or fields where there's a lot of competition for entry to apprenticeships, an associate degree or certificate may help. Related training in the military may also improve your chances of entry.

Fitness. You probably need a statement from a doctor that you are physically capable of doing the job. Keep in mind that the 1990 Americans with Disabilities Act (ADA) forbids employers from discriminating against people who have disabilities and who can perform the work tasks if provided with reasonable accommodations. This law applies to apprentices just as much as it applies to any other kind of worker. Therefore, if you have a disability, your doctor should specify what accommodations would allow you to perform the kind of job you are aiming for. A few jobs, such as Municipal Fire Fighter, require you to pass a specific fitness test—for example, you may need to be able to lift and carry a certain weight.

Residency status. You may be required to be a citizen of the United States, but in some cases you need to demonstrate only that your residency status allows you to work here.

Transportation. You need to demonstrate that you have a way of getting to the worksite. In jobs where the worksite may shift locations frequently or may be in out-of-the-way locations (for example, in many construction jobs), you may be required to have a valid driver's license and access to a car.

Aptitude. You may need to pass a test of your aptitude for the work tasks. For example, if the job involves a lot of delicate work with your hands, you may need to demonstrate good fine motor coordination. For some construction jobs, you may be required to have no debilitating fear of heights.

Interview. Like most jobs, apprenticeships usually require you to be interviewed. Keep in mind that you are asking the apprenticeship committee to invest in you (the apprenticeship is like an "industry scholarship" that may be worth $40,000–$150,000), so you need to convince the interviewers that you are genuinely interested in the job and that you are determined to complete the requirements. The interviewers may mention some of the difficult or unpleasant aspects of the job to judge whether you are easily discouraged. You should be informed about the nature of the job so that you can point out the aspects of the job that attract you. The interviewers may want additional clarification of some of the requirements mentioned above (for example, your academic background) and probably will require the names, addresses, and phone numbers of at least three people not related to you who can comment on your character and ability.

The point system. Most often, there are more candidates for an apprenticeship than there are openings in the program, and the apprenticeship committee is required to follow a fair procedure for selecting the top contenders. The committee may award candidates a certain number of points for their ability to meet some of the requirements listed above. For example, a candidate may receive x points for education, y points for aptitude, and z points for the interview. The candidates with the greatest number of points are the first to be taken on as apprentices when openings become available.

Waiting period. If there is a lot of competition, the industry is in a slump, or your point score is not among the highest, you may have to wait for weeks, months, or even years to be admitted to an apprenticeship. You probably can improve your chances by taking related courses or by working at related jobs and then re-applying. With these activities on your resume, you are likely to have a better point score for education and give a more impressive interview. At the very least, your experiences will give you a clearer picture of whether the job you are aiming for is a good choice for you.

What Are the Requirements for Completing an Apprenticeship?

When you begin an apprenticeship, you and the sponsor sign an apprenticeship agreement, and this brief document (typically one page) references a longer document called the apprenticeship standards. You should examine this standards document even before you apply for the apprenticeship because it spells out all the requirements for the apprenticeship and tells you what to expect. (In Appendix A, you can see an outline of a typical standards document and comments on typical requirements, and Appendix B contains excerpts from standards documents.)

Worksite learning. Most apprenticeships require you to complete a certain number of hours of worksite learning, typically 2,000 hours per year. That may seem like a lot of time, but it represents an eight-hour day, a five-day week, and a work year that gives you two weeks off for vacation and holidays. Most apprenticeships require a total of four years. A smaller number of apprenticeships require two or three years. Some require as little as one year or as much as six years. (See Part II for the years required for each nationally registered apprenticeship.)

A small but growing number of apprenticeships require you to achieve "competence" rather than log a specific number of hours. They use assessments that measure how far you have progressed toward mastering the work and determine when you are fully qualified. If you are a quick learner, you can complete such a program faster than other apprentices. If you enter the program with some experience and skills from either work, military training, or a partially completed apprenticeship in another trade, you may be able to skip some of the entry-level learning. Also, the credential you receive from such a program assures employers that you have demonstrated all the required skills and have not simply "paid your dues."

Classroom learning. Typically you are required to complete 144 hours of classroom learning per year, which is equivalent to taking two classes during each academic session. Keep in mind that you will have to take these classes and do your studying in the evening, not during the workday. You may be excused from some courses if you have acquired relevant classroom training in college or in the military. In some apprenticeship programs, you enroll in an associate degree program and receive your degree at the same time you become a journey worker. This is particularly common in fields where you need to be licensed and the license requires the degree.

Things you may pay for. Although apprentices earn pay at the worksite, they may have to pay certain apprenticeship-related expenses out of their own pockets. For example, they may have to buy a set of basic tools for the job. They may have to buy protective clothing, work boots, goggles, or other necessary gear. Sometimes they must pay for the night classes that they are required to take, although all or part of these costs may be waived by the local community college or covered by veterans' benefits, the program sponsor, or the state. If the worksite is unionized, apprentices are likely to have to pay union dues, although often at a reduced rate. You should investigate these requirements before you sign up for the apprenticeship.

Why Might Apprenticeship Be a Good Choice?

One of the most important reasons for apprenticing has been mentioned already: You earn as you learn. Of course, in some industries you could simply take a low-level job and acquire skills by watching what the more advanced workers do. But in a registered apprenticeship, you are taken through several job rotations so that you learn the full range of skills for the job. You get personal attention as you learn—the average number of apprentices per program is about eight. When you consider that these eight people would be in different stages of apprenticeship and therefore would probably not be working at the same worksite or on the same kind of task, you can appreciate the individual attention that you can get in this form of learning. (Compare this to a classroom in a trade school.)

Furthermore, your work performance in an apprenticeship is documented—you have a written record of all the work tasks you have performed and all the skills you have mastered. This documentation is portable, which means that any employer in the U.S. will accept it as proof of your status as a fully qualified worker. An apprenticeship also plugs you into a network of journey workers and employers. These personal contacts can help you find jobs when you complete the apprenticeship and for years to come.

Finally, consider how useful apprenticeship may be as part of your long-term career path. For many people, the apprenticeship and the job it leads to as a journey worker are only the first steps in a career path with unlimited potential. The president of the ironworkers union for western Washington state, who started out as an apprentice, likes to point out that when he speaks to a high-school class, he's the highest-paid person in the building. Others who started in construction trades are now managing contracting businesses, selling building supplies, or teaching vocational education. Likewise, in other industries where people apprentice, there are countless opportunities for ambitious and resourceful people, especially those who have a knack for acquiring new skills on the job.

What Can Go Wrong in an Apprenticeship?

During the first few months of an apprenticeship, some apprentices become discouraged when they compare their status to that of the journey workers. Their wages are so much lower, and the work tasks they do may seem menial by comparison.

In addition, a few apprentices may find that they cannot handle the demands of the workplace or of the classroom—or perhaps they do not care enough about the job to try. Most apprenticeships begin with a probationary period of a few months during which the program sponsor can terminate someone's participation in the program without having to show cause. After the probationary period, apprentices still need to perform their work satisfactorily and maintain a certain minimum grade-point average in the classes.

If the industry is in a slump, apprentices are often the first workers to be laid off. When that happens, they usually have a guarantee that they can resume their apprenticeship when there is work for them, but the layoff pushes back the date when they become a journey worker. It also leaves them without wages, and they may have trouble finding some other job if it is known that they will quit that new job as soon as they have a chance to resume their apprenticeship.

During the last year of an apprenticeship, apprentices have enough work experience and skills that outside employers may tempt them with job offers and cause them to consider quitting the program before completion. In such cases, the apprentices would do well to remember that the job being offered may be temporary, whereas journey worker status is permanent.

How Can I Find an Apprenticeship?

Some apprenticeships are advertised in the "help wanted" section of the newspaper. But when there is enough competition for openings, there may be no need to advertise. Instead, it's up to you to identify the available apprenticeship and apply for it. Here are some places to investigate:

- Union locals in your community
- Medium-sized to large employers in your community
- Your state's Job Service (see the blue pages of your telephone book)
- A school or college career counseling office
- A military recruitment office (see the blue pages of your telephone book), since some apprenticeships are offered as part of military training
- America's Job Bank (http://www.jobsearch.org/)
- Your state's office that registers apprenticeships. In some states, this is the State Apprenticeship Council (see the blue pages of your telephone book or http://www.nastad.net/index.cfm?page=3). In other states, it is the Bureau of Apprenticeship and Training (see the blue pages of your telephone book or http://www.doleta.gov/atels_bat/stateoffices.cfm). For a full listing, see Appendix C.
- The searchable database of sponsors (who may or may not have apprenticeships open at present) at the Apprenticeship Training, Employer and Labor Services Sponsors Website (http://bat.doleta.gov/).

You may also find it useful to ask journey workers in the field that interests you, especially those who have recently completed an apprenticeship. This is particularly important if you are looking for an unusual apprenticeship—for example, Fur Finisher, Harpsichord Maker, Horseshoer, or Wine Maker—one that is available in only a highly limited number of places.

How Can I Investigate an Apprenticeship Program?

The single best way to learn about the good and bad aspects of an apprenticeship program is to speak to apprentices who are enrolled in it and to journey workers who have completed it. Any apprenticeship program that you are considering should be willing to provide you with names and phone numbers of people to contact. Ask them how thorough the training was and how much personal attention they received. Also ask for their impressions of future job openings in the field—is this an industry that is growing in your community?

Give a careful reading to the apprenticeship standards document, which specifies the obligations that both you and the sponsor agree to. Appendix A shows the major headings of a typical standards document and points out what you should expect to find, and Appendix B contains excerpts from sample standards documents.

Perhaps you're wondering whether union apprenticeship programs (about one-third of existing programs) have any advantage over nonunion programs. This can vary, but a study of the construction industry in Kentucky found that union programs had a completion rate that was almost twice that of nonunion programs, had twice as many male minority and female apprentices enrolled, and had twice as many male minority and female apprentices achieving journey worker status.

PART II

Master List of Nationally Registered Apprenticeships

Apprenticeship is being introduced to more industries each year. It is truly impressive to see all the available apprenticeships listed in one place, which is what this section of the book does. But keep in mind that not every apprenticeship is presently available within your geographic area; in fact, a few apprenticeships are offered at only one location in the United States.

The following table contains the list of apprenticeships in the Registered Apprenticeship Information System (RAIS), updated as of mid-2004. The apprenticeships are ordered alphabetically within the interest fields of the *Guide for Occupational Exploration* (for more about these interest fields, see Part III). For each apprenticeship, you may see the RAIS code number, the RAIS title, the number of years for completion, and the title of the job that is linked to it in the Department of Labor's O*NET database. In Part IV you can find detailed information about many of these O*NET jobs.

Exceptions:

- O*NET jobs that are marked with * usually require a college degree, so apprenticeship is not considered the normal entry route. These jobs therefore were not considered for inclusion among the top 250 apprenticeable jobs and are not described in Part IV.

- O*NET jobs that are marked with ‡ met all the criteria for inclusion in this book except that they were ranked 251 or lower. They also are not described in Part IV.

So if you find an apprenticeship here that interests you and that is not marked with * or ‡, look up the information about the related O*NET job in Part IV, where the jobs are arranged alphabetically.

Interest Field: Arts, Entertainment, and Media

RAIS Code	RAIS Apprenticeship Title	Years	Title of Related O*NET Job
0862	Actor	2	Actors
0011	Artificial-Glass-Eye Maker	5	Glass Blowers, Molders, Benders, and Finishers
0879	Audio Operator	2	Broadcast Technicians
0640	Bank-Note Designer	5	Commercial and Industrial Designers*
0955	Camera Operator	3	Camera Operators, Television, Video, and Motion Picture
0037	Cartoonist, Motion Pictures	3	Cartoonists
0081	Cloth Designer	4	Commercial and Industrial Designers*
0013	Commercial Designer	4	Commercial and Industrial Designers*
0082	Decorator	4	Merchandise Displayers and Window Trimmers
0970	Director, Television	2	Directors—Stage, Motion Pictures, Television, and Radio*
0098	Display Designer	4	Exhibit Designers*
0324	Displayer, Merchandise	1	Merchandise Displayers and Window Trimmers
0679	Dot Etcher	5	Dot Etchers
0617	Electronic Prepress System Operator	5	Desktop Publishers
0178	Engraver	2	Engravers/Carvers‡
0705	Engraver I	5	Precision Etchers and Engravers, Hand or Machine‡
0146	Engraver, Block	4	Precision Etchers and Engravers, Hand or Machine‡
0806	Engraver, Hand, Hard Metals	4	Precision Etchers and Engravers, Hand or Machine‡
0147	Engraver, Hand, Soft Metals	4	Precision Etchers and Engravers, Hand or Machine‡
0179	Engraver, Pantograph I	4	Pantograph Engravers‡
0148	Engraver, Picture	1	Precision Etchers and Engravers, Hand or Machine‡
0175	Etcher, Hand	5	Photoengravers‡
0182	Etcher, Photoengraving	4	Photoengravers‡
0960	Field Engineer	4	Broadcast Technicians
0127	Film or Videotape Editor	4	Film and Video Editors*
0202	Floral Designer	1	Floral Designers
0224	Fur Designer	4	Fashion Designers*
0225	Furniture Designer	4	Commercial and Industrial Designers*
0218	Glass Bender	4	Glass Blowers, Molders, Benders, and Finishers
0219	Glass Blower	3	Glass Blowers, Molders, Benders, and Finishers
0768	Glass Blower, Laboratory Apparatus	4	Glass Blowers, Molders, Benders, and Finishers
0243	Glass-Blowing-Lathe Operator	4	Glass Blowers, Molders, Benders, and Finishers
0010	Graphic Designer	1.5	Graphic Designers*
0240	Illustrator	4	Painters and Illustrators
0016	Industrial Designer	4	Commercial and Industrial Designers*
0265	Interior Designer	2	Interior Designers*
0276	Light Technician	4	Audio and Video Equipment Technicians

Interest Field: Arts, Entertainment, and Media

RAIS Code	RAIS Apprenticeship Title	Years	Title of Related O*NET Job
0340	Model Maker, Pottery and Porcelain	2	Potters
0626	Painter	1	Painters and Illustrators
0392	Paste-Up Artist	3	Paste-Up Workers
0399	Photoengraver	5	Photoengravers‡
0400	Photoengraving Finisher	5	Photoengravers‡
0401	Photoengraving Printer	5	Photoengravers‡
0402	Photoengraving Proofer	5	Photoengravers‡
0685	Photographer, Lithographic	5	Camera Operators
0405	Photographer, Photoengraving	6	Photoengravers‡
0403	Photographer, Still	3	Professional Photographers
0439	Pottery-Machine Operator	3	Potters
0913	Program Assistant	3	Producers*
0952	Radio Station Operator	4	Radio Operators‡
0926	Recording Engineer	2	Sound Engineering Technicians
0472	Retoucher, Photoengraving	5	Photoengravers‡
0795	Roller Engraver, Hand	2	Engravers, Hand‡
0447	Siderographer	5	Precision Etchers and Engravers, Hand or Machine‡
0523	Sketch Maker II	4	Precision Etchers and Engravers, Hand or Machine‡
0527	Sound Mixer	4	Sound Engineering Technicians
0521	Stage Technician	3	Audio and Video Equipment Technicians
0382	Stained Glass Artist	4	Commercial and Industrial Designers*
0562	Taxidermist (Professional and Kindred)	3	Craft Artists*
0494	Wardrobe Supervisor	2	Costume Attendants

*Jobs marked with * usually require college and are not included in Parts III or IV. Jobs marked with ‡ were ranked 251 or lower and are not included in Parts III or IV.*

Interest Field: Science, Math, and Engineering

RAIS Code	RAIS Apprenticeship Title	Years	Title of Related O*NET Job
0875	Assembler, Electromechanical	4	Electro-Mechanical Technicians*
0895	Calibration Laboratory Technician	4	Calibration and Instrumentation Technicians*
0050	Chemical Laboratory Technician	4	Chemical Technicians*
0969	Chemical-Engineering Technician	4	Chemical Technicians*
0053	Chief of Party	4	Surveying Technicians

(continued)

(continued)

Interest Field: Science, Math, and Engineering

RAIS Code	RAIS Apprenticeship Title	Years	Title of Related O*NET Job
0811	Computer Programmer	2	Computer Programmers*
0630	Dairy Technologist	4	Biological Technicians*
0106	Design Drafter, Electromechanisms	4	Electronic Drafters
0108	Detailer	4	Mechanical Drafters
0113	Die Designer	4	Mechanical Drafters
0126	Drafter, Architectural	4	Architectural Drafters*
0018	Drafter, Automotive Design	4	Mechanical Drafters
0019	Drafter, Automotive Design Layout	4	Mechanical Drafters
0109	Drafter, Cartographic	4	Cartographers and Photogrammetrists*
0128	Drafter, Civil	4	Civil Drafters
0129	Drafter, Commercial	4	Architectural Drafters*
0130	Drafter, Detail	4	Mechanical Drafters
0131	Drafter, Electrical	4	Electrical Drafters*
0995	Drafter, Electronic	4	Electronic Drafters
0133	Drafter, Heating and Ventilating	4	Architectural Drafters*
0134	Drafter, Landscape	4	Architectural Drafters*
0135	Drafter, Marine	4	Architectural Drafters*
0136	Drafter, Mechanical	4	Mechanical Drafters
0111	Drafter, Plumbing	4	Architectural Drafters*
0139	Drafter, Structural	3	Architectural Drafters*
0140	Drafter, Tool Design	4	Mechanical Drafters
1054	E-Commerce Specialist	competency	Computer Specialists, All Other
0155	Electrical Technician	4	Electrical Engineering Technicians*
0157	Electrical-Instrument Repairer	3	Calibration and Instrumentation Technicians*
0167	Electromechanical Technician	3	Electro-Mechanical Technicians*
0169	Electronics Technician	4	Electronics Engineering Technicians*
0764	Engineering Assistant, Mechanical Equipment	4	Mechanical Drafters
0648	Environmental Analyst	3.5	Environmental Scientists and Specialists, Including Health*
0965	Estimator and Drafter	4	Electrical Drafters*
0207	Foundry Metallurgist	4	Materials Engineers*
0217	Geodetic Computator	2	Mapping Technicians
0257	Heat-Transfer Technician	4	Mechanical Engineering Technicians*
0236	Horticulturist	3	Plant Scientists*
0259	Industrial Engineering Technician	4	Industrial Engineering Technicians*
1060	Information Assurance (IA) Specialist	3	Computer Security Specialists*

Interest Field: Science, Math, and Engineering

RAIS Code	RAIS Apprenticeship Title	Years	Title of Related O*NET Job
0941	Inspector, Building	3	Construction and Building Inspectors
0644	Instrument Mechanic (Any Industry)	4	Calibration and Instrumentation Technicians*
0996	Instrument Mechanic, Weapons System	4	Calibration and Instrumentation Technicians*
0775	Instrument Repairer (Any Industry)	4	Calibration and Instrumentation Technicians*
0252	Instrument Technician (Utilities)	4	Calibration and Instrumentation Technicians*
0255	Instrumentation Technician	4	Calibration and Instrumentation Technicians*
1038	Internetworking Technician	2.5	Network Systems and Data Communications Analysts*
1059	IT Generalist	1.5	Computer Specialists, All Other
1048	IT Project Manager	competency	Computer and Information Systems Managers*
0267	Laboratory Assistant	3	Environmental Science and Protection Technicians, Including Health*
0621	Laboratory Assistant, Metallurgical	2	Engineering Technicians, Except Drafters, All Other*
0268	Laboratory Technician	1	Chemical Technicians*
0269	Laboratory Tester	2	Chemical Technicians*
0328	Materials Engineer	5	Materials Engineers*
0777	Mechanical-Engineering Technician	4	Mechanical Engineering Technicians*
0940	Meteorologist	3	Atmospheric and Space Scientists*
1029	Mine Inspector (Government) Coal	4	Mining and Geological Engineers, Including Mining Safety Engineers*
1028	Mine Inspector (Government) Metal/Nonmetal	4	Mining and Geological Engineers, Including Mining Safety Engineers*
1030	Mold Designer (Plastics Industry)	2	Mechanical Drafters
1010	Nondestructive Tester	1	Engineering Technicians, Except Drafters, All Other*
0368	Optomechanical Technician	4	Mechanical Engineering Technicians*
0546	Photogrammetric Technician	3	Mapping Technicians
0949	Programmer, Engineering and Scientific	4	Computer Programmers*
0462	Quality Control Technician	2	Industrial Engineering Technicians*
0788	Research Mechanic	4	Aerospace Engineering and Operations Technicians*
0450	Soil-Conservation Technician	3	Soil Conservationists*
0551	Surveyor Assistant, Instruments	2	Surveying Technicians
0190	Test Equipment Mechanic	5	Aerospace Engineering and Operations Technicians*
0482	Test-Engine Operator, Geologic Samples	2	Geological Sample Test Technicians*
0956	Tester, Geologic Samples	3	Geological Sample Test Technicians*

*Jobs marked with * usually require college and are not included in Parts III or IV. Jobs marked with ‡ were ranked 251 or lower and are not included in Parts III or IV.*

(continued)

(continued)

Interest Field: Science, Math, and Engineering

RAIS Code	RAIS Apprenticeship Title	Years	Title of Related O*NET Job
0587	Tool Design Checker	4	Mechanical Engineering Technicians*
0580	Tool Designer	4	Mechanical Engineers*
0690	Tool Programmer, Numerical Control	3	Numerical Tool and Process Control Programmers
0001	Weather Observer	2	Life, Physical, and Social Science Technicians, All Other*
0498	Welding Technician	4	Engineering Technicians, Except Drafters, All Other*
0499	Wind Tunnel Mechanic	4	Aerospace Engineering and Operations Technicians*

*Jobs marked with * usually require college and are not included in Parts III or IV. Jobs marked with ‡ were ranked 251 or lower and are not included in Parts III or IV.*

Interest Field: Plants and Animals

RAIS Code	RAIS Apprenticeship Title	Years	Title of Related O*NET Job
0703	Agricultural Service Worker	2	Pesticide Handlers, Sprayers, and Applicators, Vegetation
0871	Animal Trainer	2	Animal Trainers
0886	Beekeeper	2	Farmers and Ranchers
1000	Exterminator, Termite	2	Pest Control Workers
0177	Farmer, General	1	Farmers and Ranchers
0981	Farmworker, General I	2	Agricultural Equipment Operators
1024	Fish Hatchery Worker	2	Farmworkers, Farm and Ranch Animals‡
0934	Greenskeeper II	2	Landscaping and Groundskeeping Workers
1001	Horse Trainer	1	Animal Trainers
0235	Horseshoer	2	Nonfarm Animal Caretakers
0271	Landscape Gardener	4	Landscaping and Groundskeeping Workers
0574	Landscape Management Technician	1	Landscaping and Groundskeeping Workers
0571	Landscape Technician	2	Landscaping and Groundskeeping Workers
0900	Logger, All-Round	3	Fallers‡
0595	Tree Surgeon	3	Tree Trimmers and Pruners
0607	Tree Trimmer (Line Clear)	2	Tree Trimmers and Pruners

*Jobs marked with * usually require college and are not included in Parts III or IV. Jobs marked with ‡ were ranked 251 or lower and are not included in Parts III or IV.*

Interest Field: Law, Law Enforcement, and Public Safety

RAIS Code	RAIS Apprenticeship Title	Years	Title of Related O*NET Job
0863	Aircraft-Armament Mechanic (Government Service)	4	Artillery and Missile Crew Members‡
0531	Arson and Bomb Investigator	2	Fire Investigators*
0851	Correction Officer	1	Correctional Officers and Jailers
0730	Emergency Medical Technician	3	Emergency Medical Technicians and Paramedics
0535	Fire Apparatus Engineer	3	Municipal Fire Fighters
0576	Fire Captain	3	Municipal Fire Fighting and Prevention Supervisors
0541	Fire Engineer	1	Municipal Fire Fighters
0195	Fire Fighter	3	Municipal Fire Fighters
0192	Fire Fighter, Crash, Fire, and Rescue	1	Municipal Fire Fighters
0516	Fire Inspector	4	Fire Inspectors
0754	Fire Medic	3	Municipal Fire Fighters
0193	Fire-Control Mechanic	1	Artillery and Missile Crew Members‡
0902	Fish and Game Warden	2	Fish and Game Wardens
0695	Guard, Security	1.5	Security Guards
0992	Inspector, Quality Assurance	2	Government Property Inspectors and Investigators
0579	Investigator, Private	1	Private Detectives and Investigators
0372	Ordnance Artificer (Government Services)	1.5	Artillery and Missile Crew Members‡
1003	Paralegal	3	Paralegals and Legal Assistants*
0543	Paramedic	2	Emergency Medical Technicians and Paramedics
0437	Police Officer I	2	Police Patrol Officers
1058	Production Controller	competency	Emergency Management Specialists
1007	Radiation Monitor	4	Nuclear Monitoring Technicians*
0707	Safety Inspector/Technician	3	Occupational Health and Safety Specialists*
0544	Wildland Fire Fighter Specialist	1	Forest Fire Fighters

*Jobs marked with * usually require college and are not included in Parts III or IV. Jobs marked with ‡ were ranked 251 or lower and are not included in Parts III or IV.*

Interest Field: Mechanics, Installers, and Repairers

RAIS Code	RAIS Apprenticeship Title	Years	Title of Related O*NET Job
0990	Air and Hydronic Balancing Technician	3	Heating and Air Conditioning Mechanics
0002	Air-Conditioning Installer-Servicer, Window Unit	3	Electric Home Appliance and Power Tool Repairers
0686	Air-Conditioning Mechanic, Auto Service	1	Automotive Specialty Technicians
0003	Aircraft Mechanic, Electrical and Radio	4	Avionics Technicians
0867	Aircraft-Photographic-Equipment Mechanic	4	Camera and Photographic Equipment Repairers‡
0005	Airframe-and-Power-Plant Mechanic	4	Airframe-and-Power-Plant Mechanics
0012	Artificial-Plastic-Eye Maker	5	Medical Appliance Technicians
0878	Assembly Technician	2	Office Machine and Cash Register Servicers
0880	Audio-Video Repairer	2	Electronic Home Entertainment Equipment Installers and Repairers
0821	Automated Equipment Engineer-Technician	4	Millwrights
0021	Automatic-Equipment Technician	4	Communication Equipment Mechanics, Installers, and Repairers
0023	Automobile Mechanic	4	Automotive Master Mechanics
0024	Automobile-Body Repairer	4	Automotive Body and Related Repairers
0784	Automobile-Radiator Mechanic	2	Automotive Specialty Technicians
1034A	Automotive Technician Specialist	competency	Automotive Specialty Technicians
0836	Automotive-Cooling-System Diagnostic Technician	2	Automotive Specialty Technicians
0882	Automotive-Generator-and-Starter Repairer	2	Electric Motor and Switch Assemblers and Repairers
0027	Automotive-Maintenance-Equipment Servicer	4	Industrial Machinery Mechanics
0605	Aviation Safety Equipment Technician	4	Installation, Maintenance, and Repair Workers, All Other
0599	Aviation Support Equipment Repairer	4	Industrial Machinery Mechanics
0464	Avionics Technician	4	Electrical and Electronics Repairers, Commercial and Industrial Equipment
0029	Bakery-Machine Mechanic	3	Industrial Machinery Mechanics
0885	Battery Repairer	2	Battery Repairers
0888	Biomedical Equipment Technician	4	Medical Equipment Repairers
0892	Brake Repairer	2	Automotive Specialty Technicians
0056	Cable Installer-Repairer	3	Electrical Power-Line Installers and Repairers
0058	Cable Splicer	4	Electrical Power-Line Installers and Repairers
0566	Cable Television Installer	1	Telecommunications Line Installers and Repairers

Interest Field: Mechanics, Installers, and Repairers

RAIS Code	RAIS Apprenticeship Title	Years	Title of Related O*NET Job
0062	Camera Repairer	2	Camera and Photographic Equipment Repairers‡
0790	Canal-Equipment Mechanic	2	Industrial Machinery Mechanics
0642	Car Repairer	4	Rail Car Repairers
0896	Carburetor Mechanic	4	Automotive Specialty Technicians
0072	Cash-Register Servicer	3	Office Machine and Cash Register Servicers
0076	Central-Office Installer	4	Central Office and PBX Installers and Repairers
0077	Central-Office Repairer	4	Central Office and PBX Installers and Repairers
0609	Coin-Machine-Service Repairer	3	Coin, Vending, and Amusement Machine Servicers and Repairers
0086	Composing-Room Machinist	6	Industrial Machinery Mechanics
0336	Construction-Equipment Mechanic	4	Mobile Heavy Equipment Mechanics, Except Engines
0693	Control Equipment Electrician-Technician	5	Electrical and Electronics Repairers, Commercial and Industrial Equipment
0066	Conveyor-Maintenance Mechanic	2	Industrial Machinery Mechanics
0634	Cooling Tower Technician	2	Industrial Machinery Mechanics
0920	Corrosion-Control Fitter	4	Electrical and Electronics Repairers, Powerhouse, Substation, and Relay
1008	Customer Service Representative	3	Gas Appliance Repairers
0099	Dairy-Equipment Repairer	3	Farm Equipment Mechanics‡
0650	Dental-Equipment Installer and Servicer	3	Medical Equipment Repairers
0085	Dictating-Transcribing-Machine Servicer	3	Office Machine and Cash Register Servicers
0124	Diesel Mechanic	4	Bus and Truck Mechanics and Diesel Engine Specialists
0104	Door-Closer Mechanic	3	Mechanical Door Repairers
0154	Electrical-Appliance Repairer	3	Electric Home Appliance and Power Tool Repairers
0156	Electrical-Appliance Servicer	3	Electric Home Appliance and Power Tool Repairers
0160	Electrician, Aircraft	4	Avionics Technicians
0161	Electrician, Automotive	2	Electronic Equipment Installers and Repairers, Motor Vehicles
0162	Electrician, Locomotive	4	Electrical and Electronics Installers and Repairers, Transportation Equipment
0163	Electrician, Powerhouse	4	Electrical and Electronics Repairers, Powerhouse, Substation, and Relay
0164	Electrician, Radio	4	Radio Mechanics‡
0166	Electrician, Substation	3	Electrical and Electronics Repairers, Powerhouse, Substation, and Relay

*Jobs marked with * usually require college and are not included in Parts III or IV. Jobs marked with ‡ were ranked 251 or lower and are not included in Parts III or IV.*

(continued)

(continued)

Interest Field: Mechanics, Installers, and Repairers

RAIS Code	RAIS Apprenticeship Title	Years	Title of Related O*NET Job
0330	Electric-Meter Installer I	4	Electric Meter Installers and Repairers
0151	Electric-Meter Repairer	4	Electric Meter Installers and Repairers
0829	Electric-Motor Assembler and Tester	4	Electric Motor and Switch Assemblers and Repairers
0149	Electric-Motor Repairer	4	Electric Motor and Switch Assemblers and Repairers
0150	Electric-Tool Repairer	4	Electric Home Appliance and Power Tool Repairers
0132	Electric-Track-Switch Maintainer	4	Signal and Track Switch Repairers
0168	Electromedical-Equipment Repairer	2	Medical Equipment Repairers
1041	Electronic Systems Technician	4	Communication Equipment Mechanics, Installers, and Repairers
0137	Electronic-Organ Technician	2	Electronic Home Entertainment Equipment Installers and Repairers
0171	Electronic-Production-Line-Maintenance Mechanic	4	Industrial Machinery Mechanics
0170	Electronics Mechanic	4	Data Processing Equipment Repairers
0906	Electronic-Sales-and-Service Technician	4	Electrical and Electronics Repairers, Commercial and Industrial Equipment
0173	Elevator Constructor	4	Elevator Installers and Repairers
0174	Elevator Repairer	4	Elevator Installers and Repairers
0176	Engine Repairer, Service	4	Outdoor Power Equipment and Other Small Engine Mechanics
0165	Equipment Installer (Telephone and Telegraph)	4	Communication Equipment Mechanics, Installers, and Repairers
0672	Facilities Locator	2	Helpers—Installation, Maintenance, and Repair Workers
0187	Farm-Equipment Mechanic I	3	Farm Equipment Mechanics‡
0789	Farm-Equipment Mechanic II	4	Farm Equipment Mechanics‡
0916	Field Service Engineer	2	Electrical and Electronics Repairers, Commercial and Industrial Equipment
0203	Forge-Shop-Machine Repairer	3	Industrial Machinery Mechanics
0215	Fretted-Instrument Repairer	3	Stringed Instrument Repairers and Tuners‡
0209	Front-End Mechanic	4	Automotive Specialty Technicians
0922	Fuel-Injection Servicer	4	Automotive Specialty Technicians
0610	Fuel-System-Maintenance Worker	2	Industrial Machinery Mechanics
0794	Furnace Installer	3	Heating and Air Conditioning Mechanics
0678	Furnace Installer-and-Repairer, Hot Air	4	Heating and Air Conditioning Mechanics
0594	Gas Utility Worker	2	Valve and Regulator Repairers
0917	Gas-Appliance Servicer	3	Gas Appliance Repairers
0230	Gas-Engine Repairer	4	Outdoor Power Equipment and Other Small Engine Mechanics

Interest Field: Mechanics, Installers, and Repairers

RAIS Code	RAIS Apprenticeship Title	Years	Title of Related O*NET Job
0331	Gas-Meter Mechanic I	3	Meter Mechanics
0232	Gas-Regulator Repairer	3	Valve and Regulator Repairers
0714	Glass Installer, Automobile Service	2	Automotive Glass Installers and Repairers
0637	Heating-and-Air-Conditioning Installer-Servicer	3	Heating and Air Conditioning Mechanics
0651	Hydraulic Repairer	4	Industrial Machinery Mechanics
0783	Hydraulic-Press Servicer	2	Industrial Machinery Mechanics
0237	Hydroelectric-Machinery Mechanic	3	Industrial Machinery Mechanics
1037	Industrial Machine System Technician	2	Industrial Machinery Mechanics
0691	Laundry-Machine Mechanic	3	Industrial Machinery Mechanics
0281	Line Erector	3	Electrical Power-Line Installers and Repairers
0282	Line Installer-Repairer	4	Telecommunications Line Installers and Repairers
0283	Line Maintainer	4	Electrical Power-Line Installers and Repairers
0284	Line Repairer	3	Electrical Power-Line Installers and Repairers
0289	Locksmith	4	Locksmiths and Safe Repairers
0299	Logging-Equipment Mechanic	4	Mobile Heavy Equipment Mechanics, Except Engines
1050	Lubrication Servicer Materials Disposal Technician	2	Installation, Maintenance, and Repair Workers, All Other
0302	Machine Fixer (Carpet and Rug)	4	Industrial Machinery Mechanics
0292	Machine Repairer, Maintenance	4	Industrial Machinery Mechanics
0293	Machinery Erector	4	Millwrights
0297	Machinist, Linotype	4	Industrial Machinery Mechanics
0298	Machinist, Marine Engine	4	Bus and Truck Mechanics and Diesel Engine Specialists
0191	Machinist, Motion-Picture Equipment	2	Camera and Photographic Equipment Repairers‡
0308	Maintenance Mechanic, Any Industry	4	Industrial Machinery Mechanics
0022	Maintenance Mechanic, Bus and Truck	4	Bus and Truck Mechanics and Diesel Engine Specialists
0020	Maintenance Mechanic, Compressed-Gas Plant	4	Industrial Machinery Mechanics
0307	Maintenance Mechanic, Grain and Feed	2	Industrial Machinery Mechanics
0309	Maintenance Mechanic, Telephone	3	Station Installers and Repairers, Telephone
0310	Maintenance Repairer, Building	2	Maintenance and Repair Workers, General
0311	Maintenance Repairer, Industrial	4	Maintenance and Repair Workers, General
0946	Marine-Services Technician	3	Maintenance and Repair Workers, General
0319	Mechanic, Endless Track Vehicle	4	Mobile Heavy Equipment Mechanics, Except Engines
0153	Mechanic, Industrial Truck	4	Bus and Truck Mechanics and Diesel Engine Specialists

*Jobs marked with * usually require college and are not included in Parts III or IV. Jobs marked with ‡ were ranked 251 or lower and are not included in Parts III or IV.*

(continued)

(continued)

Interest Field: Mechanics, Installers, and Repairers

RAIS Code	RAIS Apprenticeship Title	Years	Title of Related O*NET Job
0337	Mechanical-Unit Repairer	4	Rail Car Repairers
0329	Meteorological-Equipment Repairer	4	Electrical and Electronics Repairers, Commercial and Industrial Equipment
0332	Meter Repairer	3	Meter Mechanics
0335	Millwright	4	Millwrights
0350	Mine-Car Repairer	2	Rail Car Repairers
0355	Motorboat Mechanic	3	Motorboat Mechanics
0356	Motorcycle Repairer	3	Motorcycle Mechanics
0359	Office-Machine Servicer	3	Office Machine and Cash Register Servicers
0966	Oil-Burner-Servicer-and-Installer	2	Heating and Air Conditioning Mechanics
0364	Oil-Field Equipment Mechanic	2	Bus and Truck Mechanics and Diesel Engine Specialists
0250	Optical-Instrument Assembler	2	Optical Instrument Assemblers‡
0377	Optician, Optical Goods	4	Optical Instrument Assemblers‡
0911	Orthotics Technician	1	Medical Appliance Technicians
0378	Outboard-Motor Mechanic	2	Motorboat Mechanics
0384	Overhauler (Textile)	2	Industrial Machinery Mechanics
0381	Painter, Transportation Equipment	3	Painters, Transportation Equipment
0924	Photographic Equipment Technician	3	Camera and Photographic Equipment Repairers‡
0563	Photographic-Equipment-Maintenance Technician	3	Camera and Photographic Equipment Repairers‡
0408	Piano Technician	4	Keyboard Instrument Repairers and Tuners‡
0793	Piano Tuner	3	Keyboard Instrument Repairers and Tuners‡
0387	Pinsetter Adjuster, Automatic	3	Industrial Machinery Mechanics
0985	Pinsetter Mechanic, Automatic	2	Maintenance Workers, Machinery
0388	Pipe-Organ Tuner and Repairer	4	Keyboard Instrument Repairers and Tuners‡
0434	Pneumatic-Tool Repairer	4	Industrial Machinery Mechanics
0435	Pneumatic-Tube Repairer	2	Industrial Machinery Mechanics
0443	Powerhouse Mechanic	4	Industrial Machinery Mechanics
0441	Power-Saw Mechanic	3	Outdoor Power Equipment and Other Small Engine Mechanics
0442	Power-Transformer Repairer	4	Transformer Repairers
0646	Private-Branch-Exchange Installer	4	Central Office and PBX Installers and Repairers
1006	Private-Branch-Exchange Repairer	4	Central Office and PBX Installers and Repairers
0456	Propulsion-Motor-and-Generator Repairer	4	Electric Motor and Switch Assemblers and Repairers
0376	Prosthetics Technician	4	Medical Appliance Technicians
0419	Pump Erector (Construction)	2	Industrial Machinery Mechanics

Interest Field: Mechanics, Installers, and Repairers

RAIS Code	RAIS Apprenticeship Title	Years	Title of Related O*NET Job
0933	Pump Servicer	3	Industrial Machinery Mechanics
0465	Radio Mechanic	3	Radio Mechanics‡
0466	Radio Repairer	4	Electronic Home Entertainment Equipment Installers and Repairers
0666	Refrigeration Mechanic	3	Refrigeration Mechanics
0918	Refrigeration Unit Repairer	3	Refrigeration Mechanics
0975	Relay Technician	2	Electrical and Electronics Repairers, Powerhouse, Substation, and Relay
0674	Repairer I	4	Industrial Machinery Mechanics
0421	Repairer, Handtools	3	Hand and Portable Power Tool Repairers
0997	Repairer, Heavy	2	Automotive Master Mechanics
0807	Repairer, Recreational Vehicle	4	Recreational Vehicle Service Technicians
0422	Repairer, Welding Equipment	2	Industrial Machinery Mechanics
1005	Repairer, Welding Systems and Equipment	3	Industrial Machinery Mechanics
0425	Rocket-Engine-Component Mechanic	4	Aircraft Engine Specialists
0485	Rubberizing Mechanic	4	Industrial Machinery Mechanics
0488	Safe-and-Vault Service Mechanic	4	Locksmiths and Safe Repairers
0497	Scale Mechanic	4	Industrial Machinery Mechanics
0446	Service Mechanic (Automobile Manufacturing)	2	Automotive Body and Related Repairers
0615	Service Planner (Light; Heat)	4	Helpers—Installation, Maintenance, and Repair Workers
0508	Sewing-Machine Repairer	3	Industrial Machinery Mechanics
0942	Signal Maintainer	4	Signal and Track Switch Repairers
0525	Small-Engine Mechanic	2	Outdoor Power Equipment and Other Small Engine Mechanics
0528	Sound Technician	3	Communication Equipment Mechanics, Installers, and Repairers
0533	Spring Repairer, Hand	4	Automotive Specialty Technicians
0647	Station Installer-and-Repairer	4	Station Installers and Repairers, Telephone
0467	Stoker Erector-and-Servicer	4	Industrial Machinery Mechanics
0560	Tape-Recorder Repairer	4	Electronic Home Entertainment Equipment Installers and Repairers
0552	Technician, Submarine Cable Equipment	2	Communication Equipment Mechanics, Installers, and Repairers

*Jobs marked with * usually require college and are not included in Parts III or IV. Jobs marked with ‡ were ranked 251 or lower and are not included in Parts III or IV.*

(continued)

(continued)

Interest Field: Mechanics, Installers, and Repairers

RAIS Code	RAIS Apprenticeship Title	Years	Title of Related O*NET Job
0618	Telecommunications Technician	4	Communication Equipment Mechanics, Installers, and Repairers
0565	Television-and-Radio Repairer	4	Electronic Home Entertainment Equipment Installers and Repairers
0589	Tractor Mechanic	4	Bus and Truck Mechanics and Diesel Engine Specialists
0590	Transformer Repairer	4	Transformer Repairers
0592	Transmission Mechanic	2	Automotive Master Mechanics
0847	Treatment-Plant Mechanic	3	Industrial Machinery Mechanics
0858	Trouble Shooter II	3	Electrical Power-Line Installers and Repairers
0598	Truck-Body Builder	4	Automotive Body and Related Repairers
0600	Tune-Up Mechanic	2	Automotive Specialty Technicians
1034	Undercar Specialist	2	Automotive Specialty Technicians
0616	Watch Repairer	4	Watch Repairers‡
0357	Wind-Instrument Repairer	4	Reed or Wind Instrument Repairers and Tuners‡

*Jobs marked with * usually require college and are not included in Parts III or IV. Jobs marked with ‡ were ranked 251 or lower and are not included in Parts III or IV.*

Interest Field: Construction, Mining, and Drilling

RAIS Code	RAIS Apprenticeship Title	Years	Title of Related O*NET Job
0861	Acoustical Carpenter	4	Ceiling Tile Installers
0105	Architectural Coatings Finisher	3	Painters, Construction and Maintenance
0872	Asphalt-Paving-Machine Operator	3	Paving, Surfacing, and Tamping Equipment Operators
0877	Assembler, Metal Building	2	Structural Iron and Steel Workers
0036	Boatbuilder, Wood	4	Boat Builders and Shipwrights
0038	Boilerhouse Mechanic	3	Boilermakers
0039	Boilermaker Fitter	4	Boilermakers
0040	Boilermaker I	3	Boilermakers
0041	Boilermaker II	3	Boilermakers
0051	Bricklayer (Brick and Tile)	4	Brickmasons and Blockmasons
0052	Bricklayer (Construction)	3	Brickmasons and Blockmasons
0706	Bricklayer, Firebrick and Refractory Tile	4	Brickmasons and Blockmasons
0067	Carpenter	4	Construction Carpenters
0653	Carpenter, Interior Systems	4	Construction Carpenters
0068	Carpenter, Maintenance	4	Construction Carpenters

Interest Field: Construction, Mining, and Drilling

RAIS Code	RAIS Apprenticeship Title	Years	Title of Related O*NET Job
0762	Carpenter, Mold	6	Construction Carpenters
1009	Carpenter, Piledriver	4	Rough Carpenters
0069	Carpenter, Rough	4	Rough Carpenters
0070	Carpenter, Ship	4	Ship Carpenters and Joiners
0071	Carpet Layer	3	Carpet Installers
0073	Casket Assembler	3	Carpenter Assemblers and Repairers
0075	Cement Mason	2	Cement Masons and Concrete Finishers
0849	Chimney Repairer	1	Brickmasons and Blockmasons
0661	Construction Craft Laborer	2	Construction Laborers
0091	Coppersmith	4	Pipe Fitters
0095	Cork Insulator, Refrigeration Plant	4	Insulation Workers, Floor, Ceiling, and Wall
0125	Drilling-Machine Operator	3	Mine Cutting and Channeling Machine Operators‡
0145	Dry-Wall Applicator	2	Drywall Installers
0159	Electrician (Construction)	4	Electricians
0771	Electrician (Ship-Boat Manufacturing)	4	Electricians
0158	Electrician (Water Transportation)	4	Electricians
0643	Electrician, Maintenance	4	Electricians
0138	Elevating-Grader Operator	2	Grader, Bulldozer, and Scraper Operators
0711	Fence Erector	3	Fence Erectors
0199	Floor Layer	3	Floor Layers, Except Carpet, Wood, and Hard Tiles
0201	Floor-Covering Layer	3	Floor Layers, Except Carpet, Wood, and Hard Tiles
0206	Form Builder	2	Rough Carpenters
0964	Gas-Main Fitter	4	Pipe Fitters
0221	Glazier	3	Glaziers
0222	Glazier, Stained Glass	4	Glaziers
0591	Hazardous-Waste Material Technician	2	Construction and Related Workers, All Other
0909	Insulation Worker	4	Insulation Workers, Floor, Ceiling, and Wall
0264	Joiner	4	Ship Carpenters and Joiners
0272	Lather	3	Construction Carpenters
1049	Maintenance Technician, Municipal	2	Construction Laborers
0973	Marble Finisher	2	Helpers—Brickmasons, Blockmasons, Stonemasons, and Tile and Marble Setters‡
0313	Marble Setter	3	Stonemasons
0354	Miner I (Mine and Quarry)	1	Helpers—Extraction Workers‡

*Jobs marked with * usually require college and are not included in Parts III or IV. Jobs marked with ‡ were ranked 251 or lower and are not included in Parts III or IV.*

(continued)

(continued)

Interest Field: Construction, Mining, and Drilling

RAIS Code	RAIS Apprenticeship Title	Years	Title of Related O*NET Job
0352	Monument Setter	4	Stonemasons
0353	Mosaic Worker	3	Tile and Marble Setters
0932	Motor-Grader Operator	3	Grader, Bulldozer, and Scraper Operators
0692	Neon-Sign Servicer	4	Electricians
0365	Operating Engineer	3	Operating Engineers
0373	Ornamental-Iron Worker	3	Construction and Related Workers, All Other
0379	Painter	1	Painters, Construction and Maintenance
0385	Painter, Shipyard	3	Painters, Construction and Maintenance
0390	Paperhanger	2	Paperhangers
1042	Pavement Striper	2	Painters, Construction and Maintenance
0411	Pipe Coverer and Insulator	4	Insulation Workers, Mechanical
0414A	Pipe Fitter — Sprinkler Fitter	4	Pipe Fitters
0414	Pipe Fitter, Construction	4	Pipe Fitters
0412	Pipe Fitter, Ship and Boat	4	Pipe Fitters
0423	Plasterer	2	Plasterers and Stucco Masons
0432	Plumber	4	Plumbers
0455	Prop Maker	4	Construction Carpenters
0416	Prospecting Driller	2	Rotary Drill Operators, Oil and Gas
0459	Protective-Signal Installer	4	Electricians
0006	Protective-Signal Repairer	3	Electricians
0471	Reinforcing-Metal Worker	3	Reinforcing Iron and Rebar Workers
0564	Residential Carpenter	2	Construction Carpenters
1022	Residential Wireperson	2.4	Electricians
0474	Rigger (Any Industry)	3	Riggers
0473	Rigger (Ship-Boat Manufacturing)	2	Riggers
0480	Roofer	2	Roofers
0493	Sandblaster, Stone	3	Stone Cutters and Carvers
0510	Sheet-Metal Worker	4	Sheet Metal Workers
0979	Shipwright	4	Boat Builders and Shipwrights
0517	Sign Erector I	3	Construction and Related Workers, All Other
0449	Soft-Tile Setter	3	Floor Layers, Except Carpet, Wood, and Hard Tiles
0460	Steam Service Inspector	4	Pipe Fitters
0539	Stone Carver	3	Stone Cutters and Carvers
0542	Stonecutter, Hand	3	Stone Cutters and Carvers
0540	Stonemason	3	Stonemasons
0545	Street-Light Servicer	4	Electricians

Interest Field: Construction, Mining, and Drilling

RAIS Code	RAIS Apprenticeship Title	Years	Title of Related O*NET Job
0669	Structural-Steel Worker	3	Structural Iron and Steel Workers
0558	Tank Setter	2	Structural Iron and Steel Workers
0561	Taper	2	Tapers
0972	Terrazzo Finisher	2	Terrazzo Workers and Finishers
0568	Terrazzo Worker	3	Terrazzo Workers and Finishers
0971	Tile Finisher	2	Helpers—Brickmasons, Blockmasons, Stonemasons, and Tile and Marble Setters‡
0573	Tile Setter	3	Tile and Marble Setters
0680	Tuckpointer, Cleaner, Caulker	3	Construction Laborers
0629	Well-Drill Operator	4	Well and Core Drill Operators

Interest Field: Transportation

RAIS Code	RAIS Apprenticeship Title	Years	Title of Related O*NET Job
1043	Able Seaman	1.4	Able Seamen‡
1046	Air Transport Pilot	3.4	Commercial Pilots
0724	Ambulance Attendant	1	Ambulance Drivers and Attendants, Except Emergency Medical Technicians
1032	Construction Driver	4	Truck Drivers, Heavy
0117	Dredge Operator	4	Dredge Operators
0287	Locomotive Engineer	2	Locomotive Engineers
0623	Pilot, Ship	3	Pilots, Ship*
0980	Truck Driver, Heavy	3	Truck Drivers, Heavy

*Jobs marked with * usually require college and are not included in Parts III or IV. Jobs marked with ‡ were ranked 251 or lower and are not included in Parts III or IV.*

Interest Field: Industrial Production

RAIS Code	RAIS Apprenticeship Title	Years	Title of Related O*NET Job
0860	Accordion Maker	4	Cabinetmakers and Bench Carpenters
0865	Aircraft Mechanic, Armament (Aircraft Manufacturing)	4	Aircraft Systems Assemblers, Precision‡

(continued)

(continued)

Interest Field: Industrial Production

RAIS Code	RAIS Apprenticeship Title	Years	Title of Related O*NET Job
0866	Aircraft Mechanic, Plumbing and Hydraulics	4	Aircraft Systems Assemblers, Precision‡
0868	Airplane Coverer	4	Production Workers, All Other
0004	Airplane Inspector	3	Mechanical Inspectors
0873	Assembler, Aircraft Power Plant	2	Engine and Other Machine Assemblers‡
0874	Assembler, Aircraft, Structures and Surfaces	4	Aircraft Structure Assemblers, Precision‡
0876	Assembler-Installer, General	2	Aircraft Structure Assemblers, Precision‡
0903	Assistant Press Operator	2	Printing Press Machine Operators and Tenders
0779	Auger Press Operator, Manual Control	2	Extruding, Forming, Pressing, and Compacting Machine Operators and Tenders‡
0881	Automobile Tester	4	Mechanical Inspectors
0638	Automobile-Repair-Service Estimator	4	Mechanical Inspectors
0028	Baker (Bakery Products)	3	Bakers, Manufacturing
0884	Batch-And-Furnace Operator	4	Furnace, Kiln, Oven, Drier, and Kettle Operators and Tenders‡
0031	Bench Hand	2	Bench Workers, Jewelry‡
0887	Ben-Day Artist	6	Precision Printing Workers
0033	Bindery Worker	4	Bindery Machine Operators and Tenders‡
0026	Bindery-Machine Setter	4	Bindery Machine Setters and Set-Up Operators‡
0035	Blacksmith	4	Metal Workers and Plastic Workers, All Other
0889	Blocker and Cutter, Contact Lens	1	Precision Lens Grinders and Polishers‡
0815	Boiler Operator	4	Stationary Engineers
0047	Bookbinder	5	Bookbinders‡
0891	Bracelet and Brooch Maker	4	Bench Workers, Jewelry‡
0893	Brilliandeer-Lopper	3	Gem and Diamond Workers‡
0662	Butcher, All-Round	3	Slaughterers and Meat Packers
0054	Buttermaker	1.2	Separating, Filtering, Clarifying, Precipitating, and Still Machine Setters, Operators, and Tenders
0055	Cabinetmaker	4	Cabinetmakers and Bench Carpenters
0059	Cable Tester	4	Electrical and Electronic Inspectors and Testers
1031	Calibrator, Military (Instruments and Apparatus)	2	Precision Devices Inspectors and Testers
0065	Candy Maker	3	Food Batchmakers
0641	Canvas Worker	3	Production Workers, All Other
0898	Card Grinder	4	Tool Grinders, Filers, and Sharpeners‡
0899	Carpet Cutter (Retail Trade)	1	Cutters and Trimmers, Hand‡

Interest Field: Industrial Production

RAIS Code	RAIS Apprenticeship Title	Years	Title of Related O*NET Job
0042	Carver, Hand	4	Cabinetmakers and Bench Carpenters
0043	Casing-in-Line Setter	4	Bindery Machine Setters and Set-Up Operators‡
0074	Caster	2	Bench Workers, Jewelry‡
0044	Caster	2	Metal Molding, Coremaking, and Casting Machine Operators and Tenders
0046	Cell Maker	1	Molding and Casting Workers
0049	Chaser	4	Silversmiths‡
0078	Cheesemaker	2	Food Batchmakers
0791	Chemical Operator III	3	Chemical Equipment Controllers and Operators
0057	Chief Operator	3	Chemical Plant and System Operators
0060	Clarifying-Plant Operator	1	Water and Liquid Waste Treatment Plant and System Operators
1025	Coating-Machine Operator I	1	Coating, Painting, and Spraying Machine Operators and Tenders
0084	Colorist, Photography	2	Photographic Retouchers and Restorers‡
0061	Complaint Inspector	4	Electrical and Electronic Inspectors and Testers
0087	Compositor	4	Hand Compositors and Typesetters
0904	Contour Wire Specialist, Denture	4	Dental Laboratory Technicians‡
0557	Conveyor-System Operator	1	Conveyor Operators and Tenders
0094	Coremaker	4	Foundry Mold and Coremakers‡
0991	Cupola Tender	3	Metal-Refining Furnace Operators and Tenders‡
0613	Cutter, Machine I	3	Cutters and Trimmers, Hand‡
0080	Cylinder Grinder	5	Tool Grinders, Filers, and Sharpeners‡
0677	Cylinder-Press Operator	4	Letterpress Setters and Set-Up Operators
0100	Decorator (Glass Manufacturing; Glass Products)	4	Painting, Coating, and Decorating Workers
0102	Dental Ceramist	2	Dental Laboratory Technicians‡
0103	Dental-Laboratory Technician	3	Dental Laboratory Technicians‡
0107	Designer and Patternmaker	2	Fabric and Apparel Patternmakers‡
0083	Diamond Selector (Jewelry-Silver)	4	Gem and Diamond Workers‡
0114	Die Finisher	4	Tool and Die Makers
0668	Die Maker, Bench, Stamping	4	Tool and Die Makers
0115	Die Maker, Jewelry and Silver	4	Tool and Die Makers
0654	Die Maker, Paper Goods	4	Tool and Die Makers

*Jobs marked with * usually require college and are not included in Parts III or IV. Jobs marked with ‡ were ranked 251 or lower and are not included in Parts III or IV.*

(continued)

(continued)

Interest Field: Industrial Production

RAIS Code	RAIS Apprenticeship Title	Years	Title of Related O*NET Job
0118	Die Maker, Stamping	3	Tool and Die Makers
0119	Die Maker, Trim	4	Tool and Die Makers
0939	Die Maker, Wire Drawing	3	Tool and Die Makers
0120	Die Polisher	1	Tool Grinders, Filers, and Sharpeners‡
0121	Die Setter	2	Forging Machine Setters, Operators, and Tenders, Metal and Plastic‡
0122	Die Sinker	4	Tool and Die Makers
0093	Diesel-Engine Tester	4	Mechanical Inspectors
0957	Dragline Operator	1	Dragline Operators
0905	Electric-Distribution Checker	2	Electrical and Electronic Inspectors and Testers
0792	Electric-Meter Tester	4	Precision Devices Inspectors and Testers
0927	Electric-Motor-and-Generator Assembler	2	Engine and Other Machine Assemblers‡
0652	Electric-Sign Assembler	4	Electrical and Electronic Equipment Assemblers‡
0570	Electronics Tester	3	Electrical and Electronic Inspectors and Testers
0967	Electronics Utility Worker	4	Production Workers, All Other
1036	Electrostatic Powder Coating Technician	4	Coating, Painting, and Spraying Machine Setters and Set-Up Operators
0172	Electrotyper	5	Electrotypers and Stereotypers
0704	Embosser	2	Embossing Machine Set-Up Operators
0684	Embossing-Press Operator	4	Embossing Machine Set-Up Operators
0143	Engine Turner	2	Bench Workers, Jewelry‡
0249	Engineering Model Maker	4	Model Makers, Metal and Plastic
0142	Engine-Lathe Set-Up Operator	2	Lathe and Turning Machine Tool Setters, Operators, and Tenders, Metal and Plastic
0782	Engine-Lathe Set-Up Operator, Tool	2	Lathe and Turning Machine Tool Setters, Operators, and Tenders, Metal and Plastic
0963	Engraver, Machine	4	Engraver Set-Up Operators
0915	Engraving-Press Operator	3	Engraver Set-Up Operators
0180	Envelope-Folding-Machine Adjuster	3	Paper Goods Machine Setters, Operators, and Tenders
0183	Experimental Assembler	2	Materials Inspectors
0184	Experimental Mechanic	4	Model Makers, Metal and Plastic
0185	Extruder Operator	1	Extruding and Drawing Machine Setters, Operators, and Tenders, Metal and Plastic
0833	Fabricator-Assembler, Metal Products	4	Metal Fabricators, Structural Metal Products
0808	Fastener Technologist	3	Forging Machine Setters, Operators, and Tenders, Metal and Plastic‡
0921	Film Developer	3	Photographic Processing Machine Operators‡

Interest Field: Industrial Production

RAIS Code	RAIS Apprenticeship Title	Years	Title of Related O*NET Job
0907	Film Laboratory Technician	3	Photographic Processing Machine Operators‡
0908	Film Laboratory Technician I	3	Film Laboratory Technicians‡
0181	Finisher, Denture	1	Dental Laboratory Technicians‡
0188	Firer, Kiln	3	Furnace, Kiln, Oven, Drier, and Kettle Operators and Tenders‡
1052	Firer, Marine	1	Boiler Operators and Tenders, Low Pressure
0197	Fitter (Machine Shop)	2	Fitters, Structural Metal—Precision
0189	Fitter I (Any Industry)	3	Fitters, Structural Metal—Precision
0198	Fixture Maker	2	Machinists
0194	Folding-Machine Operator	2	Bindery Machine Setters and Set-Up Operators‡
0196	Forging-Press Operator I	1	Forging Machine Setters, Operators, and Tenders, Metal and Plastic‡
0200	Former, Hand (Any Industry)	2	Metal Fabricators, Structural Metal Products
0048	Forming-Machine Operator	4	Extruding, Forming, Pressing, and Compacting Machine Setters and Set-Up Operators‡
0204	Fourdrinier-Machine Operator	3	Separating, Filtering, Clarifying, Precipitating, and Still Machine Setters, Operators, and Tenders
0208	Four-Slide-Machine Setter	2	Combination Machine Tool Setters and Set-Up Operators, Metal and Plastic
0211	Freezer Operator	1	Cooling and Freezing Equipment Operators and Tenders‡
0220	Fur Cutter	2	Cutters and Trimmers, Hand‡
0210	Fur Finisher	2	Sewing Machine Operators, Garment‡
0944	Furnace Operator	4	Metal-Refining Furnace Operators and Tenders‡
0212	Furniture Finisher	3	Furniture Finishers‡
0228	Gang Sawyer, Stone	2	Stone Sawyers
0226	Gauger	2	Gaugers
0241	Gear Hobber Set-Up Operator	4	Combination Machine Tool Setters and Set-Up Operators, Metal and Plastic
0234	Gear-Cutting-Machine Set-Up Operator (Machine Shop)	3	Combination Machine Tool Setters and Set-Up Operators, Metal and Plastic
0664	Gear-Cutting-Machine Set-Up Operator, Tool (Machine Shop)	3	Combination Machine Tool Setters and Set-Up Operators, Metal and Plastic
0242	Gem Cutter	3	Gem and Diamond Workers‡
0984	Grader	4	Production Inspectors, Testers, Graders, Sorters, Samplers, Weighers

Jobs marked with * usually require college and are not included in Parts III or IV. Jobs marked with ‡ were ranked 251 or lower and are not included in Parts III or IV.

(continued)

(continued)

Interest Field: Industrial Production

RAIS Code	RAIS Apprenticeship Title	Years	Title of Related O*NET Job
0244	Grinder I (Clock and Watch)	4	Grinding, Honing, Lapping, and Deburring Machine Set-Up Operators‡
0671	Grinder Operator, Tool	4	Tool Grinders, Filers, and Sharpeners‡
0635	Grinder Set-Up Operator, Jig	4	Grinding, Honing, Lapping, and Deburring Machine Set-Up Operators‡
0974	Grinder Set-Up Operator, Universal	4	Tool Grinders, Filers, and Sharpeners‡
0229	Gunsmith	4	Combination Machine Tool Setters and Set-Up Operators, Metal and Plastic
0248	Harpsichord Maker	2	Cabinetmakers and Bench Carpenters
0253	Hat-Block Maker (Woodworking)	3	Cabinetmakers and Bench Carpenters
0831	Head Sawyer	3	Sawing Machine Setters and Set-Up Operators‡
0233	Heat Treater I	4	Heat Treating, Annealing, and Tempering Machine Operators and Tenders, Metal and Plastic‡
0947	Heavy Forger	4	Forging Machine Setters, Operators, and Tenders, Metal and Plastic‡
0238	Hydroelectric-Station Operator	3	Power Generating Plant Operators, Except Auxiliary Equipment Operators
0239	Hydrometer Calibrator	2	Precision Devices Inspectors and Testers
0246	Injection-Molding-Machine Operator	1	Plastic Molding and Casting Machine Setters and Set-Up Operators
0968	Inspector, Electromechanical	4	Precision Devices Inspectors and Testers
0697	Inspector, Metal Fabricating	4	Materials Inspectors
0581	Inspector, Motor Vehicles	4	Motor Vehicle Inspectors
0380	Inspector, Outside Production	4	Materials Inspectors
0424	Inspector, Precision	2	Precision Devices Inspectors and Testers
0636	Inspector, Set-Up and Lay-Out	4	Materials Inspectors
0251	Instrument Maker	4	Machinists
0254	Instrument-Maker and Repairer	5	Machinists
0270	Jacquard-Loom Weaver	4	Textile Knitting and Weaving Machine Setters, Operators, and Tenders‡
0258	Jacquard-Plate Maker	1	Textile Knitting and Weaving Machine Setters, Operators, and Tenders‡
0260	Jeweler	2	Jewelers‡
0261	Jig Builder (Wooden Container)	2	Model Makers, Wood‡
0262	Job Printer	4	Job Printers
0266	Kiln Operator	3	Furnace, Kiln, Oven, Drier, and Kettle Operators and Tenders‡

Interest Field: Industrial Production

RAIS Code	RAIS Apprenticeship Title	Years	Title of Related O*NET Job
0273	Knitter Mechanic	4	Textile Knitting and Weaving Machine Setters, Operators, and Tenders‡
0850	Knitting-Machine Fixer	4	Textile Knitting and Weaving Machine Setters, Operators, and Tenders‡
0275	Last-Model Maker	4	Cabinetmakers and Bench Carpenters
0554	Lay-Out Technician	4	Precision Lens Grinders and Polishers‡
0825	Lay-Out Worker I	4	Lay-Out Workers, Metal and Plastic
0274	Lead Burner	4	Welder-Fitters
0280	Letterer (Professional and Kindred)	2	Precision Printing Workers
0279	Liner (Pottery and Porcelain)	3	Painting, Coating, and Decorating Workers
0063	Lithographic Platemaker	4	Platemakers
0683	Lithograph-Press Operator, Tinware	4	Design Printing Machine Setters and Set-Up Operators
1047	Load Dispatcher	4	Power Distributors and Dispatchers
0290	Loft Worker (Ship-Boat Manufacturing)	4	Model Makers, Wood‡
0841	Loom Fixer	3	Textile Knitting and Weaving Machine Setters, Operators, and Tenders‡
0301	Machine Assembler	2	Engine and Other Machine Assemblers‡
0291	Machine Builder	2	Engine and Other Machine Assemblers‡
0305	Machine Fixer	3	Textile Winding, Twisting, and Drawing Out Machine Setters, Operators, and Tenders‡
0511	Machine Operator I	1	Combination Machine Tool Setters and Set-Up Operators, Metal and Plastic
0938	Machine Setter (Any Industry)	4	Combination Machine Tool Setters and Set-Up Operators, Metal and Plastic
0317	Machine Setter (Clock and Watch)	4	Combination Machine Tool Setters and Set-Up Operators, Metal and Plastic
0263	Machine Setter (Machine Shop)	3	Combination Machine Tool Setters and Set-Up Operators, Metal and Plastic
0321	Machine Setter (Woodworking)	4	Woodworking Machine Setters and Set-Up Operators, Except Sawing‡
0958	Machine Set-Up Operator	2	Combination Machine Tool Setters and Set-Up Operators, Metal and Plastic
0327	Machine Set-Up Operator, Paper Goods	4	Paper Goods Machine Setters, Operators, and Tenders
0659	Machine Try-Out Setter	4	Combination Machine Tool Setters and Set-Up Operators, Metal and Plastic

*Jobs marked with * usually require college and are not included in Parts III or IV. Jobs marked with ‡ were ranked 251 or lower and are not included in Parts III or IV.*

(continued)

(continued)

Interest Field: Industrial Production

RAIS Code	RAIS Apprenticeship Title	Years	Title of Related O*NET Job
0296	Machinist	4	Machinists
0294	Machinist, Automotive	4	Machinists
0295	Machinist, Experimental	4	Machinists
0300	Machinist, Outside (Ship-Boat Manufacturing)	4	Machinists
0303	Machinist, Wood	4	Cabinetmakers and Bench Carpenters
0306	Maintenance Machinist	4	Machinists
0325	Metal Fabricator	4	Metal Fabricators, Structural Metal Products
0333	Miller, Wet Process	3	Crushing, Grinding, and Polishing Machine Setters, Operators, and Tenders‡
0334	Milling-Machine Set-Up Operator I	2	Milling and Planing Machine Setters, Operators, and Tenders, Metal and Plastic‡
0358	Mock-Up Builder	4	Model Makers, Metal and Plastic
0339	Model Builder (Furniture)	2	Model Makers, Metal and Plastic
0491	Model Maker (Automobile Manufacturing)	4	Model Makers, Metal and Plastic
0363	Model Maker (Clock and Watch)	4	Model Makers, Metal and Plastic
0773	Model Maker II (Jewelry-Silver)	4	Model and Mold Makers, Jewelry‡
0341	Model Maker, Aircraft	4	Model Makers, Wood‡
0780	Model Maker, Firearms	4	Model Makers, Metal and Plastic
0342	Model Maker, Wood	4	Model Makers, Wood‡
0343	Model-And-Mold Maker, Brick	2	Production Workers, All Other
0344	Model-And-Mold Maker, Plaster	4	Production Workers, All Other
0345	Mold Maker (Pottery and Porcelain)	3	Mold Makers, Hand
0346	Mold Maker I (Jewelry-Silver)	4	Model and Mold Makers, Jewelry‡
0347	Mold Maker II (Jewelry-Silver)	2	Model and Mold Makers, Jewelry‡
0116	Mold Maker, Die-Casting and Plastic Molding	4	Tool and Die Makers
0348	Mold Setter	1	Plastic Molding and Casting Machine Setters and Set-Up Operators
0349	Molder	4	Foundry Mold and Coremakers‡
0351	Molder, Pattern	4	Precision Pattern and Die Casters, Nonferrous Metals
0931	Multi-Operation-Forming-Machine Setter	4	Metal Workers and Plastic Workers, All Other
0371	Multi-Operation-Machine Operator	3	Forging Machine Setters, Operators, and Tenders, Metal and Plastic‡
0845	Numerical Control Machine Operator	4	Numerical Control Machine Tool Operators and Tenders, Metal and Plastic
0361	Offset-Press Operator I	4	Offset Lithographic Press Setters and Set-Up Operators

Interest Field: Industrial Production

RAIS Code	RAIS Apprenticeship Title	Years	Title of Related O*NET Job
0959	Operational Test Mechanic	3	Materials Inspectors
0032	Optician, Retail Trade	5	Precision Lens Grinders and Polishers‡
0374	Ornamental-Metal Worker	4	Combination Machine Tool Setters and Set-Up Operators, Metal and Plastic
0375	Orthodontic Technician	2	Dental Laboratory Technicians‡
0383	Painter, Hand (Any Industry)	3	Painting, Coating, and Decorating Workers
0386	Painter, Sign	4	Production Workers, All Other
0389	Pantograph-Machine Set-Up Operator	2	Milling and Planing Machine Setters, Operators, and Tenders, Metal and Plastic‡
0710	Patternmaker (Furniture; Garment; Textile Products, Not Elsewhere Classified)	3	Fabric and Apparel Patternmakers‡
0394	Patternmaker (Metal Production, Not Elsewhere Classified)	4	Patternmakers, Metal and Plastic‡
0796	Patternmaker (Stonework)	4	Patternmakers, Metal and Plastic‡
0857	Patternmaker, All-Around	5	Patternmakers, Metal and Plastic‡
0395	Patternmaker, Metal	5	Patternmakers, Metal and Plastic‡
0396	Patternmaker, Metal, Bench	5	Patternmakers, Metal and Plastic‡
0397	Patternmaker, Plaster	3	Production Workers, All Other
0923	Patternmaker, Plastics	3	Patternmakers, Metal and Plastic‡
0398	Patternmaker, Wood	5	Patternmakers, Wood
0982	Pewter Caster	3	Pewter Casters and Finishers‡
0986	Pewter Fabricator	4	Pewter Casters and Finishers‡
0983	Pewter Finisher	2	Pewter Casters and Finishers‡
0988	Pewterer	2	Pewter Casters and Finishers‡
0912	Photograph Retoucher	3	Photographic Retouchers and Restorers‡
0407	Photographic-Plate Maker	4	Platemakers
0417	Pipe-Organ Builder	3	Cabinetmakers and Bench Carpenters
0961	Plant Operator	3	Crushing, Grinding, and Polishing Machine Setters, Operators, and Tenders‡
0393	Plant Operator, Furnace Process	4	Chemical Plant and System Operators
0404	Plaster-Pattern Caster	5	Precision Mold and Pattern Casters, Except Nonferrous Metals
0660	Plastic Process Technician	4	Plastic Molding and Casting Machine Setters and Set-Up Operators

*Jobs marked with * usually require college and are not included in Parts III or IV. Jobs marked with ‡ were ranked 251 or lower and are not included in Parts III or IV.*

(continued)

(continued)

Interest Field: Industrial Production

RAIS Code	RAIS Apprenticeship Title	Years	Title of Related O*NET Job
0426	Plastic Tool Maker	4	Tool and Die Makers
0843	Plastic-Fixture Builder	4	Tool and Die Makers
0186	Plastics Fabricator	2	Production Workers, All Other
0427	Plate Finisher	6	Plate Finishers
0430	Platen-Press Operator	4	Letterpress Setters and Set-Up Operators
0431	Plater	3	Electrolytic Plating and Coating Machine Setters and Set-Up Operators, Metal and Plastic‡
0901	Pony Edger	2	Sawing Machine Operators and Tenders‡
0440	Power-Plant Operator	4	Power Generating Plant Operators, Except Auxiliary Equipment Operators
0410	Precision Assembler	3	Aircraft Systems Assemblers, Precision‡
0962	Precision Assembler, Bench	2	Electromechanical Equipment Assemblers‡
0277	Precision-Lens Grinder	4	Precision Lens Grinders and Polishers‡
0928	Press Operator, Heavy Duty	4	Press and Press Brake Machine Setters and Set-Up Operators, Metal and Plastic
0452	Printer, Plastic	4	Design Printing Machine Setters and Set-Up Operators
0451	Printer-Slotter Operator	4	Printing Press Machine Operators and Tenders
1023	Production Finisher	2	Coating, Painting, and Spraying Machine Setters and Set-Up Operators
1027	Production Technologist	competency	Team Assemblers
0413	Projection Printer	4	Photographic Reproduction Technicians‡
0288	Proof-Press Operator	5	Printing Press Machine Operators and Tenders
0415	Proofsheet Corrector	4	Hand Compositors and Typesetters
0846	Prototype Model Maker	4	Model Makers, Metal and Plastic
0950	Pumper-Gauger	1	Tank Car, Truck, and Ship Loaders‡
0461	Purification Operator II	4	Separating, Filtering, Clarifying, Precipitating, and Still Machine Setters, Operators, and Tenders
0936	Quality-Control Inspector	2	Materials Inspectors
0468	Radiographer	4	Materials Inspectors
0420	Recovery Operator (Paper and Pulp)	1	Separating, Filtering, Clarifying, Precipitating, and Still Machine Setters, Operators, and Tenders
0852	Refinery Operator	3	Petroleum Refinery and Control Panel Operators
0687	Relay Tester	4	Electrical and Electronic Inspectors and Testers
0092	Reproduction Technician	1	Photographic Reproduction Technicians‡
0475	Rocket-Motor Mechanic	4	Machinists
0428	Roll-Threader Operator	1	Rolling Machine Setters, Operators, and Tenders, Metal and Plastic‡

Interest Field: Industrial Production

RAIS Code	RAIS Apprenticeship Title	Years	Title of Related O*NET Job
0481	Rotogravure-Press Operator	4	Printing Press Machine Operators and Tenders
0429	Rubber Tester	4	Materials Inspectors
0484	Rubber-Stamp Maker	4	Molding and Casting Workers
0490	Sample Maker, Appliances	4	Model Makers, Metal and Plastic
0495	Saw Filer	4	Tool Grinders, Filers, and Sharpeners‡
0496	Saw Maker	3	Tool and Die Makers
0855	Scanner Operator	2	Scanner Operators
0520	Screen Printer	2	Painting, Coating, and Decorating Workers
0500	Screw-Machine Operator, Multiple Spindle	4	Lathe and Turning Machine Tool Setters, Operators, and Tenders, Metal and Plastic
0444	Screw-Machine Operator, Single Spindle	3	Lathe and Turning Machine Tool Setters, Operators, and Tenders, Metal and Plastic
0502	Screw-Machine Set-Up Operator	4	Lathe and Turning Machine Tool Setters, Operators, and Tenders, Metal and Plastic
0506	Screw-Machine Set-Up Operator, Single Spindle	3	Lathe and Turning Machine Tool Setters, Operators, and Tenders, Metal and Plastic
0611	Ship Propeller Finisher	3	Metal Fabricators, Structural Metal Products
0513	Shipfitter (Ship-Boat Manufacturing)	4	Lay-Out Workers, Metal and Plastic
0524	Shop Optician, Benchroom	4	Precision Lens Grinders and Polishers‡
0526	Shop Optician, Surface Room	4	Precision Lens Grinders and Polishers‡
0518	Sign Writer, Hand	1	Production Workers, All Other
0519	Silk-Screen Cutter	3	Cutters and Trimmers, Hand‡
0522	Silversmith II	3	Silversmiths‡
0448	Sketch Maker I (Printing and Publishing)	5	Precision Printing Workers
0453	Solderer, Jewelry	3	Bench Workers, Jewelry‡
0530	Spinner, Hand	3	Lathe and Turning Machine Tool Setters, Operators, and Tenders, Metal and Plastic
0457	Spring Coiling Machine Setter	4	Press and Press Brake Machine Setters and Set-Up Operators, Metal and Plastic
0532	Spring Maker	4	Combination Machine Tool Setters and Set-Up Operators, Metal and Plastic
0534	Spring-Manufacturing Set-Up Technician	4	Combination Machine Tool Setters and Set-Up Operators, Metal and Plastic
0536	Stationary Engineer	4	Stationary Engineers

*Jobs marked with * usually require college and are not included in Parts III or IV. Jobs marked with ‡ were ranked 251 or lower and are not included in Parts III or IV.*

(continued)

(continued)

Interest Field: Industrial Production

RAIS Code	RAIS Apprenticeship Title	Years	Title of Related O*NET Job
0785	Steel-Die Printer	4	Embossing Machine Set-Up Operators
0463	Stencil Cutter	2	Production Workers, All Other
0538	Stereotyper	6	Electrotypers and Stereotypers
0017	Stone Polisher, Machine	3	Buffing and Polishing Set-Up Operators‡
0312	Stone Setter	4	Bench Workers, Jewelry‡
0470	Stone-Lathe Operator	3	Cutting and Slicing Machine Operators and Tenders
0726	Stripper	5	Strippers
0064	Stripper, Lithographic II	4	Strippers
0553	Substation Operator	4	Power Distributors and Dispatchers
0478	Surface-Plate Finisher	2	Crushing, Grinding, and Polishing Machine Setters, Operators, and Tenders‡
0801	Switchboard Operator, Utilities	3	Power Distributors and Dispatchers
0559	Tap-and-Die-Maker Technician	4	Tool and Die Makers
0567	Template Maker	4	Patternmakers, Metal and Plastic‡
0123	Template Maker, Extrusion Die	4	Patternmakers, Metal and Plastic‡
0483	Test Technician	5	Machinists
0572	Testing-and-Regulating Technician	4	Electrical and Electronic Inspectors and Testers
0489	Thermometer Tester	1	Production Inspectors, Testers, Graders, Sorters, Samplers, Weighers
0575	Tinter (Paint and Varnish)	2	Mixing and Blending Machine Setters, Operators, and Tenders
0205	Tool Builder	4	Model Makers, Metal and Plastic
0582	Tool Grinder I	3	Tool Grinders, Filers, and Sharpeners‡
0584	Tool Maker	4	Tool and Die Makers
0585	Tool Maker, Bench	4	Tool and Die Makers
0586	Tool-and-Die Maker	4	Tool and Die Makers
0765	Tool-Grinder Operator	4	Tool Grinders, Filers, and Sharpeners‡
0588	Tool-Machine Set-Up Operator	3	Combination Machine Tool Setters and Set-Up Operators, Metal and Plastic
0805	Trouble Locator, Test Desk	2	Electrical and Electronic Inspectors and Testers
0014	Truck-Crane Operator	3	Crane and Tower Operators
0601	Turbine Operator	4	Power Generating Plant Operators, Except Auxiliary Equipment Operators
1021	Turret-Lathe Set-Up Operator, Tool	4	Lathe and Turning Machine Tool Setters, Operators, and Tenders, Metal and Plastic
0492	Violin Maker, Hand	4	Cabinetmakers and Bench Carpenters
0612	Wallpaper Printer I	4	Design Printing Machine Setters and Set-Up Operators

Interest Field: Industrial Production

RAIS Code	RAIS Apprenticeship Title	Years	Title of Related O*NET Job
0614	Waste-Treatment Operator	2	Water and Liquid Waste Treatment Plant and System Operators
0507	Wastewater-Treatment-Plant Operator	2	Water and Liquid Waste Treatment Plant and System Operators
0619	Water-Treatment-Plant Operator	3	Water and Liquid Waste Treatment Plant and System Operators
0667	Web-Press Operator	4	Letterpress Setters and Set-Up Operators
0620	Welder, Arc	4	Welders and Cutters
0622	Welder, Combination	3	Welders and Cutters
0627	Welder-Fitter	4	Welder-Fitters
0945	Welding-Machine Operator, Arc	3	Welding Machine Setters and Set-Up Operators
0034	Wine Maker	2	Industrial Production Managers*
0501	Wire Sawyer	2	Stone Sawyers
0504	Wire Weaver, Cloth	4	Textile Knitting and Weaving Machine Setters, Operators, and Tenders‡
0633	Wirer, Office Machines	2	Electrical and Electronic Equipment Assemblers‡
0505	Wood-Turning-Lathe Operator	1	Woodworking Machine Operators and Tenders, Except Sawing‡
0919	X-Ray-Equipment Tester	2	Precision Devices Inspectors and Testers

Interest Field: Business Detail

RAIS Code	RAIS Apprenticeship Title	Years	Title of Related O*NET Job
0870	Alarm Operator	1	Police, Fire, and Ambulance Dispatchers
0676	Computer Operator	3	Computer Operators
0817	Computer Peripheral Equipment Operator	1	Computer Operators
0681	Dispatcher, Service	2	Dispatchers, Except Police, Fire, and Ambulance
0800	Legal Secretary	1	Legal Secretaries
0286	Linotype Operator	5	Typesetting and Composing Machine Operators and Tenders
0304	Mailer	4	Mail Clerks, Except Mail Machine Operators and Postal Service‡

*Jobs marked with * usually require college and are not included in Parts III or IV. Jobs marked with ‡ were ranked 251 or lower and are not included in Parts III or IV.*

(continued)

(continued)

Interest Field: Business Detail

RAIS Code	RAIS Apprenticeship Title	Years	Title of Related O*NET Job
0856	Material Coordinator	2	Production, Planning, and Expediting Clerks
0751	Medical Secretary	1	Medical Secretaries
0367	Monotype-Keyboard Operator	3	Typesetting and Composing Machine Operators and Tenders
1033	Office Manager/Administrative Services	2	Administrative Services Managers*
0285	Photocomposing-Perforator-Machine Operator	2	Data Entry Keyers
0596	Post-Office Clerk	2	Postal Service Clerks
0445	Script Supervisor	1	Secretaries, Except Legal, Medical, and Executive
0366	Supercargo	2	Production, Planning, and Expediting Clerks
1002	Telecommunicator	4	Police, Fire, and Ambulance Dispatchers
0951	Telegraphic-Typewriter Operator	3	Word Processors and Typists
1055	Teller (Financial)	1	Tellers
0655	Transportation Clerk	1.5	Cargo and Freight Agents
1004	Tumor Registrar	2	Medical Records and Health Information Technicians*

Interest Field: Sales and Marketing

RAIS Code	RAIS Apprenticeship Title	Years	Title of Related O*NET Job
0578	Manager, Retail Store	3	First-Line Supervisors/Managers of Retail Sales Workers
0753	Salesperson, Parts	2	Parts Salespersons

Interest Field: Recreation, Travel, and Other Personal Services

RAIS Code	RAIS Apprenticeship Title	Years	Title of Related O*NET Job
0007	Alteration Tailor	2	Shop and Alteration Tailors‡
0639	Automobile Upholsterer	3	Upholsterers‡
0776	Baker (Hotel and Restaurant)	3	Bakers, Bread and Pastry
0883	Baker, Pizza	1	Cooks, Fast Food
0030	Barber	1	Barbers‡
0608	Bartender	1	Bartenders
0890	Bootmaker, Hand	1	Shoe and Leather Workers and Repairers‡

Interest Field: Recreation, Travel, and Other Personal Services

RAIS Code	RAIS Apprenticeship Title	Years	Title of Related O*NET Job
0894	Butcher, Meat	3	Butchers and Meat Cutters
0897	Card Cutter, Jacquard	4	Textile, Apparel, and Furnishings Workers, All Other‡
1053	Chief Cook (Water Transportation)	2	Chefs and Head Cooks
0090	Cook (Any Industry)	2	Cooks, Institution and Cafeteria
0663	Cook (Hotel and Restaurant)	3	Cooks, Restaurant
0722	Cook, Pastry	3	Bakers, Bread and Pastry
0096	Cosmetologist	1	Hairdressers, Hairstylists, and Cosmetologists
0314	Custom Tailor	4	Custom Tailors‡
0144	Dressmaker	4	Custom Tailors‡
0649	Dry Cleaner	3	Laundry and Drycleaning Machine Operators and Tenders, Except Pressing
0665	Embalmer	2	Embalmers
0213	Furniture Upholsterer	4	Upholsterers‡
0214	Furrier	4	Custom Tailors‡
0245	Harness Maker	3	Shoe and Leather Workers and Repairers‡
1035	Hotel Associate	2	Hotel, Motel, and Resort Desk Clerks
0943	Housekeeper, Commercial, Residential, or Industrial	1	Maids and Housekeeping Cleaners
0935	Leather Stamper	1	Shoe and Leather Workers and Repairers‡
0593	Manager, Food Service	3	Food Service Managers
0316	Meat Cutter	3	Butchers and Meat Cutters
0688	Multi-Story Window/Building Exterior Cleaner	3	Janitors and Cleaners, Except Maids and Housekeeping Cleaners
0910	Orthopedic-Boot-and-Shoe Designer and Maker	5	Shoe and Leather Workers and Repairers‡
0433	Rug Cleaner, Hand	1	Building Cleaning Workers, All Other
0487	Saddle Maker	2	Shoe and Leather Workers and Repairers‡
0436	Sample Stitcher	4	Shop and Alteration Tailors‡
0514	Shoe Repairer	3	Shoe and Leather Workers and Repairers‡
0812	Shoemaker, Custom	3	Shoe and Leather Workers and Repairers‡
0515	Shop Tailor	4	Shop and Alteration Tailors‡
0838	Swimming-Pool Servicer	2	Janitors and Cleaners, Except Maids and Housekeeping Cleaners
0097	Upholsterer (Aircraft Manufacturing)	2	Upholsterers‡
0606	Upholsterer, Inside (Furniture)	3	Upholsterers‡

*Jobs marked with * usually require college and are not included in Parts III or IV. Jobs marked with ‡ were ranked 251 or lower and are not included in Parts III or IV.*

Interest Field: Education and Social Service

RAIS Code	RAIS Apprenticeship Title	Years	Title of Related O*NET Job
0840	Child Care Development Specialist	2	Child Care Workers
0569	Counselor	2	Educational, Vocational, and School Counselors*
1040	Direct Support Specialist, Human Services	competency	Social and Human Service Assistants
0657	Teacher Aide I	2	Teacher Assistants

Interest Field: General Management and Support

RAIS Code	RAIS Apprenticeship Title	Years	Title of Related O*NET Job
1057	Career Development Technician	2	Employment, Recruitment, and Placement Specialists*
0820	Director, Funeral	2	Funeral Directors*
1056	Facility Manager	competency	Property, Real Estate, and Community Association Managers*
0632	Logistics Engineer	4	Logisticians*
0948	Purchasing Agent	4	Purchasing Agents, Except Wholesale, Retail, and Farm Products*
1039	Youth Development Practitioner	1.7	Employment Interviewers, Private or Public Employment Service*

Interest Field: Medical and Health Services

RAIS Code	RAIS Apprenticeship Title	Years	Title of Related O*NET Job
0101	Dental Assistant	1	Dental Assistants
0602	Health Care Sanitary Technician	1	Health Technologists and Technicians, All Other
0323	Medical-Laboratory Technician	2	Medical and Clinical Laboratory Technicians*
0824	Nurse Assistant	1	Nursing Aides, Orderlies, and Attendants
0837	Nurse, Licensed Practical	1	Licensed Practical and Licensed Vocational Nurses
0089	Optician, Dispensing	2	Opticians, Dispensing
0458	Orthotist	4	Orthotists and Prosthetists*
0844	Pharmacist Assistant	1	Pharmacy Technicians
0406	Podiatric Assistant	2	Medical Assistants
0418	Prosthetist	4	Orthotists and Prosthetists*
1051	Surgical Technologist	competency	Surgical Technologists

*Jobs marked with * usually require college and are not included in Parts III or IV. Jobs marked with ‡ were ranked 251 or lower and are not included in Parts III or IV.*

PART III

The Best Jobs Lists: Jobs You Can Enter Through Apprenticeship

This part contains a lot of interesting lists, and it's a good place for you to start using the book. Here are some suggestions for using the lists to explore career options:

⑥ The Table of Contents at the beginning of this book presents a complete listing of the list titles in this section. You can browse the lists or use the Table of Contents to find those that interest you most.

⑥ We gave the lists clear titles, so most require little explanation. We provide comments for each group of lists.

⑥ As you review the lists, one or more of the jobs may appeal to you enough that you want to seek additional information. As this happens, mark that job (or, if someone else will be using this book, write it on a separate sheet of paper) so that you can look up the description of the job in Part IV.

⑥ Keep in mind that all jobs in these lists meet our basic criteria for being included in this book. All lists, therefore, emphasize occupations with high pay, high growth, or large numbers of openings. These measures are easily quantified and are often presented in lists of best jobs in the newspapers and other media. While earnings, growth, and openings are important, there are other factors to consider in your career planning. For example, location, liking the people you work with, having an opportunity to serve others, and enjoying your work are a few of many factors that may define the ideal job for you. These measures are difficult or impossible to quantify and thus are not used in this book, so you will need to consider the importance of these issues yourself.

⑥ All data used to create these lists comes from the U.S. Department of Labor. The earnings figures are based on the average annual pay received by full-time workers. Because the earnings represent the national averages, actual pay rates can vary greatly by location, amount of previous work experience, and other factors, including journey worker status.

Best Jobs Overall: Apprenticeable Jobs with the Highest Pay, Fastest Growth, and Most Openings

The four lists that follow are the most important lists in this book. The first list presents the apprenticeable jobs with the highest combined scores for pay, growth, and number of openings. This is a very appealing list because it represents jobs with the very highest quantifiable measures from our labor market. Three additional lists present apprenticeable jobs with the highest scores in each of three measures: annual earnings, projected percentage growth, and largest number of openings. As you review these lists, keep in mind that the lists include jobs with the highest measures from a database of jobs that included all major jobs that are linked to registered apprenticeships and don't usually require a college degree. Jobs that did not make it onto the list of 250 best apprenticeable jobs are not included in the descriptions in Part IV, although they are named in the list of all registered apprenticeships in Part II.

The 250 Best Apprenticeable Jobs

This is the list that most people want to see first. It includes the 250 jobs you can enter through apprenticeship that have the highest overall combined ratings for earnings, projected growth, and number of openings. (The section in the introduction called "How the Best Apprenticeable Jobs in This Book Were Selected" explains in detail how we rated jobs to assemble this list.)

You'll notice a wide variety of jobs on the list. Among the top 20 are jobs in protective services, construction, high tech, business services, transportation, and health care.

Police Patrol Officers was the occupation with the best total score, and it is on the top of the list. The other occupations follow in descending order based on their total scores. Many jobs had tied scores and are simply listed one after another, so there are often only very small or even no differences between the scores of jobs that are near each other on the list. All other jobs lists in this book (except the jobs linked to the 25 Most Popular Apprenticeships list) use these jobs as their source list. You can find descriptions for each of these jobs in Part IV, beginning on page 121.

Job	Annual Earnings	Percent Growth	Annual Openings
The 250 Best Apprenticeable Jobs			
1. Police Patrol Officers	$44,020	24.7%	67,000
2. Computer Specialists, All Other	$54,070	36.5%	27,000
3. Electricians	$41,680	23.4%	65,000
4. Pipe Fitters	$40,950	18.7%	56,000
5. Plumbers	$40,950	18.7%	56,000

The 250 Best Apprenticeable Jobs

Job	Annual Earnings	Percent Growth	Annual Openings
6. Heating and Air Conditioning Mechanics	$35,160	31.8%	35,000
7. Refrigeration Mechanics	$35,160	31.8%	35,000
8. Truck Drivers, Heavy	$33,310	19.0%	299,000
9. Legal Secretaries	$35,660	18.8%	39,000
10. Correctional Officers and Jailers	$33,160	24.2%	49,000
11. Licensed Practical and Licensed Vocational Nurses	$32,390	20.2%	105,000
12. Forest Fire Fighters	$37,060	20.7%	29,000
13. Municipal Fire Fighters	$37,060	20.7%	29,000
14. Sheet Metal Workers	$35,000	19.8%	30,000
15. Municipal Fire Fighting and Prevention Supervisors	$57,000	18.7%	8,000
16. Telecommunications Line Installers and Repairers	$39,540	18.8%	13,000
17. Production, Planning, and Expediting Clerks	$34,820	14.1%	51,000
18. Food Service Managers	$37,260	11.5%	58,000
19. Brickmasons and Blockmasons	$41,550	14.2%	21,000
20. Boat Builders and Shipwrights	$34,250	10.1%	193,000
21. Carpenter Assemblers and Repairers	$34,250	10.1%	193,000
22. Construction Carpenters	$34,250	10.1%	193,000
23. Rough Carpenters	$34,250	10.1%	193,000
24. Ship Carpenters and Joiners	$34,250	10.1%	193,000
25. Ceiling Tile Installers	$33,670	21.4%	17,000
26. Drywall Installers	$33,670	21.4%	17,000
27. Maintenance and Repair Workers, General	$29,800	16.3%	155,000
28. Cement Masons and Concrete Finishers	$30,780	26.1%	24,000
29. Surgical Technologists	$32,130	27.9%	13,000
30. Welder-Fitters	$29,640	17.0%	71,000
31. Welders and Cutters	$29,640	17.0%	71,000
32. Bus and Truck Mechanics and Diesel Engine Specialists	$34,970	14.2%	28,000
33. Government Property Inspectors and Investigators	$46,780	9.8%	20,000
34. Roofers	$30,020	18.6%	38,000
35. Grader, Bulldozer, and Scraper Operators	$35,030	10.4%	45,000
36. Operating Engineers	$35,030	10.4%	45,000
37. Dental Assistants	$27,700	42.5%	35,000
38. Construction and Building Inspectors	$42,650	13.8%	10,000
39. Automotive Master Mechanics	$31,130	12.4%	100,000
40. Automotive Specialty Technicians	$31,130	12.4%	100,000

(continued)

(continued)

The 250 Best Apprenticeable Jobs

Job	Annual Earnings	Percent Growth	Annual Openings
41. Structural Iron and Steel Workers	$40,730	15.9%	9,000
42. Data Processing Equipment Repairers	$33,780	15.1%	19,000
43. Office Machine and Cash Register Servicers	$33,780	15.1%	19,000
44. Aircraft Engine Specialists	$43,560	11.0%	12,000
45. Airframe-and-Power-Plant Mechanics	$43,560	11.0%	12,000
46. Automotive Body and Related Repairers	$33,140	13.2%	23,000
47. Tapers	$39,130	20.8%	5,000
48. Costume Attendants	$25,410	27.8%	66,000
49. Medical Assistants	$24,170	58.9%	78,000
50. Painters, Transportation Equipment	$34,100	17.5%	9,000
51. First-Line Supervisors/Managers of Retail Sales Workers	$30,680	9.1%	251,000
52. Tile and Marble Setters	$35,610	26.5%	4,000
53. Carpet Installers	$32,900	16.8%	10,000
54. Electrical and Electronics Repairers, Commercial and Industrial Equipment	$42,200	10.3%	10,000
55. Emergency Management Specialists	$45,090	28.2%	2,000
56. Elevator Installers and Repairers	$55,960	17.1%	3,000
57. Social and Human Service Assistants	$23,860	48.7%	63,000
58. Installation, Maintenance, and Repair Workers, All Other	$33,010	12.2%	22,000
59. Private Detectives and Investigators	$30,410	25.3%	9,000
60. Water and Liquid Waste Treatment Plant and System Operators	$33,910	16.0%	9,000
61. Dispatchers, Except Police, Fire, and Ambulance	$30,390	14.4%	28,000
62. Painters, Construction and Maintenance	$29,360	11.6%	69,000
63. Mapping Technicians	$29,520	23.1%	10,000
64. Surveying Technicians	$29,520	23.1%	10,000
65. Security Guards	$19,660	31.9%	228,000
66. Nursing Aides, Orderlies, and Attendants	$20,490	24.9%	302,000
67. Chefs and Head Cooks	$28,750	15.8%	33,000
68. Emergency Medical Technicians and Paramedics	$24,440	33.1%	32,000
69. Machinists	$33,090	8.2%	30,000
70. Mobile Heavy Equipment Mechanics, Except Engines	$36,800	9.6%	12,000
71. Pharmacy Technicians	$22,760	28.8%	39,000
72. Medical Secretaries	$26,000	17.2%	50,000
73. Glaziers	$32,310	17.2%	7,000
74. Teacher Assistants	$19,000	23.0%	259,000
75. Landscaping and Groundskeeping Workers	$19,940	22.0%	203,000

The 250 Best Apprenticeable Jobs

Job	Annual Earnings	Percent Growth	Annual Openings
76. Health Technologists and Technicians, All Other	$49,710	18.9%	1,000
77. Industrial Machinery Mechanics	$38,440	5.5%	19,000
78. Sound Engineering Technicians	$38,290	25.5%	2,000
79. Electric Meter Installers and Repairers	$42,540	12.0%	5,000
80. Meter Mechanics	$42,540	12.0%	5,000
81. Valve and Regulator Repairers	$42,540	12.0%	5,000
82. Audio and Video Equipment Technicians	$30,810	26.7%	5,000
83. Cartoonists	$35,420	16.5%	4,000
84. Painters and Illustrators	$35,420	16.5%	4,000
85. Desktop Publishers	$31,590	29.2%	4,000
86. Construction Laborers	$24,670	14.2%	166,000
87. Medical Equipment Repairers	$37,960	14.8%	4,000
88. Cargo and Freight Agents	$31,990	15.5%	8,000
89. Plasterers and Stucco Masons	$33,060	13.5%	8,000
90. Central Office and PBX Installers and Repairers	$48,230	–0.6%	23,000
91. Communication Equipment Mechanics, Installers, and Repairers	$48,230	–0.6%	23,000
92. Station Installers and Repairers, Telephone	$48,230	–0.6%	23,000
93. Janitors and Cleaners, Except Maids and Housekeeping Cleaners	$18,410	18.3%	454,000
94. Commercial Pilots	$49,830	14.9%	2,000
95. Construction and Related Workers, All Other	$22,900	32.0%	17,000
96. Motor Vehicle Inspectors	$49,590	7.7%	5,000
97. Dragline Operators	$32,150	8.9%	14,000
98. Cooks, Restaurant	$19,260	15.9%	211,000
99. Crane and Tower Operators	$37,150	10.8%	5,000
100. Hotel, Motel, and Resort Desk Clerks	$17,450	23.9%	46,000
101. Insulation Workers, Floor, Ceiling, and Wall	$29,190	15.8%	9,000
102. Insulation Workers, Mechanical	$29,190	15.8%	9,000
103. Helpers—Installation, Maintenance, and Repair Workers	$21,240	20.3%	33,000
104. Civil Drafters	$37,690	4.2%	14,000
105. Floor Layers, Except Carpet, Wood, and Hard Tiles	$34,840	13.4%	4,000
106. Camera Operators, Television, Video, and Motion Picture	$34,330	13.4%	4,000
107. Police, Fire, and Ambulance Dispatchers	$28,290	12.7%	15,000
108. Model Makers, Metal and Plastic	$43,470	14.6%	1,000
109. Electrical Power-Line Installers and Repairers	$48,960	1.6%	9,000
110. Millwrights	$42,390	5.3%	7,000

(continued)

(continued)

The 250 Best Apprenticeable Jobs

Job	Annual Earnings	Percent Growth	Annual Openings
111. Opticians, Dispensing	$26,350	18.2%	10,000
112. Nonfarm Animal Caretakers	$17,190	22.2%	32,000
113. Tree Trimmers and Pruners	$25,630	18.6%	11,000
114. Reinforcing Iron and Rebar Workers	$34,950	16.7%	2,000
115. Riggers	$33,800	14.3%	3,000
116. Electrical and Electronic Inspectors and Testers	$27,750	4.7%	87,000
117. Materials Inspectors	$27,750	4.7%	87,000
118. Mechanical Inspectors	$27,750	4.7%	87,000
119. Precision Devices Inspectors and Testers	$27,750	4.7%	87,000
120. Production Inspectors, Testers, Graders, Sorters, Samplers, Weighers	$27,750	4.7%	87,000
121. Fire Inspectors	$44,250	11.6%	1,000
122. Numerical Tool and Process Control Programmers	$38,330	13.0%	2,000
123. Numerical Control Machine Tool Operators and Tenders, Metal and Plastic	$29,420	9.3%	11,000
124. Mechanical Drafters	$41,520	1.9%	9,000
125. Pest Control Workers	$24,990	17.0%	11,000
126. Production Workers, All Other	$22,260	11.3%	67,000
127. Hairdressers, Hairstylists, and Cosmetologists	$18,700	14.7%	68,000
128. Paving, Surfacing, and Tamping Equipment Operators	$29,240	12.6%	8,000
129. Design Printing Machine Setters and Set-Up Operators	$29,340	4.6%	30,000
130. Embossing Machine Set-Up Operators	$29,340	4.6%	30,000
131. Engraver Set-Up Operators	$29,340	4.6%	30,000
132. Letterpress Setters and Set-Up Operators	$29,340	4.6%	30,000
133. Offset Lithographic Press Setters and Set-Up Operators	$29,340	4.6%	30,000
134. Precision Printing Workers	$29,340	4.6%	30,000
135. Printing Press Machine Operators and Tenders	$29,340	4.6%	30,000
136. Professional Photographers	$25,050	13.6%	18,000
137. Child Care Workers	$16,430	11.7%	406,000
138. Slaughterers and Meat Packers	$20,420	18.1%	23,000
139. Actors	$26,460	17.7%	8,000
140. Coin, Vending, and Amusement Machine Servicers and Repairers	$27,800	15.2%	7,000
141. Building Cleaning Workers, All Other	$20,990	16.1%	24,000
142. Recreational Vehicle Service Technicians	$27,270	21.8%	4,000
143. Job Printers	$30,850	9.2%	7,000
144. Dredge Operators	$27,800	8.9%	14,000

The 250 Best Apprenticeable Jobs

Job	Annual Earnings	Percent Growth	Annual Openings
145. Locksmiths and Safe Repairers	$28,760	21.0%	3,000
146. Stonemasons	$34,000	14.1%	2,000
147. Tellers	$20,670	9.4%	127,000
148. Press and Press Brake Machine Setters and Set-Up Operators, Metal and Plastic	$25,210	6.8%	37,000
149. Maids and Housekeeping Cleaners	$16,600	9.2%	352,000
150. Fitters, Structural Metal—Precision	$28,990	6.2%	14,000
151. Metal Fabricators, Structural Metal Products	$28,990	6.2%	14,000
152. Coating, Painting, and Spraying Machine Operators and Tenders	$25,720	9.4%	17,000
153. Coating, Painting, and Spraying Machine Setters and Set-Up Operators	$25,720	9.4%	17,000
154. Mechanical Door Repairers	$29,620	21.8%	1,000
155. Laundry and Drycleaning Machine Operators and Tenders, Except Pressing	$16,920	12.3%	47,000
156. Lay-Out Workers, Metal and Plastic	$31,970	15.6%	1,000
157. Metal Workers and Plastic Workers, All Other	$28,400	6.6%	11,000
158. Electrical and Electronics Installers and Repairers, Transportation Equipment	$39,300	7.1%	2,000
159. Bakers, Bread and Pastry	$20,990	11.2%	29,000
160. Bakers, Manufacturing	$20,990	11.2%	29,000
161. Electronic Drafters	$41,730	0.7%	5,000
162. Motorboat Mechanics	$29,170	18.3%	2,000
163. Combination Machine Tool Setters and Set-Up Operators, Metal and Plastic	$29,050	8.3%	8,000
164. Chemical Equipment Controllers and Operators	$38,740	–3.8%	8,000
165. Maintenance Workers, Machinery	$33,000	5.9%	5,000
166. Boiler Operators and Tenders, Low Pressure	$43,420	0.3%	4,000
167. Extruding and Drawing Machine Setters, Operators, and Tenders, Metal and Plastic	$26,450	7.1%	14,000
168. Stationary Engineers	$43,420	0.3%	4,000
169. Fish and Game Wardens	$41,380	7.1%	1,000
170. Power Generating Plant Operators, Except Auxiliary Equipment Operators	$50,860	0.3%	3,000
171. Cabinetmakers and Bench Carpenters	$24,550	9.4%	15,000
172. Avionics Technicians	$43,110	3.4%	3,000
173. Bartenders	$15,040	8.6%	100,000

(continued)

(continued)

The 250 Best Apprenticeable Jobs

Job	Annual Earnings	Percent Growth	Annual Openings
174. Conveyor Operators and Tenders	$24,690	12.4%	9,000
175. Well and Core Drill Operators	$32,540	7.7%	3,000
176. Metal Molding, Coremaking, and Casting Machine Operators and Tenders	$23,930	8.9%	18,000
177. Plastic Molding and Casting Machine Setters and Set-Up Operators	$23,930	8.9%	18,000
178. Postal Service Clerks	$39,790	–0.5%	5,000
179. Secretaries, Except Legal, Medical, and Executive	$25,420	–2.9%	254,000
180. Cutting and Slicing Machine Operators and Tenders	$26,060	6.6%	12,000
181. Stone Sawyers	$26,060	6.6%	12,000
182. Outdoor Power Equipment and Other Small Engine Mechanics	$24,820	18.9%	3,000
183. Painting, Coating, and Decorating Workers	$21,650	17.6%	6,000
184. Tool and Die Makers	$42,990	0.4%	3,000
185. Broadcast Technicians	$28,090	11.3%	4,000
186. Locomotive Engineers	$45,990	–7.2%	4,000
187. Embalmers	$34,350	8.3%	1,000
188. Floral Designers	$19,660	12.4%	13,000
189. Motorcycle Mechanics	$27,630	18.7%	1,000
190. Ambulance Drivers and Attendants, Except Emergency Medical Technicians	$19,000	26.7%	4,000
191. Merchandise Displayers and Window Trimmers	$22,030	11.3%	10,000
192. Electrical and Electronics Repairers, Powerhouse, Substation, and Relay	$52,040	–0.6%	2,000
193. Computer Operators	$29,970	–16.7%	27,000
194. Gas Appliance Repairers	$29,890	5.5%	5,000
195. Gaugers	$49,970	–11.0%	3,000
196. Petroleum Refinery and Control Panel Operators	$49,970	–11.0%	3,000
197. Boilermakers	$43,240	1.7%	2,000
198. Battery Repairers	$32,310	5.3%	3,000
199. Cooks, Fast Food	$14,450	4.9%	165,000
200. Electric Home Appliance and Power Tool Repairers	$32,310	5.3%	3,000
201. Electric Motor and Switch Assemblers and Repairers	$32,310	5.3%	3,000
202. Hand and Portable Power Tool Repairers	$32,310	5.3%	3,000
203. Paperhangers	$32,040	5.9%	3,000
204. Transformer Repairers	$32,310	5.3%	3,000
205. Chemical Plant and System Operators	$44,050	–12.3%	4,000

The 250 Best Apprenticeable Jobs

Job	Annual Earnings	Percent Growth	Annual Openings
206. Medical Appliance Technicians	$27,890	16.1%	1,000
207. Team Assemblers	$23,180	−1.6%	143,000
208. Welding Machine Setters and Set-Up Operators	$29,110	0.9%	10,000
209. Rail Car Repairers	$39,610	4.5%	1,000
210. Paper Goods Machine Setters, Operators, and Tenders	$28,920	−2.8%	16,000
211. Electronic Home Entertainment Equipment Installers and Repairers	$27,340	8.6%	5,000
212. Lathe and Turning Machine Tool Setters, Operators, and Tenders, Metal and Plastic	$30,300	0.8%	7,000
213. Terrazzo Workers and Finishers	$27,710	15.2%	1,000
214. Separating, Filtering, Clarifying, Precipitating, and Still Machine Setters, Operators, and Tenders	$31,720	0.8%	5,000
215. Automotive Glass Installers and Repairers	$27,160	10.7%	3,000
216. Power Distributors and Dispatchers	$55,010	−3.0%	1,000
217. Pesticide Handlers, Sprayers, and Applicators, Vegetation	$25,490	9.7%	5,000
218. Cooks, Institution and Cafeteria	$18,300	2.1%	121,000
219. Animal Trainers	$22,350	14.3%	4,000
220. Parts Salespersons	$24,510	−2.0%	37,000
221. Patternmakers, Wood	$29,650	11.8%	fewer than 500
222. Fence Erectors	$22,580	13.4%	4,000
223. Word Processors and Typists	$27,150	−38.6%	45,000
224. Data Entry Keyers	$22,600	−5.4%	72,000
225. Food Batchmakers	$21,900	7.2%	10,000
226. Mixing and Blending Machine Setters, Operators, and Tenders	$27,940	−6.5%	14,000
227. Agricultural Equipment Operators	$17,880	7.3%	14,000
228. Signal and Track Switch Repairers	$43,690	−3.1%	1,000
229. Farmers and Ranchers	$24,076	−20.6%	118,000
230. Glass Blowers, Molders, Benders, and Finishers	$24,780	6.4%	6,000
231. Mold Makers, Hand	$24,780	6.4%	6,000
232. Molding and Casting Workers	$24,780	6.4%	6,000
233. Potters	$24,780	6.4%	6,000
234. Precision Mold and Pattern Casters, Except Nonferrous Metals	$24,780	6.4%	6,000
235. Precision Pattern and Die Casters, Nonferrous Metals	$24,780	6.4%	6,000
236. Rotary Drill Operators, Oil and Gas	$34,910	1.5%	2,000
237. Stone Cutters and Carvers	$24,780	6.4%	6,000

(continued)

(continued)

The 250 Best Apprenticeable Jobs

Job	Annual Earnings	Percent Growth	Annual Openings
238. Camera Operators	$31,660	–11.2%	6,000
239. Dot Etchers	$31,660	–11.2%	6,000
240. Electrotypers and Stereotypers	$31,660	–11.2%	6,000
241. Hand Compositors and Typesetters	$31,660	–11.2%	6,000
242. Paste-Up Workers	$31,660	–11.2%	6,000
243. Photoengravers	$31,660	–11.2%	6,000
244. Plate Finishers	$31,660	–11.2%	6,000
245. Platemakers	$31,660	–11.2%	6,000
246. Scanner Operators	$31,660	–11.2%	6,000
247. Strippers	$31,660	–11.2%	6,000
248. Typesetting and Composing Machine Operators and Tenders	$31,660	–11.2%	6,000
249. Butchers and Meat Cutters	$25,570	–2.5%	21,000
250. Electronic Equipment Installers and Repairers, Motor Vehicles	$26,280	14.8%	1,000

The 100 Best-Paying Apprenticeable Jobs

Of the 250 jobs that met our criteria for this book, this list shows the 100 with the highest earnings. This is a popular list, for obvious reasons.

If you look at the descriptions of these jobs in Part IV, you'll notice that the number of years required to complete the apprenticeship varies quite a lot. There is not a very strong link between the number of years of apprenticeship and the amount of pay. But note that the highest-paying job on the list, Municipal Fire Fighting and Prevention Supervisors, requires more than just the three-year apprenticeship called Fire Captain; to qualify for the Fire Captain apprenticeship, you must previously have logged some years of experience as a Municipal Fire Fighter, which itself requires a three-year apprenticeship.

Among the top 25, technology is a common factor: Several of the jobs are in the energy industry, communications, or transportation.

As you review this list, keep in mind what we said earlier about how earnings can vary by region of the country, amount of experience, and many other factors. For example, when you have journey worker status in an occupation, you are likely to be paid more than the average amount listed here because this amount is based on the earnings of *everyone* working in the job, including apprentices and those who learned informally.

The 100 Best-Paying Apprenticeable Jobs

Job	Annual Earnings
1. Municipal Fire Fighting and Prevention Supervisors	$57,000
2. Elevator Installers and Repairers	$55,960
3. Power Distributors and Dispatchers	$55,010
4. Computer Specialists, All Other	$54,070
5. Electrical and Electronics Repairers, Powerhouse, Substation, and Relay	$52,040
6. Power Generating Plant Operators, Except Auxiliary Equipment Operators	$50,860
7. Gaugers	$49,970
8. Petroleum Refinery and Control Panel Operators	$49,970
9. Commercial Pilots	$49,830
10. Health Technologists and Technicians, All Other	$49,710
11. Motor Vehicle Inspectors	$49,590
12. Electrical Power-Line Installers and Repairers	$48,960
13. Central Office and PBX Installers and Repairers	$48,230
14. Communication Equipment Mechanics, Installers, and Repairers	$48,230
15. Station Installers and Repairers, Telephone	$48,230
16. Government Property Inspectors and Investigators	$46,780
17. Locomotive Engineers	$45,990
18. Emergency Management Specialists	$45,090
19. Fire Inspectors	$44,250
20. Chemical Plant and System Operators	$44,050
21. Police Patrol Officers	$44,020
22. Signal and Track Switch Repairers	$43,690
23. Aircraft Engine Specialists	$43,560
24. Airframe-and-Power-Plant Mechanics	$43,560
25. Model Makers, Metal and Plastic	$43,470
26. Boiler Operators and Tenders, Low Pressure	$43,420
27. Stationary Engineers	$43,420
28. Boilermakers	$43,240
29. Avionics Technicians	$43,110
30. Tool and Die Makers	$42,990
31. Construction and Building Inspectors	$42,650
32. Electric Meter Installers and Repairers	$42,540
33. Meter Mechanics	$42,540
34. Valve and Regulator Repairers	$42,540
35. Millwrights	$42,390
36. Electrical and Electronics Repairers, Commercial and Industrial Equipment	$42,200
37. Electronic Drafters	$41,730

(continued)

(continued)

The 100 Best-Paying Apprenticeable Jobs

Job	Annual Earnings
38. Electricians	$41,680
39. Brickmasons and Blockmasons	$41,550
40. Mechanical Drafters	$41,520
41. Fish and Game Wardens	$41,380
42. Pipe Fitters	$40,950
43. Plumbers	$40,950
44. Structural Iron and Steel Workers	$40,730
45. Postal Service Clerks	$39,790
46. Rail Car Repairers	$39,610
47. Telecommunications Line Installers and Repairers	$39,540
48. Electrical and Electronics Installers and Repairers, Transportation Equipment	$39,300
49. Tapers	$39,130
50. Chemical Equipment Controllers and Operators	$38,740
51. Industrial Machinery Mechanics	$38,440
52. Numerical Tool and Process Control Programmers	$38,330
53. Sound Engineering Technicians	$38,290
54. Medical Equipment Repairers	$37,960
55. Civil Drafters	$37,690
56. Food Service Managers	$37,260
57. Crane and Tower Operators	$37,150
58. Forest Fire Fighters	$37,060
59. Municipal Fire Fighters	$37,060
60. Mobile Heavy Equipment Mechanics, Except Engines	$36,800
61. Legal Secretaries	$35,660
62. Tile and Marble Setters	$35,610
63. Cartoonists	$35,420
64. Painters and Illustrators	$35,420
65. Heating and Air Conditioning Mechanics	$35,160
66. Refrigeration Mechanics	$35,160
67. Grader, Bulldozer, and Scraper Operators	$35,030
68. Operating Engineers	$35,030
69. Sheet Metal Workers	$35,000
70. Bus and Truck Mechanics and Diesel Engine Specialists	$34,970
71. Reinforcing Iron and Rebar Workers	$34,950
72. Rotary Drill Operators, Oil and Gas	$34,910
73. Floor Layers, Except Carpet, Wood, and Hard Tiles	$34,840
74. Production, Planning, and Expediting Clerks	$34,820

The 100 Best-Paying Apprenticeable Jobs

Job	Annual Earnings
75. Embalmers	$34,350
76. Camera Operators, Television, Video, and Motion Picture	$34,330
77. Boat Builders and Shipwrights	$34,250
78. Carpenter Assemblers and Repairers	$34,250
79. Construction Carpenters	$34,250
80. Rough Carpenters	$34,250
81. Ship Carpenters and Joiners	$34,250
82. Painters, Transportation Equipment	$34,100
83. Stonemasons	$34,000
84. Water and Liquid Waste Treatment Plant and System Operators	$33,910
85. Riggers	$33,800
86. Data Processing Equipment Repairers	$33,780
87. Office Machine and Cash Register Servicers	$33,780
88. Ceiling Tile Installers	$33,670
89. Drywall Installers	$33,670
90. Truck Drivers, Heavy	$33,310
91. Correctional Officers and Jailers	$33,160
92. Automotive Body and Related Repairers	$33,140
93. Machinists	$33,090
94. Plasterers and Stucco Masons	$33,060
95. Installation, Maintenance, and Repair Workers, All Other	$33,010
96. Maintenance Workers, Machinery	$33,000
97. Carpet Installers	$32,900
98. Well and Core Drill Operators	$32,540
99. Licensed Practical and Licensed Vocational Nurses	$32,390
100. Glaziers	$32,310

The 100 Fastest-Growing Apprenticeable Jobs

Of the 250 jobs that met our criteria for this book, this list shows the 100 that are projected to have the highest percentage increase in the number of people employed through 2012.

Note that seven of the top 25 jobs are in the health care field, an industry that is growing quickly and that will provide many opportunities. A large number of the highest-ranked jobs, even in non–health care fields, involve the human touch—providing services to people directly and in person. These jobs are growing so fast partly because they can't be done by computers or by overseas workers.

The 100 Fastest-Growing Apprenticeable Jobs

Job	Percent Growth
1. Medical Assistants	58.9%
2. Social and Human Service Assistants	48.7%
3. Dental Assistants	42.5%
4. Computer Specialists, All Other	36.5%
5. Emergency Medical Technicians and Paramedics	33.1%
6. Construction and Related Workers, All Other	32.0%
7. Security Guards	31.9%
8. Heating and Air Conditioning Mechanics	31.8%
9. Refrigeration Mechanics	31.8%
10. Desktop Publishers	29.2%
11. Pharmacy Technicians	28.8%
12. Emergency Management Specialists	28.2%
13. Surgical Technologists	27.9%
14. Costume Attendants	27.8%
15. Ambulance Drivers and Attendants, Except Emergency Medical Technicians	26.7%
16. Audio and Video Equipment Technicians	26.7%
17. Tile and Marble Setters	26.5%
18. Cement Masons and Concrete Finishers	26.1%
19. Sound Engineering Technicians	25.5%
20. Private Detectives and Investigators	25.3%
21. Nursing Aides, Orderlies, and Attendants	24.9%
22. Police Patrol Officers	24.7%
23. Correctional Officers and Jailers	24.2%
24. Hotel, Motel, and Resort Desk Clerks	23.9%
25. Electricians	23.4%
26. Mapping Technicians	23.1%
27. Surveying Technicians	23.1%
28. Teacher Assistants	23.0%
29. Nonfarm Animal Caretakers	22.2%
30. Landscaping and Groundskeeping Workers	22.0%
31. Mechanical Door Repairers	21.8%
32. Recreational Vehicle Service Technicians	21.8%
33. Ceiling Tile Installers	21.4%
34. Drywall Installers	21.4%
35. Locksmiths and Safe Repairers	21.0%
36. Tapers	20.8%
37. Forest Fire Fighters	20.7%

The 100 Fastest-Growing Apprenticeable Jobs

Job	Percent Growth
38. Municipal Fire Fighters	20.7%
39. Helpers—Installation, Maintenance, and Repair Workers	20.3%
40. Licensed Practical and Licensed Vocational Nurses	20.2%
41. Sheet Metal Workers	19.8%
42. Truck Drivers, Heavy	19.0%
43. Health Technologists and Technicians, All Other	18.9%
44. Outdoor Power Equipment and Other Small Engine Mechanics	18.9%
45. Legal Secretaries	18.8%
46. Telecommunications Line Installers and Repairers	18.8%
47. Motorcycle Mechanics	18.7%
48. Municipal Fire Fighting and Prevention Supervisors	18.7%
49. Pipe Fitters	18.7%
50. Plumbers	18.7%
51. Roofers	18.6%
52. Tree Trimmers and Pruners	18.6%
53. Janitors and Cleaners, Except Maids and Housekeeping Cleaners	18.3%
54. Motorboat Mechanics	18.3%
55. Opticians, Dispensing	18.2%
56. Slaughterers and Meat Packers	18.1%
57. Actors	17.7%
58. Painting, Coating, and Decorating Workers	17.6%
59. Painters, Transportation Equipment	17.5%
60. Glaziers	17.2%
61. Medical Secretaries	17.2%
62. Elevator Installers and Repairers	17.1%
63. Pest Control Workers	17.0%
64. Welder-Fitters	17.0%
65. Welders and Cutters	17.0%
66. Carpet Installers	16.8%
67. Reinforcing Iron and Rebar Workers	16.7%
68. Cartoonists	16.5%
69. Painters and Illustrators	16.5%
70. Maintenance and Repair Workers, General	16.3%
71. Building Cleaning Workers, All Other	16.1%
72. Medical Appliance Technicians	16.1%
73. Water and Liquid Waste Treatment Plant and System Operators	16.0%
74. Cooks, Restaurant	15.9%

(continued)

(continued)

The 100 Fastest-Growing Apprenticeable Jobs

Job	Percent Growth
75. Structural Iron and Steel Workers	15.9%
76. Chefs and Head Cooks	15.8%
77. Insulation Workers, Floor, Ceiling, and Wall	15.8%
78. Insulation Workers, Mechanical	15.8%
79. Lay-Out Workers, Metal and Plastic	15.6%
80. Cargo and Freight Agents	15.5%
81. Coin, Vending, and Amusement Machine Servicers and Repairers	15.2%
82. Terrazzo Workers and Finishers	15.2%
83. Data Processing Equipment Repairers	15.1%
84. Office Machine and Cash Register Servicers	15.1%
85. Commercial Pilots	14.9%
86. Electronic Equipment Installers and Repairers, Motor Vehicles	14.8%
87. Medical Equipment Repairers	14.8%
88. Hairdressers, Hairstylists, and Cosmetologists	14.7%
89. Model Makers, Metal and Plastic	14.6%
90. Dispatchers, Except Police, Fire, and Ambulance	14.4%
91. Animal Trainers	14.3%
92. Riggers	14.3%
93. Brickmasons and Blockmasons	14.2%
94. Bus and Truck Mechanics and Diesel Engine Specialists	14.2%
95. Construction Laborers	14.2%
96. Production, Planning, and Expediting Clerks	14.1%
97. Stonemasons	14.1%
98. Construction and Building Inspectors	13.8%
99. Professional Photographers	13.6%
100. Plasterers and Stucco Masons	13.5%

The 100 Apprenticeable Jobs with the Most Openings

Of the 250 jobs that met our criteria for this book, this list shows the 100 jobs that are projected to have the largest number of job openings per year.

Jobs with many openings present several advantages that may be attractive to you. Because there are many openings, these jobs can be easier to obtain, particularly for those just entering the job market. These jobs may also offer more opportunities to move from one employer to another with relative ease. Though some of these jobs have average or below-average pay, some also pay quite well and can provide good long-term career opportunities or the ability to move up to more responsible roles.

It is interesting to note that high technology does not play a large role among most of the top 25 jobs on this list. Therefore it is not really true that nowadays you must master high-tech skills to be employable. In fact, most of these jobs have so many openings precisely because they require hands-on work and workers cannot be replaced by technology. Most of these jobs also require on-site work, sometimes in-person work, and therefore cannot be exported overseas.

The 100 Apprenticeable Jobs with the Most Openings

Job	Annual Openings
1. Janitors and Cleaners, Except Maids and Housekeeping Cleaners	454,000
2. Child Care Workers	406,000
3. Maids and Housekeeping Cleaners	352,000
4. Nursing Aides, Orderlies, and Attendants	302,000
5. Truck Drivers, Heavy	299,000
6. Teacher Assistants	259,000
7. Secretaries, Except Legal, Medical, and Executive	254,000
8. First-Line Supervisors/Managers of Retail Sales Workers	251,000
9. Security Guards	228,000
10. Cooks, Restaurant	211,000
11. Landscaping and Groundskeeping Workers	203,000
12. Boat Builders and Shipwrights	193,000
13. Carpenter Assemblers and Repairers	193,000
14. Construction Carpenters	193,000
15. Rough Carpenters	193,000
16. Ship Carpenters and Joiners	193,000
17. Construction Laborers	166,000
18. Cooks, Fast Food	165,000
19. Maintenance and Repair Workers, General	155,000
20. Team Assemblers	143,000
21. Tellers	127,000
22. Cooks, Institution and Cafeteria	121,000
23. Farmers and Ranchers	118,000
24. Licensed Practical and Licensed Vocational Nurses	105,000
25. Automotive Master Mechanics	100,000
26. Automotive Specialty Technicians	100,000
27. Bartenders	100,000
28. Electrical and Electronic Inspectors and Testers	87,000

(continued)

(continued)

The 100 Apprenticeable Jobs with the Most Openings

Job	Annual Openings
29. Materials Inspectors	87,000
30. Mechanical Inspectors	87,000
31. Precision Devices Inspectors and Testers	87,000
32. Production Inspectors, Testers, Graders, Sorters, Samplers, Weighers	87,000
33. Medical Assistants	78,000
34. Data Entry Keyers	72,000
35. Welder-Fitters	71,000
36. Welders and Cutters	71,000
37. Painters, Construction and Maintenance	69,000
38. Hairdressers, Hairstylists, and Cosmetologists	68,000
39. Police Patrol Officers	67,000
40. Production Workers, All Other	67,000
41. Costume Attendants	66,000
42. Electricians	65,000
43. Social and Human Service Assistants	63,000
44. Food Service Managers	58,000
45. Pipe Fitters	56,000
46. Plumbers	56,000
47. Production, Planning, and Expediting Clerks	51,000
48. Medical Secretaries	50,000
49. Correctional Officers and Jailers	49,000
50. Laundry and Drycleaning Machine Operators and Tenders, Except Pressing	47,000
51. Hotel, Motel, and Resort Desk Clerks	46,000
52. Grader, Bulldozer, and Scraper Operators	45,000
53. Operating Engineers	45,000
54. Word Processors and Typists	45,000
55. Legal Secretaries	39,000
56. Pharmacy Technicians	39,000
57. Roofers	38,000
58. Parts Salespersons	37,000
59. Press and Press Brake Machine Setters and Set-Up Operators, Metal and Plastic	37,000
60. Dental Assistants	35,000
61. Heating and Air Conditioning Mechanics	35,000
62. Refrigeration Mechanics	35,000
63. Chefs and Head Cooks	33,000
64. Helpers—Installation, Maintenance, and Repair Workers	33,000

The 100 Apprenticeable Jobs with the Most Openings

Job	Annual Openings
65. Emergency Medical Technicians and Paramedics	32,000
66. Nonfarm Animal Caretakers	32,000
67. Design Printing Machine Setters and Set-Up Operators	30,000
68. Embossing Machine Set-Up Operators	30,000
69. Engraver Set-Up Operators	30,000
70. Letterpress Setters and Set-Up Operators	30,000
71. Machinists	30,000
72. Offset Lithographic Press Setters and Set-Up Operators	30,000
73. Precision Printing Workers	30,000
74. Printing Press Machine Operators and Tenders	30,000
75. Sheet Metal Workers	30,000
76. Bakers, Bread and Pastry	29,000
77. Bakers, Manufacturing	29,000
78. Forest Fire Fighters	29,000
79. Municipal Fire Fighters	29,000
80. Bus and Truck Mechanics and Diesel Engine Specialists	28,000
81. Dispatchers, Except Police, Fire, and Ambulance	28,000
82. Computer Operators	27,000
83. Computer Specialists, All Other	27,000
84. Building Cleaning Workers, All Other	24,000
85. Cement Masons and Concrete Finishers	24,000
86. Automotive Body and Related Repairers	23,000
87. Central Office and PBX Installers and Repairers	23,000
88. Communication Equipment Mechanics, Installers, and Repairers	23,000
89. Slaughterers and Meat Packers	23,000
90. Station Installers and Repairers, Telephone	23,000
91. Installation, Maintenance, and Repair Workers, All Other	22,000
92. Brickmasons and Blockmasons	21,000
93. Butchers and Meat Cutters	21,000
94. Government Property Inspectors and Investigators	20,000
95. Data Processing Equipment Repairers	19,000
96. Industrial Machinery Mechanics	19,000
97. Office Machine and Cash Register Servicers	19,000
98. Metal Molding, Coremaking, and Casting Machine Operators and Tenders	18,000
99. Plastic Molding and Casting Machine Setters and Set-Up Operators	18,000
100. Professional Photographers	18,000

Best Apprenticeable Jobs Based on Personality Types

Several popular career assessment inventories organize jobs into groupings based on personality types. The most-used system is one that presents six personality types: Realistic, Investigative, Artistic, Social, Enterprising, and Conventional. This system is used in the *Self-Directed Search (SDS)*, developed by John Holland, and many other inventories.

If you have used one of these career exploration systems, the following lists may help. Even if you have not, you may find the concept of personality types—and the jobs that are related to them—helpful to you.

We've broken down the list of 250 top apprenticeable jobs into five of the six personality types (there were none linked to the Investigative type) and ranked the jobs within each grouping based on their total combined scores for earnings, growth, and annual openings.

Here are brief descriptions for each of the six personality types:

- **Artistic.** These occupations frequently involve working with forms, designs, and patterns. They often require self-expression, and the work can be done without following a clear set of rules.

- **Conventional.** These occupations frequently involve following set procedures and routines. These occupations can include working with data and details more than with ideas. Usually there is a clear line of authority to follow.

- **Enterprising.** These occupations frequently involve starting up and carrying out projects. These occupations can involve leading people and making many decisions. They sometimes require risk taking and often deal with business.

- **Investigative.** These occupations frequently involve working with ideas and require an extensive amount of thinking. These occupations can involve searching for facts and figuring out problems mentally. Note that **none of the top 250 apprenticeable jobs is associated with this personality type.** A college education is usually needed to acquire the research skills required for "investigative" work.

- **Realistic.** These occupations frequently involve work activities that include practical, hands-on problems and solutions. They often deal with plants, animals, and real-world materials like wood, tools, and machinery. Many of the occupations require working outside and do not involve a lot of paperwork or working closely with others.

- **Social.** These occupations frequently involve working with, communicating with, and teaching people. These occupations often involve helping or providing service to others.

Best Jobs for Artistic Personality Types

Job	Annual Earnings	Percent Growth	Annual Openings
1. Costume Attendants	$25,410	27.8%	66,000
2. Cartoonists	$35,420	16.5%	4,000
3. Painters and Illustrators	$35,420	16.5%	4,000
4. Camera Operators, Television, Video, and Motion Picture	$34,330	13.4%	4,000
5. Professional Photographers	$25,050	13.6%	18,000
6. Actors	$26,460	17.7%	8,000
7. Floral Designers	$19,660	12.4%	13,000
8. Merchandise Displayers and Window Trimmers	$22,030	11.3%	10,000

Best Jobs for Conventional Personality Types

Job	Annual Earnings	Percent Growth	Annual Openings
1. Legal Secretaries	$35,660	18.8%	39,000
2. Production, Planning, and Expediting Clerks	$34,820	14.1%	51,000
3. Construction and Building Inspectors	$42,650	13.8%	10,000
4. Dispatchers, Except Police, Fire, and Ambulance	$30,390	14.4%	28,000
5. Mapping Technicians	$29,520	23.1%	10,000
6. Pharmacy Technicians	$22,760	28.8%	39,000
7. Medical Secretaries	$26,000	17.2%	50,000
8. Audio and Video Equipment Technicians	$30,810	26.7%	5,000
9. Cargo and Freight Agents	$31,990	15.5%	8,000
10. Hotel, Motel, and Resort Desk Clerks	$17,450	23.9%	46,000
11. Fire Inspectors	$44,250	11.6%	1,000
12. Tellers	$20,670	9.4%	127,000
13. Postal Service Clerks	$39,790	−0.5%	5,000
14. Secretaries, Except Legal, Medical, and Executive	$25,420	−2.9%	254,000
15. Computer Operators	$29,970	−16.7%	27,000
16. Word Processors and Typists	$27,150	−38.6%	45,000
17. Data Entry Keyers	$22,600	−5.4%	72,000

Best Jobs for Enterprising Personality Types

Job	Annual Earnings	Percent Growth	Annual Openings
1. Food Service Managers	$37,260	11.5%	58,000
2. Government Property Inspectors and Investigators	$46,780	9.8%	20,000
3. First-Line Supervisors/Managers of Retail Sales Workers	$30,680	9.1%	251,000
4. Private Detectives and Investigators	$30,410	25.3%	9,000
5. Chefs and Head Cooks	$28,750	15.8%	33,000
6. Opticians, Dispensing	$26,350	18.2%	10,000
7. Hairdressers, Hairstylists, and Cosmetologists	$18,700	14.7%	68,000
8. Bartenders	$15,040	8.6%	100,000
9. Parts Salespersons	$24,510	–2.0%	37,000

Best Jobs for Realistic Personality Types

Job	Annual Earnings	Percent Growth	Annual Openings
1. Electricians	$41,680	23.4%	65,000
2. Pipe Fitters	$40,950	18.7%	56,000
3. Plumbers	$40,950	18.7%	56,000
4. Heating and Air Conditioning Mechanics	$35,160	31.8%	35,000
5. Refrigeration Mechanics	$35,160	31.8%	35,000
6. Truck Drivers, Heavy	$33,310	19.0%	299,000
7. Correctional Officers and Jailers	$33,160	24.2%	49,000
8. Forest Fire Fighters	$37,060	20.7%	29,000
9. Municipal Fire Fighters	$37,060	20.7%	29,000
10. Sheet Metal Workers	$35,000	19.8%	30,000
11. Municipal Fire Fighting and Prevention Supervisors	$57,000	18.7%	8,000
12. Telecommunications Line Installers and Repairers	$39,540	18.8%	13,000
13. Brickmasons and Blockmasons	$41,550	14.2%	21,000
14. Boat Builders and Shipwrights	$34,250	10.1%	193,000
15. Carpenter Assemblers and Repairers	$34,250	10.1%	193,000
16. Construction Carpenters	$34,250	10.1%	193,000
17. Rough Carpenters	$34,250	10.1%	193,000
18. Ship Carpenters and Joiners	$34,250	10.1%	193,000
19. Ceiling Tile Installers	$33,670	21.4%	17,000
20. Drywall Installers	$33,670	21.4%	17,000
21. Maintenance and Repair Workers, General	$29,800	16.3%	155,000
22. Cement Masons and Concrete Finishers	$30,780	26.1%	24,000

Best Jobs for Realistic Personality Types

Job	Annual Earnings	Percent Growth	Annual Openings
23. Surgical Technologists	$32,130	27.9%	13,000
24. Welder-Fitters	$29,640	17.0%	71,000
25. Welders and Cutters	$29,640	17.0%	71,000
26. Bus and Truck Mechanics and Diesel Engine Specialists	$34,970	14.2%	28,000
27. Roofers	$30,020	18.6%	38,000
28. Grader, Bulldozer, and Scraper Operators	$35,030	10.4%	45,000
29. Operating Engineers	$35,030	10.4%	45,000
30. Automotive Master Mechanics	$31,130	12.4%	100,000
31. Automotive Specialty Technicians	$31,130	12.4%	100,000
32. Structural Iron and Steel Workers	$40,730	15.9%	9,000
33. Data Processing Equipment Repairers	$33,780	15.1%	19,000
34. Office Machine and Cash Register Servicers	$33,780	15.1%	19,000
35. Aircraft Engine Specialists	$43,560	11.0%	12,000
36. Airframe-and-Power-Plant Mechanics	$43,560	11.0%	12,000
37. Automotive Body and Related Repairers	$33,140	13.2%	23,000
38. Tapers	$39,130	20.8%	5,000
39. Painters, Transportation Equipment	$34,100	17.5%	9,000
40. Tile and Marble Setters	$35,610	26.5%	4,000
41. Carpet Installers	$32,900	16.8%	10,000
42. Electrical and Electronics Repairers, Commercial and Industrial Equipment	$42,200	10.3%	10,000
43. Elevator Installers and Repairers	$55,960	17.1%	3,000
44. Water and Liquid Waste Treatment Plant and System Operators	$33,910	16.0%	9,000
45. Painters, Construction and Maintenance	$29,360	11.6%	69,000
46. Surveying Technicians	$29,520	23.1%	10,000
47. Machinists	$33,090	8.2%	30,000
48. Mobile Heavy Equipment Mechanics, Except Engines	$36,800	9.6%	12,000
49. Glaziers	$32,310	17.2%	7,000
50. Landscaping and Groundskeeping Workers	$19,940	22.0%	203,000
51. Industrial Machinery Mechanics	$38,440	5.5%	19,000
52. Sound Engineering Technicians	$38,290	25.5%	2,000
53. Electric Meter Installers and Repairers	$42,540	12.0%	5,000
54. Meter Mechanics	$42,540	12.0%	5,000
55. Valve and Regulator Repairers	$42,540	12.0%	5,000
56. Desktop Publishers	$31,590	29.2%	4,000
57. Construction Laborers	$24,670	14.2%	166,000

(continued)

(continued)

Best Jobs for Realistic Personality Types

Job	Annual Earnings	Percent Growth	Annual Openings
58. Medical Equipment Repairers	$37,960	14.8%	4,000
59. Plasterers and Stucco Masons	$33,060	13.5%	8,000
60. Central Office and PBX Installers and Repairers	$48,230	–0.6%	23,000
61. Communication Equipment Mechanics, Installers, and Repairers	$48,230	–0.6%	23,000
62. Station Installers and Repairers, Telephone	$48,230	–0.6%	23,000
63. Janitors and Cleaners, Except Maids and Housekeeping Cleaners	$18,410	18.3%	454,000
64. Commercial Pilots	$49,830	14.9%	2,000
65. Motor Vehicle Inspectors	$49,590	7.7%	5,000
66. Dragline Operators	$32,150	8.9%	14,000
67. Cooks, Restaurant	$19,260	15.9%	211,000
68. Crane and Tower Operators	$37,150	10.8%	5,000
69. Insulation Workers, Floor, Ceiling, and Wall	$29,190	15.8%	9,000
70. Insulation Workers, Mechanical	$29,190	15.8%	9,000
71. Helpers—Installation, Maintenance, and Repair Workers	$21,240	20.3%	33,000
72. Civil Drafters	$37,690	4.2%	14,000
73. Floor Layers, Except Carpet, Wood, and Hard Tiles	$34,840	13.4%	4,000
74. Model Makers, Metal and Plastic	$43,470	14.6%	1,000
75. Electrical Power-Line Installers and Repairers	$48,960	1.6%	9,000
76. Millwrights	$42,390	5.3%	7,000
77. Nonfarm Animal Caretakers	$17,190	22.2%	32,000
78. Tree Trimmers and Pruners	$25,630	18.6%	11,000
79. Reinforcing Iron and Rebar Workers	$34,950	16.7%	2,000
80. Riggers	$33,800	14.3%	3,000
81. Electrical and Electronic Inspectors and Testers	$27,750	4.7%	87,000
82. Materials Inspectors	$27,750	4.7%	87,000
83. Mechanical Inspectors	$27,750	4.7%	87,000
84. Precision Devices Inspectors and Testers	$27,750	4.7%	87,000
85. Production Inspectors, Testers, Graders, Sorters, Samplers, Weighers	$27,750	4.7%	87,000
86. Numerical Tool and Process Control Programmers	$38,330	13.0%	2,000
87. Numerical Control Machine Tool Operators and Tenders, Metal and Plastic	$29,420	9.3%	11,000
88. Mechanical Drafters	$41,520	1.9%	9,000
89. Pest Control Workers	$24,990	17.0%	11,000
90. Paving, Surfacing, and Tamping Equipment Operators	$29,240	12.6%	8,000

Best Jobs for Realistic Personality Types

Job	Annual Earnings	Percent Growth	Annual Openings
91. Design Printing Machine Setters and Set-Up Operators	$29,340	4.6%	30,000
92. Embossing Machine Set-Up Operators	$29,340	4.6%	30,000
93. Engraver Set-Up Operators	$29,340	4.6%	30,000
94. Letterpress Setters and Set-Up Operators	$29,340	4.6%	30,000
95. Offset Lithographic Press Setters and Set-Up Operators	$29,340	4.6%	30,000
96. Precision Printing Workers	$29,340	4.6%	30,000
97. Printing Press Machine Operators and Tenders	$29,340	4.6%	30,000
98. Slaughterers and Meat Packers	$20,420	18.1%	23,000
99. Coin, Vending, and Amusement Machine Servicers and Repairers	$27,800	15.2%	7,000
100. Recreational Vehicle Service Technicians	$27,270	21.8%	4,000
101. Job Printers	$30,850	9.2%	7,000
102. Dredge Operators	$27,800	8.9%	14,000
103. Locksmiths and Safe Repairers	$28,760	21.0%	3,000
104. Stonemasons	$34,000	14.1%	2,000
105. Press and Press Brake Machine Setters and Set-Up Operators, Metal and Plastic	$25,210	6.8%	37,000
106. Maids and Housekeeping Cleaners	$16,600	9.2%	352,000
107. Fitters, Structural Metal—Precision	$28,990	6.2%	14,000
108. Metal Fabricators, Structural Metal Products	$28,990	6.2%	14,000
109. Coating, Painting, and Spraying Machine Operators and Tenders	$25,720	9.4%	17,000
110. Coating, Painting, and Spraying Machine Setters and Set-Up Operators	$25,720	9.4%	17,000
111. Mechanical Door Repairers	$29,620	21.8%	1,000
112. Laundry and Drycleaning Machine Operators and Tenders, Except Pressing	$16,920	12.3%	47,000
113. Lay-Out Workers, Metal and Plastic	$31,970	15.6%	1,000
114. Electrical and Electronics Installers and Repairers, Transportation Equipment	$39,300	7.1%	2,000
115. Bakers, Bread and Pastry	$20,990	11.2%	29,000
116. Bakers, Manufacturing	$20,990	11.2%	29,000
117. Electronic Drafters	$41,730	0.7%	5,000
118. Motorboat Mechanics	$29,170	18.3%	2,000
119. Combination Machine Tool Setters and Set-Up Operators, Metal and Plastic	$29,050	8.3%	8,000
120. Chemical Equipment Controllers and Operators	$38,740	–3.8%	8,000
121. Maintenance Workers, Machinery	$33,000	5.9%	5,000

(continued)

(continued)

Best Jobs for Realistic Personality Types

Job	Annual Earnings	Percent Growth	Annual Openings
122. Boiler Operators and Tenders, Low Pressure	$43,420	0.3%	4,000
123. Extruding and Drawing Machine Setters, Operators, and Tenders, Metal and Plastic	$26,450	7.1%	14,000
124. Stationary Engineers	$43,420	0.3%	4,000
125. Fish and Game Wardens	$41,380	7.1%	1,000
126. Power Generating Plant Operators, Except Auxiliary Equipment Operators	$50,860	0.3%	3,000
127. Cabinetmakers and Bench Carpenters	$24,550	9.4%	15,000
128. Avionics Technicians	$43,110	3.4%	3,000
129. Conveyor Operators and Tenders	$24,690	12.4%	9,000
130. Well and Core Drill Operators	$32,540	7.7%	3,000
131. Metal Molding, Coremaking, and Casting Machine Operators and Tenders	$23,930	8.9%	18,000
132. Plastic Molding and Casting Machine Setters and Set-Up Operators	$23,930	8.9%	18,000
133. Cutting and Slicing Machine Operators and Tenders	$26,060	6.6%	12,000
134. Stone Sawyers	$26,060	6.6%	12,000
135. Outdoor Power Equipment and Other Small Engine Mechanics	$24,820	18.9%	3,000
136. Painting, Coating, and Decorating Workers	$21,650	17.6%	6,000
137. Tool and Die Makers	$42,990	0.4%	3,000
138. Broadcast Technicians	$28,090	11.3%	4,000
139. Locomotive Engineers	$45,990	−7.2%	4,000
140. Embalmers	$34,350	8.3%	1,000
141. Motorcycle Mechanics	$27,630	18.7%	1,000
142. Electrical and Electronics Repairers, Powerhouse, Substation, and Relay	$52,040	−0.6%	2,000
143. Gas Appliance Repairers	$29,890	5.5%	5,000
144. Gaugers	$49,970	−11.0%	3,000
145. Petroleum Refinery and Control Panel Operators	$49,970	−11.0%	3,000
146. Boilermakers	$43,240	1.7%	2,000
147. Battery Repairers	$32,310	5.3%	3,000
148. Cooks, Fast Food	$14,450	4.9%	165,000
149. Electric Home Appliance and Power Tool Repairers	$32,310	5.3%	3,000
150. Electric Motor and Switch Assemblers and Repairers	$32,310	5.3%	3,000
151. Hand and Portable Power Tool Repairers	$32,310	5.3%	3,000
152. Paperhangers	$32,040	5.9%	3,000
153. Transformer Repairers	$32,310	5.3%	3,000

Best Jobs for Realistic Personality Types

Job	Annual Earnings	Percent Growth	Annual Openings
154. Chemical Plant and System Operators	$44,050	–12.3%	4,000
155. Medical Appliance Technicians	$27,890	16.1%	1,000
156. Welding Machine Setters and Set-Up Operators	$29,110	0.9%	10,000
157. Rail Car Repairers	$39,610	4.5%	1,000
158. Paper Goods Machine Setters, Operators, and Tenders	$28,920	–2.8%	16,000
159. Electronic Home Entertainment Equipment Installers and Repairers	$27,340	8.6%	5,000
160. Lathe and Turning Machine Tool Setters, Operators, and Tenders, Metal and Plastic	$30,300	0.8%	7,000
161. Terrazzo Workers and Finishers	$27,710	15.2%	1,000
162. Separating, Filtering, Clarifying, Precipitating, and Still Machine Setters, Operators, and Tenders	$31,720	0.8%	5,000
163. Automotive Glass Installers and Repairers	$27,160	10.7%	3,000
164. Power Distributors and Dispatchers	$55,010	–3.0%	1,000
165. Pesticide Handlers, Sprayers, and Applicators, Vegetation	$25,490	9.7%	5,000
166. Cooks, Institution and Cafeteria	$18,300	2.1%	121,000
167. Patternmakers, Wood	$29,650	11.8%	fewer than 500
168. Fence Erectors	$22,580	13.4%	4,000
169. Food Batchmakers	$21,900	7.2%	10,000
170. Mixing and Blending Machine Setters, Operators, and Tenders	$27,940	–6.5%	14,000
171. Agricultural Equipment Operators	$17,880	7.3%	14,000
172. Signal and Track Switch Repairers	$43,690	–3.1%	1,000
173. Farmers and Ranchers	$24,076	–20.6%	118,000
174. Glass Blowers, Molders, Benders, and Finishers	$24,780	6.4%	6,000
175. Mold Makers, Hand	$24,780	6.4%	6,000
176. Molding and Casting Workers	$24,780	6.4%	6,000
177. Potters	$24,780	6.4%	6,000
178. Precision Mold and Pattern Casters, Except Nonferrous Metals	$24,780	6.4%	6,000
179. Precision Pattern and Die Casters, Nonferrous Metals	$24,780	6.4%	6,000
180. Rotary Drill Operators, Oil and Gas	$34,910	1.5%	2,000
181. Stone Cutters and Carvers	$24,780	6.4%	6,000
182. Camera Operators	$31,660	–11.2%	6,000
183. Dot Etchers	$31,660	–11.2%	6,000
184. Electrotypers and Stereotypers	$31,660	–11.2%	6,000
185. Hand Compositors and Typesetters	$31,660	–11.2%	6,000
186. Paste-Up Workers	$31,660	–11.2%	6,000
187. Photoengravers	$31,660	–11.2%	6,000

(continued)

(continued)

Best Jobs for Realistic Personality Types

Job	Annual Earnings	Percent Growth	Annual Openings
188. Plate Finishers	$31,660	−11.2%	6,000
189. Platemakers	$31,660	−11.2%	6,000
190. Scanner Operators	$31,660	−11.2%	6,000
191. Strippers	$31,660	−11.2%	6,000
192. Typesetting and Composing Machine Operators and Tenders	$31,660	−11.2%	6,000
193. Butchers and Meat Cutters	$25,570	−2.5%	21,000
194. Electronic Equipment Installers and Repairers, Motor Vehicles	$26,280	14.8%	1,000

Best Jobs for Social Personality Types

Job	Annual Earnings	Percent Growth	Annual Openings
1. Police Patrol Officers	$44,020	24.7%	67,000
2. Licensed Practical and Licensed Vocational Nurses	$32,390	20.2%	105,000
3. Dental Assistants	$27,700	42.5%	35,000
4. Medical Assistants	$24,170	58.9%	78,000
5. Social and Human Service Assistants	$23,860	48.7%	63,000
6. Security Guards	$19,660	31.9%	228,000
7. Nursing Aides, Orderlies, and Attendants	$20,490	24.9%	302,000
8. Emergency Medical Technicians and Paramedics	$24,440	33.1%	32,000
9. Teacher Assistants	$19,000	23.0%	259,000
10. Police, Fire, and Ambulance Dispatchers	$28,290	12.7%	15,000
11. Child Care Workers	$16,430	11.7%	406,000
12. Ambulance Drivers and Attendants, Except Emergency Medical Technicians	$19,000	26.7%	4,000
13. Animal Trainers	$22,350	14.3%	4,000

Best Apprenticeable Jobs Based on Interests

The lists that follow organize the 250 apprenticeable jobs that met the criteria for this book into 13 of the 14 interest areas that are used in a variety of career exploration systems. The lists provide a very useful way to identify jobs quickly based on your interests.

The lists can help you identify jobs that are related to ones you have had in the past or that require similar skills to those you want to use in the future. Within each interest grouping, occupations are arranged in order of their total scores based on earnings, growth, and number of openings.

This system of interest areas is called the *Guide for Occupational Exploration*, or *GOE*, and it was developed by the U.S. Department of Labor as an intuitive way to assist in career exploration. The lists that follow use the revised *GOE* groupings as presented in the *Guide for Occupational Exploration*, Third Edition, published by JIST.

Brief descriptions follow for each of the 14 interest areas in the *GOE* system. Simply look for the area or areas that interest you most and then use the lists in this section to identify apprenticeable jobs that are likely to interest you. Then, as with most of our lists, simply look up the job description in Part IV for the jobs that interest you most. Note that the descriptions for each of the interest areas may mention sample jobs that are not among those described in this book.

- **Arts, Entertainment, and Media**—*An interest in creatively expressing feelings or ideas, in communicating news or information, or in performing.* You can satisfy this interest in several creative, verbal, or performing activities. For example, if you enjoy literature, perhaps writing or editing would appeal to you. Do you prefer to work in the performing arts? If so, you could direct or perform in drama, music, or dance. If you especially enjoy the visual arts, you could become a critic in painting, sculpture, or ceramics. You may want to use your hands to create or decorate products. You may prefer to model clothes or develop sets for entertainment. Or you may want to participate in sports professionally, as an athlete or coach.

- **Science, Math, and Engineering**—*An interest in discovering, collecting, and analyzing information about the natural world; in applying scientific research findings to problems in medicine, the life sciences, and the natural sciences; in imagining and manipulating quantitative data; and in applying technology to manufacturing, transportation, mining, and other economic activities.* You can satisfy this interest by working with the knowledge and processes of the sciences. You may enjoy researching and developing new knowledge in mathematics, or perhaps solving problems in the physical or life sciences would appeal to you. You may wish to study engineering and help create new machines, processes, and structures. If you want to work with scientific equipment and procedures, you could seek a job in a research or testing laboratory.

- **Plants and Animals**—*An interest in working with plants and animals, usually outdoors.* You can satisfy this interest by working in farming, forestry, fishing, and related fields. You may like doing physical work outdoors, such as on a farm. You may enjoy animals; perhaps training or taking care of animals would appeal to you. If you have management ability, you could own, operate, or manage a farm or related business.

- **Law, Law Enforcement, and Public Safety**—*An interest in upholding people's rights or in protecting people and property by using authority, inspecting, or monitoring.* You can satisfy this by working in law, law enforcement, fire fighting, and related fields. For example, if you enjoy mental challenge and intrigue, you could investigate crimes or fires for a living. If you enjoy working with verbal skills, you may want to defend citizens in court or research deeds, wills, and other legal documents. You may prefer to fight fires and respond to other emergencies. Or, if you want more routine work, perhaps a job in guarding or patrolling would appeal to you; if you have management ability, you could seek a leadership position in law enforcement and the protective services.

⊚ **Mechanics, Installers, and Repairers**—*An interest in applying mechanical and electrical/electronic principles to practical situations by use of machines or hand tools.* You can satisfy this interest working with a variety of tools, technologies, materials, and settings. If you enjoy making machines run efficiently or fixing them when they break down, you could seek a job installing or repairing such devices as copiers, aircraft engines, automobiles, or watches. You may instead prefer to deal directly with certain materials and find work cutting and shaping metal or wood. Or if electricity and electronics interest you, you could install cables, troubleshoot telephone networks, or repair videocassette recorders. If you prefer routine or physical work in settings other than factories, perhaps work repairing tires or batteries would appeal to you.

⊚ **Construction, Mining, and Drilling**—*An interest in assembling components of buildings and other structures or in using mechanical devices to drill or excavate.* If construction interests you, you can find fulfillment in the many building projects that are being undertaken at all times. If you like to organize and plan, you can find careers in management. On the other hand, you can play a more direct role in putting up and finishing buildings by doing jobs such as plumbing, carpentry, masonry, painting, or roofing. You may like working at a mine or oilfield, operating the powerful drilling or digging equipment. There are also other jobs that let you put your hands to the task.

⊚ **Transportation**—*An interest in operations that move people or materials.* You can satisfy this interest by managing a transportation service, by helping vehicles keep on their assigned schedules and routes, or by driving or piloting a vehicle. If you enjoy taking responsibility, perhaps managing a rail line would appeal to you. If you work well with details and can take pressure on the job, you might consider being an air traffic controller. Or would you rather get out on the highway, on the water, or up in the air? If so, then you could drive a truck from state to state, sail down the Mississippi on a barge, or fly a crop duster over a cornfield. If you prefer to stay closer to home, you could drive a delivery van, taxi, or school bus. You can use your physical strength to load freight and arrange it so it gets to its destination in one piece.

⊚ **Industrial Production**—*An interest in repetitive, concrete, organized activities most often done in a factory setting.* You can satisfy this interest by working in one of many industries that mass-produce goods or for a utility that distributes electric power, gas, etc. You may enjoy manual work, using your hands or hand tools. Perhaps you prefer to operate machines. You may like to inspect, sort, count, or weigh products. Using your training and experience to set up machines or supervise other workers may appeal to you.

⊚ **Business Detail**—*An interest in organized, clearly defined activities requiring accuracy and attention to details, primarily in an office setting.* You can satisfy this interest in a variety of jobs in which you attend to the details of a business operation. You may enjoy using your math skills; if so, perhaps a job in billing, computing, or financial record-keeping would satisfy you. If you prefer to deal with people, you may want a job in which you meet the public, talk on the telephone, or supervise other workers. You may like to do word processing on a computer, turn out copies on a duplicating machine, or work out sums on a calculator. Perhaps a job in filing or recording would satisfy you. Or you may wish to use your training and experience to manage an office.

- **Sales and Marketing**—*An interest in bringing others to a particular point of view by personal persuasion, using sales and promotional techniques.* You can satisfy this interest in a variety of sales and marketing jobs. If you like using technical knowledge of science or agriculture, you may enjoy selling technical products or services. Or perhaps you are more interested in selling business-related services such as insurance coverage, advertising space, or investment opportunities. Real estate offers several kinds of sales jobs. Perhaps you'd rather work with something you can pick up and show to people. You may work in stores, sales offices, or customers' homes.

- **Recreation, Travel, and Other Personal Services**—*An interest in catering to the personal wishes and needs of others so that they may enjoy cleanliness, good food and drink, comfortable lodging away from home, and enjoyable recreation.* You can satisfy this interest by providing services for the convenience, feeding, and pampering of others in hotels, restaurants, airplanes, etc. If you enjoy improving the appearance of others, perhaps working in the hair and beauty care field would satisfy you. You may wish to provide personal services such as taking care of small children, tailoring garments, or ushering. Or you may use your knowledge of the field to manage workers who are providing these services.

- **Education and Social Service**—*An interest in teaching people or improving their social or spiritual well-being.* You can satisfy this interest by teaching students, who may be preschoolers, retirees, or any age in between. Or, if you are interested in helping people sort out their complicated lives, you may find fulfillment as a counselor, social worker, or religious worker. Working in a museum or library may give you opportunities to expand people's understanding of the world. If you also have an interest in business, you may find satisfaction in managerial work in this field.

- **General Management and Support**—*An interest in making an organization run smoothly.* Note that **none of the top 250 apprenticeable jobs is associated with this interest field.** A college education is usually needed to acquire the skills required for jobs in this field.

- **Medical and Health Services**—*An interest in helping people be healthy.* You can satisfy this interest by working in a health care team as a doctor, therapist, or nurse. You might specialize in one of the many different parts of the body or types of care, or you might be a generalist who deals with the whole patient. If you like technology, you might find satisfaction working with X rays, one of the electronic means of diagnosis, or clinical laboratory testing. You might work with healthy people, helping them stay in condition through exercise and eating right. If you like to organize, analyze, and plan, a managerial role might be right for you.

Best Jobs for People Interested in Arts, Entertainment, and Media

Job	Annual Earnings	Percent Growth	Annual Openings
1. Costume Attendants	$25,410	27.8%	66,000
2. Sound Engineering Technicians	$38,290	25.5%	2,000
3. Audio and Video Equipment Technicians	$30,810	26.7%	5,000
4. Cartoonists	$35,420	16.5%	4,000
5. Painters and Illustrators	$35,420	16.5%	4,000
6. Desktop Publishers	$31,590	29.2%	4,000
7. Camera Operators, Television, Video, and Motion Picture	$34,330	13.4%	4,000
8. Professional Photographers	$25,050	13.6%	18,000
9. Actors	$26,460	17.7%	8,000
10. Broadcast Technicians	$28,090	11.3%	4,000
11. Floral Designers	$19,660	12.4%	13,000
12. Merchandise Displayers and Window Trimmers	$22,030	11.3%	10,000
13. Glass Blowers, Molders, Benders, and Finishers	$24,780	6.4%	6,000
14. Potters	$24,780	6.4%	6,000
15. Camera Operators	$31,660	–11.2%	6,000
16. Dot Etchers	$31,660	–11.2%	6,000
17. Paste-Up Workers	$31,660	–11.2%	6,000
18. Photoengravers	$31,660	–11.2%	6,000

Best Jobs for People Interested in Science, Math, and Engineering

Job	Annual Earnings	Percent Growth	Annual Openings
1. Computer Specialists, All Other	$54,070	36.5%	27,000
2. Construction and Building Inspectors	$42,650	13.8%	10,000
3. Mapping Technicians	$29,520	23.1%	10,000
4. Surveying Technicians	$29,520	23.1%	10,000
5. Civil Drafters	$37,690	4.2%	14,000
6. Numerical Tool and Process Control Programmers	$38,330	13.0%	2,000
7. Mechanical Drafters	$41,520	1.9%	9,000
8. Electronic Drafters	$41,730	0.7%	5,000

Best Jobs for People Interested in Plants and Animals

Job	Annual Earnings	Percent Growth	Annual Openings
1. Landscaping and Groundskeeping Workers	$19,940	22.0%	203,000
2. Nonfarm Animal Caretakers	$17,190	22.2%	32,000
3. Tree Trimmers and Pruners	$25,630	18.6%	11,000
4. Pest Control Workers	$24,990	17.0%	11,000
5. Pesticide Handlers, Sprayers, and Applicators, Vegetation	$25,490	9.7%	5,000
6. Animal Trainers	$22,350	14.3%	4,000
7. Agricultural Equipment Operators	$17,880	7.3%	14,000
8. Farmers and Ranchers	$24,076	−20.6%	118,000

Best Jobs for People Interested in Law, Law Enforcement, and Public Safety

Job	Annual Earnings	Percent Growth	Annual Openings
1. Police Patrol Officers	$44,020	24.7%	67,000
2. Correctional Officers and Jailers	$33,160	24.2%	49,000
3. Forest Fire Fighters	$37,060	20.7%	29,000
4. Municipal Fire Fighters	$37,060	20.7%	29,000
5. Municipal Fire Fighting and Prevention Supervisors	$57,000	18.7%	8,000
6. Government Property Inspectors and Investigators	$46,780	9.8%	20,000
7. Emergency Management Specialists	$45,090	28.2%	2,000
8. Private Detectives and Investigators	$30,410	25.3%	9,000
9. Security Guards	$19,660	31.9%	228,000
10. Emergency Medical Technicians and Paramedics	$24,440	33.1%	32,000
11. Fire Inspectors	$44,250	11.6%	1,000
12. Fish and Game Wardens	$41,380	7.1%	1,000

Best Jobs for People Interested in Being Mechanics, Installers, and Repairers

Job	Annual Earnings	Percent Growth	Annual Openings
1. Heating and Air Conditioning Mechanics	$35,160	31.8%	35,000
2. Refrigeration Mechanics	$35,160	31.8%	35,000
3. Telecommunications Line Installers and Repairers	$39,540	18.8%	13,000
4. Maintenance and Repair Workers, General	$29,800	16.3%	155,000
5. Bus and Truck Mechanics and Diesel Engine Specialists	$34,970	14.2%	28,000
6. Automotive Master Mechanics	$31,130	12.4%	100,000
7. Automotive Specialty Technicians	$31,130	12.4%	100,000
8. Data Processing Equipment Repairers	$33,780	15.1%	19,000
9. Office Machine and Cash Register Servicers	$33,780	15.1%	19,000
10. Aircraft Engine Specialists	$43,560	11.0%	12,000
11. Airframe-and-Power-Plant Mechanics	$43,560	11.0%	12,000
12. Automotive Body and Related Repairers	$33,140	13.2%	23,000
13. Painters, Transportation Equipment	$34,100	17.5%	9,000
14. Electrical and Electronics Repairers, Commercial and Industrial Equipment	$42,200	10.3%	10,000
15. Elevator Installers and Repairers	$55,960	17.1%	3,000
16. Installation, Maintenance, and Repair Workers, All Other	$33,010	12.2%	22,000
17. Mobile Heavy Equipment Mechanics, Except Engines	$36,800	9.6%	12,000
18. Industrial Machinery Mechanics	$38,440	5.5%	19,000
19. Electric Meter Installers and Repairers	$42,540	12.0%	5,000
20. Meter Mechanics	$42,540	12.0%	5,000
21. Valve and Regulator Repairers	$42,540	12.0%	5,000
22. Medical Equipment Repairers	$37,960	14.8%	4,000
23. Central Office and PBX Installers and Repairers	$48,230	−0.6%	23,000
24. Communication Equipment Mechanics, Installers, and Repairers	$48,230	−0.6%	23,000
25. Station Installers and Repairers, Telephone	$48,230	−0.6%	23,000
26. Helpers—Installation, Maintenance, and Repair Workers	$21,240	20.3%	33,000
27. Electrical Power-Line Installers and Repairers	$48,960	1.6%	9,000
28. Millwrights	$42,390	5.3%	7,000
29. Coin, Vending, and Amusement Machine Servicers and Repairers	$27,800	15.2%	7,000
30. Recreational Vehicle Service Technicians	$27,270	21.8%	4,000
31. Locksmiths and Safe Repairers	$28,760	21.0%	3,000
32. Mechanical Door Repairers	$29,620	21.8%	1,000

Best Jobs for People Interested in Being Mechanics, Installers, and Repairers

Job	Annual Earnings	Percent Growth	Annual Openings
33. Electrical and Electronics Installers and Repairers, Transportation Equipment	$39,300	7.1%	2,000
34. Motorboat Mechanics	$29,170	18.3%	2,000
35. Maintenance Workers, Machinery	$33,000	5.9%	5,000
36. Avionics Technicians	$43,110	3.4%	3,000
37. Outdoor Power Equipment and Other Small Engine Mechanics	$24,820	18.9%	3,000
38. Motorcycle Mechanics	$27,630	18.7%	1,000
39. Electrical and Electronics Repairers, Powerhouse, Substation, and Relay	$52,040	–0.6%	2,000
40. Gas Appliance Repairers	$29,890	5.5%	5,000
41. Battery Repairers	$32,310	5.3%	3,000
42. Electric Home Appliance and Power Tool Repairers	$32,310	5.3%	3,000
43. Electric Motor and Switch Assemblers and Repairers	$32,310	5.3%	3,000
44. Hand and Portable Power Tool Repairers	$32,310	5.3%	3,000
45. Transformer Repairers	$32,310	5.3%	3,000
46. Medical Appliance Technicians	$27,890	16.1%	1,000
47. Rail Car Repairers	$39,610	4.5%	1,000
48. Electronic Home Entertainment Equipment Installers and Repairers	$27,340	8.6%	5,000
49. Automotive Glass Installers and Repairers	$27,160	10.7%	3,000
50. Signal and Track Switch Repairers	$43,690	–3.1%	1,000
51. Electronic Equipment Installers and Repairers, Motor Vehicles	$26,280	14.8%	1,000

Best Jobs for People Interested in Construction, Mining, and Drilling

Job	Annual Earnings	Percent Growth	Annual Openings
1. Electricians	$41,680	23.4%	65,000
2. Pipe Fitters	$40,950	18.7%	56,000
3. Plumbers	$40,950	18.7%	56,000
4. Sheet Metal Workers	$35,000	19.8%	30,000
5. Brickmasons and Blockmasons	$41,550	14.2%	21,000
6. Boat Builders and Shipwrights	$34,250	10.1%	193,000
7. Carpenter Assemblers and Repairers	$34,250	10.1%	193,000

(continued)

(continued)

Best Jobs for People Interested in Construction, Mining, and Drilling

Job	Annual Earnings	Percent Growth	Annual Openings
8. Construction Carpenters	$34,250	10.1%	193,000
9. Rough Carpenters	$34,250	10.1%	193,000
10. Ship Carpenters and Joiners	$34,250	10.1%	193,000
11. Ceiling Tile Installers	$33,670	21.4%	17,000
12. Drywall Installers	$33,670	21.4%	17,000
13. Cement Masons and Concrete Finishers	$30,780	26.1%	24,000
14. Roofers	$30,020	18.6%	38,000
15. Grader, Bulldozer, and Scraper Operators	$35,030	10.4%	45,000
16. Operating Engineers	$35,030	10.4%	45,000
17. Structural Iron and Steel Workers	$40,730	15.9%	9,000
18. Tapers	$39,130	20.8%	5,000
19. Tile and Marble Setters	$35,610	26.5%	4,000
20. Carpet Installers	$32,900	16.8%	10,000
21. Painters, Construction and Maintenance	$29,360	11.6%	69,000
22. Glaziers	$32,310	17.2%	7,000
23. Construction Laborers	$24,670	14.2%	166,000
24. Plasterers and Stucco Masons	$33,060	13.5%	8,000
25. Construction and Related Workers, All Other	$22,900	32.0%	17,000
26. Insulation Workers, Floor, Ceiling, and Wall	$29,190	15.8%	9,000
27. Insulation Workers, Mechanical	$29,190	15.8%	9,000
28. Floor Layers, Except Carpet, Wood, and Hard Tiles	$34,840	13.4%	4,000
29. Reinforcing Iron and Rebar Workers	$34,950	16.7%	2,000
30. Riggers	$33,800	14.3%	3,000
31. Paving, Surfacing, and Tamping Equipment Operators	$29,240	12.6%	8,000
32. Stonemasons	$34,000	14.1%	2,000
33. Well and Core Drill Operators	$32,540	7.7%	3,000
34. Boilermakers	$43,240	1.7%	2,000
35. Paperhangers	$32,040	5.9%	3,000
36. Terrazzo Workers and Finishers	$27,710	15.2%	1,000
37. Fence Erectors	$22,580	13.4%	4,000
38. Rotary Drill Operators, Oil and Gas	$34,910	1.5%	2,000
39. Stone Cutters and Carvers	$24,780	6.4%	6,000

Best Jobs for People Interested in Transportation

Job	Annual Earnings	Percent Growth	Annual Openings
1. Truck Drivers, Heavy	$33,310	19.0%	299,000
2. Commercial Pilots	$49,830	14.9%	2,000
3. Dredge Operators	$27,800	8.9%	14,000
4. Locomotive Engineers	$45,990	−7.2%	4,000
5. Ambulance Drivers and Attendants, Except Emergency Medical Technicians	$19,000	26.7%	4,000

Best Jobs for People Interested in Industrial Production

Job	Annual Earnings	Percent Growth	Annual Openings
1. Welder-Fitters	$29,640	17.0%	71,000
2. Welders and Cutters	$29,640	17.0%	71,000
3. Water and Liquid Waste Treatment Plant and System Operators	$33,910	16.0%	9,000
4. Machinists	$33,090	8.2%	30,000
5. Motor Vehicle Inspectors	$49,590	7.7%	5,000
6. Dragline Operators	$32,150	8.9%	14,000
7. Crane and Tower Operators	$37,150	10.8%	5,000
8. Model Makers, Metal and Plastic	$43,470	14.6%	1,000
9. Electrical and Electronic Inspectors and Testers	$27,750	4.7%	87,000
10. Materials Inspectors	$27,750	4.7%	87,000
11. Mechanical Inspectors	$27,750	4.7%	87,000
12. Precision Devices Inspectors and Testers	$27,750	4.7%	87,000
13. Production Inspectors, Testers, Graders, Sorters, Samplers, Weighers	$27,750	4.7%	87,000
14. Numerical Control Machine Tool Operators and Tenders, Metal and Plastic	$29,420	9.3%	11,000
15. Production Workers, All Other	$22,260	11.3%	67,000
16. Design Printing Machine Setters and Set-Up Operators	$29,340	4.6%	30,000
17. Embossing Machine Set-Up Operators	$29,340	4.6%	30,000
18. Engraver Set-Up Operators	$29,340	4.6%	30,000
19. Letterpress Setters and Set-Up Operators	$29,340	4.6%	30,000
20. Offset Lithographic Press Setters and Set-Up Operators	$29,340	4.6%	30,000
21. Precision Printing Workers	$29,340	4.6%	30,000
22. Printing Press Machine Operators and Tenders	$29,340	4.6%	30,000

(continued)

(continued)

Best Jobs for People Interested in Industrial Production

Job	Annual Earnings	Percent Growth	Annual Openings
23. Slaughterers and Meat Packers	$20,420	18.1%	23,000
24. Job Printers	$30,850	9.2%	7,000
25. Press and Press Brake Machine Setters and Set-Up Operators, Metal and Plastic	$25,210	6.8%	37,000
26. Fitters, Structural Metal—Precision	$28,990	6.2%	14,000
27. Metal Fabricators, Structural Metal Products	$28,990	6.2%	14,000
28. Coating, Painting, and Spraying Machine Operators and Tenders	$25,720	9.4%	17,000
29. Coating, Painting, and Spraying Machine Setters and Set-Up Operators	$25,720	9.4%	17,000
30. Lay-Out Workers, Metal and Plastic	$31,970	15.6%	1,000
31. Metal Workers and Plastic Workers, All Other	$28,400	6.6%	11,000
32. Bakers, Manufacturing	$20,990	11.2%	29,000
33. Combination Machine Tool Setters and Set-Up Operators, Metal and Plastic	$29,050	8.3%	8,000
34. Chemical Equipment Controllers and Operators	$38,740	–3.8%	8,000
35. Boiler Operators and Tenders, Low Pressure	$43,420	0.3%	4,000
36. Extruding and Drawing Machine Setters, Operators, and Tenders, Metal and Plastic	$26,450	7.1%	14,000
37. Stationary Engineers	$43,420	0.3%	4,000
38. Power Generating Plant Operators, Except Auxiliary Equipment Operators	$50,860	0.3%	3,000
39. Cabinetmakers and Bench Carpenters	$24,550	9.4%	15,000
40. Conveyor Operators and Tenders	$24,690	12.4%	9,000
41. Metal Molding, Coremaking, and Casting Machine Operators and Tenders	$23,930	8.9%	18,000
42. Plastic Molding and Casting Machine Setters and Set-Up Operators	$23,930	8.9%	18,000
43. Cutting and Slicing Machine Operators and Tenders	$26,060	6.6%	12,000
44. Stone Sawyers	$26,060	6.6%	12,000
45. Painting, Coating, and Decorating Workers	$21,650	17.6%	6,000
46. Tool and Die Makers	$42,990	0.4%	3,000
47. Gaugers	$49,970	–11.0%	3,000
48. Petroleum Refinery and Control Panel Operators	$49,970	–11.0%	3,000
49. Chemical Plant and System Operators	$44,050	–12.3%	4,000
50. Team Assemblers	$23,180	–1.6%	143,000

Best Jobs for People Interested in Industrial Production

Job	Annual Earnings	Percent Growth	Annual Openings
51. Welding Machine Setters and Set-Up Operators	$29,110	0.9%	10,000
52. Paper Goods Machine Setters, Operators, and Tenders	$28,920	–2.8%	16,000
53. Lathe and Turning Machine Tool Setters, Operators, and Tenders, Metal and Plastic	$30,300	0.8%	7,000
54. Separating, Filtering, Clarifying, Precipitating, and Still Machine Setters, Operators, and Tenders	$31,720	0.8%	5,000
55. Power Distributors and Dispatchers	$55,010	–3.0%	1,000
56. Patternmakers, Wood	$29,650	11.8%	fewer than 500
57. Food Batchmakers	$21,900	7.2%	10,000
58. Mixing and Blending Machine Setters, Operators, and Tenders	$27,940	–6.5%	14,000
59. Mold Makers, Hand	$24,780	6.4%	6,000
60. Molding and Casting Workers	$24,780	6.4%	6,000
61. Precision Mold and Pattern Casters, Except Nonferrous Metals	$24,780	6.4%	6,000
62. Precision Pattern and Die Casters, Nonferrous Metals	$24,780	6.4%	6,000
63. Electrotypers and Stereotypers	$31,660	–11.2%	6,000
64. Hand Compositors and Typesetters	$31,660	–11.2%	6,000
65. Plate Finishers	$31,660	–11.2%	6,000
66. Platemakers	$31,660	–11.2%	6,000
67. Scanner Operators	$31,660	–11.2%	6,000
68. Strippers	$31,660	–11.2%	6,000

Best Jobs for People Interested in Business Detail

Job	Annual Earnings	Percent Growth	Annual Openings
1. Legal Secretaries	$35,660	18.8%	39,000
2. Production, Planning, and Expediting Clerks	$34,820	14.1%	51,000
3. Dispatchers, Except Police, Fire, and Ambulance	$30,390	14.4%	28,000
4. Medical Secretaries	$26,000	17.2%	50,000
5. Cargo and Freight Agents	$31,990	15.5%	8,000
6. Police, Fire, and Ambulance Dispatchers	$28,290	12.7%	15,000
7. Tellers	$20,670	9.4%	127,000
8. Postal Service Clerks	$39,790	–0.5%	5,000
9. Secretaries, Except Legal, Medical, and Executive	$25,420	–2.9%	254,000
10. Computer Operators	$29,970	–16.7%	27,000
11. Word Processors and Typists	$27,150	–38.6%	45,000
12. Data Entry Keyers	$22,600	–5.4%	72,000
13. Typesetting and Composing Machine Operators and Tenders	$31,660	–11.2%	6,000

Best Jobs for People Interested in Sales and Marketing

Job	Annual Earnings	Percent Growth	Annual Openings
1. First-Line Supervisors/Managers of Retail Sales Workers	$30,680	9.1%	251,000
2. Parts Salespersons	$24,510	–2.0%	37,000

Best Jobs for People Interested in Recreation, Travel, and Other Personal Services

Job	Annual Earnings	Percent Growth	Annual Openings
1. Food Service Managers	$37,260	11.5%	58,000
2. Chefs and Head Cooks	$28,750	15.8%	33,000
3. Janitors and Cleaners, Except Maids and Housekeeping Cleaners	$18,410	18.3%	454,000
4. Cooks, Restaurant	$19,260	15.9%	211,000
5. Hotel, Motel, and Resort Desk Clerks	$17,450	23.9%	46,000
6. Hairdressers, Hairstylists, and Cosmetologists	$18,700	14.7%	68,000
7. Building Cleaning Workers, All Other	$20,990	16.1%	24,000
8. Maids and Housekeeping Cleaners	$16,600	9.2%	352,000

Best Jobs for People Interested in Recreation, Travel, and Other Personal Services

Job	Annual Earnings	Percent Growth	Annual Openings
9. Laundry and Drycleaning Machine Operators and Tenders, Except Pressing	$16,920	12.3%	47,000
10. Bakers, Bread and Pastry	$20,990	11.2%	29,000
11. Bartenders	$15,040	8.6%	100,000
12. Embalmers	$34,350	8.3%	1,000
13. Cooks, Fast Food	$14,450	4.9%	165,000
14. Cooks, Institution and Cafeteria	$18,300	2.1%	121,000
15. Butchers and Meat Cutters	$25,570	–2.5%	21,000

Best Jobs for People Interested in Education and Social Service

Job	Annual Earnings	Percent Growth	Annual Openings
1. Social and Human Service Assistants	$23,860	48.7%	63,000
2. Teacher Assistants	$19,000	23.0%	259,000
3. Child Care Workers	$16,430	11.7%	406,000

Best Jobs for People Interested in Medical and Health Services

Job	Annual Earnings	Percent Growth	Annual Openings
1. Licensed Practical and Licensed Vocational Nurses	$32,390	20.2%	105,000
2. Surgical Technologists	$32,130	27.9%	13,000
3. Dental Assistants	$27,700	42.5%	35,000
4. Medical Assistants	$24,170	58.9%	78,000
5. Nursing Aides, Orderlies, and Attendants	$20,490	24.9%	302,000
6. Pharmacy Technicians	$22,760	28.8%	39,000
7. Health Technologists and Technicians, All Other	$49,710	18.9%	1,000
8. Opticians, Dispensing	$26,350	18.2%	10,000

Best Apprenticeable Jobs Based on Number of Years Required

The lists that follow organize the 250 apprenticeable jobs that met the criteria for this book according to how many years are required to reach journey worker status. Note that for many occupations, more than one apprenticeship program is available as an entry route, and sometimes the different programs have different durations. For example, Water and Liquid Waste Treatment Plant and System Operators may learn their skills in any of the following apprenticeship programs: Clarifying-Plant Operator (requiring one year), Wastewater-Treatment-Plant Operator (two years), Waste-Treatment Operator (two years), or Water-Treatment-Plant Operator (three years). Therefore, this job is listed below among "Best Jobs with Apprenticeships that Take as Little as One Year," and the "Years Required" column lists "1, 2, or 3."

Best Jobs with Apprenticeships that Take as Little as One Year

Job	Annual Earnings	Percent Growth	Annual Openings	Years Required
1. Computer Specialists, All Other	$54,070	36.5%	27,000	1.5 or competency
2. Legal Secretaries	$35,660	18.8%	39,000	1
3. Correctional Officers and Jailers	$33,160	24.2%	49,000	1
4. Licensed Practical and Licensed Vocational Nurses	$32,390	20.2%	105,000	1
5. Forest Fire Fighters	$37,060	20.7%	29,000	1
6. Municipal Fire Fighters	$37,060	20.7%	29,000	1 or 3
7. Telecommunications Line Installers and Repairers	$39,540	18.8%	13,000	1 or 4
8. Brickmasons and Blockmasons	$41,550	14.2%	21,000	1, 3, or 4
9. Dental Assistants	$27,700	42.5%	35,000	1
10. Automotive Specialty Technicians	$31,130	12.4%	100,000	1, 2, 4, or competency
11. Private Detectives and Investigators	$30,410	25.3%	9,000	1
12. Water and Liquid Waste Treatment Plant and System Operators	$33,910	16.0%	9,000	1, 2, or 3
13. Painters, Construction and Maintenance	$29,360	11.6%	69,000	1, 2, or 3
14. Security Guards	$19,660	31.9%	228,000	1.5
15. Nursing Aides, Orderlies, and Attendants	$20,490	24.9%	302,000	1
16. Pharmacy Technicians	$22,760	28.8%	39,000	1
17. Medical Secretaries	$26,000	17.2%	50,000	1
18. Landscaping and Groundskeeping Workers	$19,940	22.0%	203,000	1, 2, or 4
19. Health Technologists and Technicians, All Other	$49,710	18.9%	1,000	1
20. Painters and Illustrators	$35,420	16.5%	4,000	1 or 4

Best Jobs with Apprenticeships that Take as Little as One Year

Job	Annual Earnings	Percent Growth	Annual Openings	Years Required
21. Cargo and Freight Agents	$31,990	15.5%	8,000	1.5
22. Dragline Operators	$32,150	8.9%	14,000	1
23. Police, Fire, and Ambulance Dispatchers	$28,290	12.7%	15,000	1 or 4
24. Production Inspectors, Testers, Graders, Sorters, Samplers, Weighers	$27,750	4.7%	87,000	1 or 4
25. Production Workers, All Other	$22,260	11.3%	67,000	1, 2, 3, or 4
26. Hairdressers, Hairstylists, and Cosmetologists	$18,700	14.7%	68,000	1
27. Building Cleaning Workers, All Other	$20,990	16.1%	24,000	1
28. Tellers	$20,670	9.4%	127,000	1
29. Maids and Housekeeping Cleaners	$16,600	9.2%	352,000	1
30. Coating, Painting, and Spraying Machine Operators and Tenders	$25,720	9.4%	17,000	1
31. Combination Machine Tool Setters and Set-Up Operators, Metal and Plastic	$29,050	8.3%	8,000	1, 2, 3, or 4
32. Boiler Operators and Tenders, Low Pressure	$43,420	0.3%	4,000	1
33. Extruding and Drawing Machine Setters, Operators, and Tenders, Metal and Plastic	$26,450	7.1%	14,000	1
34. Bartenders	$15,040	8.6%	100,000	1
35. Conveyor Operators and Tenders	$24,690	12.4%	9,000	1
36. Plastic Molding and Casting Machine Setters and Set-Up Operators	$23,930	8.9%	18,000	1 or 4
37. Secretaries, Except Legal, Medical, and Executive	$25,420	–2.9%	254,000	1
38. Floral Designers	$19,660	12.4%	13,000	1
39. Ambulance Drivers and Attendants, Except Emergency Medical Technicians	$19,000	26.7%	4,000	1
40. Merchandise Displayers and Window Trimmers	$22,030	11.3%	10,000	1 or 4
41. Computer Operators	$29,970	–16.7%	27,000	1 or 3
42. Cooks, Fast Food	$14,450	4.9%	165,000	1
43. Medical Appliance Technicians	$27,890	16.1%	1,000	1, 4, or 5
44. Separating, Filtering, Clarifying, Precipitating, and Still Machine Setters, Operators, and Tenders	$31,720	0.8%	5,000	1, 1.2, 3, or 4
45. Animal Trainers	$22,350	14.3%	4,000	1 or 2
46. Farmers and Ranchers	$24,076	–20.6%	118,000	1 or 2
47. Molding and Casting Workers	$24,780	6.4%	6,000	1 or 4

Best Jobs with Apprenticeships that Take as Little as Two Years

Job	Annual Earnings	Percent Growth	Annual Openings	Years Required
1. Police Patrol Officers	$44,020	24.7%	67,000	2
2. Electricians	$41,680	23.4%	65,000	2.4, 3, or 4
3. Heating and Air Conditioning Mechanics	$35,160	31.8%	35,000	2, 3, or 4
4. Production, Planning, and Expediting Clerks	$34,820	14.1%	51,000	2
5. Construction Carpenters	$34,250	10.1%	193,000	2, 3, 4, or 6
6. Rough Carpenters	$34,250	10.1%	193,000	2 or 4
7. Drywall Installers	$33,670	21.4%	17,000	2
8. Maintenance and Repair Workers, General	$29,800	16.3%	155,000	2, 3, or 4
9. Cement Masons and Concrete Finishers	$30,780	26.1%	24,000	2
10. Bus and Truck Mechanics and Diesel Engine Specialists	$34,970	14.2%	28,000	2 or 4
11. Government Property Inspectors and Investigators	$46,780	9.8%	20,000	2
12. Roofers	$30,020	18.6%	38,000	2
13. Grader, Bulldozer, and Scraper Operators	$35,030	10.4%	45,000	2 or 3
14. Automotive Master Mechanics	$31,130	12.4%	100,000	2 or 4
15. Structural Iron and Steel Workers	$40,730	15.9%	9,000	2 or 3
16. Office Machine and Cash Register Servicers	$33,780	15.1%	19,000	2 or 3
17. Automotive Body and Related Repairers	$33,140	13.2%	23,000	2 or 4
18. Tapers	$39,130	20.8%	5,000	2
19. Costume Attendants	$25,410	27.8%	66,000	2
20. Medical Assistants	$24,170	58.9%	78,000	2
21. Electrical and Electronics Repairers, Commercial and Industrial Equipment	$42,200	10.3%	10,000	2, 4, or 5
22. Installation, Maintenance, and Repair Workers, All Other	$33,010	12.2%	22,000	2 or 4
23. Dispatchers, Except Police, Fire, and Ambulance	$30,390	14.4%	28,000	2
24. Mapping Technicians	$29,520	23.1%	10,000	2 or 3
25. Surveying Technicians	$29,520	23.1%	10,000	2 or 4
26. Chefs and Head Cooks	$28,750	15.8%	33,000	2
27. Emergency Medical Technicians and Paramedics	$24,440	33.1%	32,000	2 or 3
28. Machinists	$33,090	8.2%	30,000	2, 4, or 5
29. Teacher Assistants	$19,000	23.0%	259,000	2
30. Industrial Machinery Mechanics	$38,440	5.5%	19,000	2, 3, 4, or 6
31. Sound Engineering Technicians	$38,290	25.5%	2,000	2 or 4
32. Valve and Regulator Repairers	$42,540	12.0%	5,000	2 or 3
33. Construction Laborers	$24,670	14.2%	166,000	2 or 3

Best Jobs with Apprenticeships that Take as Little as Two Years

Job	Annual Earnings	Percent Growth	Annual Openings	Years Required
34. Medical Equipment Repairers	$37,960	14.8%	4,000	2, 3, or 4
35. Plasterers and Stucco Masons	$33,060	13.5%	8,000	2
36. Communication Equipment Mechanics, Installers, and Repairers	$48,230	–0.6%	23,000	2, 3, or 4
37. Janitors and Cleaners, Except Maids and Housekeeping Cleaners	$18,410	18.3%	454,000	2 or 3
38. Construction and Related Workers, All Other	$22,900	32.0%	17,000	2 or 3
39. Hotel, Motel, and Resort Desk Clerks	$17,450	23.9%	46,000	2
40. Helpers—Installation, Maintenance, and Repair Workers	$21,240	20.3%	33,000	2 or 4
41. Model Makers, Metal and Plastic	$43,470	14.6%	1,000	2 or 4
42. Opticians, Dispensing	$26,350	18.2%	10,000	2
43. Nonfarm Animal Caretakers	$17,190	22.2%	32,000	2
44. Tree Trimmers and Pruners	$25,630	18.6%	11,000	2 or 3
45. Riggers	$33,800	14.3%	3,000	2 or 3
46. Electrical and Electronic Inspectors and Testers	$27,750	4.7%	87,000	2, 3, or 4
47. Materials Inspectors	$27,750	4.7%	87,000	2, 3, or 4
48. Precision Devices Inspectors and Testers	$27,750	4.7%	87,000	2 or 4
49. Mechanical Drafters	$41,520	1.9%	9,000	2 or 4
50. Pest Control Workers	$24,990	17.0%	11,000	2
51. Embossing Machine Set-Up Operators	$29,340	4.6%	30,000	2 or 4
52. Precision Printing Workers	$29,340	4.6%	30,000	2, 5, or 6
53. Printing Press Machine Operators and Tenders	$29,340	4.6%	30,000	2, 4, or 5
54. Child Care Workers	$16,430	11.7%	406,000	2
55. Actors	$26,460	17.7%	8,000	2
56. Fitters, Structural Metal—Precision	$28,990	6.2%	14,000	2 or 3
57. Metal Fabricators, Structural Metal Products	$28,990	6.2%	14,000	2, 3, or 4
58. Coating, Painting, and Spraying Machine Setters and Set-Up Operators	$25,720	9.4%	17,000	2 or 4
59. Motorboat Mechanics	$29,170	18.3%	2,000	2 or 3
60. Maintenance Workers, Machinery	$33,000	5.9%	5,000	2
61. Fish and Game Wardens	$41,380	7.1%	1,000	2
62. Cabinetmakers and Bench Carpenters	$24,550	9.4%	15,000	2, 3, or 4
63. Metal Molding, Coremaking, and Casting Machine Operators and Tenders	$23,930	8.9%	18,000	2
64. Postal Service Clerks	$39,790	–0.5%	5,000	2
65. Stone Sawyers	$26,060	6.6%	12,000	2

(continued)

(continued)

Best Jobs with Apprenticeships that Take as Little as Two Years

Job	Annual Earnings	Percent Growth	Annual Openings	Years Required
66. Outdoor Power Equipment and Other Small Engine Mechanics	$24,820	18.9%	3,000	2, 3, or 4
67. Painting, Coating, and Decorating Workers	$21,650	17.6%	6,000	2, 3, or 4
68. Broadcast Technicians	$28,090	11.3%	4,000	2 or 4
69. Locomotive Engineers	$45,990	−7.2%	4,000	2
70. Embalmers	$34,350	8.3%	1,000	2
71. Electrical and Electronics Repairers, Powerhouse, Substation, and Relay	$52,040	−0.6%	2,000	2, 3, or 4
72. Gaugers	$49,970	−11.0%	3,000	2
73. Battery Repairers	$32,310	5.3%	3,000	2
74. Electric Motor and Switch Assemblers and Repairers	$32,310	5.3%	3,000	2 or 4
75. Paperhangers	$32,040	5.9%	3,000	2
76. Rail Car Repairers	$39,610	4.5%	1,000	2 or 4
77. Electronic Home Entertainment Equipment Installers and Repairers	$27,340	8.6%	5,000	2 or 4
78. Lathe and Turning Machine Tool Setters, Operators, and Tenders, Metal and Plastic	$30,300	0.8%	7,000	2, 3, or 4
79. Terrazzo Workers and Finishers	$27,710	15.2%	1,000	2 or 3
80. Automotive Glass Installers and Repairers	$27,160	10.7%	3,000	2
81. Pesticide Handlers, Sprayers, and Applicators, Vegetation	$25,490	9.7%	5,000	2
82. Cooks, Institution and Cafeteria	$18,300	2.1%	121,000	2
83. Parts Salespersons	$24,510	−2.0%	37,000	2
84. Data Entry Keyers	$22,600	−5.4%	72,000	2
85. Food Batchmakers	$21,900	7.2%	10,000	2 or 3
86. Mixing and Blending Machine Setters, Operators, and Tenders	$27,940	−6.5%	14,000	2
87. Agricultural Equipment Operators	$17,880	7.3%	14,000	2
88. Potters	$24,780	6.4%	6,000	2 or 3
89. Rotary Drill Operators, Oil and Gas	$34,910	1.5%	2,000	2
90. Scanner Operators	$31,660	−11.2%	6,000	2
91. Electronic Equipment Installers and Repairers, Motor Vehicles	$26,280	14.8%	1,000	2

Best Jobs with Apprenticeships that Take as Little as Three Years

Job	Annual Earnings	Percent Growth	Annual Openings	Years Required
1. Refrigeration Mechanics	$35,160	31.8%	35,000	3
2. Truck Drivers, Heavy	$33,310	19.0%	299,000	3 or 4
3. Municipal Fire Fighting and Prevention Supervisors	$57,000	18.7%	8,000	3
4. Food Service Managers	$37,260	11.5%	58,000	3
5. Carpenter Assemblers and Repairers	$34,250	10.1%	193,000	3
6. Welders and Cutters	$29,640	17.0%	71,000	3 or 4
7. Operating Engineers	$35,030	10.4%	45,000	3
8. Construction and Building Inspectors	$42,650	13.8%	10,000	3
9. Painters, Transportation Equipment	$34,100	17.5%	9,000	3
10. First-Line Supervisors/Managers of Retail Sales Workers	$30,680	9.1%	251,000	3
11. Tile and Marble Setters	$35,610	26.5%	4,000	3
12. Carpet Installers	$32,900	16.8%	10,000	3
13. Glaziers	$32,310	17.2%	7,000	3 or 4
14. Meter Mechanics	$42,540	12.0%	5,000	3
15. Audio and Video Equipment Technicians	$30,810	26.7%	5,000	3 or 4
16. Cartoonists	$35,420	16.5%	4,000	3
17. Station Installers and Repairers, Telephone	$48,230	–0.6%	23,000	3 or 4
18. Commercial Pilots	$49,830	14.9%	2,000	3.4
19. Cooks, Restaurant	$19,260	15.9%	211,000	3
20. Crane and Tower Operators	$37,150	10.8%	5,000	3
21. Floor Layers, Except Carpet, Wood, and Hard Tiles	$34,840	13.4%	4,000	3
22. Camera Operators, Television, Video, and Motion Picture	$34,330	13.4%	4,000	3
23. Electrical Power-Line Installers and Repairers	$48,960	1.6%	9,000	3 or 4
24. Reinforcing Iron and Rebar Workers	$34,950	16.7%	2,000	3
25. Mechanical Inspectors	$27,750	4.7%	87,000	3 or 4
26. Numerical Tool and Process Control Programmers	$38,330	13.0%	2,000	3
27. Paving, Surfacing, and Tamping Equipment Operators	$29,240	12.6%	8,000	3
28. Engraver Set-Up Operators	$29,340	4.6%	30,000	3 or 4
29. Professional Photographers	$25,050	13.6%	18,000	3
30. Slaughterers and Meat Packers	$20,420	18.1%	23,000	3
31. Coin, Vending, and Amusement Machine Servicers and Repairers	$27,800	15.2%	7,000	3

(continued)

(continued)

Best Jobs with Apprenticeships that Take as Little as Three Years

Job	Annual Earnings	Percent Growth	Annual Openings	Years Required
32. Stonemasons	$34,000	14.1%	2,000	3 or 4
33. Mechanical Door Repairers	$29,620	21.8%	1,000	3
34. Laundry and Drycleaning Machine Operators and Tenders, Except Pressing	$16,920	12.3%	47,000	3
35. Bakers, Bread and Pastry	$20,990	11.2%	29,000	3
36. Bakers, Manufacturing	$20,990	11.2%	29,000	3
37. Chemical Equipment Controllers and Operators	$38,740	–3.8%	8,000	3
38. Power Generating Plant Operators, Except Auxiliary Equipment Operators	$50,860	0.3%	3,000	3 or 4
39. Cutting and Slicing Machine Operators and Tenders	$26,060	6.6%	12,000	3
40. Tool and Die Makers	$42,990	0.4%	3,000	3 or 4
41. Motorcycle Mechanics	$27,630	18.7%	1,000	3
42. Gas Appliance Repairers	$29,890	5.5%	5,000	3
43. Petroleum Refinery and Control Panel Operators	$49,970	–11.0%	3,000	3
44. Boilermakers	$43,240	1.7%	2,000	3 or 4
45. Electric Home Appliance and Power Tool Repairers	$32,310	5.3%	3,000	3 or 4
46. Hand and Portable Power Tool Repairers	$32,310	5.3%	3,000	3
47. Chemical Plant and System Operators	$44,050	–12.3%	4,000	3 or 4
48. Welding Machine Setters and Set-Up Operators	$29,110	0.9%	10,000	3
49. Paper Goods Machine Setters, Operators, and Tenders	$28,920	–2.8%	16,000	3 or 4
50. Power Distributors and Dispatchers	$55,010	–3.0%	1,000	3 or 4
51. Fence Erectors	$22,580	13.4%	4,000	3
52. Word Processors and Typists	$27,150	–38.6%	45,000	3
53. Glass Blowers, Molders, Benders, and Finishers	$24,780	6.4%	6,000	3, 4, or 5
54. Mold Makers, Hand	$24,780	6.4%	6,000	3
55. Stone Cutters and Carvers	$24,780	6.4%	6,000	3
56. Paste-Up Workers	$31,660	–11.2%	6,000	3
57. Typesetting and Composing Machine Operators and Tenders	$31,660	–11.2%	6,000	3 or 5
58. Butchers and Meat Cutters	$25,570	–2.5%	21,000	3

Best Jobs with Apprenticeships that Take as Little as Four Years

Job	Annual Earnings	Percent Growth	Annual Openings	Years Required
1. Pipe Fitters	$40,950	18.7%	56,000	4
2. Plumbers	$40,950	18.7%	56,000	4
3. Sheet Metal Workers	$35,000	19.8%	30,000	4
4. Boat Builders and Shipwrights	$34,250	10.1%	193,000	4
5. Ship Carpenters and Joiners	$34,250	10.1%	193,000	4
6. Ceiling Tile Installers	$33,670	21.4%	17,000	4
7. Welder-Fitters	$29,640	17.0%	71,000	4
8. Data Processing Equipment Repairers	$33,780	15.1%	19,000	4
9. Aircraft Engine Specialists	$43,560	11.0%	12,000	4
10. Airframe-and-Power-Plant Mechanics	$43,560	11.0%	12,000	4
11. Elevator Installers and Repairers	$55,960	17.1%	3,000	4
12. Mobile Heavy Equipment Mechanics, Except Engines	$36,800	9.6%	12,000	4
13. Electric Meter Installers and Repairers	$42,540	12.0%	5,000	4
14. Central Office and PBX Installers and Repairers	$48,230	–0.6%	23,000	4
15. Motor Vehicle Inspectors	$49,590	7.7%	5,000	4
16. Insulation Workers, Floor, Ceiling, and Wall	$29,190	15.8%	9,000	4
17. Insulation Workers, Mechanical	$29,190	15.8%	9,000	4
18. Civil Drafters	$37,690	4.2%	14,000	4
19. Millwrights	$42,390	5.3%	7,000	4
20. Fire Inspectors	$44,250	11.6%	1,000	4
21. Numerical Control Machine Tool Operators and Tenders, Metal and Plastic	$29,420	9.3%	11,000	4
22. Design Printing Machine Setters and Set-Up Operators	$29,340	4.6%	30,000	4
23. Letterpress Setters and Set-Up Operators	$29,340	4.6%	30,000	4
24. Offset Lithographic Press Setters and Set-Up Operators	$29,340	4.6%	30,000	4
25. Recreational Vehicle Service Technicians	$27,270	21.8%	4,000	4
26. Job Printers	$30,850	9.2%	7,000	4
27. Dredge Operators	$27,800	8.9%	14,000	4
28. Locksmiths and Safe Repairers	$28,760	21.0%	3,000	4
29. Press and Press Brake Machine Setters and Set-Up Operators, Metal and Plastic	$25,210	6.8%	37,000	4
30. Lay-Out Workers, Metal and Plastic	$31,970	15.6%	1,000	4
31. Metal Workers and Plastic Workers, All Other	$28,400	6.6%	11,000	4
32. Electrical and Electronics Installers and Repairers, Transportation Equipment	$39,300	7.1%	2,000	4

(continued)

(continued)

Best Jobs with Apprenticeships that Take as Little as Four Years

Job	Annual Earnings	Percent Growth	Annual Openings	Years Required
33. Electronic Drafters	$41,730	0.7%	5,000	4
34. Stationary Engineers	$43,420	0.3%	4,000	4
35. Avionics Technicians	$43,110	3.4%	3,000	4
36. Well and Core Drill Operators	$32,540	7.7%	3,000	4
37. Transformer Repairers	$32,310	5.3%	3,000	4
38. Signal and Track Switch Repairers	$43,690	–3.1%	1,000	4
39. Precision Pattern and Die Casters, Nonferrous Metals	$24,780	6.4%	6,000	4
40. Hand Compositors and Typesetters	$31,660	–11.2%	6,000	4
41. Photoengravers	$31,660	–11.2%	6,000	4, 5, or 6
42. Platemakers	$31,660	–11.2%	6,000	4
43. Strippers	$31,660	–11.2%	6,000	4 or 5

Best Jobs with Apprenticeships that Take as Little as Five Years

Job	Annual Earnings	Percent Growth	Annual Openings	Years Required
1. Desktop Publishers	$31,590	29.2%	4,000	5
2. Patternmakers, Wood	$29,650	11.8%	fewer than 500	5
3. Precision Mold and Pattern Casters, Except Nonferrous Metals	$24,780	6.4%	6,000	5
4. Camera Operators	$31,660	–11.2%	6,000	5
5. Dot Etchers	$31,660	–11.2%	6,000	5
6. Electrotypers and Stereotypers	$31,660	–11.2%	6,000	5 or 6

Best Jobs with Apprenticeships that Take Six Years

Job	Annual Earnings	Percent Growth	Annual Openings
1. Plate Finishers	$31,660	–11.2%	6,000

Best Jobs with Apprenticeships with a Duration Based on Attaining Competency

Job	Annual Earnings	Percent Growth	Annual Openings
1. Surgical Technologists	$32,130	27.9%	13,000
2. Emergency Management Specialists	$45,090	28.2%	2,000
3. Social and Human Service Assistants	$23,860	48.7%	63,000
4. Team Assemblers	$23,180	–1.6%	143,000

Apprenticeable Jobs with the Highest Percentage of Women and Men

Apprenticeship is often mistakenly thought of as an all-male preserve. The continuing use (in some places—not in this book) of the term "journeyman" has not helped. It is true that the best available statistics suggest that only about 7 percent of apprentices are women. On the other hand, does this low turnout of women mean that women are being discouraged or rather that women are not interested? The answer is not at all clear. Where there is interest, there sometimes is opportunity—some employers and unions have been moving aggressively for inclusion of women in apprenticeships.

Therefore, as you look over the following lists of apprenticeable jobs with a high percentage of women and men, you should not regard the lists as intended to restrict women or men from considering apprenticeship options. In fact, one reason for including these lists is exactly the opposite. We hope the lists help people see possibilities that they might not otherwise have considered. For example, we suggest that women browse the lists of apprenticeable jobs that employ high percentages of men. Many of these occupations pay quite well, and women who want to do them and are willing to undertake the necessary apprenticeships should consider them.

We created the lists by sorting the jobs that met the criteria for this book and including only those employing 70 percent or more of women or men. Of the 250 best apprenticeable jobs, 16 met this criterion for women and 181 for men.

In the following lists, if you compare the apprenticeable occupations employing a high percentage of women with those employing a high percentage of men, you may notice some distinct differences beyond the obvious. For example, you may notice that the jobs with the highest percentage of women tend to cluster into certain industries. The following chart, based on 2003 data from 31 states, shows an estimation of how the distribution varies among different industries:

Figure 2: Gender distribution among industries, 2003.

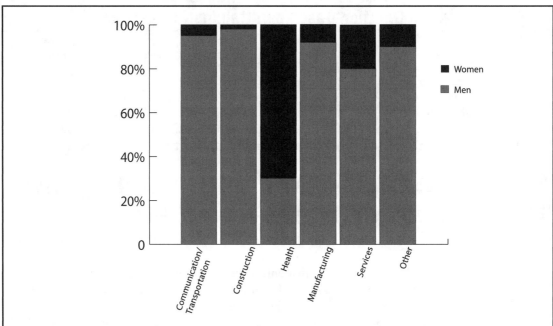

You may also notice in the following lists that the jobs with a high percentage of women are growing somewhat faster than those with a high percentage of men. We've done the math and discovered that the difference is an average growth rate of 16 percent for the jobs that employ mostly women versus an average rate of 11 percent for the jobs that employ mostly men. The number of annual job openings shows a similar pattern. Occupations with a high percentage of men average 28,389 openings per year, while almost five times that number of openings, 140,250, are projected on average for occupations with a high percentage of women.

This discrepancy might explain why men have had more problems than women in adapting to an economy dominated by service and information-based jobs. Many women may simply be better prepared for these jobs, possessing more appropriate skills for the jobs that are now growing rapidly and have more job openings.

On the other hand, you may notice that on average the jobs with a high percentage of men have higher wages (an average of $33,452) than do the jobs with a high percentage of women ($24,242). This indicates that women interested in improving their earnings may want to consider jobs traditionally dominated by men. Remember that a time-honored gender imbalance is not always a barrier to women. As noted earlier, some apprenticeship programs are seeking female recruits to counterbalance a traditional male dominance.

Apprenticeable Jobs with the Highest Percentage of Women

Job	Percent Women
1. Dental Assistants	97.1%
2. Legal Secretaries	96.5%
3. Medical Secretaries	96.5%
4. Secretaries, Except Legal, Medical, and Executive	96.5%
5. Child Care Workers	94.7%
6. Licensed Practical and Licensed Vocational Nurses	93.0%
7. Word Processors and Typists	93.0%
8. Teacher Assistants	91.6%
9. Hairdressers, Hairstylists, and Cosmetologists	90.3%
10. Tellers	89.7%
11. Medical Assistants	88.0%
12. Nursing Aides, Orderlies, and Attendants	87.8%
13. Maids and Housekeeping Cleaners	87.6%
14. Data Entry Keyers	81.8%
15. Pharmacy Technicians	80.7%
16. Surgical Technologists	80.7%

Best Apprenticeable Jobs Overall Employing 70 Percent or More Women

Job	Percent Women	Annual Earnings	Percent Growth	Annual Openings
1. Legal Secretaries	96.5%	$35,660	18.8%	39,000
2. Licensed Practical and Licensed Vocational Nurses	93.0%	$32,390	20.2%	105,000
3. Surgical Technologists	80.7%	$32,130	27.9%	13,000
4. Dental Assistants	97.1%	$27,700	42.5%	35,000
5. Medical Assistants	88.0%	$24,170	58.9%	78,000
6. Nursing Aides, Orderlies, and Attendants	87.8%	$20,490	24.9%	302,000
7. Pharmacy Technicians	80.7%	$22,760	28.8%	39,000
8. Medical Secretaries	96.5%	$26,000	17.2%	50,000

(continued)

(continued)

Best Apprenticeable Jobs Overall Employing 70 Percent or More Women

Job	Percent Women	Annual Earnings	Percent Growth	Annual Openings
9. Teacher Assistants	91.6%	$19,000	23.0%	259,000
10. Hairdressers, Hairstylists, and Cosmetologists	90.3%	$18,700	14.7%	68,000
11. Child Care Workers	94.7%	$16,430	11.7%	406,000
12. Tellers	89.7%	$20,670	9.4%	127,000
13. Maids and Housekeeping Cleaners	87.6%	$16,600	9.2%	352,000
14. Secretaries, Except Legal, Medical, and Executive	96.5%	$25,420	–2.9%	254,000
15. Word Processors and Typists	93.0%	$27,150	–38.6%	45,000
16. Data Entry Keyers	81.8%	$22,600	–5.4%	72,000

Apprenticeable Jobs with the Highest Percentage of Men

Job	Percent Men
1. Rail Car Repairers	99.0%
2. Mobile Heavy Equipment Mechanics, Except Engines	99.0%
3. Stonemasons	98.9%
4. Brickmasons and Blockmasons	98.9%
5. Bus and Truck Mechanics and Diesel Engine Specialists	98.8%
6. Cement Masons and Concrete Finishers	98.7%
7. Rotary Drill Operators, Oil and Gas	98.7%
8. Terrazzo Workers and Finishers	98.7%
9. Plasterers and Stucco Masons	98.6%
10. Elevator Installers and Repairers	98.6%
11. Well and Core Drill Operators	98.5%
12. Roofers	98.4%
13. Motorboat Mechanics	98.3%
14. Outdoor Power Equipment and Other Small Engine Mechanics	98.3%
15. Pipe Fitters	98.3%
16. Riggers	98.3%
17. Plumbers	98.3%
18. Recreational Vehicle Service Technicians	98.3%
19. Motorcycle Mechanics	98.3%
20. Dredge Operators	98.2%
21. Heating and Air Conditioning Mechanics	98.2%
22. Dragline Operators	98.2%
23. Refrigeration Mechanics	98.2%

Apprenticeable Jobs with the Highest Percentage of Men

Job	Percent Men
24. Automotive Specialty Technicians	98.1%
25. Boat Builders and Shipwrights	98.1%
26. Ship Carpenters and Joiners	98.1%
27. Carpenter Assemblers and Repairers	98.1%
28. Automotive Master Mechanics	98.1%
29. Rough Carpenters	98.1%
30. Construction Carpenters	98.1%
31. Automotive Body and Related Repairers	97.9%
32. Operating Engineers	97.8%
33. Millwrights	97.8%
34. Grader, Bulldozer, and Scraper Operators	97.8%
35. Structural Iron and Steel Workers	97.6%
36. Reinforcing Iron and Rebar Workers	97.6%
37. Carpet Installers	97.5%
38. Tile and Marble Setters	97.5%
39. Floor Layers, Except Carpet, Wood, and Hard Tiles	97.5%
40. Fence Erectors	97.4%
41. Electricians	97.4%
42. Ceiling Tile Installers	97.3%
43. Drywall Installers	97.3%
44. Tapers	97.3%
45. Electrical Power-Line Installers and Repairers	97.3%
46. Gas Appliance Repairers	97.1%
47. Municipal Fire Fighting and Prevention Supervisors	97.0%
48. Automotive Glass Installers and Repairers	97.0%
49. Tool and Die Makers	96.9%
50. Boilermakers	96.8%
51. Boiler Operators and Tenders, Low Pressure	96.7%
52. Stationary Engineers	96.7%
53. Crane and Tower Operators	96.6%
54. Construction Laborers	96.5%
55. Municipal Fire Fighters	96.4%
56. Forest Fire Fighters	96.4%
57. Construction and Related Workers, All Other	96.3%
58. Industrial Machinery Mechanics	96.2%
59. Commercial Pilots	96.1%

(continued)

(continued)

Apprenticeable Jobs with the Highest Percentage of Men

Job	Percent Men
60. Locomotive Engineers	96.0%
61. Insulation Workers, Floor, Ceiling, and Wall	95.9%
62. Insulation Workers, Mechanical	95.9%
63. Maintenance and Repair Workers, General	95.9%
64. Electronic Home Entertainment Equipment Installers and Repairers	95.8%
65. Sheet Metal Workers	95.8%
66. Glaziers	95.6%
67. Electric Motor and Switch Assemblers and Repairers	95.5%
68. Battery Repairers	95.5%
69. Transformer Repairers	95.5%
70. Hand and Portable Power Tool Repairers	95.5%
71. Electric Home Appliance and Power Tool Repairers	95.5%
72. Paving, Surfacing, and Tamping Equipment Operators	95.4%
73. Fitters, Structural Metal—Precision	95.3%
74. Electronic Equipment Installers and Repairers, Motor Vehicles	95.3%
75. Metal Fabricators, Structural Metal Products	95.3%
76. Meter Mechanics	95.1%
77. Valve and Regulator Repairers	95.1%
78. Mechanical Door Repairers	95.1%
79. Aircraft Engine Specialists	95.1%
80. Airframe-and-Power-Plant Mechanics	95.1%
81. Electric Meter Installers and Repairers	95.1%
82. Machinists	94.7%
83. Water and Liquid Waste Treatment Plant and System Operators	94.5%
84. Maintenance Workers, Machinery	94.4%
85. Electrical and Electronics Repairers, Powerhouse, Substation, and Relay	94.1%
86. Electrical and Electronics Repairers, Commercial and Industrial Equipment	94.1%
87. Truck Drivers, Heavy	94.1%
88. Electrical and Electronics Installers and Repairers, Transportation Equipment	94.1%
89. Pest Control Workers	93.7%
90. Telecommunications Line Installers and Repairers	93.5%
91. Locksmiths and Safe Repairers	93.0%
92. Cabinetmakers and Bench Carpenters	93.0%
93. Signal and Track Switch Repairers	92.9%
94. Installation, Maintenance, and Repair Workers, All Other	92.9%
95. Power Generating Plant Operators, Except Auxiliary Equipment Operators	92.6%
96. Welder-Fitters	92.6%

Apprenticeable Jobs with the Highest Percentage of Men

Job	Percent Men
97. Gaugers	92.6%
98. Power Distributors and Dispatchers	92.6%
99. Petroleum Refinery and Control Panel Operators	92.6%
100. Welding Machine Setters and Set-Up Operators	92.6%
101. Welders and Cutters	92.6%
102. Chemical Plant and System Operators	92.6%
103. Painters, Construction and Maintenance	92.6%
104. Landscaping and Groundskeeping Workers	92.4%
105. Tree Trimmers and Pruners	92.4%
106. Pesticide Handlers, Sprayers, and Applicators, Vegetation	92.4%
107. Mapping Technicians	91.1%
108. Surveying Technicians	91.1%
109. Helpers—Installation, Maintenance, and Repair Workers	90.8%
110. Construction and Building Inspectors	90.2%
111. Fire Inspectors	90.0%
112. Lay-Out Workers, Metal and Plastic	89.8%
113. Parts Salespersons	89.6%
114. Avionics Technicians	88.9%
115. Patternmakers, Wood	88.9%
116. Numerical Tool and Process Control Programmers	88.0%
117. Numerical Control Machine Tool Operators and Tenders, Metal and Plastic	88.0%
118. Medical Equipment Repairers	87.9%
119. Lathe and Turning Machine Tool Setters, Operators, and Tenders, Metal and Plastic	87.6%
120. Central Office and PBX Installers and Repairers	87.0%
121. Communication Equipment Mechanics, Installers, and Repairers	87.0%
122. Station Installers and Repairers, Telephone	87.0%
123. Police Patrol Officers	86.9%
124. Data Processing Equipment Repairers	86.5%
125. Office Machine and Cash Register Servicers	86.5%
126. Separating, Filtering, Clarifying, Precipitating, and Still Machine Setters, Operators, and Tenders	85.9%
127. Chemical Equipment Controllers and Operators	85.9%
128. Sound Engineering Technicians	85.8%
129. Broadcast Technicians	85.8%
130. Audio and Video Equipment Technicians	85.8%
131. Mixing and Blending Machine Setters, Operators, and Tenders	85.6%
132. Farmers and Ranchers	85.4%

(continued)

(continued)

Apprenticeable Jobs with the Highest Percentage of Men

Job	Percent Men
133. Model Makers, Metal and Plastic	85.2%
134. Conveyor Operators and Tenders	84.4%
135. Ambulance Drivers and Attendants, Except Emergency Medical Technicians	83.9%
136. Motor Vehicle Inspectors	83.8%
137. Coating, Painting, and Spraying Machine Operators and Tenders	83.2%
138. Painters, Transportation Equipment	83.2%
139. Coating, Painting, and Spraying Machine Setters and Set-Up Operators	83.2%
140. Painting, Coating, and Decorating Workers	83.2%
141. Design Printing Machine Setters and Set-Up Operators	82.2%
142. Letterpress Setters and Set-Up Operators	82.2%
143. Offset Lithographic Press Setters and Set-Up Operators	82.2%
144. Engraver Set-Up Operators	82.2%
145. Printing Press Machine Operators and Tenders	82.2%
146. Precision Printing Workers	82.2%
147. Embossing Machine Set-Up Operators	82.2%
148. Extruding and Drawing Machine Setters, Operators, and Tenders, Metal and Plastic	82.1%
149. Camera Operators, Television, Video, and Motion Picture	81.1%
150. Chefs and Head Cooks	80.8%
151. Coin, Vending, and Amusement Machine Servicers and Repairers	80.2%
152. Mechanical Drafters	80.1%
153. Electronic Drafters	80.1%
154. Civil Drafters	80.1%
155. Molding and Casting Workers	79.6%
156. Stone Cutters and Carvers	79.6%
157. Precision Mold and Pattern Casters, Except Nonferrous Metals	79.6%
158. Precision Pattern and Die Casters, Nonferrous Metals	79.6%
159. Mold Makers, Hand	79.6%
160. Potters	79.6%
161. Glass Blowers, Molders, Benders, and Finishers	79.6%
162. Security Guards	79.0%
163. Embalmers	77.9%
164. Plastic Molding and Casting Machine Setters and Set-Up Operators	77.6%
165. Metal Molding, Coremaking, and Casting Machine Operators and Tenders	77.6%
166. Job Printers	77.5%
167. Butchers and Meat Cutters	76.3%
168. Slaughterers and Meat Packers	76.3%

Apprenticeable Jobs with the Highest Percentage of Men

Job	Percent Men
169. Agricultural Equipment Operators	75.4%
170. Correctional Officers and Jailers	74.0%
171. Cutting and Slicing Machine Operators and Tenders	73.1%
172. Stone Sawyers	73.1%
173. Cargo and Freight Agents	73.1%
174. Paper Goods Machine Setters, Operators, and Tenders	72.8%
175. Press and Press Brake Machine Setters and Set-Up Operators, Metal and Plastic	71.9%
176. Metal Workers and Plastic Workers, All Other	71.5%
177. Combination Machine Tool Setters and Set-Up Operators, Metal and Plastic	71.5%
178. Fish and Game Wardens	71.0%
179. Paperhangers	70.3%
180. Building Cleaning Workers, All Other	70.1%
181. Janitors and Cleaners, Except Maids and Housekeeping Cleaners	70.1%

Best Apprenticeable Jobs Overall Employing 70 Percent or More Men

Job	Percent Men	Annual Earnings	Percent Growth	Annual Openings
1. Police Patrol Officers	86.9%	$44,020	24.7%	67,000
2. Electricians	97.4%	$41,680	23.4%	65,000
3. Pipe Fitters	98.3%	$40,950	18.7%	56,000
4. Plumbers	98.3%	$40,950	18.7%	56,000
5. Heating and Air Conditioning Mechanics	98.2%	$35,160	31.8%	35,000
6. Refrigeration Mechanics	98.2%	$35,160	31.8%	35,000
7. Truck Drivers, Heavy	94.1%	$33,310	19.0%	299,000
8. Correctional Officers and Jailers	74.0%	$33,160	24.2%	49,000
9. Forest Fire Fighters	96.4%	$37,060	20.7%	29,000
10. Municipal Fire Fighters	96.4%	$37,060	20.7%	29,000
11. Sheet Metal Workers	95.8%	$35,000	19.8%	30,000
12. Municipal Fire Fighting and Prevention Supervisors	97.0%	$57,000	18.7%	8,000
13. Telecommunications Line Installers and Repairers	93.5%	$39,540	18.8%	13,000
14. Brickmasons and Blockmasons	98.9%	$41,550	14.2%	21,000
15. Boat Builders and Shipwrights	98.1%	$34,250	10.1%	193,000
16. Carpenter Assemblers and Repairers	98.1%	$34,250	10.1%	193,000
17. Construction Carpenters	98.1%	$34,250	10.1%	193,000

(continued)

Best Apprenticeable Jobs Overall Employing 70 Percent or More Men

Job	Percent Men	Annual Earnings	Percent Growth	Annual Openings
18. Rough Carpenters	98.1%	$34,250	10.1%	193,000
19. Ship Carpenters and Joiners	98.1%	$34,250	10.1%	193,000
20. Ceiling Tile Installers	97.3%	$33,670	21.4%	17,000
21. Drywall Installers	97.3%	$33,670	21.4%	17,000
22. Maintenance and Repair Workers, General	95.9%	$29,800	16.3%	155,000
23. Cement Masons and Concrete Finishers	98.7%	$30,780	26.1%	24,000
24. Welder-Fitters	92.6%	$29,640	17.0%	71,000
25. Welders and Cutters	92.6%	$29,640	17.0%	71,000
26. Bus and Truck Mechanics and Diesel Engine Specialists	98.8%	$34,970	14.2%	28,000
27. Roofers	98.4%	$30,020	18.6%	38,000
28. Grader, Bulldozer, and Scraper Operators	97.8%	$35,030	10.4%	45,000
29. Operating Engineers	97.8%	$35,030	10.4%	45,000
30. Construction and Building Inspectors	90.2%	$42,650	13.8%	10,000
31. Automotive Master Mechanics	98.1%	$31,130	12.4%	100,000
32. Automotive Specialty Technicians	98.1%	$31,130	12.4%	100,000
33. Structural Iron and Steel Workers	97.6%	$40,730	15.9%	9,000
34. Data Processing Equipment Repairers	86.5%	$33,780	15.1%	19,000
35. Office Machine and Cash Register Servicers	86.5%	$33,780	15.1%	19,000
36. Aircraft Engine Specialists	95.1%	$43,560	11.0%	12,000
37. Airframe-and-Power-Plant Mechanics	95.1%	$43,560	11.0%	12,000
38. Automotive Body and Related Repairers	97.9%	$33,140	13.2%	23,000
39. Tapers	97.3%	$39,130	20.8%	5,000
40. Painters, Transportation Equipment	83.2%	$34,100	17.5%	9,000
41. Tile and Marble Setters	97.5%	$35,610	26.5%	4,000
42. Carpet Installers	97.5%	$32,900	16.8%	10,000
43. Electrical and Electronics Repairers, Commercial and Industrial Equipment	94.1%	$42,200	10.3%	10,000
44. Elevator Installers and Repairers	98.6%	$55,960	17.1%	3,000
45. Installation, Maintenance, and Repair Workers, All Other	92.9%	$33,010	12.2%	22,000
46. Water and Liquid Waste Treatment Plant and System Operators	94.5%	$33,910	16.0%	9,000
47. Painters, Construction and Maintenance	92.6%	$29,360	11.6%	69,000
48. Mapping Technicians	91.1%	$29,520	23.1%	10,000
49. Surveying Technicians	91.1%	$29,520	23.1%	10,000
50. Security Guards	79.0%	$19,660	31.9%	228,000
51. Chefs and Head Cooks	80.8%	$28,750	15.8%	33,000

Best Apprenticeable Jobs Overall Employing 70 Percent or More Men

Job	Percent Men	Annual Earnings	Percent Growth	Annual Openings
52. Machinists	94.7%	$33,090	8.2%	30,000
53. Mobile Heavy Equipment Mechanics, Except Engines	99.0%	$36,800	9.6%	12,000
54. Glaziers	95.6%	$32,310	17.2%	7,000
55. Landscaping and Groundskeeping Workers	92.4%	$19,940	22.0%	203,000
56. Industrial Machinery Mechanics	96.2%	$38,440	5.5%	19,000
57. Sound Engineering Technicians	85.8%	$38,290	25.5%	2,000
58. Electric Meter Installers and Repairers	95.1%	$42,540	12.0%	5,000
59. Meter Mechanics	95.1%	$42,540	12.0%	5,000
60. Valve and Regulator Repairers	95.1%	$42,540	12.0%	5,000
61. Audio and Video Equipment Technicians	85.8%	$30,810	26.7%	5,000
62. Construction Laborers	96.5%	$24,670	14.2%	166,000
63. Medical Equipment Repairers	87.9%	$37,960	14.8%	4,000
64. Cargo and Freight Agents	73.1%	$31,990	15.5%	8,000
65. Plasterers and Stucco Masons	98.6%	$33,060	13.5%	8,000
66. Central Office and PBX Installers and Repairers	87.0%	$48,230	–0.6%	23,000
67. Communication Equipment Mechanics, Installers, and Repairers	87.0%	$48,230	–0.6%	23,000
68. Station Installers and Repairers, Telephone	87.0%	$48,230	–0.6%	23,000
69. Janitors and Cleaners, Except Maids and Housekeeping Cleaners	70.1%	$18,410	18.3%	454,000
70. Commercial Pilots	96.1%	$49,830	14.9%	2,000
71. Construction and Related Workers, All Other	96.3%	$22,900	32.0%	17,000
72. Motor Vehicle Inspectors	83.8%	$49,590	7.7%	5,000
73. Dragline Operators	98.2%	$32,150	8.9%	14,000
74. Crane and Tower Operators	96.6%	$37,150	10.8%	5,000
75. Insulation Workers, Floor, Ceiling, and Wall	95.9%	$29,190	15.8%	9,000
76. Insulation Workers, Mechanical	95.9%	$29,190	15.8%	9,000
77. Helpers—Installation, Maintenance, and Repair Workers	90.8%	$21,240	20.3%	33,000
78. Civil Drafters	80.1%	$37,690	4.2%	14,000
79. Floor Layers, Except Carpet, Wood, and Hard Tiles	97.5%	$34,840	13.4%	4,000
80. Camera Operators, Television, Video, and Motion Picture	81.1%	$34,330	13.4%	4,000
81. Model Makers, Metal and Plastic	85.2%	$43,470	14.6%	1,000
82. Electrical Power-Line Installers and Repairers	97.3%	$48,960	1.6%	9,000
83. Millwrights	97.8%	$42,390	5.3%	7,000
84. Tree Trimmers and Pruners	92.4%	$25,630	18.6%	11,000

(continued)

(continued)

Best Apprenticeable Jobs Overall Employing 70 Percent or More Men

Job	Percent Men	Annual Earnings	Percent Growth	Annual Openings
85. Reinforcing Iron and Rebar Workers	97.6%	$34,950	16.7%	2,000
86. Riggers	98.3%	$33,800	14.3%	3,000
87. Fire Inspectors	90.0%	$44,250	11.6%	1,000
88. Numerical Tool and Process Control Programmers	88.0%	$38,330	13.0%	2,000
89. Numerical Control Machine Tool Operators and Tenders, Metal and Plastic	88.0%	$29,420	9.3%	11,000
90. Mechanical Drafters	80.1%	$41,520	1.9%	9,000
91. Pest Control Workers	93.7%	$24,990	17.0%	11,000
92. Paving, Surfacing, and Tamping Equipment Operators	95.4%	$29,240	12.6%	8,000
93. Design Printing Machine Setters and Set-Up Operators	82.2%	$29,340	4.6%	30,000
94. Embossing Machine Set-Up Operators	82.2%	$29,340	4.6%	30,000
95. Engraver Set-Up Operators	82.2%	$29,340	4.6%	30,000
96. Letterpress Setters and Set-Up Operators	82.2%	$29,340	4.6%	30,000
97. Offset Lithographic Press Setters and Set-Up Operators	82.2%	$29,340	4.6%	30,000
98. Precision Printing Workers	82.2%	$29,340	4.6%	30,000
99. Printing Press Machine Operators and Tenders	82.2%	$29,340	4.6%	30,000
100. Slaughterers and Meat Packers	76.3%	$20,420	18.1%	23,000
101. Coin, Vending, and Amusement Machine Servicers and Repairers	80.2%	$27,800	15.2%	7,000
102. Building Cleaning Workers, All Other	70.1%	$20,990	16.1%	24,000
103. Recreational Vehicle Service Technicians	98.3%	$27,270	21.8%	4,000
104. Job Printers	77.5%	$30,850	9.2%	7,000
105. Dredge Operators	98.2%	$27,800	8.9%	14,000
106. Locksmiths and Safe Repairers	93.0%	$28,760	21.0%	3,000
107. Stonemasons	98.9%	$34,000	14.1%	2,000
108. Press and Press Brake Machine Setters and Set-Up Operators, Metal and Plastic	71.9%	$25,210	6.8%	37,000
109. Fitters, Structural Metal—Precision	95.3%	$28,990	6.2%	14,000
110. Metal Fabricators, Structural Metal Products	95.3%	$28,990	6.2%	14,000
111. Coating, Painting, and Spraying Machine Operators and Tenders	83.2%	$25,720	9.4%	17,000
112. Coating, Painting, and Spraying Machine Setters and Set-Up Operators	83.2%	$25,720	9.4%	17,000
113. Mechanical Door Repairers	95.1%	$29,620	21.8%	1,000
114. Lay-Out Workers, Metal and Plastic	89.8%	$31,970	15.6%	1,000
115. Metal Workers and Plastic Workers, All Other	71.5%	$28,400	6.6%	11,000

Best Apprenticeable Jobs Overall Employing 70 Percent or More Men

Job	Percent Men	Annual Earnings	Percent Growth	Annual Openings
116. Electrical and Electronics Installers and Repairers, Transportation Equipment	94.1%	$39,300	7.1%	2,000
117. Electronic Drafters	80.1%	$41,730	0.7%	5,000
118. Motorboat Mechanics	98.3%	$29,170	18.3%	2,000
119. Combination Machine Tool Setters and Set-Up Operators, Metal and Plastic	71.5%	$29,050	8.3%	8,000
120. Chemical Equipment Controllers and Operators	85.9%	$38,740	−3.8%	8,000
121. Maintenance Workers, Machinery	94.4%	$33,000	5.9%	5,000
122. Boiler Operators and Tenders, Low Pressure	96.7%	$43,420	0.3%	4,000
123. Extruding and Drawing Machine Setters, Operators, and Tenders, Metal and Plastic	82.1%	$26,450	7.1%	14,000
124. Stationary Engineers	96.7%	$43,420	0.3%	4,000
125. Fish and Game Wardens	71.0%	$41,380	7.1%	1,000
126. Power Generating Plant Operators, Except Auxiliary Equipment Operators	92.6%	$50,860	0.3%	3,000
127. Cabinetmakers and Bench Carpenters	93.0%	$24,550	9.4%	15,000
128. Avionics Technicians	88.9%	$43,110	3.4%	3,000
129. Conveyor Operators and Tenders	84.4%	$24,690	12.4%	9,000
130. Well and Core Drill Operators	98.5%	$32,540	7.7%	3,000
131. Metal Molding, Coremaking, and Casting Machine Operators and Tenders	77.6%	$23,930	8.9%	18,000
132. Plastic Molding and Casting Machine Setters and Set-Up Operators	77.6%	$23,930	8.9%	18,000
133. Cutting and Slicing Machine Operators and Tenders	73.1%	$26,060	6.6%	12,000
134. Stone Sawyers	73.1%	$26,060	6.6%	12,000
135. Outdoor Power Equipment and Other Small Engine Mechanics	98.3%	$24,820	18.9%	3,000
136. Painting, Coating, and Decorating Workers	83.2%	$21,650	17.6%	6,000
137. Tool and Die Makers	96.9%	$42,990	0.4%	3,000
138. Broadcast Technicians	85.8%	$28,090	11.3%	4,000
139. Locomotive Engineers	96.0%	$45,990	−7.2%	4,000
140. Embalmers	77.9%	$34,350	8.3%	1,000
141. Motorcycle Mechanics	98.3%	$27,630	18.7%	1,000
142. Ambulance Drivers and Attendants, Except Emergency Medical Technicians	83.9%	$19,000	26.7%	4,000
143. Electrical and Electronics Repairers, Powerhouse, Substation, and Relay	94.1%	$52,040	−0.6%	2,000
144. Gas Appliance Repairers	97.1%	$29,890	5.5%	5,000

(continued)

(continued)

Best Apprenticeable Jobs Overall Employing 70 Percent or More Men

Job	Percent Men	Annual Earnings	Percent Growth	Annual Openings
145. Gaugers	92.6%	$49,970	–11.0%	3,000
146. Petroleum Refinery and Control Panel Operators	92.6%	$49,970	–11.0%	3,000
147. Boilermakers	96.8%	$43,240	1.7%	2,000
148. Battery Repairers	95.5%	$32,310	5.3%	3,000
149. Electric Home Appliance and Power Tool Repairers	95.5%	$32,310	5.3%	3,000
150. Electric Motor and Switch Assemblers and Repairers	95.5%	$32,310	5.3%	3,000
151. Hand and Portable Power Tool Repairers	95.5%	$32,310	5.3%	3,000
152. Paperhangers	70.3%	$32,040	5.9%	3,000
153. Transformer Repairers	95.5%	$32,310	5.3%	3,000
154. Chemical Plant and System Operators	92.6%	$44,050	–12.3%	4,000
155. Welding Machine Setters and Set-Up Operators	92.6%	$29,110	0.9%	10,000
156. Rail Car Repairers	99.0%	$39,610	4.5%	1,000
157. Paper Goods Machine Setters, Operators, and Tenders	72.8%	$28,920	–2.8%	16,000
158. Electronic Home Entertainment Equipment Installers and Repairers	95.8%	$27,340	8.6%	5,000
159. Lathe and Turning Machine Tool Setters, Operators, and Tenders, Metal and Plastic	87.6%	$30,300	0.8%	7,000
160. Terrazzo Workers and Finishers	98.7%	$27,710	15.2%	1,000
161. Separating, Filtering, Clarifying, Precipitating, and Still Machine Setters, Operators, and Tenders	85.9%	$31,720	0.8%	5,000
162. Automotive Glass Installers and Repairers	97.0%	$27,160	10.7%	3,000
163. Power Distributors and Dispatchers	92.6%	$55,010	–3.0%	1,000
164. Pesticide Handlers, Sprayers, and Applicators, Vegetation	92.4%	$25,490	9.7%	5,000
165. Parts Salespersons	89.6%	$24,510	–2.0%	37,000
166. Patternmakers, Wood	88.9%	$29,650	11.8%	fewer than 500
167. Fence Erectors	97.4%	$22,580	13.4%	4,000
168. Mixing and Blending Machine Setters, Operators, and Tenders	85.6%	$27,940	–6.5%	14,000
169. Agricultural Equipment Operators	75.4%	$17,880	7.3%	14,000
170. Signal and Track Switch Repairers	92.9%	$43,690	–3.1%	1,000
171. Farmers and Ranchers	85.4%	$24,076	–20.6%	118,000
172. Glass Blowers, Molders, Benders, and Finishers	79.6%	$24,780	6.4%	6,000
173. Mold Makers, Hand	79.6%	$24,780	6.4%	6,000
174. Molding and Casting Workers	79.6%	$24,780	6.4%	6,000
175. Potters	79.6%	$24,780	6.4%	6,000

Best Appriceable Jobs Overall Employing 70 Percent or More Men

Job	Percent Men	Annual Earnings	Percent Growth	Annual Openings
176. Precision Mold and Pattern Casters, Except Nonferrous Metals	79.6%	$24,780	6.4%	6,000
177. Precision Pattern and Die Casters, Nonferrous Metals	79.6%	$24,780	6.4%	6,000
178. Rotary Drill Operators, Oil and Gas	98.7%	$34,910	1.5%	2,000
179. Stone Cutters and Carvers	79.6%	$24,780	6.4%	6,000
180. Butchers and Meat Cutters	76.3%	$25,570	–2.5%	21,000
181. Electronic Equipment Installers and Repairers, Motor Vehicles	95.3%	$26,280	14.8%	1,000

Most Popular Apprenticeships

As you scan the following lists, keep in mind that they are based on somewhat limited information. The statistics on the most popular apprenticeships are derived from the Registered Apprenticeship Information System of the U.S. Department of Labor, which gets input from only 31 states. Thus it does not represent the entire country and may not be a good reflection of conditions in your state and locality. Furthermore, it is based on 2003 data, and the ranking is known to vary from one year to another. For example, in 2002 Roofer was in ninth place, not eleventh. Elevator Constructor was not even among the top 25 in 2002 or 2001. Nevertheless, the top five have not varied over the three most recent years for which we have figures.

The list with the "Best 24 Jobs Linked to the 25 Most Popular Apprenticeships" contains only 24 jobs because two of the apprenticeships are linked to the same occupation, Electricians.

The 25 Most Popular Apprenticeships

Apprenticeship	Job	Total Active Apprentices Enrolled	Number of Active Apprenticeship Programs	Average Enrollment per Program
1. Electrician, Construction	Electricians	46,519	3,496	13.3
2. Carpenter	Construction Carpenters	26,019	658	39.5
3. Plumber	Plumbers	16,317	2,336	7.0
4. Pipe Fitter, Construction	Pipe Fitters	15,127	957	15.8
5. Electrician, Maintenance	Electricians	9,722	1,145	8.5

(continued)

(continued)

The 25 Most Popular Apprenticeships

Apprenticeship	Job	Total Active Apprentices Enrolled	Number of Active Apprentice- ship Programs	Average Enrollment per Program
6. Sheet Metal Worker	Sheet Metal Workers	9,492	746	12.7
7. Electronics Mechanic	Data Processing Equipment Repairers	9,380	82	114.4
8. Structural-Steel Worker	Structural Iron and Steel Workers	6,322	171	37.0
9. Construction Craft Laborer	Construction Laborers	5,475	67	81.7
10. Bricklayer, Construction	Brickmasons and Blockmasons	4,823	288	16.7
11. Roofer	Roofers	4,794	191	25.1
12. Painter, Construction	Painters, Construction and Maintenance	4,144	353	11.7
13. Maintenance Mechanic, Any Industry	Industrial Machinery Mechanics	4,022	849	4.7
14. Operating Engineer	Operating Engineers	3,914	154	25.4
15. Elevator Constructor	Elevator Installers and Repairers	3,893	52	74.9
16. Boilermaker	Boilermakers	3,787	57	66.4
17. Electrician, Aircraft	Avionics Technicians	3,638	3	1212.7
18. Cook, Any Industry	Cooks, Institution and Cafeteria	3,031	172	17.6
19. Machinist	Machinists	3,020	2,071	1.5
20. Millwright	Millwrights	2,963	574	5.2
21. Heating/Air-Conditioner-Installer	Heating and Air Conditioning Mechanics	2,847	728	3.9
22. Power Plant Operator	Power Generating Plant Operators, Except Auxiliary Equipment Operators	2,702	69	39.2
23. Tool and Die Maker	Tool and Die Makers	2,691	2,202	1.2
24. Cook, Hotel and Restaurant	Cooks, Restaurant	2,610	542	4.8
25. Child Care Development Specialist	Child Care Workers	2,390	908	2.6

The Best 24 Jobs Linked to the 25 Most Popular Apprenticeships

Job	Annual Earnings	Percent Growth	Annual Openings
1. Electricians	$41,680	23.4%	65,000
2. Pipe Fitters	$40,950	18.7%	56,000
3. Plumbers	$40,950	18.7%	56,000
4. Heating and Air Conditioning Mechanics	$35,160	31.8%	35,000
5. Sheet Metal Workers	$35,000	19.8%	30,000
6. Brickmasons and Blockmasons	$41,550	14.2%	21,000
7. Construction Carpenters	$34,250	10.1%	193,000
8. Roofers	$30,020	18.6%	38,000
9. Operating Engineers	$35,030	10.4%	45,000
10. Data Processing Equipment Repairers	$33,780	15.1%	19,000
11. Structural Iron and Steel Workers	$40,730	15.9%	9,000
12. Elevator Installers and Repairers	$55,960	17.1%	3,000
13. Painters, Construction and Maintenance	$29,360	11.6%	69,000
14. Machinists	$33,090	8.2%	30,000
15. Industrial Machinery Mechanics	$38,440	5.5%	19,000
16. Construction Laborers	$24,670	14.2%	166,000
17. Cooks, Restaurant	$19,260	15.9%	211,000
18. Millwrights	$42,390	5.3%	7,000
19. Child Care Workers	$16,430	11.7%	406,000
20. Avionics Technicians	$43,110	3.4%	3,000
21. Power Generating Plant Operators, Except Auxiliary Equipment Operators	$50,860	0.3%	3,000
22. Boilermakers	$43,240	1.7%	2,000
23. Tool and Die Makers	$42,990	0.4%	3,000
24. Cooks, Institution and Cafeteria	$18,300	2.1%	121,000

PART IV

Descriptions of the 250 Best Apprenticeable Jobs

This part provides descriptions for all the jobs included in one or more of the lists in Part III. The book's introduction gives more details on how to use and interpret the job descriptions, but here are the highlights, along with some additional information.

- The job descriptions that follow met our criteria for inclusion in this book, as we describe in the Introduction. The jobs in this book can be entered via a registered apprenticeship and scored among the 250 highest for earnings, projected growth, and number of job openings. Many good jobs do not meet one or more of these criteria, but we think the jobs that do are the best ones to consider in your career planning.

- Keep in mind that although every job in this book can be entered via a registered apprenticeship *somewhere* in the United States, it is not likely that apprenticeships for *all* of these jobs are available in your area. For example, where you live Police Patrol Officers may be required to get a college degree. Follow the suggestions under "How Can I Find an Apprenticeship?" in Part I to investigate what apprenticeships are available in your area.

- The job descriptions are arranged in alphabetical order by job title. This approach allows you to find a description quickly if you know its title from one of the lists in Part III. If you have not browsed the lists in Part III, consider spending some time there. The lists are interesting and will help you identify job titles that you can look up in the descriptions that follow.

- Refer to the Introduction, beginning on page 1, for details on interpreting the job descriptions' content.

- The *GOE* job description section includes a subsection titled Other Apprenticeable Jobs in This Work Group to help you identify similar jobs. Not all of the jobs listed here are among the top 250.

◉ When reviewing the descriptions, keep in mind that the jobs meet our criteria for being among the top 250 jobs based on their total scores for earnings, growth, and number of openings—but one or more of these measures may not be among the highest. For example, an occupation that has high pay may be included, even though growth rate and number of job openings are below average.

"Well," you might ask, "doesn't this mean that at least some 'bad' jobs are described in this part?" Our answer is yes and no. Some jobs with high scores for all measures, such as Police Patrol Officers—the apprenticeable job with the highest total for pay, growth, and number of openings—would be a very bad job for people who dislike or are not good at that sort of work. On the other hand, many people love working as Animal Trainers even though that job has lower earnings, a lower projected growth rate, and fewer openings. Descriptions for both jobs are included in this book.

Most likely, somewhere an ex-cop works as an animal trainer and loves it. Some who do so may even have figured out how to make more money (say, by running a training business), have a more flexible schedule, have more fun, or have other advantages not available to police patrol officers.

The point is that each job is right for somebody, perhaps at a certain time in their lives. We are all likely to change careers and jobs several times, and it's not always money that motivates us. So browse the job descriptions that follow and know that somewhere there is a good place for you. We hope you find it.

Actors

- ◎ Growth: 17.7%
- ◎ Annual Job Openings: 8,000
- ◎ Annual Earnings: $26,460
- ◎ Percentage of Women: 42.4%

Related Apprenticeship	Years
Actor	2

Play parts in stage, television, radio, video, or motion picture productions for entertainment, information, or instruction. Interpret serious or comic role by speech, gesture, and body movement to entertain or inform audience. May dance and sing. Attend auditions and casting calls in order to audition for roles. Collaborate with other actors as part of an ensemble. Learn about characters in scripts and their relationships to each other in order to develop role interpretations. Perform humorous and serious interpretations of emotions, actions, and situations, using body movements, facial expressions, and gestures. Portray and interpret roles, using speech, gestures, and body movements in order to entertain, inform, or instruct radio, film, television, or live audiences. Sing and/or dance during dramatic or comedic performances. Study and rehearse roles from scripts in order to interpret, learn, and memorize lines, stunts, and cues as directed. Work closely with directors, other actors, and playwrights to find the interpretation most suited to the role. Manipulate strings, wires, rods, or fingers to animate puppets or dummies in synchronization with talking, singing, or recorded programs. Perform original and stock tricks of illusion to entertain and mystify audiences, occasionally including audience members as participants. Promote productions using means such as interviews about plays or movies. Read from scripts or books to narrate action or to inform or entertain audiences, utilizing few or no stage props. Tell jokes; perform comic dances, songs, and skits; impersonate mannerisms and voices of others; contort face; and use other devices to amuse audiences. Work with other crewmembers responsible for lighting, costumes, makeup, and props. Write original or adapted material for dramas, comedies, puppet shows, narration, or other performances. Construct puppets and ventriloquist dummies and sew accessory clothing, using hand tools and machines. Dress in comical clown costumes and makeup and perform comedy routines to entertain audiences. Introduce performances and performers in order to stimulate excitement and coordinate smooth transition of acts during events. Prepare and perform action stunts for motion picture, television, or stage productions. **SKILLS**—Speaking; Monitoring; Social Perceptiveness; Repairing; Coordination; Active Learning; Equipment Maintenance; Reading Comprehension.

GOE—Interest Area: 01. Arts, Entertainment, and Media. **Work Group:** 01.05 Performing Arts. **Other Apprenticeable Jobs in This Work Group:** Directors—Stage, Motion Pictures, Television, and Radio. **PERSONALITY TYPE:** Artistic. Artistic occupations frequently involve working with forms, designs, and patterns. They often require self-expression, and the work can be done without following a clear set of rules.

RELATED KNOWLEDGE/COURSES—Fine Arts: Knowledge of the theory and techniques required to compose, produce, and perform works of music, dance, visual arts, drama, and sculpture. **Communications and Media:**

Knowledge of media production, communication, and dissemination techniques and methods. This includes alternative ways to inform and entertain via written, oral, and visual media. **English Language:** Knowledge of the structure and content of the English language, including the meaning and spelling of words, rules of composition, and grammar.

WORK ENVIRONMENT—Outdoors; extremely bright or inadequate lighting; standing; very hot or cold; sitting; walking and running.

Agricultural Equipment Operators

- Growth: 7.3%
- Annual Job Openings: 14,000
- Annual Earnings: $17,880
- Percentage of Women: 24.6%

Related Apprenticeship	Years
Farmworker, General I	2

Drive and control farm equipment to till soil and to plant, cultivate, and harvest crops. May perform tasks such as crop baling or hay bucking. May operate stationary equipment to perform post-harvest tasks, such as husking, shelling, threshing, and ginning. Drives tractor with implements to plow, plant, cultivate, or harvest crops and to move trailers for crop harvest. Drives truck to haul harvested crops, supplies, tools, or farm workers. Adjusts, repairs, lubricates, and services farm machinery and notifies supervisor or appropriate personnel when machinery malfunctions. Loads hoppers, containers, or conveyor to feed machine with products, using suction gates, shovel, or pitchfork. Thins, hoes, weeds, or prunes row crops, fruit trees, or vines, using hand implements. Positions boxes or attaches bags at discharge end of machinery to catch products, places lids on boxes, and closes sacks. Discards diseased or rotting product and guides product on conveyor to regulate flow through machine. Attaches farm implements, such as plow, disc, sprayer, or harvester, to tractor, using bolts and mechanic's hand tools. Observes and listens to machinery operation to detect equipment malfunction and removes obstruction to avoid damage to product or machinery. Sprays fertilizer or pesticide solutions, using hand sprayer, to control insects, fungus and weed growth, and diseases. Drives truck, or tractor with trailer attached, alongside crew loading crop or adjacent to harvesting machine. Oversees work crew engaged in planting, weeding, or harvesting activities. Hand-picks fruit, such as apples, oranges, or strawberries. Weighs crop-filled containers and records weights and other identifying information. Loads and unloads crops or containers of materials manually or using conveyors, hand-truck, forklift, or transfer auger. Mixes specified materials or chemicals and dumps solutions, powders, or seeds into planter or sprayer machinery. Irrigates soil, using portable pipe or ditch system, and maintains ditch or pipe and pumps. Walks beside or rides on planting machine while inserting plants in planter mechanism at specified intervals. Manipulates controls to set, activate, and regulate mechanisms on machinery such as self-propelled machines, conveyors, separators, cleaners, and dryers. **SKILLS**—Repairing; Equipment Maintenance; Operation Monitoring; Operation and Control; Management of Personnel Resources; Technology Design; Time Management; Science.

GOE—**Interest Area:** 03. Plants and Animals. **Work Group:** 03.03 Hands-on Work in Plants and Animals. **Other Apprenticeable Jobs in This Work Group:** Fallers; Farmworkers, Farm and Ranch Animals; Landscaping and Groundskeeping Workers; Pest Control Workers; Pesticide Handlers, Sprayers, and Applicators, Vegetation; Tree Trimmers and Pruners. **PERSONALITY TYPE:** Realistic. Realistic occupations frequently involve work activities that include practical, hands-on problems and solutions. They often deal with plants, animals, and real-world materials like wood, tools, and machinery. Many of the occupations require working outside and do not involve a lot of paperwork or working closely with others.

RELATED KNOWLEDGE/COURSES—Food Production: Knowledge of techniques and equipment for planting, growing, and harvesting food products (both plant and animal) for consumption, including storage/handling techniques. **Mechanical Devices:** Knowledge of machines and tools, including their designs, uses, repair, and maintenance. **Chemistry:** Knowledge of the chemical composition, structure, and properties of substances and of the chemical processes and transformations that they undergo. This includes uses of chemicals, their danger signs, production techniques, and disposal methods. **Physics:** Knowledge and prediction of physical principles and laws and their interrelationships and applications to understanding fluid, material, and atmospheric dynamics and mechanical, electrical, atomic, and subatomic structures and processes. **Transportation:** Knowledge of principles and methods for moving people or goods by air, rail, sea, or road, including the relative costs and benefits. **Foreign Language:** Knowledge of the structure and content of a foreign (non-English) language, including the meaning and spelling of words, rules of composition and grammar, and pronunciation.

WORK ENVIRONMENT—Outdoors; hazardous equipment; minor burns, cuts, bites, or stings; very hot or cold; hazardous conditions.

Aircraft Engine Specialists

- Growth: 11.0%
- Annual Job Openings: 12,000
- Annual Earnings: $43,560
- Percentage of Women: 4.9%

Related Apprenticeship	Years
Rocket-Engine-Component Mechanic	4

Repair and maintain the operating condition of aircraft engines. Includes helicopter engine mechanics. Replaces or repairs worn, defective, or damaged components, using hand tools, gauges, and testing equipment. Tests engine operation, using test equipment such as ignition analyzer, compression checker, distributor timer, and ammeter, to identify malfunction. Listens to operating engine to detect and diagnose malfunctions, such as sticking or burned valves. Reassembles engine and installs engine in aircraft. Disassembles and inspects engine parts, such as turbine blades and cylinders, for wear, warping, cracks, and leaks. Removes engine from aircraft, using hoist or forklift truck. Services, repairs, and rebuilds aircraft structures, such as wings, fuselage, rigging, and surface and hydraulic controls, using hand or power tools and equipment. Adjusts, repairs, or replaces electrical wiring system and aircraft accessories. Reads and interprets manufacturers' maintenance manuals, service bulletins, and other specifications to determine feasibility and methods of repair. Services and maintains aircraft and related apparatus by performing activities such as flushing crankcase, cleaning screens, and lubricating moving parts. **SKILLS**—Equipment Maintenance; Repairing; Installation; Troubleshooting; Operation Monitoring; Quality Control Analysis; Judgment and Decision Making; Equipment Selection.

GOE—Interest Area: 05. Mechanics, Installers, and Repairers. **Work Group:** 05.03 Mechanical Work. **Other Apprenticeable Jobs in This Work Group:** Airframe-and-Power-Plant Mechanics; Automotive Body and Related Repairers; Automotive Glass Installers and Repairers; Automotive Master Mechanics; Automotive Specialty Technicians; Bus and Truck Mechanics and Diesel Engine Specialists; Camera and Photographic Equipment Repairers; Coin, Vending, and Amusement Machine Servicers and Repairers; Farm Equipment Mechanics; Gas Appliance Repairers; Hand and Portable Power Tool Repairers; Heating and Air Conditioning Mechanics; Helpers—Installation, Maintenance, and Repair Workers; Industrial Machinery Mechanics; Installation, Maintenance, and Repair Workers, All Other; Keyboard Instrument Repairers and Tuners; Locksmiths and Safe Repairers; Maintenance and Repair Workers, General; Maintenance Workers, Machinery; Mechanical Door Repairers; Medical Appliance Technicians; Medical Equipment Repairers; Meter Mechanics; Millwrights; Mobile Heavy Equipment Mechanics,

Except Engines; Motorboat Mechanics; Motorcycle Mechanics; Optical Instrument Assemblers; Outdoor Power Equipment and Other Small Engine Mechanics; Painters, Transportation Equipment; Rail Car Repairers; Recreational Vehicle Service Technicians; Reed or Wind Instrument Repairers and Tuners; Refrigeration Mechanics; Stringed Instrument Repairers and Tuners; Valve and Regulator Repairers; Watch Repairers. **PERSONALITY TYPE:** Realistic. Realistic occupations frequently involve work activities that include practical, hands-on problems and solutions. They often deal with plants, animals, and real-world materials like wood, tools, and machinery. Many of the occupations require working outside and do not involve a lot of paperwork or working closely with others.

RELATED KNOWLEDGE/COURSES—Mechanical Devices: Knowledge of machines and tools, including their designs, uses, repair, and maintenance. **Engineering and Technology:** Knowledge of the practical application of engineering science and technology. This includes applying principles, techniques, procedures, and equipment to the design and production of various goods and services. **Physics:** Knowledge and prediction of physical principles and laws and their interrelationships and applications to understanding fluid, material, and atmospheric dynamics and mechanical, electrical, atomic, and subatomic structures and processes. **Building and Construction:** Knowledge of the materials, methods, and tools involved in the construction or repair of houses, buildings, or other structures, such as highways and roads. **Computers and Electronics:** Knowledge of circuit boards, processors, chips, electronic equipment, and computer hardware and software, including applications and programming. **Mathematics:** Knowledge of arithmetic, algebra, geometry, calculus, and statistics and their applications.

WORK ENVIRONMENT—Hazardous equipment; minor burns, cuts, bites, or stings; hazardous conditions; outdoors; sounds, noise levels are distracting or uncomfortable; climbing ladders, scaffolds, or poles.

Airframe-and-Power-Plant Mechanics

- Growth: 11.0%
- Annual Job Openings: 12,000
- Annual Earnings: $43,560
- Percentage of Women: 4.9%

Related Apprenticeship	Years
Airframe-and-Power-Plant Mechanic	4

Inspect, test, repair, maintain, and service aircraft. Adjusts, aligns, and calibrates aircraft systems, using hand tools, gauges, and test equipment. Examines and inspects engines or other components for cracks, breaks, or leaks. Disassembles and inspects parts for wear, warping, or other defects. Assembles and installs electrical, plumbing, mechanical, hydraulic, and structural components and accessories, using hand tools and power tools. Services and maintains aircraft systems by performing tasks such as flushing crankcase, cleaning screens, greasing moving parts, and checking brakes. Repairs, replaces, and rebuilds aircraft structures, functional components, and parts, such as wings and fuselage, rigging, and hydraulic units. Tests engine and system operations, using testing equipment, and listens to engine sounds to detect and diagnose malfunctions. Removes engine from aircraft or installs engine, using hoist or forklift truck. Modifies aircraft structures, space vehicles, systems, or components, following drawings, engineering orders, and technical publications. Reads and interprets aircraft maintenance manuals and specifications to determine feasibility and method of repairing or replacing malfunctioning or damaged components. **SKILLS**—Equipment Maintenance; Installation; Repairing; Troubleshooting; Operation Monitoring; Quality Control Analysis; Science; Equipment Selection.

GOE—Interest Area: 05. Mechanics, Installers, and Repairers. **Work Group:** 05.03 Mechanical Work. **Other Apprenticeable Jobs in This Work Group:** Aircraft Engine Specialists; Automotive Body and Related Repairers; Automotive Glass Installers and Repairers; Automotive Master Mechanics; Automotive Specialty Technicians; Bus and Truck Mechanics and Diesel Engine Specialists; Camera and Photographic Equipment Repairers; Coin, Vending, and Amusement Machine Servicers and Repairers; Farm Equipment Mechanics; Gas Appliance Repairers; Hand and Portable Power Tool Repairers; Heating and Air Conditioning Mechanics; Helpers—Installation, Maintenance, and Repair Workers; Industrial Machinery Mechanics; Installation, Maintenance, and Repair Workers, All Other; Keyboard Instrument Repairers and Tuners; Locksmiths and Safe Repairers; Maintenance and Repair Workers, General; Maintenance Workers, Machinery; Mechanical Door Repairers; Medical Appliance Technicians; Medical Equipment Repairers; Meter Mechanics; Millwrights; Mobile Heavy Equipment Mechanics, Except

Engines; Motorboat Mechanics; Motorcycle Mechanics; Optical Instrument Assemblers; Outdoor Power Equipment and Other Small Engine Mechanics; Painters, Transportation Equipment; Rail Car Repairers; Recreational Vehicle Service Technicians; Reed or Wind Instrument Repairers and Tuners; Refrigeration Mechanics; Stringed Instrument Repairers and Tuners; Valve and Regulator Repairers; Watch Repairers. **PERSONALITY TYPE:** Realistic. Realistic occupations frequently involve work activities that include practical, hands-on problems and solutions. They often deal with plants, animals, and real-world materials like wood, tools, and machinery. Many of the occupations require working outside and do not involve a lot of paperwork or working closely with others.

RELATED KNOWLEDGE/COURSES—Mechanical Devices: Knowledge of machines and tools, including their designs, uses, repair, and maintenance. **Engineering and Technology:** Knowledge of the practical application of engineering science and technology. This includes applying principles, techniques, procedures, and equipment to the design and production of various goods and services. **Building and Construction:** Knowledge of the materials, methods, and tools involved in the construction or repair of houses, buildings, or other structures, such as highways and roads. **Design:** Knowledge of design techniques, tools, and principles involved in production of precision technical plans, blueprints, drawings, and models. **Physics:** Knowledge and prediction of physical principles and laws and their interrelationships and applications to understanding fluid, material, and atmospheric dynamics and mechanical, electrical, atomic, and subatomic structures and processes. **Public Safety and Security:** Knowledge of relevant equipment, policies, procedures, and strategies to promote effective local, state, or national security operations for the protection of people, data, property, and institutions.

WORK ENVIRONMENT—Hazardous equipment; spend time kneeling, crouching, stooping, or crawling; common protective or safety equipment; very hot or cold; spend time bending or twisting the body.

Ambulance Drivers and Attendants, Except Emergency Medical Technicians

- Growth: 26.7%
- Annual Job Openings: 4,000
- Annual Earnings: $19,000
- Percentage of Women: 16.1%

Related Apprenticeship	Years
Ambulance Attendant	1

Drive ambulance or assist ambulance driver in transporting sick, injured, or convalescent persons. Assist in lifting patients. Accompany and assist emergency medical technicians on calls. Administer first aid such as bandaging, splinting, and administering oxygen. Drive ambulances or assist ambulance drivers in transporting sick, injured, or convalescent persons. Place patients on stretchers and load stretchers into ambulances, usually with assistance from other attendants. Remove and replace soiled linens and equipment in order to maintain sanitary conditions. Replace supplies and disposable items on ambulances. Report facts concerning accidents or emergencies to hospital personnel or law enforcement officials. Earn and maintain appropriate certifications. Restrain or shackle violent patients. **SKILLS**—Service Orientation; Operation and Control; Persuasion; Coordination; Speaking; Active Listening; Critical Thinking; Operation Monitoring.

GOE—Interest Area: 07. Transportation. **Work Group:** 07.07 Other Services Requiring Driving. **Other Apprenticeable Jobs in This Work Group:** No other apprenticeable jobs in this group. **PERSONALITY TYPE:** Social. Social occupations frequently involve working with, communicating with, and teaching people. These occupations often involve helping or providing service to others.

RELATED KNOWLEDGE/COURSES—Medicine and Dentistry: Knowledge of the information and techniques needed to diagnose and treat human injuries, diseases, and deformities. This includes symptoms, treatment alternatives, drug properties and interactions, and preventive health-care measures. **Geography:** Knowledge of principles and methods for describing the features of land, sea, and air masses, including their physical characteristics; locations; interrelationships; and distribution of plant, animal, and human life. **Transportation:** Knowledge of principles and methods for moving people or goods by air, rail, sea, or road, including the relative costs and benefits. **Customer and Personal Service:** Knowledge of principles and processes for providing customer and personal services. This includes customer needs assessment, meeting quality standards for services, and evaluation of customer satisfaction. **Biology:** Knowledge of plant and animal organisms and their tissues, cells, functions, interdependencies, and interactions with each

other and the environment. **Public Safety and Security:** Knowledge of relevant equipment, policies, procedures, and strategies to promote effective local, state, or national security operations for the protection of people, data, property, and institutions. **Telecommunications:** Knowledge of transmission, broadcasting, switching, control, and operation of telecommunications systems.

WORK ENVIRONMENT—Disease or infections; outdoors; contaminants; common protective or safety equipment; hazardous conditions.

Animal Trainers

- Growth: 14.3%
- Annual Job Openings: 4,000
- Annual Earnings: $22,350
- Percentage of Women: 46.6%

Related Apprenticeship	Years
Horse Trainer	1
Animal Trainer	2

Train animals for riding, harness, security, performance, obedience, or assisting persons with disabilities. Accustom animals to human voice and contact; condition animals to respond to commands. Train animals according to prescribed standards for show or competition. May train animals to carry pack loads or work as part of pack team. Train dogs in human-assistance or property protection duties. Train horses or other equines for riding, harness, show, racing, or other work, using knowledge of breed characteristics, training methods, performance standards, and the peculiarities of each animal. Administer prescribed medications to animals. Advise animal owners regarding the purchase of specific animals. Arrange for mating of stallions and mares and assist mares during foaling. Keep records documenting animal health, diet, and behavior. Place tack or harnesses on horses in order to accustom horses to the feel of equipment. Retrain horses to break bad habits, such as kicking, bolting, and resisting bridling and grooming. Talk to and interact with animals in order to familiarize them to human voices and contact. Use oral, spur, rein, and/or hand commands in order to condition horses to carry riders or to pull horse-drawn equipment. Instruct jockeys in handling specific horses during races. Organize and conduct animal shows. Conduct training programs in order to develop and maintain desired animal behaviors for competition, entertainment, obedience, security, riding, and related areas. Cue or signal animals during performances. Evaluate animals in order to determine their temperaments, abilities, and aptitude for training. Feed and exercise animals and provide other general care such as cleaning and maintaining holding and performance areas. Observe animals' physical conditions in order to detect illness or unhealthy conditions requiring medical care. Train and rehearse animals, according to scripts, for motion picture, television, film, stage, or circus performances. **SKILLS**—Instructing; Learning Strategies; Monitoring; Persuasion; Social Perceptiveness; Systems Evaluation; Active Learning; Coordination; Systems Analysis.

GOE—Interest Area: 03. Plants and Animals. **Work Group:** 03.02 Animal Care and Training. **Other Apprenticeable Jobs in This Work Group:** Nonfarm Animal Caretakers. **PER-**SONALITY TYPE: Social. Social occupations frequently involve working with, communicating with, and teaching people. These occupations often involve helping or providing service to others.

RELATED KNOWLEDGE/COURSES— Education and Training: Knowledge of principles and methods for curriculum and training design, teaching and instruction for individuals and groups, and the measurement of training effects. **Biology:** Knowledge of plant and animal organisms and their tissues, cells, functions, interdependencies, and interactions with each other and the environment. **Customer and Personal Service:** Knowledge of principles and processes for providing customer and personal services. This includes customer needs assessment, meeting quality standards for services, and evaluation of customer satisfaction. **Sales and Marketing:** Knowledge of principles and methods for showing, promoting, and selling products or services. This includes marketing strategy and tactics, product demonstration, sales techniques, and sales control systems. **Public Safety and Security:** Knowledge of relevant equipment, policies, procedures, and strategies to promote effective local, state, or national security operations for the protection of people, data, property, and institutions. **Medicine and Dentistry:** Knowledge of the information and techniques needed to diagnose and treat human injuries, diseases, and deformities. This includes symptoms, treatment alternatives, drug properties and interactions, and preventive health-care measures.

WORK ENVIRONMENT—Minor burns, cuts, bites, or stings; spend time kneeling, crouching, stooping, or crawling; disease or infections; outdoors; walking and running.

Audio and Video Equipment Technicians

⊚ Growth: 26.7%

⊚ Annual Job Openings: 5,000

⊚ Annual Earnings: $30,810

⊚ Percentage of Women: 14.2%

Related Apprenticeship	Years
Stage Technician	3
Light Technician	4

Set up or set up and operate audio and video equipment, including microphones, sound speakers, video screens, projectors, video monitors, recording equipment, connecting wires and cables, sound and mixing boards, and related electronic equipment, for concerts, sports events, meetings and conventions, presentations, and news conferences. May also set up and operate associated spotlights and other custom lighting systems. Compress, digitize, duplicate, and store audio and video data. Control the lights and sound of events, such as live concerts, before and after performances, and during intermissions. Design layouts of audio and video equipment and perform upgrades and maintenance. Diagnose and resolve media system problems in classrooms. Install, adjust, and operate electronic equipment used to record, edit, and transmit radio and television programs, cable programs, and motion pictures. Maintain inventories of audio- and videotapes and related supplies. Meet with directors and senior members of camera crews to discuss assignments and determine filming sequences, camera movements, and picture composition. Mix and regulate sound inputs and feeds or coordinate audio feeds with television pictures. Monitor incoming and outgoing pictures and sound feeds to ensure quality and notify directors of any possible problems. Obtain, set up, and load videotapes for scheduled productions or broadcasts. Perform minor repairs and routine cleaning of audio and video equipment. Record and edit audio material, such as movie soundtracks, using audio recording and editing equipment. Record and label contents of exposed film. Switch sources of video input from one camera or studio to another, from film to live programming, or from network to local programming. Conduct training sessions on selection, use, and design of audiovisual materials and on operation of presentation equipment. Construct and position properties, sets, lighting equipment, and other equipment. Determine formats, approaches, content, levels, and mediums to effectively meet objectives within budgetary constraints, utilizing research, knowledge, and training. Develop manuals, texts, workbooks, or related materials for use in conjunction with production materials or for training. Direct and coordinate activities of assistants and other personnel during production. Edit videotapes by erasing and removing portions of programs and adding video and/or sound as required. Inform users of audio- and videotaping service policies and procedures. Locate and secure settings, properties, effects, and other production necessities. **SKILLS**—Learning Strategies; Instructing; Writing; Operations Analysis; Management of Financial Resources; Complex Problem Solving; Management of Material Resources; Management of Personnel Resources.

GOE—Interest Area: 01. Arts, Entertainment, and Media. **Work Group:** 01.08 Media Technology. **Other Apprenticeable Jobs in This Work Group:** Broadcast Technicians; Camera Operators, Television, Video, and Motion Picture; Film and Video Editors; Professional Photographers; Radio Operators; Sound Engineering Technicians. **PERSONALITY TYPE:** Conventional. Conventional occupations frequently involve following set procedures and routines. These occupations can include working with data and details more than with ideas. Usually there is a clear line of authority to follow.

RELATED KNOWLEDGE/COURSES— Communications and Media: Knowledge of media production, communication, and dissemination techniques and methods. This includes alternative ways to inform and entertain via written, oral, and visual media. **Education and Training:** Knowledge of principles and methods for curriculum and training design, teaching and instruction for individuals and groups, and the measurement of training effects. **Telecommunications:** Knowledge of transmission, broadcasting, switching, control, and operation of telecommunications systems. **Fine Arts:** Knowledge of the theory and techniques required to compose, produce, and perform works of music, dance, visual arts, drama, and sculpture. **Administration and Management:** Knowledge of business and management principles involved in strategic planning, resource allocation, human resources modeling, leadership technique, production methods, and coordination of people and resources. **Economics and Accounting:** Knowledge of economic and accounting principles and practices, the financial markets, banking, and the analysis and reporting of financial data.

WORK ENVIRONMENT—Spend time kneeling, crouching, stooping, or crawling; spend time bending or twisting the body; sitting; indoors; standing; walking and running.

Automotive Body and Related Repairers

- Growth: 13.2%
- Annual Job Openings: 23,000
- Annual Earnings: $33,140
- Percentage of Women: 2.1%

Related Apprenticeship	Years
Service Mechanic (Automobile Manufacturing)	2
Automobile-Body Repairer	4
Truck-Body Builder	4

Repair and refinish automotive vehicle bodies and straighten vehicle frames. File, grind, sand, and smooth filled or repaired surfaces, using power tools and hand tools. Sand body areas to be painted and cover bumpers, windows, and trim with masking tape or paper to protect them from the paint. Follow supervisors' instructions as to which parts to restore or replace and how much time the job should take. Remove damaged sections of vehicles, using metal-cutting guns, air grinders, and wrenches, and install replacement parts, using wrenches or welding equipment. Cut and tape plastic separating film to outside repair areas in order to avoid damaging surrounding surfaces during repair procedure and remove tape and wash surfaces after repairs are complete. Prime and paint repaired surfaces, using paint sprayguns and motorized sanders. Inspect repaired vehicles for dimensional accuracy and test drive them to ensure proper alignment and handling. Mix polyester resins and hardeners to be used in restoring damaged areas. Chain or clamp frames and sections to alignment machines that use hydraulic pressure to align damaged components. Fill small dents that cannot be worked out with plastic or solder. Fit and weld replacement parts into place, using wrenches and welding equipment, and grind down welds to smooth them, using power grinders and other tools. Position dolly blocks against surfaces of dented areas and beat opposite surfaces to remove dents, using hammers. Remove damaged panels and identify the family and properties of the plastic used on a vehicle. Review damage reports, prepare or review repair cost estimates, and plan work to be performed. Remove small pits and dimples in body metal, using pick hammers and punches. Remove upholstery, accessories, electrical window-and-seat-operating equipment, and trim in order to gain access to vehicle bodies and fenders. Clean work areas, using air hoses, in order to remove damaged material and discarded fiberglass strips used in repair procedures. Adjust or align headlights, wheels, and brake systems. Apply heat to plastic panels, using hot-air welding guns or immersion in hot water, and press the softened panels back into shape by hand. **SKILLS—** Repairing; Equipment Maintenance; Installation; Troubleshooting; Learning Strategies; Equipment Selection; Negotiation; Management of Financial Resources.

GOE—Interest Area: 05. Mechanics, Installers, and Repairers. **Work Group:** 05.03 Mechanical Work. **Other Apprenticeable Jobs in This Work Group:** Aircraft Engine Specialists; Airframe-and-Power-Plant Mechanics; Automotive Glass Installers and Repairers; Automotive Master Mechanics; Automotive Specialty Technicians; Bus and Truck Mechanics and Diesel Engine Specialists; Camera and Photographic Equipment Repairers; Coin, Vending, and Amusement Machine Servicers and Repairers; Farm Equipment Mechanics; Gas Appliance Repairers; Hand and Portable Power Tool Repairers; Heating and Air Conditioning Mechanics; Helpers—Installation, Maintenance, and Repair Workers; Industrial Machinery Mechanics; Installation, Maintenance, and Repair Workers, All Other; Keyboard Instrument Repairers and Tuners; Locksmiths and Safe Repairers; Maintenance and Repair Workers, General; Maintenance Workers, Machinery; Mechanical Door Repairers; Medical Appliance Technicians; Medical Equipment Repairers; Meter Mechanics; Millwrights; Mobile Heavy Equipment Mechanics, Except Engines; Motorboat Mechanics; Motorcycle Mechanics; Optical Instrument Assemblers; Outdoor Power Equipment and Other Small Engine Mechanics; Painters, Transportation Equipment; Rail Car Repairers; Recreational Vehicle Service Technicians; Reed or Wind Instrument Repairers and Tuners; Refrigeration Mechanics; Stringed Instrument Repairers and Tuners; Valve and Regulator Repairers; Watch Repairers. **PERSONALITY TYPE:** Realistic. Realistic occupations frequently involve work activities that include practical, hands-on problems and solutions. They often deal with plants, animals, and real-world materials like wood, tools, and machinery. Many of the occupations require working outside and do not involve a lot of paperwork or working closely with others.

RELATED KNOWLEDGE/COURSES— **Mechanical Devices:** Knowledge of machines and tools, including their designs, uses, repair, and maintenance. **Customer and Personal Service:** Knowledge of principles and processes for providing customer and personal services. This includes customer needs assessment, meeting quality standards for services, and evaluation of customer satisfaction. **Building and Construction:** Knowledge of the materials, methods, and tools involved in the construction or repair of houses, buildings, or other structures, such as highways and roads. **Administration and Management:** Knowledge of business and management principles involved in strategic planning, resource allocation, human resources modeling, leadership technique, production methods, and coordination of people and resources. **Chemistry:** Knowledge of the chemical composition, structure, and properties of substances and of the chemical processes and transformations that they undergo. This includes uses of chemicals, their danger signs, production techniques, and disposal methods. **Transportation:** Knowledge of principles and methods for moving people or goods by air, rail, sea, or road, including the relative costs and benefits. **Production and Processing:** Knowledge of raw materials, production processes, quality control, costs, and other techniques for maximizing the effective manufacture and distribution of goods.

WORK ENVIRONMENT—Contaminants; sounds, noise levels are distracting or uncomfortable; hazardous conditions; minor burns, cuts, bites, or stings; hazardous equipment.

Automotive Glass Installers and Repairers

- Growth: 10.7%
- Annual Job Openings: 3,000
- Annual Earnings: $27,160
- Percentage of Women: 3.1%

Related Apprenticeship	Years
Glass Installer, Automobile Service	2

Replace or repair broken windshields and window glass in motor vehicles. Prime all scratches on pinchwelds with primer and allow primed scratches to dry. Remove all dirt, foreign matter, and loose glass from damaged areas; then apply primer along windshield or window edges and allow it to dry. Remove all moldings, clips, windshield wipers, screws, bolts, and inside A-pillar moldings; then lower headliners prior to beginning installation or repair work. Remove broken or damaged glass windshields or window glass from motor vehicles, using hand tools to remove screws from frames holding glass. Replace all moldings, clips, windshield wipers, and any other parts that were removed prior to glass replacement or repair. Replace or adjust motorized or manual window-raising mechanisms. Select appropriate tools, safety equipment, and parts according to job requirements. Cut flat safety glass according to specified patterns or perform precision pattern-making and glass-cutting to custom-fit replacement windows. Allow all glass parts installed with urethane ample time to cure, taking temperature and humidity into account. Apply a bead of urethane around the perimeter of each pinch-weld and dress the remaining urethane on the pinchwelds so that it is of uniform level and thickness all the way around. Check for moisture or contamination in damaged areas, dry out any moisture prior to making repairs, and keep damaged areas dry until repairs are complete. Cool or warm glass in the event of temperature extremes. Hold cut or uneven edges of glass against automated abrasive belts in order to shape or smooth edges. Install new foam dams on pinchwelds if required. Install replacement glass in vehicles after old glass has been removed and all necessary preparations have been made. Install rubber-channeling strips around edges of glass or frames in order to weatherproof windows or to prevent rattling. Install, repair, and replace safety glass and related materials, such as backglass heating elements, on vehicles and equipment. Obtain windshields or windows for specific automobile makes and models from stock and examine them for defects prior to installation. **SKILLS**—Installation; Repairing; Technology Design.

GOE—**Interest Area:** 05. Mechanics, Installers, and Repairers. **Work Group:** 05.03 Mechanical Work. **Other Apprenticeable Jobs in This Work Group:** Aircraft Engine Specialists; Air-frame-and-Power-Plant Mechanics; Automotive Body and Related Repairers; Automotive Master Mechanics; Automotive Specialty Technicians; Bus and Truck Mechanics and Diesel Engine Specialists; Camera and Photographic Equipment Repairers; Coin, Vending, and Amusement Machine Servicers and Repairers; Farm Equipment Mechanics; Gas Appliance Repairers; Hand and Portable Power Tool Repairers; Heating and Air Conditioning Mechanics; Helpers—Installation, Mainte-

nance, and Repair Workers; Industrial Machinery Mechanics; Installation, Maintenance, and Repair Workers, All Other; Keyboard Instrument Repairers and Tuners; Locksmiths and Safe Repairers; Maintenance and Repair Workers, General; Maintenance Workers, Machinery; Mechanical Door Repairers; Medical Appliance Technicians; Medical Equipment Repairers; Meter Mechanics; Millwrights; Mobile Heavy Equipment Mechanics, Except Engines; Motorboat Mechanics; Motorcycle Mechanics; Optical Instrument Assemblers; Outdoor Power Equipment and Other Small Engine Mechanics; Painters, Transportation Equipment; Rail Car Repairers; Recreational Vehicle Service Technicians; Reed or Wind Instrument Repairers and Tuners; Refrigeration Mechanics; Stringed Instrument Repairers and Tuners; Valve and Regulator Repairers; Watch Repairers. **PERSONALITY TYPE:** Realistic. Realistic occupations frequently involve work activities that include practical, hands-on problems and solutions. They often deal with plants, animals, and real-world materials like wood, tools, and machinery. Many of the occupations require working outside and do not involve a lot of paperwork or working closely with others.

RELATED KNOWLEDGE/COURSES—**Mechanical Devices:** Knowledge of machines and tools, including their designs, uses, repair, and maintenance. **Engineering and Technology:** Knowledge of the practical application of engineering science and technology. This includes applying principles, techniques, procedures, and equipment to the design and production of various goods and services.

WORK ENVIRONMENT—Common protective or safety equipment; minor burns, cuts, bites, or stings; outdoors; standing; using hands on objects, tools, or controls.

Automotive Master Mechanics

- Growth: 12.4%
- Annual Job Openings: 100,000
- Annual Earnings: $31,130
- Percentage of Women: 1.9%

Related Apprenticeship	*Years*
Repairer, Heavy	2
Transmission Mechanic	2
Automobile Mechanic	4

Repair automobiles, trucks, buses, and other vehicles. Master mechanics repair virtually any part on the vehicle or specialize in the transmission system. Examine vehicles to determine extent of damage or malfunctions. Test drive vehicles and test components and systems, using equipment such as infrared engine analyzers, compression gauges, and computerized diagnostic devices. Repair, reline, replace, and adjust brakes. Review work orders and discuss work with supervisors. Follow checklists to ensure all important parts are examined, including belts, hoses, steering systems, spark plugs, brake and fuel systems, wheel bearings, and other potentially troublesome areas. Plan work procedures, using charts, technical manuals, and experience. Test and adjust repaired systems to meet manufacturers' performance specifications. Confer with customers to obtain descriptions of vehicle problems and to discuss work to be performed and future repair requirements. Perform routine and scheduled maintenance services such as oil changes, lubrications, and tune-ups. Disassemble units and inspect parts for wear, using micrometers, calipers, and gauges. Overhaul or replace carburetors, blowers, generators, distributors, starters, and pumps. Repair and service air conditioning, heating, engine-cooling, and electrical systems. Repair or replace parts such as pistons, rods, gears, valves, and bearings. Tear down, repair, and rebuild faulty assemblies such as power systems, steering systems, and linkages. Rewire ignition systems, lights, and instrument panels. Repair radiator leaks. Install and repair accessories such as radios, heaters, mirrors, and windshield wipers. Repair manual and automatic transmissions. Repair or replace shock absorbers. Align vehicles' front ends. Rebuild parts such as crankshafts and cylinder blocks. **SKILLS**—Troubleshooting; Repairing; Equipment Maintenance; Installation; Active Learning; Complex Problem Solving; Instructing; Equipment Selection.

GOE—Interest Area: 05. Mechanics, Installers, and Repairers. **Work Group:** 05.03 Mechanical Work. **Other Apprenticeable Jobs in This Work Group:** Aircraft Engine Specialists; Airframe-and-Power-Plant Mechanics; Automotive Body and Related Repairers; Automotive Glass Installers and Repairers; Automotive Specialty Technicians; Bus and Truck Mechanics and Diesel Engine Specialists; Camera and Photographic Equipment Repairers; Coin, Vending, and Amusement Machine Servicers and Repairers; Farm Equipment Mechanics; Gas Appliance Repairers; Hand and Portable Power Tool Repairers; Heating and Air Conditioning Mechanics; Helpers—Installation, Maintenance, and Repair Workers; Industrial Machinery Mechanics; Installation, Maintenance, and Repair Workers, All Other; Keyboard Instrument Repairers and Tuners; Locksmiths and

Safe Repairers; Maintenance and Repair Workers, General; Maintenance Workers, Machinery; Mechanical Door Repairers; Medical Appliance Technicians; Medical Equipment Repairers; Meter Mechanics; Millwrights; Mobile Heavy Equipment Mechanics, Except Engines; Motorboat Mechanics; Motorcycle Mechanics; Optical Instrument Assemblers; Outdoor Power Equipment and Other Small Engine Mechanics; Painters, Transportation Equipment; Rail Car Repairers; Recreational Vehicle Service Technicians; Reed or Wind Instrument Repairers and Tuners; Refrigeration Mechanics; Stringed Instrument Repairers and Tuners; Valve and Regulator Repairers; Watch Repairers. **PERSONALITY TYPE:** Realistic. Realistic occupations frequently involve work activities that include practical, hands-on problems and solutions. They often deal with plants, animals, and real-world materials like wood, tools, and machinery. Many of the occupations require working outside and do not involve a lot of paperwork or working closely with others.

RELATED KNOWLEDGE/COURSES—Mechanical Devices: Knowledge of machines and tools, including their designs, uses, repair, and maintenance. **Computers and Electronics:** Knowledge of circuit boards, processors, chips, electronic equipment, and computer hardware and software, including applications and programming. **Physics:** Knowledge and prediction of physical principles and laws and their interrelationships and applications to understanding fluid, material, and atmospheric dynamics and mechanical, electrical, atomic, and subatomic structures and processes. **Customer and Personal Service:** Knowledge of principles and processes for providing customer and personal services. This includes customer needs assessment, meeting quality standards for services, and evaluation of customer satisfaction. **Education and Train-**

ing: Knowledge of principles and methods for curriculum and training design, teaching and instruction for individuals and groups, and the measurement of training effects. **Engineering and Technology:** Knowledge of the practical application of engineering science and technology. This includes applying principles, techniques, procedures, and equipment to the design and production of various goods and services.

WORK ENVIRONMENT—Contaminants; sounds, noise levels are distracting or uncomfortable; in an enclosed vehicle or equipment; cramped work space, awkward positions; hazardous conditions; minor burns, cuts, bites, or stings.

Automotive Specialty Technicians

- Growth: 12.4%
- Annual Job Openings: 100,000
- Annual Earnings: $31,130
- Percentage of Women: 1.9%

Related Apprenticeship	Years
Air-Conditioning Mechanic, Auto Service	1
Automobile-Radiator Mechanic	2
Automotive-Cooling-System Diagnostic Technician	2
Automotive Technician Specialist	competency

Brake Repairer	2
Tune-Up Mechanic	2
Undercar Specialist	2
Carburetor Mechanic	4

Repair only one system or component on a vehicle, such as brakes, suspension, or radiator. Align and repair wheels, axles, frames, torsion bars, and steering mechanisms of automobiles, using special alignment equipment and wheel-balancing machines. Examine vehicles, compile estimates of repair costs, and secure customers' approval to perform repairs. Install and repair air conditioners and service components such as compressors, condensers, and controls. Rebuild, repair, and test automotive fuel injection units. Remove and replace defective mufflers and tailpipes. Repair and rebuild clutch systems. Repair and replace automobile leaf springs. Repair and replace defective ball joint suspensions, brake shoes, and wheel bearings. Repair, overhaul, and adjust automobile brake systems. Repair, replace, and adjust defective carburetor parts and gasoline filters. Test electronic computer components in automobiles to ensure that they are working properly. Tune automobile engines to ensure proper and efficient functioning. Use electronic test equipment to locate and correct malfunctions in fuel, ignition, and emissions control systems. Convert vehicle fuel systems from gasoline to butane gas operations and repair and service operating butane fuel units. Inspect and test new vehicles for damage and then record findings so that necessary repairs can be made. Repair, install, and adjust hydraulic and electromagnetic automatic lift mechanisms used to raise and lower automobile windows, seats, and tops. **SKILLS**—Installation; Repairing; Troubleshooting; Equipment Maintenance; Technology Design; Quality Control Analysis; Operation Monitoring; Operation and Control; Management of Material Resources.

GOE—**Interest Area:** 05. Mechanics, Installers, and Repairers. **Work Group:** 05.03 Mechanical Work. **Other Apprenticeable Jobs in This Work Group:** Aircraft Engine Specialists; Airframe-and-Power-Plant Mechanics; Automotive Body and Related Repairers; Automotive Glass Installers and Repairers; Automotive Master Mechanics; Bus and Truck Mechanics and Diesel Engine Specialists; Camera and Photographic Equipment Repairers; Coin, Vending, and Amusement Machine Servicers and Repairers; Farm Equipment Mechanics; Gas Appliance Repairers; Hand and Portable Power Tool Repairers; Heating and Air Conditioning Mechanics; Helpers—Installation, Maintenance, and Repair Workers; Industrial Machinery Mechanics; Installation, Maintenance, and Repair Workers, All Other; Keyboard Instrument Repairers and Tuners; Locksmiths and Safe Repairers; Maintenance and Repair Workers, General; Maintenance Workers, Machinery; Mechanical Door Repairers; Medical Appliance Technicians; Medical Equipment Repairers; Meter Mechanics; Millwrights; Mobile Heavy Equipment Mechanics, Except Engines; Motorboat Mechanics; Motorcycle Mechanics; Optical Instrument Assemblers; Outdoor Power Equipment and Other Small Engine Mechanics; Painters, Transportation Equipment; Rail Car Repairers; Recreational Vehicle Service Technicians; Reed or Wind Instrument Repairers and Tuners; Refrigeration Mechanics; Stringed Instrument Repairers and Tuners; Valve and Regulator Repairers; Watch Repairers. **PERSONALITY TYPE:** Realistic. Realistic occupations frequently involve work activities that include practical, hands-on problems and solutions. They often deal with plants, animals, and real-world materials like wood, tools, and machinery. Many of the occupations require working outside and do not involve a lot of paperwork or working closely with others.

RELATED KNOWLEDGE/COURSES—**Mechanical Devices:** Knowledge of machines and tools, including their designs, uses, repair, and maintenance. **Computers and Electronics:** Knowledge of circuit boards, processors, chips, electronic equipment, and computer hardware and software, including applications and programming. **Design:** Knowledge of design techniques, tools, and principles involved in production of precision technical plans, blueprints, drawings, and models. **Engineering and Technology:** Knowledge of the practical application of engineering science and technology. This includes applying principles, techniques, procedures, and equipment to the design and production of various goods and services. **Physics:** Knowledge and prediction of physical principles and laws and their interrelationships and applications to understanding fluid, material, and atmospheric dynamics and mechanical, electrical, atomic, and subatomic structures and processes. **Chemistry:** Knowledge of the chemical composition, structure, and properties of substances and of the chemical processes and transformations that they undergo. This includes uses of chemicals, their danger signs, production techniques, and disposal methods.

WORK ENVIRONMENT—Common protective or safety equipment; contaminants; spend time kneeling, crouching, stooping, or crawling; hazardous equipment; minor burns, cuts, bites, or stings; standing.

Avionics Technicians

- ⌬ Growth: 3.4%
- ⌬ Annual Job Openings: 3,000
- ⌬ Annual Earnings: $43,110
- ⌬ Percentage of Women: 11.2%

Related Apprenticeship	*Years*
Aircraft Mechanic, Electrical and Radio	4
Electrician, Aircraft	4

(This is one of the most popular apprenticeable jobs.)

Install, inspect, test, adjust, or repair avionics equipment, such as radar, radio, navigation, and missile control systems in aircraft or space vehicles. Adjust, repair, or replace malfunctioning components or assemblies, using hand tools and/or soldering irons. Assemble components such as switches, electrical controls, and junction boxes, using hand tools and soldering irons. Connect components to assemblies such as radio systems, instruments, magnetos, inverters, and in-flight refueling systems, using hand tools and soldering irons. Install electrical and electronic components, assemblies, and systems in aircraft, using hand tools, power tools, and/or soldering irons. Interpret flight test data in order to diagnose malfunctions and systemic performance problems. Lay out installation of aircraft assemblies and systems, following documentation such as blueprints, manuals, and wiring diagrams. Test and troubleshoot instruments, components, and assemblies, using circuit testers, oscilloscopes, and voltmeters. Assemble prototypes or models of circuits, instruments, and systems so that they can be used for testing. Coordinate work with that of engineers, technicians, and other aircraft maintenance personnel. Fabricate parts and test aids as required. Keep records of maintenance and repair work. Operate computer-aided drafting and design applications to design avionics system modifications. Set up and operate ground support and test equipment to perform functional flight tests of electrical and electronic systems. **SKILLS**—Repairing; Installation; Equipment Maintenance; Troubleshooting; Operation Monitoring; Science; Operation and Control; Quality Control Analysis.

GOE—**Interest Area:** 05. Mechanics, Installers, and Repairers. **Work Group:** 05.02 Electrical and Electronic Systems. **Other Apprenticeable Jobs in This Work Group:** Battery Repairers; Central Office and PBX Installers and Repairers; Communication Equipment Mechanics, Installers, and Repairers; Data Processing Equipment Repairers; Electric Home Appliance and Power Tool Repairers; Electric Meter Installers and Repairers; Electric Motor and Switch Assemblers and Repairers; Electrical and Electronics Installers and Repairers, Transportation Equipment; Electrical and Electronics Repairers, Commercial and Industrial Equipment; Electrical and Electronics Repairers, Powerhouse, Substation, and Relay; Electrical Power-Line Installers and Repairers; Electronic Equipment Installers and Repairers, Motor Vehicles; Electronic Home Entertainment Equipment Installers and Repairers; Elevator Installers and Repairers; Installation, Maintenance, and Repair Workers, All Other; Office Machine and Cash Register Servicers; Radio Mechanics; Signal and Track Switch Repairers; Station Installers and Repairers, Telephone; Telecommunications Line Installers and Repair-

ers; Transformer Repairers. **PERSONALITY TYPE:** Realistic. Realistic occupations frequently involve work activities that include practical, hands-on problems and solutions. They often deal with plants, animals, and real-world materials like wood, tools, and machinery. Many of the occupations require working outside and do not involve a lot of paperwork or working closely with others.

RELATED KNOWLEDGE/COURSES—**Computers and Electronics:** Knowledge of circuit boards, processors, chips, electronic equipment, and computer hardware and software, including applications and programming. **Physics:** Knowledge and prediction of physical principles and laws and their interrelationships and applications to understanding fluid, material, and atmospheric dynamics and mechanical, electrical, atomic, and subatomic structures and processes. **Design:** Knowledge of design techniques, tools, and principles involved in production of precision technical plans, blueprints, drawings, and models. **Engineering and Technology:** Knowledge of the practical application of engineering science and technology. This includes applying principles, techniques, procedures, and equipment to the design and production of various goods and services. **Telecommunications:** Knowledge of transmission, broadcasting, switching, control, and operation of telecommunications systems. **Mechanical Devices:** Knowledge of machines and tools, including their designs, uses, repair, and maintenance.

WORK ENVIRONMENT—Hazardous conditions; spend time kneeling, crouching, stooping, or crawling; common protective or safety equipment; using hands on objects, tools, or controls; sounds, noise levels are distracting or uncomfortable; cramped work space, awkward positions.

Bakers, Bread and Pastry

- Growth: 11.2%
- Annual Job Openings: 29,000
- Annual Earnings: $20,990
- Percentage of Women: 49.7%

Related Apprenticeship	Years
Baker (Hotel and Restaurant)	3
Cook, Pastry	3

Mix and bake ingredients according to recipes to produce small quantities of breads, pastries, and other baked goods for consumption on premises or for sale as specialty baked goods. Weighs and measures ingredients, using measuring cups and spoons. Mixes ingredients to form dough or batter by hand or using electric mixer. Rolls and shapes dough, using rolling pin, and cuts dough in uniform portions with knife, divider, or cookie cutter. Molds dough in desired shapes, places dough in greased or floured pans, and trims overlapping edges with knife. Mixes and cooks pie filling, pours filling into pie shells, and tops filling with meringue or cream. Checks production schedule to determine variety and quantity of goods to bake. Spreads or sprinkles toppings on loaves or specialties and places dough in oven, using long-handled paddle (peel). Covers filling with top crust, places pies in oven, and adjusts drafts or thermostatic controls to regulate oven temperatures. Mixes ingredients to make icings; decorates cakes and pastries; and blends colors for icings, shaped ornaments, and statuaries. Cuts, peels, and prepares fruit for pie fillings. **SKILLS**—None met the criteria.

GOE—Interest Area: 11. Recreation, Travel, and Other Personal Services. **Work Group:** 11.05 Food and Beverage Services. **Other Apprenticeable Jobs in This Work Group:** Bartenders; Butchers and Meat Cutters; Chefs and Head Cooks; Cooks, Fast Food; Cooks, Institution and Cafeteria; Cooks, Restaurant. **PERSONALITY TYPE:** Realistic. Realistic occupations frequently involve work activities that include practical, hands-on problems and solutions. They often deal with plants, animals, and real-world materials like wood, tools, and machinery. Many of the occupations require working outside and do not involve a lot of paperwork or working closely with others.

RELATED KNOWLEDGE/COURSES—Food Production: Knowledge of techniques and equipment for planting, growing, and harvesting food products (both plant and animal) for consumption, including storage/handling techniques. **Production and Processing:** Knowledge of raw materials, production processes, quality control, costs, and other techniques for maximizing the effective manufacture and distribution of goods. **Sales and Marketing:** Knowledge of principles and methods for showing, promoting, and selling products or services. This includes marketing strategy and tactics, product demonstration, sales techniques, and sales control systems.

WORK ENVIRONMENT—Standing; indoors; minor burns, cuts, bites, or stings; spend time making repetitive motions; very hot or cold.

Bakers, Manufacturing

◎ Growth: 11.2%

◎ Annual Job Openings: 29,000

◎ Annual Earnings: $20,990

◎ Percentage of Women: 49.7%

Related Apprenticeship	*Years*
Baker (Bakery Products)	3

Mix and bake ingredients according to recipes to produce breads, pastries, and other baked goods. Goods are produced in large quantities for sale through establishments such as grocery stores. Generally, high-volume production equipment is used. Measures flour and other ingredients to prepare batters, dough, fillings, and icings, using scale and graduated containers. Places dough in pans, in molds, or on sheets and bakes dough in oven or on grill. Dumps ingredients into mixing-machine bowl or steam kettle to mix or cook ingredients according to specific instructions. Decorates cakes. Applies glace, icing, or other topping to baked goods, using spatula or brush. Rolls, cuts, and shapes dough to form sweet rolls, pie crusts, tarts, cookies, and related products prior to baking. Observes color of products being baked and adjusts oven temperature. Develops new recipes for cakes and icings. SKILLS—Operation Monitoring.

GOE—Interest Area: 08. Industrial Production. Work Group: 08.03 Production Work. Other Apprenticeable Jobs in This Work Group: Bindery Machine Operators and Tenders; Chemical Equipment Controllers and Operators; Coating, Painting, and Spraying Machine Operators and Tenders; Cooling and Freezing Equipment Operators and Tenders; Crushing, Grinding, and Polishing Machine Setters, Operators, and Tenders; Cutters and Trimmers, Hand; Cutting and Slicing Machine Operators and Tenders; Design Printing Machine Setters and Set-Up Operators; Electrolytic Plating and Coating Machine Setters and Set-Up Operators, Metal and Plastic; Electrotypers and Stereotypers; Embossing Machine Set-Up Operators; Engraver Set-Up Operators; Extruding, Forming, Pressing, and Compacting Machine Operators and Tenders; Fabric and Apparel Patternmakers; Film Laboratory Technicians; Fitters, Structural Metal—Precision; Food Batchmakers; Furnace, Kiln, Oven, Drier, and Kettle Operators and Tenders; Hand Compositors and Typesetters; Job Printers; Letterpress Setters and Set-Up Operators; Metal Fabricators, Structural Metal Products; Metal-Refining Furnace Operators and Tenders; Mixing and Blending Machine Setters, Operators, and Tenders; Mold Makers, Hand; Molding and Casting Workers; Numerical Control Machine Tool Operators and Tenders, Metal and Plastic; Offset Lithographic Press Setters and Set-Up Operators; Painting, Coating, and Decorating Workers; Photographic Processing Machine Operators; Photographic Reproduction Technicians; Photographic Retouchers and Restorers; Plate Finishers; Platemakers; Precision Printing Workers; Printing Press Machine Operators and Tenders; Production Workers, All Other; Sawing Machine Operators and Tenders; Sawing Machine Setters and Set-Up Operators; Scanner Operators; Separating, Filtering, Clarifying, Precipitating, and Still Machine Setters, Operators, and Tenders; Sewing Machine Operators, Garment; Slaughterers and Meat Packers; Stone Sawyers; Strippers; Team Assemblers; Welder-Fitters; Welders and Cutters; Woodworking Machine Operators and Tenders, Except Sawing. **PERSONALITY TYPE:** Realistic. Realistic occupations frequently involve work activities that include practical, hands-on problems and solutions. They often deal with plants, animals, and real-world materials like wood, tools, and machinery. Many of the occupations require working outside and do not involve a lot of paperwork or working closely with others.

RELATED KNOWLEDGE/COURSES—Production and Processing: Knowledge of raw materials, production processes, quality control, costs, and other techniques for maximizing the effective manufacture and distribution of goods. **Food Production:** Knowledge of techniques and equipment for planting, growing, and harvesting food products (both plant and animal) for consumption, including storage/handling techniques.

WORK ENVIRONMENT—Minor burns, cuts, bites, or stings; very hot or cold; indoors; standing; spend time making repetitive motions.

Bartenders

◎ Growth: 8.6%

◎ Annual Job Openings: 100,000

◎ Annual Earnings: $15,040

◎ Percentage of Women: 53.7%

Related Apprenticeship	*Years*
Bartender	1

Mix and serve drinks to patrons directly or through waitstaff. Collect money for drinks served. Check identification of customers in order to verify age requirements for purchase of alcohol. Balance cash receipts. Attempt to limit problems and liability related to customers' excessive drinking by taking steps such as persuading customers to stop drinking or ordering taxis or other transportation for intoxicated patrons. Clean glasses, utensils, and bar equipment. Take beverage orders from serving staff or directly from patrons. Serve wine and bottled or draft beer. Clean bars, work areas, and tables. Mix ingredients, such as liquor, soda, water, sugar, and bitters, in order to prepare cocktails and other drinks. Serve snacks or food items to customers seated at the bar. Order or requisition liquors and supplies. Ask customers who become loud and obnoxious to leave or physically remove them. Slice and pit fruit for garnishing drinks. Arrange bottles and glasses to make attractive displays. Plan, organize, and control the operations of a cocktail lounge or bar. Supervise the work of bar staff and other bartenders. Plan bar menus. Prepare appetizers, such as pickles, cheese, and cold meats. **SKILLS—**Social Perceptiveness; Persuasion; Service Orientation; Learning Strategies; Negotiation; Critical Thinking; Speaking; Instructing.

GOE—Interest Area: 11. Recreation, Travel, and Other Personal Services. **Work Group:** 11.05 Food and Beverage Services. **Other Apprenticeable Jobs in This Work Group:** Bakers, Bread and Pastry; Butchers and Meat Cutters; Chefs and Head Cooks; Cooks, Fast Food; Cooks, Institution and Cafeteria; Cooks, Restaurant. **PERSONALITY TYPE:** Enterprising. Enterprising occupations frequently involve starting up and carrying out projects. These occupations can involve leading people and making many decisions. They sometimes require risk taking and often deal with business.

RELATED KNOWLEDGE/COURSES— **Customer and Personal Service:** Knowledge of principles and processes for providing customer and personal services. This includes customer needs assessment, meeting quality standards for services, and evaluation of customer satisfaction. **Psychology:** Knowledge of human behavior and performance; individual differences in ability, personality, and interests; learning and motivation; psychological research methods; and the assessment and treatment of behavioral and affective disorders. **Sales and Marketing:** Knowledge of principles and methods for showing, promoting, and selling products or services. This includes marketing strategy and tactics, product demonstration, sales techniques, and sales control systems. **Food Production:** Knowledge of techniques and equipment for planting, growing, and harvesting food products (both plant and animal) for consumption, including storage/handling techniques. **Sociology and Anthropology:** Knowledge of group behavior and dynamics, societal trends and influences, human migrations, ethnicity, and cultures and their history and origins. **Philosophy and Theology:** Knowledge of different philosophical systems and religions. This includes their basic principles, values, ethics, ways of thinking, customs, and practices and their impact on human culture.

WORK ENVIRONMENT—Physical proximity; walking and running; standing; sounds, noise levels are distracting or uncomfortable; contaminants.

Battery Repairers

- Growth: 5.3%
- Annual Job Openings: 3,000
- Annual Earnings: $32,310
- Percentage of Women: 4.5%

Related Apprenticeship	*Years*
Battery Repairer	2

Inspect, repair, recharge, and replace batteries. Inspects electrical connections, wiring charging relays, charging resistance box, and storage batteries, following wiring diagram. Removes and disassembles cells and cathode assembly, using tension handles, prybars, and hoist, and cuts wires to faulty cells. Inspects battery for defects, such as dented cans, damaged carbon rods and terminals, and defective seals. Tests condition, fluid level, and specific gravity of electrolyte cells, using voltmeter, hydrometer, and thermometer. Secures cell on rocker mechanism or attaches assemblies, using bolts or cement. Positions and levels, or signals worker to position and level, cell, anode, or cathode, using hoist and leveling jacks. Installs recharged or repaired battery or cells, using hand tools. Cleans cells, cell assemblies, glassware, leads, electrical connections, and battery poles, using scraper, steam, water, emery cloth, power grinder, or acid. Disconnects electrical leads and removes battery, using hand tools and hoist. Adds water and acid to battery cells to obtain specified concentration. Repairs or adjusts defective parts, using hand tools or power tools. Replaces defective parts, such as cell plates, fuses, lead parts, switches, wires, anodes, cathodes, and rheostat. Connects battery to battery charger and adjusts rheostat to start flow of electricity into battery. Fabricates and assembles electrolytic cell parts for storage batteries. Compiles operating and maintenance records. Seals joints with putty, mortar, and asbestos, using putty extruder and knife. Repairs battery-charging equipment. Measures cathode blade and anode, using ruler, and rate of mercury flow, using stopwatch. **SKILLS**—Repairing; Installation; Troubleshooting; Equipment Maintenance; Quality Control Analysis; Science; Operation and Control; Equipment Selection.

GOE—Interest Area: 05. Mechanics, Installers, and Repairers. **Work Group:** 05.02 Electrical and Electronic Systems. **Other Apprenticeable Jobs in This Work Group:** Avionics Technicians; Central Office and PBX Installers and Repairers; Communication Equipment Mechanics, Installers, and Repairers; Data Processing Equipment Repairers; Electric Home Appliance and Power Tool Repairers; Electric Meter Installers and Repairers; Electric Motor and Switch Assemblers and Repairers; Electrical and Electronics Installers and Repairers, Transportation Equipment; Electrical and Electronics Repairers, Commercial and Industrial Equipment; Electrical and Electronics Repairers, Powerhouse, Substation, and Relay; Electrical Power-Line Installers and Repairers; Electronic Equipment Installers and Repairers, Motor Vehicles; Electronic Home Entertainment Equipment Installers and Repairers; Elevator Installers and Repairers; Installation, Maintenance, and Repair Workers, All Other; Office Machine and Cash Register Servicers; Radio Mechanics; Signal and Track Switch Repairers; Station Installers and Repairers, Telephone; Telecommunications Line Installers and Repairers; Transformer Repairers. **PERSONALITY TYPE:** Realistic. Realistic occupations frequently involve work activities that include practical, hands-on problems and solutions.

They often deal with plants, animals, and real-world materials like wood, tools, and machinery. Many of the occupations require working outside and do not involve a lot of paperwork or working closely with others.

RELATED KNOWLEDGE/COURSES— Computers and Electronics: Knowledge of circuit boards, processors, chips, electronic equipment, and computer hardware and software, including applications and programming. **Mechanical Devices:** Knowledge of machines and tools, including their designs, uses, repair, and maintenance. **Chemistry:** Knowledge of the chemical composition, structure, and properties of substances and of the chemical processes and transformations that they undergo. This includes uses of chemicals, their danger signs, production techniques, and disposal methods. **Engineering and Technology:** Knowledge of the practical application of engineering science and technology. This includes applying principles, techniques, procedures, and equipment to the design and production of various goods and services.

WORK ENVIRONMENT—Minor burns, cuts, bites, or stings; spend time kneeling, crouching, stooping, or crawling; cramped work space, awkward positions; hazardous conditions; contaminants.

Boat Builders and Shipwrights

- Growth: 10.1%
- Annual Job Openings: 193,000
- Annual Earnings: $34,250
- Percentage of Women: 1.9%

Related Apprenticeship	Years
Boatbuilder, Wood	4
Shipwright	4

Construct and repair ships or boats according to blueprints. Cuts and forms parts, such as keel, ribs, sidings, and support structures and blocks, using woodworking hand tools and power tools. Constructs and shapes wooden frames, structures, and other parts according to blueprint specifications, using hand tools, power tools, and measuring instruments. Attaches metal parts, such as fittings, plates, and bulkheads, to ship, using brace and bits, augers, and wrenches. Establishes dimensional reference points on layout and hull to make template of parts and locate machinery and equipment. Smoothes and finishes ship surfaces, using power sander, broadax, adz, and paint, and waxes and buffs surface to specified finish. Cuts out defect, using power tools and hand tools, and fits and secures replacement part, using caulking gun, adhesive, or hand tools. Assembles and installs hull timbers and other structures in ship, using adhesive, measuring instruments, and hand tools or power tools. Measures and marks dimensional lines on lumber, following template and using scriber. Consults with customer or supervisor and reads blueprint to determine necessary repairs. Attaches hoist to sections of hull and directs hoist operator to align parts over blocks according to layout of boat. Marks outline of boat on building dock, shipway, or mold loft according to blueprint specifications, using measuring instruments and crayon. Inspects boat to determine location and extent of defect. Positions and secures support structures on construction area. **SKILLS**—Installation; Repairing; Opera-tions Analysis; Technology Design; Equipment Maintenance; Equipment Selection; Mathematics; Quality Control Analysis.

GOE—Interest Area: 06. Construction, Mining, and Drilling. **Work Group:** 06.02 Construction. **Other Apprenticeable Jobs in This Work Group:** Boilermakers; Brickmasons and Blockmasons; Carpet Installers; Ceiling Tile Installers; Cement Masons and Concrete Finishers; Construction and Related Workers, All Other; Construction Carpenters; Drywall Installers; Electricians; Fence Erectors; Floor Layers, Except Carpet, Wood, and Hard Tiles; Glaziers; Grader, Bulldozer, and Scraper Operators; Insulation Workers, Floor, Ceiling, and Wall; Insulation Workers, Mechanical; Operating Engineers; Painters, Construction and Maintenance; Paperhangers; Paving, Surfacing, and Tamping Equipment Operators; Pipe Fitters; Plasterers and Stucco Masons; Plumbers; Reinforcing Iron and Rebar Workers; Riggers; Roofers; Rough Carpenters; Sheet Metal Workers; Ship Carpenters and Joiners; Stone Cutters and Carvers; Stonemasons; Structural Iron and Steel Workers; Tapers; Terrazzo Workers and Finishers; Tile and Marble Setters. **PERSONALITY TYPE:** Realistic. Realistic occupations frequently involve work activities that include practical, hands-on problems and solutions. They often deal with plants, animals, and real-world materials like wood, tools, and machinery. Many of the occupations require working outside and do not involve a lot of paperwork or working closely with others.

RELATED KNOWLEDGE/COURSES—Building and Construction: Knowledge of the materials, methods, and tools involved in the construction or repair of houses, buildings, or other structures, such as highways and roads. **Design:** Knowledge of design techniques, tools, and principles involved in production of precision technical plans, blueprints, drawings, and models. **Mechanical Devices:** Knowledge of machines and tools, including their designs, uses, repair, and maintenance. **Engineering and Technology:** Knowledge of the practical application of engineering science and technology. This includes applying principles, techniques, procedures, and equipment to the design and production of various goods and services. **Production and Processing:** Knowledge of raw materials, production processes, quality control, costs, and other techniques for maximizing the effective manufacture and distribution of goods. **Physics:** Knowledge and prediction of physical principles and laws and their interrelationships and applications to understanding fluid, material, and atmospheric dynamics and mechanical, electrical, atomic, and subatomic structures and processes.

WORK ENVIRONMENT—Outdoors; climbing ladders, scaffolds, or poles; standing; hazardous equipment; spend time kneeling, crouching, stooping, or crawling; common protective or safety equipment.

Boiler Operators and Tenders, Low Pressure

- Growth: 0.3%
- Annual Job Openings: 4,000
- Annual Earnings: $43,420
- Percentage of Women: 3.3%

Related Apprenticeship	*Years*
Firer, Marine	1

Operate or tend low-pressure stationary steam boilers and auxiliary steam equipment, such as pumps, compressors, and air conditioning equipment, to supply steam heat for office buildings, apartment houses, or industrial establishments; to maintain steam at specified pressure aboard marine vessels; or to generate and supply compressed air for operation of pneumatic tools, hoists, and air lances. Tends boilers and equipment to supply and maintain steam or heat for buildings, marine vessels, or operation of pneumatic tools. Cleans and maintains heating and steam boilers and equipment, using hand tools. Records test results on specified form and gives to worker or supervisor. Tests sample quality to ensure sample meets specifications, using testing devices. Moves controls and observes gauges to regulate heat and steam. Installs burners and auxiliary equipment, using hand tools. Shovels coal or coke into firebox to feed fuel, using hand tools. Obtains samples from designated location on boiler and carries samples to testing laboratory. Ignites fuel in burner, using torch or flame. SKILLS—Installation; Equipment Maintenance; Operation Monitoring; Operation and Control; Repairing; Troubleshooting; Equipment Selection; Quality Control Analysis.

GOE—Interest Area: 08. Industrial Production. Work Group: 08.06 Systems Operation. Other Apprenticeable Jobs in This Work Group: Chemical Plant and System Operators; Gaugers; Petroleum Refinery and Control Panel Operators; Power Distributors and Dispatchers; Power Generating Plant Operators, Except Auxiliary Equipment Operators; Stationary Engineers; Water and Liquid Waste Treatment Plant and System Operators. **PERSONALITY TYPE:** Realistic. Realistic occupations frequently involve work activities that include practical, hands-on problems and solutions. They often deal with plants, animals, and real-world materials like wood, tools, and machinery. Many of the occupations require working outside and do not involve a lot of paperwork or working closely with others.

RELATED KNOWLEDGE/COURSES—**Mechanical Devices:** Knowledge of machines and tools, including their designs, uses, repair, and maintenance. **Physics:** Knowledge and prediction of physical principles and laws and their interrelationships and applications to understanding fluid, material, and atmospheric dynamics and mechanical, electrical, atomic, and subatomic structures and processes. **Production and Processing:** Knowledge of raw materials, production processes, quality control, costs, and other techniques for maximizing the effective manufacture and distribution of goods. **Engineering and Technology:** Knowledge of the practical application of engineering science and technology. This includes applying principles, techniques, procedures, and equipment to the design and production of various goods and services. **Public Safety and Security:** Knowledge of relevant equipment, policies, procedures, and strategies to promote effective local, state, or national security operations for the protection of people, data, property, and institutions. **Clerical Practices:** Knowledge of administrative and clerical procedures and systems, such as word processing, managing files and records, stenography and transcription, designing forms, and other office procedures and terminology.

WORK ENVIRONMENT—Very hot or cold; hazardous equipment; minor burns, cuts, bites, or stings; hazardous conditions; sounds, noise levels are distracting or uncomfortable; contaminants.

Boilermakers

- Growth: 1.7%
- Annual Job Openings: 2,000
- Annual Earnings: $43,240
- Percentage of Women: 3.2%

Related Apprenticeship	Years
Boilerhouse Mechanic	3
Boilermaker I	3
Boilermaker II	3
Boilermaker Fitter	4

(This is one of the most popular apprenticeable jobs.)

Construct, assemble, maintain, and repair stationary steam boilers and boiler house auxiliaries. Align structures or plate sections to assemble boiler frame tanks or vats, following blueprints. Work involves use of hand and power tools, plumb bobs, levels, wedges, dogs, or turnbuckles. Assist in testing assembled vessels. Direct cleaning of boilers and boiler furnaces. Inspect and repair boiler fittings, such as safety valves, regulators, automatic-control mechanisms, water columns, and auxiliary machines. Bell, bead with power hammers, or weld pressure vessel tube ends in order to ensure leakproof joints. Bolt or arc-weld pressure vessel structures and parts together, using wrenches and welding equipment. Examine boilers, pressure vessels, tanks, and vats to locate defects such as leaks, weak spots, and defective sections so that they can be repaired. Inspect assembled vessels and individual components, such as tubes, fittings, valves, controls, and auxiliary mechanisms, to locate any defects. Install manholes, handholes, taps, tubes, valves, gauges, and feedwater connections in drums of water tube boilers, using hand tools. Install refractory bricks and other heat-resistant materials in fireboxes of pressure vessels. Lay out plate, sheet steel, or other heavy metal and locate and mark bending and cutting lines, using protractors, compasses, and drawing instruments or templates. Locate and mark reference points for columns or plates on boiler foundations, following blueprints and using straightedges, squares, transits, and measuring instruments. Position, align, and secure structural parts and related assemblies to boiler frames, tanks, or vats of pressure vessels, following blueprints. Repair or replace defective pressure vessel parts, such as safety valves and regulators, using torches, jacks, caulking hammers, power saws, threading dies, welding equipment, and metalworking machinery. Shape seams, joints, and irregular edges of pressure vessel sections and structural parts in order to attain specified fit of parts, using cutting torches, hammers, files, and metalworking machines. Straighten or reshape bent pressure vessel plates and structure parts, using hammers, jacks, and torches. Study blueprints to determine locations, relationships, and dimensions of parts. Assemble large vessels in an on-site fabrication shop prior to installation in order to ensure proper fit. Attach rigging and signal crane or hoist operators to lift heavy frame and plate sections and other parts into place. Clean pressure vessel equipment, using scrapers, wire brushes, and cleaning solvents.

Shape and fabricate parts, such as stacks, uptakes, and chutes, in order to adapt pressure vessels, heat exchangers, and piping to premises, using heavy-metalworking machines such as brakes, rolls, and drill presses. **SKILLS**—Installation; Repairing; Equipment Maintenance; Troubleshooting; Quality Control Analysis; Technology Design; Operation Monitoring; Systems Analysis.

GOE—Interest Area: 06. Construction, Mining, and Drilling. **Work Group:** 06.02 Construction. **Other Apprenticeable Jobs in This Work Group:** Boat Builders and Shipwrights; Brickmasons and Blockmasons; Carpet Installers; Ceiling Tile Installers; Cement Masons and Concrete Finishers; Construction and Related Workers, All Other; Construction Carpenters; Drywall Installers; Electricians; Fence Erectors; Floor Layers, Except Carpet, Wood, and Hard Tiles; Glaziers; Grader, Bulldozer, and Scraper Operators; Insulation Workers, Floor, Ceiling, and Wall; Insulation Workers, Mechanical; Operating Engineers; Painters, Construction and Maintenance; Paperhangers; Paving, Surfacing, and Tamping Equipment Operators; Pipe Fitters; Plasterers and Stucco Masons; Plumbers; Reinforcing Iron and Rebar Workers; Riggers; Roofers; Rough Carpenters; Sheet Metal Workers; Ship Carpenters and Joiners; Stone Cutters and Carvers; Stonemasons; Structural Iron and Steel Workers; Tapers; Terrazzo Workers and Finishers; Tile and Marble Setters. **PERSONALITY TYPE:** Realistic. Realistic occupations frequently involve work activities that include practical, hands-on problems and solutions. They often deal with plants, animals, and real-world materials like wood, tools, and machinery. Many of the occupations require working outside and do not involve a lot of paperwork or working closely with others.

RELATED KNOWLEDGE/COURSES—Mechanical Devices: Knowledge of machines and tools, including their designs, uses, repair, and maintenance. Building and Construction: Knowledge of the materials, methods, and tools involved in the construction or repair of houses, buildings, or other structures, such as highways and roads. Engineering and Technology: Knowledge of the practical application of engineering science and technology. This includes applying principles, techniques, procedures, and equipment to the design and production of various goods and services. Physics: Knowledge and prediction of physical principles and laws and their interrelationships and applications to understanding fluid, material, and atmospheric dynamics and mechanical, electrical, atomic, and subatomic structures and processes. Public Safety and Security: Knowledge of relevant equipment, policies, procedures, and strategies to promote effective local, state, or national security operations for the protection of people, data, property, and institutions. Design: Knowledge of design techniques, tools, and principles involved in production of precision technical plans, blueprints, drawings, and models.

WORK ENVIRONMENT—Hazardous equipment; minor burns, cuts, bites, or stings; common protective or safety equipment; sounds, noise levels are distracting or uncomfortable; using hands on objects, tools, or controls.

FURTHER INFORMATION—Contact a local joint union-management apprenticeship committee or the nearest office of your state employment service or apprenticeship agency (see Appendix C). To identify the local union office, contact International Brotherhood of Boilermakers, Iron Ship Builders, Blacksmiths, Forgers, and Helpers, 753 State Ave., Suite 570, Kansas City, KS 66101.

Brickmasons and Blockmasons

- ◉ Growth: 14.2%
- ◉ Annual Job Openings: 21,000
- ◉ Annual Earnings: $41,550
- ◉ Percentage of Women: 1.1%

Related Apprenticeship	Years
Chimney Repairer	1
Bricklayer (Construction)	3
Bricklayer (Brick and Tile)	4
Bricklayer, Firebrick and Refractory Tile	4

(This is one of the most popular apprenticeable jobs.)

Lay and bind building materials, such as brick, structural tile, concrete block, cinder block, glass block, and terra-cotta block, with mortar and other substances to construct or repair walls, partitions, arches, sewers, and other structures. Construct corners by fastening in plumb position a corner pole or building a corner pyramid of bricks and then filling in between the corners, using a line from corner to corner to guide each course, or layer, of brick. Fasten or fuse brick or other building material to structure with wire clamps, anchor holes, torch, or cement. Interpret blueprints and drawings to determine specifications and to calculate the materials required. Lay and align bricks, blocks, or tiles to build or repair structures or high-temperature equipment, such as cupola, kilns, ovens, or furnaces. Measure distance from reference points and mark guidelines to lay out work, using plumb bobs and levels. Mix specified amounts of sand, clay, dirt, or mortar powder with water to form refractory mixtures. Remove burned or damaged brick or mortar, using sledgehammer, crowbar, chipping gun, or chisel. Apply and smooth mortar or other mixture over work surface. Break or cut bricks, tiles, or blocks to size, using trowel edge, hammer, or power saw. Calculate angles and courses and determine vertical and horizontal alignment of courses. Remove excess mortar with trowels and hand tools and finish mortar joints with jointing tools for a sealed, uniform appearance. Clean working surface to remove scale, dust, soot, or chips of brick and mortar, using broom, wire brush, or scraper. Examine brickwork or structure to determine need for repair. Spray or spread refractory material over brickwork to protect against deterioration. **SKILLS**—Repairing; Mathematics; Equipment Selection; Equipment Maintenance; Installation; Science.

GOE—Interest Area: 06. Construction, Mining, and Drilling. **Work Group:** 06.02 Construction. **Other Apprenticeable Jobs in This Work Group:** Boat Builders and Shipwrights; Boilermakers; Carpet Installers; Ceiling Tile Installers; Cement Masons and Concrete Finishers; Construction and Related Workers, All Other; Construction Carpenters; Drywall Installers; Electricians; Fence Erectors; Floor Layers, Except Carpet, Wood, and Hard Tiles; Glaziers; Grader, Bulldozer, and Scraper Operators; Insulation Workers, Floor, Ceiling, and Wall; Insulation Workers, Mechanical; Operating Engineers; Painters, Construction and Maintenance; Paperhangers; Paving, Surfacing, and Tamping Equipment Operators; Pipe Fit-

ters; Plasterers and Stucco Masons; Plumbers; Reinforcing Iron and Rebar Workers; Riggers; Roofers; Rough Carpenters; Sheet Metal Workers; Ship Carpenters and Joiners; Stone Cutters and Carvers; Stonemasons; Structural Iron and Steel Workers; Tapers; Terrazzo Workers and Finishers; Tile and Marble Setters. **PERSONALITY TYPE:** Realistic. Realistic occupations frequently involve work activities that include practical, hands-on problems and solutions. They often deal with plants, animals, and real-world materials like wood, tools, and machinery. Many of the occupations require working outside and do not involve a lot of paperwork or working closely with others.

RELATED KNOWLEDGE/COURSES— Building and Construction: Knowledge of the materials, methods, and tools involved in the construction or repair of houses, buildings, or other structures, such as highways and roads. **Mechanical Devices:** Knowledge of machines and tools, including their designs, uses, repair, and maintenance.

WORK ENVIRONMENT—Outdoors; standing; contaminants; spend time making repetitive motions; very hot or cold.

FURTHER INFORMATION—Contact a local joint union-management apprenticeship committee or the nearest office of your state employment service or apprenticeship agency (see Appendix C). To identify the local union office, contact International Union of Bricklayers and Allied Craftworkers, 1776 I St. NW, Washington, DC 20006.

Broadcast Technicians

- Growth: 11.3%
- Annual Job Openings: 4,000
- Annual Earnings: $28,090
- Percentage of Women: 14.2%

Related Apprenticeship	Years
Audio Operator	2
Field Engineer	4

Set up, operate, and maintain the electronic equipment used to transmit radio and television programs. Control audio equipment to regulate volume level and quality of sound during radio and television broadcasts. Operate radio transmitter to broadcast radio and television programs. Align antennae with receiving dishes in order to obtain the clearest signal for transmission of broadcasts from field locations. Control audio equipment in order to regulate the volume and sound quality during radio and television broadcasts. Monitor strength, clarity, and reliability of incoming and outgoing signals and adjust equipment as necessary to maintain quality broadcasts. Observe monitors and converse with station personnel in order to determine audio and video levels and to ascertain that programs are airing. Preview scheduled programs to ensure that signals are functioning and programs are ready for transmission. Regulate the fidelity, brightness, and contrast of video transmissions, using video console control panels. Report equipment problems and ensure that repairs are made; make emergency repairs to equipment when necessary

and possible. Schedule programming and/or read television programming logs in order to determine which programs are to be recorded or aired. Select sources from which programming will be received or through which programming will be transmitted. Set up and operate portable field transmission equipment outside the studio. Substitute programs in cases where signals fail. Design and modify equipment to employer specifications. Determine the number, type, and approximate location of microphones needed for best sound recording or transmission quality and position them appropriately. Discuss production requirements with clients. Edit broadcast material electronically, using computers. Give technical directions to other personnel during filming. Maintain programming logs as required by station management and the Federal Communications Commission. Organize recording sessions and prepare areas such as radio booths and television stations for recording. Perform preventive and minor equipment maintenance, using hand tools. Prepare reports outlining past and future programs, including content. Record sound onto tape or film for radio or television, checking its quality and making adjustments where necessary. Instruct trainees in how to use television production equipment, how to film events, and how to copy/edit graphics or sound onto videotape. **SKILLS**—Instructing; Technology Design; Installation; Troubleshooting; Learning Strategies; Writing; Management of Material Resources; Operation Monitoring; Systems Analysis.

GOE—Interest Area: 01. Arts, Entertainment, and Media. **Work Group:** 01.08 Media Technology. **Other Apprenticeable Jobs in This Work Group:** Audio and Video Equipment Technicians; Camera Operators, Television, Video, and Motion Picture; Film and Video

Editors; Professional Photographers; Radio Operators; Sound Engineering Technicians. **PERSONALITY TYPE:** Realistic. Realistic occupations frequently involve work activities that include practical, hands-on problems and solutions. They often deal with plants, animals, and real-world materials like wood, tools, and machinery. Many of the occupations require working outside and do not involve a lot of paperwork or working closely with others.

RELATED KNOWLEDGE/COURSES— Telecommunications: Knowledge of transmission, broadcasting, switching, control, and operation of telecommunications systems. **Geography:** Knowledge of principles and methods for describing the features of land, sea, and air masses, including their physical characteristics; locations; interrelationships; and distribution of plant, animal, and human life. **Computers and Electronics:** Knowledge of circuit boards, processors, chips, electronic equipment, and computer hardware and software, including applications and programming. **Communications and Media:** Knowledge of media production, communication, and dissemination techniques and methods. This includes alternative ways to inform and entertain via written, oral, and visual media. **Transportation:** Knowledge of principles and methods for moving people or goods by air, rail, sea, or road, including the relative costs and benefits. **Education and Training:** Knowledge of principles and methods for curriculum and training design, teaching and instruction for individuals and groups, and the measurement of training effects.

WORK ENVIRONMENT—Outdoors; standing; extremely bright or inadequate lighting; hazardous conditions; hazardous equipment.

Building Cleaning Workers, All Other

- Growth: 16.1%
- Annual Job Openings: 24,000
- Annual Earnings: $20,990
- Percentage of Women: 29.9%

Related Apprenticeship	Years
Rug Cleaner, Hand	1

All building cleaning workers not listed separately. **SKILLS**—No data available.

GOE—Interest Area: 11. Recreation, Travel, and Other Personal Services. **Work Group:** 11.07 Cleaning and Building Services. **Other Apprenticeable Jobs in This Work Group:** Janitors and Cleaners, Except Maids and Housekeeping Cleaners; Maids and Housekeeping Cleaners. **PERSONALITY TYPE:** No data available.

RELATED KNOWLEDGE/COURSES—No data available.

WORK ENVIRONMENT—No data available.

Bus and Truck Mechanics and Diesel Engine Specialists

- ◎ Growth: 14.2%
- ◎ Annual Job Openings: 28,000
- ◎ Annual Earnings: $34,970
- ◎ Percentage of Women: 1.2%

Related Apprenticeship	*Years*
Oil-Field Equipment Mechanic	2
Diesel Mechanic	4
Machinist, Marine Engine	4
Maintenance Mechanic, Bus and Truck	4
Mechanic, Industrial Truck	4
Tractor Mechanic	4

Diagnose, adjust, repair, or overhaul trucks, buses, and all types of diesel engines. Includes mechanics working primarily with automobile diesel engines. Use handtools such as screwdrivers, pliers, wrenches, pressure gauges, and precision instruments, as well as power tools such as pneumatic wrenches, lathes, welding equipment, and jacks and hoists. Inspect brake systems, steering mechanisms, wheel bearings, and other important parts to ensure that they are in proper operating condition. Perform routine maintenance such as changing oil, checking batteries, and lubricating equipment and machinery. Adjust and reline brakes, align

wheels, tighten bolts and screws, and reassemble equipment. Raise trucks, buses, and heavy parts or equipment, using hydraulic jacks or hoists. Test-drive trucks and buses to diagnose malfunctions or to ensure that they are working properly. Inspect, test, and listen to defective equipment to diagnose malfunctions, using test instruments such as handheld computers, motor analyzers, chassis charts, and pressure gauges. Examine and adjust protective guards, loose bolts, and specified safety devices. Inspect and verify dimensions and clearances of parts to ensure conformance to factory specifications. Specialize in repairing and maintaining parts of the engine, such as fuel injection systems. Attach test instruments to equipment and read dials and gauges in order to diagnose malfunctions. Rewire ignition systems, lights, and instrument panels. Recondition and replace parts, pistons, bearings, gears, and valves. Repair and adjust seats, doors, and windows and install and repair accessories. Inspect, repair, and maintain automotive and mechanical equipment and machinery such as pumps and compressors. Disassemble and overhaul internal combustion engines, pumps, generators, transmissions, clutches, and differential units. Rebuild gas and/or diesel engines. Align front ends and suspension systems. SKILLS—Equipment Maintenance; Repairing; Troubleshooting; Installation; Learning Strategies; Instructing; Technology Design; Social Perceptiveness; Coordination.

GOE—Interest Area: 05. Mechanics, Installers, and Repairers. **Work Group:** 05.03 Mechanical Work. **Other Apprenticeable Jobs in This Work Group:** Aircraft Engine Specialists; Airframe-and-Power-Plant Mechanics; Automotive Body and Related Repairers; Automotive Glass Installers and Repairers; Automotive Master Mechanics; Automotive Specialty Technicians;

Camera and Photographic Equipment Repairers; Coin, Vending, and Amusement Machine Servicers and Repairers; Farm Equipment Mechanics; Gas Appliance Repairers; Hand and Portable Power Tool Repairers; Heating and Air Conditioning Mechanics; Helpers—Installation, Maintenance, and Repair Workers; Industrial Machinery Mechanics; Installation, Maintenance, and Repair Workers, All Other; Keyboard Instrument Repairers and Tuners; Locksmiths and Safe Repairers; Maintenance and Repair Workers, General; Maintenance Workers, Machinery; Mechanical Door Repairers; Medical Appliance Technicians; Medical Equipment Repairers; Meter Mechanics; Millwrights; Mobile Heavy Equipment Mechanics, Except Engines; Motorboat Mechanics; Motorcycle Mechanics; Optical Instrument Assemblers; Outdoor Power Equipment and Other Small Engine Mechanics; Painters, Transportation Equipment; Rail Car Repairers; Recreational Vehicle Service Technicians; Reed or Wind Instrument Repairers and Tuners; Refrigeration Mechanics; Stringed Instrument Repairers and Tuners; Valve and Regulator Repairers; Watch Repairers. **PERSONALITY TYPE:** Realistic. Realistic occupations frequently involve work activities that include practical, hands-on problems and solutions. They often deal with plants, animals, and real-world materials like wood, tools, and machinery. Many of the occupations require working outside and do not involve a lot of paperwork or working closely with others.

RELATED KNOWLEDGE/COURSES— **Mechanical Devices:** Knowledge of machines and tools, including their designs, uses, repair, and maintenance. **Public Safety and Security:** Knowledge of relevant equipment, policies, procedures, and strategies to promote effective local, state, or national security operations for the protection of people, data, property, and institutions. **Transportation:** Knowledge of principles and methods for moving people or goods by air, rail, sea, or road, including the relative costs and benefits. **Engineering and Technology:** Knowledge of the practical application of engineering science and technology. This includes applying principles, techniques, procedures, and equipment to the design and production of various goods and services. **Law and Government:** Knowledge of laws, legal codes, court procedures, precedents, government regulations, executive orders, agency rules, and the democratic political process. **Chemistry:** Knowledge of the chemical composition, structure, and properties of substances and of the chemical processes and transformations that they undergo. This includes uses of chemicals, their danger signs, production techniques, and disposal methods.

WORK ENVIRONMENT—Sounds, noise levels are distracting or uncomfortable; contaminants; extremely bright or inadequate lighting; very hot or cold; hazardous conditions.

Butchers and Meat Cutters

- ◎ Growth: –2.5%
- ◎ Annual Job Openings: 21,000
- ◎ Annual Earnings: $25,570
- ◎ Percentage of Women: 23.7%

Related Apprenticeship	Years
Butcher, Meat	3
Meat Cutter	3

Cut, trim, or prepare consumer-sized portions of meat for use or sale in retail establishments. Cure, smoke, tenderize, and preserve meat. Cut, trim, bone, tie, and grind meats, such as beef, pork, poultry, and fish, to prepare meat in cooking form. Prepare and place meat cuts and products in display counter so they will appear attractive and catch the shopper's eye. Prepare special cuts of meat ordered by customers. Shape, lace, and tie roasts, using boning knife, skewer, and twine. Total sales and collect money from customers. Wrap, weigh, label, and price cuts of meat. Estimate requirements and order or requisition meat supplies to maintain inventories. Negotiate with representatives from supply companies to determine order details. Receive, inspect, and store meat upon delivery to ensure meat quality. Record quantity of meat received and issued to cooks and/or keep records of meat sales. Supervise other butchers or meat cutters. **SKILLS**—Management of Personnel Resources; Management of Financial Resources.

GOE—Interest Area: 11. Recreation, Travel, and Other Personal Services. **Work Group:** 11.05 Food and Beverage Services. **Other Apprenticeable Jobs in This Work Group:** Bakers, Bread and Pastry; Bartenders; Chefs and Head Cooks; Cooks, Fast Food; Cooks, Institution and Cafeteria; Cooks, Restaurant. **PERSONALITY TYPE:** Realistic. Realistic occupations frequently involve work activities that include practical, hands-on problems and solutions. They often deal with plants, animals, and real-world materials like wood, tools, and machinery. Many of the occupations require working outside and do not involve a lot of paperwork or working closely with others.

RELATED KNOWLEDGE/COURSES— Food Production: Knowledge of techniques and equipment for planting, growing, and harvesting food products (both plant and animal) for consumption, including storage/handling techniques. **Sales and Marketing:** Knowledge of principles and methods for showing, promoting, and selling products or services. This includes marketing strategy and tactics, product demonstration, sales techniques, and sales control systems. **Biology:** Knowledge of plant and animal organisms and their tissues, cells, functions, interdependencies, and interactions with each other and the environment.

WORK ENVIRONMENT—Minor burns, cuts, bites, or stings; standing; hazardous equipment; indoors; spend time making repetitive motions.

Cabinetmakers and Bench Carpenters

- Growth: 9.4%
- Annual Job Openings: 15,000
- Annual Earnings: $24,550
- Percentage of Women: 7.0%

Related Apprenticeship	Years
Harpsichord Maker	2
Hat-Block Maker (Woodworking)	3

Pipe-Organ Builder	3
Accordion Maker	4
Cabinetmaker	4
Carver, Hand	4
Last-Model Maker	4

Cut, shape, and assemble wooden articles or set up and operate a variety of woodworking machines, such as power saws, jointers, and mortisers, to surface, cut, or shape lumber or to fabricate parts for wood products. Sets up and operates machines, including power saws, jointers, mortisers, tenoners, molders, and shapers, to cut and shape woodstock. Marks dimensions of parts on paper or lumber stock, following blueprints, and matches lumber for color, grain, and texture. Studies blueprints, drawings, and written specifications of articles to be constructed or repaired and plans sequence of performing such operations. Installs hardware, such as hinges, catches, and drawer pulls, using hand tools. Dips, brushes, or sprays assembled articles with protective or decorative materials, such as stain, varnish, or lacquer. Sands and scrapes surfaces and joints of articles to prepare articles for finishing. Bores holes for insertion of screws or dowel by hand or using boring machine. Trims component parts of joints to ensure snug fit, using hand tools, such as planes, chisels, or wood files. Glues, fits, and clamps parts and subassemblies together to form complete unit. Drives nails or other fasteners to joints of articles to prepare articles for finishing. **SKILLS**—Installation; Operation and Control; Equipment Selection; Equipment Maintenance.

GOE—Interest Area: 08. Industrial Production. **Work Group:** 08.05 Woodworking Technology. **Other Appriceable Jobs in This Work Group:** Furniture Finishers; Model Makers, Wood; Patternmakers, Wood. **PERSONALITY TYPE:** Realistic. Realistic occupations frequently involve work activities that include practical, hands-on problems and solutions. They often deal with plants, animals, and real-world materials like wood, tools, and machinery. Many of the occupations require working outside and do not involve a lot of paperwork or working closely with others.

RELATED KNOWLEDGE/COURSES— Building and Construction: Knowledge of the materials, methods, and tools involved in the construction or repair of houses, buildings, or other structures, such as highways and roads. **Design:** Knowledge of design techniques, tools, and principles involved in production of precision technical plans, blueprints, drawings, and models. **Engineering and Technology:** Knowledge of the practical application of engineering science and technology. This includes applying principles, techniques, procedures, and equipment to the design and production of various goods and services. **Production and Processing:** Knowledge of raw materials, production processes, quality control, costs, and other techniques for maximizing the effective manufacture and distribution of goods. **Mechanical Devices:** Knowledge of machines and tools, including their designs, uses, repair, and maintenance.

WORK ENVIRONMENT—Spend time kneeling, crouching, stooping, or crawling; hazardous equipment; using hands on objects, tools, or controls; spend time bending or twisting the body; standing.

Camera Operators

- Growth: −11.2%
- Annual Job Openings: 6,000
- Annual Earnings: $31,660
- Percentage of Women: 47.6%

Related Apprenticeship	*Years*
Photographer, Lithographic	5

Operate process camera and related darkroom equipment to photograph and develop negatives of material to be printed. Feeds film into automatic film processor that develops, fixes, washes, and dries film. Measures original layouts and determines proportions needed to make reduced or enlarged photographic prints for pasteup. Exposes high-contrast film for predetermined exposure time. Immerses film in series of chemical baths to develop images and hangs film on rack to dry. Performs exposure tests to determine line, halftone, and color reproduction exposure lengths for various photographic factors. Mounts material to be photographed on copyboard of camera. Measures density of continuous-tone images to be photographed to set exposure time for halftone images. Selects and installs screens and filters in camera to produce desired effects. Adjusts camera settings, lights, and lens. **SKILLS**—Technology Design; Equipment Selection; Operations Analysis; Operation and Control; Quality Control Analysis; Installation.

GOE—Interest Area: 01. Arts, Entertainment, and Media. **Work Group:** 01.07 Graphic Arts. **Other Apprenticeable Jobs in This Work**

Group: Desktop Publishers; Dot Etchers; Engravers, Hand; Engravers/Carvers; Pantograph Engravers; Paste-Up Workers; Photoengravers; Precision Etchers and Engravers, Hand or Machine. **PERSONALITY TYPE:** Realistic. Realistic occupations frequently involve work activities that include practical, hands-on problems and solutions. They often deal with plants, animals, and real-world materials like wood, tools, and machinery. Many of the occupations require working outside and do not involve a lot of paperwork or working closely with others.

RELATED KNOWLEDGE/COURSES—Fine Arts: Knowledge of the theory and techniques required to compose, produce, and perform works of music, dance, visual arts, drama, and sculpture. **Chemistry:** Knowledge of the chemical composition, structure, and properties of substances and of the chemical processes and transformations that they undergo. This includes uses of chemicals, their danger signs, production techniques, and disposal methods.

WORK ENVIRONMENT—Indoors; extremely bright or inadequate lighting; spend time bending or twisting the body; standing; using hands on objects, tools, or controls.

Camera Operators, Television, Video, and Motion Picture

- Growth: 13.4%
- Annual Job Openings: 4,000
- Annual Earnings: $34,330
- Percentage of Women: 18.9%

Related Apprenticeship	*Years*
Camera Operator	3

Operate television, video, or motion picture camera to photograph images or scenes for various purposes, such as TV broadcasts, advertising, video production, or motion pictures. Adjust positions and controls of cameras, printers, and related equipment in order to change focus, exposure, and lighting. Compose and frame each shot, applying the technical aspects of light, lenses, film, filters, and camera settings in order to achieve the effects sought by directors. Confer with directors, sound and lighting technicians, electricians, and other crew members to discuss assignments and determine filming sequences, desired effects, camera movements, and lighting requirements. Observe sets or locations for potential problems and to determine filming and lighting requirements. Operate television or motion picture cameras to record scenes for television broadcasts, advertising, or motion pictures. Operate zoom lenses, changing images according to specifications and rehearsal instructions. Read and analyze work orders and specifications to determine locations of subject material, work procedures, sequences of operations, and machine setups. Read charts and compute ratios to determine variables such as lighting, shutter angles, filter factors, and camera distances. Reload camera magazines with fresh raw film stock. Select and assemble cameras, accessories, equipment, and film stock to be used during filming, using knowledge of filming techniques, requirements, and computations. Set up cameras, optical printers, and related equipment to produce photographs and special effects. Test, clean, and maintain equipment to ensure proper working condition. Use cameras in any of several different camera mounts, such as stationary, track-mounted, or crane-mounted. View films to resolve problems of exposure control, subject and camera movement, changes in subject distance, and related variables. Download exposed film for shipment to processing labs. Gather and edit raw footage on location to send to television affiliates for broadcast, using electronic news-gathering or film-production equipment. Instruct camera operators regarding camera setups, angles, distances, movement, and variables and cues for starting and stopping filming. Label and record contents of exposed film and note details on report forms. **SKILLS**—Technology Design; Operation and Control; Operation Monitoring; Instructing; Equipment Selection; Operations Analysis; Quality Control Analysis; Management of Material Resources.

GOE—Interest Area: 01. Arts, Entertainment, and Media. **Work Group:** 01.08 Media Technology. **Other Apprenticeable Jobs in This Work Group:** Audio and Video Equipment Technicians; Broadcast Technicians; Film and Video Editors; Professional Photographers; Radio Operators; Sound Engineering Technicians. **PERSONALITY TYPE:** Artistic. Artistic occupations frequently involve working with forms, designs, and patterns. They often require self-expression, and the work can be done without following a clear set of rules.

RELATED KNOWLEDGE/COURSES— Fine Arts: Knowledge of the theory and techniques required to compose, produce, and perform works of music, dance, visual arts, drama, and sculpture. **Communications and Media:** Knowledge of media production, communication, and dissemination techniques and methods. This includes alternative ways to inform and entertain via written, oral, and visual media. **Telecommunications:** Knowledge of transmission, broadcasting, switching, control,

C

and operation of telecommunications systems. **Physics:** Knowledge and prediction of physical principles and laws and their interrelationships and applications to understanding fluid, material, and atmospheric dynamics and mechanical, electrical, atomic, and subatomic structures and processes. **Design:** Knowledge of design techniques, tools, and principles involved in production of precision technical plans, blueprints, drawings, and models. **Mathematics:** Knowledge of arithmetic, algebra, geometry, calculus, and statistics and their applications.

WORK ENVIRONMENT—High places; outdoors; extremely bright or inadequate lighting; climbing ladders, scaffolds, or poles; very hot or cold; using hands on objects, tools, or controls.

Cargo and Freight Agents

- Growth: 15.5%
- Annual Job Openings: 8,000
- Annual Earnings: $31,990
- Percentage of Women: 26.9%

Related Apprenticeship	Years
Transportation Clerk	1.5

Expedite and route movement of incoming and outgoing cargo and freight shipments in airline, train, and trucking terminals and shipping docks. Take orders from customers and arrange pickup of freight and cargo for delivery to loading platform. Prepare and examine

bills of lading to determine shipping charges and tariffs. Negotiate and arrange transport of goods with shipping or freight companies. Notify consignees, passengers, or customers of the arrival of freight or baggage and arrange for delivery. Retrieve stored items and trace lost shipments as necessary. Route received goods to first available flight or to appropriate storage areas or departments, using forklifts, handtrucks, or other equipment. Assemble containers and crates used to transport items such as machines or vehicles. Attach address labels, identification codes, and shipping instructions to containers. Coordinate and supervise activities of workers engaged in packing and shipping merchandise. Advise clients on transportation and payment methods. Arrange insurance coverage for goods. Check import/export documentation to determine cargo contents and classify goods into different fee or tariff groups, using a tariff coding system. Contact vendors and/or claims adjustment departments in order to resolve problems with shipments or contact service depots to arrange for repairs. Determine method of shipment and prepare bills of lading, invoices, and other shipping documents. Direct delivery trucks to shipping doors or designated marshalling areas and help load and unload goods safely. Direct or participate in cargo loading in order to ensure completeness of load and even distribution of weight. Enter shipping information into a computer by hand or by using a hand-held scanner that reads bar codes on goods. Estimate freight or postal rates and record shipment costs and weights. Inspect and count items received and check them against invoices or other documents, recording shortages and rejecting damaged goods. Keep records of all goods shipped, received, and stored. Inspect trucks and vans to ensure cleanliness when shipping such items as grain, flour, and milk. Install straps, braces, and padding to loads in order to prevent shifting or damage during shipment. Maintain a supply of packing materials. Obtain flight numbers, airplane numbers, and names of crew members from dispatchers and record data on airplane flight papers. Open cargo containers and unwrap contents, using steel cutters, crowbars, or other hand tools. **SKILLS**—Service Orientation; Operation and Control; Coordination.

GOE—Interest Area: 09. Business Detail. **Work Group:** 09.08 Records and Materials Processing. **Other Apprenticeable Jobs in This Work Group:** Mail Clerks, Except Mail Machine Operators and Postal Service. **PERSONALITY TYPE:** Conventional. Conventional occupations frequently involve following set procedures and routines. These occupations can include working with data and details more than with ideas. Usually there is a clear line of authority to follow.

RELATED KNOWLEDGE/COURSES—Transportation: Knowledge of principles and methods for moving people or goods by air, rail, sea, or road, including the relative costs and benefits. **Clerical Practices:** Knowledge of administrative and clerical procedures and systems, such as word processing, managing files and records, stenography and transcription, designing forms, and other office procedures and terminology. **Geography:** Knowledge of principles and methods for describing the features of land, sea, and air masses, including their physical characteristics; locations; interrelationships; and distribution of plant, animal, and human life. **Telecommunications:** Knowledge of transmission, broadcasting, switching, control, and operation of telecommunications systems. **Customer and Personal Service:** Knowledge of principles and processes for pro-

viding customer and personal services. This includes customer needs assessment, meeting quality standards for services, and evaluation of customer satisfaction. **Public Safety and Security:** Knowledge of relevant equipment, policies, procedures, and strategies to promote effective local, state, or national security operations for the protection of people, data, property, and institutions.

WORK ENVIRONMENT—Sounds, noise levels are distracting or uncomfortable; walking and running; outdoors; standing; very hot or cold.

Carpenter Assemblers and Repairers

- ◎ Growth: 10.1%
- ◎ Annual Job Openings: 193,000
- ◎ Annual Earnings: $34,250
- ◎ Percentage of Women: 1.9%

Related Apprenticeship	Years
Casket Assembler	3

Perform a variety of tasks requiring a limited knowledge of carpentry, such as applying siding and weatherboard to building exteriors or assembling and erecting prefabricated buildings. Measures and marks location of studs, leaders, and receptacle openings, using tape measure, template, and marker. Cuts sidings and moldings, sections of weatherboard, openings in sheetrock, and lumber, using hand tools and power tools. Lays out and aligns materials on worktable or in assembly jig according to specified instructions. Removes surface defects, using knife, scraper, wet sponge, electric iron, and sanding tools. Trims overlapping edges of wood or weatherboard, using portable router or power saw and hand tools. Installs prefabricated windows and doors; insulation; wall, ceiling, and floor panels; or siding, using adhesives, hoists, hand tools, and power tools. Aligns and fastens materials together, using hand tools and power tools, to form building or bracing. Repairs or replaces defective locks, hinges, cranks, and pieces of wood, using glue, hand tools, and power tools. Applies stain, paint, or crayons to defects and filters to touch up the repaired area. Directs crane operator in positioning floor, wall, ceiling, and roof panel on house foundation. Moves panel or roof section to other work stations or to storage or shipping area, using electric hoist. Studies blueprints, specification sheets, and drawings to determine style and type of window or wall panel required. Fills cracks, seams, depressions, and nail holes with filler. Examines wood surfaces for defects, such as nicks, cracks, or blisters. Measures cut materials to determine conformance to specifications, using tape measure. Realigns windows and screens to fit casements and oils moving parts. **SKILLS**—Repairing; Installation; Equipment Maintenance; Management of Material Resources; Operation and Control.

GOE—Interest Area: 06. Construction, Mining, and Drilling. **Work Group:** 06.04 Hands-on Work in Construction, Extraction, and Maintenance. **Other Apprenticeable Jobs in This Work Group:** Construction Laborers; Helpers—Brickmasons, Blockmasons, Stonemasons, and Tile and Marble Setters; Helpers—Extraction Workers. **PERSONALITY TYPE:** Realistic. Realistic occupations frequently involve work activities that include practical, hands-on problems and solutions. They often deal with plants, animals, and real-world materials like wood, tools, and machinery. Many of the occupations require working outside and do not involve a lot of paperwork or working closely with others.

RELATED KNOWLEDGE/COURSES— Building and Construction: Knowledge of the materials, methods, and tools involved in the construction or repair of houses, buildings, or other structures, such as highways and roads. **Design:** Knowledge of design techniques, tools, and principles involved in production of precision technical plans, blueprints, drawings, and models. **Engineering and Technology:** Knowledge of the practical application of engineering science and technology. This includes applying principles, techniques, procedures, and equipment to the design and production of various goods and services. **Mechanical Devices:** Knowledge of machines and tools, including their designs, uses, repair, and maintenance.

WORK ENVIRONMENT—Hazardous equipment; high places; climbing ladders, scaffolds, or poles; spend time kneeling, crouching, stooping, or crawling; sounds, noise levels are distracting or uncomfortable; cramped work space, awkward positions.

Carpet Installers

- Growth: 16.8%
- Annual Job Openings: 10,000
- Annual Earnings: $32,900
- Percentage of Women: 2.5%

Related Apprenticeship	Years
Carpet Layer	3

Lay and install carpet from rolls or blocks on floors. Install padding and trim flooring materials. Join edges of carpet and seam edges where necessary, by sewing or by using tape with glue and heated carpet iron. Cut and trim carpet to fit along wall edges, openings, and projections, finishing the edges with a wall trimmer. Inspect the surface to be covered to determine its condition and correct any imperfections that might show through carpet or cause carpet to wear unevenly. Roll out, measure, mark, and cut carpeting to size with a carpet knife, following floor sketches and allowing extra carpet for final fitting. Plan the layout of the carpet, allowing for expected traffic patterns and placing seams for best appearance and longest wear. Stretch carpet to align with walls and ensure a smooth surface and press carpet in place over tack strips or use staples, tape, tacks, or glue to hold carpet in place. Take measurements and study floor sketches to calculate the area to be carpeted and the amount of material needed. Cut carpet padding to size and install padding, following prescribed method. Install carpet on some floors using adhesive, following prescribed method. Nail tack strips around area to be carpeted or use old strips to attach edges of new carpet. Fasten metal treads across door openings or where carpet meets flooring to hold carpet in place. Measure, cut, and install tackless strips along the baseboard or wall. Draw building diagrams and record dimensions. Move furniture from area to be carpeted and remove old carpet and padding. Cut and bind material. **SKILLS—**Installation; Equipment Selection; Repairing; Management of Personnel Resources; Coordination; Learning Strategies; Instructing; Complex Problem Solving.

GOE—Interest Area: 06. Construction, Mining, and Drilling. **Work Group:** 06.02 Construction. **Other Apprenticeable Jobs in This Work Group:** Boat Builders and Shipwrights; Boilermakers; Brickmasons and Blockmasons; Ceiling Tile Installers; Cement Masons and Concrete Finishers; Construction and Related Workers, All Other; Construction Carpenters; Drywall Installers; Electricians; Fence Erectors; Floor Layers, Except Carpet, Wood, and Hard Tiles; Glaziers; Grader, Bulldozer, and Scraper Operators; Insulation Workers, Floor, Ceiling, and Wall; Insulation Workers, Mechanical; Operating Engineers; Painters, Construction and Maintenance; Paperhangers; Paving, Surfacing, and Tamping Equipment Operators; Pipe Fitters; Plasterers and Stucco Masons; Plumbers; Reinforcing Iron and Rebar Workers; Riggers; Roofers; Rough Carpenters; Sheet Metal Workers; Ship Carpenters and Joiners; Stone Cutters and Carvers; Stonemasons; Structural Iron and Steel Workers; Tapers; Terrazzo Workers and Finishers; Tile and Marble Setters. **PERSONALITY TYPE:** Realistic. Realistic occupations frequently involve work activities that include practical, hands-on problems and solutions. They often deal with plants, animals, and real-world materials like wood, tools, and machinery. Many of the occupations require working outside and do not involve a lot of paperwork or working closely with others.

RELATED KNOWLEDGE/COURSES—Public Safety and Security: Knowledge of relevant equipment, policies, procedures, and strategies to promote effective local, state, or national security operations for the protection of people, data, property, and institutions. **Customer and Personal Service:** Knowledge of principles and processes for providing customer and personal services. This includes customer needs assessment, meeting quality standards for services, and evaluation of customer satisfaction. **Sales and Marketing:** Knowledge of principles and methods for showing, promoting, and selling products or services. This includes marketing strategy and tactics, product demonstration, sales techniques, and sales control systems. **Transportation:** Knowledge of principles and methods for moving people or goods by air, rail, sea, or road, including the relative costs and benefits. **Personnel and Human Resources:** Knowledge of principles and procedures for personnel recruitment, selection, training, compensation and benefits, labor relations and negotiation, and personnel information systems. **Building and Construction:** Knowledge of the materials, methods, and tools involved in the construction or repair of houses, buildings, or other structures, such as highways and roads.

WORK ENVIRONMENT—Very hot or cold; spend time kneeling, crouching, stooping, or crawling; keeping or regaining balance; minor burns, cuts, bites, or stings; extremely bright or inadequate lighting.

Cartoonists

- ⊚ Growth: 16.5%
- ⊚ Annual Job Openings: 4,000
- ⊚ Annual Earnings: $35,420
- ⊚ Percentage of Women: 47.1%

Related Apprenticeship	Years
Cartoonist, Motion Pictures	3

Create original artwork by using any of a wide variety of mediums and techniques, such as painting and sculpture. Sketches and submits cartoon or animation for approval. Develops personal ideas for cartoons, comic strips, or animations or reads written material to develop ideas. Makes changes and corrections to cartoon, comic strip, or animation as necessary. Creates and prepares sketches and model drawings of characters, providing details from memory, live models, manufactured products, or reference material. Renders sequential drawings of characters or other subject material that become animated when photographed and projected at specific speed. Develops color patterns and moods and paints background layouts to dramatize action for animated cartoon scenes. Discusses ideas for cartoons, comic strips, or animations with editor or publisher's representative. Labels each section with designated colors when colors are used. **SKILLS**—Operations Analysis; Active Listening.

GOE—Interest Area: 01. Arts, Entertainment, and Media. **Work Group:** 01.04 Visual Arts. **Other Apprenticeable Jobs in This Work Group:** Commercial and Industrial Designers; Exhibit Designers; Fashion Designers; Floral Designers; Graphic Designers; Interior Designers; Merchandise Displayers and Window Trimmers; Painters and Illustrators. **PERSONALITY TYPE:** Artistic. Artistic occupations frequently involve working with forms, designs, and patterns. They often require self-expression, and the work can be done without following a clear set of rules.

RELATED KNOWLEDGE/COURSES—Fine Arts: Knowledge of the theory and techniques required to compose, produce, and perform works of music, dance, visual arts, drama, and sculpture. **Communications and Media:** Knowledge of media production, communication, and dissemination techniques and methods. This includes alternative ways to inform and entertain via written, oral, and visual media. **Sales and Marketing:** Knowledge of principles and methods for showing, promoting, and selling products or services. This includes marketing strategy and tactics, product demonstration, sales techniques, and sales control systems. **Design:** Knowledge of design techniques, tools, and principles involved in production of precision technical plans, blueprints, drawings, and models. **Telecommunications:** Knowledge of transmission, broadcasting, switching, control, and operation of telecommunications systems.

WORK ENVIRONMENT—Sitting; indoors; spend time making repetitive motions.

Ceiling Tile Installers

- ◉ Growth: 21.4%
- ◉ Annual Job Openings: 17,000
- ◉ Annual Earnings: $33,670
- ◉ Percentage of Women: 2.7%

Related Apprenticeship	Years
Acoustical Carpenter	4

Apply or mount acoustical tiles or blocks, strips, or sheets of shock-absorbing materials to ceilings and walls of buildings to reduce or reflect sound. Materials may be of decorative quality. Includes lathers who fasten wooden, metal, or rockboard lath to walls, ceilings, or partitions of buildings to provide support base for plaster, fire-proofing, or acoustical material. Applies acoustical tiles or shock-absorbing materials to ceilings and walls of buildings to reduce or reflect sound and to decorate rooms. Washes concrete surfaces with washing soda and zinc sulfate solution before mounting tile to increase adhesive qualities of surfaces. Inspects furrings, mechanical mountings, and masonry surface for plumbness and level, using spirit or water level. Hangs dry lines (stretched string) to wall molding to guide positioning of main runners. Nails or screws molding to wall to support and seals joint between ceiling tile and wall. Scribes and cuts edges of tile to fit wall where wall molding is not specified. Nails channels or wood furring strips to surfaces to provide mounting for tile. Measures and marks surface to lay out work according to blueprints and drawings. Cuts tiles for fixture and borders, using keyhole saw, and inserts tiles into supporting framework. Applies cement to back of tile and presses tile into place, aligning with layout marks and joints of previously laid tile. **SKILLS**—None met the criteria.

GOE—**Interest Area:** 06. Construction, Mining, and Drilling. **Work Group:** 06.02 Construction. **Other Apprenticeable Jobs in This Work Group:** Boat Builders and Shipwrights; Boilermakers; Brickmasons and Blockmasons; Carpet Installers; Cement Masons and Concrete Finishers; Construction and Related Workers, All Other; Construction Carpenters; Drywall Installers; Electricians; Fence Erectors; Floor Layers, Except Carpet, Wood, and Hard Tiles; Glaziers; Grader, Bulldozer, and Scraper Operators; Insulation Workers, Floor, Ceiling, and Wall; Insulation Workers, Mechanical; Operating Engineers; Painters, Construction and Maintenance; Paperhangers; Paving, Surfacing, and Tamping Equipment Operators; Pipe Fitters; Plasterers and Stucco Masons; Plumbers; Reinforcing Iron and Rebar Workers; Riggers; Roofers; Rough Carpenters; Sheet Metal Workers; Ship Carpenters and Joiners; Stone Cutters and Carvers; Stonemasons; Structural Iron and Steel Workers; Tapers; Terrazzo Workers and Finishers; Tile and Marble Setters. **PERSONALITY TYPE:** Realistic. Realistic occupations frequently involve work activities that include practical, hands-on problems and solutions. They often deal with plants, animals, and real-world materials like wood, tools, and machinery. Many of the occupations require working outside and do not involve a lot of paperwork or working closely with others.

RELATED KNOWLEDGE/COURSES— **Building and Construction:** Knowledge of the materials, methods, and tools involved in the construction or repair of houses, buildings, or other structures, such as highways and roads. **Design:** Knowledge of design techniques, tools, and principles involved in production of precision technical plans, blueprints, drawings, and models. **Mathematics:** Knowledge of arithmetic, algebra, geometry, calculus, and statistics and their applications. **Physics:** Knowledge and prediction of physical principles and laws and their interrelationships and applications to understanding fluid, material, and atmospheric dynamics and mechanical, electrical, atomic, and subatomic structures and processes.

WORK ENVIRONMENT—Minor burns, cuts, bites, or stings; climbing ladders, scaffolds, or poles; hazardous equipment; common protective or safety equipment; high places.

Cement Masons and Concrete Finishers

- Growth: 26.1%
- Annual Job Openings: 24,000
- Annual Earnings: $30,780
- Percentage of Women: 1.4%

Related Apprenticeship	*Years*
Cement Mason	2

Smooth and finish surfaces of poured concrete, such as floors, walks, sidewalks, roads, or curbs, using a variety of hand and power tools. Align forms for sidewalks, curbs, or gutters; patch voids; use saws to cut expansion joints. Check the forms that hold the concrete to see that they are properly constructed. Chip, scrape, and grind high spots, ridges, and rough projections to finish concrete, using pneumatic chisels, power grinders, or hand tools. Clean chipped area, using wire brush, and feel and observe surface to determine if it is rough or uneven. Mix cement, sand, and water to produce concrete, grout, or slurry, using hoe, trowel, tamper, scraper, or concrete-mixing machine. Mold expansion joints and edges, using edging tools, jointers, and straightedge. Monitor how the wind, heat, or cold affect the curing of the concrete throughout the entire process. Set the forms that hold concrete to the desired pitch and depth and align them. Apply hardening and sealing compounds to cure surface of concrete and waterproof or restore surface. Apply muriatic acid to clean surface and rinse with water. Spread, level, and smooth concrete, using rake, shovel, hand or power trowel, hand or power screed, and float. Waterproof or restore concrete surfaces, using appropriate compounds. Wet concrete surface and rub with stone to smooth surface and obtain specified finish. Wet surface to prepare for bonding, fill holes and cracks with grout or slurry, and smooth, using trowel. Build wooden molds and clamp molds around area to be repaired, using hand tools. Cut out damaged areas, drill holes for reinforcing rods, and position reinforcing rods to repair concrete, using power saw and drill. Direct the casting of the concrete and supervise laborers who use shovels or special tools to spread it. Install anchor bolts, steel plates, door sills, and other fixtures in freshly poured concrete and/or pattern or stamp the surface to provide a decorative finish. Polish surface, using polishing or surfacing machine. Produce rough concrete surface, using broom. Push roller over surface to embed chips in surface. Signal truck driver to position truck to facilitate pouring concrete; move chute to direct concrete on forms. Sprinkle colored marble or stone chips, powdered steel, or coloring powder over surface to produce prescribed finish. **SKILLS**—Technology Design; Repairing; Operations Analysis; Installation; Science; Equipment Maintenance.

GOE—Interest Area: 06. Construction, Mining, and Drilling. **Work Group:** 06.02 Construction. **Other Apprenticeable Jobs in This Work Group:** Boat Builders and Shipwrights; Boilermakers; Brickmasons and Blockmasons; Carpet Installers; Ceiling Tile Installers; Construction and Related Workers, All Other; Construction Carpenters; Drywall Installers; Electricians; Fence Erectors; Floor Layers, Except Carpet, Wood, and Hard Tiles; Glaziers; Grader, Bulldozer, and Scraper Operators; Insu-

lation Workers, Floor, Ceiling, and Wall; Insulation Workers, Mechanical; Operating Engineers; Painters, Construction and Maintenance; Paperhangers; Paving, Surfacing, and Tamping Equipment Operators; Pipe Fitters; Plasterers and Stucco Masons; Plumbers; Reinforcing Iron and Rebar Workers; Riggers; Roofers; Rough Carpenters; Sheet Metal Workers; Ship Carpenters and Joiners; Stone Cutters and Carvers; Stonemasons; Structural Iron and Steel Workers; Tapers; Terrazzo Workers and Finishers; Tile and Marble Setters. **PERSONALITY TYPE:** Realistic. Realistic occupations frequently involve work activities that include practical, hands-on problems and solutions. They often deal with plants, animals, and real-world materials like wood, tools, and machinery. Many of the occupations require working outside and do not involve a lot of paperwork or working closely with others.

RELATED KNOWLEDGE/COURSES— Building and Construction: Knowledge of the materials, methods, and tools involved in the construction or repair of houses, buildings, or other structures, such as highways and roads. **Engineering and Technology:** Knowledge of the practical application of engineering science and technology. This includes applying principles, techniques, procedures, and equipment to the design and production of various goods and services. **Design:** Knowledge of design techniques, tools, and principles involved in production of precision technical plans, blueprints, drawings, and models. **Mechanical Devices:** Knowledge of machines and tools, including their designs, uses, repair, and maintenance. **Geography:** Knowledge of principles and methods for describing the features of land, sea, and air masses, including their physical characteristics; locations; interrelationships; and distribution of plant, animal, and human life. **Fine Arts:** Knowledge of the theory and techniques required to compose, produce, and perform works of music, dance, visual arts, drama, and sculpture.

WORK ENVIRONMENT—Outdoors; spend time kneeling, crouching, stooping, or crawling; spend time bending or twisting the body; very hot or cold; climbing ladders, scaffolds, or poles; keeping or regaining balance.

Central Office and PBX Installers and Repairers

- Growth: –0.6%
- Annual Job Openings: 23,000
- Annual Earnings: $48,230
- Percentage of Women: 13.0%

Related Apprenticeship	Years
Central-Office Installer	4
Central-Office Repairer	4
Private-Branch-Exchange Installer	4
Private-Branch-Exchange Repairer	4

Test, analyze, and repair telephone or telegraph circuits and equipment at a central office location, using test meters and hand tools. Analyze and repair defects in communications equipment on customers' premises, using circuit diagrams, polarity probes, meters, and a telephone test set. May install equipment. Tests circuits and components of malfunctioning telecommunication equipment to isolate source of malfunction, using test instruments and circuit diagrams. Analyzes test readings, computer printouts, and trouble reports to determine method of repair. Tests and adjusts installed equipment to ensure circuit continuity and operational performance, using test instruments. Connects wires to equipment, using hand tools, soldering iron, or wire wrap gun. Installs preassembled or partially assembled switching equipment, switchboards, wiring frames, and power apparatus according to floor plans. Retests repaired equipment to ensure that malfunction has been corrected. Repairs or replaces defective components, such as switches, relays, amplifiers, and circuit boards, using hand tools and soldering iron. Removes and remakes connections on wire distributing frame to change circuit layout, following diagrams. Routes cables and trunklines from entry points to specified equipment, following diagrams. Enters codes to correct programming of electronic switching systems. SKILLS—Installation; Repairing; Troubleshooting; Technology Design; Operation Monitoring; Equipment Maintenance; Science; Quality Control Analysis.

GOE—**Interest Area:** 05. Mechanics, Installers, and Repairers. **Work Group:** 05.02 Electrical and Electronic Systems. **Other Apprenticeable Jobs in This Work Group:** Avionics Technicians; Battery Repairers; Communication Equipment Mechanics, Installers, and Repairers; Data Processing Equipment Repairers; Electric Home Appliance and Power Tool Repairers; Electric Meter Installers and Repairers; Electric Motor and Switch Assemblers and

Repairers; Electrical and Electronics Installers and Repairers, Transportation Equipment; Electrical and Electronics Repairers, Commercial and Industrial Equipment; Electrical and Electronics Repairers, Powerhouse, Substation, and Relay; Electrical Power-Line Installers and Repairers; Electronic Equipment Installers and Repairers, Motor Vehicles; Electronic Home Entertainment Equipment Installers and Repairers; Elevator Installers and Repairers; Installation, Maintenance, and Repair Workers, All Other; Office Machine and Cash Register Servicers; Radio Mechanics; Signal and Track Switch Repairers; Station Installers and Repairers, Telephone; Telecommunications Line Installers and Repairers; Transformer Repairers. **PERSONALITY TYPE:** Realistic. Realistic occupations frequently involve work activities that include practical, hands-on problems and solutions. They often deal with plants, animals, and real-world materials like wood, tools, and machinery. Many of the occupations require working outside and do not involve a lot of paperwork or working closely with others.

RELATED KNOWLEDGE/COURSES— Telecommunications: Knowledge of transmission, broadcasting, switching, control, and operation of telecommunications systems. **Computers and Electronics:** Knowledge of circuit boards, processors, chips, electronic equipment, and computer hardware and software, including applications and programming. **Design:** Knowledge of design techniques, tools, and principles involved in production of precision technical plans, blueprints, drawings, and models. **Engineering and Technology:** Knowledge of the practical application of engineering science and technology. This includes applying principles, techniques, procedures, and equipment to the design and production of various

goods and services. **Physics:** Knowledge and prediction of physical principles and laws and their interrelationships and applications to understanding fluid, material, and atmospheric dynamics and mechanical, electrical, atomic, and subatomic structures and processes.

WORK ENVIRONMENT—Sitting; spend time kneeling, crouching, stooping, or crawling; hazardous conditions; hazardous equipment; climbing ladders, scaffolds, or poles.

Chefs and Head Cooks

- Growth: 15.8%
- Annual Job Openings: 33,000
- Annual Earnings: $28,750
- Percentage of Women: 19.2%

Related Apprenticeship	*Years*
Chief Cook (Water Transportation)	2

Direct the preparation, seasoning, and cooking of salads, soups, fish, meats, vegetables, desserts, or other foods. May plan and price menu items, order supplies, and keep records and accounts. May participate in cooking. Prepare and cook foods of all types, either on a regular basis or for special guests or functions. Supervise and coordinate activities of cooks and workers engaged in food preparation. Collaborate with other personnel to plan and develop recipes and menus, taking into account such factors as seasonal availability of ingredients and the likely number of customers. Check the quality of raw and cooked food products to ensure that standards are met. Check the quantity and quality of received products. Demonstrate new cooking techniques and equipment to staff. Determine how food should be presented and create decorative food displays. Determine production schedules and staff requirements necessary to ensure timely delivery of services. Estimate amounts and costs of required supplies, such as food and ingredients. Inspect supplies, equipment, and work areas to ensure conformance to established standards. Instruct cooks and other workers in the preparation, cooking, garnishing, and presentation of food. Monitor sanitation practices to ensure that employees follow standards and regulations. Order or requisition food and other supplies needed to ensure efficient operation. Recruit and hire staff, including cooks and other kitchen workers. Analyze recipes to assign prices to menu items, based on food, labor, and overhead costs. Arrange for equipment purchases and repairs. Meet with customers to discuss menus for special occasions such as weddings, parties, and banquets. Meet with sales representatives in order to negotiate prices and order supplies. Record production and operational data on specified forms. Coordinate planning, budgeting, and purchasing for all the food operations within establishments such as clubs, hotels, or restaurant chains. Plan, direct, and supervise the food preparation and cooking activities of multiple kitchens or restaurants in an establishment such as a restaurant chain, hospital, or hotel. **SKILLS**—Management of Financial Resources; Management of Material Resources; Management of Personnel Resources; Coordination; Instructing; Time Management; Systems Evaluation; Learning Strategies; Negotiation.

GOE—Interest Area: 11. Recreation, Travel, and Other Personal Services. **Work Group:** 11.05 Food and Beverage Services. **Other Apprenticeable Jobs in This Work Group:** Bakers, Bread and Pastry; Bartenders; Butchers and Meat Cutters; Cooks, Fast Food; Cooks, Institution and Cafeteria; Cooks, Restaurant. **PERSONALITY TYPE:** Enterprising. Enterprising occupations frequently involve starting up and carrying out projects. These occupations can involve leading people and making many decisions. They sometimes require risk taking and often deal with business.

RELATED KNOWLEDGE/COURSES— Administration and Management: Knowledge of business and management principles involved in strategic planning, resource allocation, human resources modeling, leadership technique, production methods, and coordination of people and resources. **Personnel and Human Resources:** Knowledge of principles and procedures for personnel recruitment, selection, training, compensation and benefits, labor relations and negotiation, and personnel information systems. **Education and Training:** Knowledge of principles and methods for curriculum and training design, teaching and instruction for individuals and groups, and the measurement of training effects. **Economics and Accounting:** Knowledge of economic and accounting principles and practices, the financial markets, banking, and the analysis and reporting of financial data. **Biology:** Knowledge of plant and animal organisms and their tissues, cells, functions, interdependencies, and interactions with each other and the environment. **Production and Processing:** Knowledge of raw materials, production processes, quality control, costs, and other techniques for maximizing the effective manufacture and distribution of goods. **Food Production:** Knowledge of techniques and equipment for planting, growing, and harvesting food products (both plant and animal) for consumption, including storage/handling techniques.

WORK ENVIRONMENT—Minor burns, cuts, bites, or stings; hazardous equipment; standing; using hands on objects, tools, or controls; very hot or cold.

Chemical Equipment Controllers and Operators

- ◉ Growth: –3.8%
- ◉ Annual Job Openings: 8,000
- ◉ Annual Earnings: $38,740
- ◉ Percentage of Women: 14.1%

Related Apprenticeship	Years
Chemical Operator III	3

Control or operate equipment to control chemical changes or reactions in the processing of industrial or consumer products. Typical equipment used are reaction kettles, catalytic converters, continuous or batch treating equipment, saturator tanks, electrolytic cells, reactor vessels, recovery units, and fermentation chambers. Sets and adjusts indicating, controlling, or timing devices, such as gauging instruments, thermostat, gas analyzers, or recording calorimeter. Moves controls to adjust feed and flow of liquids and gases through equipment in specified sequence. Adjusts controls to regulate temperature, pressure, and time of prescribed reaction according to knowledge of equipment and process. Opens valves or operates pumps to admit or drain specified amounts of materials, impurities, or treating agents to or from equipment. Starts pumps, agitators, reactors, blowers, or automatic feed of materials. Monitors gauges, recording instruments, flowmeters, or product to regulate or maintain specified conditions. Mixes chemicals according to proportion tables or prescribed formulas. Records operational data, such as temperature, pressure, ingredients used, processing time, or test results, in operating log. Flushes or cleans equipment, using steamhose or mechanical reamer. Draws samples of product and sends to laboratory for analysis. Tests sample for specific gravity, chemical characteristics, pH level, concentration, or viscosity. Patrols and inspects equipment or unit to detect leaks and malfunctions. Weighs or measures specified amounts of materials. Reads plant specifications to ascertain product, ingredient, and prescribed modifications of plant procedures. Dumps or scoops prescribed solid, granular, or powdered materials into equipment. Adds treating or neutralizing agent to product and pumps product through filter or centrifuge to remove impurities or precipitate product. Directs activities of workers assisting in control or verification of process or in unloading materials. Makes minor repairs and lubricates and maintains equipment, using hand tools. Operates or tends auxiliary equipment, such as heaters, scrubbers, filters, or driers, to prepare or further process materials. SKILLS—Operation Monitoring; Science; Operation and Control; Quality Control Analysis; Management of Personnel Resources; Equipment Maintenance; Repairing; Mathematics; Time Management.

GOE—Interest Area: 08. Industrial Production. **Work Group:** 08.03 Production Work. **Other Apprenticeable Jobs in This Work Group:** Bakers, Manufacturing; Bindery Machine Operators and Tenders; Coating, Painting, and Spraying Machine Operators and Tenders; Cooling and Freezing Equipment Operators and Tenders; Crushing, Grinding, and Polishing Machine Setters, Operators, and Tenders; Cutters and Trimmers, Hand; Cutting and Slicing Machine Operators and Tenders; Design Printing Machine Setters and Set-Up Operators; Electrolytic Plating and Coating Machine Setters and Set-Up Operators, Metal and Plastic; Electrotypers and Stereotypers; Embossing Machine Set-Up Operators; Engraver Set-Up Operators; Extruding, Forming, Pressing, and Compacting Machine Operators and Tenders; Fabric and Apparel Patternmakers; Film Laboratory Technicians; Fitters, Structural Metal—Precision; Food Batchmakers; Furnace, Kiln, Oven, Drier, and Kettle Operators and Tenders; Hand Compositors and Typesetters; Job Printers; Letterpress Setters and Set-Up Operators; Metal Fabricators, Structural Metal Products; Metal-Refining Furnace Operators and Tenders; Mixing and Blending Machine Setters, Operators, and Tenders; Mold Makers, Hand; Molding and Casting Workers; Numerical Control Machine Tool Operators and Tenders, Metal and Plastic; Offset Lithographic Press Setters and Set-Up Operators; Painting, Coating, and Decorating Workers; Photographic Processing Machine Operators; Photographic Reproduction Technicians; Photographic Retouchers and Restorers; Plate Finishers; Platemakers; Precision Printing Workers; Printing Press Machine Operators and Tenders; Production Workers, All Other; Sawing Machine Operators and Tenders; Sawing Machine Setters and Set-Up Operators; Scanner Operators; Separating, Filtering, Clarifying, Precipitating, and Still Machine Setters, Operators, and Tenders; Sewing Machine Operators, Garment; Slaughterers and Meat Packers; Stone Sawyers; Strippers; Team Assemblers; Welder-Fitters; Welders and Cutters; Woodworking Machine Operators and Tenders, Except Sawing. **PERSONALITY TYPE:** Realistic. Realistic occupations frequently involve work activities that include practical, hands-on problems and solutions. They often deal with plants, animals, and real-world materials like wood, tools, and machinery. Many of the occupations require working outside and do not involve a lot of paperwork or working closely with others.

RELATED KNOWLEDGE/COURSES— Chemistry: Knowledge of the chemical composition, structure, and properties of substances and of the chemical processes and transformations that they undergo. This includes uses of chemicals, their danger signs, production techniques, and disposal methods. **Mechanical Devices:** Knowledge of machines and tools, including their designs, uses, repair, and maintenance. **Public Safety and Security:** Knowledge of relevant equipment, policies, procedures, and strategies to promote effective local, state, or national security operations for the protection of people, data, property, and institutions. **Telecommunications:** Knowledge of transmission, broadcasting, switching, control, and operation of telecommunications systems. **Engineering and Technology:** Knowledge of the practical application of engineering science and technology. This includes applying principles, techniques, procedures, and equipment to the design and production of various goods and services. **Production and Processing:** Knowledge of raw materials, production processes, quality control, costs, and other techniques for maximizing the effective manufacture and distribution of goods.

WORK ENVIRONMENT—Hazardous conditions; common protective or safety equipment; minor burns, cuts, bites, or stings; indoors; hazardous equipment.

Chemical Plant and System Operators

- Growth: –12.3%
- Annual Job Openings: 4,000
- Annual Earnings: $44,050
- Percentage of Women: 7.4%

Related Apprenticeship	Years
Chief Operator	3
Plant Operator, Furnace Process	4

Control or operate an entire chemical process or system of machines. Calculate material requirements or yields according to formulas. Control or operate chemical processes or systems of machines, using panelboards, control boards, or semi-automatic equipment. Draw samples of products and conduct quality control tests in order to monitor processing and to ensure that standards are met. Gauge tank levels, using calibrated rods. Interpret chemical reactions visible through sight glasses or on television monitors and review laboratory test reports for process adjustments. Monitor recording instruments, flowmeters, panel lights, and other indicators and listen for warning signals in order to verify conformity of process conditions. Move control settings to make necessary adjustments on equipment units affecting speeds of chemical reactions, quality, and yields. Notify maintenance, stationary-engineering, and other auxiliary personnel to correct equipment malfunctions and to adjust power, steam, water, or air supplies. Patrol work areas to ensure that solutions in tanks and troughs are not in danger of overflowing. Record operating data such as process conditions, test results, and instrument readings. Regulate or shut down equipment during emergency situations as directed by supervisory personnel. Start pumps to wash and rinse reactor vessels; to exhaust gases and vapors; to regulate the flow of oil, steam, air, and perfume to towers; and to add products to converter or blending vessels. Turn valves to regulate flow of products or byproducts through agitator tanks, storage drums, or neutralizer tanks. Confer with technical and supervisory personnel to report or resolve conditions affecting safety, efficiency, and product quality. Defrost frozen valves, using steam hoses. Direct workers engaged in operating machinery that regulates the flow of materials and products. Inspect operating units such as towers, soap-spray storage tanks, scrubbers, collectors, and driers to ensure that all are functioning and to maintain maximum efficiency. Repair and replace damaged equipment. Supervise the cleaning of towers, strainers, and spray tips. **SKILLS**—Operation Monitoring; Operation and Control; Science; Troubleshooting; Quality Control Analysis; Mathematics; Systems Analysis; Equipment Maintenance.

GOE—Interest Area: 08. Industrial Production. **Work Group:** 08.06 Systems Operation. **Other Apprenticeable Jobs in This Work Group:** Boiler Operators and Tenders, Low Pressure; Gaugers; Petroleum Refinery and Control Panel Operators; Power Distributors and Dispatchers; Power Generating Plant Operators, Except Auxiliary Equipment Operators; Stationary Engineers; Water and Liquid Waste Treatment Plant and System Operators. **PERSONALITY TYPE:** Realistic. Realistic occupations frequently involve work activities that include practical, hands-on problems and solutions. They often deal with plants, animals, and real-world materials like wood, tools, and machinery. Many of the occupations require working outside and do not involve a lot of paperwork or working closely with others.

RELATED KNOWLEDGE/COURSES—**Production and Processing:** Knowledge of raw materials, production processes, quality control, costs, and other techniques for maximizing the effective manufacture and distribution of goods. **Chemistry:** Knowledge of the chemical composition, structure, and properties of substances and of the chemical processes and transformations that they undergo. This includes uses of chemicals, their danger signs, production techniques, and disposal methods. **Public Safety and Security:** Knowledge of relevant equipment, policies, procedures, and strategies to promote effective local, state, or national security operations for the protection of people, data, property, and institutions. **Mechanical Devices:** Knowledge of machines and tools, including their designs, uses, repair, and maintenance. **Engineering and Technology:** Knowledge of the practical application of engineering science and technology. This includes applying principles, techniques, procedures, and equipment to the design and production of various goods and services. **Mathematics:** Knowledge of arithmetic, algebra, geometry, calculus, and statistics and their applications.

WORK ENVIRONMENT—Hazardous conditions; common protective or safety equipment; standing; sitting; walking and running.

Child Care Workers

- Growth: 11.7%
- Annual Job Openings: 406,000
- Annual Earnings: $16,430
- Percentage of Women: 94.7%

Related Apprenticeship	*Years*
Child Care Development Specialist	2

(This is one of the most popular apprenticeable jobs.)

Attend to children at schools, businesses, private households, and child care institutions. Perform a variety of tasks, such as dressing, feeding, bathing, and overseeing play. Support children's emotional and social development, encouraging understanding of others and positive self-concepts. Care for children in institutional setting, such as group homes, nursery schools, private businesses, or schools for the handicapped. Sanitize toys and play equipment. Discipline children and recommend or initiate other measures to control behavior, such as caring for own clothing and picking up toys and books. Identify signs of emotional or developmental problems in children and bring them to parents' or guardians' attention. Observe and monitor children's play activities. Keep records on individual children, including daily observations and information about activities, meals served, and medications administered. Instruct children in health and personal habits such as eating, resting, and toilet habits. Read to children and teach them simple painting, drawing, handicrafts, and songs. Organize and participate in recreational activities, such as games. Assist in preparing food for children, serve meals and refreshments to children, and regulate rest periods. Organize and store toys and materials to ensure order in activity areas. Operate in-house daycare centers within businesses. Sterilize bottles and prepare formulas. Provide counseling or therapy to mentally disturbed, delinquent, or handicapped children. Dress children and change diapers. Help children with homework and school work. Perform housekeeping duties such as laundry, cleaning, dishwashing, and changing of linens. Accompany children to and from school, on outings, and to medical appointments. **SKILLS**—Learning Strategies; Social Perceptiveness; Negotiation; Service Orientation; Persuasion; Time Management; Critical Thinking; Monitoring; Instructing.

GOE—**Interest Area:** 12. Education and Social Service. **Work Group:** 12.03 Educational Services. **Other Apprenticeable Jobs in This Work Group:** Educational, Vocational, and School Counselors; Teacher Assistants. **PERSONALITY TYPE:** Social. Social occupations frequently involve working with, communicating with, and teaching people. These occupations often involve helping or providing service to others.

RELATED KNOWLEDGE/COURSES—**Customer and Personal Service:** Knowledge of principles and processes for providing customer and personal services. This includes customer needs assessment, meeting quality standards for services, and evaluation of customer satisfaction. **Psychology:** Knowledge of human behavior and performance; individual differences in ability, personality, and interests; learning and motivation; psychological research methods; and the assessment and treatment of behavioral

and affective disorders. **Sociology and Anthropology:** Knowledge of group behavior and dynamics, societal trends and influences, human migrations, ethnicity, and cultures and their history and origins. **Public Safety and Security:** Knowledge of relevant equipment, policies, procedures, and strategies to promote effective local, state, or national security operations for the protection of people, data, property, and institutions. **Philosophy and Theology:** Knowledge of different philosophical systems and religions. This includes their basic principles, values, ethics, ways of thinking, customs, and practices and their impact on human culture. **Education and Training:** Knowledge of principles and methods for curriculum and training design, teaching and instruction for individuals and groups, and the measurement of training effects.

WORK ENVIRONMENT—Physical proximity; sounds, noise levels are distracting or uncomfortable; minor burns, cuts, bites, or stings; spend time kneeling, crouching, stooping, or crawling; sitting.

Civil Drafters

- Growth: 4.2%
- Annual Job Openings: 14,000
- Annual Earnings: $37,690
- Percentage of Women: 19.9%

Related Apprenticeship	Years
Drafter, Civil	4

Prepare drawings and topographical and relief maps used in civil engineering projects, such as highways, bridges, pipelines, flood control projects, and water and sewerage control systems. Produce drawings using computer-assisted drafting systems (CAD) or drafting machines or by hand, using compasses, dividers, protractors, triangles, and other drafting devices. Draft plans and detailed drawings for structures, installations, and construction projects such as highways, sewage disposal systems, and dikes, working from sketches or notes. Draw maps, diagrams, and profiles, using cross-sections and surveys, to represent elevations, topographical contours, subsurface formations, and structures. Correlate, interpret, and modify data obtained from topographical surveys, well logs, and geophysical prospecting reports. Finish and duplicate drawings and documentation packages according to required mediums and specifications for reproduction, using blueprinting, photography, or other duplicating methods. Review rough sketches, drawings, specifications, and other engineering data received from civil engineers to ensure that they conform to design concepts. Supervise and train other technologists, technicians, and drafters. Supervise or conduct field surveys, inspections, or technical investigations to obtain data required to revise construction drawings. Determine the order of work and method of presentation, such as orthographic or isometric drawing. Calculate excavation tonnage and prepare graphs and fill-hauling diagrams for use in earth-moving operations. Explain drawings to production or construction teams and provide adjustments as necessary. Locate and identify symbols located on topographical surveys to denote geological and geophysical formations or oil field installations. **SKILLS**—Mathematics; Instructing; Coordination; Operations Analysis; Time Management; Active Learning; Technology Design; Active Listening.

GOE—Interest Area: 02. Science, Math, and Engineering. **Work Group:** 02.08 Engineering Technology. **Other Apprenticeable Jobs in This Work Group:** Aerospace Engineering and Operations Technicians; Architectural Drafters; Calibration and Instrumentation Technicians; Cartographers and Photogrammetrists; Construction and Building Inspectors; Electrical Drafters; Electrical Engineering Technicians; Electro-Mechanical Technicians; Electronic Drafters; Electronics Engineering Technicians; Engineering Technicians, Except Drafters, All Other; Industrial Engineering Technicians; Mapping Technicians; Mechanical Drafters; Mechanical Engineering Technicians; Numerical Tool and Process Control Programmers; Surveying Technicians. **PERSONALITY TYPE:** Realistic. Realistic occupations frequently involve work activities that include practical, hands-on problems and solutions. They often deal with plants, animals, and real-world materials like wood, tools, and machinery. Many of the occupations require working outside and do not involve a lot of paperwork or working closely with others.

RELATED KNOWLEDGE/COURSES— Design: Knowledge of design techniques, tools, and principles involved in production of precision technical plans, blueprints, drawings, and models. **Engineering and Technology:** Knowledge of the practical application of engineering science and technology. This includes applying principles, techniques, procedures, and equipment to the design and production of various goods and services. **Computers and Electronics:** Knowledge of circuit boards, processors, chips, electronic equipment, and computer hardware and software, including applications and programming. **Geography:** Knowledge of principles and methods for describing the features of land, sea, and air masses, including their physical characteristics; locations; interrelationships; and distribution of plant, animal, and human life. **Mathematics:** Knowledge of arithmetic, algebra, geometry, calculus, and statistics and their applications. **Public Safety and Security:** Knowledge of relevant equipment, policies, procedures, and strategies to promote effective local, state, or national security operations for the protection of people, data, property, and institutions. **Law and Government:** Knowledge of laws, legal codes, court procedures, precedents, government regulations, executive orders, agency rules, and the democratic political process.

WORK ENVIRONMENT—Sitting; physical proximity; sounds, noise levels are distracting or uncomfortable; indoors; extremely bright or inadequate lighting.

Coating, Painting, and Spraying Machine Operators and Tenders

- ☺ Growth: 9.4%
- ☺ Annual Job Openings: 17,000
- ☺ Annual Earnings: $25,720
- ☺ Percentage of Women: 16.8%

Related Apprenticeship	Years
Coating-Machine Operator I	1

Coating Machine Operators and Tenders: Operate or tend machines to coat any of a wide variety of items: Coat food products with sugar, chocolate, or butter; coat paper and paper products with chemical solutions, wax, or glazes; or coat fabric with rubber or plastic. Painting and Spraying Machine Operators and Tenders: Operate or tend machines to spray or paint decorative, protective, or other coating or finish, such as adhesive, lacquer, paint, stain, latex, preservative, oil, or other solutions. May apply coating or finish to any of a wide variety of items or materials, such as wood and wood products, ceramics, and glass. Includes workers who apply coating or finish to materials preparatory to further processing or to consumer use. Observes machine operation and gauges to detect defects or deviations from standards. Fills hopper, reservoir, trough, or pan with material used to coat, paint, or spray, using conveyor or pail. Measures and mixes specified quantities of substances to create coatings, paints, or sprays. Threads or feeds item or product through or around machine rollers and dryers. Examines, measures, weighs, or tests sample product to ensure conformance to specifications. Cleans machine, equipment, and work area, using water, solvents, and other cleaning aids. Records production data. Transfers completed item or product from machine to drying or storage area, using handcart, handtruck, or crane. Places item or product on feedrack, spindle, or reel strand to coat, paint, or spray, using hands, hoist, or trucklift. Aligns or fastens machine parts such as rollers, guides, brushes, and blades to secure roll, using hand tools. Attaches specified hose or nozzle to machine, using wrench and pliers. Starts and stops operation of machine, using lever or button. Turns dial, handwheel, valve, or switch to control and adjust temperature, speed, and flow of product or machine. **SKILLS**—Operation Monitoring; Operation and Control; Technology Design; Equipment Maintenance.

GOE—Interest Area: 08. Industrial Production. **Work Group:** 08.03 Production Work. **Other Apprenticeable Jobs in This Work Group:** Bakers, Manufacturing; Bindery Machine Operators and Tenders; Chemical Equipment Controllers and Operators; Cooling and Freezing Equipment Operators and Tenders; Crushing, Grinding, and Polishing Machine Setters, Operators, and Tenders; Cutters and Trimmers, Hand; Cutting and Slicing Machine Operators and Tenders; Design Printing Machine Setters and Set-Up Operators; Electrolytic Plating and Coating Machine Setters and Set-Up Operators, Metal and Plastic; Electrotypers and Stereotypers; Embossing Machine Set-Up Operators; Engraver Set-Up Operators; Extruding, Forming, Pressing, and Compacting Machine Operators and Tenders; Fabric and Apparel Patternmakers; Film Laboratory Technicians; Fitters, Structural Metal—Precision; Food Batchmakers; Furnace, Kiln, Oven, Drier, and Kettle Operators and Tenders; Hand Compositors and Typesetters; Job Printers; Letterpress Setters and Set-Up Operators; Metal Fabricators, Structural Metal Products; Metal-Refining Furnace Operators and Tenders; Mixing and Blending Machine Setters, Operators, and Tenders; Mold Makers, Hand; Molding and Casting Workers; Numerical Control Machine Tool Operators and Tenders, Metal and Plastic; Offset Lithographic Press Setters and Set-Up Operators; Painting, Coating, and Decorating Workers; Photographic Processing Machine Operators; Photographic Reproduction Technicians; Photographic Retouchers and Restorers; Plate Finishers; Platemakers; Precision Printing Workers; Printing Press Machine Operators and Tenders; Production Workers, All Other; Sawing Machine Operators and Tenders; Sawing Machine Setters and Set-Up Operators; Scanner Operators; Separating, Filtering, Clarifying, Precipitating, and Still Machine Setters, Operators, and Tenders; Sewing Machine Operators, Garment; Slaughterers and Meat Packers; Stone Sawyers; Strippers; Team Assemblers; Welder-Fitters; Welders and Cutters; Woodworking Machine Operators and Tenders, Except Sawing. **PERSONALITY TYPE:** Realistic. Realistic occupations frequently involve work activities that include practical, hands-on problems and solutions. They often deal with plants, animals, and real-world materials like wood, tools, and machinery. Many of the occupations require working outside and do not involve a lot of paperwork or working closely with others.

RELATED KNOWLEDGE/COURSES—**Chemistry:** Knowledge of the chemical composition, structure, and properties of substances and of the chemical processes and transformations that they undergo. This includes uses of chemicals, their danger signs, production techniques, and disposal methods. **Production and Processing:** Knowledge of raw materials, production processes, quality control, costs, and other techniques for maximizing the effective manufacture and distribution of goods. **Physics:** Knowledge and prediction of physical principles and laws and their interrelationships and applications to understanding fluid, material, and atmospheric dynamics and mechanical, electrical, atomic, and subatomic structures and processes. **Engineering and Technology:** Knowledge of the practical application of engineering science and technology. This includes applying principles, techniques, procedures, and equipment to the design and production of various goods and services.

Mechanical Devices: Knowledge of machines and tools, including their designs, uses, repair, and maintenance. **Food Production:** Knowledge of techniques and equipment for planting, growing, and harvesting food products (both plant and animal) for consumption, including storage/handling techniques.

WORK ENVIRONMENT—Hazardous conditions; contaminants; common protective or safety equipment; hazardous equipment; standing; spend time making repetitive motions.

Coating, Painting, and Spraying Machine Setters and Set-Up Operators

- Growth: 9.4%
- Annual Job Openings: 17,000
- Annual Earnings: $25,720
- Percentage of Women: 16.8%

Related Apprenticeship	Years
Production Finisher	2
Electrostatic Powder Coating Technician	4

Set up or set up and operate machines to coat or paint any of a wide variety of products, such as food products; glassware; and cloth, ceramic, metal, plastic, paper, and wood products, with lacquer, silver and copper solution, rubber, paint, varnish, glaze, enamel, oil, or rustproofing materials. Sets up and operates machines to paint or coat products with such materials as silver and copper solution, rubber, paint, glaze, oil, or rust-proofing materials. Removes materials, parts, or workpieces from painting or coating machines, using hand tools. Records operational data on specified forms. Cleans and maintains coating and painting machines, using hand tools. Measures thickness and quality of coating, using micrometer. Examines and tests solutions, paints, products, and workpieces to ensure specifications are met. Observes and adjusts loaded workpiece or machine according to specifications. Selects and loads materials, parts, and workpieces on machine, using hand tools. Starts pumps to mix solutions and to activate coating or painting machines. Operates auxiliary machines or equipment used on the coating or painting process. Weighs or measures chemicals, coatings, or paints and adds to machine. Turns valves and adjusts controls to regulate speed of conveyor, temperature, air pressure and circulation, and flow or spray of coating or paint. SKILLS—Operation Monitoring; Operation and Control; Equipment Maintenance; Installation; Equipment Selection; Quality Control Analysis.

GOE—Interest Area: 08. Industrial Production. Work Group: 08.02 Production Technology. Other Apprenticeable Jobs in This Work Group: Aircraft Structure Assemblers, Precision; Aircraft Systems Assemblers, Precision; Bench Workers, Jewelry; Bindery Machine Setters and Set-Up Operators; Bookbinders; Buffing and Polishing Set-Up Operators; Combination Machine Tool Setters and Set-Up Operators, Metal and Plastic; Dental Laboratory Technicians; Electrical and Electronic Equipment Assemblers; Electrical and Electronic Inspectors and Testers; Electromechanical Equipment Assemblers; Engine and Other Machine Assemblers; Extruding and Drawing Machine Setters, Operators, and Tenders, Metal and Plastic; Extruding, Forming, Pressing, and Compacting Machine Setters and Set-Up Operators; Forging Machine Setters, Operators, and Tenders, Metal and Plastic; Foundry Mold and Coremakers; Gem and Diamond Workers; Grinding, Honing, Lapping, and Deburring Machine Set-Up Operators; Heat Treating, Annealing, and Tempering Machine Operators and Tenders, Metal and Plastic; Jewelers; Lathe and Turning Machine Tool Setters, Operators, and Tenders, Metal and Plastic; Materials Inspectors; Mechanical Inspectors; Metal Molding, Coremaking, and Casting Machine Operators and Tenders; Milling and Planing Machine Setters, Operators, and Tenders, Metal and Plastic; Model and Mold Makers, Jewelry; Motor Vehicle Inspectors; Paper Goods Machine Setters, Operators, and Tenders; Pewter Casters and Finishers; Plastic Molding and Casting Machine Setters and Set-Up Operators; Precision Devices Inspectors and Testers; Precision Lens Grinders and Polishers; Precision Mold and Pattern Casters, except Nonferrous Metals; Precision Pattern and Die Casters, Nonferrous Metals; Press and Press Brake Machine Setters and Set-Up Operators, Metal and Plastic; Production Inspectors, Testers, Graders, Sorters, Samplers, Weighers; Production Workers, All Other; Rolling Machine Setters, Operators, and Tenders, Metal and Plastic; Silversmiths; Textile Knitting and Weaving Machine Setters, Operators, and Tenders; Textile Winding, Twisting, and Drawing Out Machine Setters, Operators, and Tenders; Welding Machine Setters and Set-Up Operators; Woodworking Machine Setters and Set-Up Operators, Except Sawing. **PERSONALITY TYPE:** Realistic. Realistic occupations frequently involve work activities that include practical, hands-on problems and solutions. They often deal with plants, animals, and real-world materials like wood, tools, and machinery. Many of the occupations require working outside and do not involve a lot of paperwork or working closely with others.

RELATED KNOWLEDGE/COURSES—Production and Processing: Knowledge of raw materials, production processes, quality control, costs, and other techniques for maximizing the effective manufacture and distribution of goods. **Chemistry:** Knowledge of the chemical composition, structure, and properties of substances and of the chemical processes and transformations that they undergo. This includes uses of chemicals, their danger signs, production techniques, and disposal methods. **Mechanical Devices:** Knowledge of machines and tools, including their designs, uses, repair, and maintenance. **Physics:** Knowledge and prediction of physical principles and laws and their interrelationships and applications to understanding fluid, material, and atmospheric dynamics and mechanical, electrical, atomic, and subatomic structures and processes. **Clerical Practices:** Knowledge of administrative and clerical procedures and systems, such as word processing, managing files and records, stenography and transcription, designing forms, and other office procedures and terminology.

WORK ENVIRONMENT—Hazardous conditions; contaminants; common protective or safety equipment; hazardous equipment; standing.

Coin, Vending, and Amusement Machine Servicers and Repairers

- Growth: 15.2%
- Annual Job Openings: 7,000
- Annual Earnings: $27,800
- Percentage of Women: 19.8%

Related Apprenticeship	Years
Coin-Machine-Service Repairer	3

Install, service, adjust, or repair coin, vending, or amusement machines, including video games, jukeboxes, pinball machines, and slot machines. Adjusts and repairs vending machines and meters and replaces defective mechanical and electrical parts, using hand tools, soldering iron, and diagrams. Tests dispensing, coin-handling, electrical, refrigeration, carbonation, or ice-making systems of machine. Examines and inspects vending machines and meters to determine cause of malfunction. Disassembles and assembles machines, following specifications and using hand tools and power tools. Cleans and oils parts with soap and water, gasoline, kerosene, or carbon tetrachloride. Replenishes vending machines with ingredients or products. Shellacs or paints dial markings or mechanisms' exterior, using brush or spray gun. Collects coins from machine and makes settlements with concessionaires. Keeps records of machine maintenance and repair. **SKILLS—** Repairing; Equipment Maintenance; Installa-tion; Troubleshooting; Quality Control Analysis; Operation Monitoring.

GOE—Interest Area: 05. Mechanics, Installers, and Repairers. **Work Group:** 05.03 Mechanical Work. **Other Apprenticeable Jobs in This Work Group:** Aircraft Engine Specialists; Airframe-and-Power-Plant Mechanics; Automotive Body and Related Repairers; Automotive Glass Installers and Repairers; Automotive Master Mechanics; Automotive Specialty Technicians; Bus and Truck Mechanics and Diesel Engine Specialists; Camera and Photographic Equipment Repairers; Farm Equipment Mechanics; Gas Appliance Repairers; Hand and Portable Power Tool Repairers; Heating and Air Conditioning Mechanics; Helpers—Installation, Maintenance, and Repair Workers; Industrial Machinery Mechanics; Installation, Maintenance, and Repair Workers, All Other; Keyboard Instrument Repairers and Tuners; Locksmiths and Safe Repairers; Maintenance and Repair Workers, General; Maintenance Workers, Machinery; Mechanical Door Repairers; Medical Appliance Technicians; Medical Equipment Repairers; Meter Mechanics; Millwrights; Mobile Heavy Equipment Mechanics, Except Engines; Motorboat Mechanics; Motorcycle Mechanics; Optical Instrument Assemblers; Outdoor Power Equipment and Other Small Engine Mechanics; Painters, Transportation Equipment; Rail Car Repairers; Recreational Vehicle Service Technicians; Reed or Wind Instrument Repairers and Tuners; Refrigeration Mechanics; Stringed Instrument Repairers and Tuners; Valve and Regulator Repairers; Watch Repairers. **PERSONALITY TYPE:** Realistic. Realistic occupations frequently involve work activities that include practical, hands-on problems and solutions. They often deal with plants, animals, and real-world materials like wood, tools, and machinery. Many of the occupations require working outside and do not involve a lot of paperwork or working closely with others.

RELATED KNOWLEDGE/COURSES—**Mechanical Devices:** Knowledge of machines and tools, including their designs, uses, repair, and maintenance. **Engineering and Technology:** Knowledge of the practical application of engineering science and technology. This includes applying principles, techniques, procedures, and equipment to the design and production of various goods and services.

WORK ENVIRONMENT—Spend time kneeling, crouching, stooping, or crawling; spend time bending or twisting the body; spend time making repetitive motions; standing; walking and running.

Combination Machine Tool Setters and Set-Up Operators, Metal and Plastic

- Growth: 8.3%
- Annual Job Openings: 8,000
- Annual Earnings: $29,050
- Percentage of Women: 28.5%

Related Apprenticeship	Years
Machine Operator I	1
Four-Slide-Machine Setter	2
Machine Set-Up Operator	2
Gear-Cutting-Machine Set-Up Operator (Machine Shop)	3
Gear-Cutting-Machine Set-Up Operator, Tool (Machine Shop)	3
Machine Setter (Machine Shop)	3
Tool-Machine Set-Up Operator	3

Set up or set up and operate more than one type of cutting or forming machine tool, such as gear hobbers, lathes, press brakes, shearing, and boring machines. Sets up and operates lathes, cutters, borers, millers, grinders, presses, drills, and auxiliary machines to make metallic and plastic workpieces. Computes data, such as gear dimensions and machine settings, applying knowledge of shop mathematics. Instructs operators or other workers in machine setup and operation. Records operational data such as pressure readings, length of stroke, feeds, and speeds. Makes minor electrical and mechanical repairs and adjustments to machines and notifies supervisor when major service is required. Lifts, positions, and secures workpieces in holding devices, using hoists and hand tools. Inspects first-run workpieces and verifies conformance to specifications to check accuracy of machine setup. Measures and marks reference points and cutting lines on workpiece, using traced templates, compasses, and rules. Moves controls or mounts gears, cams, or templates in machine to set feed rate and cutting speed, depth, and angle. Selects, installs, and adjusts alignment of drills, cutters, dies, guides, and holding devices, using template, measuring instruments, and hand tools. Starts machine and turns handwheels or valves to engage feeding, cooling, and lubricating mechanisms. Reads blueprint or job order to determine product specifications and tooling instructions and to plan operational sequences. Monitors machine operation and moves controls to align and adjust position of workpieces and action of cutting tools. **SKILLS**—Operation Monitoring; Equipment Maintenance; Quality Control Analysis; Operation and Control; Installation; Repairing; Instructing; Troubleshooting.

GOE—Interest Area: 08. Industrial Production. **Work Group:** 08.02 Production Technology. **Other Apprenticeable Jobs in This Work Group:** Aircraft Structure Assemblers, Precision; Aircraft Systems Assemblers, Precision; Bench Workers, Jewelry; Bindery Machine Setters and Set-Up Operators; Bookbinders; Buffing and Polishing Set-Up Operators; Coating, Painting, and Spraying Machine Setters and Set-Up Operators; Dental Laboratory Technicians; Electrical and Electronic Equipment Assemblers; Electrical and Electronic Inspectors and Testers; Electromechanical Equipment Assemblers; Engine and Other Machine Assemblers; Extruding and Drawing Machine Setters, Operators, and Tenders, Metal and Plastic; Extruding, Forming, Pressing, and Compacting Machine Setters and Set-Up Operators; Forging Machine Setters, Operators, and Tenders, Metal and Plastic; Foundry Mold and Coremakers; Gem and Diamond Workers; Grinding, Honing, Lapping, and Deburring Machine Set-Up Operators; Heat Treating, Annealing, and Tempering Machine Operators and Tenders, Metal and Plastic; Jewelers; Lathe and Turning Machine Tool Setters, Operators, and Tenders, Metal and Plastic; Materials Inspectors; Mechanical Inspectors; Metal Molding, Coremaking, and Casting Machine Operators and Tenders; Milling and Planing Machine Setters, Operators, and Tenders, Metal and Plastic; Model and Mold Makers, Jewelry; Motor Vehicle Inspectors; Paper Goods Machine Setters, Operators, and Tenders; Pewter Casters and Finishers; Plastic Molding and Casting Machine Setters and Set-Up Operators; Precision Devices Inspectors and Testers; Precision Lens Grinders and Polishers; Precision Mold and Pattern Casters, except Nonferrous Metals; Precision Pattern and Die Casters, Nonferrous Metals; Press and Press Brake Machine Setters and Set-Up Operators, Metal and Plastic; Production Inspectors, Testers, Graders, Sorters, Samplers, Weighers; Production Workers, All Other; Rolling Machine Setters, Operators, and Tenders, Metal and Plastic; Silversmiths; Textile Knitting and Weaving Machine Setters, Operators, and Tenders; Textile Winding, Twisting, and Drawing Out Machine Setters, Operators, and Tenders; Welding Machine Setters and Set-Up Operators; Woodworking Machine Setters and Set-Up Operators, Except Sawing. **PERSONALITY TYPE:** Realistic. Realistic occupations frequently involve work activities that include practical, hands-on problems and solutions. They often deal with plants, animals, and real-world materials like wood, tools, and machinery. Many of the occupations require working outside and do not involve a lot of paperwork or working closely with others.

RELATED KNOWLEDGE/COURSES— Mechanical Devices: Knowledge of machines and tools, including their designs, uses, repair, and maintenance. **Design:** Knowledge of design techniques, tools, and principles involved in production of precision technical plans, blueprints, drawings, and models. **Production and Processing:** Knowledge of raw materials, production processes, quality control, costs, and other techniques for maximizing the effective manufacture and distribution of goods. **Educa-**

tion and Training: Knowledge of principles and methods for curriculum and training design, teaching and instruction for individuals and groups, and the measurement of training effects. **Building and Construction:** Knowledge of the materials, methods, and tools involved in the construction or repair of houses, buildings, or other structures, such as highways and roads. **Public Safety and Security:** Knowledge of relevant equipment, policies, procedures, and strategies to promote effective local, state, or national security operations for the protection of people, data, property, and institutions.

WORK ENVIRONMENT—Hazardous equipment; common protective or safety equipment; sounds, noise levels are distracting or uncomfortable; minor burns, cuts, bites, or stings; indoors; standing.

Commercial Pilots

- Growth: 14.9%
- Annual Job Openings: 2,000
- Annual Earnings: $49,830
- Percentage of Women: 4.0%

Related Apprenticeship	Years
Air Transport Pilot	3.4

Pilot and navigate the flight of small fixed or rotary winged aircraft, primarily for the transport of cargo and passengers. Requires Commercial Rating. Check aircraft prior to flights to ensure that the engines, controls, instru- ments, and other systems are functioning properly. Check baggage or cargo to ensure that it has been loaded correctly. Choose routes, altitudes, and speeds that will provide the fastest, safest, and smoothest flights. Consider airport altitudes, outside temperatures, plane weights, and wind speeds and directions in order to calculate the speed needed to become airborne. Contact control towers for takeoff clearances, arrival instructions, and other information, using radio equipment. Coordinate flight activities with ground crews and air-traffic control and inform crew members of flight and test procedures. File instrument flight plans with air traffic control so that flights can be coordinated with other air traffic. Monitor engine operation, fuel consumption, and functioning of aircraft systems during flights. Obtain and review data such as load weights, fuel supplies, weather conditions, and flight schedules in order to determine flight plans and to see if changes might be necessary. Order changes in fuel supplies, loads, routes, or schedules to ensure safety of flights. Plan and formulate flight activities and test schedules and prepare flight evaluation reports. Plan flights, following government and company regulations, using aeronautical charts and navigation instruments. Request changes in altitudes or routes as circumstances dictate. Start engines, operate controls, and pilot airplanes to transport passengers, mail, or freight while adhering to flight plans, regulations, and procedures. Use instrumentation to pilot aircraft when visibility is poor. Check the flight performance of new and experimental planes. Conduct in-flight tests and evaluations at specified altitudes and in all types of weather in order to determine the receptivity and other characteristics of equipment and systems. Co-pilot aircraft or perform captain's duties if required. Fly with other pilots or pilot-license applicants to evaluate their proficiency. Instruct other pilots and student pilots in aircraft operations. Perform minor aircraft maintenance and repair work or arrange for major maintenance. **SKILLS—** Operation and Control; Operation Monitoring; Instructing; Science; Coordination; Systems Evaluation; Judgment and Decision Making; Learning Strategies; Systems Analysis.

GOE—Interest Area: 07. Transportation. **Work Group:** 07.03 Air Vehicle Operation. **Other Apprenticeable Jobs in This Work Group:** No other apprenticeable jobs in this group. **PERSONALITY TYPE:** Realistic. Realistic occupations frequently involve work activities that include practical, hands-on problems and solutions. They often deal with plants, animals, and real-world materials like wood, tools, and machinery. Many of the occupations require working outside and do not involve a lot of paperwork or working closely with others.

RELATED KNOWLEDGE/COURSES— Transportation: Knowledge of principles and methods for moving people or goods by air, rail, sea, or road, including the relative costs and benefits. **Geography:** Knowledge of principles and methods for describing the features of land, sea, and air masses, including their physical characteristics; locations; interrelationships; and distribution of plant, animal, and human life. **Public Safety and Security:** Knowledge of relevant equipment, policies, procedures, and strategies to promote effective local, state, or national security operations for the protection of people, data, property, and institutions. **Education and Training:** Knowledge of principles and methods for curriculum and training design, teaching and instruction for individuals and groups, and the measurement of training effects. **Mechanical Devices:** Knowledge of machines and tools, including their designs, uses, repair, and maintenance. **Computers and**

Electronics: Knowledge of circuit boards, processors, chips, electronic equipment, and computer hardware and software, including applications and programming. **Physics:** Knowledge and prediction of physical principles and laws and their interrelationships and applications to understanding fluid, material, and atmospheric dynamics and mechanical, electrical, atomic, and subatomic structures and processes.

WORK ENVIRONMENT—High places; exposed to whole-body vibration; sitting; hazardous equipment; hazardous conditions.

Communication Equipment Mechanics, Installers, and Repairers

- Growth: –0.6%
- Annual Job Openings: 23,000
- Annual Earnings: $48,230
- Percentage of Women: 13.0%

Related Apprenticeship	Years
Technician, Submarine Cable Equipment	2
Sound Technician	3
Automatic-Equipment Technician	4
Electronic Systems Technician	4

Equipment Installer
(Telephone and Telegraph)   4

Telecommunications
Technician   4

Install, maintain, test, and repair communication cables and equipment. Examines and tests malfunctioning equipment to determine defects, using blueprints and electrical measuring instruments. Tests installed equipment for conformance to specifications, using test equipment. Assembles and installs communication equipment, such as data communication lines and equipment, computer systems, and antennas and towers, using hand tools. Repairs, replaces, or adjusts defective components. Disassembles equipment to adjust, repair, or replace parts, using hand tools. Evaluates quality of performance of installed equipment by observance and using test equipment. Digs holes or trenches. Answers customers' inquiries or complaints. Cleans and maintains tools, test equipment, and motor vehicle. Communicates with base, using telephone or two-way radio to receive instructions or technical advice or to report unauthorized use of equipment. Demonstrates equipment and instructs customer in use of equipment. Determines viability of site through observation and discusses site location and construction requirements with customer. Measures distance from landmarks to identify exact installation site. Climbs poles and ladders; constructs pole, roof mounts, or reinforcements; and mixes concrete to enable equipment installation. Plans layout and installation of data communications equipment. Reviews work orders, building permits, manufacturer's instructions, and ordinances to move, change, install, repair, or remove communication equipment. Adjusts or modifies equipment in accor-

dance with customer request or to enhance performance of equipment. Performs routine maintenance on equipment, which includes adjustment, repair, and painting. Measures, cuts, splices, connects, solders, and installs wires and cables. **SKILLS**—Repairing; Installation; Troubleshooting; Equipment Maintenance; Technology Design; Quality Control Analysis; Operation Monitoring; Operation and Control.

GOE—Interest Area: 05. Mechanics, Installers, and Repairers. **Work Group:** 05.02 Electrical and Electronic Systems. **Other Apprenticeable Jobs in This Work Group:** Avionics Technicians; Battery Repairers; Central Office and PBX Installers and Repairers; Data Processing Equipment Repairers; Electric Home Appliance and Power Tool Repairers; Electric Meter Installers and Repairers; Electric Motor and Switch Assemblers and Repairers; Electrical and Electronics Installers and Repairers, Transportation Equipment; Electrical and Electronics Repairers, Commercial and Industrial Equipment; Electrical and Electronics Repairers, Powerhouse, Substation, and Relay; Electrical Power-Line Installers and Repairers; Electronic Equipment Installers and Repairers, Motor Vehicles; Electronic Home Entertainment Equipment Installers and Repairers; Elevator Installers and Repairers; Installation, Maintenance, and Repair Workers, All Other; Office Machine and Cash Register Servicers; Radio Mechanics; Signal and Track Switch Repairers; Station Installers and Repairers, Telephone; Telecommunications Line Installers and Repairers; Transformer Repairers. **PERSONALITY TYPE:** Realistic. Realistic occupations frequently involve work activities that include practical, hands-on problems and solutions. They often deal with plants, animals, and real-world materials like wood, tools, and machinery. Many of the occupations require working outside and do not involve a lot of paperwork or working closely with others.

RELATED KNOWLEDGE/COURSES— **Telecommunications:** Knowledge of transmission, broadcasting, switching, control, and operation of telecommunications systems. **Computers and Electronics:** Knowledge of circuit boards, processors, chips, electronic equipment, and computer hardware and software, including applications and programming. **Design:** Knowledge of design techniques, tools, and principles involved in production of precision technical plans, blueprints, drawings, and models. **Mechanical Devices:** Knowledge of machines and tools, including their designs, uses, repair, and maintenance. **Engineering and Technology:** Knowledge of the practical application of engineering science and technology. This includes applying principles, techniques, procedures, and equipment to the design and production of various goods and services.

WORK ENVIRONMENT—Hazardous conditions; high places; outdoors; climbing ladders, scaffolds, or poles; common protective or safety equipment.

Computer Operators

◎ Growth: –16.7%

◎ Annual Job Openings: 27,000

◎ Annual Earnings: $29,970

◎ Percentage of Women: 52.3%

Related Apprenticeship	*Years*
Computer Peripheral Equipment Operator	1
Computer Operator	3

Monitor and control electronic computer and peripheral electronic data processing equipment to process business, scientific, engineering, and other data according to operating instructions. May enter commands at a computer terminal and set controls on computer and peripheral devices. Monitor and respond to operating and error messages. Clear equipment at end of operating run and review schedule to determine next assignment. Enter commands, using computer terminal, and activate controls on computer and peripheral equipment to integrate and operate equipment. Load peripheral equipment with selected materials for operating runs or oversee loading of peripheral equipment by peripheral equipment operators. Monitor the system for equipment failure or errors in performance. Notify supervisor or computer maintenance technicians of equipment malfunctions. Read job set-up instructions to determine equipment to be used; order of use; material to be loaded, such as disks and paper; and control settings. Record information such as computer operating time, problems that occurred, and actions taken. Respond to program error messages by finding and correcting problems or terminating the program. Retrieve, separate, and sort program output as needed and send data to specified users. Type command on keyboard to transfer encoded data from memory unit to magnetic tape and assist in labeling, classifying, cataloging, and maintaining tapes. Answer telephone calls to assist computer users encountering problems. Help programmers and systems analysts test and debug new programs. Oversee the operation of computer hardware systems, including coordinating and scheduling the use of computer terminals and networks to ensure efficient use. Supervise and train peripheral equipment operators and computer operator trainees. Operate encoding machine to trace coordinates on documents such as maps or drawings and to encode document points into computer. Operate spreadsheet programs and other types of software to load and manipulate data and to produce reports. **SKILLS**—Troubleshooting; Programming; Reading Comprehension; Active Listening; Equipment Selection; Critical Thinking; Speaking; Operation Monitoring.

GOE—Interest Area: 09. Business Detail. **Work Group:** 09.09 Clerical Machine Operation. **Other Apprenticeable Jobs in This Work Group:** Data Entry Keyers; Postal Service Clerks; Typesetting and Composing Machine Operators and Tenders; Word Processors and Typists. **PERSONALITY TYPE:** Conventional. Conventional occupations frequently involve following set procedures and routines. These occupations can include working with data and details more than with ideas. Usually there is a clear line of authority to follow.

RELATED KNOWLEDGE/COURSES— **Computers and Electronics:** Knowledge of circuit boards, processors, chips, electronic equipment, and computer hardware and software, including applications and programming. **Clerical Practices:** Knowledge of administrative and clerical procedures and systems, such as word processing, managing files and records, stenography and transcription, designing forms, and other office procedures and terminology. **Customer and Personal Service:** Knowledge of

principles and processes for providing customer and personal services. This includes customer needs assessment, meeting quality standards for services, and evaluation of customer satisfaction. **Telecommunications:** Knowledge of transmission, broadcasting, switching, control, and operation of telecommunications systems. **Communications and Media:** Knowledge of media production, communication, and dissemination techniques and methods. This includes alternative ways to inform and entertain via written, oral, and visual media. **English Language:** Knowledge of the structure and content of the English language, including the meaning and spelling of words, rules of composition, and grammar.

WORK ENVIRONMENT—Sitting; indoors; spend time making repetitive motions.

Computer Specialists, All Other

- Growth: 36.5%
- Annual Job Openings: 27,000
- Annual Earnings: $54,070
- Percentage of Women: 33.2%

Related Apprenticeship	Years
IT Generalist	1.5
E-Commerce Specialist	competency

All computer specialists not listed separately. SKILLS—No data available.

GOE—Interest Area: 02. Science, Math, and Engineering. Work Group: 02.06 Computer Systems and Technology. Other Apprenticeable Jobs in This Work Group: Computer Programmers; Computer Security Specialists; Network Systems and Data Communications Analysts. PERSONALITY TYPE: No data available.

RELATED KNOWLEDGE/COURSES—No data available.

WORK ENVIRONMENT—No data available.

Construction and Building Inspectors

@ Growth: 13.8%

@ Annual Job Openings: 10,000

@ Annual Earnings: $42,650

@ Percentage of Women: 9.8%

Related Apprenticeship	Years
Inspector, Building	3

Inspect structures, using engineering skills to determine structural soundness and compliance with specifications, building codes, and other regulations. Inspections may be general in nature or may be limited to a specific area, such as electrical systems or plumbing. Use survey instruments, metering devices, tape measures, and test equipment, such as concrete strength measurers, to perform inspections. Inspect bridges, dams, highways, buildings, wiring, plumbing, electrical circuits, sewers, heating systems, and foundations during and after construction for structural quality, general safety, and conformance to specifications and codes. Maintain daily logs and supplement inspection records with photographs. Review and interpret plans, blueprints, site layouts, specifications, and construction methods to ensure compliance to legal requirements and safety regulations. Inspect and monitor construction sites to ensure adherence to safety standards, building codes, and specifications. Measure dimensions and verify level, alignment, and elevation of structures and fixtures to ensure compliance to building plans and codes. Issue violation notices and stop-work orders, conferring with owners, violators, and authorities to explain regulations and recommend rectifications. Issue permits for construction, relocation, demolition, and occupancy. Approve and sign plans that meet required specifications. Compute estimates of work completed or of needed renovations or upgrades and approve payment for contractors. Monitor installation of plumbing, wiring, equipment, and appliances to ensure that installation is performed properly and is in compliance with applicable regulations. Examine lifting and conveying devices, such as elevators, escalators, moving sidewalks, lifts and hoists, inclined railways, ski lifts, and amusement rides, to ensure safety and proper functioning. Train, direct, and supervise other construction inspectors. Evaluate premises for cleanliness, including proper garbage disposal and lack of vermin infestation. SKILLS—Persuasion; Time Management; Negotiation; Instructing; Active Listening; Active Learning; Coordination; Service Orientation.

GOE—Interest Area: 02. Science, Math, and Engineering. Work Group: 02.08 Engineering Technology. Other Apprenticeable Jobs in This

Work Group: Aerospace Engineering and Operations Technicians; Architectural Drafters; Calibration and Instrumentation Technicians; Cartographers and Photogrammetrists; Civil Drafters; Electrical Drafters; Electrical Engineering Technicians; Electro-Mechanical Technicians; Electronic Drafters; Electronics Engineering Technicians; Engineering Technicians, Except Drafters, All Other; Industrial Engineering Technicians; Mapping Technicians; Mechanical Drafters; Mechanical Engineering Technicians; Numerical Tool and Process Control Programmers; Surveying Technicians. **PERSONALITY TYPE:** Conventional. Conventional occupations frequently involve following set procedures and routines. These occupations can include working with data and details more than with ideas. Usually there is a clear line of authority to follow.

RELATED KNOWLEDGE/COURSES— **Building and Construction:** Knowledge of the materials, methods, and tools involved in the construction or repair of houses, buildings, or other structures, such as highways and roads. **Design:** Knowledge of design techniques, tools, and principles involved in production of precision technical plans, blueprints, drawings, and models. **Engineering and Technology:** Knowledge of the practical application of engineering science and technology. This includes applying principles, techniques, procedures, and equipment to the design and production of various goods and services. **Customer and Personal Service:** Knowledge of principles and processes for providing customer and personal services. This includes customer needs assessment, meeting quality standards for services, and evaluation of customer satisfaction. **Public Safety and Security:** Knowledge of relevant equipment, policies, procedures, and strategies to promote effective local, state, or national security operations for the protection of people, data, property, and

institutions. **Administration and Management:** Knowledge of business and management principles involved in strategic planning, resource allocation, human resources modeling, leadership technique, production methods, and coordination of people and resources. **Computers and Electronics:** Knowledge of circuit boards, processors, chips, electronic equipment, and computer hardware and software, including applications and programming.

WORK ENVIRONMENT—Outdoors; sounds, noise levels are distracting or uncomfortable; in an enclosed vehicle or equipment; very hot or cold; contaminants.

Construction and Related Workers, All Other

- ◉ Growth: 32.0%
- ◉ Annual Job Openings: 17,000
- ◉ Annual Earnings: $22,900
- ◉ Percentage of Women: 3.7%

Related Apprenticeship	Years
Hazardous-Waste Material Technician	2
Ornamental-Iron Worker	3
Sign Erector I	3

All construction and related workers not listed separately. SKILLS—No data available.

GOE—**Interest Area:** 06. Construction, Mining, and Drilling. **Work Group:** 06.02 Construction. **Other Apprenticeable Jobs in This Work Group:** Boat Builders and Shipwrights; Boilermakers; Brickmasons and Blockmasons; Carpet Installers; Ceiling Tile Installers; Cement Masons and Concrete Finishers; Construction Carpenters; Drywall Installers; Electricians; Fence Erectors; Floor Layers, Except Carpet, Wood, and Hard Tiles; Glaziers; Grader, Bulldozer, and Scraper Operators; Insulation Workers, Floor, Ceiling, and Wall; Insulation Workers, Mechanical; Operating Engineers; Painters, Construction and Maintenance; Paperhangers; Paving, Surfacing, and Tamping Equipment Operators; Pipe Fitters; Plasterers and Stucco Masons; Plumbers; Reinforcing Iron and Rebar Workers; Riggers; Roofers; Rough Carpenters; Sheet Metal Workers; Ship Carpenters and Joiners; Stone Cutters and Carvers; Stonemasons; Structural Iron and Steel Workers; Tapers; Terrazzo Workers and Finishers; Tile and Marble Setters. **PERSONALITY TYPE:** No data available.

RELATED KNOWLEDGE/COURSES—No data available.

WORK ENVIRONMENT—No data available.

Construction Carpenters

- Growth: 10.1%
- Annual Job Openings: 193,000
- Annual Earnings: $34,250
- Percentage of Women: 1.9%

Related Apprenticeship	Years
Residential Carpenter	2
Lather	3
Carpenter	4
Carpenter, Interior Systems	4
Carpenter, Maintenance	4
Prop Maker	4
Carpenter, Mold	6

(This is one of the most popular apprenticeable jobs.)

Construct, erect, install, and repair structures and fixtures of wood, plywood, and wallboard, using carpenter's hand tools and power tools. Measure and mark cutting lines on materials, using ruler, pencil, chalk, and marking gauge. Follow established safety rules and regulations and maintain a safe and clean environment. Verify trueness of structure, using plumb bob and level. Shape or cut materials to specified measurements, using hand tools, machines, or power saw. Study specifications in blueprints, sketches, or building plans to prepare project layout and determine dimensions and materials required. Assemble and fasten materials to make framework or props, using hand tools and wood screws, nails, dowel pins, or glue. Build or repair cabinets, doors, frameworks, floors, and other wooden fixtures used in buildings, using woodworking machines, carpenter's hand tools, and power tools. Erect scaffolding and ladders for assembling structures above ground level. Remove damaged or defective parts or sections of structures and repair or replace, using hand tools. Install structures and fixtures, such as

C

windows, frames, floorings, and trim, or hardware, using carpenter's hand and power tools. Select and order lumber and other required materials. Maintain records, document actions, and present written progress reports. Finish surfaces of woodwork or wallboard in houses and buildings, using paint, hand tools, and paneling. Prepare cost estimates for clients or employers. Arrange for subcontractors to deal with special areas such as heating and electrical wiring work. **SKILLS**—Management of Personnel Resources; Management of Financial Resources; Management of Material Resources; Equipment Maintenance; Repairing; Service Orientation; Quality Control Analysis; Time Management.

GOE—**Interest Area:** 06. Construction, Mining, and Drilling. **Work Group:** 06.02 Construction. **Other Apprenticeable Jobs in This Work Group:** Boat Builders and Shipwrights; Boilermakers; Brickmasons and Blockmasons; Carpet Installers; Ceiling Tile Installers; Cement Masons and Concrete Finishers; Drywall Installers; Electricians; Fence Erectors; Floor Layers, Except Carpet, Wood, and Hard Tiles; Glaziers; Grader, Bulldozer, and Scraper Operators; Insulation Workers, Floor, Ceiling, and Wall; Insulation Workers, Mechanical; Operating Engineers; Painters, Construction and Maintenance; Paperhangers; Paving, Surfacing, and Tamping Equipment Operators; Pipe Fitters; Plasterers and Stucco Masons; Plumbers; Reinforcing Iron and Rebar Workers; Riggers; Roofers; Rough Carpenters; Sheet Metal Workers; Ship Carpenters and Joiners; Stone Cutters and Carvers; Stonemasons; Structural Iron and Steel Workers; Tapers; Terrazzo Workers and Finishers; Tile and Marble Setters. **PERSONALITY TYPE:** Realistic. Realistic occupations frequently involve work activities that include practical, hands-on problems and

solutions. They often deal with plants, animals, and real-world materials like wood, tools, and machinery. Many of the occupations require working outside and do not involve a lot of paperwork or working closely with others.

RELATED KNOWLEDGE/COURSES— **Building and Construction:** Knowledge of the materials, methods, and tools involved in the construction or repair of houses, buildings, or other structures, such as highways and roads. **Production and Processing:** Knowledge of raw materials, production processes, quality control, costs, and other techniques for maximizing the effective manufacture and distribution of goods. **Engineering and Technology:** Knowledge of the practical application of engineering science and technology. This includes applying principles, techniques, procedures, and equipment to the design and production of various goods and services. **Public Safety and Security:** Knowledge of relevant equipment, policies, procedures, and strategies to promote effective local, state, or national security operations for the protection of people, data, property, and institutions. **Design:** Knowledge of design techniques, tools, and principles involved in production of precision technical plans, blueprints, drawings, and models. **Mechanical Devices:** Knowledge of machines and tools, including their designs, uses, repair, and maintenance.

WORK ENVIRONMENT—Sounds, noise levels are distracting or uncomfortable; hazardous equipment; very hot or cold; contaminants; outdoors.

FURTHER INFORMATION—Contact a local joint union-management apprenticeship committee or the nearest office of your state employment service or apprenticeship agency (see Appendix C). To identify the local union office, contact United Brotherhood of Carpenters and

Joiners of America, 50 F St. NW, Washington, DC 20001. Internet: http://www.carpenters.org.

Construction Laborers

- Growth: 14.2%
- Annual Job Openings: 166,000
- Annual Earnings: $24,670
- Percentage of Women: 3.5%

Related Apprenticeship	Years
Construction Craft Laborer	2
Maintenance Technician, Municipal	2
Tuckpointer, Cleaner, Caulker	3

(This is one of the most popular apprenticeable jobs.)

Perform tasks involving physical labor at building, highway, and heavy construction projects; tunnel and shaft excavations; and demolition sites. May operate hand and power tools of all types: air hammers, earth tampers, cement mixers, small mechanical hoists, surveying and measuring equipment, and a variety of other equipment and instruments. May clean and prepare sites; dig trenches; set braces to support the sides of excavations; erect scaffolding; clean up rubble and debris; and remove asbestos, lead, and other hazardous waste materials. May assist other craft workers. Tends pumps, compressors, and generators to provide power for tools, machinery, and equipment or to heat and move materials such as asphalt. Lubricates, cleans, and repairs machinery, equipment, and tools. Mixes ingredients to create compounds used to cover or clean surfaces. Loads and unloads trucks and hauls and hoists materials. Erects and disassembles scaffolding, shoring, braces, and other temporary structures. Builds and positions forms for pouring concrete and dismantles forms after use, using saws, hammers, nails, or bolts. Measures, marks, and records openings and distances to lay out area to be graded or to erect building structures. Smooths and finishes freshly poured cement or concrete, using float, trowel, screed, or powered cement-finishing tool. Applies caulking compounds by hand or with caulking gun to seal crevices. Positions, joins, aligns, and seals structural components, such as concrete wall sections and pipes. Digs ditches and levels earth to grade specifications, using pick and shovel. Signals equipment operators to facilitate alignment, movement, and adjustment of machinery, equipment, and materials. Grinds, scrapes, sands, or polishes surfaces such as concrete, marble, terrazzo, or wood flooring, using abrasive tools or machines. Mixes concrete, using portable mixer. Razes buildings and salvages useful materials. Sprays materials such as water, sand, steam, vinyl, paint, or stucco through hose to clean, coat, or seal surfaces. Tends machine that pumps concrete, grout, cement, sand, plaster, or stucco through spray gun for application to ceilings and walls. Mops, brushes, or spreads paints, cleaning solutions, or other compounds over surfaces to clean or provide protection. Cleans construction site to eliminate possible hazards. SKILLS—Equipment Maintenance.

GOE—Interest Area: 06. Construction, Mining, and Drilling. Work Group: 06.04 Hands-on Work in Construction, Extraction, and Maintenance. **Other Apprenticeable Jobs in This Work Group:** Carpenter Assemblers and Repairers; Helpers—Brickmasons, Blockmasons, Stonemasons, and Tile and Marble Setters; Helpers—Extraction Workers. **PERSONALITY TYPE:** Realistic. Realistic occupations frequently involve work activities that include practical, hands-on problems and solutions. They often deal with plants, animals, and real-world materials like wood, tools, and machinery. Many of the occupations require working outside and do not involve a lot of paperwork or working closely with others.

RELATED KNOWLEDGE/COURSES— **Building and Construction:** Knowledge of the materials, methods, and tools involved in the construction or repair of houses, buildings, or other structures, such as highways and roads. **Mechanical Devices:** Knowledge of machines and tools, including their designs, uses, repair, and maintenance. **Production and Processing:** Knowledge of raw materials, production processes, quality control, costs, and other techniques for maximizing the effective manufacture and distribution of goods. **Engineering and Technology:** Knowledge of the practical application of engineering science and technology. This includes applying principles, techniques, procedures, and equipment to the design and production of various goods and services. **Physics:** Knowledge and prediction of physical principles and laws and their interrelationships and applications to understanding fluid, material, and atmospheric dynamics and mechanical, electrical, atomic, and subatomic structures and processes. **Design:** Knowledge of design techniques, tools, and principles involved in production of precision technical plans, blueprints, drawings, and models. **Chemistry:** Knowledge of the chemical composition,

structure, and properties of substances and of the chemical processes and transformations that they undergo. This includes uses of chemicals, their danger signs, production techniques, and disposal methods.

WORK ENVIRONMENT—Outdoors; hazardous equipment; minor burns, cuts, bites, or stings; very hot or cold; standing.

Conveyor Operators and Tenders

- Growth: 12.4%
- Annual Job Openings: 9,000
- Annual Earnings: $24,690
- Percentage of Women: 15.6%

Related Apprenticeship	Years
Conveyor-System Operator	1

Control or tend conveyors or conveyor systems that move materials or products to and from stockpiles, processing stations, departments, or vehicles. May control speed and routing of materials or products. Inform supervisors of equipment malfunctions that need to be addressed. Load, unload, or adjust materials or products on conveyors by hand; by using lifts, hoists, and scoops; or by opening gates, chutes, or hoppers. Manipulate controls, levers, and valves to start pumps, auxiliary equipment, or conveyors and to adjust equipment positions, speeds, timing, and material flows. Observe conveyor operations and monitor lights, dials, and gauges in order to maintain specified operating levels and to detect equipment malfunctions. Observe packages moving along conveyors in order to identify packages and to detect defective packaging. Position deflector bars, gates, chutes, or spouts to divert flow of materials from one conveyor onto another conveyor. Press console buttons to deflect packages to predetermined accumulators or reject lines. Read production and delivery schedules and confer with supervisors to determine sorting and transfer procedures, arrangement of packages on pallets, and destinations of loaded pallets. Stop equipment or machinery and clear jams, using poles, bars, and hand tools, or remove damaged materials from conveyors. Weigh or measure materials and products, using scales or other measuring instruments, or read scales on conveyors that continually weigh products in order to verify specified tonnages and prevent overloads. Affix identifying information to materials or products, using hand tools. Clean, sterilize, and maintain equipment, machinery, and work stations, using hand tools, shovels, brooms, chemicals, hoses, and lubricants. Collect samples of materials or products, checking them to ensure conformance to specifications or sending them to laboratories for analysis. Contact workers in work stations or other departments to request movement of materials, products, or machinery or to notify them of incoming shipments and their estimated delivery times. Distribute materials, supplies, and equipment to work stations, using lifts and trucks. Join sections of conveyor frames at temporary working areasand connect power units. Measure dimensions of bundles, using rulers, and cut battens to required sizes, using power saws. **SKILLS**—Equipment Maintenance; Operation Monitoring; Operation and Control; Repairing; Troubleshooting.

GOE—Interest Area: 08. Industrial Production. **Work Group:** 08.07 Hands-on Work: Loading, Moving, Hoisting, and Conveying. **Other Apprenticeable Jobs in This Work Group:** Crane and Tower Operators; Dragline Operators; Tank Car, Truck, and Ship Loaders. **PERSONALITY TYPE:** Realistic. Realistic occupations frequently involve work activities that include practical, hands-on problems and solutions. They often deal with plants, animals, and real-world materials like wood, tools, and machinery. Many of the occupations require working outside and do not involve a lot of paperwork or working closely with others.

RELATED KNOWLEDGE/COURSES— Production and Processing: Knowledge of raw materials, production processes, quality control, costs, and other techniques for maximizing the effective manufacture and distribution of goods. **Mechanical Devices:** Knowledge of machines and tools, including their designs, uses, repair, and maintenance.

WORK ENVIRONMENT—Spend time making repetitive motions; contaminants; hazardous equipment; using hands on objects, tools, or controls; spend time bending or twisting the body.

Cooks, Fast Food

- Growth: 4.9%
- Annual Job Openings: 165,000
- Annual Earnings: $14,450
- Percentage of Women: 44.3%

Related Apprenticeship	Years
Baker, Pizza	1

Prepare and cook food in a fast-food restaurant with a limited menu. Duties of the cooks are limited to preparation of a few basic items and normally involve operating large-volume single-purpose cooking equipment. Clean food preparation areas, cooking surfaces, and utensils. Cook and package batches of food, such as hamburgers and fried chicken, which are prepared to order or kept warm until sold. Cook the exact number of items ordered by each customer, working on several different orders simultaneously. Maintain sanitation, health, and safety standards in work areas. Measure ingredients required for specific food items being prepared. Mix ingredients such as pancake or waffle batters. Operate large-volume cooking equipment such as grills, deep-fat fryers, or griddles. Precook items such as bacon in order to prepare them for later use. Prepare and serve beverages such as coffee and fountain drinks. Prepare specialty foods such as pizzas, fish and chips, sandwiches, and tacos, following specific methods that usually require short preparation time. Read food order slips or receive verbal instructions as to food required by patron and prepare and cook food according to instructions. Verify that prepared food meets requirements for quality and quantity. Wash, cut, and prepare foods designated for cooking. Clean, stock, and restock workstations and display cases. Order and take delivery of supplies. Prepare dough, following recipe. Schedule activities and equipment use with managers, using information about daily menus to help coordinate cooking times. Serve orders to customers at windows, counters, or tables. Take food and drink orders and receive payment from customers. **SKILLS**—None met the criteria.

GOE—Interest Area: 11. Recreation, Travel, and Other Personal Services. **Work Group:** 11.05 Food and Beverage Services. **Other Apprenticeable Jobs in This Work Group:** Bakers, Bread and Pastry; Bartenders; Butchers and Meat Cutters; Chefs and Head Cooks; Cooks, Institution and Cafeteria; Cooks, Restaurant. **PERSONALITY TYPE:** Realistic. Realistic occupations frequently involve work activities that include practical, hands-on problems and solutions. They often deal with plants, animals, and real-world materials like wood, tools, and machinery. Many of the occupations require working outside and do not involve a lot of paperwork or working closely with others.

RELATED KNOWLEDGE/COURSES— Customer and Personal Service: Knowledge of principles and processes for providing customer and personal services. This includes customer needs assessment, meeting quality standards for services, and evaluation of customer satisfaction. **Economics and Accounting:** Knowledge of economic and accounting principles and practices, the financial markets, banking, and the analysis and reporting of financial data.

WORK ENVIRONMENT—Standing; minor burns, cuts, bites, or stings; indoors; spend time making repetitive motions; very hot or cold.

Cooks, Institution and Cafeteria

- Growth: 2.1%
- Annual Job Openings: 121,000
- Annual Earnings: $18,300
- Percentage of Women: 44.3%

Related Apprenticeship	*Years*
Cook (Any Industry)	2

(This is one of the most popular apprenticeable jobs.)

Prepare and cook large quantities of food for institutions, such as schools, hospitals, or cafeterias. Cook foodstuffs according to menus, special dietary or nutritional restrictions, and numbers of portions to be served. Clean and inspect galley equipment, kitchen appliances, and work areas in order to ensure cleanliness and functional operation. Direct activities of one or more workers who assist in preparing and serving meals. Bake breads, rolls, and other pastries. Clean, cut, and cook meat, fish, and poultry. Compile and maintain records of food use and expenditures. Determine meal prices based on calculations of ingredient prices. Requisition food supplies, kitchen equipment, and appliances, based on estimates of future needs. Apportion and serve food to facility residents, employees, or patrons. Monitor menus and spending in order to ensure that meals are prepared economically. Monitor use of government food commodities to ensure that proper procedures are followed. Plan menus that are varied, nutritionally balanced, and appetizing, taking advantage of foods in season and local availability. Take inventory of supplies and equipment. Train new employees. Wash pots, pans, dishes, utensils, and other cooking equipment. **SKILLS**—Management of Financial Resources; Management of Personnel Resources; Management of Material Resources; Active Learning; Service Orientation; Critical Thinking; Operation Monitoring; Coordination.

GOE—Interest Area: 11. Recreation, Travel, and Other Personal Services. **Work Group:** 11.05 Food and Beverage Services. **Other Apprenticeable Jobs in This Work Group:** Bakers, Bread and Pastry; Bartenders; Butchers and Meat Cutters; Chefs and Head Cooks; Cooks, Fast Food; Cooks, Restaurant. **PERSONALITY TYPE:** Realistic. Realistic occupations frequently involve work activities that include practical, hands-on problems and solutions. They often deal with plants, animals, and real-world materials like wood, tools, and machinery. Many of the occupations require working outside and do not involve a lot of paperwork or working closely with others.

RELATED KNOWLEDGE/COURSES—Customer and Personal Service: Knowledge of principles and processes for providing customer and personal services. This includes customer needs assessment, meeting quality standards for services, and evaluation of customer satisfaction. **Administration and Management:** Knowledge of business and management principles involved in strategic planning, resource allocation, human resources modeling, leadership technique, production methods, and coordination of people and resources. **Food Production:** Knowledge of techniques and equipment for planting, growing, and harvesting food products (both plant and animal) for consumption, including storage/

handling techniques. **Economics and Accounting:** Knowledge of economic and accounting principles and practices, the financial markets, banking, and the analysis and reporting of financial data. **Personnel and Human Resources:** Knowledge of principles and procedures for personnel recruitment, selection, training, compensation and benefits, labor relations and negotiation, and personnel information systems. **Clerical Practices:** Knowledge of administrative and clerical procedures and systems, such as word processing, managing files and records, stenography and transcription, designing forms, and other office procedures and terminology. **Production and Processing:** Knowledge of raw materials, production processes, quality control, costs, and other techniques for maximizing the effective manufacture and distribution of goods.

WORK ENVIRONMENT—Standing; indoors; minor burns, cuts, bites, or stings; using hands on objects, tools, or controls; very hot or cold.

FURTHER INFORMATION—Contact a local joint union-management apprenticeship committee or the nearest office of your state employment service or apprenticeship agency (see Appendix C). Or contact American Culinary Federation, 180 Center Place Way, St. Augustine, FL 32095. Internet: http://www.acfchefs.org.

Cooks, Restaurant

- ☞ Growth: 15.9%
- ☞ Annual Job Openings: 211,000
- ☞ Annual Earnings: $19,260
- ☞ Percentage of Women: 44.3%

Related Apprenticeship	*Years*
Cook (Hotel and Restaurant)	3

(This is one of the most popular apprenticeable jobs.)

Prepare, season, and cook soups, meats, vegetables, desserts, or other foodstuffs in restaurants. May order supplies, keep records and accounts, price items on menu, or plan menu. Inspect food preparation and serving areas to ensure observance of safe, sanitary food-handling practices. Turn or stir foods to ensure even cooking. Season and cook food according to recipes or personal judgment and experience. Observe and test foods to determine if they have been cooked sufficiently, using methods such as tasting, smelling, or piercing them with utensils. Weigh, measure, and mix ingredients according to recipes or personal judgment, using various kitchen utensils and equipment. Portion, arrange, and garnish food and serve food to waiters or patrons. Regulate temperature of ovens, broilers, grills, and roasters. Substitute for or assist other cooks during emergencies or rush periods. Bake, roast, broil, and steam meats, fish, vegetables, and other foods. Wash, peel, cut, and seed fruits and vegetables to prepare them for consumption. Estimate expected food consumption; then requisition or purchase supplies or procure food from storage. Carve and trim meats such as beef, veal, ham, pork, and lamb for hot or cold service or for sandwiches. Coordinate and supervise work of kitchen staff. Consult with supervisory staff to plan menus, taking into consideration factors such as costs and special-event needs. Butcher and dress animals, fowl, or shellfish or cut and bone meat prior to cooking.

Bake breads, rolls, cakes, and pastries. Prepare relishes and hors d'oeuvres. Keep records and accounts. Plan and price menu items. **SKILLS**—Equipment Maintenance; Instructing; Time Management; Active Learning; Learning Strategies; Management of Personnel Resources; Social Perceptiveness; Troubleshooting.

GOE—**Interest Area:** 11. Recreation, Travel, and Other Personal Services. **Work Group:** 11.05 Food and Beverage Services. **Other Apprenticeable Jobs in This Work Group:** Bakers, Bread and Pastry; Bartenders; Butchers and Meat Cutters; Chefs and Head Cooks; Cooks, Fast Food; Cooks, Institution and Cafeteria. **PERSONALITY TYPE:** Realistic. Realistic occupations frequently involve work activities that include practical, hands-on problems and solutions. They often deal with plants, animals, and real-world materials like wood, tools, and machinery. Many of the occupations require working outside and do not involve a lot of paperwork or working closely with others.

RELATED KNOWLEDGE/COURSES—**Food Production:** Knowledge of techniques and equipment for planting, growing, and harvesting food products (both plant and animal) for consumption, including storage/handling techniques. **Customer and Personal Service:** Knowledge of principles and processes for providing customer and personal services. This includes customer needs assessment, meeting quality standards for services, and evaluation of customer satisfaction. **Production and Processing:** Knowledge of raw materials, production processes, quality control, costs, and other techniques for maximizing the effective manufacture and distribution of goods. **Education and Training:** Knowledge of principles and methods

for curriculum and training design, teaching and instruction for individuals and groups, and the measurement of training effects. **Foreign Language:** Knowledge of the structure and content of a foreign (non-English) language, including the meaning and spelling of words, rules of composition and grammar, and pronunciation. **Chemistry:** Knowledge of the chemical composition, structure, and properties of substances and of the chemical processes and transformations that they undergo. This includes uses of chemicals, their danger signs, production techniques, and disposal methods.

WORK ENVIRONMENT—Very hot or cold; minor burns, cuts, bites, or stings; physical proximity; sounds, noise levels are distracting or uncomfortable; standing.

FURTHER INFORMATION—Contact a local joint union-management apprenticeship committee or the nearest office of your state employment service or apprenticeship agency (see Appendix C). Or contact American Culinary Federation, 180 Center Place Way, St. Augustine, FL 32095. Internet: http://www.acfchefs.org.

Correctional Officers and Jailers

- ◉ Growth: 24.2%
- ◉ Annual Job Openings: 49,000
- ◉ Annual Earnings: $33,160
- ◉ Percentage of Women: 26.0%

Related Apprenticeship	Years
Correction Officer	1

Guard inmates in penal or rehabilitative institution in accordance with established regulations and procedures. May guard prisoners in transit between jail, courtroom, prison, or other point. Includes deputy sheriffs and police who spend the majority of their time guarding prisoners in correctional institutions. Monitor conduct of prisoners according to established policies, regulations, and procedures in order to prevent escape or violence. Inspect conditions of locks, window bars, grills, doors, and gates at correctional facilities in order to ensure that they will prevent escapes. Search prisoners, cells, and vehicles for weapons, valuables, or drugs. Guard facility entrances in order to screen visitors. Search for and recapture escapees. Inspect mail for the presence of contraband. Take prisoners into custody and escort to locations within and outside of facility, such as visiting room, courtroom, or airport. Record information such as prisoner identification, charges, and incidences of inmate disturbance. Use weapons, handcuffs, and physical force to maintain discipline and order among prisoners. Conduct fire, safety, and sanitation inspections. Provide to supervisors oral and written reports of the quality and quantity of work performed by inmates, inmate disturbances and rule violations, and unusual occurrences. Settle disputes between inmates. Drive passenger vehicles and trucks used to transport inmates to other institutions, courtrooms, hospitals, and work sites. Arrange daily schedules for prisoners, including library visits, work assignments, family visits, and counseling appointments. Assign duties to inmates, providing instructions as needed. Issue clothing, tools, and other authorized items to inmates. Serve meals and distribute commissary items to prisoners. Investigate crimes that have occurred within an institution or assist police in their investigations of crimes and inmates. Maintain records of prisoners' identification and charges. Supervise and coordinate work of other correctional service officers. Sponsor inmate recreational activities, such as newspapers and self-help groups. **SKILLS**—Social Perceptiveness; Persuasion; Negotiation; Instructing; Monitoring; Speaking; Active Listening; Writing; Critical Thinking.

GOE—Interest Area: 04. Law, Law Enforcement, and Public Safety. **Work Group:** 04.03 Law Enforcement. **Other Apprenticeable Jobs in This Work Group:** Fire Investigators; Fish and Game Wardens; Police Patrol Officers; Private Detectives and Investigators; Security Guards. **PERSONALITY TYPE:** Realistic. Realistic occupations frequently involve work activities that include practical, hands-on problems and solutions. They often deal with plants, animals, and real-world materials like wood, tools, and machinery. Many of the occupations require working outside and do not involve a lot of paperwork or working closely with others.

RELATED KNOWLEDGE/COURSES— Public Safety and Security: Knowledge of relevant equipment, policies, procedures, and strategies to promote effective local, state, or national security operations for the protection of people, data, property, and institutions. **Psychology:** Knowledge of human behavior and performance; individual differences in ability, personality, and interests; learning and motivation; psychological research methods; and the assessment and treatment of behavioral and affective disorders. **Law and Government:** Knowledge of laws, legal codes, court procedures, precedents, government regulations, executive orders, agency rules, and the democratic political process. **Philosophy and Theology:** Knowledge of different philosophical systems and religions. This includes their basic principles, values, ethics, ways of thinking, customs, and practices and their impact on human culture. **Sociology and Anthropology:** Knowledge of group behavior and dynamics, societal trends and influences, human migrations, ethnicity, and cultures and their history and origins. **Education and Training:** Knowledge of principles and methods for curriculum and training design, teaching and instruction for individuals and groups, and the measurement of training effects.

WORK ENVIRONMENT—Sounds, noise levels are distracting or uncomfortable; physical proximity; contaminants; very hot or cold; disease or infections.

Costume Attendants

- Growth: 27.8%
- Annual Job Openings: 66,000
- Annual Earnings: $25,410
- Percentage of Women: 38.2%

Related Apprenticeship	Years
Wardrobe Supervisor	2

Select, fit, and take care of costumes for cast members and aid entertainers. Recommend vendors and monitor their work. Review scripts or other production information in order to determine a story's locale and period, as well as the number of characters and required costumes. Study books, pictures, and examples of period clothing in order to determine styles worn during specific periods in history. Arrange costumes in order of use to facilitate quick-change procedures for performances. Assign lockers to employees and maintain locker rooms, dressing rooms, wig rooms, and costume storage and laundry areas. Care for non-clothing items such as flags, table skirts, and draperies. Check the appearance of costumes on stage and under lights in order to determine whether desired effects are being achieved. Clean and press costumes before and after performances and perform any minor repairs. Collaborate with production designers, costume designers, and other production staff in order to discuss and execute costume design details. Create worksheets for dressing lists, show notes, and costume checks. Distribute costumes and related equipment and keep records of item status. Examine costume fit on cast members and sketch or write notes for alterations. Inventory stock in order to determine types and conditions of available costuming. Monitor, maintain, and secure inventories of costumes, wigs, and makeup, providing keys or access to assigned directors, costume designers, and wardrobe mistresses/masters. Provide assistance to cast members in wearing costumes or assign cast dressers to assist specific cast members with costume changes. Return borrowed or rented items when productions are complete and return other items to storage. Design and construct costumes or send them to tailors for construction, major repairs, or alterations. Direct the work of wardrobe crews during dress rehearsals and performances. Participate in the hiring, training, scheduling, and supervision of alteration workers. Provide managers with budget recommendations and take responsibility for budgetary line items related to costumes, storage, and makeup needs. Purchase, rent, or

C

requisition costumes and other wardrobe necessities. **SKILLS**—Management of Financial Resources; Management of Material Resources; Repairing; Time Management.

GOE—Interest Area: 01. Arts, Entertainment, and Media. **Work Group:** 01.09 Modeling and Personal Appearance. **Other Apprenticeable Jobs in This Work Group:** No other apprenticeable jobs in this group. **PERSONALITY TYPE:** Artistic. Artistic occupations frequently involve working with forms, designs, and patterns. They often require self-expression, and the work can be done without following a clear set of rules.

RELATED KNOWLEDGE/COURSES— Fine Arts: Knowledge of the theory and techniques required to compose, produce, and perform works of music, dance, visual arts, drama, and sculpture. **Design:** Knowledge of design techniques, tools, and principles involved in production of precision technical plans, blueprints, drawings, and models. **Sociology and Anthropology:** Knowledge of group behavior and dynamics, societal trends and influences, human migrations, ethnicity, and cultures and their history and origins. **Geography:** Knowledge of principles and methods for describing the features of land, sea, and air masses, including their physical characteristics; locations; interrelationships; and distribution of plant, animal, and human life. **History and Archeology:** Knowledge of historical events and their causes, indicators, and effects on civilizations and cultures.

WORK ENVIRONMENT—Indoors; spend time kneeling, crouching, stooping, or crawling; standing; sitting; using hands on objects, tools, or controls; spend time bending or twisting the body.

Crane and Tower Operators

- Growth: 10.8%
- Annual Job Openings: 5,000
- Annual Earnings: $37,150
- Percentage of Women: 3.4%

Related Apprenticeship	*Years*
Truck-Crane Operator	3

Operate mechanical boom and cable or tower and cable equipment to lift and move materials, machines, or products in many directions. Determine load weights and check them against lifting capacities in order to prevent overload. Direct helpers engaged in placing blocking and outrigging under cranes. Load and unload bundles from trucks and move containers to storage bins, using moving equipment. Move levers, depress foot pedals, and turn dials to operate cranes, cherry pickers, electromagnets, or other moving equipment for lifting, moving, and placing loads. Review daily work and delivery schedules to determine orders, sequences of deliveries, and special loading instructions. Weigh bundles, using floor scales, and record weights for company records. Clean, lubricate, and maintain mechanisms such as cables, pulleys, and grappling devices, making repairs as necessary. Direct truck drivers backing vehicles into loading bays and cover, uncover, and secure loads for delivery. Inspect and adjust crane mechanisms and lifting accessories in order to prevent malfunctions and damage. Inspect bundle packaging for conformance to regulations and customer requirements and remove and batch packaging tickets. Inspect cables and grappling devices for wear and install or replace cables as needed. **SKILLS**—Operation and Control; Repairing; Installation; Equipment Maintenance; Operation Monitoring; Equipment Selection; Coordination.

GOE—**Interest Area:** 08. Industrial Production. **Work Group:** 08.07 Hands-on Work: Loading, Moving, Hoisting, and Conveying. **Other Apprenticeable Jobs in This Work Group:** Conveyor Operators and Tenders; Dragline Operators; Tank Car, Truck, and Ship Loaders. **PERSONALITY TYPE:** Realistic. Realistic occupations frequently involve work activities that include practical, hands-on problems and solutions. They often deal with plants, animals, and real-world materials like wood, tools, and machinery. Many of the occupations require working outside and do not involve a lot of paperwork or working closely with others.

RELATED KNOWLEDGE/COURSES— **Mechanical Devices:** Knowledge of machines and tools, including their designs, uses, repair, and maintenance. **Transportation:** Knowledge of principles and methods for moving people or goods by air, rail, sea, or road, including the relative costs and benefits. **Clerical Practices:** Knowledge of administrative and clerical procedures and systems, such as word processing, managing files and records, stenography and transcription, designing forms, and other office procedures and terminology. **Building and Construction:** Knowledge of the materials, methods, and tools involved in the construction or repair of houses, buildings, or other structures, such as highways and roads.

WORK ENVIRONMENT—Outdoors; hazardous equipment; climbing ladders, scaffolds, or poles; exposed to whole-body vibration; high places.

Cutting and Slicing Machine Operators and Tenders

- Growth: 6.6%
- Annual Job Openings: 12,000
- Annual Earnings: $26,060
- Percentage of Women: 26.9%

Related Apprenticeship	Years
Stone-Lathe Operator	3

Operate or tend machines to cut or slice any of a wide variety of products or materials, such as tobacco, food, paper, roofing slate, glass, stone, rubber, cork, and insulating material. Starts cutting machine by pressing button, pulling lever, or depressing pedal to cut stock, following markings or specifications. Stops cutting machine when necessary, by pulling lever, pressing button, or depressing pedal, and removes debris. Observes cutting machine in operation to ensure even flow of stock and to detect jamming, improper feeding, or foreign materials. Feeds stock into cutting machine, onto conveyor, or under cutting blades by threading, guiding, pushing, or turning handwheel. Marks cutting lines or identifying information on stock, using marking pencil, ruler, or scribe. Stacks and sorts cut material according to type and size for packaging, further processing, or shipping. Moves stock or scrap to and from machine transporting, either manually or using cart, handtruck, or lift truck. Records data concerning amount and type of stock cut from duties performed, including weight, length, and width. Cleans and lubricates cutting machine, conveyors, blades, saws, or knives, using steam hose, scrapers, brush, or oil cans. Cuts stock manually to prepare for machine cutting, using tools such as knife, cleaver, handsaw, or hammer and chisel. Sharpens cutting blades, knives, or saws, using file, bench grinder, or honing stone. Examines and measures stock to ensure conformance to specifications, using ruler, gauge, micrometer or scale, and removes defects. Installs or replaces cutting knives, blades, or wheels in cutting machine, using hand tools. Positions stock along cutting lines, or against stops, on bed of scoring or cutting machine. Reads work order or receives oral instructions regarding specifications for stock to be cut. Adjusts feeding guides, blades, settings, or speed to regulate specified depth, length, or width of material, using hand tools or hands. **SKILLS**—Operation Monitoring; Operation and Control; Installation; Equipment Maintenance; Troubleshooting.

GOE—Interest Area: 08. Industrial Production. **Work Group:** 08.03 Production Work. **Other Apprenticeable Jobs in This Work Group:** Bakers, Manufacturing; Bindery Machine Operators and Tenders; Chemical Equipment Controllers and Operators; Coating, Painting, and Spraying Machine Operators and Tenders; Cooling and Freezing Equipment Operators and Tenders; Crushing, Grinding, and Polishing Machine Setters, Operators, and Tenders; Cutters and Trimmers, Hand; Design Printing Machine Setters and Set-Up Operators; Electrolytic Plating and Coating Machine Setters and Set-Up Operators, Metal and Plastic; Electrotypers and Stereotypers; Embossing Machine Set-Up Operators; Engraver Set-Up Operators; Extruding, Forming, Pressing, and Compacting Machine Operators and Tenders;

Fabric and Apparel Patternmakers; Film Laboratory Technicians; Fitters, Structural Metal—Precision; Food Batchmakers; Furnace, Kiln, Oven, Drier, and Kettle Operators and Tenders; Hand Compositors and Typesetters; Job Printers; Letterpress Setters and Set-Up Operators; Metal Fabricators, Structural Metal Products; Metal-Refining Furnace Operators and Tenders; Mixing and Blending Machine Setters, Operators, and Tenders; Mold Makers, Hand; Molding and Casting Workers; Numerical Control Machine Tool Operators and Tenders, Metal and Plastic; Offset Lithographic Press Setters and Set-Up Operators; Painting, Coating, and Decorating Workers; Photographic Processing Machine Operators; Photographic Reproduction Technicians; Photographic Retouchers and Restorers; Plate Finishers; Platemakers; Precision Printing Workers; Printing Press Machine Operators and Tenders; Production Workers, All Other; Sawing Machine Operators and Tenders; Sawing Machine Setters and Set-Up Operators; Scanner Operators; Separating, Filtering, Clarifying, Precipitating, and Still Machine Setters, Operators, and Tenders; Sewing Machine Operators, Garment; Slaughterers and Meat Packers; Stone Sawyers; Strippers; Team Assemblers; Welder-Fitters; Welders and Cutters; Woodworking Machine Operators and Tenders, Except Sawing. **PERSONALITY TYPE:** Realistic. Realistic occupations frequently involve work activities that include practical, hands-on problems and solutions. They often deal with plants, animals, and real-world materials like wood, tools, and machinery. Many of the occupations require working outside and do not involve a lot of paperwork or working closely with others.

RELATED KNOWLEDGE/COURSES—Production and Processing: Knowledge of raw materials, production processes, quality control, costs, and other techniques for maximizing the effective manufacture and distribution of goods. **Mechanical Devices:** Knowledge of machines and tools, including their designs, uses, repair, and maintenance. **Food Production:** Knowledge of techniques and equipment for planting, growing, and harvesting food products (both plant and animal) for consumption, including storage/handling techniques. **Design:** Knowledge of design techniques, tools, and principles involved in production of precision technical plans, blueprints, drawings, and models. **Physics:** Knowledge and prediction of physical principles and laws and their interrelationships and applications to understanding fluid, material, and atmospheric dynamics and mechanical, electrical, atomic, and subatomic structures and processes.

WORK ENVIRONMENT—Hazardous equipment; minor burns, cuts, bites, or stings; common protective or safety equipment; using hands on objects, tools, or controls; indoors; standing.

Data Entry Keyers

- ◉ Growth: –5.4%
- ◉ Annual Job Openings: 72,000
- ◉ Annual Earnings: $22,600
- ◉ Percentage of Women: 81.8%

Related Apprenticeship	Years
Photocomposing-Perforator-Machine Operator	2

Operate data entry device, such as keyboard or photo-composing perforator. Duties may include verifying data and preparing materials for printing. Compare data with source documents or re-enter data in verification format to detect errors. Compile, sort, and verify the accuracy of data before it is entered. Locate and correct data entry errors or report them to supervisors. Maintain logs of activities and completed work. Read source documents such as canceled checks, sales reports, or bills and enter data in specific data fields or onto tapes or disks for subsequent entry, using keyboards or scanners. Load machines with required input or output media, such as paper, cards, disks, tape, or Braille media. Resolve garbled or indecipherable messages, using cryptographic procedures and equipment. Select materials needed to complete work assignments. Store completed documents in appropriate locations. **SKILLS**—Reading Comprehension.

GOE—**Interest Area:** 09. Business Detail. **Work Group:** 09.09 Clerical Machine Operation. **Other Apprenticeable Jobs in This Work Group:** Computer Operators; Postal Service Clerks; Typesetting and Composing Machine Operators and Tenders; Word Processors and Typists. **PERSONALITY TYPE:** Conventional. Conventional occupations frequently involve following set procedures and routines. These occupations can include working with data and details more than with ideas. Usually there is a clear line of authority to follow.

RELATED KNOWLEDGE/COURSES—**Clerical Practices:** Knowledge of administrative and clerical procedures and systems, such as word processing, managing files and records, stenography and transcription, designing forms, and other office procedures and terminology. **Computers and Electronics:** Knowledge of circuit boards, processors, chips, electronic equipment, and computer hardware and software, including applications and programming.

WORK ENVIRONMENT—Spend time making repetitive motions; sitting; indoors; using hands on objects, tools, or controls.

Data Processing Equipment Repairers

- Growth: 15.1%
- Annual Job Openings: 19,000
- Annual Earnings: $33,780
- Percentage of Women: 13.5%

Related Apprenticeship	Years
Electronics Mechanic	4

(This is one of the most popular apprenticeable jobs.)

Repair, maintain, and install computer hardware such as peripheral equipment and word processing systems. Replaces defective components and wiring. Tests faulty equipment and applies knowledge of functional operation of electronic units and systems to diagnose cause of malfunction. Aligns, adjusts, and calibrates equipment according to specifications. Calibrates testing instruments. Adjusts mechanical parts, using hand tools and soldering iron. Converses with equipment operators to ascertain problems with equipment before breakdown or cause of breakdown. Tests electronic components and circuits to locate defects, using oscil-

loscopes, signal generators, ammeters, and voltmeters. Maintains records of repairs, calibrations, and tests. Enters information into computer to copy program from one electronic component to another or to draw, modify, or store schematics. **SKILLS**—Installation; Repairing; Troubleshooting; Equipment Maintenance; Science; Operation Monitoring; Quality Control Analysis; Operation and Control.

GOE—Interest Area: 05. Mechanics, Installers, and Repairers. **Work Group:** 05.02 Electrical and Electronic Systems. **Other Apprenticeable Jobs in This Work Group:** Avionics Technicians; Battery Repairers; Central Office and PBX Installers and Repairers; Communication Equipment Mechanics, Installers, and Repairers; Electric Home Appliance and Power Tool Repairers; Electric Meter Installers and Repairers; Electric Motor and Switch Assemblers and Repairers; Electrical and Electronics Installers and Repairers, Transportation Equipment; Electrical and Electronics Repairers, Commercial and Industrial Equipment; Electrical and Electronics Repairers, Powerhouse, Substation, and Relay; Electrical Power-Line Installers and Repairers; Electronic Equipment Installers and Repairers, Motor Vehicles; Electronic Home Entertainment Equipment Installers and Repairers; Elevator Installers and Repairers; Installation, Maintenance, and Repair Workers, All Other; Office Machine and Cash Register Servicers; Radio Mechanics; Signal and Track Switch Repairers; Station Installers and Repairers, Telephone; Telecommunications Line Installers and Repairers; Transformer Repairers. **PERSONALITY TYPE:** Realistic. Realistic occupations frequently involve work activities that include practical, hands-on problems and solutions. They often deal with plants, animals, and real-world materials like wood, tools, and machinery. Many of the occupations require working outside and do not involve a lot of paperwork or working closely with others.

RELATED KNOWLEDGE/COURSES— Computers and Electronics: Knowledge of circuit boards, processors, chips, electronic equipment, and computer hardware and software, including applications and programming. **Telecommunications:** Knowledge of transmission, broadcasting, switching, control, and operation of telecommunications systems. **Design:** Knowledge of design techniques, tools, and principles involved in production of precision technical plans, blueprints, drawings, and models. **Mechanical Devices:** Knowledge of machines and tools, including their designs, uses, repair, and maintenance. **Engineering and Technology:** Knowledge of the practical application of engineering science and technology. This includes applying principles, techniques, procedures, and equipment to the design and production of various goods and services. **Physics:** Knowledge and prediction of physical principles and laws and their interrelationships and applications to understanding fluid, material, and atmospheric dynamics and mechanical, electrical, atomic, and subatomic structures and processes.

WORK ENVIRONMENT—Indoors; hazardous conditions; spend time kneeling, crouching, stooping, or crawling; using hands on objects, tools, or controls; sitting.

Dental Assistants

- Growth: 42.5%
- Annual Job Openings: 35,000
- Annual Earnings: $27,700
- Percentage of Women: 97.1%

Related Apprenticeship	*Years*
Dental Assistant	1

Assist dentist, set up patient and equipment, and keep records. Prepare patient, sterilize and disinfect instruments, set up instrument trays, prepare materials, and assist dentist during dental procedures. Expose dental diagnostic X rays. Record treatment information in patient records. Take and record medical and dental histories and vital signs of patients. Provide postoperative instructions prescribed by dentist. Assist dentist in management of medical and dental emergencies. Pour, trim, and polish study casts. Instruct patients in oral hygiene and plaque control programs. Make preliminary impressions for study casts and occlusal registrations for mounting study casts. Clean and polish removable appliances. Clean teeth, using dental instruments. Apply protective coating of fluoride to teeth. Fabricate temporary restorations and custom impressions from preliminary impressions. Schedule appointments, prepare bills and receive payment for dental services, complete insurance forms, and maintain records, manually or using computer. **SKILLS**—Social Perceptiveness; Equipment Maintenance; Instructing; Service Orientation; Time Management; Persuasion; Management of Material Resources; Learning Strategies; Operation and Control.

GOE—Interest Area: 14. Medical and Health Services. **Work Group:** 14.03 Dentistry. **Other Apprenticeable Jobs in This Work Group:** No other apprenticeable jobs in this group. **PERSONALITY TYPE:** Social. Social occupations frequently involve working with, communicating with, and teaching people. These occupations often involve helping or providing service to others.

D

RELATED KNOWLEDGE/COURSES—
Medicine and Dentistry: Knowledge of the
information and techniques needed to diagnose
and treat human injuries, diseases, and deformities. This includes symptoms, treatment alternatives, drug properties and interactions, and
preventive health-care measures. **Customer and
Personal Service:** Knowledge of principles and
processes for providing customer and personal
services. This includes customer needs assessment, meeting quality standards for services,
and evaluation of customer satisfaction. **Clerical Practices:** Knowledge of administrative and
clerical procedures and systems, such as word
processing, managing files and records, stenography and transcription, designing forms, and
other office procedures and terminology.
Chemistry: Knowledge of the chemical composition, structure, and properties of substances
and of the chemical processes and transformations that they undergo. This includes uses of
chemicals, their danger signs, production techniques, and disposal methods. **Psychology:**
Knowledge of human behavior and performance; individual differences in ability, personality, and interests; learning and motivation;
psychological research methods; and the assessment and treatment of behavioral and affective
disorders. **Computers and Electronics:** Knowledge of circuit boards, processors, chips, electronic equipment, and computer hardware and
software, including applications and programming. **Public Safety and Security:** Knowledge
of relevant equipment, policies, procedures, and
strategies to promote effective local, state, or
national security operations for the protection
of people, data, property, and institutions.

WORK ENVIRONMENT—Physical proxim-
ity; contaminants; disease or infections; sounds,
noise levels are distracting or uncomfortable;
extremely bright or inadequate lighting; sitting.

Design Printing Machine Setters and Set-Up Operators

- Growth: 4.6%
- Annual Job Openings: 30,000
- Annual Earnings: $29,340
- Percentage of Women: 17.8%

Related Apprenticeship	*Years*
Lithograph-Press Operator, Tinware	4
Printer, Plastic	4
Wallpaper Printer I	4

**Set up or set up and operate machines to print
designs on materials.** Installs printing plates,
cylinders, or rollers on machine, using hand
tools and gauges. Measures and records amount
of product produced. Repairs or replaces worn
or broken parts, using hand tools. Cleans and
lubricates equipment. Inspects product to
detect defects. Mixes colors of paint according
to formulas. Adjusts and changes gears, using
hand tools. Fills reservoirs with paint or ink.
Adjusts feed guides, gauges, and rollers, using
hand tools. Monitors machines and gauges to
ensure and maintain standards. SKILLS—
Repairing; Operation Monitoring; Equipment
Maintenance; Operation and Control; Technology Design; Installation; Troubleshooting;
Equipment Selection.

GOE—Interest Area: 08. Industrial Production.
Work Group: 08.03 Production Work. **Other**

Apprenticeable Jobs in This Work Group: Bakers, Manufacturing; Bindery Machine Operators and Tenders; Chemical Equipment Controllers and Operators; Coating, Painting, and Spraying Machine Operators and Tenders; Cooling and Freezing Equipment Operators and Tenders; Crushing, Grinding, and Polishing Machine Setters, Operators, and Tenders; Cutters and Trimmers, Hand; Cutting and Slicing Machine Operators and Tenders; Electrolytic Plating and Coating Machine Setters and Set-Up Operators, Metal and Plastic; Electrotypers and Stereotypers; Embossing Machine Set-Up Operators; Engraver Set-Up Operators; Extruding, Forming, Pressing, and Compacting Machine Operators and Tenders; Fabric and Apparel Patternmakers; Film Laboratory Technicians; Fitters, Structural Metal—Precision; Food Batchmakers; Furnace, Kiln, Oven, Drier, and Kettle Operators and Tenders; Hand Compositors and Typesetters; Job Printers; Letterpress Setters and Set-Up Operators; Metal Fabricators, Structural Metal Products; Metal-Refining Furnace Operators and Tenders; Mixing and Blending Machine Setters, Operators, and Tenders; Mold Makers, Hand; Molding and Casting Workers; Numerical Control Machine Tool Operators and Tenders, Metal and Plastic; Offset Lithographic Press Setters and Set-Up Operators; Painting, Coating, and Decorating Workers; Photographic Processing Machine Operators; Photographic Reproduction Technicians; Photographic Retouchers and Restorers; Plate Finishers; Platemakers; Precision Printing Workers; Printing Press Machine Operators and Tenders; Production Workers, All Other; Sawing Machine Operators and Tenders; Sawing Machine Setters and Set-Up Operators; Scanner Operators; Separating, Filtering, Clarifying, Precipitating, and Still Machine Setters, Operators, and Tenders; Sewing Machine Operators, Garment; Slaughterers and Meat Packers; Stone Sawyers; Strippers; Team Assemblers; Welder-Fitters; Welders and Cutters; Woodworking Machine Operators and Tenders, Except Sawing. **PERSONALITY TYPE:** Realistic. Realistic occupations frequently involve work activities that include practical, hands-on problems and solutions. They often deal with plants, animals, and real-world materials like wood, tools, and machinery. Many of the occupations require working outside and do not involve a lot of paperwork or working closely with others.

RELATED KNOWLEDGE/COURSES—Mechanical Devices: Knowledge of machines and tools, including their designs, uses, repair, and maintenance. **Engineering and Technology:** Knowledge of the practical application of engineering science and technology. This includes applying principles, techniques, procedures, and equipment to the design and production of various goods and services. **Production and Processing:** Knowledge of raw materials, production processes, quality control, costs, and other techniques for maximizing the effective manufacture and distribution of goods.

WORK ENVIRONMENT—Hazardous equipment; spend time making repetitive motions; indoors; common protective or safety equipment; spend time kneeling, crouching, stooping, or crawling; spend time bending or twisting the body.

Desktop Publishers

- Growth: 29.2%
- Annual Job Openings: 4,000
- Annual Earnings: $31,590
- Percentage of Women: 65.9%

Related Apprenticeship	Years
Electronic Prepress System Operator	5

Format typescript and graphic elements, using computer software, to produce publication-ready material. Check preliminary and final proofs for errors and make necessary corrections. Operate desktop publishing software and equipment to design, lay out, and produce camera-ready copy. View monitors for visual representation of work in progress and for instructions and feedback throughout process, making modifications as necessary. Enter text into computer keyboard and select the size and style of type, column width, and appropriate spacing for printed materials. Store copies of publications on paper, magnetic tape, film, or diskette. Position text and art elements from a variety of databases in a visually appealing way in order to design print or Web pages, using knowledge of type styles and size and layout patterns. Enter digitized data into electronic prepress system computer memory, using scanner, camera, keyboard, or mouse. Edit graphics and photos, using pixel or bitmap editing, airbrushing, masking, or image retouching. Import text and art elements such as electronic clip art or electronic files from photographs that have been scanned or produced with a digital camera, using computer software. Prepare sample layouts for approval, using computer software. Study layout or other design instructions to determine work to be done and sequence of operations. Load floppy disks or tapes containing information into system. Convert various types of files for printing or for the Internet, using computer software. Enter data, such as coordinates of images and color specifications, into system to retouch and make color corrections. Select number of colors and determine color separations. Transmit, deliver, or mail publication master to printer for production into film and plates. Collaborate with graphic artists, editors, and writers to produce master copies according to design specifications. Create special effects such as vignettes, mosaics, and image combining and add elements such as sound and animation to electronic publications. **SKILLS**—Time Management; Service Orientation; Instructing; Active Listening; Operation and Control; Operations Analysis; Technology Design; Reading Comprehension; Writing.

GOE—Interest Area: 01. Arts, Entertainment, and Media. **Work Group:** 01.07 Graphic Arts. **Other Apprenticeable Jobs in This Work Group:** Camera Operators; Dot Etchers; Engravers, Hand; Engravers/Carvers; Pantograph Engravers; Paste-Up Workers; Photoengravers; Precision Etchers and Engravers, Hand or Machine. **PERSONALITY TYPE:** Realistic. Realistic occupations frequently involve work activities that include practical, hands-on problems and solutions. They often deal with plants, animals, and real-world materials like wood, tools, and machinery. Many of the occupations require working outside and do not involve a lot of paperwork or working closely with others.

RELATED KNOWLEDGE/COURSES— Computers and Electronics: Knowledge of circuit boards, processors, chips, electronic equipment, and computer hardware and software, including applications and programming. **Production and Processing:** Knowledge of raw materials, production processes, quality control, costs, and other techniques for maximizing the effective manufacture and distribution of goods. **Customer and Personal Service:** Knowledge of principles and processes for providing customer and personal services. This includes customer needs assessment, meeting quality standards for services, and evaluation of customer satisfaction. **English Language:** Knowledge of the structure and content of the English language, including the meaning and spelling of words, rules of composition, and grammar. **Clerical Practices:** Knowledge of administrative and clerical procedures and systems, such as word processing, managing files and records, stenography and transcription, designing forms, and other office procedures and terminology. **Administration and Management:** Knowledge of business and management principles involved in strategic planning, resource allocation, human resources modeling, leadership technique, production methods, and coordination of people and resources.

WORK ENVIRONMENT—Sitting; physical proximity; indoors; sounds, noise levels are distracting or uncomfortable; contaminants.

Dispatchers, Except Police, Fire, and Ambulance

- Growth: 14.4%
- Annual Job Openings: 28,000
- Annual Earnings: $30,390
- Percentage of Women: 53.1%

Related Apprenticeship	*Years*
Dispatcher, Service	2

Schedule and dispatch workers, work crews, equipment, or service vehicles for conveyance of materials, freight, or passengers or for normal installation, service, or emergency repairs rendered outside the place of business. Duties may include using radio, telephone, or computer to transmit assignments and compiling statistics and reports on work progress. Schedule and dispatch workers, work crews, equipment, or service vehicles to appropriate locations according to customer requests, specifications, or needs, using radios or telephones. Arrange for necessary repairs in order to restore service and schedules. Relay work orders, messages, and information to or from work crews, supervisors, and field inspectors using telephones or two-way radios. Confer with customers or supervising personnel in order to address questions, problems, and requests for service or equipment. Prepare daily work and run schedules. Receive or prepare work orders. Oversee all communications within specifically assigned territories. Monitor personnel and/or equipment locations and utilization in order to coordinate service and schedules. Record and maintain files and records of customer requests, work or services performed, charges, expenses, inventory, and other dispatch information. Determine types or amounts of equipment, vehicles, materials, or personnel required according to work orders or specifications. Advise personnel about traffic problems such as construction areas, accidents, congestion, weather conditions, and other hazards. Ensure timely and efficient movement of trains according to train orders and schedules. Order supplies and equipment and issue them to personnel. **SKILLS**—Service Orientation; Learning Strategies; Operations Analysis; Instructing; Management of Personnel Resources; Critical Thinking; Time Management; Social Perceptiveness.

GOE—**Interest Area:** 09. Business Detail. **Work Group:** 09.06 Communications. **Other Apprenticeable Jobs in This Work Group:** Police, Fire, and Ambulance Dispatchers. **PERSONALITY TYPE:** Conventional. Conventional occupations frequently involve following set procedures and routines. These occupations can include working with data and details more than with ideas. Usually there is a clear line of authority to follow.

RELATED KNOWLEDGE/COURSES— Transportation: Knowledge of principles and methods for moving people or goods by air, rail, sea, or road, including the relative costs and benefits. **Clerical Practices:** Knowledge of administrative and clerical procedures and systems, such as word processing, managing files and records, stenography and transcription, designing forms, and other office procedures and terminology. **Public Safety and Security:** Knowledge of relevant equipment, policies, procedures, and strategies to promote effective local, state, or national security operations for the protection of people, data, property, and institutions. **Customer and Personal Service:** Knowledge of principles and processes for providing customer and personal services. This includes customer needs assessment, meeting quality standards for services, and evaluation of customer satisfaction. **Computers and Electronics:** Knowledge of circuit boards, processors, chips, electronic equipment, and computer hardware and software, including applications and programming. **Communications and Media:** Knowledge of media production, communication, and dissemination techniques and methods. This includes alternative ways to inform and entertain via written, oral, and visual media.

WORK ENVIRONMENT—Sitting; sounds, noise levels are distracting or uncomfortable; physical proximity; contaminants; very hot or cold.

Dot Etchers

- Growth: –11.2%
- Annual Job Openings: 6,000
- Annual Earnings: $31,660
- Percentage of Women: 47.6%

Related Apprenticeship	Years
Dot Etcher	5

Increase or reduce size of photographic dots by chemical or photomechanical methods to make color corrections on halftone negatives or positives to be used in preparation of lithographic printing plates. Places masks over separation negatives or positives and exposes film for specified time, using contact frame and automatic film processor to reduce size of photographic dots to increase or reduce color. Prepares photographic masks to protect areas of film not needing correction, using contact frame and automatic film processor or by manually cutting masking material to correct color by photomechanical method. Compares proof print of color separation negative or positive with customer's original copy and standard color chart to determine accuracy of reproduction. Examines film on light table to determine specified color and color balance, using magnifying glass or densitometer. Identifies and marks color discrepancies on print and film. Applies opaque to defective areas of film to block out blemishes and pinholes. Determines extent of correction and exposure length needed based on experience or predetermined exposure and color charts. Prepares dyes and other chemical solutions according to standard and applies solution to inaccurately colored areas of film to correct color by chemical method. Blocks out or modifies color shades of film, using template, brushes, and opaque. **SKILLS**—Equipment Selection; Operations Analysis.

GOE—Interest Area: 01. Arts, Entertainment, and Media. **Work Group:** 01.07 Graphic Arts. **Other Apprenticeable Jobs in This Work Group:** Camera Operators; Desktop Publishers; Engravers, Hand; Engravers/Carvers; Pantograph Engravers; Paste-Up Workers; Photoengravers; Precision Etchers and Engravers, Hand or Machine. **PERSONALITY TYPE:** Realistic. Realistic occupations frequently involve work activities that include practical, hands-on problems and solutions. They often deal with plants, animals, and real-world materials like wood, tools, and machinery. Many of the occupations require working outside and do not involve a lot of paperwork or working closely with others.

RELATED KNOWLEDGE/COURSES— **Fine Arts:** Knowledge of the theory and techniques required to compose, produce, and perform works of music, dance, visual arts, drama, and sculpture. **Chemistry:** Knowledge of the chemical composition, structure, and properties of substances and of the chemical processes and transformations that they undergo. This includes uses of chemicals, their danger signs, production techniques, and disposal methods. **Production and Processing:** Knowledge of raw materials, production processes, quality control, costs, and other techniques for maximizing the effective manufacture and distribution of goods.

WORK ENVIRONMENT—Extremely bright or inadequate lighting; sitting; using hands on objects, tools, or controls; exposed to radiation; hazardous conditions.

Dragline Operators

- Growth: 8.9%
- Annual Job Openings: 14,000
- Annual Earnings: $32,150
- Percentage of Women: 1.8%

Related Apprenticeship	Years
Dragline Operator	1

Operate power-driven crane equipment with dragline bucket to excavate or move sand, gravel, mud, or other materials. Moves controls to position boom, lower and drag bucket through material, and release material at unloading point. Directs workers engaged in placing blocks and outriggers to prevent capsizing of machine when lifting heavy loads. Drives machine to work site. **SKILLS**—Operation and Control; Operation Monitoring; Coordination.

GOE—Interest Area: 08. Industrial Production. **Work Group:** 08.07 Hands-on Work: Loading, Moving, Hoisting, and Conveying. **Other Apprenticeable Jobs in This Work Group:** Conveyor Operators and Tenders; Crane and Tower Operators; Tank Car, Truck, and Ship Loaders. **PERSONALITY TYPE:**

Realistic. Realistic occupations frequently involve work activities that include practical, hands-on problems and solutions. They often deal with plants, animals, and real-world materials like wood, tools, and machinery. Many of the occupations require working outside and do not involve a lot of paperwork or working closely with others.

RELATED KNOWLEDGE/COURSES— Building and Construction: Knowledge of the materials, methods, and tools involved in the construction or repair of houses, buildings, or other structures, such as highways and roads. **Transportation:** Knowledge of principles and methods for moving people or goods by air, rail, sea, or road, including the relative costs and benefits. **Physics:** Knowledge and prediction of physical principles and laws and their interrelationships and applications to understanding fluid, material, and atmospheric dynamics and mechanical, electrical, atomic, and subatomic structures and processes. **Public Safety and Security:** Knowledge of relevant equipment, policies, procedures, and strategies to promote effective local, state, or national security operations for the protection of people, data, property, and institutions. **Engineering and Technology:** Knowledge of the practical application of engineering science and technology. This includes applying principles, techniques, procedures, and equipment to the design and production of various goods and services. **Mechanical Devices:** Knowledge of machines and tools, including their designs, uses, repair, and maintenance.

WORK ENVIRONMENT—Outdoors; exposed to whole-body vibration; hazardous equipment; extremely bright or inadequate lighting; very hot or cold.

Dredge Operators

- Growth: 8.9%
- Annual Job Openings: 14,000
- Annual Earnings: $27,800
- Percentage of Women: 1.8%

Related Apprenticeship	Years
Dredge Operator	4

Operate dredge to remove sand, gravel, or other materials from lakes, rivers, or streams and to excavate and maintain navigable channels in waterways. Starts and stops engines to operate equipment. Directs workers placing shore anchors and cables, laying additional pipes from dredge to shore, and pumping water from pontoons. Lowers anchor pole to verify depth of excavation, using winch, or scans depth gauge to determine depth of excavation. Moves levers to position dredge for excavation, engage hydraulic pump, raise and lower suction boom, and control rotation of cutterhead. Starts power winch that draws in or lets out cable to change position of dredge or pulls in and lets out cable manually. **SKILLS**—Operation Monitoring; Operation and Control; Management of Personnel Resources; Coordination.

GOE—Interest Area: 07. Transportation. **Work Group:** 07.04 Water Vehicle Operation. **Other Apprenticeable Jobs in This Work Group:** Able Seamen; Pilots, Ship. **PERSONALITY TYPE:** Realistic. Realistic occupations frequently involve work activities that include practical, hands-on problems and solutions.

They often deal with plants, animals, and real-world materials like wood, tools, and machinery. Many of the occupations require working outside and do not involve a lot of paperwork or working closely with others.

RELATED KNOWLEDGE/COURSES— **Engineering and Technology:** Knowledge of the practical application of engineering science and technology. This includes applying principles, techniques, procedures, and equipment to the design and production of various goods and services. **Mechanical Devices:** Knowledge of machines and tools, including their designs, uses, repair, and maintenance. **Physics:** Knowledge and prediction of physical principles and laws and their interrelationships and applications to understanding fluid, material, and atmospheric dynamics and mechanical, electrical, atomic, and subatomic structures and processes. **Transportation:** Knowledge of principles and methods for moving people or goods by air, rail, sea, or road, including the relative costs and benefits. **Geography:** Knowledge of principles and methods for describing the features of land, sea, and air masses, including their physical characteristics; locations; interrelationships; and distribution of plant, animal, and human life. **Public Safety and Security:** Knowledge of relevant equipment, policies, procedures, and strategies to promote effective local, state, or national security operations for the protection of people, data, property, and institutions.

WORK ENVIRONMENT—Outdoors; hazardous equipment; exposed to whole-body vibration; sounds, noise levels are distracting or uncomfortable; minor burns, cuts, bites, or stings; using hands on objects, tools, or controls.

Drywall Installers

- Growth: 21.4%
- Annual Job Openings: 17,000
- Annual Earnings: $33,670
- Percentage of Women: 2.7%

Related Apprenticeship	Years
Dry-Wall Applicator	2

Apply plasterboard or other wallboard to ceilings and interior walls of buildings. Trims rough edges from wallboard to maintain even joints, using knife. Fits and fastens wallboard or sheetrock into specified position, using hand tools, portable power tools, or adhesive. Measures and marks cutting lines on framing, drywall, and trim, using tape measure, straightedge or square, and marking devices. Installs blanket insulation between studs and tacks plastic moisture barrier over insulation. Removes plaster, drywall, or paneling, using crowbar and hammer. Assembles and installs metal framing and decorative trim for windows, doorways, and bents. Reads blueprints and other specifications to determine method of installation, work procedures, and material and tool requirements. Lays out reference lines and points, computes position of framing and furring channels, and marks position, using chalkline. Suspends angle iron grid and channel iron from ceiling, using wire. Installs horizontal and vertical metal or wooden studs for attachment of wallboard on interior walls, using hand tools. Cuts metal or wood framing, angle and channel iron, and trim to size, using cutting tools. Cuts openings into board for electrical outlets, windows, vents, or fixtures, using keyhole saw or other cutting tools. **SKILLS**—Installation; Equipment Selection.

GOE—**Interest Area:** 06. Construction, Mining, and Drilling. **Work Group:** 06.02 Construction. **Other Apprenticeable Jobs in This Work Group:** Boat Builders and Shipwrights; Boilermakers; Brickmasons and Blockmasons; Carpet Installers; Ceiling Tile Installers; Cement Masons and Concrete Finishers; Construction and Related Workers, All Other; Construction Carpenters; Electricians; Fence Erectors; Floor Layers, Except Carpet, Wood, and Hard Tiles; Glaziers; Grader, Bulldozer, and Scraper Operators; Insulation Workers, Floor, Ceiling, and Wall; Insulation Workers, Mechanical; Operating Engineers; Painters, Construction and Maintenance; Paperhangers; Paving, Surfacing, and Tamping Equipment Operators; Pipe Fitters; Plasterers and Stucco Masons; Plumbers; Reinforcing Iron and Rebar Workers; Riggers; Roofers; Rough Carpenters; Sheet Metal Workers; Ship Carpenters and Joiners; Stone Cutters and Carvers; Stonemasons; Structural Iron and Steel Workers; Tapers; Terrazzo Workers and Finishers; Tile and Marble Setters. **PERSONALITY TYPE:** Realistic. Realistic occupations frequently involve work activities that include practical, hands-on problems and solutions. They often deal with plants, animals, and real-world materials like wood, tools, and machinery. Many of the occupations require working outside and do not involve a lot of paperwork or working closely with others.

RELATED KNOWLEDGE/COURSES— **Building and Construction:** Knowledge of the materials, methods, and tools involved in the construction or repair of houses, buildings, or other structures, such as highways and roads. **Design:** Knowledge of design techniques, tools, and principles involved in production of precision technical plans, blueprints, drawings, and models. **Engineering and Technology:** Knowledge of the practical application of engineering science and technology. This includes applying principles, techniques, procedures, and equipment to the design and production of various goods and services. **Mechanical Devices:** Knowledge of machines and tools, including their designs, uses, repair, and maintenance.

WORK ENVIRONMENT—Climbing ladders, scaffolds, or poles; contaminants; cramped work space, awkward positions; hazardous equipment; minor burns, cuts, bites, or stings.

Electric Home Appliance and Power Tool Repairers

- Growth: 5.3%
- Annual Job Openings: 3,000
- Annual Earnings: $32,310
- Percentage of Women: 4.5%

Related Apprenticeship	Years
Air-Conditioning Installer-Servicer, Window Unit	3
Electrical-Appliance Repairer	3
Electrical-Appliance Servicer	3
Electric-Tool Repairer	4

Repair, adjust, and install all types of electric household appliances. Disassembles appliance to examine specific mechanical and electrical parts to diagnose problem. Replaces worn and defective parts, such as switches, bearings, transmissions, belts, gears, circuit boards, or defective wiring. Connects appliance to power source and uses test instruments to calibrate timers and thermostats and to adjust contact points. Traces electrical circuits, following diagram, to locate shorts and grounds, using electrical circuit testers. Cleans, lubricates, and touches up minor scratches on newly installed or repaired appliance. Measures and performs minor carpentry procedures to area where appliance is to be installed. Records nature of maintenance or repair in log and returns to business office for further assignments. Maintains stock of parts used in on-site installation, maintenance, and repair of appliance. Instructs customer regarding operation and care of appliance and provides emergency service number. Observes and examines appliance during operation to detect specific malfunction, such as loose parts or leaking fluid. Reassembles unit, making necessary adjustments to ensure efficient operation. **SKILLS**—Installation; Troubleshooting; Repairing; Equipment Maintenance; Technology Design; Operation Monitoring; Quality Control Analysis; Service Orientation.

GOE—**Interest Area:** 05. Mechanics, Installers, and Repairers. **Work Group:** 05.02 Electrical and Electronic Systems. **Other Apprenticeable Jobs in This Work Group:** Avionics Technicians; Battery Repairers; Central Office and PBX Installers and Repairers; Communication Equipment Mechanics, Installers, and Repairers; Data Processing Equipment Repairers; Electric Meter Installers and Repairers; Electric Motor and Switch Assemblers and Repairers; Electrical and Electronics Installers and Repair-

ers, Transportation Equipment; Electrical and Electronics Repairers, Commercial and Industrial Equipment; Electrical and Electronics Repairers, Powerhouse, Substation, and Relay; Electrical Power-Line Installers and Repairers; Electronic Equipment Installers and Repairers, Motor Vehicles; Electronic Home Entertainment Equipment Installers and Repairers; Elevator Installers and Repairers; Installation, Maintenance, and Repair Workers, All Other; Office Machine and Cash Register Servicers; Radio Mechanics; Signal and Track Switch Repairers; Station Installers and Repairers, Telephone; Telecommunications Line Installers and Repairers; Transformer Repairers. **PERSONALITY TYPE:** Realistic. Realistic occupations frequently involve work activities that include practical, hands-on problems and solutions. They often deal with plants, animals, and real-world materials like wood, tools, and machinery. Many of the occupations require working outside and do not involve a lot of paperwork or working closely with others.

RELATED KNOWLEDGE/COURSES— **Mechanical Devices:** Knowledge of machines and tools, including their designs, uses, repair, and maintenance. **Building and Construction:** Knowledge of the materials, methods, and tools involved in the construction or repair of houses, buildings, or other structures, such as highways and roads. **Engineering and Technology:** Knowledge of the practical application of engineering science and technology. This includes applying principles, techniques, procedures, and equipment to the design and production of various goods and services. **Design:** Knowledge of design techniques, tools, and principles involved in production of precision technical plans, blueprints, drawings, and models. **Computers and Electronics:** Knowledge of circuit boards, processors, chips, electronic equipment, and computer hardware and software, including applications and programming. **Physics:** Knowledge and prediction of physical principles and laws and their interrelationships and applications to understanding fluid, material, and atmospheric dynamics and mechanical, electrical, atomic, and subatomic structures and processes.

WORK ENVIRONMENT—Using hands on objects, tools, or controls; indoors; sitting; spend time kneeling, crouching, stooping, or crawling; hazardous equipment.

Electric Meter Installers and Repairers

@ Growth: 12.0%

@ Annual Job Openings: 5,000

@ Annual Earnings: $42,540

@ Percentage of Women: 4.8%

Related Apprenticeship	Years
Electric-Meter Installer I	4
Electric-Meter Repairer	4

Install electric meters on customers' premises or on pole. Test meters and perform necessary repairs. Turn current on/off by connecting/ disconnecting service drop. Mounts and installs meter and other electric equipment, such as time clocks, transformers, and circuit breakers, using electrician's hand tools. Inspects and tests electric meters, relays, and power to detect cause of malfunction and inaccuracy, using hand tools and testing equipment. Splices and connects cable from meter or current transformer to pull box or switchboard, using hand tools, to provide power. Disconnects and removes electric power meters when defective or when customer accounts are in default, using hand tools. Records meter reading and installation data on meter cards, work orders, or field service orders. Cleans meter parts, using chemical solutions, brushes, sandpaper, and soap and water. Makes adjustments to meter components, such as setscrews or timing mechanism, to conform to specifications. Repairs electric meters and components, such as transformers and relays, and changes faulty or incorrect wiring, using hand tools. SKILLS—Installation; Troubleshooting; Repairing; Equipment Maintenance; Technology Design; Science; Quality Control Analysis; Operation Monitoring.

GOE—Interest Area: 05. Mechanics, Installers, and Repairers. Work Group: 05.02 Electrical and Electronic Systems. Other Apprenticeable Jobs in This Work Group: Avionics Technicians; Battery Repairers; Central Office and PBX Installers and Repairers; Communication Equipment Mechanics, Installers, and Repairers; Data Processing Equipment Repairers; Electric Home Appliance and Power Tool Repairers; Electric Motor and Switch Assemblers and Repairers; Electrical and Electronics Installers and Repairers, Transportation Equipment; Electrical and Electronics Repairers, Commercial and Industrial Equipment; Electrical and Electronics Repairers, Powerhouse, Substation, and Relay; Electrical Power-Line Installers and Repairers; Electronic Equipment Installers and Repairers, Motor Vehicles; Electronic Home Entertainment Equipment Installers and Repairers; Elevator Installers and Repairers; Installation, Maintenance, and

Repair Workers, All Other; Office Machine and Cash Register Servicers; Radio Mechanics; Signal and Track Switch Repairers; Station Installers and Repairers, Telephone; Telecommunications Line Installers and Repairers; Transformer Repairers. **PERSONALITY TYPE:** Realistic. Realistic occupations frequently involve work activities that include practical, hands-on problems and solutions. They often deal with plants, animals, and real-world materials like wood, tools, and machinery. Many of the occupations require working outside and do not involve a lot of paperwork or working closely with others.

RELATED KNOWLEDGE/COURSES— Mechanical Devices: Knowledge of machines and tools, including their designs, uses, repair, and maintenance. **Computers and Electronics:** Knowledge of circuit boards, processors, chips, electronic equipment, and computer hardware and software, including applications and programming. **Engineering and Technology:** Knowledge of the practical application of engineering science and technology. This includes applying principles, techniques, procedures, and equipment to the design and production of various goods and services. **Design:** Knowledge of design techniques, tools, and principles involved in production of precision technical plans, blueprints, drawings, and models. **Geography:** Knowledge of principles and methods for describing the features of land, sea, and air masses, including their physical characteristics; locations; interrelationships; and distribution of plant, animal, and human life. **Foreign Language:** Knowledge of the structure and content of a foreign (non-English) language, including the meaning and spelling of words, rules of composition and grammar, and pronunciation.

WORK ENVIRONMENT—Hazardous conditions; outdoors; minor burns, cuts, bites, or stings; climbing ladders, scaffolds, or poles; high places; hazardous equipment.

Electric Motor and Switch Assemblers and Repairers

- Growth: 5.3%
- Annual Job Openings: 3,000
- Annual Earnings: $32,310
- Percentage of Women: 4.5%

Related Apprenticeship	Years
Automotive-Generator-and-Starter Repairer	2
Electric-Motor Assembler and Tester	4
Electric-Motor Repairer	4
Propulsion-Motor-and-Generator Repairer	4

Test, repair, rebuild, and assemble electric motors, generators, and equipment. Assembles electrical parts, such as alternators, generators, starting devices, and switches, following schematic drawings, using hand, machine, and power tools. Repairs and rebuilds defective mechanical parts in electric motors, generators, and related equipment, using hand tools and power tools. Rewinds coils on core while core is in slots or makes replacement coils, using coil-winding machine. Rewires electrical systems and repairs or replaces electrical accessories.

Installs, secures, and aligns parts, using hand tools, welding equipment, and electrical meters. Replaces defective parts, such as coil leads, carbon brushes, and connecting wires, using soldering equipment. Tests for overheating, using speed gauges and thermometers. Reassembles repaired electric motors to specified requirements and ratings, using hand tools and electrical meters. Records repairs required, parts used, and labor time. Refaces, reams, and polishes commutators and machine parts to specified tolerances, using machine tools. Cuts and forms insulation and inserts insulation into armature, rotor, or stator slots. Inspects parts for wear or damage or reads work order or schematic drawings to determine required repairs. Tests charges and replaces batteries. Adjusts working parts, such as fan belt tension, voltage output, contacts, and springs, using hand tools, and verifies corrections, using gauges. Cuts and removes parts, such as defective coils and insulation. Measures velocity, horsepower, r.p.m., amperage, circuitry, and voltage of unit or parts, using electrical meters and mechanical testing devices. Disassembles defective unit, using hand tools. Lifts units or parts, such as motors or generators, using crane or chain hoist. Scrapes and cleans units or parts, using cleaning solvent, and lubricates moving parts. **SKILLS**—Installation; Repairing; Science; Troubleshooting; Technology Design; Equipment Maintenance; Operation Monitoring; Quality Control Analysis.

GOE—Interest Area: 05. Mechanics, Installers, and Repairers. **Work Group:** 05.02 Electrical and Electronic Systems. **Other Apprenticeable Jobs in This Work Group:** Avionics Technicians; Battery Repairers; Central Office and PBX Installers and Repairers; Communication Equipment Mechanics, Installers, and Repairers; Data Processing Equipment Repairers; Electric Home Appliance and Power Tool Repairers; Electric Meter Installers and Repairers; Electrical and Electronics Installers and Repairers, Transportation Equipment; Electrical and Electronics Repairers, Commercial and Industrial Equipment; Electrical and Electronics Repairers, Powerhouse, Substation, and Relay; Electrical Power-Line Installers and Repairers; Electronic Equipment Installers and Repairers, Motor Vehicles; Electronic Home Entertainment Equipment Installers and Repairers; Elevator Installers and Repairers; Installation, Maintenance, and Repair Workers, All Other; Office Machine and Cash Register Servicers; Radio Mechanics; Signal and Track Switch Repairers; Station Installers and Repairers, Telephone; Telecommunications Line Installers and Repairers; Transformer Repairers. **PERSONALITY TYPE:** Realistic. Realistic occupations frequently involve work activities that include practical, hands-on problems and solutions. They often deal with plants, animals, and real-world materials like wood, tools, and machinery. Many of the occupations require working outside and do not involve a lot of paperwork or working closely with others.

RELATED KNOWLEDGE/COURSES— Mechanical Devices: Knowledge of machines and tools, including their designs, uses, repair, and maintenance. **Computers and Electronics:** Knowledge of circuit boards, processors, chips, electronic equipment, and computer hardware and software, including applications and programming. **Design:** Knowledge of design techniques, tools, and principles involved in production of precision technical plans, blueprints, drawings, and models. **Engineering and Technology:** Knowledge of the practical application of engineering science and technology. This includes applying principles, techniques, procedures, and equipment to the design and production of various goods and services. **Pub-**

lic Safety and Security: Knowledge of relevant equipment, policies, procedures, and strategies to promote effective local, state, or national security operations for the protection of people, data, property, and institutions. **Foreign Language:** Knowledge of the structure and content of a foreign (non-English) language, including the meaning and spelling of words, rules of composition and grammar, and pronunciation.

WORK ENVIRONMENT—Hazardous equipment; hazardous conditions; using hands on objects, tools, or controls; minor burns, cuts, bites, or stings; common protective or safety equipment.

Electrical and Electronic Inspectors and Testers

- ◎ Growth: 4.7%
- ◎ Annual Job Openings: 87,000
- ◎ Annual Earnings: $27,750
- ◎ Percentage of Women: 45.7%

Related Apprenticeship	Years
Electric-Distribution Checker	2
Trouble Locator, Test Desk	2
Electronics Tester	3
Cable Tester	4
Complaint Inspector	4
Relay Tester	4
Testing-and-Regulating Technician	4

Inspect and test electrical and electronic systems, such as radar navigational equipment, computer memory units, and television and radio transmitters, using precision measuring instruments. Tests and measures finished products, components, or assemblies for functioning, operation, accuracy, or assembly to verify adherence to functional specifications. Reads dials and meters to verify functioning of equipment according to specifications. Analyzes and interprets blueprints, sample data, and other materials to determine, change, or measure specifications or inspection and testing procedures. Marks items for acceptance or rejection, records test results and inspection data, and compares findings with specifications to ensure conformance to standards. Inspects materials, products, and work in progress for conformance to specifications and adjusts process or assembly equipment to meet standards. Computes and/or calculates sample data and test results. Confers with vendors and others regarding inspection results; recommends corrective procedures; and compiles reports of results, recommendations, and needed repairs. Writes and installs computer programs to control test equipment. Installs, positions, or connects new or replacement parts, components, and instruments. Reviews maintenance records to ensure that plant equipment functions properly. Disassembles defective parts and components. Cleans and maintains test equipment and instruments to ensure proper functioning. Positions or directs other workers to position products, components, or parts for testing. Operates or tends machinery and equipment and uses hand tools. Examines and adjusts or repairs finished products and components or parts. **SKILLS**—Installation; Programming; Quality Control Analysis; Troubleshooting; Equipment Maintenance; Operation Monitoring; Repairing; Science.

GOE—**Interest Area:** 08. Industrial Production. **Work Group:** 08.02 Production Technology. **Other Apprenticeable Jobs in This Work Group:** Aircraft Structure Assemblers, Precision; Aircraft Systems Assemblers, Precision; Bench Workers, Jewelry; Bindery Machine Setters and Set-Up Operators; Bookbinders; Buffing and Polishing Set-Up Operators; Coating, Painting, and Spraying Machine Setters and Set-Up Operators; Combination Machine Tool Setters and Set-Up Operators, Metal and Plastic; Dental Laboratory Technicians; Electrical and Electronic Equipment Assemblers; Electromechanical Equipment Assemblers; Engine and Other Machine Assemblers; Extruding and Drawing Machine Setters, Operators, and Tenders, Metal and Plastic; Extruding, Forming, Pressing, and Compacting Machine Setters and Set-Up Operators; Forging Machine Setters, Operators, and Tenders, Metal and Plastic; Foundry Mold and Coremakers; Gem and Diamond Workers; Grinding, Honing, Lapping, and Deburring Machine Set-Up Operators; Heat Treating, Annealing, and Tempering Machine Operators and Tenders, Metal and Plastic; Jewelers; Lathe and Turning Machine Tool Setters, Operators, and Tenders, Metal and Plastic; Materials Inspectors; Mechanical Inspectors; Metal Molding, Coremaking, and Casting Machine Operators and Tenders; Milling and Planing Machine Setters, Operators, and Tenders, Metal and Plastic; Model and Mold Makers, Jewelry; Motor Vehicle Inspectors; Paper Goods Machine Setters, Operators, and Tenders; Pewter Casters and Finishers; Plastic Molding and Casting Machine Setters and Set-Up Operators; Precision Devices Inspectors and Testers; Precision Lens Grinders and Polishers; Precision Mold and Pattern Casters, except Nonferrous Metals; Precision Pattern and Die Casters, Nonferrous Metals; Press and Press Brake Machine Setters and Set-Up Operators, Metal and Plastic; Production Inspectors, Testers, Graders, Sorters, Samplers, Weighers; Production Workers, All Other; Rolling Machine Setters, Operators, and Tenders, Metal and Plastic; Silversmiths; Textile Knitting and Weaving Machine Setters, Operators, and Tenders; Textile Winding, Twisting, and Drawing Out Machine Setters, Operators, and Tenders; Welding Machine Setters and Set-Up Operators; Woodworking Machine Setters and Set-Up Operators, Except Sawing. **PERSONALITY TYPE:** Realistic. Realistic occupations frequently involve work activities that include practical, hands-on problems and solutions. They often deal with plants, animals, and real-world materials like wood, tools, and machinery. Many of the occupations require working outside and do not involve a lot of paperwork or working closely with others.

RELATED KNOWLEDGE/COURSES—**Computers and Electronics:** Knowledge of circuit boards, processors, chips, electronic equipment, and computer hardware and software, including applications and programming. **Telecommunications:** Knowledge of transmission, broadcasting, switching, control, and operation of telecommunications systems. **Design:** Knowledge of design techniques, tools, and principles involved in production of precision technical plans, blueprints, drawings, and models. **Mechanical Devices:** Knowledge of machines and tools, including their designs, uses, repair, and maintenance. **Engineering and Technology:** Knowledge of the practical application of engineering science and technology. This includes applying principles, techniques, procedures, and equipment to the design and production of various goods and services. **Production and Processing:** Knowledge of raw materials, production processes, quality control, costs, and other techniques for maximizing the effective manufacture and distribution of goods.

WORK ENVIRONMENT—Common protective or safety equipment; hazardous conditions; hazardous equipment; walking and running; standing.

Electrical and Electronics Installers and Repairers, Transportation Equipment

- Growth: 7.1%
- Annual Job Openings: 2,000
- Annual Earnings: $39,300
- Percentage of Women: 5.9%

Related Apprenticeship	Years
Electrician, Locomotive	4

Install, adjust, or maintain mobile electronics communication equipment, including sound, sonar, security, navigation, and surveillance systems on trains, watercraft, or other mobile equipment. Adjust, repair, or replace defective wiring and relays in ignition, lighting, air-conditioning, and safety control systems, using electrician's tools. Cut openings and drill holes for fixtures, outlet boxes, and fuse holders, using electric drills and routers. Inspect and test electrical systems and equipment to locate and diagnose malfunctions, using visual inspections, testing devices, and computer software. Install electrical equipment such as air-conditioning, heating, or ignition systems and components such as generator brushes and commutators, using hand tools. Install fixtures, outlets, terminal boards, switches, and wall boxes, using hand tools. Install new fuses, electrical cables, or power sources as required. Locate and remove or repair circuit defects such as blown fuses or malfunctioning transistors. Measure, cut, and install frameworks and conduit to support and connect wiring, control panels, and junction boxes, using hand tools. Reassemble and test equipment after repairs. Refer to schematics and manufacturers' specifications that show connections and provide instructions on how to locate problems. Repair or rebuild equipment such as starters, generators, distributors, or door controls, using electrician's tools. Splice wires with knives or cutting pliers and solder connections to fixtures, outlets, and equipment. Confer with customers to determine the nature of malfunctions. Estimate costs of repairs based on parts and labor requirements. Maintain equipment service records. SKILLS—Repairing; Installation; Equipment Maintenance; Equipment Selection; Troubleshooting; Science; Quality Control Analysis; Operation Monitoring.

GOE—**Interest Area:** 05. Mechanics, Installers, and Repairers. **Work Group:** 05.02 Electrical and Electronic Systems. **Other Apprenticeable Jobs in This Work Group:** Avionics Technicians; Battery Repairers; Central Office and PBX Installers and Repairers; Communication Equipment Mechanics, Installers, and Repairers;

Data Processing Equipment Repairers; Electric Home Appliance and Power Tool Repairers; Electric Meter Installers and Repairers; Electric Motor and Switch Assemblers and Repairers; Electrical and Electronics Repairers, Commercial and Industrial Equipment; Electrical and Electronics Repairers, Powerhouse, Substation, and Relay; Electrical Power-Line Installers and Repairers; Electronic Equipment Installers and Repairers, Motor Vehicles; Electronic Home Entertainment Equipment Installers and Repairers; Elevator Installers and Repairers; Installation, Maintenance, and Repair Workers, All Other; Office Machine and Cash Register Servicers; Radio Mechanics; Signal and Track Switch Repairers; Station Installers and Repairers, Telephone; Telecommunications Line Installers and Repairers; Transformer Repairers. **PERSONALITY TYPE:** Realistic. Realistic occupations frequently involve work activities that include practical, hands-on problems and solutions. They often deal with plants, animals, and real-world materials like wood, tools, and machinery. Many of the occupations require working outside and do not involve a lot of paperwork or working closely with others.

RELATED KNOWLEDGE/COURSES—Mechanical Devices: Knowledge of machines and tools, including their designs, uses, repair, and maintenance. **Computers and Electronics:** Knowledge of circuit boards, processors, chips, electronic equipment, and computer hardware and software, including applications and programming. **Building and Construction:** Knowledge of the materials, methods, and tools involved in the construction or repair of houses, buildings, or other structures, such as highways and roads. **Engineering and Technology:** Knowledge of the practical application of engineering science and technology. This includes applying principles, techniques, procedures, and equipment to the design and production of various goods and services. **Public Safety and Security:** Knowledge of relevant equipment, policies, procedures, and strategies to promote effective local, state, or national security operations for the protection of people, data, property, and institutions. **Physics:** Knowledge and prediction of physical principles and laws and their interrelationships and applications to understanding fluid, material, and atmospheric dynamics and mechanical, electrical, atomic, and subatomic structures and processes.

WORK ENVIRONMENT—Hazardous equipment; hazardous conditions; spend time kneeling, crouching, stooping, or crawling; using hands on objects, tools, or controls; cramped work space, awkward positions; minor burns, cuts, bites, or stings.

Electrical and Electronics Repairers, Commercial and Industrial Equipment

- ◉ Growth: 10.3%
- ◉ Annual Job Openings: 10,000
- ◉ Annual Earnings: $42,200
- ◉ Percentage of Women: 5.9%

Related Apprenticeship	Years
Field Service Engineer	2
Avionics Technician	4

Repair, test, adjust, or install electronic equipment, such as industrial controls, transmitters, and antennas. Perform scheduled preventive maintenance tasks, such as checking, cleaning, and repairing equipment, to detect and prevent problems. Examine work orders and converse with equipment operators to detect equipment problems and to ascertain whether mechanical or human errors contributed to the problems. Set up and test industrial equipment to ensure that it functions properly. Operate equipment to demonstrate proper use and to analyze malfunctions. Test faulty equipment to diagnose malfunctions, using test equipment and software and applying knowledge of the functional operation of electronic units and systems. Repair and adjust equipment, machines, and defective components, replacing worn parts such as gaskets and seals in watertight electrical equipment. Calibrate testing instruments and installed or repaired equipment to prescribed specifications. Advise management regarding customer satisfaction, product performance, and suggestions for product improvements. Inspect components of industrial equipment for accurate assembly and installation and for defects such as loose connections and frayed wires. Study blueprints, schematics, manuals, and other specifications to determine installation procedures. Maintain equipment logs that record performance problems, repairs, calibrations, and tests. Coordinate efforts with other workers involved in installing and maintaining equipment or components. Maintain inventory of spare parts. Consult with customers, supervisors, and engineers to plan layout of equipment and to resolve problems in system operation and maintenance. Send defective units to the manufacturer or to a specialized repair shop for repair. Install repaired equipment in various settings, such as industrial or military establishments. Determine feasibility of using standardized equipment and develop specifications for equipment required to perform additional functions. Enter information into computer to copy program or to draw, modify, or store schematics, applying knowledge of software package used. Sign overhaul documents for equipment replaced or repaired. Develop or modify industrial electronic devices, circuits, and equipment according to available specifications. **SKILLS**—Installation; Troubleshooting; Repairing; Operation Monitoring; Equipment Maintenance; Operation and Control; Coordination; Systems Analysis.

GOE—Interest Area: 05. Mechanics, Installers, and Repairers. **Work Group:** 05.02 Electrical and Electronic Systems. **Other Apprenticeable Jobs in This Work Group:** Avionics Technicians; Battery Repairers; Central Office and PBX Installers and Repairers; Communication Equipment Mechanics, Installers, and Repairers; Data Processing Equipment Repairers; Electric Home Appliance and Power Tool Repairers; Electric Meter Installers and Repairers; Electric Motor and Switch Assemblers and Repairers; Electrical and Electronics Installers and Repairers, Transportation Equipment; Electrical and Electronics Repairers, Powerhouse, Substation, and Relay; Electrical Power-Line Installers and Repairers; Electronic Equipment Installers and Repairers, Motor Vehicles; Electronic Home Entertainment Equipment

Installers and Repairers; Elevator Installers and Repairers; Installation, Maintenance, and Repair Workers, All Other; Office Machine and Cash Register Servicers; Radio Mechanics; Signal and Track Switch Repairers; Station Installers and Repairers, Telephone; Telecommunications Line Installers and Repairers; Transformer Repairers. **PERSONALITY TYPE:** Realistic. Realistic occupations frequently involve work activities that include practical, hands-on problems and solutions. They often deal with plants, animals, and real-world materials like wood, tools, and machinery. Many of the occupations require working outside and do not involve a lot of paperwork or working closely with others.

RELATED KNOWLEDGE/COURSES— **Computers and Electronics:** Knowledge of circuit boards, processors, chips, electronic equipment, and computer hardware and software, including applications and programming. **Mechanical Devices:** Knowledge of machines and tools, including their designs, uses, repair, and maintenance. **Telecommunications:** Knowledge of transmission, broadcasting, switching, control, and operation of telecommunications systems. **Engineering and Technology:** Knowledge of the practical application of engineering science and technology. This includes applying principles, techniques, procedures, and equipment to the design and production of various goods and services. **Customer and Personal Service:** Knowledge of principles and processes for providing customer and personal services. This includes customer needs assessment, meeting quality standards for services, and evaluation of customer satisfaction. **Design:** Knowledge of design techniques, tools, and principles involved in production of precision technical plans, blueprints, drawings, and models.

WORK ENVIRONMENT—Sounds, noise levels are distracting or uncomfortable; cramped work space, awkward positions; hazardous conditions; physical proximity; contaminants.

Electrical and Electronics Repairers, Powerhouse, Substation, and Relay

- Growth: –0.6%
- Annual Job Openings: 2,000
- Annual Earnings: $52,040
- Percentage of Women: 5.9%

Related Apprenticeship	Years
Relay Technician	2
Electrician, Substation	3
Corrosion-Control Fitter	4
Electrician, Powerhouse	4

Inspect, test, repair, or maintain electrical equipment in generating stations, substations, and in-service relays. Analyze test data in order to diagnose malfunctions, to determine performance characteristics of systems, and to evaluate effects of system modifications. Construct, test, maintain, and repair substation relay and control systems. Consult manuals, schematics, wiring diagrams, and engineering personnel in order to troubleshoot and solve equipment problems and to determine optimum equipment functioning. Inspect and test equipment and circuits to identify malfunctions or defects, using wiring diagrams and testing devices such as ohmmeters, voltmeters, or ammeters. Open and close switches to isolate defective relays; then perform adjustments or repairs. Repair, replace, and clean equipment and components such as circuit breakers, brushes, and commutators. Run signal quality and connectivity tests for individual cables and record results. Disconnect voltage regulators, bolts, and screws and connect replacement regulators to high-voltage lines. Maintain inventories of spare parts for all equipment, requisitioning parts as necessary. Notify facility personnel of equipment shutdowns. Prepare and maintain records detailing tests, repairs, and maintenance. Schedule and supervise splicing or termination of cables in color-code order. Test insulators and bushings of equipment by inducing voltage across insulation, testing current, and calculating insulation loss. Test oil in circuit breakers and transformers for dielectric strength, refilling oil periodically. Schedule and supervise the construction and testing of special devices and the implementation of unique monitoring or control systems. Set forms and pour concrete footings for installation of heavy equipment. **SKILLS—** Equipment Maintenance; Repairing; Installation; Troubleshooting; Science; Operation Monitoring; Quality Control Analysis; Equipment Selection.

GOE—Interest Area: 05. Mechanics, Installers, and Repairers. **Work Group:** 05.02 Electrical and Electronic Systems. **Other Apprenticeable Jobs in This Work Group:** Avionics Technicians; Battery Repairers; Central Office and PBX Installers and Repairers; Communication Equipment Mechanics, Installers, and Repairers; Data Processing Equipment Repairers; Electric Home Appliance and Power Tool Repairers; Electric Meter Installers and Repairers; Electric Motor and Switch Assemblers and Repairers; Electrical and Electronics Installers and Repairers, Transportation Equipment; Electrical and Electronics Repairers, Commercial and Industrial Equipment; Electrical Power-Line Installers and Repairers; Electronic Equipment Installers and Repairers, Motor Vehicles; Electronic Home Entertainment Equipment Installers and Repairers; Elevator Installers and Repairers; Installation, Maintenance, and Repair Workers, All Other; Office Machine and Cash Register Servicers; Radio Mechanics; Signal and Track Switch Repairers; Station Installers and Repairers, Telephone; Telecommunications Line Installers and Repairers; Transformer Repairers. **PERSONALITY TYPE:** Realistic. Realistic occupations frequently involve work activities that include practical, hands-on problems and solutions. They often deal with plants, animals, and real-world materials like wood, tools, and machinery. Many of the occupations require working outside and do not involve a lot of paperwork or working closely with others.

RELATED KNOWLEDGE/COURSES— Computers and Electronics: Knowledge of circuit boards, processors, chips, electronic equipment, and computer hardware and software, including applications and programming. **Mechanical Devices:** Knowledge of machines and tools, including their designs, uses, repair, and maintenance. **Engineering and Technology:** Knowledge of the practical application of engineering science and technology. This includes applying principles, techniques, procedures, and equipment to the design and production of various goods and services. **Physics:** Knowledge and prediction of physical principles and laws and their interrelationships and applications to understanding fluid, material, and atmospheric dynamics and mechanical, electrical, atomic, and subatomic structures and processes. **Mathematics:** Knowledge of arithmetic, algebra, geometry, calculus, and statistics and their applications.

WORK ENVIRONMENT—Hazardous conditions; using hands on objects, tools, or controls; common protective or safety equipment; spend time bending or twisting the body; outdoors; hazardous equipment.

Electrical Power-Line Installers and Repairers

- Growth: 1.6%
- Annual Job Openings: 9,000
- Annual Earnings: $48,960
- Percentage of Women: 2.7%

Related Apprenticeship	Years
Cable Installer-Repairer	3
Line Erector	3
Line Repairer	3
Trouble Shooter II	3
Cable Splicer	4
Line Maintainer	4

Install or repair cables or wires used in electrical power or distribution systems. May erect poles and light- or heavy-duty transmission towers. Adhere to safety practices and procedures, such as checking equipment regularly and erecting barriers around work areas. Attach crossarms, insulators, and auxiliary equipment to poles prior to installing them. Clean, tin, and splice corresponding conductors by twisting ends together or by joining ends with metal clamps and soldering connections. Climb poles or use truck-mounted buckets to access equipment. Cut and peel lead sheathing and insulation from defective or newly installed cables and conduits prior to splicing. Identify defective sectionalizing devices, circuit breakers, fuses, voltage regulators, transformers, switches, relays, or wiring, using wiring diagrams and electrical-testing instruments. Inspect and test power lines and auxiliary equipment to locate and identify problems, using reading and testing instruments. Install, maintain, and repair electrical distribution and transmission systems, including conduits, cables, wires, and related equipment such as transformers, circuit breakers, and switches. Lay underground cable directly in trenches or string it through conduit running through the trenches. Open switches or attach grounding devices in order to remove electrical hazards from disturbed or fallen lines or to facilitate repairs. Place insulating or fireproofing materials over conductors and joints. Pull up cable by hand from large reels mounted on trucks. Replace damaged poles with new poles and straighten the poles. Splice or solder cables together or to overhead transmission lines, customer service lines, or street light lines, using hand tools, epoxies, or specialized equipment. String wire conductors and cables between poles, towers, trenches, pylons, and buildings, setting lines in place and using winches to adjust tension. Test conductors according to electrical diagrams and specifications to identify corresponding conductors and to prevent incorrect connections. Coordinate work assignment preparation and completion with other workers. Cut trenches for laying underground cables, using trenchers and cable plows. Dig holes, using augers, and set poles, using cranes and power equipment. **SKILLS—** Installation; Repairing; Troubleshooting; Equipment Maintenance; Science; Quality Control Analysis; Technology Design; Operation and Control.

GOE—Interest Area: 05. Mechanics, Installers, and Repairers. **Work Group:** 05.02 Electrical and Electronic Systems. **Other Apprenticeable Jobs in This Work Group:** Avionics Technicians; Battery Repairers; Central Office and PBX Installers and Repairers; Communication Equipment Mechanics, Installers, and Repairers; Data Processing Equipment Repairers; Electric Home Appliance and Power Tool Repairers; Electric Meter Installers and Repairers; Electric Motor and Switch Assemblers and Repairers; Electrical and Electronics Installers and Repairers, Transportation Equipment; Electrical and Electronics Repairers, Commercial and Industrial Equipment; Electrical and Electronics Repairers, Powerhouse, Substation, and Relay; Electronic Equipment Installers and Repairers, Motor Vehicles; Electronic Home Entertainment Equipment Installers and Repairers; Elevator Installers and Repairers; Installation, Maintenance, and Repair Workers, All Other; Office Machine and Cash Register Servicers; Radio Mechanics; Signal and Track Switch Repairers; Station Installers and Repairers, Telephone; Telecommunications Line Installers and Repairers; Transformer Repairers. **PERSONALITY TYPE:** Realistic. Realistic occupations frequently involve work activities that include practical, hands-on problems and solutions. They often deal with plants, animals, and real-world materials like wood, tools, and machinery. Many of the occupations require working outside and do not involve a lot of paperwork or working closely with others.

RELATED KNOWLEDGE/COURSES— Public Safety and Security: Knowledge of relevant equipment, policies, procedures, and strategies to promote effective local, state, or national security operations for the protection of people, data, property, and institutions. **Mechanical Devices:** Knowledge of machines and tools, including their designs, uses, repair, and maintenance. **Design:** Knowledge of design techniques, tools, and principles involved in production of precision technical plans, blueprints, drawings, and models. **Engineering and Technology:** Knowledge of the practical application of engineering science and technology. This includes applying principles, techniques, procedures, and equipment to the design and production of various goods and services. **Building and Construction:** Knowledge of the materials, methods, and tools involved in the construction or repair of houses, buildings, or other structures, such as highways and roads. **Computers and Electronics:** Knowledge of circuit boards, processors, chips, electronic equipment, and computer hardware and software, including applications and programming.

WORK ENVIRONMENT—Hazardous conditions; outdoors; common protective or safety equipment; high places; climbing ladders, scaffolds, or poles.

Electricians

- Growth: 23.4%
- Annual Job Openings: 65,000
- Annual Earnings: $41,680
- Percentage of Women: 2.6%

Related Apprenticeship	*Years*
Residential Wireperson	2.4
Protective-Signal Repairer	3
Electrician (Construction)	4
Electrician (Ship-Boat Manufacturing)	4
Electrician (Water Transportation)	4
Electrician, Maintenance	4
Neon-Sign Servicer	4
Protective-Signal Installer	4
Street-Light Servicer	4

(This is one of the most popular apprenticeable jobs.)

Install, maintain, and repair electrical wiring, equipment, and fixtures. Ensure that work is in accordance with relevant codes. May install or service street lights, intercom systems, or electrical control systems. Assemble, install, test, and maintain electrical or electronic wiring, equipment, appliances, apparatus, and fixtures, using hand tools and power tools. Diagnose malfunctioning systems, apparatus, and components, using test equipment and hand tools, to locate the cause of a breakdown and correct the problem. Connect wires to circuit breakers, transformers, or other components. Inspect electrical systems, equipment, and components to identify hazards, defects, and the need for adjustment or repair and to ensure compliance with codes. Advise management on whether continued operation of equipment could be hazardous. Test electrical systems and continuity of circuits in electrical wiring, equipment, and fixtures, using testing devices such as ohmmeters,

voltmeters, and oscilloscopes, to ensure compatibility and safety of system. Maintain current electrician's license or identification card to meet governmental regulations. Plan layout and installation of electrical wiring, equipment, and fixtures based on job specifications and local codes. Direct and train workers to install, maintain, or repair electrical wiring, equipment, and fixtures. Prepare sketches or follow blueprints to determine the location of wiring and equipment and to ensure conformance to building and safety codes. Use a variety of tools and equipment, such as power construction equipment; measuring devices; power tools; and testing equipment, including oscilloscopes, ammeters, and test lamps. Install ground leads and connect power cables to equipment such as motors. Perform business management duties such as maintaining records and files, preparing reports, and ordering supplies and equipment. Repair or replace wiring, equipment, and fixtures, using hand tools and power tools. Work from ladders, scaffolds, and roofs to install, maintain, or repair electrical wiring, equipment, and fixtures. Place conduit (pipes or tubing) inside designated partitions, walls, or other concealed areas and pull insulated wires or cables through the conduit to complete circuits between boxes. Construct and fabricate parts, using hand tools and specifications. **SKILLS**—Installation; Troubleshooting; Equipment Maintenance; Repairing; Technology Design; Management of Financial Resources; Equipment Selection; Operations Analysis.

GOE—Interest Area: 06. Construction, Mining, and Drilling. **Work Group:** 06.02 Construction. **Other Apprenticeable Jobs in This Work Group:** Boat Builders and Shipwrights; Boilermakers; Brickmasons and Blockmasons; Carpet Installers; Ceiling Tile Installers; Cement Masons and Concrete Finishers; Construction and Related Workers, All Other; Construction Carpenters;

Drywall Installers; Fence Erectors; Floor Layers, Except Carpet, Wood, and Hard Tiles; Glaziers; Grader, Bulldozer, and Scraper Operators; Insulation Workers, Floor, Ceiling, and Wall; Insulation Workers, Mechanical; Operating Engineers; Painters, Construction and Maintenance; Paperhangers; Paving, Surfacing, and Tamping Equipment Operators; Pipe Fitters; Plasterers and Stucco Masons; Plumbers; Reinforcing Iron and Rebar Workers; Riggers; Roofers; Rough Carpenters; Sheet Metal Workers; Ship Carpenters and Joiners; Stone Cutters and Carvers; Stonemasons; Structural Iron and Steel Workers; Tapers; Terrazzo Workers and Finishers; Tile and Marble Setters. **PERSONALITY TYPE:** Realistic. Realistic occupations frequently involve work activities that include practical, hands-on problems and solutions. They often deal with plants, animals, and real-world materials like wood, tools, and machinery. Many of the occupations require working outside and do not involve a lot of paperwork or working closely with others.

RELATED KNOWLEDGE/COURSES— Building and Construction: Knowledge of the materials, methods, and tools involved in the construction or repair of houses, buildings, or other structures, such as highways and roads. **Mechanical Devices:** Knowledge of machines and tools, including their designs, uses, repair, and maintenance. **Customer and Personal Service:** Knowledge of principles and processes for providing customer and personal services. This includes customer needs assessment, meeting quality standards for services, and evaluation of customer satisfaction. **Production and Processing:** Knowledge of raw materials, production processes, quality control, costs, and other techniques for maximizing the effective manufacture and distribution of goods. **Design:** Knowledge of design techniques, tools, and principles involved in production of precision technical plans, blue-prints, drawings, and models. **Public Safety and Security:** Knowledge of relevant equipment, policies, procedures, and strategies to promote effective local, state, or national security operations for the protection of people, data, property, and institutions.

WORK ENVIRONMENT—Very hot or cold; sounds, noise levels are distracting or uncomfortable; indoors, not environmentally controlled; extremely bright or inadequate lighting; cramped work space, awkward positions.

FURTHER INFORMATION—Contact a local joint union-management apprenticeship committee or the nearest office of your state employment service or apprenticeship agency (see Appendix C). For information about union apprenticeship programs, contact the following:

National Joint Apprenticeship Training Committee (NJATC), 301 Prince George's Blvd., Upper Marlboro, MD 20774. Internet: http://www.njatc.org.

National Electrical Contractors Association (NECA), 3 Metro Center, Suite 1100, Bethesda, MD 20814. Internet: http://www.necanet.org.

International Brotherhood of Electrical Workers (IBEW), 1125 15th St. NW, Washington, DC 20005. Internet: http://www.ibew.org.

For information about independent apprenticeship programs, contact the following:

Associated Builders and Contractors, Workforce Development Department, 4250 North Fairfax Dr., 9th Floor, Arlington, VA 22203.

Independent Electrical Contractors, Inc., 4401 Ford Ave., Suite 1100, Alexandria, VA 22302. Internet: http://www.ieci.org.

National Association of Home Builders, 1201 15th St. NW, Washington, DC 20005. Internet: http://www.nahb.org.

Home Builders Institute, 1201 15th St. NW, Washington, DC 20005. Internet: http://www.hbi.org.

Electronic Drafters

- Growth: 0.7%
- Annual Job Openings: 5,000
- Annual Earnings: $41,730
- Percentage of Women: 19.9%

Related Apprenticeship	Years
Design Drafter, Electromechanisms	4
Drafter, Electronic	4

Draw wiring diagrams, circuit board assembly diagrams, schematics, and layout drawings used for manufacture, installation, and repair of electronic equipment. Compare logic element configuration on display screen with engineering schematics and calculate figures to convert, redesign, and modify element. Consult with engineers to discuss and interpret design concepts and determine requirements of detailed working drawings. Draft detail and assembly drawings of design components, circuitry, and printed circuit boards, using computer-assisted equipment or standard drafting techniques and devices. Examine electronic schematics and supporting documents to develop, compute, and verify specifications for drafting data, such as configuration of parts, dimensions, and tolerances. Key and program specified commands and engineering specifications into computer system to change functions and test final layout. Plot electrical test points on layout sheets and draw schematics for wiring test fixture heads to frames. Review work orders and procedural manuals and confer with vendors and design staff to resolve problems and modify design. Copy drawings of printed circuit board fabrication, using print machine or blueprinting procedure. Generate computer tapes of final layout design to produce layered photo masks and photo plotting design onto film. Locate files relating to specified design project in database library, load program into computer, and record completed job data. Review blueprints to determine customer requirements and consult with assembler regarding schematics, wiring procedures, and conductor paths. Select drill size to drill test head, according to test design and specifications, and submit guide layout to designated department. Supervise and coordinate work activities of workers engaged in drafting, designing layouts, assembling, and testing printed circuit boards. Train students to use drafting machines and to prepare schematic diagrams, block diagrams, control drawings, logic diagrams, integrated circuit drawings, and interconnection diagrams. **SKILLS**—Programming; Technology Design; Operations Analysis; Mathematics; Science; Management of Material Resources; Troubleshooting; Quality Control Analysis.

GOE—Interest Area: 02. Science, Math, and Engineering. **Work Group:** 02.09 Engineering Technology. **Other Apprenticeable Jobs in This Work Group:** Aerospace Engineering and Operations Technicians; Architectural Drafters; Calibration and Instrumentation Technicians; Cartographers and Photogrammetrists; Civil Drafters; Construction and Building Inspectors; Electrical Drafters; Electrical Engineering Technicians; Electro-Mechanical Technicians; Electronics Engineering Technicians; Engineering Technicians, Except Drafters, All Other; Industrial Engineering Technicians; Mapping Technicians; Mechanical Drafters; Mechanical Engineering Technicians; Numerical Tool and Process Control Programmers; Surveying Technicians. **PERSONALITY TYPE:** Realistic. Realistic occupations frequently involve work activities that include practical, hands-on problems and solutions. They often deal with plants, animals, and real-world materials like wood, tools, and machinery. Many of the occupations require working outside and do not involve a lot of paperwork or working closely with others.

RELATED KNOWLEDGE/COURSES— Design: Knowledge of design techniques, tools, and principles involved in production of precision technical plans, blueprints, drawings, and models. **Computers and Electronics:** Knowledge of circuit boards, processors, chips, electronic equipment, and computer hardware and software, including applications and programming. **Engineering and Technology:** Knowledge of the practical application of engineering science and technology. This includes applying principles, techniques, procedures, and equipment to the design and production of various goods and services. **Mathematics:** Knowledge of arithmetic, algebra, geometry, calculus, and statistics and their applications. **Administration and Management:** Knowledge of business and management principles involved in strategic planning, resource allocation, human resources modeling, leadership technique, production methods, and coordination of people and resources. **Physics:** Knowledge and prediction of physical principles and laws and their interrelationships and applications to understanding fluid, material, and atmospheric dynamics and mechanical, electrical, atomic, and subatomic structures and processes. **Telecommunications:** Knowledge of

transmission, broadcasting, switching, control, and operation of telecommunications systems.

WORK ENVIRONMENT—Sitting; using hands on objects, tools, or controls; indoors; walking and running; spend time making repetitive motions.

Electronic Equipment Installers and Repairers, Motor Vehicles

- ◉ Growth: 14.8%
- ◉ Annual Job Openings: 1,000
- ◉ Annual Earnings: $26,280
- ◉ Percentage of Women: 4.7%

Related Apprenticeship	Years
Electrician, Automotive	2

Install, diagnose, or repair communications, sound, security, or navigation equipment in motor vehicles. Adjusts, repairs, or replaces defective wiring and relays in ignition, lighting, air-conditioning, and safety control systems, using electrician's tools. Repairs or rebuilds starters, generators, distributors, or door controls, using electrician's tools. Installs electrical equipment, such as air-conditioning, heating, or ignition systems; generator brushes; and commutators, using hand tools. Installs fixtures, outlets, terminal boards, switches, and wall

E

boxes, using hand tools. Measures, cuts, and installs framework and conduit to support and connect wiring, control panels, and junction boxes, using hand tools. Splices wires with knife or cutting pliers and solders connections to fixtures, outlets, and equipment. Visually inspects and tests electrical system or equipment, using testing devices such as oscilloscope, voltmeter, and ammeter, to determine malfunctions. Cuts openings and drills holes for fixtures, outlet boxes, and fuse holders, using electric drill and router. Confers with customer to determine nature of malfunction. Estimates cost of repairs based on parts and labor charges. **SKILLS**— Repairing; Installation; Equipment Maintenance; Equipment Selection; Troubleshooting; Science; Quality Control Analysis; Operation Monitoring.

GOE—Interest Area: 05. Mechanics, Installers, and Repairers. **Work Group:** 05.02 Electrical and Electronic Systems. **Other Apprenticeable Jobs in This Work Group:** Avionics Technicians; Battery Repairers; Central Office and PBX Installers and Repairers; Communication Equipment Mechanics, Installers, and Repairers; Data Processing Equipment Repairers; Electric Home Appliance and Power Tool Repairers; Electric Meter Installers and Repairers; Electric Motor and Switch Assemblers and Repairers; Electrical and Electronics Installers and Repairers, Transportation Equipment; Electrical and Electronics Repairers, Commercial and Industrial Equipment; Electrical and Electronics Repairers, Powerhouse, Substation, and Relay; Electrical Power-Line Installers and Repairers; Electronic Home Entertainment Equipment Installers and Repairers; Elevator Installers and Repairers; Installation, Maintenance, and Repair Workers, All Other; Office Machine and Cash Register Servicers; Radio Mechanics; Signal and Track Switch Repairers;

Station Installers and Repairers, Telephone; Telecommunications Line Installers and Repairers; Transformer Repairers. **PERSONALITY TYPE:** Realistic. Realistic occupations frequently involve work activities that include practical, hands-on problems and solutions. They often deal with plants, animals, and real-world materials like wood, tools, and machinery. Many of the occupations require working outside and do not involve a lot of paperwork or working closely with others.

RELATED KNOWLEDGE/COURSES—Mechanical Devices: Knowledge of machines and tools, including their designs, uses, repair, and maintenance. **Computers and Electronics:** Knowledge of circuit boards, processors, chips, electronic equipment, and computer hardware and software, including applications and programming. **Building and Construction:** Knowledge of the materials, methods, and tools involved in the construction or repair of houses, buildings, or other structures, such as highways and roads. **Engineering and Technology:** Knowledge of the practical application of engineering science and technology. This includes applying principles, techniques, procedures, and equipment to the design and production of various goods and services. **Public Safety and Security:** Knowledge of relevant equipment, policies, procedures, and strategies to promote effective local, state, or national security operations for the protection of people, data, property, and institutions. **Physics:** Knowledge and prediction of physical principles and laws and their interrelationships and applications to understanding fluid, material, and atmospheric dynamics and mechanical, electrical, atomic, and subatomic structures and processes.

WORK ENVIRONMENT—Hazardous equipment; hazardous conditions; spend time kneeling, crouching, stooping, or crawling; using hands on objects, tools, or controls; cramped work space, awkward positions; minor burns, cuts, bites, or stings.

Electronic Home Entertainment Equipment Installers and Repairers

◎ Growth: 8.6%

◎ Annual Job Openings: 5,000

◎ Annual Earnings: $27,340

◎ Percentage of Women: 4.2%

Related Apprenticeship	Years
Audio-Video Repairer	2
Electronic-Organ Technician	2
Radio Repairer	4
Tape-Recorder Repairer	4
Television-and-Radio Repairer	4

Repair, adjust, or install audio or television receivers, stereo systems, camcorders, video systems, or other electronic home entertainment equipment. Disassembles equipment and repairs or replaces loose, worn, or defective components and wiring, using hand tools and soldering iron. Tunes or adjusts equipment and instruments according to specifications to obtain optimum visual or auditory reception.

Tests circuits, using schematic diagrams, service manuals, and testing instruments such as voltmeters, oscilloscopes, and audiogenerators. Analyzes and tests products and parts to locate defects or source of trouble. Confers with customers to determine nature of problem or to explain repairs. Positions or mounts speakers and wires speakers to console. Computes cost estimates for labor and materials. Installs electronic equipment or instruments, such as televisions, radios, audio-visual equipment, and organs, using hand tools. Makes service calls and repairs units in customers' homes or returns unit to shop for major repair. **SKILLS**—Installation; Science; Troubleshooting; Repairing; Equipment Maintenance; Technology Design; Service Orientation; Management of Financial Resources.

GOE—Interest Area: 05. Mechanics, Installers, and Repairers. **Work Group:** 05.02 Electrical and Electronic Systems. **Other Apprenticeable Jobs in This Work Group:** Avionics Technicians; Battery Repairers; Central Office and PBX Installers and Repairers; Communication Equipment Mechanics, Installers, and Repairers; Data Processing Equipment Repairers; Electric Home Appliance and Power Tool Repairers; Electric Meter Installers and Repairers; Electric Motor and Switch Assemblers and Repairers; Electrical and Electronics Installers and Repairers, Transportation Equipment; Electrical and Electronics Repairers, Commercial and Industrial Equipment; Electrical and Electronics Repairers, Powerhouse, Substation, and Relay; Electrical Power-Line Installers and Repairers; Electronic Equipment Installers and Repairers, Motor Vehicles; Elevator Installers and Repairers; Installation, Maintenance, and Repair Workers, All Other; Office Machine and Cash Register Servicers; Radio Mechanics; Signal and Track Switch Repairers; Station

E

Installers and Repairers, Telephone; Telecommunications Line Installers and Repairers; Transformer Repairers. **PERSONALITY TYPE:** Realistic. Realistic occupations frequently involve work activities that include practical, hands-on problems and solutions. They often deal with plants, animals, and real-world materials like wood, tools, and machinery. Many of the occupations require working outside and do not involve a lot of paperwork or working closely with others.

RELATED KNOWLEDGE/COURSES— Computers and Electronics: Knowledge of circuit boards, processors, chips, electronic equipment, and computer hardware and software, including applications and programming. **Telecommunications:** Knowledge of transmission, broadcasting, switching, control, and operation of telecommunications systems. **Design:** Knowledge of design techniques, tools, and principles involved in production of precision technical plans, blueprints, drawings, and models. **Mechanical Devices:** Knowledge of machines and tools, including their designs, uses, repair, and maintenance. **Engineering and Technology:** Knowledge of the practical application of engineering science and technology. This includes applying principles, techniques, procedures, and equipment to the design and production of various goods and services. **Customer and Personal Service:** Knowledge of principles and processes for providing customer and personal services. This includes customer needs assessment, meeting quality standards for services, and evaluation of customer satisfaction.

WORK ENVIRONMENT—Climbing ladders, scaffolds, or poles; spend time bending or twisting the body; keeping or regaining balance; cramped work space, awkward positions; spend time kneeling, crouching, stooping, or crawling.

Electrotypers and Stereotypers

- Growth: –11.2%
- Annual Job Openings: 6,000
- Annual Earnings: $31,660
- Percentage of Women: 47.6%

Related Apprenticeship	Years
Electrotyper	5
Stereotyper	6

Fabricate and finish electrotype and stereotype printing plates. Inserts pins in base to register stereotype plates to key plate for mat molding. Mounts finished plates on wood or metal blocks for flatbed presses, using hammer, nails, or bonding press. Curves plates for cylinder presses, using plate-curving machine. Cuts and pastes pieces of paper-felt or cardboard in nonprinting areas of wood-fiber mat to prevent collapse during casting. Operates proof press to obtain proof of plate reproduction and registration. Examines plate to detect imperfect formation of lines, type, and halftone dots, using magnifier. Sprays plastic mold with silver solution and immerses mold in plating tank. Trims mat, using trimming machine, by aligning notches of mat with pins on trimming machine. Aligns and notches mats of color series with key color mat, using matching machine with mono-color magnifier attachment. Removes excess metal from edges, back, and nonprinting surface areas of plate, using power shear, milling machines, or routing machine. Pours metal into casting box or plated mold by hand to produce electrotype or stereotype printing plates. Drills matching holes in series of mounted color stereotype plates to be duplicated. Forms mold of composed type, using plastic sheet-molding or wood-fiber mat and hydraulic press. Corrects defects on plate, using engraver's hand tools, punches, and hammers. Operates automatic casting machine to produce electrotype or stereotype printing plates. **SKILLS**—Operation and Control; Operation Monitoring; Troubleshooting; Technology Design; Quality Control Analysis.

GOE—Interest Area: 08. Industrial Production. **Work Group:** 08.03 Production Work. **Other Apprenticeable Jobs in This Work Group:** Bakers, Manufacturing; Bindery Machine Operators and Tenders; Chemical Equipment Controllers and Operators; Coating, Painting, and Spraying Machine Operators and Tenders; Cooling and Freezing Equipment Operators and Tenders; Crushing, Grinding, and Polishing Machine Setters, Operators, and Tenders; Cutters and Trimmers, Hand; Cutting and Slicing Machine Operators and Tenders; Design Printing Machine Setters and Set-Up Operators; Electrolytic Plating and Coating Machine Setters and Set-Up Operators, Metal and Plastic; Embossing Machine Set-Up Operators; Engraver Set-Up Operators; Extruding, Forming, Pressing, and Compacting Machine Operators and Tenders; Fabric and Apparel Patternmakers; Film Laboratory Technicians; Fitters, Structural Metal—Precision; Food Batchmakers; Furnace, Kiln, Oven, Drier, and Kettle Operators and Tenders; Hand Compositors and Typesetters; Job Printers; Letterpress Setters and Set-Up Operators; Metal Fabricators, Structural Metal Products; Metal-Refining Furnace Operators and Tenders; Mixing and Blending Machine Setters, Operators, and Tenders; Mold Makers, Hand; Molding and Casting Workers; Numerical Control Machine Tool Operators and Tenders, Metal and Plastic; Offset Lithographic Press Setters and Set-Up Operators; Painting, Coating, and Decorating Workers; Photographic Processing Machine Operators; Photographic Reproduction Technicians; Photographic Retouchers and Restorers; Plate Finishers; Platemakers; Precision Printing Workers; Printing Press Machine Operators and Tenders; Production Workers, All Other; Sawing Machine Operators and Tenders; Sawing Machine Setters and Set-Up Operators; Scanner Operators; Separating, Filtering, Clarifying, Precipitating, and Still Machine Setters, Operators, and Tenders; Sewing Machine Operators, Garment; Slaughterers and Meat Packers; Stone Sawyers; Strippers; Team Assemblers; Welder-Fitters; Welders and Cutters; Woodworking Machine Operators and Tenders, Except Sawing. **PERSONALITY TYPE:** Realistic. Realistic occupations frequently involve work activities that include practical, hands-on problems and solutions. They often deal with plants, animals, and real-world materials like wood, tools, and machinery. Many of the occupations require working outside and do not involve a lot of paperwork or working closely with others.

RELATED KNOWLEDGE/COURSES— **Mechanical Devices:** Knowledge of machines and tools, including their designs, uses, repair, and maintenance. **Engineering and Technology:** Knowledge of the practical application of engineering science and technology. This includes applying principles, techniques, procedures, and equipment to the design and production of various goods and services. **Production and Processing:** Knowledge of raw materials, production processes, quality control costs, and other techniques for maximizing the effective manufacture and distribution of goods.

WORK ENVIRONMENT—Hazardous equipment; common protective or safety equipment; using hands on objects, tools, or controls; spend time making repetitive motions; sounds, noise levels are distracting or uncomfortable.

Elevator Installers and Repairers

⊚ Growth: 17.1%

⊚ Annual Job Openings: 3,000

⊚ Annual Earnings: $55,960

⊚ Percentage of Women: 1.4%

Related Apprenticeship	Years
Elevator Constructor	4
Elevator Repairer	4

(This is one of the most popular apprenticeable jobs.)

Assemble, install, repair, or maintain electric or hydraulic freight or passenger elevators, escalators, or dumbwaiters. Adjust safety controls, counterweights, door mechanisms, and components such as valves, ratchets, seals, and brake linings. Assemble electrically powered stairs, steel frameworks, and tracks and install associated motors and electrical wiring. Assemble elevator cars, installing each car's platform, walls, and doors. Assemble, install, repair, and maintain elevators, escalators, moving sidewalks, and dumbwaiters, using hand and power tools and testing devices such as test lamps,

ammeters, and voltmeters. Attach guide shoes and rollers to minimize the lateral motion of cars as they travel through shafts. Bolt or weld steel rails to the walls of shafts to guide elevators, working from scaffolding or platforms. Check that safety regulations and building codes are met and complete service reports verifying conformance to standards. Connect car frames to counterweights, using steel cables. Connect electrical wiring to control panels and electric motors. Cut prefabricated sections of framework, rails, and other components to specified dimensions. Disassemble defective units and repair or replace parts such as locks, gears, cables, and electric wiring. Inspect wiring connections, control panel hookups, door installations, and alignments and clearances of cars and hoistways to ensure that equipment will operate properly. Install electrical wires and controls by attaching conduit along shaft walls from floor to floor and then pulling plastic-covered wires through the conduit. Install outer doors and door frames at elevator entrances on each floor of a structure. Locate malfunctions in brakes, motors, switches, and signal and control systems, using test equipment. Maintain logbooks that detail all repairs and checks performed. Operate elevators to determine power demands and test power consumption to detect overload factors. Read and interpret blueprints to determine the layout of system components, frameworks, and foundations and to select installation equipment. Test newly installed equipment to ensure that it meets specifications, such as stopping at floors for set amounts of time. **SKILLS**—Installation; Repairing; Equipment Maintenance; Troubleshooting; Quality Control Analysis; Operation Monitoring; Operation and Control; Technology Design; Systems Analysis.

GOE—Interest Area: 05. Mechanics, Installers, and Repairers. **Work Group:** 05.02 Electrical and Electronic Systems. **Other Apprenticeable Jobs in This Work Group:** Avionics Technicians; Battery Repairers; Central Office and PBX Installers and Repairers; Communication Equipment Mechanics, Installers, and Repairers; Data Processing Equipment Repairers; Electric Home Appliance and Power Tool Repairers; Electric Meter Installers and Repairers; Electric Motor and Switch Assemblers and Repairers; Electrical and Electronics Installers and Repairers, Transportation Equipment; Electrical and Electronics Repairers, Commercial and Industrial Equipment; Electrical and Electronics Repairers, Powerhouse, Substation, and Relay; Electrical Power-Line Installers and Repairers; Electronic Equipment Installers and Repairers, Motor Vehicles; Electronic Home Entertainment Equipment Installers and Repairers; Installation, Maintenance, and Repair Workers, All Other; Office Machine and Cash Register Servicers; Radio Mechanics; Signal and Track Switch Repairers; Station Installers and Repairers, Telephone; Telecommunications Line Installers and Repairers; Transformer Repairers. **PERSONALITY TYPE:** Realistic. Realistic occupations frequently involve work activities that include practical, hands-on problems and solutions. They often deal with plants, animals, and real-world materials like wood, tools, and machinery. Many of the occupations require working outside and do not involve a lot of paperwork or working closely with others.

RELATED KNOWLEDGE/COURSES—

Building and Construction: Knowledge of the materials, methods, and tools involved in the construction or repair of houses, buildings, or other structures, such as highways and roads.

Mechanical Devices: Knowledge of machines and tools, including their designs, uses, repair, and maintenance. **Engineering and Technology:** Knowledge of the practical application of engineering science and technology. This includes applying principles, techniques, procedures, and equipment to the design and production of various goods and services. **Physics:** Knowledge and prediction of physical principles and laws and their interrelationships and applications to understanding fluid, material, and atmospheric dynamics and mechanical, electrical, atomic, and subatomic structures and processes. **Public Safety and Security:** Knowledge of relevant equipment, policies, procedures, and strategies to promote effective local, state, or national security operations for the protection of people, data, property, and institutions. **Computers and Electronics:** Knowledge of circuit boards, processors, chips, electronic equipment, and computer hardware and software, including applications and programming. **Telecommunications:** Knowledge of transmission, broadcasting, switching, control, and operation of telecommunications systems.

WORK ENVIRONMENT—Hazardous equipment; minor burns, cuts, bites, or stings; climbing ladders, scaffolds, or poles; hazardous conditions; high places.

FURTHER INFORMATION—Contact a local joint union-management apprenticeship committee or the nearest office of your state employment service or apprenticeship agency (see Appendix C). To identify the local union office, contact International Union of Elevator Constructors, 7154 Columbia Gateway Dr., Columbia, MD 21046. Internet: http://www.iuec.org.

E

Embalmers

- Growth: 8.3%
- Annual Job Openings: 1,000
- Annual Earnings: $34,350
- Percentage of Women: 22.0%

Related Apprenticeship	Years
Embalmer	2

Prepare bodies for interment in conformity with legal requirements. Apply cosmetics to impart lifelike appearance to the deceased. Attach trocar to pump-tube, start pump, and repeat probing to force embalming fluid into organs. Close incisions, using needles and sutures. Conform to laws of health and sanitation and ensure that legal requirements concerning embalming are met. Dress bodies and place them in caskets. Incise stomach and abdominal walls and probe internal organs, using trocar, to withdraw blood and waste matter from organs. Insert convex celluloid or cotton between eyeballs and eyelids to prevent slipping and sinking of eyelids. Join lips, using needles and thread or wire. Make incisions in arms or thighs and drain blood from circulatory system and replace it with embalming fluid, using pump. Pack body orifices with cotton saturated with embalming fluid to prevent escape of gases or waste matter. Press diaphragm to evacuate air from lungs. Reshape or reconstruct disfigured or maimed bodies when necessary, using derma-surgery techniques and materials such as clay, cotton, plaster of paris, and wax. Wash and dry bodies, using germicidal soap and towels or hot air dryers. Arrange for transport-ing the deceased to another state for interment. Assist coroners at death scenes or at autopsies, file police reports, and testify at inquests or in court if employed by a coroner. Maintain records such as itemized lists of clothing or valuables delivered with body and names of persons embalmed. Perform special procedures necessary for remains that are to be transported to other states or overseas or where death was caused by infectious disease. Supervise funeral attendants and other funeral home staff. Arrange funeral home equipment and perform general maintenance. Assist with placing caskets in hearses and organize cemetery processions. Conduct interviews to arrange for the preparation of obituary notices, to assist with the selection of caskets or urns, and to determine the location and time of burials or cremations. Direct casket and floral display placement and arrange guest seating. Perform the duties of funeral directors, including coordinating funeral activities. **SKILLS**—Social Perceptiveness; Monitoring; Management of Material Resources; Service Orientation; Equipment Selection; Judgment and Decision Making.

GOE—Interest Area: 11. Recreation, Travel, and Other Personal Services. **Work Group:** 11.08 Other Personal Services. **Other Apprenticeable Jobs in This Work Group:** No other apprenticeable jobs in this group. **PERSONALITY TYPE:** Realistic. Realistic occupations frequently involve work activities that include practical, hands-on problems and solutions. They often deal with plants, animals, and real-world materials like wood, tools, and machinery. Many of the occupations require working outside and do not involve a lot of paperwork or working closely with others.

RELATED KNOWLEDGE/COURSES—Biology: Knowledge of plant and animal organisms and their tissues, cells, functions, interdependencies, and interactions with each other and the environment. **Chemistry:** Knowledge of the chemical composition, structure, and properties of substances and of the chemical processes and transformations that they undergo. This includes uses of chemicals, their danger signs, production techniques, and disposal methods. **Customer and Personal Service:** Knowledge of principles and processes for providing customer and personal services. This includes customer needs assessment, meeting quality standards for services, and evaluation of customer satisfaction. **Medicine and Dentistry:** Knowledge of the information and techniques needed to diagnose and treat human injuries, diseases, and deformities. This includes symptoms, treatment alternatives, drug properties and interactions, and preventive health-care measures. **Law and Government:** Knowledge of laws, legal codes, court procedures, precedents, government regulations, executive orders, agency rules, and the democratic political process. **Sociology and Anthropology:** Knowledge of group behavior and dynamics, societal trends and influences, human migrations, ethnicity, and cultures and their history and origins. **Public Safety and Security:** Knowledge of relevant equipment, policies, procedures, and strategies to promote effective local, state, or national security operations for the protection of people, data, property, and institutions.

WORK ENVIRONMENT—Contaminants; common protective or safety equipment; hazardous conditions; disease or infections; indoors; using hands on objects, tools, or controls.

Embossing Machine Set-Up Operators

- Growth: 4.6%
- Annual Job Openings: 30,000
- Annual Earnings: $29,340
- Percentage of Women: 17.8%

Related Apprenticeship	Years
Embosser	2
Embossing-Press Operator	4
Steel-Die Printer	4

Set up and operate embossing machines. Sets guides to hold cover in position and adjusts table height to obtain correct depth of impression. Positions, installs, and locks embossed plate in chase and locks chase in bed of press. Makes impression of embossing to desired depth in composition on platen, trims off excess, and allows composition to harden. Stamps embossing design on workpiece, using heated work tools. Starts machine to lower ram and impress cardboard. Sets sheets singly in gauge pins and starts press. Scrapes high spots on counter die to prevent from puncturing paper. Removes and stacks embossed covers. Cuts surface of cardboard, leaving design or letters, using hand tools. Mixes embossing composition to putty-like consistency, spreads glue on paten, and applies thin pad of composition over glue. SKILLS—Installation; Equipment Maintenance; Operation and Control; Operation Monitoring; Repairing.

E

GOE—**Interest Area:** 08. Industrial Production. **Work Group:** 08.03 Production Work. **Other Apprenticeable Jobs in This Work Group:** Bakers, Manufacturing; Bindery Machine Operators and Tenders; Chemical Equipment Controllers and Operators; Coating, Painting, and Spraying Machine Operators and Tenders; Cooling and Freezing Equipment Operators and Tenders; Crushing, Grinding, and Polishing Machine Setters, Operators, and Tenders; Cutters and Trimmers, Hand; Cutting and Slicing Machine Operators and Tenders; Design Printing Machine Setters and Set-Up Operators; Electrolytic Plating and Coating Machine Setters and Set-Up Operators, Metal and Plastic; Electrotypers and Stereotypers; Engraver Set-Up Operators; Extruding, Forming, Pressing, and Compacting Machine Operators and Tenders; Fabric and Apparel Patternmakers; Film Laboratory Technicians; Fitters, Structural Metal—Precision; Food Batchmakers; Furnace, Kiln, Oven, Drier, and Kettle Operators and Tenders; Hand Compositors and Typesetters; Job Printers; Letterpress Setters and Set-Up Operators; Metal Fabricators, Structural Metal Products; Metal-Refining Furnace Operators and Tenders; Mixing and Blending Machine Setters, Operators, and Tenders; Mold Makers, Hand; Molding and Casting Workers; Numerical Control Machine Tool Operators and Tenders, Metal and Plastic; Offset Lithographic Press Setters and Set-Up Operators; Painting, Coating, and Decorating Workers; Photographic Processing Machine Operators; Photographic Reproduction Technicians; Photographic Retouchers and Restorers; Plate Finishers; Platemakers; Precision Printing Workers; Printing Press Machine Operators and Tenders; Production Workers, All Other; Sawing Machine Operators and Tenders; Sawing Machine Setters and Set-Up Operators; Scanner Operators; Separating, Filtering, Clarifying, Precipitating, and Still Machine Setters, Operators, and Tenders; Sewing Machine Operators, Garment; Slaughterers and Meat Packers; Stone Sawyers; Strippers; Team Assemblers; Welder-Fitters; Welders and Cutters; Woodworking Machine Operators and Tenders, Except Sawing. **PERSONALITY TYPE:** Realistic. Realistic occupations frequently involve work activities that include practical, hands-on problems and solutions. They often deal with plants, animals, and real-world materials like wood, tools, and machinery. Many of the occupations require working outside and do not involve a lot of paperwork or working closely with others.

RELATED KNOWLEDGE/COURSES— Production and Processing: Knowledge of raw materials, production processes, quality control, costs, and other techniques for maximizing the effective manufacture and distribution of goods. **Administration and Management:** Knowledge of business and management principles involved in strategic planning, resource allocation, human resources modeling, leadership technique, production methods, and coordination of people and resources.

WORK ENVIRONMENT—Hazardous equipment; common protective or safety equipment; using hands on objects, tools, or controls; indoors; spend time making repetitive motions.

Emergency Management Specialists

- Growth: 28.2%
- Annual Job Openings: 2,000
- Annual Earnings: $45,090
- Percentage of Women: 56.6%

Related Apprenticeship	Years
Production Controller	competency

Coordinate disaster response or crisis management activities, provide disaster preparedness training, and prepare emergency plans and procedures for natural (e.g., hurricanes, floods, earthquakes), wartime, or technological (e.g., nuclear power plant emergencies, hazardous materials spills) disasters or hostage situations. Keep informed of activities or changes that could affect the likelihood of an emergency, as well as those that could affect response efforts and details of plan implementation. Keep informed of federal, state, and local regulations affecting emergency plans and ensure that plans adhere to these regulations. Maintain and update all resource materials associated with emergency preparedness plans. Prepare emergency situation status reports that describe response and recovery efforts, needs, and preliminary damage assessments. Prepare plans that outline operating procedures to be used in response to disasters/emergencies such as hurricanes, nuclear accidents, and terrorist attacks and in recovery from these events. Propose alteration of emergency response procedures based on regulatory changes, technological changes, or knowledge gained from outcomes of previous emergency situations. Review emergency plans of individual organizations such as medical facilities in order to ensure their adequacy. Study emergency plans used elsewhere in order to gather information for plan development. Apply for federal funding for emergency management–related needs; administer such grants and report on their progress. Attend meetings, conferences, and workshops related to emergency management in order to learn new information and to develop working relationships with other emergency management specialists. Develop and implement training procedures and strategies for radiological protection, detection, and decontamination. Develop instructional materials for the public and make presentations to citizens' groups in order to provide information on emergency plans and their implementation process. Inventory and distribute nuclear, biological, and chemical detection and contamination equipment, providing instruction in its maintenance and use. Provide communities with assistance in applying for federal funding for emergency management facilities, radiological instrumentation, and other related items. Train local groups in the preparation of long-term plans that are compatible with federal and state plans. **SKILLS**—No data available.

GOE—Interest Area: 04. Law, Law Enforcement, and Public Safety. **Work Group:** 04.01 Managerial Work in Law, Law Enforcement, and Public Safety. **Other Apprenticeable Jobs in This Work Group:** Municipal Fire Fighting and Prevention Supervisors. **PERSONALITY TYPE:** No data available.

RELATED KNOWLEDGE/COURSES—No data available.

WORK ENVIRONMENT—No data available.

Emergency Medical Technicians and Paramedics

- Growth: 33.1%
- Annual Job Openings: 32,000
- Annual Earnings: $24,440
- Percentage of Women: 32.1%

Related Apprenticeship	Years
Paramedic	2
Emergency Medical Technician	3

Assess injuries, administer emergency medical care, and extricate trapped individuals. Transport injured or sick persons to medical facilities. Administer first-aid treatment and life-support care to sick or injured persons in prehospital setting. Operate equipment such as EKGs, external defibrillators, and bag-valve mask resuscitators in advanced life-support environments. Assess nature and extent of illness or injury to establish and prioritize medical procedures. Maintain vehicles and medical and communication equipment and replenish first-aid equipment and supplies. Observe, record, and report to physician the patient's condition or injury, the treatment provided, and reactions to drugs and treatment. Perform emergency diagnostic and treatment procedures, such as stomach suction, airway management, and heart monitoring, during ambulance ride. Administer drugs, orally or by injection, and perform intravenous procedures under a physician's direction. Comfort and reassure patients. Coordinate work with other emergency medical team members and police and fire department personnel. Communicate with dispatchers and treatment center personnel to provide information about situation, to arrange reception of victims, and to receive instructions for further treatment. Immobilize patient for placement on stretcher and ambulance transport, using backboard or other spinal immobilization device. Decontaminate ambulance interior following treatment of patient with infectious disease and report case to proper authorities. Drive mobile intensive care unit to specified location, following instructions from emergency medical dispatcher. Coordinate with treatment center personnel to obtain patients' vital statistics and medical history, to determine the circumstances of the emergency, and to administer emergency treatment. **SKILLS**—Equipment Maintenance; Service Orientation; Social Perceptiveness; Instructing; Coordination; Negotiation; Persuasion; Critical Thinking.

GOE—Interest Area: 04. Law, Law Enforcement, and Public Safety. **Work Group:** 04.04 Public Safety. **Other Apprenticeable Jobs in This Work Group:** Fire Inspectors; Forest Fire Fighters; Government Property Inspectors and Investigators; Municipal Fire Fighters; Nuclear Monitoring Technicians; Occupational Health and Safety Specialists. **PERSONALITY TYPE:** Social. Social occupations frequently involve working with, communicating with, and teaching people. These occupations often involve helping or providing service to others.

RELATED KNOWLEDGE/COURSES—**Customer and Personal Service:** Knowledge of principles and processes for providing customer and personal services. This includes customer needs assessment, meeting quality standards for services, and evaluation of customer satisfaction. **Medicine and Dentistry:** Knowledge of the information and techniques needed to diagnose and treat human injuries, diseases, and deformities. This includes symptoms, treatment alternatives, drug properties and interactions, and preventive health-care measures. **Psychology:** Knowledge of human behavior and performance; individual differences in ability, personality, and interests; learning and motivation; psychological research methods; and the assessment and treatment of behavioral and affective disorders. **Public Safety and Security:** Knowledge of relevant equipment, policies, procedures, and strategies to promote effective local, state, or national security operations for the protection of people, data, property, and institutions. **Chemistry:** Knowledge of the chemical composition, structure, and properties of substances and of the chemical processes and transformations that they undergo. This includes uses of chemicals, their danger signs, production techniques, and disposal methods. **Therapy and Counseling:** Knowledge of principles, methods, and procedures for diagnosis, treatment, and rehabilitation of physical and mental dysfunctions and for career counseling and guidance.

WORK ENVIRONMENT—Extremely bright or inadequate lighting; physical proximity; sounds, noise levels are distracting or uncomfortable; very hot or cold; contaminants; cramped work space, awkward positions.

Engraver Set-Up Operators

- Growth: 4.6%
- Annual Job Openings: 30,000
- Annual Earnings: $29,340
- Percentage of Women: 17.8%

Related Apprenticeship	Years
Engraving-Press Operator	3
Engraver, Machine	4

Set up and operate machines to transfer printing designs. Positions machine mechanisms and depresses levers to apply marks on roller. Aligns plate with markings on machine table and tacks to table. Turns screws to align machine components. Determines ground setting according to weight of fabric, type of design, and colors in design. Examines marks on roller to verify alignment and detect defects. Records ground setting, length of roller, width of engraving, and circumference of roller on production sheet. Measures depth of engraving and weighs diamond points, using gauges and scales. Inserts mandrel through roller and lifts into position on machine. Adjusts and tightens levers in position, using hand tools. SKILLS—Operation and Control; Installation; Operation Monitoring.

GOE—**Interest Area:** 08. Industrial Production. **Work Group:** 08.03 Production Work. **Other Apprenticeable Jobs in This Work Group:** Bakers, Manufacturing; Bindery Machine Operators and Tenders; Chemical

E

Equipment Controllers and Operators; Coating, Painting, and Spraying Machine Operators and Tenders; Cooling and Freezing Equipment Operators and Tenders; Crushing, Grinding, and Polishing Machine Setters, Operators, and Tenders; Cutters and Trimmers, Hand; Cutting and Slicing Machine Operators and Tenders; Design Printing Machine Setters and Set-Up Operators; Electrolytic Plating and Coating Machine Setters and Set-Up Operators, Metal and Plastic; Electrotypers and Stereotypers; Embossing Machine Set-Up Operators; Extruding, Forming, Pressing, and Compacting Machine Operators and Tenders; Fabric and Apparel Patternmakers; Film Laboratory Technicians; Fitters, Structural Metal—Precision; Food Batchmakers; Furnace, Kiln, Oven, Drier, and Kettle Operators and Tenders; Hand Compositors and Typesetters; Job Printers; Letterpress Setters and Set-Up Operators; Metal Fabricators, Structural Metal Products; Metal-Refining Furnace Operators and Tenders; Mixing and Blending Machine Setters, Operators, and Tenders; Mold Makers, Hand; Molding and Casting Workers; Numerical Control Machine Tool Operators and Tenders, Metal and Plastic; Offset Lithographic Press Setters and Set-Up Operators; Painting, Coating, and Decorating Workers; Photographic Processing Machine Operators; Photographic Reproduction Technicians; Photographic Retouchers and Restorers; Plate Finishers; Platemakers; Precision Printing Workers; Printing Press Machine Operators and Tenders; Production Workers, All Other; Sawing Machine Operators and Tenders; Sawing Machine Setters and Set-Up Operators; Scanner Operators; Separating, Filtering, Clarifying, Precipitating, and Still Machine Setters, Operators, and Tenders; Sewing Machine Operators, Garment; Slaughterers and Meat Packers; Stone Sawyers; Strippers; Team Assemblers; Welder-Fitters; Welders and Cutters; Woodworking Machine Operators and Tenders, Except Sawing. **PERSONALITY TYPE:** Realistic. Realistic occupations frequently involve work activities that include practical, hands-on problems and solutions. They often deal with plants, animals, and real-world materials like wood, tools, and machinery. Many of the occupations require working outside and do not involve a lot of paperwork or working closely with others.

RELATED KNOWLEDGE/COURSES— Production and Processing: Knowledge of raw materials, production processes, quality control, costs, and other techniques for maximizing the effective manufacture and distribution of goods. **Mechanical Devices:** Knowledge of machines and tools, including their designs, uses, repair, and maintenance. **Clerical Practices:** Knowledge of administrative and clerical procedures and systems, such as word processing, managing files and records, stenography and transcription, designing forms, and other office procedures and terminology.

WORK ENVIRONMENT—Hazardous equipment; minor burns, cuts, bites, or stings; indoors; using hands on objects, tools, or controls; sounds, noise levels are distracting or uncomfortable; standing.

Extruding and Drawing Machine Setters, Operators, and Tenders, Metal and Plastic

- Growth: 7.1%
- Annual Job Openings: 14,000
- Annual Earnings: $26,450
- Percentage of Women: 17.9%

Related Apprenticeship	*Years*
Extruder Operator	1

Set up, operate, or tend machines to extrude or draw thermoplastic or metal materials into tubes, rods, hoses, wire, bars, or structural shapes. Adjust controls to draw or press metal into specified shapes and diameters. Change dies on extruding machines according to production line changes. Install dies, machine screws, and sizing rings on machines that extrude thermoplastic or metal materials. Load machine hoppers with mixed materials, using augers, or stuff rolls of plastic dough into machine cylinders. Measure and examine extruded products in order to locate defects and to check for conformance to specifications; adjust controls as necessary to alter products. Replace worn dies when products vary from specifications. Select nozzles, spacers, and wire guides according to diameters and lengths of rods. Start machines and set controls to regulate vacuum, air pressure, sizing rings, and temperature and to synchronize speed of extrusion. Determine setup procedures and select machine dies and parts according to specifications. Clean work areas. Maintain an inventory of materials. Operate shearing mechanisms to cut rods to specified lengths. Reel extruded products into rolls of specified lengths and weights. Test physical properties of products with testing devices such as acid-bath testers, burst testers, and impact testers. Troubleshoot, maintain, and make minor repairs to equipment. Weigh and mix pelletized, granular, or powdered thermoplastic materials and coloring pigments. **SKILLS**—Quality Control Analysis; Operation Monitoring; Equipment Maintenance; Installation; Operation and Control; Repairing; Science; Equipment Selection.

GOE—Interest Area: 08. Industrial Production. **Work Group:** 08.02 Production Technology. **Other Apprenticeable Jobs in This Work Group:** Aircraft Structure Assemblers, Precision; Aircraft Systems Assemblers, Precision; Bench Workers, Jewelry; Bindery Machine Setters and Set-Up Operators; Bookbinders; Buffing and Polishing Set-Up Operators; Coating, Painting, and Spraying Machine Setters and Set-Up Operators; Combination Machine Tool Setters and Set-Up Operators, Metal and Plastic; Dental Laboratory Technicians; Electrical and Electronic Equipment Assemblers; Electrical and Electronic Inspectors and Testers; Electromechanical Equipment Assemblers; Engine and Other Machine Assemblers; Extruding, Forming, Pressing, and Compacting Machine Setters and Set-Up Operators; Forging Machine Setters, Operators, and Tenders, Metal and Plastic; Foundry Mold and Coremakers; Gem and Diamond Workers; Grinding, Honing, Lapping, and Deburring Machine Set-Up Operators; Heat Treating, Annealing, and Tempering Machine Operators and Tenders, Metal and Plastic; Jewelers; Lathe and Turning

E

Machine Tool Setters, Operators, and Tenders, Metal and Plastic; Materials Inspectors; Mechanical Inspectors; Metal Molding, Coremaking, and Casting Machine Operators and Tenders; Milling and Planing Machine Setters, Operators, and Tenders, Metal and Plastic; Model and Mold Makers, Jewelry; Motor Vehicle Inspectors; Paper Goods Machine Setters, Operators, and Tenders; Pewter Casters and Finishers; Plastic Molding and Casting Machine Setters and Set-Up Operators; Precision Devices Inspectors and Testers; Precision Lens Grinders and Polishers; Precision Mold and Pattern Casters, except Nonferrous Metals; Precision Pattern and Die Casters, Nonferrous Metals; Press and Press Brake Machine Setters and Set-Up Operators, Metal and Plastic; Production Inspectors, Testers, Graders, Sorters, Samplers, Weighers; Production Workers, All Other; Rolling Machine Setters, Operators, and Tenders, Metal and Plastic; Silversmiths; Textile Knitting and Weaving Machine Setters, Operators, and Tenders; Textile Winding, Twisting, and Drawing Out Machine Setters, Operators, and Tenders; Welding Machine Setters and Set-Up Operators; Woodworking Machine Setters and Set-Up Operators, Except Sawing. **PERSONALITY TYPE:** Realistic. Realistic occupations frequently involve work activities that include practical, hands-on problems and solutions. They often deal with plants, animals, and real-world materials like wood, tools, and machinery. Many of the occupations require working outside and do not involve a lot of paperwork or working closely with others.

RELATED KNOWLEDGE/COURSES—Production and Processing: Knowledge of raw materials, production processes, quality control, costs, and other techniques for maximizing the effective manufacture and distribution of goods. **Mechanical Devices:** Knowledge of machines and tools, including their designs, uses, repair, and maintenance. **Physics:** Knowledge and prediction of physical principles and laws and their interrelationships and applications to understanding fluid, material, and atmospheric dynamics and mechanical, electrical, atomic, and subatomic structures and processes. **Engineering and Technology:** Knowledge of the practical application of engineering science and technology. This includes applying principles, techniques, procedures, and equipment to the design and production of various goods and services.

WORK ENVIRONMENT—Hazardous equipment; common protective or safety equipment; sounds, noise levels are distracting or uncomfortable; indoors; standing.

Farmers and Ranchers

- Growth: –20.6%
- Annual Job Openings: 118,000
- Annual Earnings: $24,076
- Percentage of Women: 14.6%

Related Apprenticeship	Years
Farmer, General	1
Beekeeper	2

On an ownership or rental basis, operate farms, ranches, greenhouses, nurseries, timber tracts, or other agricultural production establishments that produce crops, horticultural specialties, livestock, poultry, finfish, shellfish, or animal specialties. **May plant, cultivate, harvest, perform post-harvest activities, and market crops and livestock; may hire, train, and supervise farm workers or supervise a farm labor contractor; may prepare cost, production, and other records. May maintain and operate machinery and perform physical work.** Harvests crops and collects specialty products, such as royal jelly from queen bee cells and honey from honeycombs. Sets up and operates farm machinery to till soil, plant, prune, fertilize, apply herbicides and pesticides, and haul harvested crops. Inspects growing environment to maintain optimum growing or breeding conditions. Plans harvesting, considering ripeness and maturity of crop and weather conditions. Breeds and raises stock, such as animals, poultry, honeybees, or earthworms. Arranges with buyers for sale and shipment of crops. Hires and directs workers engaged in planting, cultivating, irrigating, harvesting, and marketing crops and raising livestock. Assembles, positions, and secures structures, such as trellises or beehives, using hand tools. Lubricates, adjusts, and makes minor repairs on farm equipment, using oilcan, grease gun, and hand tools. Maintains employee and financial records. Grades and packages crop for marketing. Demonstrates and explains farm work techniques and safety regulations to workers. Installs irrigation systems and irrigates fields. Grows out-of-season crops in greenhouse or early crops in cold-frame bed or buds and grafts plant stock. Selects and purchases supplies and equipment, such as seed, tree stock, fertilizers, farm machinery, implements, livestock, and feed. Destroys diseased or superfluous crops, such as queen bee cells, bee colonies, parasites, and vermin. Determines kind and quantity of crops or livestock to be raised according to market conditions, weather, and farm size. **SKILLS**—Management of Financial Resources; Management of Personnel Resources; Installation; Equipment Selection; Management of Material Resources; Operation and Control; Equipment Maintenance; Repairing.

GOE—Interest Area: 03. Plants and Animals. **Work Group:** 03.01 Managerial Work in Plants and Animals. **Other Apprenticeable Jobs in This Work Group:** No other apprenticeable jobs in this group. **PERSONALITY TYPE:** Realistic. Realistic occupations frequently involve work activities that include practical, hands-on problems and solutions. They often deal with plants, animals, and real-world materials like wood, tools, and machinery. Many of the occupations require working outside and do not involve a lot of paperwork or working closely with others.

RELATED KNOWLEDGE/COURSES— Food Production: Knowledge of techniques and equipment for planting, growing, and harvesting food products (both plant and animal) for consumption, including storage/handling techniques. **Economics and Accounting:** Knowledge of economic and accounting principles and practices, the financial markets, banking, and the analysis and reporting of financial data. **Personnel and Human Resources:** Knowledge of principles and procedures for personnel recruitment, selection, training, compensation and benefits, labor relations and negotiation, and personnel information systems. **Production and Processing:** Knowledge of raw materials, production processes, quality control, costs, and other techniques for maximizing the effective manufacture and distribution of goods. **Sales and Marketing:** Knowledge of principles and methods for showing, promoting, and selling products or services. This includes marketing strategy and tactics, product demonstration, sales techniques, and sales control systems. **Transportation:** Knowledge of principles and methods for moving people or goods by air, rail, sea, or road, including the relative costs and benefits.

WORK ENVIRONMENT—Outdoors; hazardous equipment; minor burns, cuts, bites, or stings; using hands on objects, tools, or controls; contaminants; standing.

Fence Erectors

- Growth: 13.4%
- Annual Job Openings: 4,000
- Annual Earnings: $22,580
- Percentage of Women: 2.6%

Related Apprenticeship	*Years*
Fence Erector	3

Erect and repair metal and wooden fences and fence gates around highways, industrial establishments, residences, or farms, using hand and power tools. Sets metal or wooden post in upright position in posthole. Inserts metal tubing through rail supports. Attaches rails or tension wire along bottoms of posts to form fencing frame. Attaches fencing to frame. Nails pointed slats to rails to construct picket fence. Mixes and pours concrete around base of post or tamps soil into posthole to embed post. Blasts rock formations with dynamite to facilitate digging of postholes. Welds metal parts together, using portable gas welding equipment.

Cuts metal tubing, using pipe cutter. Lays out fence line, using tape measure, and marks positions for postholes. Aligns posts, using line or by sighting, and verifies vertical alignment of posts with plumb bob or spirit level. Digs postholes with spade, posthole digger, or power-driven auger. Saws required lengths of lumber to make rails for wooden fence. Assembles gate and fastens gate in position, using hand tools. Erects alternate panel, basket weave, and louvered fences. Nails top and bottom rails to fence posts or inserts them in slots on posts. Stretches wire, wire mesh, or chain link fencing between posts. Completes top fence rail of metal fence by connecting tube sections, using metal sleeves. Attaches fencerail support to post, using hammer and pliers. **SKILLS**—Repairing; Equipment Selection.

GOE—**Interest Area:** 06. Construction, Mining, and Drilling. **Work Group:** 06.02 Construction. **Other Apprenticeable Jobs in This Work Group:** Boat Builders and Shipwrights; Boilermakers; Brickmasons and Blockmasons; Carpet Installers; Ceiling Tile Installers; Cement Masons and Concrete Finishers; Construction and Related Workers, All Other; Construction Carpenters; Drywall Installers; Electricians; Floor Layers, Except Carpet, Wood, and Hard Tiles; Glaziers; Grader, Bulldozer, and Scraper Operators; Insulation Workers, Floor, Ceiling, and Wall; Insulation Workers, Mechanical; Operating Engineers; Painters, Construction and Maintenance; Paperhangers; Paving, Surfacing, and Tamping Equipment Operators; Pipe Fitters; Plasterers and Stucco Masons; Plumbers; Reinforcing Iron and Rebar Workers; Riggers; Roofers; Rough Carpenters; Sheet Metal Workers; Ship Carpenters and Joiners; Stone Cutters and Carvers; Stonemasons; Structural Iron and Steel Workers; Tapers; Terrazzo Workers and Finishers; Tile and Marble Setters. **PERSONALITY TYPE:** Realistic. Realistic occupations frequently involve work activities that include practical, hands-on problems and solutions. They often deal with plants, animals, and real-world materials like wood, tools, and machinery. Many of the occupations require working outside and do not involve a lot of paperwork or working closely with others.

RELATED KNOWLEDGE/COURSES— Building and Construction: Knowledge of the materials, methods, and tools involved in the construction or repair of houses, buildings, or other structures, such as highways and roads. **Geography:** Knowledge of principles and methods for describing the features of land, sea, and air masses, including their physical characteristics; locations; interrelationships; and distribution of plant, animal, and human life. **Public Safety and Security:** Knowledge of relevant equipment, policies, procedures, and strategies to promote effective local, state, or national security operations for the protection of people, data, property, and institutions. **Design:** Knowledge of design techniques, tools, and principles involved in production of precision technical plans, blueprints, drawings, and models. **Engineering and Technology:** Knowledge of the practical application of engineering science and technology. This includes applying principles, techniques, procedures, and equipment to the design and production of various goods and services. **Mechanical Devices:** Knowledge of machines and tools, including their designs, uses, repair, and maintenance.

WORK ENVIRONMENT—Outdoors; minor burns, cuts, bites, or stings; standing; using hands on objects, tools, or controls; hazardous conditions.

Fire Inspectors

- Growth: 11.6%
- Annual Job Openings: 1,000
- Annual Earnings: $44,250
- Percentage of Women: 10.1%

Related Apprenticeship	Years
Fire Inspector	4

Inspect buildings and equipment to detect fire hazards and enforce state and local regulations. Attend training classes in order to maintain current knowledge of fire prevention, safety, and firefighting procedures. Conduct fire code compliance follow-ups to ensure that corrective actions have been taken in cases where violations were found. Conduct fire exit drills to monitor and evaluate evacuation procedures. Conduct inspections and acceptance testing of newly installed fire protection systems. Develop or review fire exit plans. Identify corrective actions necessary to bring properties into compliance with applicable fire codes, laws, regulations, and standards and explain these measures to property owners or their representatives. Inspect and test fire protection and/or fire detection systems to verify that such systems are installed in accordance with appropriate laws, codes, ordinances, regulations, and standards. Inspect buildings to locate hazardous conditions and fire code violations such as accumulations of combustible material, electrical wiring problems, and inadequate or non-functional fire exits. Inspect liquefied petroleum installations, storage containers, and transportation and delivery systems for compliance with fire laws. Inspect properties that store, handle, and use hazardous materials to ensure compliance with laws, codes, and regulations and issue hazardous materials permits to facilities found in compliance. Issue permits for public assemblies. Review blueprints and plans for new or remodeled buildings in order to ensure that the structures meet fire safety codes. Search for clues as to the cause of a fire after the fire is completely extinguished. Write detailed reports of fire inspections performed, fire code violations observed, and corrective recommendations offered. Arrange for the replacement of defective fire fighting equipment and for repair of fire alarm and sprinkler systems, making minor repairs such as servicing fire extinguishers when feasible. Collect fees for permits and licenses. Develop and coordinate fire prevention programs such as false alarm billing, fire inspection reporting, and hazardous materials management. Investigate causes of fires, collecting and preparing evidence and presenting it in court when necessary. **SKILLS**—Persuasion; Service Orientation; Troubleshooting; Science; Writing; Systems Analysis; Critical Thinking; Instructing.

GOE—Interest Area: 04. Law, Law Enforcement, and Public Safety. **Work Group:** 04.04 Public Safety. **Other Apprenticeable Jobs in This Work Group:** Emergency Medical Technicians and Paramedics; Forest Fire Fighters; Government Property Inspectors and Investigators; Municipal Fire Fighters; Nuclear Monitoring Technicians; Occupational Health and Safety Specialists. **PERSONALITY TYPE:** Conventional. Conventional occupations frequently involve following set procedures and routines. These occupations can include working with data and details more than with ideas. Usually there is a clear line of authority to follow.

RELATED KNOWLEDGE/COURSES—Public Safety and Security: Knowledge of relevant equipment, policies, procedures, and strategies to promote effective local, state, or national security operations for the protection of people, data, property, and institutions. **Law and Government:** Knowledge of laws, legal codes, court procedures, precedents, government regulations, executive orders, agency rules, and the democratic political process. **Medicine and Dentistry:** Knowledge of the information and techniques needed to diagnose and treat human injuries, diseases, and deformities. This includes symptoms, treatment alternatives, drug properties and interactions, and preventive health-care measures. **Engineering and Technology:** Knowledge of the practical application of engineering science and technology. This includes applying principles, techniques, procedures, and equipment to the design and production of various goods and services. **Education and Training:** Knowledge of principles and methods for curriculum and training design, teaching and instruction for individuals and groups, and the measurement of training effects. **Mechanical Devices:** Knowledge of machines and tools, including their designs, uses, repair, and maintenance.

WORK ENVIRONMENT—Climbing ladders, scaffolds, or poles; hazardous conditions; walking and running; spend time kneeling, crouching, stooping, or crawling; outdoors; standing.

First-Line Supervisors/Managers of Retail Sales Workers

- Growth: 9.1%
- Annual Job Openings: 251,000
- Annual Earnings: $30,680
- Percentage of Women: 41.8%

Related Apprenticeship	Years
Manager, Retail Store	3

Directly supervise sales workers in a retail establishment or department. Duties may include management functions, such as purchasing, budgeting, accounting, and personnel work, in addition to supervisory duties. Provide customer service by greeting and assisting customers and responding to customer inquiries and complaints. Monitor sales activities to ensure that customers receive satisfactory service and quality goods. Assign employees to specific duties. Direct and supervise employees engaged in sales, inventory-taking, reconciling cash receipts, or performing services for customers. Inventory stock and reorder when inventory drops to a specified level. Keep records of purchases, sales, and requisitions. Enforce safety, health, and security rules. Examine products purchased for resale or received for storage to assess the condition of each product or item. Hire, train, and evaluate personnel in sales or marketing establishments, promoting or firing workers when appropriate. Perform work activities of subordinates, such as cleaning and organizing shelves and displays and selling merchandise. Establish and implement policies, goals, objectives, and procedures for their department. Instruct staff on how to handle difficult and complicated sales. Formulate pricing policies for merchandise according to profitability requirements. Estimate consumer demand and determine the types and amounts of goods to be sold. Examine merchandise to ensure that it is correctly priced and displayed and that it functions as advertised. Plan and prepare work schedules and keep records of employees' work schedules and time cards. Review inventory and sales records to prepare reports for management and budget departments. Plan and coordinate advertising campaigns and sales promotions and prepare merchandise displays and advertising copy. Confer with company officials to develop methods and procedures to increase sales, expand markets, and promote business. Establish credit policies and operating procedures. Plan budgets and authorize payments and merchandise returns. **SKILLS**—Management of Personnel Resources; Persuasion; Instructing; Time Management; Management of Financial Resources; Service Orientation; Social Perceptiveness; Negotiation.

GOE—Interest Area: 10. Sales and Marketing. **Work Group:** 10.01 Managerial Work in Sales and Marketing. **Other Apprenticeable Jobs in This Work Group:** No other apprenticeable jobs in this group. **PERSONALITY TYPE:** Enterprising. Enterprising occupations frequently involve starting up and carrying out projects. These occupations can involve leading people and making many decisions. They sometimes require risk taking and often deal with business.

RELATED KNOWLEDGE/COURSES— **Customer and Personal Service:** Knowledge of principles and processes for providing customer and personal services. This includes customer needs assessment, meeting quality standards for services, and evaluation of customer satisfaction. **Sales and Marketing:** Knowledge of principles and methods for showing, promoting, and selling products or services. This includes marketing strategy and tactics, product demonstration, sales techniques, and sales control systems. **Administration and Management:** Knowledge of business and management principles involved in strategic planning, resource allocation, human resources modeling, leadership technique, production methods, and coordination of people and resources. **Personnel and Human Resources:** Knowledge of principles and procedures for personnel recruitment, selection, training, compensation and benefits, labor relations and negotiation, and personnel information systems. **Public Safety and Security:** Knowledge of relevant equipment, policies, procedures, and strategies to promote effective local, state, or national security operations for the protection of people, data, property, and institutions. **English Language:** Knowledge of the structure and content of the English language, including the meaning and spelling of words, rules of composition, and grammar. **Communications and Media:** Knowledge of media production, communication, and dissemination techniques and methods. This includes alternative ways to inform and entertain via written, oral, and visual media.

WORK ENVIRONMENT—Physical proximity; walking and running; standing; indoors; hazardous equipment.

Fish and Game Wardens

- Growth: 7.1%
- Annual Job Openings: 1,000
- Annual Earnings: $41,380
- Percentage of Women: 29.2%

Related Apprenticeship	Years
Fish and Game Warden	2

Patrol assigned area to prevent fish and game law violations. Investigate reports of damage to crops or property by wildlife. Compile biological data. Patrols assigned area by car, boat, airplane, or horse or on foot to observe persons engaged in taking fish and game. Resurveys area and totals bag counts of hunters to determine effectiveness of control measures. Assists in promoting hunter safety training. Recommends revisions or changes in hunting and trapping regulations or seasons and animal relocation and release to obtain balance of wildlife and habitat. Seizes equipment used in fish and game law violations and arranges for disposition of fish and game illegally taken or possessed. Ensures that method and equipment used are lawful and apprehends violators. Collects and reports information on population and condition of fish and wildlife in their habitat, availability of game food and cover, and suspected pollution. Searches area of reported property damage for animal tracks, leavings, and other evidence to identify species of animal responsible. Serves warrants, makes arrests, and prepares and presents evidence in court actions. Investigates hunting accidents and reports of fish and game law violations, issues warnings or citations, and files reports. Traps beavers, dynamites beaver dams, and tranquilizes animals to implement approved control measures. Photographs extent of damage, documents other evidence, estimates financial loss, and recommends compensation. Addresses schools and civic groups to disseminate wildlife information and promote public relations. **SKILLS**—Persuasion; Negotiation; Speaking; Systems Analysis; Systems Evaluation; Social Perceptiveness; Active Listening; Critical Thinking.

GOE—Interest Area: 04. Law, Law Enforcement, and Public Safety. **Work Group:** 04.03 Law Enforcement. **Other Apprenticeable Jobs in This Work Group:** Correctional Officers and Jailers; Fire Investigators; Police Patrol Officers; Private Detectives and Investigators; Security Guards. **PERSONALITY TYPE:** Realistic. Realistic occupations frequently involve work activities that include practical, hands-on problems and solutions. They often deal with plants, animals, and real-world materials like wood, tools, and machinery. Many of the occupations require working outside and do not involve a lot of paperwork or working closely with others.

RELATED KNOWLEDGE/COURSES—**Biology:** Knowledge of plant and animal organisms and their tissues, cells, functions, interdependencies, and interactions with each other and the environment. **Law and Government:** Knowledge of laws, legal codes, court procedures, precedents, government regulations, executive orders, agency rules, and the democratic political process. **Public Safety and Security:** Knowledge of relevant equipment, policies, procedures, and strategies to promote effective local, state, or national security operations for the protection of people, data, property, and institutions. **Geography:** Knowledge of

principles and methods for describing the features of land, sea, and air masses, including their physical characteristics; locations; interrelationships; and distribution of plant, animal, and human life. **Food Production:** Knowledge of techniques and equipment for planting, growing, and harvesting food products (both plant and animal) for consumption, including storage/handling techniques. **Education and Training:** Knowledge of principles and methods for curriculum and training design, teaching and instruction for individuals and groups, and the measurement of training effects.

WORK ENVIRONMENT—Outdoors; minor burns, cuts, bites, or stings; walking and running; extremely bright or inadequate lighting; hazardous conditions.

Fitters, Structural Metal—Precision

- ◉ Growth: 6.2%
- ◉ Annual Job Openings: 14,000
- ◉ Annual Earnings: $28,990
- ◉ Percentage of Women: 4.7%

Related Apprenticeship	Years
Fitter (Machine Shop)	2
Fitter I (Any Industry)	3

Lay out, position, align, and fit together fabricated parts of structural metal products preparatory to welding or riveting. Locates reference points, using transit, and erects ladders and scaffolding to fit together large assemblies. Removes high spots and cuts bevels, using hand files, portable grinders, and cutting torch. Sets up face block, jigs, and fixtures. Examines blueprints and plans sequence of operation, applying knowledge of geometry, effects of heat, weld shrinkage, machining, and metal thickness. Tack-welds fitted parts together. Positions or tightens braces, jacks, clamps, ropes, or bolt straps or bolts parts in positions for welding or riveting. Aligns parts, using jack, turnbuckles, wedges, drift pins, pry bars, and hammer. Moves parts into position manually or by hoist or crane. Marks reference points onto floor or face block and transposes them to workpiece, using measuring devices, squares, chalk, and soapstone. Gives directions to welder to build up low spots or short pieces with weld. Heat-treats parts with acetylene torch. Straightens warped or bent parts, using sledge, hand torch, straightening press, or bulldozer. **SKILLS**—Mathematics; Equipment Selection.

GOE—Interest Area: 08. Industrial Production. **Work Group:** 08.03 Production Work. **Other Apprenticeable Jobs in This Work Group:** Bakers, Manufacturing; Bindery Machine Operators and Tenders; Chemical Equipment Controllers and Operators; Coating, Painting, and Spraying Machine Operators and Tenders; Cooling and Freezing Equipment Operators and Tenders; Crushing, Grinding, and Polishing Machine Setters, Operators, and Tenders; Cutters and Trimmers, Hand; Cutting and Slicing Machine Operators and Tenders; Design Printing Machine Setters and Set-Up Operators; Electrolytic Plating and Coating Machine Setters and Set-Up Operators, Metal and Plastic; Electrotypers and Stereotypers; Embossing Machine Set-Up Operators; Engraver Set-Up Operators; Extruding, Forming, Pressing, and Compacting Machine Operators and Tenders; Fabric and Apparel Patternmakers; Film Laboratory Technicians; Food Batchmakers; Furnace, Kiln, Oven, Drier, and Kettle Operators and Tenders; Hand Compositors and Typesetters; Job Printers; Letterpress Setters and Set-Up Operators; Metal Fabricators, Structural Metal Products; Metal-Refining Furnace Operators and Tenders; Mixing and Blending Machine Setters, Operators, and Tenders; Mold Makers, Hand; Molding and Casting Workers; Numerical Control Machine Tool Operators and Tenders, Metal and Plastic; Offset Lithographic Press Setters and Set-Up Operators; Painting, Coating, and Decorating Workers; Photographic Processing Machine Operators; Photographic Reproduction Technicians; Photographic Retouchers and Restorers; Plate Finishers; Platemakers; Precision Printing Workers; Printing Press Machine Operators and Tenders; Production Workers, All Other; Sawing Machine Operators and Tenders; Sawing Machine Setters and Set-Up Operators; Scanner Operators; Separating, Filtering, Clarifying, Precipitating, and Still Machine Setters, Operators, and Tenders; Sewing Machine Operators, Garment; Slaughterers and Meat Packers; Stone Sawyers; Strippers; Team Assemblers; Welder-Fitters; Welders and Cutters; Woodworking Machine Operators and Tenders, Except Sawing. **PERSONALITY TYPE:** Realistic. Realistic occupations frequently involve work activities that include practical, hands-on problems and solutions. They often deal with plants, animals, and real-world materials like wood, tools, and machinery. Many of the occupations require working outside and do not involve a lot of paperwork or working closely with others.

RELATED KNOWLEDGE/COURSES—
Building and Construction: Knowledge of the materials, methods, and tools involved in the construction or repair of houses, buildings, or other structures, such as highways and roads. **Mechanical Devices:** Knowledge of machines and tools, including their designs, uses, repair, and maintenance. **Physics:** Knowledge and prediction of physical principles and laws and their interrelationships and applications to understanding fluid, material, and atmospheric dynamics and mechanical, electrical, atomic, and subatomic structures and processes. **Design:** Knowledge of design techniques, tools, and principles involved in production of precision technical plans, blueprints, drawings, and models. **Mathematics:** Knowledge of arithmetic, algebra, geometry, calculus, and statistics and their applications. **Production and Processing:** Knowledge of raw materials, production processes, quality control, costs, and other techniques for maximizing the effective manufacture and distribution of goods. **Engineering and Technology:** Knowledge of the practical application of engineering science and technology. This includes applying principles, techniques, procedures, and equipment to the design and production of various goods and services.

WORK ENVIRONMENT—Hazardous equipment; minor burns, cuts, bites, or stings; common protective or safety equipment; sounds, noise levels are distracting or uncomfortable; climbing ladders, scaffolds, or poles.

Floor Layers, Except Carpet, Wood, and Hard Tiles

- Growth: 13.4%
- Annual Job Openings: 4,000
- Annual Earnings: $34,840
- Percentage of Women: 2.5%

Related Apprenticeship	Years
Floor Layer	3
Floor-Covering Layer	3
Soft-Tile Setter	3

Apply blocks, strips, or sheets of shock-absorbing, sound-deadening, or decorative coverings to floors. Cut flooring material to fit around obstructions. Determine traffic areas and decide location of seams. Form a smooth foundation by stapling plywood or Masonite over the floor or by brushing waterproof compound onto surface and filling cracks with plaster, putty, or grout to seal pores. Heat and soften floor covering materials to patch cracks or fit floor coverings around irregular surfaces, using blowtorch. Inspect surface to be covered to ensure that it is firm and dry. Lay out, position, and apply shock-absorbing, sound-deadening, or decorative coverings to floors, walls, and cabinets, following guidelines to keep courses straight and create designs. Measure and mark guidelines on surfaces or foundations, using chalk lines and dividers. Apply adhesive cement to floor or wall material to join and adhere foundation material. Cut covering and foundation materials according to blueprints and sketches. Remove excess cement to clean finished surface. Roll and press sheet wall and floor covering into cement base to smooth and finish surface, using hand roller. Sweep, scrape, sand, or chip dirt and irregularities to clean base surfaces, correcting imperfections that may show through the covering. Trim excess covering materials, tack edges, and join sections of covering material to form tight joint. Disconnect and remove appliances, light fixtures, and worn floor and wall covering from floors, walls, and cabinets. **SKILLS**—Installation; Repairing.

GOE—**Interest Area:** 06. Construction, Mining, and Drilling. **Work Group:** 06.02 Construction. **Other Apprenticeable Jobs in This Work Group:** Boat Builders and Shipwrights; Boilermakers; Brickmasons and Blockmasons; Carpet Installers; Ceiling Tile Installers; Cement Masons and Concrete Finishers; Construction and Related Workers, All Other; Construction Carpenters; Drywall Installers; Electricians; Fence Erectors; Glaziers; Grader, Bulldozer, and Scraper Operators; Insulation Workers, Floor, Ceiling, and Wall; Insulation Workers, Mechanical; Operating Engineers; Painters, Construction and Maintenance; Paperhangers; Paving, Surfacing, and Tamping Equipment Operators; Pipe Fitters; Plasterers and Stucco Masons; Plumbers; Reinforcing Iron and Rebar Workers; Riggers; Roofers; Rough Carpenters; Sheet Metal Workers; Ship Carpenters and Joiners; Stone Cutters and Carvers; Stonemasons; Structural Iron and Steel Workers; Tapers; Terrazzo Workers and Finishers; Tile and Marble Setters. **PERSONALITY TYPE:** Realistic. Realistic occupations frequently involve work activities that include practical, hands-on problems and solutions. They often deal with plants, animals, and real-world materials like wood, tools, and machinery. Many of the occupations require working outside and do not involve a lot of paperwork or working closely with others.

RELATED KNOWLEDGE/COURSES— **Building and Construction:** Knowledge of the materials, methods, and tools involved in the construction or repair of houses, buildings, or other structures, such as highways and roads. **Design:** Knowledge of design techniques, tools, and principles involved in production of precision technical plans, blueprints, drawings, and models.

WORK ENVIRONMENT—Spend time kneeling, crouching, stooping, or crawling; spend time bending or twisting the body; minor burns, cuts, bites, or stings; indoors; cramped work space, awkward positions.

Floral Designers

- Growth: 12.4%
- Annual Job Openings: 13,000
- Annual Earnings: $19,660
- Percentage of Women: 55.4%

Related Apprenticeship	*Years*
Floral Designer	1

Design, cut, and arrange live, dried, or artificial flowers and foliage. Confer with clients regarding price and type of arrangement desired and the date, time, and place of delivery. Plan arrangement according to client's requirements, utilizing knowledge of design and properties of materials, or select appropriate standard design pattern. Water plants and cut, condition, and clean flowers and foliage for storage. Select flora and foliage for arrangements, working with numerous combinations to synthesize and develop new creations. Order and purchase flowers and supplies from wholesalers and growers. Wrap and price completed arrangements. Trim material and arrange bouquets, wreaths, terrariums, and other items, using trimmers, shapers, wire, pins, floral tape, foam, and other materials. Perform office and retail service duties such as keeping financial records, serving customers, answering telephones, selling giftware items, and receiving payment. Inform customers about the care, maintenance, and handling of various flowers and foliage, indoor plants, and other items. Decorate or supervise the decoration of buildings, halls, churches, or other facilities for parties, weddings, and other occasions. Perform general cleaning duties in the store to ensure the shop is clean and tidy. Unpack stock as it comes into the shop. Create and change in-store and window displays, designs, and looks to enhance a shop's image. Conduct classes or demonstrations or train other workers. Grow flowers for use in arrangements or for sale in shop. **SKILLS**—Management of Financial Resources; Management of Material Resources; Service Orientation; Time Management; Social Perceptiveness; Instructing; Management of Personnel Resources; Learning Strategies.

GOE—**Interest Area:** 01. Arts, Entertainment, and Media. **Work Group:** 01.04 Visual Arts. **Other Apprenticeable Jobs in This Work Group:** Cartoonists; Commercial and Industrial Designers; Exhibit Designers; Fashion Designers; Graphic Designers; Interior Designers; Merchandise Displayers and Window Trimmers; Painters and Illustrators. **PERSONALITY TYPE:** Artistic. Artistic occupations frequently involve working with forms, designs, and patterns. They often require self-expression, and the work can be done without following a clear set of rules.

RELATED KNOWLEDGE/COURSES— **Customer and Personal Service:** Knowledge of principles and processes for providing customer and personal services. This includes customer needs assessment, meeting quality standards for services, and evaluation of customer satisfaction. **Sales and Marketing:** Knowledge of principles and methods for showing, promoting, and selling products or services. This includes marketing strategy and tactics, product demonstration, sales techniques, and sales control systems. **Fine Arts:** Knowledge of the theory and techniques required to compose, produce, and perform works of music, dance, visual arts, drama, and sculpture. **Personnel and Human Resources:** Knowledge of principles and procedures for personnel recruitment, selection, training, compensation and benefits, labor relations and negotiation, and personnel information systems. **Production and Processing:** Knowledge of raw materials, production processes, quality control, costs, and other techniques for maximizing the effective manufacture and distribution of goods. **Design:** Knowledge of design techniques, tools, and principles involved in production of precision technical plans, blueprints, drawings, and models.

WORK ENVIRONMENT—Physical proximity; standing; in an enclosed vehicle or equipment; minor burns, cuts, bites, or stings; very hot or cold.

Food Batchmakers

- Growth: 7.2%
- Annual Job Openings: 10,000
- Annual Earnings: $21,900
- Percentage of Women: 55.8%

Related Apprenticeship	Years
Cheesemaker	2
Candy Maker	3

Set up and operate equipment that mixes or blends ingredients used in the manufacturing of food products. Includes candy makers and cheese makers. Determine mixing sequences, based on knowledge of temperature effects and of the solubility of specific ingredients. Examine, feel, and taste product samples during production in order to evaluate quality, color, texture, flavor, and bouquet and document the results. Fill processing or cooking containers, such as kettles, rotating cookers, pressure cookers, or vats, with ingredients by opening valves, by starting pumps or injectors, or by hand. Follow recipes to produce food products of specified flavor, texture, clarity, bouquet, and/or color. Manipulate products, by hand or using machines, in order to separate, spread, knead, spin, cast, cut, pull, or roll products. Mix or blend ingredients according to recipes, using a paddle or an agitator or by controlling vats that heat and mix ingredients. Modify cooking and forming operations based on the results of sampling processes, adjusting time cycles and ingredients in order to achieve desired qualities such as firmness or texture. Observe and listen to

equipment in order to detect possible malfunctions, such as leaks or plugging, and report malfunctions or undesirable tastes to supervisors. Observe gauges and thermometers to determine if the mixing chamber temperature is within specified limits and turn valves to control the temperature. Press switches and turn knobs to start, adjust, and regulate equipment such as beaters, extruders, discharge pipes, and salt pumps. Select and measure or weigh ingredients, using English or metric measures and balance scales. Set up, operate, and tend equipment that cooks, mixes, blends, or processes ingredients in the manufacturing of food products according to formulas or recipes. Test food product samples for moisture content, acidity level, specific gravity, and/or butter-fat content and continue processing until desired levels are reached. Turn valve controls to start equipment and to adjust operation in order to maintain product quality. Clean and sterilize vats and factory processing areas. Cool food product batches on slabs or in water-cooled kettles. Formulate and/or modify recipes for specific kinds of food products. **SKILLS**—Science; Instructing; Operation and Control.

GOE—Interest Area: 08. Industrial Production. **Work Group:** 08.03 Production Work. **Other Apprenticeable Jobs in This Work Group:** Bakers, Manufacturing; Bindery Machine Operators and Tenders; Chemical Equipment Controllers and Operators; Coating, Painting, and Spraying Machine Operators and Tenders; Cooling and Freezing Equipment Operators and Tenders; Crushing, Grinding, and Polishing Machine Setters, Operators, and Tenders; Cutters and Trimmers, Hand; Cutting and Slicing Machine Operators and Tenders; Design Printing Machine Setters and Set-Up Operators; Electrolytic Plating and Coating

Machine Setters and Set-Up Operators, Metal and Plastic; Electrotypers and Stereotypers; Embossing Machine Set-Up Operators; Engraver Set-Up Operators; Extruding, Forming, Pressing, and Compacting Machine Operators and Tenders; Fabric and Apparel Patternmakers; Film Laboratory Technicians; Fitters, Structural Metal—Precision; Furnace, Kiln, Oven, Drier, and Kettle Operators and Tenders; Hand Compositors and Typesetters; Job Printers; Letterpress Setters and Set-Up Operators; Metal Fabricators, Structural Metal Products; Metal-Refining Furnace Operators and Tenders; Mixing and Blending Machine Setters, Operators, and Tenders; Mold Makers, Hand; Molding and Casting Workers; Numerical Control Machine Tool Operators and Tenders, Metal and Plastic; Offset Lithographic Press Setters and Set-Up Operators; Painting, Coating, and Decorating Workers; Photographic Processing Machine Operators; Photographic Reproduction Technicians; Photographic Retouchers and Restorers; Plate Finishers; Platemakers; Precision Printing Workers; Printing Press Machine Operators and Tenders; Production Workers, All Other; Sawing Machine Operators and Tenders; Sawing Machine Setters and Set-Up Operators; Scanner Operators; Separating, Filtering, Clarifying, Precipitating, and Still Machine Setters, Operators, and Tenders; Sewing Machine Operators, Garment; Slaughterers and Meat Packers; Stone Sawyers; Strippers; Team Assemblers; Welder-Fitters; Welders and Cutters; Woodworking Machine Operators and Tenders, Except Sawing. **PERSONALITY TYPE:** Realistic. Realistic occupations frequently involve work activities that include practical, hands-on problems and solutions. They often deal with plants, animals, and real-world materials like wood, tools, and machinery. Many of the occupations require working outside and do not involve a lot of paperwork or working closely with others.

RELATED KNOWLEDGE/COURSES— Food Production: Knowledge of techniques and equipment for planting, growing, and harvesting food products (both plant and animal) for consumption, including storage/handling techniques. **Production and Processing:** Knowledge of raw materials, production processes, quality control, costs, and other techniques for maximizing the effective manufacture and distribution of goods.

WORK ENVIRONMENT—Standing; indoors; spend time making repetitive motions; using hands on objects, tools, or controls; very hot or cold.

Food Service Managers

- Growth: 11.5%
- Annual Job Openings: 58,000
- Annual Earnings: $37,260
- Percentage of Women: 44.6%

Related Apprenticeship	Years
Manager, Food Service	3

Plan, direct, or coordinate activities of an organization or department that serves food and beverages. Test cooked food by tasting and smelling it in order to ensure palatability and flavor conformity. Investigate and resolve complaints regarding food quality, service, or accommodations. Schedule and receive food and beverage deliveries, checking delivery contents in order to verify product quality and quantity. Monitor food preparation methods, portion sizes, and garnishing and presentation of food in order to ensure that food is prepared and presented in an acceptable manner. Monitor budgets and payroll records and review financial transactions in order to ensure that expenditures are authorized and budgeted. Schedule staff hours and assign duties. Monitor compliance with health and fire regulations regarding food preparation and serving and building maintenance in lodging and dining facilities. Coordinate assignments of cooking personnel in order to ensure economical use of food and timely preparation. Keep records required by government agencies regarding sanitation and food subsidies when appropriate. Establish standards for personnel performance and customer service. Estimate food, liquor, wine, and other beverage consumption in order to anticipate amounts to be purchased or requisitioned. Review work procedures and operational problems in order to determine ways to improve service, performance, and/or safety. Perform some food preparation or service tasks such as cooking, clearing tables, and serving food and drinks when necessary. Maintain food and equipment inventories and keep inventory records. Organize and direct worker training programs, resolve personnel problems, hire new staff, and evaluate employee performance in dining and lodging facilities. Order and purchase equipment and supplies. Review menus and analyze recipes in order to determine labor and overhead costs and assign prices to menu items. Record the number, type, and cost of items sold in order to determine which items may be unpopular or less profitable. Assess staffing needs and recruit staff using methods such as newspaper advertisements or attendance at job fairs. Arrange for equipment maintenance and repairs and coordinate a variety of services such as waste removal and pest control. **SKILLS**—Management of Personnel Resources; Management of Financial Resources; Time Management; Instructing; Service Orientation; Learning Strategies; Monitoring; Social Perceptiveness; Negotiation.

GOE—Interest Area: 11. Recreation, Travel, and Other Personal Services. **Work Group:** 11.01 Managerial Work in Recreation, Travel, and Other Personal Services. **Other Apprenticeable Jobs in This Work Group:** No other apprenticeable jobs in this group. **PERSONALITY TYPE:** Enterprising. Enterprising occupations frequently involve starting up and carrying out projects. These occupations can involve leading people and making many decisions. They sometimes require risk taking and often deal with business.

RELATED KNOWLEDGE/COURSES— **Customer and Personal Service:** Knowledge of principles and processes for providing customer and personal services. This includes customer needs assessment, meeting quality standards for services, and evaluation of customer satisfaction. **Sales and Marketing:** Knowledge of principles and methods for showing, promoting, and selling products or services. This includes marketing strategy and tactics, product demonstration, sales techniques, and sales control systems. **Food Production:** Knowledge of techniques and equipment for planting, growing, and harvesting food products (both plant and animal) for consumption, including storage/handling techniques. **Production and Processing:** Knowledge of raw materials, production processes, quality control, costs, and other techniques for maximizing the effective manufacture and distribution of goods. **Administration and Management:** Knowledge of business and management principles involved in strategic planning, resource allocation, human resources modeling, leadership technique, production methods, and coordination of people and resources. **Personnel and Human Resources:** Knowledge of principles and procedures for personnel recruitment, selection, training, compensation and benefits, labor relations and negotiation, and personnel information systems.

WORK ENVIRONMENT—Very hot or cold; physical proximity; walking and running; sounds, noise levels are distracting or uncomfortable; minor burns, cuts, bites, or stings.

Forest Fire Fighters

- Growth: 20.7%
- Annual Job Openings: 29,000
- Annual Earnings: $37,060
- Percentage of Women: 3.6%

Related Apprenticeship	Years
Wildland Fire Fighter Specialist	1

Control and suppress fires in forests or vacant public land. Collaborate with other firefighters as a member of a firefighting crew. Establish water supplies, connect hoses, and direct water onto fires. Extinguish flames and embers to suppress fires, using shovels or engine- or hand-driven water or chemical pumps. Fell trees, cut and clear brush, and dig trenches in order to create firelines, using axes, chainsaws, or shovels. Maintain contact with fire dispatchers at all times in order to notify them of the need for additional firefighters and supplies or to detail any difficulties encountered. Operate pumps connected to high-pressure hoses. Orient self in relation to fire, using compass and map, and collect supplies and equipment dropped by parachute. Participate in physical training in order to maintain high levels of physical fitness. Patrol burned areas after fires to locate and eliminate hot spots that may restart fires. Test and maintain tools, equipment, jump gear and parachutes in order to ensure readiness for fire suppression activities. Observe forest areas from fire lookout towers in order to spot potential problems. Organize fire caches, positioning equipment for the most effective response. Parachute from aircraft into remote areas for initial attack on wildland fires. Participate in fire prevention and inspection programs. Perform forest maintenance and improvement tasks such as cutting brush, planting trees, building trails and marking timber. Rescue fire victims, and administer emergency medical aid. Take action to contain any hazardous chemicals that could catch fire, leak, or spill. Transport personnel and cargo to and from fire areas. Drop weighted paper streamers from aircraft to determine the speed and direction of the wind at fire sites. Inform and educate the public about fire prevention. Maintain fire equipment and firehouse living quarters. Maintain knowledge of current firefighting practices by participating in drills and by attending seminars, conventions, and conferences. Serve as fully trained lead helicopter crewmember and as helispot manager. **SKILLS**—Service Orientation; Coordination; Technology Design; Science; Critical Thinking; Systems Analysis; Social Perceptiveness; Monitoring; Management of Material Resources.

GOE—Interest Area: 04. Law, Law Enforcement, and Public Safety. Work Group: 04.04 Public Safety. Other Apprenticeable Jobs in This Work Group: Emergency Medical Technicians and Paramedics; Fire Inspectors; Government Property Inspectors and Investigators; Municipal Fire Fighters; Nuclear Monitoring Technicians; Occupational Health and Safety Specialists. PERSONALITY TYPE: Realistic. Realistic occupations frequently involve work activities that include practical, hands-on problems and solutions. They often deal with plants, animals, and real-world materials like wood, tools, and machinery. Many of the occupations require working outside and do not involve a lot of paperwork or working closely with others.

RELATED KNOWLEDGE/COURSES— Public Safety and Security: Knowledge of relevant equipment, policies, procedures, and strategies to promote effective local, state, or national security operations for the protection of people, data, property, and institutions. Transportation: Knowledge of principles and methods for moving people or goods by air, rail, sea, or road, including the relative costs and benefits. Telecommunications: Knowledge of transmission, broadcasting, switching, control, and operation of telecommunications systems. Geography: Knowledge of principles and methods for describing the features of land, sea, and air masses, including their physical characteristics; locations; interrelationships; and distribution of plant, animal, and human life. Biology: Knowledge of plant and animal organisms and their tissues, cells, functions, interdependencies, and interactions with each other and the environment. Medicine and Dentistry: Knowledge of the information and techniques needed to diagnose and treat human injuries, diseases, and deformities. This includes symptoms, treatment

alternatives, drug properties and interactions, and preventive health-care measures. Therapy and Counseling: Knowledge of principles, methods, and procedures for diagnosis, treatment, and rehabilitation of physical and mental dysfunctions and for career counseling and guidance.

WORK ENVIRONMENT—Specialized protective or safety equipment; outdoors; common protective or safety equipment; very hot or cold; minor burns, cuts, bites, or stings.

Gas Appliance Repairers

- ◎ Growth: 5.5%
- ◎ Annual Job Openings: 5,000
- ◎ Annual Earnings: $29,890
- ◎ Percentage of Women: 2.9%

Related Apprenticeship	Years
Customer Service Representative	3
Gas-Appliance Servicer	3

Repair and install gas appliances and equipment, such as ovens, dryers, and hot water heaters. Measures, cuts, and threads pipe and connects it to feeder lines and equipment or appliance, using rule and hand tools. Tests and examines pipelines and equipment to locate leaks and faulty connections and to determine pressure and flow of gas. Assembles new or reconditioned appliances. Dismantles meters and regulators, and replaces defective pipes, thermocouples, thermostats, valves, and indicator spindles, using hand tools. **SKILLS—** Repairing; Installation; Troubleshooting; Operation Monitoring; Equipment Maintenance; Operation and Control; Quality Control Analysis; Systems Evaluation.

GOE—Interest Area: 05. Mechanics, Installers, and Repairers. **Work Group:** 05.03 Mechanical Work. **Other Apprenticeable Jobs in This Work Group:** Aircraft Engine Specialists; Airframe-and-Power-Plant Mechanics; Automotive Body and Related Repairers; Automotive Glass Installers and Repairers; Automotive Master Mechanics; Automotive Specialty Technicians; Bus and Truck Mechanics and Diesel Engine Specialists; Camera and Photographic Equipment Repairers; Coin, Vending, and Amusement Machine Servicers and Repairers; Farm Equipment Mechanics; Hand and Portable Power Tool Repairers; Heating and Air Conditioning Mechanics; Helpers—Installation, Maintenance, and Repair Workers; Industrial Machinery Mechanics; Installation, Maintenance, and Repair Workers, All Other; Keyboard Instrument Repairers and Tuners; Locksmiths and Safe Repairers; Maintenance and Repair Workers, General; Maintenance Workers, Machinery; Mechanical Door Repairers; Medical Appliance Technicians; Medical Equipment Repairers; Meter Mechanics; Millwrights; Mobile Heavy Equipment Mechanics, Except Engines; Motorboat Mechanics; Motorcycle Mechanics; Optical Instrument Assemblers; Outdoor Power Equipment and Other Small Engine Mechanics; Painters, Transportation Equipment; Rail Car Repairers; Recreational Vehicle Service Technicians; Reed or Wind Instrument Repairers and Tuners; Refrig-

eration Mechanics; Stringed Instrument Repairers and Tuners; Valve and Regulator Repairers; Watch Repairers. **PERSONALITY TYPE:** Realistic. Realistic occupations frequently involve work activities that include practical, hands-on problems and solutions. They often deal with plants, animals, and real-world materials like wood, tools, and machinery. Many of the occupations require working outside and do not involve a lot of paperwork or working closely with others.

RELATED KNOWLEDGE/COURSES— Mechanical Devices: Knowledge of machines and tools, including their designs, uses, repair, and maintenance. **Physics:** Knowledge and prediction of physical principles and laws and their interrelationships and applications to understanding fluid, material, and atmospheric dynamics and mechanical, electrical, atomic, and subatomic structures and processes. **Building and Construction:** Knowledge of the materials, methods, and tools involved in the construction or repair of houses, buildings, or other structures, such as highways and roads. **Chemistry:** Knowledge of the chemical composition, structure, and properties of substances and of the chemical processes and transformations that they undergo. This includes uses of chemicals, their danger signs, production techniques, and disposal methods. **Engineering and Technology:** Knowledge of the practical application of engineering science and technology. This includes applying principles, techniques, procedures, and equipment to the design and production of various goods and services. **Public Safety and Security:** Knowledge of relevant equipment, policies, procedures, and strategies to promote effective local, state, or national security operations for the protection of people, data, property, and institutions.

WORK ENVIRONMENT—Hazardous conditions; spend time kneeling, crouching, stooping, or crawling; minor burns, cuts, bites, or stings; using hands on objects, tools, or controls; contaminants; cramped work space, awkward positions.

Gaugers

- Growth: –11.0%
- Annual Job Openings: 3,000
- Annual Earnings: $49,970
- Percentage of Women: 7.4%

Related Apprenticeship	Years
Gauger	2

Gauge and test oil in storage tanks. Regulate flow of oil into pipelines at wells, tank farms, refineries, and marine and rail terminals, following prescribed standards and regulations. Gauges quality of oil in storage tanks before and after delivery, using calibrated steel tape and conversion. Regulates flow of products into pipelines, using automated pumping equipment. Reads automatic gauges at specified intervals to determine flow rate of oil into or from tanks and amount of oil in tanks. Operates pumps, teletype, and mobile radio. Turns bleeder valves or lowers sample container into tank to obtain oil sample. Lowers thermometer into tanks to obtain temperature reading. Reports leaks or defective valves to maintenance. Tightens connections with wrenches and greases and oils valves, using grease gum and oil can. Inspects pipelines, valves, and flanges to detect malfunctions, such as loose connections and leaks. Clamps seal around valves to secure tanks. Records meter and pressure readings at gas well. Records readings and test results. Calculates test results, using standard formulas. Gauges tank containing petroleum and natural gas byproducts, such as condensate or natural gasoline. Starts pumps and opens valves to regulate flow of oil into and out of tanks, according to delivery schedules. Tests oil to determine amount of bottom sediment, water, and foreign materials, using centrifugal tester. SKILLS—Operation Monitoring; Equipment Maintenance; Operation and Control; Science; Troubleshooting; Mathematics; Quality Control Analysis; Repairing.

GOE—Interest Area: 08. Industrial Production. Work Group: 08.06 Systems Operation. Other Apprenticeable Jobs in This Work Group: Boiler Operators and Tenders, Low Pressure; Chemical Plant and System Operators; Petroleum Refinery and Control Panel Operators; Power Distributors and Dispatchers; Power Generating Plant Operators, Except Auxiliary Equipment Operators; Stationary Engineers; Water and Liquid Waste Treatment Plant and System Operators. PERSONALITY TYPE: Realistic. Realistic occupations frequently involve work activities that include practical, hands-on problems and solutions. They often deal with plants, animals, and real-world materials like wood, tools, and machinery. Many of the occupations require working outside and do not involve a lot of paperwork or working closely with others.

RELATED KNOWLEDGE/COURSES—Mechanical Devices: Knowledge of machines and tools, including their designs, uses, repair, and maintenance. **Physics:** Knowledge and prediction of physical principles and laws and their interrelationships and applications to understanding fluid, material, and atmospheric dynamics and mechanical, electrical, atomic, and subatomic structures and processes. **Engineering and Technology:** Knowledge of the practical application of engineering science and technology. This includes applying principles, techniques, procedures, and equipment to the design and production of various goods and services. **Public Safety and Security:** Knowledge of relevant equipment, policies, procedures, and strategies to promote effective local, state, or national security operations for the protection of people, data, property, and institutions. **Production and Processing:** Knowledge of raw materials, production processes, quality control, costs, and other techniques for maximizing the effective manufacture and distribution of goods. **Mathematics:** Knowledge of arithmetic, algebra, geometry, calculus, and statistics and their applications.

WORK ENVIRONMENT—Hazardous conditions; contaminants; outdoors; common protective or safety equipment; climbing ladders, scaffolds, or poles.

Glass Blowers, Molders, Benders, and Finishers

- ◉ Growth: 6.4%
- ◉ Annual Job Openings: 6,000
- ◉ Annual Earnings: $24,780
- ◉ Percentage of Women: 20.4%

Related Apprenticeship	Years
Glass Blower	3
Glass Bender	4
Glass Blower, Laboratory Apparatus	4
Glass-Blowing-Lathe Operator	4
Artificial-Glass-Eye Maker	5

Shape molten glass according to patterns. Shapes, bends, or joins sections of glass, using paddles, pressing and flattening hand tools, or cork. Blows tubing into specified shape, using compressed air or own breath. Places glass into die or mold of press and controls press to form products, such as, glassware components or optical blanks. Dips end of blowpipe into molten glass to collect gob on pipe head or cuts gob from molten glass, using sheers. Preheats or melts glass pieces or anneals or cools glass products and components, using ovens and refractory powder. Heats glass to pliable stage, using gas flame or oven. Cuts length of tubing to specified size, using file or cutting wheel. Inspects and measures product to verify conformance to specifications, using instruments, such as micrometers, calipers, magnifier, and ruler. Examines gob of molten glass for imperfections, utilizing knowledge of molten glass characteristics. Strikes neck of finished article to separate article from blowpipe. Determines type and quantity of glass required to fabricate product. Adjusts press stroke length and pressure, and regulates oven temperatures according to glass type processed. Develops sketch of glass product into blueprint specifications, applying knowledge of glass technology and glass blowing. **SKILLS**—None met the criteria.

GOE—Interest Area: 01. Arts, Entertainment, and Media. **Work Group:** 01.06 Craft Arts. **Other Apprenticeable Jobs in This Work Group:** Craft Artists; Potters. **PERSONALITY TYPE:** Realistic. Realistic occupations frequently involve work activities that include practical, hands-on problems and solutions. They often deal with plants, animals, and real-world materials like wood, tools, and machinery. Many of the occupations require working outside and do not involve a lot of paperwork or working closely with others.

RELATED KNOWLEDGE/COURSES—Production and Processing: Knowledge of raw materials, production processes, quality control, costs, and other techniques for maximizing the effective manufacture and distribution of goods. **Physics:** Knowledge and prediction of physical principles and laws and their interrelationships and applications to understanding fluid, material, and atmospheric dynamics and mechanical, electrical, atomic, and subatomic structures and processes. **Design:** Knowledge of design techniques, tools, and principles involved in production of precision technical plans, blueprints, drawings, and models. **Engineering and Technology:** Knowledge of the practical application of engineering science and technology. This includes applying principles, techniques, procedures, and equipment to the design and production of various goods and services. **Fine Arts:** Knowledge of the theory and techniques required to compose, produce, and perform works of music, dance, visual arts, drama, and sculpture.

WORK ENVIRONMENT—Very hot or cold; minor burns, cuts, bites, or stings; standing; indoors; spend time making repetitive motions.

Glaziers

- Growth: 17.2%
- Annual Job Openings: 7,000
- Annual Earnings: $32,310
- Percentage of Women: 4.4%

Related Apprenticeship	Years
Glazier	3
Glazier, Stained Glass	4

Install glass in windows, skylights, store fronts, and display cases, or on surfaces, such as building fronts, interior walls, ceilings, and tabletops. Loads and arranges mirrors on truck, following sequence of deliveries. Measures, cuts, fits, and presses anti-glare adhesive film to glass or sprays glass with tinting solution to prevent light glare. Fastens glass panes into wood sash and spreads and smoothes putty around edge of pane with knife to seal joints. Installs pre-assembled framework for windows or doors designed to be fitted with glass panels, including stained glass windows, using hand tools. Marks outline or pattern on glass, cuts glass, and breaks off excess glass by hand or with notched tool. Sets glass doors into frame and bolts metal hinges, handles, locks, and other hardware onto glass doors. Attaches backing and leveling devices to wall surface, using nails and screws, and cuts mounting strips and moldings to required lengths. Assembles, fits, and attaches metal-framed glass enclosures for showers or bathtubs to framing around bath enclosure. Measures mirror and dimensions of area to be covered and determines plumb of walls or ceilings, using plumb-line and level. Attaches mounting strips and moldings to surface and applies mastic cement, putty, or screws to secure mirrors into position. Covers mirrors with protective material to prevent damage. Drives truck to installation site and unloads mirrors, equipment, and tools. Moves furniture to clear work site and covers floors and furnishings with drop cloths. **SKILLS**—Installation; Technology Design; Repairing; Mathematics; Operations Analysis.

GOE—**Interest Area:** 06. Construction, Mining, and Drilling. **Work Group:** 06.02 Construction. **Other Apprenticeable Jobs in This Work Group:** Boat Builders and Shipwrights; Boilermakers; Brickmasons and Blockmasons; Carpet Installers; Ceiling Tile Installers; Cement Masons and Concrete Finishers; Construction and Related Workers, All Other; Construction Carpenters; Drywall Installers; Electricians; Fence Erectors; Floor Layers, Except Carpet, Wood, and Hard Tiles; Grader, Bulldozer, and Scraper Operators; Insulation Workers, Floor, Ceiling, and Wall; Insulation Workers, Mechanical; Operating Engineers; Painters, Construction and Maintenance; Paperhangers; Paving, Surfacing, and Tamping Equipment Operators; Pipe Fitters; Plasterers and Stucco Masons; Plumbers; Reinforcing Iron and Rebar Workers; Riggers; Roofers; Rough Carpenters; Sheet Metal Workers; Ship Carpenters and Joiners; Stone Cutters and Carvers; Stonemasons; Structural Iron and Steel Workers; Tapers; Terrazzo Workers and Finishers; Tile and Marble Setters. **PERSONALITY TYPE:** Realistic. Realistic occupations frequently involve work activities that include practical, hands-on problems and solutions. They often deal with plants, animals, and real-world materials like wood, tools, and machinery. Many of the occupations require working outside and do not involve a lot of paperwork or working closely with others.

RELATED KNOWLEDGE/COURSES—**Building and Construction:** Knowledge of the materials, methods, and tools involved in the construction or repair of houses, buildings, or other structures, such as highways and roads. **Production and Processing:** Knowledge of raw materials, production processes, quality control, costs, and other techniques for maximizing the effective manufacture and distribution of goods. **Design:** Knowledge of design techniques, tools, and principles involved in production of precision technical plans, blueprints, drawings, and models. **Geography:** Knowledge of principles and methods for describing the features of land, sea, and air masses, including their physical characteristics; locations; interrelationships; and distribution of plant, animal, and human life. **Engineering and Technology:** Knowledge of the practical application of engineering science and technology. This includes applying principles, techniques, procedures, and equipment to the design and production of various goods and services. **Transportation:** Knowledge of principles and methods for moving people or goods by air, rail, sea, or road, including the relative costs and benefits.

WORK ENVIRONMENT—Minor burns, cuts, bites, or stings; climbing ladders, scaffolds, or poles; spend time kneeling, crouching, stooping, or crawling; keeping or regaining balance; common protective or safety equipment.

Government Property Inspectors and Investigators

- ◎ Growth: 9.8%
- ◎ Annual Job Openings: 20,000
- ◎ Annual Earnings: $46,780
- ◎ Percentage of Women: 47.1%

Related Apprenticeship	Years
Inspector, Quality Assurance	2

Investigate or inspect government property to ensure compliance with contract agreements and government regulations. Investigates regulated activities to detect violation of law relating to such activities as revenue collection, employment practices, or fraudulent benefit claims. Inspects manufactured or processed products to ensure compliance with contract specifications and legal requirements. Examines records, reports, and documents to establish facts and detect discrepancies. Investigates character of applicant for special license or permit and misuses of license or permit. Inspects government-owned equipment and materials in hands of private contractors to prevent waste, damage, theft, and other irregularities. Locates and interviews plaintiffs, witnesses, or representatives of business or government to gather facts relevant to inspection or alleged violation. Submits samples of product to government laboratory for testing as indicated by departmental procedures. Testifies in court or at administrative proceedings concerning findings of investigation. Prepares correspondence, reports of inspections or investigations, and recommendations for administrative or legal authorities. **SKILLS—** Negotiation; Speaking; Judgment and Decision Making; Systems Analysis; Writing; Critical Thinking; Reading Comprehension; Systems Evaluation.

GOE—Interest Area: 04. Law, Law Enforcement, and Public Safety. **Work Group:** 04.04 Public Safety. **Other Apprenticeable Jobs in This Work Group:** Emergency Medical Technicians and Paramedics; Fire Inspectors; Forest Fire Fighters; Municipal Fire Fighters; Nuclear Monitoring Technicians; Occupational Health and Safety Specialists. **PERSONALITY TYPE:** Enterprising. Enterprising occupations frequently involve starting up and carrying out projects. These occupations can involve leading people and making many decisions. They sometimes require risk taking and often deal with business.

RELATED KNOWLEDGE/COURSES— Law and Government: Knowledge of laws, legal codes, court procedures, precedents, government regulations, executive orders, agency rules, and the democratic political process. **Personnel and Human Resources:** Knowledge of principles and procedures for personnel recruitment, selection, training, compensation and benefits, labor relations and negotiation, and personnel information systems. **Public Safety and Security:** Knowledge of relevant equipment, policies, procedures, and strategies to promote effective local, state, or national security operations for the protection of people, data, property, and institutions. **English Language:** Knowledge of the structure and content of the English language, including the meaning and spelling of words, rules of composition, and grammar. **Communications and Media:** Knowledge of media production, communication, and dissemination techniques and methods. This includes alternative ways to inform and entertain via written, oral, and visual media. **Production and Processing:** Knowledge of raw materials, production processes, quality control, costs, and other techniques for maximizing the effective manufacture and distribution of goods.

WORK ENVIRONMENT—Walking and running; standing; extremely bright or inadequate lighting; sounds, noise levels are distracting or uncomfortable; very hot or cold; sitting.

Grader, Bulldozer, and Scraper Operators

- Growth: 10.4%
- Annual Job Openings: 45,000
- Annual Earnings: $35,030
- Percentage of Women: 2.2%

Related Apprenticeship	*Years*
Elevating-Grader Operator	2
Motor-Grader Operator	3

Operate machines or vehicles equipped with blades to remove, distribute, level, or grade earth. Starts engine, moves throttle, switches, and levers, and depresses pedals to operate machines, equipment, and attachments. Drives equipment in successive passes over working area to achieve specified result, such as grade terrain or remove, dump, or spread earth and rock. Aligns machine, cutterhead, or depth gauge marker with reference stakes and guidelines on ground or positions equipment following hand signals of assistant. Fastens bulldozer blade or other attachment to tractor, using hitches. Greases, oils, and performs minor repairs on tractor, using grease gun, oilcans, and hand tools. Signals operator to guide movement of tractor-drawn machine. Connects hydraulic hoses, belts, mechanical linkage, or power take-off shaft to tractor. **SKILLS**—Operation and Control; Repairing; Operation Monitoring; Equipment Maintenance; Equipment Selection; Installation.

GOE—Interest Area: 06. Construction, Mining, and Drilling. **Work Group:** 06.02 Construction. **Other Apprenticeable Jobs in This Work Group:** Boat Builders and Shipwrights; Boilermakers; Brickmasons and Blockmasons; Carpet Installers; Ceiling Tile Installers; Cement Masons and Concrete Finishers; Construction and Related Workers, All Other; Construction Carpenters; Drywall Installers; Electricians; Fence Erectors; Floor Layers, Except Carpet, Wood, and Hard Tiles; Glaziers; Insulation Workers, Floor, Ceiling, and Wall; Insulation Workers, Mechanical; Operating Engineers; Painters, Construction and Maintenance; Paperhangers; Paving, Surfacing, and Tamping Equipment Operators; Pipe Fitters; Plasterers and Stucco Masons; Plumbers; Reinforcing Iron and Rebar Workers; Riggers; Roofers; Rough Carpenters; Sheet Metal Workers; Ship Carpenters and Joiners; Stone Cutters and Carvers; Stonemasons; Structural Iron and Steel Workers; Tapers; Terrazzo Workers and Finishers; Tile and Marble Setters. **PERSONALITY TYPE:** Realistic. Realistic occupations frequently involve work activities that include practical, hands-on problems and solutions. They often deal with plants, animals, and real-world materials like wood, tools, and machinery. Many of the occupations require working outside and do not involve a lot of paperwork or working closely with others.

RELATED KNOWLEDGE/COURSES—**Mechanical Devices:** Knowledge of machines and tools, including their designs, uses, repair, and maintenance. **Transportation:** Knowledge of principles and methods for moving people or goods by air, rail, sea, or road, including the relative costs and benefits. **Physics:** Knowledge and prediction of physical principles and laws and their interrelationships and applications to understanding fluid, material, and atmospheric dynamics and mechanical, electrical, atomic, and subatomic structures and processes.

WORK ENVIRONMENT—Outdoors; exposed to whole-body vibration; hazardous equipment; sounds, noise levels are distracting or uncomfortable; very hot or cold.

Hairdressers, Hairstylists, and Cosmetologists

- ⑤ Growth: 14.7%
- ⑤ Annual Job Openings: 68,000
- ⑤ Annual Earnings: $18,700
- ⑤ Percentage of Women: 90.3%

Related Apprenticeship	*Years*
Cosmetologist	1

Provide beauty services, such as shampooing, cutting, coloring, and styling hair, and massaging and treating scalp. May also apply makeup, dress wigs, perform hair removal, and provide nail and skin care services. Keep work stations clean and sanitize tools such as scissors and combs. Cut, trim and shape hair or hairpieces, based on customers' instructions, hair type and facial features, using clippers, scissors, trimmers and razors. Analyze patrons' hair and other physical features to determine and recommend beauty treatment or suggest hair styles. Schedule client appointments. Bleach, dye, or tint hair, using applicator or brush. Update and maintain customer information records, such as beauty services provided. Shampoo, rinse, condition and dry hair and scalp or hairpieces with water, liquid soap, or other solutions. Operate cash registers to receive payments from patrons. Demonstrate and sell hair care products and cosmetics. Develop new styles and techniques. Apply water, setting, straightening or waving solutions to hair and use curlers, rollers, hot combs and curling irons to press and curl hair. Comb, brush, and spray hair or wigs to set style. Shape eyebrows and remove facial hair, using depilatory cream, tweezers, electrolysis or wax. Administer therapeutic medication and advise patron to seek medical treatment for chronic or contagious scalp conditions. Massage and treat scalp for hygienic and remedial purposes, using hands, fingers, or vibrating equipment. Shave, trim and shape beards and moustaches. Train or supervise other hairstylists, hairdressers and assistants. Recommend and explain the use of cosmetics, lotions, and creams to soften and lubricate skin and enhance and restore natural appearance. Give facials to patrons, using special compounds such as lotions and creams. Clean, shape, and polish fingernails and toenails, using files and nail polish. Apply artificial fingernails. **SKILLS**—Learning Strategies; Social Perceptiveness; Time Management; Service Orientation; Management of Financial Resources; Persuasion; Science; Active Learning; Operations Analysis.

GOE—**Interest Area:** 11. Recreation, Travel, and Other Personal Services. **Work Group:** 11.04 Barber and Beauty Services. **Other Apprenticeable Jobs in This Work Group:** Barbers. **PERSONALITY TYPE:** Enterprising. Enterprising occupations frequently involve starting up and carrying out projects. These occupations can involve leading people and making many decisions. They sometimes require risk taking and often deal with business.

RELATED KNOWLEDGE/COURSES—**Customer and Personal Service:** Knowledge of principles and processes for providing customer and personal services. This includes customer needs assessment, meeting quality standards for services, and evaluation of customer satisfaction. **Chemistry:** Knowledge of the chemical composition, structure, and properties of substances and of the chemical processes and transformations that they undergo. This includes uses of chemicals, their danger signs, production techniques, and disposal methods. **Sales and Marketing:** Knowledge of principles and methods for showing, promoting, and selling products or services. This includes marketing strategy and tactics, product demonstration, sales techniques, and sales control systems. **Education and Training:** Knowledge of principles and methods for

curriculum and training design, teaching and instruction for individuals and groups, and the measurement of training effects. **Administration and Management:** Knowledge of business and management principles involved in strategic planning, resource allocation, human resources modeling, leadership technique, production methods, and coordination of people and resources. **English Language:** Knowledge of the structure and content of the English language, including the meaning and spelling of words, rules of composition, and grammar.

WORK ENVIRONMENT—Contaminants; physical proximity; hazardous conditions; minor burns, cuts, bites, or stings; standing.

Hand and Portable Power Tool Repairers

- Growth: 5.3%
- Annual Job Openings: 3,000
- Annual Earnings: $32,310
- Percentage of Women: 4.5%

Related Apprenticeship	Years
Repairer, Handtools	3

Repair and adjust hand and power tools. Repairs or replaces tools and defective parts, such as handles, vises, pliers, or metal buckets, using soldering tool, gas torch, power tools, or hand tools. Examines and tests tools to determine defects or cause of malfunction, using hand and power tools, observation, and experience. Disassembles and reassembles tools, using hand tools, power tools, or arbor press. Verifies and adjusts alignment and dimensions of parts, using gauges and tracing lathe. Records nature and extent of repairs performed. Maintains stock of parts. Cleans polishing and buffing wheels, using steam cleaning machine, to remove abrasives and bonding materials and salvages cloth from wheel. Sprays, brushes, or recoats surface of polishing wheel and places it in oven to dry. Sharpens tools, such as picks, shovels, screwdrivers, and scoops, using bench grinder and emery wheel. **SKILLS**—Repairing; Equipment Maintenance; Technology Design; Management of Material Resources; Operation and Control; Troubleshooting; Quality Control Analysis; Installation.

GOE—Interest Area: 05. Mechanics, Installers, and Repairers. **Work Group:** 05.03 Mechanical Work. **Other Apprenticeable Jobs in This Work Group:** Aircraft Engine Specialists; Airframe-and-Power-Plant Mechanics; Automotive Body and Related Repairers; Automotive Glass Installers and Repairers; Automotive Master Mechanics; Automotive Specialty Technicians; Bus and Truck Mechanics and Diesel Engine Specialists; Camera and Photographic Equipment Repairers; Coin, Vending, and Amusement Machine Servicers and Repairers; Farm Equipment Mechanics; Gas Appliance Repairers; Heating and Air Conditioning Mechanics; Helpers—Installation, Maintenance, and Repair Workers; Industrial Machinery Mechanics; Installation, Maintenance, and Repair Workers, All Other; Keyboard Instrument Repairers and Tuners; Locksmiths and Safe Repairers; Maintenance and Repair Workers, General; Maintenance Workers, Machinery; Mechanical Door Repairers; Medical Appliance Technicians; Medical Equipment Repairers; Meter Mechanics; Millwrights; Mobile Heavy

Equipment Mechanics, Except Engines; Motorboat Mechanics; Motorcycle Mechanics; Optical Instrument Assemblers; Outdoor Power Equipment and Other Small Engine Mechanics; Painters, Transportation Equipment; Rail Car Repairers; Recreational Vehicle Service Technicians; Reed or Wind Instrument Repairers and Tuners; Refrigeration Mechanics; Stringed Instrument Repairers and Tuners; Valve and Regulator Repairers; Watch Repairers. **PERSONALITY TYPE:** Realistic. Realistic occupations frequently involve work activities that include practical, hands-on problems and solutions. They often deal with plants, animals, and real-world materials like wood, tools, and machinery. Many of the occupations require working outside and do not involve a lot of paperwork or working closely with others.

RELATED KNOWLEDGE/COURSES— Mechanical Devices: Knowledge of machines and tools, including their designs, uses, repair, and maintenance. **Engineering and Technology:** Knowledge of the practical application of engineering science and technology. This includes applying principles, techniques, procedures, and equipment to the design and production of various goods and services. **Clerical Practices:** Knowledge of administrative and clerical procedures and systems, such as word processing, managing files and records, stenography and transcription, designing forms, and other office procedures and terminology. **Design:** Knowledge of design techniques, tools, and principles involved in production of precision technical plans, blueprints, drawings, and models.

WORK ENVIRONMENT—Common protective or safety equipment; hazardous equipment; using hands on objects, tools, or controls; minor burns, cuts, bites, or stings; spend time making repetitive motions.

Hand Compositors and Typesetters

☺ Growth: –11.2%
☺ Annual Job Openings: 6,000
☺ Annual Earnings: $31,660
☺ Percentage of Women: 47.6%

Related Apprenticeship	Years
Compositor	4
Proofsheet Corrector	4

Set up and arrange type by hand. Assemble and lock setup of type, cuts, and headings. Pull proofs. Inserts spacers between words or units to balance and justify lines. Arranges galleys of linotype slugs (takes) in sequence on correction table. Transfers type from stick to galley when setup is complete. Cleans type after use and distributes it to specified boxes in type case. Removes incorrect portion and manually inserts corrections. Compares symbols on proof with galley symbol, and reads portion of text to locate positions for insertion of corrected slugs. Compares corrected type slugs against proof to detect errors. Measures copy with line gauge to determine length of line. Prepares proof copy of setup, using proof press. Inserts lead, slugs, or lines of quads between lines to adjust length of setup. Arranges, groups, and locks galley setups of type, cuts, and headings in chases, according to dummy makeup sheet. Selects type from type case and sets it in compositional sequence, reading from copy. **SKILLS**—None met the criteria.

GOE—Interest Area: 08. Industrial Production. **Work Group:** 08.03 Production Work. **Other Apprenticeable Jobs in This Work Group:** Bakers, Manufacturing; Bindery Machine Operators and Tenders; Chemical Equipment Controllers and Operators; Coating, Painting, and Spraying Machine Operators and Tenders; Cooling and Freezing Equipment Operators and Tenders; Crushing, Grinding, and Polishing Machine Setters, Operators, and Tenders; Cutters and Trimmers, Hand; Cutting and Slicing Machine Operators and Tenders; Design Printing Machine Setters and Set-Up Operators; Electrolytic Plating and Coating Machine Setters and Set-Up Operators, Metal and Plastic; Electrotypers and Stereotypers; Embossing Machine Set-Up Operators; Engraver Set-Up Operators; Extruding, Forming, Pressing, and Compacting Machine Operators and Tenders; Fabric and Apparel Patternmakers; Film Laboratory Technicians; Fitters, Structural Metal—Precision; Food Batchmakers; Furnace, Kiln, Oven, Drier, and Kettle Operators and Tenders; Job Printers; Letterpress Setters and Set-Up Operators; Metal Fabricators, Structural Metal Products; Metal-Refining Furnace Operators and Tenders; Mixing and Blending Machine Setters, Operators, and Tenders; Mold Makers, Hand; Molding and Casting Workers; Numerical Control Machine Tool Operators and Tenders, Metal and Plastic; Offset Lithographic Press Setters and Set-Up Operators; Painting, Coating, and Decorating Workers; Photographic Processing Machine Operators; Photographic Reproduction Technicians; Photographic Retouchers and Restorers; Plate Finishers; Platemakers; Precision Printing Workers; Printing Press Machine Operators and Tenders; Production Workers, All Other; Sawing Machine Operators and Tenders; Sawing Machine Setters and Set-Up Operators; Scanner

Operators; Separating, Filtering, Clarifying, Precipitating, and Still Machine Setters, Operators, and Tenders; Sewing Machine Operators, Garment; Slaughterers and Meat Packers; Stone Sawyers; Strippers; Team Assemblers; Welder-Fitters; Welders and Cutters; Woodworking Machine Operators and Tenders, Except Sawing. **PERSONALITY TYPE:** Realistic. Realistic occupations frequently involve work activities that include practical, hands-on problems and solutions. They often deal with plants, animals, and real-world materials like wood, tools, and machinery. Many of the occupations require working outside and do not involve a lot of paperwork or working closely with others.

RELATED KNOWLEDGE/COURSES— Production and Processing: Knowledge of raw materials, production processes, quality control, costs, and other techniques for maximizing the effective manufacture and distribution of goods. **Communications and Media:** Knowledge of media production, communication, and dissemination techniques and methods. This includes alternative ways to inform and entertain via written, oral, and visual media. **English Language:** Knowledge of the structure and content of the English language, including the meaning and spelling of words, rules of composition, and grammar. **Clerical Practices:** Knowledge of administrative and clerical procedures and systems, such as word processing, managing files and records, stenography and transcription, designing forms, and other office procedures and terminology.

WORK ENVIRONMENT—Indoors; hazardous equipment; using hands on objects, tools, or controls; sounds, noise levels are distracting or uncomfortable; sitting; spend time making repetitive motions.

Health Technologists and Technicians, All Other

- ⊚ Growth: 18.9%
- ⊚ Annual Job Openings: 1,000
- ⊚ Annual Earnings: $49,710
- ⊚ Percentage of Women: 36.6%

Related Apprenticeship	Years
Health Care Sanitary Technician	1

All health technologists and technicians not listed separately. **SKILLS**—No data available.

GOE—Interest Area: 14. Medical and Health Services. **Work Group:** 14.05 Medical Technology. **Other Apprenticeable Jobs in This Work Group:** Medical and Clinical Laboratory Technicians; Orthotists and Prosthetists. **PERSONALITY TYPE:** No data available.

RELATED KNOWLEDGE/COURSES—No data available.

WORK ENVIRONMENT—No data available.

Heating and Air Conditioning Mechanics

- Growth: 31.8%
- Annual Job Openings: 35,000
- Annual Earnings: $35,160
- Percentage of Women: 1.8%

Related Apprenticeship	Years
Oil-Burner-Servicer-and-Installer	2
Air and Hydronic Balancing Technician	3
Furnace Installer	3
Heating-and-Air-Conditioning Installer-Servicer	3
Furnace Installer-and-Repairer, Hot Air	4

(This is one of the most popular apprenticeable jobs.)

Install, service, and repair heating and air conditioning systems in residences and commercial establishments. Obtain and maintain required certification(s). Comply with all applicable standards, policies, and procedures, including safety procedures and the maintenance of a clean work area. Repair or replace defective equipment, components, or wiring. Test electrical circuits and components for continuity, using electrical test equipment. Reassemble and test equipment following repairs. Inspect and test system to verify system compliance with plans and specifications and to detect and locate malfunctions. Discuss heating-cooling system malfunctions with users to isolate problems or to verify that malfunctions have been corrected. Record and report all faults, deficiencies, and other unusual occurrences, as well as the time and materials expended on work orders. Test pipe or tubing joints and connections for leaks, using pressure gauge or soap-and-water solution. Adjust system controls to setting recommended by manufacturer to balance system, using hand tools. Recommend, develop, and perform preventive and general maintenance procedures such as cleaning, power-washing and vacuuming equipment, oiling parts, and changing filters. Lay out and connect electrical wiring between controls and equipment according to wiring diagram, using electrician's hand tools. Install auxiliary components to heating-cooling equipment, such as expansion and discharge valves, air ducts, pipes, blowers, dampers, flues and stokers, following blueprints. Assist with other work in coordination with repair and maintenance teams. Install, connect, and adjust thermostats, humidistats and timers, using hand tools. Generate work orders that address deficiencies in need of correction. Join pipes or tubing to equipment and to fuel, water, or refrigerant source, to form complete circuit. Assemble, position and mount heating or cooling equipment, following blueprints. Study blueprints, design specifications, and manufacturers' recommendations to ascertain the configuration of heating or cooling equipment components and to ensure the proper installation of components. Cut and drill holes in floors, walls, and roof to install equipment, using power saws and drills. **SKILLS**—Installation; Repairing; Equipment Maintenance; Troubleshooting; Coordination; Negotiation; Systems Evaluation; Persuasion.

GOE—**Interest Area:** 05. Mechanics, Installers, and Repairers. **Work Group:** 05.03 Mechanical Work. **Other Apprenticeable Jobs in This Work Group:** Aircraft Engine Specialists; Airframe-and-Power-Plant Mechanics; Automotive Body and Related Repairers; Automotive Glass Installers and Repairers; Automotive Master Mechanics; Automotive Specialty Technicians; Bus and Truck Mechanics and Diesel Engine Specialists; Camera and Photographic Equipment Repairers; Coin, Vending, and Amusement Machine Servicers and Repairers; Farm Equipment Mechanics; Gas Appliance Repairers; Hand and Portable Power Tool Repairers; Helpers—Installation, Maintenance, and Repair Workers; Industrial Machinery Mechanics; Installation, Maintenance, and Repair Workers, All Other; Keyboard Instrument Repairers and Tuners; Locksmiths and Safe Repairers; Maintenance and Repair Workers, General; Maintenance Workers, Machinery; Mechanical Door Repairers; Medical Appliance Technicians; Medical Equipment Repairers; Meter Mechanics; Millwrights; Mobile Heavy Equipment Mechanics, Except Engines; Motorboat Mechanics; Motorcycle Mechanics; Optical Instrument Assemblers; Outdoor Power Equipment and Other Small Engine Mechanics; Painters, Transportation Equipment; Rail Car Repairers; Recreational Vehicle Service Technicians; Reed or Wind Instrument Repairers and Tuners; Refrigeration Mechanics; Stringed Instrument Repairers and Tuners; Valve and Regulator Repairers; Watch Repairers. **PERSONALITY TYPE:** Realistic. Realistic occupations frequently involve work activities that include practical, hands-on problems and solutions. They often deal with plants, animals, and real-world materials like wood, tools, and machinery. Many of the occupations require working outside and do not involve a lot of paperwork or working closely with others.

RELATED KNOWLEDGE/COURSES—Mechanical Devices: Knowledge of machines and tools, including their designs, uses, repair, and maintenance. **Building and Construction:** Knowledge of the materials, methods, and tools involved in the construction or repair of houses, buildings, or other structures, such as highways and roads. **Design:** Knowledge of design techniques, tools, and principles involved in production of precision technical plans, blueprints, drawings, and models. **Customer and Personal Service:** Knowledge of principles and processes for providing customer and personal services. This includes customer needs assessment, meeting quality standards for services, and evaluation of customer satisfaction. **Engineering and Technology:** Knowledge of the practical application of engineering science and technology. This includes applying principles, techniques, procedures, and equipment to the design and production of various goods and services. **Physics:** Knowledge and prediction of physical principles and laws and their interrelationships and applications to understanding fluid, material, and atmospheric dynamics and mechanical, electrical, atomic, and subatomic structures and processes.

WORK ENVIRONMENT—Hazardous conditions; very hot or cold; contaminants; sounds, noise levels are distracting or uncomfortable; cramped work space, awkward positions.

Helpers—Installation, Maintenance, and Repair Workers

- Growth: 20.3%
- Annual Job Openings: 33,000
- Annual Earnings: $21,240
- Percentage of Women: 9.3%

Related Apprenticeship	Years
Facilities Locator	2
Service Planner (Light; Heat)	4

Help installation, maintenance, and repair workers in maintenance, parts replacement, and repair of vehicles, industrial machinery, and electrical and electronic equipment. Perform duties, such as furnishing tools, materials, and supplies to other workers; cleaning work area, machines, and tools; and holding materials or tools for other workers. Tend and observe equipment and machinery in order to verify efficient and safe operation. Examine and test machinery, equipment, components, and parts for defects, and to ensure proper functioning. Adjust, connect, or disconnect wiring, piping, tubing, and other parts, using hand tools or power tools. Install or replace machinery, equipment, and new or replacement parts and instruments, using hand tools or power tools. Clean or lubricate vehicles, machinery, equipment, instruments, tools, work areas, and other objects, using hand tools, power tools, and cleaning equipment. Apply protective materials to equipment, components, and parts in order to prevent defects and corrosion. Transfer tools, parts, equipment, and supplies to and from work stations and other areas. Disassemble broken or defective equipment in order to facilitate repair); reassemble equipment when repairs are complete. Assemble and maintain physical structures, using hand tools or power tools. Provide assistance to more skilled workers involved in the adjustment, maintenance, part replacement, and repair of tools, equipment, and machines. Position vehicles, machinery, equipment, physical structures, and other objects for assembly or installation, using hand tools, power tools, and moving equipment. Hold or supply tools, parts, equipment, and supplies for other workers. Prepare work stations so mechanics and repairers can conduct work. **SKILLS**—Installation; Operation Monitoring; Repairing; Equipment Maintenance; Troubleshooting; Operations Analysis; Persuasion; Service Orientation.

GOE—Interest Area: 05. Mechanics, Installers, and Repairers. **Work Group:** 05.03 Mechanical Work. **Other Apprenticeable Jobs in This Work Group:** Aircraft Engine Specialists; Airframe-and-Power-Plant Mechanics; Automotive Body and Related Repairers; Automotive Glass Installers and Repairers; Automotive Master Mechanics; Automotive Specialty Technicians; Bus and Truck Mechanics and Diesel Engine Specialists; Camera and Photographic Equipment Repairers; Coin, Vending, and Amusement Machine Servicers and Repairers; Farm Equipment Mechanics; Gas Appliance Repairers; Hand and Portable Power Tool Repairers; Heating and Air Conditioning Mechanics; Industrial Machinery Mechanics; Installation, Maintenance, and Repair Workers, All Other; Keyboard Instrument Repairers and Tuners;

Locksmiths and Safe Repairers; Maintenance and Repair Workers, General; Maintenance Workers, Machinery; Mechanical Door Repairers; Medical Appliance Technicians; Medical Equipment Repairers; Meter Mechanics; Millwrights; Mobile Heavy Equipment Mechanics, Except Engines; Motorboat Mechanics; Motorcycle Mechanics; Optical Instrument Assemblers; Outdoor Power Equipment and Other Small Engine Mechanics; Painters, Transportation Equipment; Rail Car Repairers; Recreational Vehicle Service Technicians; Reed or Wind Instrument Repairers and Tuners; Refrigeration Mechanics; Stringed Instrument Repairers and Tuners; Valve and Regulator Repairers; Watch Repairers. **PERSONALITY TYPE:** Realistic. Realistic occupations frequently involve work activities that include practical, hands-on problems and solutions. They often deal with plants, animals, and real-world materials like wood, tools, and machinery. Many of the occupations require working outside and do not involve a lot of paperwork or working closely with others.

RELATED KNOWLEDGE/COURSES— Mechanical Devices: Knowledge of machines and tools, including their designs, uses, repair, and maintenance. **Engineering and Technology:** Knowledge of the practical application of engineering science and technology. This includes applying principles, techniques, procedures, and equipment to the design and production of various goods and services. **Design:** Knowledge of design techniques, tools, and principles involved in production of precision technical plans, blueprints, drawings, and models. **Chemistry:** Knowledge of the chemical composition, structure, and properties of substances and of the chemical processes and transformations that they undergo. This includes uses of chemicals, their danger signs, production techniques, and disposal methods. **Public**

Safety and Security: Knowledge of relevant equipment, policies, procedures, and strategies to promote effective local, state, or national security operations for the protection of people, data, property, and institutions. **Building and Construction:** Knowledge of the materials, methods, and tools involved in the construction or repair of houses, buildings, or other structures, such as highways and roads.

WORK ENVIRONMENT—Hazardous conditions; hazardous equipment; sounds, noise levels are distracting or uncomfortable; extremely bright or inadequate lighting; very hot or cold.

Hotel, Motel, and Resort Desk Clerks

- ◎ Growth: 23.9%
- ◎ Annual Job Openings: 46,000
- ◎ Annual Earnings: $17,450
- ◎ Percentage of Women: 68.9%

Related Apprenticeship	*Years*
Hotel Associate	2

Accommodate hotel, motel, and resort patrons by registering and assigning rooms to guests, issuing room keys, transmitting and receiving messages, keeping records of occupied rooms and guests' accounts, making and confirming reservations, and presenting statements to and collecting payments from departing guests. Greet, register, and assign rooms to guests of hotels or motels. Verify customers' credit, and establish how the customer will pay for the accommodation. Keep records of room availability and guests' accounts, manually or using computers. Compute bills, collect payments, and make change for guests. Perform simple bookkeeping activities, such as balancing cash accounts. Issue room keys and escort instructions to bellhops. Review accounts and charges with guests during the check out process. Post charges, such as those for rooms, food, liquor, or telephone calls, to ledgers manually or by using computers. Transmit and receive messages, using telephones or telephone switchboards. Contact housekeeping or maintenance staff when guests report problems. Make and confirm reservations. Answer inquiries pertaining to hotel services, registration of guests, and shopping, dining, entertainment, and travel directions. Record guest comments or complaints, referring customers to managers as necessary. Advise housekeeping staff when rooms have been vacated and are ready for cleaning. Arrange tours, taxis, and restaurants for customers. Deposit guests' valuables in hotel safes or safe-deposit boxes. Date-stamp, sort, and rack incoming mail and messages. **SKILLS—** Service Orientation; Instructing; Learning Strategies; Critical Thinking; Persuasion; Social Perceptiveness; Active Listening; Negotiation.

GOE—**Interest Area:** 11. Recreation, Travel, and Other Personal Services. **Work Group:** 11.03 Transportation and Lodging Services. **Other Apprenticeable Jobs in This Work Group:** No other apprenticeable jobs in this group. **PERSONALITY TYPE:** Conventional. Conventional occupations frequently involve following set procedures and routines. These occupations can include working with data and

details more than with ideas. Usually there is a clear line of authority to follow.

RELATED   KNOWLEDGE/COURSES— **Customer and Personal Service:** Knowledge of principles and processes for providing customer and personal services. This includes customer needs assessment, meeting quality standards for services, and evaluation of customer satisfaction. **Clerical Practices:** Knowledge of administrative and clerical procedures and systems, such as word processing, managing files and records, stenography and transcription, designing forms, and other office procedures and terminology. **Sales and Marketing:** Knowledge of principles and methods for showing, promoting, and selling products or services. This includes marketing strategy and tactics, product demonstration, sales techniques, and sales control systems. **Computers and Electronics:** Knowledge of circuit boards, processors, chips, electronic equipment, and computer hardware and software, including applications and programming. **Administration and Management:** Knowledge of business and management principles involved in strategic planning, resource allocation, human resources modeling, leadership technique, production methods, and coordination of people and resources. **Geography:** Knowledge of principles and methods for describing the features of land, sea, and air masses, including their physical characteristics; locations; interrelationships; and distribution of plant, animal, and human life.

WORK ENVIRONMENT—Physical proximity; sounds, noise levels are distracting or uncomfortable; standing; very hot or cold; sitting.

Industrial Machinery Mechanics

- Growth: 5.5%
- Annual Job Openings: 19,000
- Annual Earnings: $38,440
- Percentage of Women: 3.8%

Related Apprenticeship	Years
Canal-Equipment Mechanic	2
Conveyor-Maintenance Mechanic	2
Cooling Tower Technician	2
Fuel-System-Maintenance Worker	2
Hydraulic-Press Servicer	2
Industrial Machine System Technician	2
Maintenance Mechanic, Grain and Feed	2
Rubberizing Mechanic	4
Scale Mechanic	4

(This is one of the most popular apprenticeable jobs.)

Repair, install, adjust, or maintain industrial production and processing machinery or refinery and pipeline distribution systems. Confers with operators and observes, tests, and evaluates operation of machinery and equipment to diagnose cause of malfunction. Disassembles machinery and equipment to remove parts and make repairs. Repairs, replaces, adjusts, and aligns components of machinery and equipment. Fabricates replacement parts. Test-runs repaired machinery and equipment to verify adequacy of repairs. Cleans and lubricates parts, equipment, and machinery. Examines parts for defects, such as breakage or excessive wear. Welds to repair broken metal parts, fabricate new parts, and assemble new equipment. Records repairs and maintenance performed. Enters codes and instructions to program computer-controlled machinery. Repairs and replaces electrical wiring and components of machinery. Orders or requisitions parts and materials. **SKILLS**—Equipment Maintenance; Repairing; Troubleshooting; Operation Monitoring; Quality Control Analysis; Installation; Technology Design; Operation and Control.

GOE—Interest Area: 05. Mechanics, Installers, and Repairers. **Work Group:** 05.03 Mechanical Work. **Other Apprenticeable Jobs in This Work Group:** Aircraft Engine Specialists; Airframe-and-Power-Plant Mechanics; Automotive Body and Related Repairers; Automotive Glass Installers and Repairers; Automotive Master Mechanics; Automotive Specialty Technicians; Bus and Truck Mechanics and Diesel Engine Specialists; Camera and Photographic Equipment Repairers; Coin, Vending, and Amusement Machine Servicers and Repairers; Farm Equipment Mechanics; Gas Appliance Repairers; Hand and Portable Power Tool Repairers; Heating and Air Conditioning Mechanics; Helpers—Installation, Maintenance, and Repair Workers; Installation, Maintenance, and Repair Workers, All Other; Keyboard Instrument Repairers and Tuners; Locksmiths and Safe Repairers; Maintenance and Repair Workers, General; Maintenance Workers, Machinery; Mechanical Door Repairers; Medical Appliance Technicians; Medical Equipment

Repairers; Meter Mechanics; Millwrights; Mobile Heavy Equipment Mechanics, Except Engines; Motorboat Mechanics; Motorcycle Mechanics; Optical Instrument Assemblers; Outdoor Power Equipment and Other Small Engine Mechanics; Painters, Transportation Equipment; Rail Car Repairers; Recreational Vehicle Service Technicians; Reed or Wind Instrument Repairers and Tuners; Refrigeration Mechanics; Stringed Instrument Repairers and Tuners; Valve and Regulator Repairers; Watch Repairers. **PERSONALITY TYPE:** Realistic. Realistic occupations frequently involve work activities that include practical, hands-on problems and solutions. They often deal with plants, animals, and real-world materials like wood, tools, and machinery. Many of the occupations require working outside and do not involve a lot of paperwork or working closely with others.

RELATED KNOWLEDGE/COURSES—Mechanical Devices: Knowledge of machines and tools, including their designs, uses, repair, and maintenance. **Engineering and Technology:** Knowledge of the practical application of engineering science and technology. This includes applying principles, techniques, procedures, and equipment to the design and production of various goods and services. **Computers and Electronics:** Knowledge of circuit boards, processors, chips, electronic equipment, and computer hardware and software, including applications and programming. **Physics:** Knowledge and prediction of physical principles and laws and their interrelationships and applications to understanding fluid, material, and atmospheric dynamics and mechanical, electrical, atomic, and subatomic structures and processes. **Public Safety and Security:** Knowledge of relevant equipment, policies, procedures, and strategies to promote effective local, state, or national security operations for the protection of people, data, property, and institutions. **Production and Processing:** Knowledge of raw materials, production processes, quality control, costs, and other techniques for maximizing the effective manufacture and distribution of goods. **Design:** Knowledge of design techniques, tools, and principles involved in production of precision technical plans, blueprints, drawings, and models.

WORK ENVIRONMENT—Hazardous equipment; common protective or safety equipment; sounds, noise levels are distracting or uncomfortable; minor burns, cuts, bites, or stings; spend time kneeling, crouching, stooping, or crawling; using hands on objects, tools, or controls.

Installation, Maintenance, and Repair Workers, All Other

- Growth: 12.2%
- Annual Job Openings: 22,000
- Annual Earnings: $33,010
- Percentage of Women: 7.0%

Related Apprenticeship	Years
Lubrication Servicer Materials Disposal Technician	2
Aviation Safety Equipment Technician	4

All mechanical, installation, and repair workers and helpers not listed separately. **SKILLS**—No data available.

GOE—Interest Area: 05. Mechanics, Installers, and Repairers. **Work Group:** 05.02 Electrical and Electronic Systems; 05.03 Mechanical Work. **Other Apprenticeable Jobs in This Work Group:** Aircraft Engine Specialists; Airframe-and-Power-Plant Mechanics; Automotive Body and Related Repairers; Automotive Glass Installers and Repairers; Automotive Master Mechanics; Automotive Specialty Technicians; Avionics Technicians; Battery Repairers; Bus and Truck Mechanics and Diesel Engine Specialists; Camera and Photographic Equipment Repairers; Central Office and PBX Installers and Repairers; Coin, Vending, and Amusement Machine Servicers and Repairers; Communication Equipment Mechanics, Installers, and Repairers; Data Processing Equipment Repairers; Electric Home Appliance and Power Tool Repairers; Electric Meter Installers and Repairers; Electric Motor and Switch Assemblers and Repairers; Electrical and Electronics Installers and Repairers, Transportation Equipment; Electrical and Electronics Repairers, Commercial and Industrial Equipment; Electrical and Electronics Repairers, Powerhouse, Substation, and Relay; Electrical Power-Line Installers and Repairers; Electronic Equipment Installers and Repairers, Motor Vehicles; Electronic Home Entertainment Equipment Installers and Repairers; Elevator Installers and Repairers; Farm Equipment Mechanics; Gas Appliance Repairers; Hand and Portable Power Tool Repairers; Heating and Air Conditioning Mechanics; Helpers—Installation, Maintenance, and Repair Workers; Industrial Machinery Mechanics; Keyboard Instrument Repairers and Tuners; Locksmiths and Safe Repairers; Maintenance and Repair Workers, General; Maintenance Workers, Machinery; Mechanical Door Repairers; Medical Appliance Technicians; Medical Equipment Repairers; Meter Mechanics; Millwrights; Mobile Heavy Equipment Mechanics, Except Engines; Motorboat Mechanics; Motorcycle Mechanics; Office Machine and Cash Register Servicers; Optical Instrument Assemblers; Outdoor Power Equipment and Other Small Engine Mechanics; Painters, Transportation Equipment; Radio Mechanics; Rail Car Repairers; Recreational Vehicle Service Technicians; Reed or Wind Instrument Repairers and Tuners; Refrigeration Mechanics; Signal and Track Switch Repairers; Station Installers and Repairers, Telephone; Stringed Instrument Repairers and Tuners; Telecommunications Line Installers and Repairers; Transformer Repairers; Valve and Regulator Repairers; Watch Repairers. **PERSONALITY TYPE:** No data available.

RELATED KNOWLEDGE/COURSES—No data available.

WORK ENVIRONMENT—No data available.

Insulation Workers, Floor, Ceiling, and Wall

- Growth: 15.8%
- Annual Job Openings: 9,000
- Annual Earnings: $29,190
- Percentage of Women: 4.1%

Related Apprenticeship	*Years*
Cork Insulator, Refrigeration Plant	4
Insulation Worker	4

Line and cover structures with insulating materials. May work with batt, roll, or blown insulation materials. Fits, wraps, or attaches insulating materials to structures of surfaces, using hand tools or wires, following blueprint specifications. Fills blower hopper with insulating materials. Covers, seals or finishes insulated surfaces or access holes with plastic covers, canvas ships, sealant, tape, cement or asphalt mastic. Reads blueprints and selects appropriate insulation, based on the heat retaining or excluding characteristics of the material. Measures and cuts insulation for covering surfaces, using tape measure, handsaw, knife or scissors. Moves controls, buttons, or levers to start blower and regulate flow of materials through nozzle. Prepare surfaces for insulation application by brushing or spreading on adhesives, cement, or asphalt or attaching metal pins to surfaces. Evenly distributes insulating materials into small spaces within floors, ceilings, or walls, using blower and hose attachments or cement mortar. **SKILLS**—Installation.

GOE—Interest Area: 06. Construction, Mining, and Drilling. **Work Group:** 06.02 Construction. **Other Apprenticeable Jobs in This Work Group:** Boat Builders and Shipwrights; Boilermakers; Brickmasons and Blockmasons; Carpet Installers; Ceiling Tile Installers; Cement Masons and Concrete Finishers; Construction and Related Workers, All Other; Construction Carpenters; Drywall Installers; Electricians; Fence Erectors; Floor Layers, Except Carpet, Wood, and Hard Tiles; Glaziers; Grader, Bulldozer, and Scraper Operators; Insulation Workers, Mechanical; Operating Engineers; Painters, Construction and Maintenance; Paperhangers; Paving, Surfacing, and Tamping Equipment Operators; Pipe Fitters; Plasterers and Stucco Masons; Plumbers; Reinforcing Iron and Rebar Workers; Riggers; Roofers; Rough Carpenters; Sheet Metal Workers; Ship Carpenters and Joiners; Stone Cutters and Carvers; Stonemasons; Structural Iron and Steel Workers; Tapers; Terrazzo Workers and Finishers; Tile and Marble Setters. **PERSONALITY TYPE:** Realistic. Realistic occupations frequently involve work activities that include practical, hands-on problems and solutions. They often deal with plants, animals, and real-world materials like wood, tools, and machinery. Many of the occupations require working outside and do not involve a lot of paperwork or working closely with others.

RELATED KNOWLEDGE/COURSES— Building and Construction: Knowledge of the materials, methods, and tools involved in the construction or repair of houses, buildings, or other structures, such as highways and roads. **Mechanical Devices:** Knowledge of machines and tools, including their designs, uses, repair, and maintenance.

WORK ENVIRONMENT—Common protective or safety equipment; standing; contaminants; high places; climbing ladders, scaffolds, or poles; spend time bending or twisting the body.

Insulation Workers, Mechanical

- Growth: 15.8%
- Annual Job Openings: 9,000
- Annual Earnings: $29,190
- Percentage of Women: 4.1%

Related Apprenticeship	Years
Pipe Coverer and Insulator	4

Apply insulating materials to pipes or ductwork, or other mechanical systems in order to help control and maintain temperature. Fits, wraps, or attaches insulating materials to structures of surfaces, using hand tools or wires, following blueprint specifications. Fills blower hopper with insulating materials. Covers, seals or finishes insulated surfaces or access holes with plastic covers, canvas ships, sealant, tape, cement or asphalt mastic. Reads blueprints and selects appropriate insulation, based on the heat retaining or excluding characteristics of the material. Measures and cuts insulation for covering surfaces, using tape measure, handsaw, knife or scissors. Moves controls, buttons, or levers to start blower and regulate flow of materials through nozzle. Prepare surfaces for insulation application by brushing or spreading on adhesives, cement, or asphalt or attaching metal pins to surfaces. Evenly distributes insulating materials into small spaces within floors, ceilings, or walls, using blower and hose attachments or cement mortar. **SKILLS**—Installation.

GOE—Interest Area: 06. Construction, Mining, and Drilling. **Work Group:** 06.02 Construction. **Other Apprenticeable Jobs in This Work Group:** Boat Builders and Shipwrights; Boilermakers; Brickmasons and Blockmasons; Carpet Installers; Ceiling Tile Installers; Cement Masons and Concrete Finishers; Construction and Related Workers, All Other; Construction Carpenters; Drywall Installers; Electricians; Fence Erectors; Floor Layers, Except Carpet, Wood, and Hard Tiles; Glaziers; Grader, Bulldozer, and Scraper Operators; Insulation Workers, Floor, Ceiling, and Wall; Operating Engineers; Painters, Construction and Maintenance; Paperhangers; Paving, Surfacing, and Tamping Equipment Operators; Pipe Fitters; Plasterers and Stucco Masons; Plumbers; Reinforcing Iron and Rebar Workers; Riggers; Roofers; Rough Carpenters; Sheet Metal Workers; Ship Carpenters and Joiners; Stone Cutters and Carvers; Stonemasons; Structural Iron and Steel Workers; Tapers; Terrazzo Workers and Finishers; Tile and Marble Setters. **PERSONALITY TYPE:** Realistic. Realistic occupations frequently involve work activities that include practical, hands-on problems and solutions. They often deal with plants, animals, and real-world materials like wood, tools, and machinery. Many of the occupations require working outside and do not involve a lot of paperwork or working closely with others.

RELATED KNOWLEDGE/COURSES— Building and Construction: Knowledge of the materials, methods, and tools involved in the construction or repair of houses, buildings, or other structures, such as highways and roads. **Mechanical Devices:** Knowledge of machines and tools, including their designs, uses, repair, and maintenance.

WORK ENVIRONMENT—Common protective or safety equipment; standing; contaminants; high places; climbing ladders, scaffolds, or poles; spend time bending or twisting the body.

FURTHER INFORMATION—Contact a local joint union-management apprenticeship committee or the nearest office of your state employment service or apprenticeship agency (see Appendix C). Or contact National Tooling and Machining Association, 9300 Livingston Rd., Fort Washington, MD 20744. Internet: http://www.ntma.org.

Janitors and Cleaners, Except Maids and Housekeeping Cleaners

- Growth: 18.3%
- Annual Job Openings: 454,000
- Annual Earnings: $18,410
- Percentage of Women: 29.9%

Related Apprenticeship	Years
Swimming-Pool Servicer	2
Multi-Story Window/Building Exterior Cleaner	3

Keep buildings in clean and orderly condition. Perform heavy cleaning duties, such as cleaning floors, shampooing rugs, washing walls and glass, and removing rubbish. Duties may include tending furnace and boiler, performing routine maintenance activities, notifying management of need for repairs, and cleaning snow or debris from sidewalk. Spray insecticides and fumigants to prevent insect and rodent infestation. Clean building floors by sweeping, mopping, scrubbing, or vacuuming them. Gather and empty trash. Service, clean, and supply restrooms. Clean and polish furniture and fixtures. Clean windows, glass partitions, and mirrors, using soapy water or other cleaners, sponges, and squeegees. Dust furniture, walls, machines, and equipment. Make adjustments and minor repairs to heating, cooling, ventilating, plumbing, and electrical systems. Mix water and detergents or acids in containers to prepare cleaning solutions, according to specifications. Steam-clean or shampoo carpets. Strip, seal, finish, and polish floors. Clean and restore building interiors damaged by fire, smoke, or water, using commercial cleaning equipment. Clean chimneys, flues, and connecting pipes, using power and hand tools. Clean laboratory equipment, such as glassware and metal instruments, using solvents, brushes, rags, and power cleaning equipment. Drive vehicles required to perform or travel to cleaning work, including vans, industrial trucks, or industrial vacuum cleaners. Follow procedures for the use of chemical cleaners and power equipment, in order to prevent damage to floors and fixtures. Monitor building security and safety by performing such tasks as locking doors after operating hours and checking electrical appliance use to ensure that hazards are not created. Move heavy furniture, equipment, and supplies, either manually or by using hand trucks. Mow and trim lawns and shrubbery, using mowers and hand and power trimmers, and clear debris from grounds. Notify managers concerning the need for major repairs or additions to building operating systems. Remove snow from sidewalks, driveways, and parking areas, using snowplows, snow blowers, and snow shovels, and spread snow melting chemicals. Requisition supplies and equipment needed for cleaning and maintenance duties. Set up, arrange, and remove decorations, tables, chairs, ladders, and scaffolding to prepare facilities for events such as banquets and meetings. **SKILLS**—Repairing; Equipment Maintenance; Installation; Troubleshooting.

GOE—**Interest Area:** 11. Recreation, Travel, and Other Personal Services. **Work Group:** 11.07 Cleaning and Building Services. **Other Apprenticeable Jobs in This Work Group:** Building Cleaning Workers, All Other; Maids and Housekeeping Cleaners. **PERSONALITY TYPE:** Realistic. Realistic occupations frequently involve work activities that include practical, hands-on problems and solutions. They often deal with plants, animals, and real-world materials like wood, tools, and machinery. Many of the occupations require working outside and do not involve a lot of paperwork or working closely with others.

RELATED KNOWLEDGE/COURSES—**Mechanical Devices:** Knowledge of machines and tools, including their designs, uses, repair, and maintenance. **Chemistry:** Knowledge of the chemical composition, structure, and properties of substances and of the chemical processes and transformations that they undergo. This includes uses of chemicals, their danger signs, production techniques, and disposal methods. **Building and Construction:** Knowledge of the materials, methods, and tools involved in the construction or repair of houses, buildings, or other structures, such as highways and roads. **Transportation:** Knowledge of principles and methods for moving people or goods by air, rail, sea, or road, including the relative costs and benefits. **Public Safety and Security:** Knowl-

edge of relevant equipment, policies, procedures, and strategies to promote effective local, state, or national security operations for the protection of people, data, property, and institutions. **Customer and Personal Service:** Knowledge of principles and processes for providing customer and personal services. This includes customer needs assessment, meeting quality standards for services, and evaluation of customer satisfaction.

WORK ENVIRONMENT—Contaminants; hazardous conditions; very hot or cold; climbing ladders, scaffolds, or poles; standing.

Job Printers

- Growth: 9.2%
- Annual Job Openings: 7,000
- Annual Earnings: $30,850
- Percentage of Women: 22.5%

Related Apprenticeship	*Years*
Job Printer	4

Set type according to copy; operate press to print job order; and read proof for errors and clarity of impression and correct imperfections. Job printers are often found in small establishments where work combines several job skills. Clean ink rollers after runs are completed. Design and set up product compositions and page layouts. Examine proofs or printed sheets in order to detect errors and to evaluate the adequacy of impression clarity. Fill ink fountains and move levers to adjust the flow of ink. Operate cylinder or automatic platen presses to print job orders. Reset type to correct typographical errors. Set feed guides according to sizes and thicknesses of paper. Insert spacers between words and leads between lines. Lay forms on proof presses; then ink type, fasten paper to press rollers, and pull rollers over forms to make proof copies. Place chases over type, insert quoins, and lock chases to hold type in place. Position forms (type in locked chases) on beds of presses; then tighten clamps, using wrenches. Remove assembled type from galleys and place type on composing stones. Select type from type cases, and insert type in printers' sticks to reproduce material in copy. Slide type from sticks into galleys. Tap typefaces with hammers to improve the quality of impressions. **SKILLS**—Operation and Control; Operation Monitoring; Quality Control Analysis; Equipment Maintenance.

GOE—**Interest Area:** 08. Industrial Production. **Work Group:** 08.03 Production Work. **Other Apprenticeable Jobs in This Work Group:** Bakers, Manufacturing; Bindery Machine Operators and Tenders; Chemical Equipment Controllers and Operators; Coating, Painting, and Spraying Machine Operators and Tenders; Cooling and Freezing Equipment Operators and Tenders; Crushing, Grinding, and Polishing Machine Setters, Operators, and Tenders; Cutters and Trimmers, Hand; Cutting and Slicing Machine Operators and Tenders; Design Printing Machine Setters and Set-Up Operators; Electrolytic Plating and Coating Machine Setters and Set-Up Operators, Metal and Plastic; Electrotypers and Stereotypers; Embossing Machine Set-Up Operators; Engraver Set-Up Operators; Extruding, Forming, Pressing, and Compacting Machine Operators and Tenders; Fabric and Apparel Patternmakers; Film Laboratory Technicians; Fitters, Structural Metal—Precision; Food Batchmakers; Furnace, Kiln, Oven, Drier, and Kettle Operators and Tenders; Hand Compositors and Typesetters; Letterpress Setters and Set-Up Operators; Metal Fabricators, Structural Metal Products; Metal-Refining Furnace Operators and Tenders; Mixing and Blending Machine Setters, Operators, and Tenders; Mold Makers, Hand; Molding and Casting Workers; Numerical Control Machine Tool Operators and Tenders, Metal and Plastic; Offset Lithographic Press Setters and Set-Up Operators; Painting, Coating, and Decorating Workers; Photographic Processing Machine Operators; Photographic Reproduction Technicians; Photographic Retouchers and Restorers; Plate Finishers; Platemakers; Precision Printing Workers; Printing Press Machine Operators and Tenders; Production Workers, All Other; Sawing Machine Operators and Tenders; Sawing Machine Setters and Set-Up Operators; Scanner Operators; Separating, Filtering, Clarifying, Precipitating, and Still Machine Setters, Operators, and Tenders; Sewing Machine Operators, Garment; Slaughterers and Meat Packers; Stone Sawyers; Strippers; Team Assemblers; Welder-Fitters; Welders and Cutters; Woodworking Machine Operators and Tenders, Except Sawing. **PERSONALITY TYPE:** Realistic. Realistic occupations frequently involve work activities that include practical, hands-on problems and solutions. They often deal with plants, animals, and real-world materials like wood, tools, and machinery. Many of the occupations require working outside and do not involve a lot of paperwork or working closely with others.

RELATED KNOWLEDGE/COURSES—**Production and Processing:** Knowledge of raw materials, production processes, quality control, costs, and other techniques for maximizing the effective manufacture and distribution of goods. **Communications and Media:** Knowledge of media production, communication, and dissemination techniques and methods. This includes alternative ways to inform and entertain via written, oral, and visual media. **English Language:** Knowledge of the structure and content of the English language, including the meaning and spelling of words, rules of composition, and grammar. **Mechanical Devices:** Knowledge of machines and tools, including their designs, uses, repair, and maintenance. **Clerical Practices:** Knowledge of administrative and clerical procedures and systems, such as word processing, managing files and records, stenography and transcription, designing forms, and other office procedures and terminology.

WORK ENVIRONMENT—Hazardous equipment; hazardous conditions; contaminants; indoors; sounds, noise levels are distracting or uncomfortable.

Landscaping and Groundskeeping Workers

◉ Growth: 22.0%
◉ Annual Job Openings: 203,000
◉ Annual Earnings: $19,940
◉ Percentage of Women: 7.6%

Related Apprenticeship	Years
Landscape Management Technician	1
Greenskeeper II	2
Landscape Technician	2
Landscape Gardener	4

Landscape or maintain grounds of property using hand or power tools or equipment. Workers typically perform a variety of tasks, which may include any combination of the following: sod laying, mowing, trimming, planting, watering, fertilizing, digging, raking, sprinkler installation, and installation of mortarless segmental concrete masonry wall units. Care for established lawns by mulching, aerating, weeding, grubbing and removing thatch, and trimming and edging around flower beds, walks, and walls. Mix and spray or spread fertilizers, herbicides, or insecticides onto grass, shrubs, and trees, using hand or automatic sprayers or spreaders. Mow and edge lawns, using power mowers and edgers. Plant seeds, bulbs, foliage, flowering plants, grass, ground covers, trees, and shrubs, and apply mulch for protection, using gardening tools. Attach wires from planted trees to support stakes. Decorate gardens with stones and plants. Follow planned landscaping designs to determine where to lay sod, sow grass, or plant flowers and foliage. Gather and remove litter. Haul or spread topsoil, and spread straw over seeded soil to hold soil in place. Maintain irrigation systems, including winterizing the systems and starting them up in spring. Plan and cultivate lawns and gardens. Prune and trim trees, shrubs, and hedges, using shears, pruners, or chain saws. Rake, mulch, and compost leaves. Trim and pick flowers, and clean flower beds. Water lawns, trees, and plants, using portable sprinkler systems, hoses, or watering cans. Advise customers on plant selection and care. Build forms, and mix and pour cement to form garden borders. Install rock gardens, ponds, decks, drainage systems, irrigation systems, retaining walls, fences, planters, and/or playground equipment. Maintain and repair tools, equipment, and structures such as buildings, greenhouses, fences, and benches, using hand and power tools. Provide proper upkeep of sidewalks, driveways, parking lots, fountains, planters, burial sites, and other grounds features. Shovel snow from walks, driveways, and parking lots, and spread salt in those areas. Use irrigation methods to adjust the amount of water consumption and to prevent waste. Care for artificial turf fields, periodically removing the turf and replacing cushioning pads, and vacuuming and disinfecting the turf after use to prevent the growth of harmful bacteria. Care for natural turf fields, making sure the underlying soil has the required composition to allow proper drainage and to support the grasses used on the fields. SKILLS—Equipment Maintenance; Repairing; Operation and Control; Installation.

GOE—Interest Area: 03. Plants and Animals. Work Group: 03.03 Hands-on Work in Plants and Animals. Other Apprenticeable Jobs in This Work Group: Agricultural Equipment Operators; Fallers; Farmworkers, Farm and Ranch Animals; Pest Control Workers; Pesticide Handlers, Sprayers, and Applicators, Vegetation; Tree Trimmers and Pruners. PERSONALITY TYPE: Realistic. Realistic occupations frequently involve work activities that include practical, hands-on problems and solutions. They often deal with plants, animals, and real-world materials like wood, tools, and machinery. Many of the occupations require working outside and do not involve a lot of paperwork or working closely with others.

RELATED KNOWLEDGE/COURSES—Chemistry: Knowledge of the chemical composition, structure, and properties of substances and of the chemical processes and transformations that they undergo. This includes uses of chemicals, their danger signs, production techniques, and disposal methods. Building and Construction: Knowledge of the materials, methods, and tools involved in the construction or repair of houses, buildings, or other structures, such as highways and roads. Mechanical Devices: Knowledge of machines and tools, including their designs, uses, repair, and maintenance.

WORK ENVIRONMENT—Outdoors; walking and running; spend time kneeling, crouching, stooping, or crawling; spend time bending or twisting the body; minor burns, cuts, bites, or stings.

Lathe and Turning Machine Tool Setters, Operators, and Tenders, Metal and Plastic

- Growth: 0.8%
- Annual Job Openings: 7,000
- Annual Earnings: $30,300
- Percentage of Women: 12.4%

Related Apprenticeship	Years
Engine-Lathe Set-Up Operator	2
Engine-Lathe Set-Up Operator, Tool	2

Screw-Machine Operator, Single Spindle	3
Screw-Machine Set-Up Operator, Single Spindle	3
Spinner, Hand	3
Screw-Machine Operator, Multiple Spindle	4
Screw-Machine Set-Up Operator	4
Turret-Lathe Set-Up Operator, Tool	4

Set up, operate, or tend lathe and turning machines to turn, bore, thread, form, or face metal or plastic materials, such as wire, rod, or bar stock. Installs holding fixtures, cams, gears, and stops to control stock and tool movement, using hand tools, power tools, and measuring instruments. Selects cutting tools and tooling instructions, according to knowledge of metal properties and shop mathematics, or written specifications. Observes operation and stops machine to inspect finished workpiece and verify conformance with specifications of first-run, using measuring instruments. Studies blueprint, layout, or chart, to visualize work and determine materials needed, sequence of operations, dimensions, and tooling instructions. Lifts metal stock or workpiece manually or using hoist, and positions and secures it in machine, using fasteners and hand tools. Replaces worn tools and sharpens dull cutting tools and dies. Computes unspecified dimensions and machine settings, using knowledge of metal properties and shop mathematics. Moves controls to set cutting speeds and depths, and feed rates and to position tool in relation to workplace. Cranks machine through cycle, stopping to adjust tool positions and machine controls, to ensure specified timing, clearance, and tolerances. Mounts attachments, such as relieving or tracing attachments, to perform operations, such as duplicating contours of template or trimming workpiece. Positions, secures, and aligns cutting tools in toolholders on machine, using hand tools, and verifies their position with measuring instruments. Moves toolholder manually or by turning handwheel, or engages automatic feeding mechanism, to feed tools to and along workpiece. Starts machine, and turns valve handle to direct flow of coolant on work area or coats disk with spinning compound. **SKILLS—**Equipment Maintenance; Installation; Technology Design; Operation Monitoring; Operation and Control; Operations Analysis; Repairing; Quality Control Analysis.

GOE—Interest Area: 08. Industrial Production. **Work Group:** 08.02 Production Technology. **Other Apprenticeable Jobs in This Work Group:** Aircraft Structure Assemblers, Precision; Aircraft Systems Assemblers, Precision; Bench Workers, Jewelry; Bindery Machine Setters and Set-Up Operators; Bookbinders; Buffing and Polishing Set-Up Operators; Coating, Painting, and Spraying Machine Setters and Set-Up Operators; Combination Machine Tool Setters and Set-Up Operators, Metal and Plastic; Dental Laboratory Technicians; Electrical and Electronic Equipment Assemblers; Electrical and Electronic Inspectors and Testers; Electromechanical Equipment Assemblers; Engine and Other Machine Assemblers; Extruding and Drawing Machine Setters, Operators, and Tenders, Metal and Plastic; Extruding, Forming, Pressing, and Compacting Machine Setters and Set-Up Operators; Forging Machine Setters, Operators, and Tenders, Metal and Plastic; Foundry Mold and Coremakers; Gem and Diamond Workers; Grinding, Honing, Lapping, and Deburring Machine Set-Up Operators; Heat Treating, Annealing, and Tempering Machine Operators and Tenders, Metal and Plastic; Jewelers; Materials Inspectors; Mechanical Inspectors; Metal Molding, Coremaking, and Casting Machine Operators and Tenders; Milling and Planing Machine Setters, Operators, and Tenders, Metal and Plastic; Model and Mold Makers, Jewelry; Motor Vehicle Inspectors; Paper Goods Machine Setters, Operators, and Tenders; Pewter Casters and Finishers; Plastic Molding and Casting Machine Setters and Set-Up Operators; Precision Devices Inspectors and Testers; Precision Lens Grinders and Polishers; Precision Mold and Pattern Casters, except Nonferrous Metals; Precision Pattern and Die Casters, Nonferrous Metals; Press and Press Brake Machine Setters and Set-Up Operators, Metal and Plastic; Production Inspectors, Testers, Graders, Sorters, Samplers, Weighers; Production Workers, All Other; Rolling Machine Setters, Operators, and Tenders, Metal and Plastic; Silversmiths; Textile Knitting and Weaving Machine Setters, Operators, and Tenders; Textile Winding, Twisting, and Drawing Out Machine Setters, Operators, and Tenders; Welding Machine Setters and Set-Up Operators; Woodworking Machine Setters and Set-Up Operators, Except Sawing. **PERSONALITY TYPE:** Realistic. Realistic occupations frequently involve work activities that include practical, hands-on problems and solutions. They often deal with plants, animals, and real-world materials like wood, tools, and machinery. Many of the occupations require working outside and do not involve a lot of paperwork or working closely with others.

RELATED KNOWLEDGE/COURSES— Production and Processing: Knowledge of raw materials, production processes, quality control, costs, and other techniques for maximizing the effective manufacture and distribution of goods. **Mechanical Devices:** Knowledge of machines and tools, including their designs, uses, repair, and maintenance. **Engineering and Technology:** Knowledge of the practical application of engineering science and technology. This includes applying principles, techniques, procedures, and equipment to the design and production of various goods and services. **Physics:** Knowledge and prediction of physical principles and laws and their interrelationships and applications to understanding fluid, material, and atmospheric dynamics and mechanical, electrical, atomic, and subatomic structures and processes. **Design:** Knowledge of design techniques, tools, and principles involved in production of precision technical plans, blueprints, drawings, and models. **Mathematics:** Knowledge of arithmetic, algebra, geometry, calculus, and statistics and their applications.

WORK ENVIRONMENT—Hazardous equipment; common protective or safety equipment; sounds, noise levels are distracting or uncomfortable; using hands on objects, tools, or controls; indoors.

Laundry and Drycleaning Machine Operators and Tenders, Except Pressing

- Growth: 12.3%
- Annual Job Openings: 47,000
- Annual Earnings: $16,920
- Percentage of Women: 59.7%

Related Apprenticeship	Years
Dry Cleaner	3

Operate or tend washing or dry-cleaning machines to wash or dry-clean commercial, industrial, or household articles, such as cloth garments, suede, leather, furs, blankets, draperies, fine linens, rugs, and carpets. Sorts and counts articles removed from dryer and folds, wraps, or hangs items for airing out, pick-up, or delivery. Examines and sorts articles to be cleaned into lots, according to color, fabric, dirt content, and cleaning technique required. Pre-soaks, sterilizes, scrubs, spot-cleans, and dries contaminated or stained articles, using neutralizer solutions and portable machines. Washes, dry cleans, or glazes delicate articles or fur garment linings by hand, using mild detergent or dry cleaning solutions. Removes or directs other workers to remove items from washer or dry cleaning machine and into extractor or tumbler. Tends variety of automatic machines that comb and polish furs; clean, sterilize, and fluff feathers and blankets; and roll and package towels. Mixes and adds detergents, dyes, bleach, starch, and other solutions and chemicals to clean, color, dry, or stiffen articles. Loads or directs other workers to load articles into washer or dry cleaning machine. Starts pumps to operate distilling system that drains and reclaims dry cleaning solvents. Adjusts switches to tend and regulate equipment that fumigates and removes foreign matter from furs. Cleans machine filters and lubricates equipment. Mends and sews articles, using hand stitching, adhesive patch, or power sewing machine. Hangs curtains, drapes, blankets, pants, and other garments on stretch frames to dry, and transports items between specified locations. Irons or presses articles, fabrics, and furs, using hand iron or pressing machine. Starts washer, dry cleaner, drier, or extractor, and turns valves or levers to regulate and monitor cleaning or drying operations. Receives and marks articles for laundry or dry cleaning with identifying code number or name, using hand or machine marker. SKILLS— Operation Monitoring; Equipment Maintenance; Operation and Control; Installation.

GOE—Interest Area: 11. Recreation, Travel, and Other Personal Services. Work Group: 11.06 Apparel, Shoes, Leather, and Fabric Care. Other Apprenticeable Jobs in This Work Group: Custom Tailors; Shoe and Leather Workers and Repairers; Shop and Alteration Tailors; Textile, Apparel, and Furnishings Workers, All Other; Upholsterers. PERSONALITY TYPE: Realistic. Realistic occupations frequently involve work activities that include practical, hands-on problems and solutions. They often deal with plants, animals, and real-world materials like wood, tools, and machinery. Many of the occupations require working outside and do not involve a lot of paperwork or working closely with others.

RELATED KNOWLEDGE/COURSES— Chemistry: Knowledge of the chemical composition, structure, and properties of substances and of the chemical processes and transformations that they undergo. This includes uses of chemicals, their danger signs, production techniques, and disposal methods. Production and Processing: Knowledge of raw materials, production processes, quality control, costs, and other techniques for maximizing the effective manufacture and distribution of goods. Customer and Personal Service: Knowledge of principles and processes for providing customer and personal services. This includes customer needs assessment, meeting quality standards for services, and evaluation of customer satisfaction. **Mechanical Devices:** Knowledge of machines and tools, including their designs, uses, repair, and maintenance.

WORK ENVIRONMENT—Hazardous equipment; very hot or cold; hazardous conditions; contaminants; using hands on objects, tools, or controls.

Lay-Out Workers, Metal and Plastic

@ Growth: 15.6%

@ Annual Job Openings: 1,000

@ Annual Earnings: $31,970

@ Percentage of Women: 10.3%

Related Apprenticeship	Years
Lay-Out Worker I	4
Shipfitter (Ship-Boat Manufacturing)	4

Lay out reference points and dimensions on metal or plastic stock or workpieces, such as sheets, plates, tubes, structural shapes, castings, or machine parts, for further processing. Includes shipfitters. Compute layout dimensions, and determine and mark reference points on metal stock or workpieces for further processing, such as welding and assembly. Design and prepare templates of wood, paper, or metal. Fit and align fabricated parts to be welded or assembled. Lay out and fabricate metal structural parts such as plates, bulkheads, and

frames. Locate center lines and verify template positions, using measuring instruments such as gauge blocks, height gauges, and dial indicators. Mark curves, lines, holes, dimensions, and welding symbols onto workpieces, using scribes, soapstones, punches, and hand drills. Plan and develop layouts from blueprints and templates, applying knowledge of trigonometry, design, effects of heat, and properties of metals. Plan locations and sequences of cutting, drilling, bending, rolling, punching, and welding operations, using compasses, protractors, dividers, and rules. Add dimensional details to blueprints or drawings made by other workers. Apply pigment to layout surfaces, using paint brushes. Brace parts in position within hulls or ships for riveting or welding. Inspect machined parts to verify conformance to specifications. Install doors, hatches, brackets, and clips. Lift and position workpieces in relation to surface plates, manually or with hoists, and using parallel blocks and angle plates. **SKILLS**—Mathematics; Technology Design; Operations Analysis; Science; Equipment Selection; Quality Control Analysis.

GOE—**Interest Area:** 08. Industrial Production. **Work Group:** 08.04 Metal and Plastics Machining Technology. **Other Apprenticeable Jobs in This Work Group:** Machinists; Metal Workers and Plastic Workers, All Other; Model Makers, Metal and Plastic; Patternmakers, Metal and Plastic; Tool and Die Makers; Tool Grinders, Filers, and Sharpeners. **PERSONALITY TYPE:** Realistic. Realistic occupations frequently involve work activities that include practical, hands-on problems and solutions. They often deal with plants, animals, and real-world materials like wood, tools, and machinery. Many of the occupations require working outside and do not involve a lot of paperwork or working closely with others.

RELATED KNOWLEDGE/COURSES—
Design: Knowledge of design techniques, tools, and principles involved in production of precision technical plans, blueprints, drawings, and models. **Production and Processing:** Knowledge of raw materials, production processes, quality control, costs, and other techniques for maximizing the effective manufacture and distribution of goods. **Mathematics:** Knowledge of arithmetic, algebra, geometry, calculus, and statistics and their applications. **Physics:** Knowledge and prediction of physical principles and laws and their interrelationships and applications to understanding fluid, material, and atmospheric dynamics and mechanical, electrical, atomic, and subatomic structures and processes. **Engineering and Technology:** Knowledge of the practical application of engineering science and technology. This includes applying principles, techniques, procedures, and equipment to the design and production of various goods and services. **Chemistry:** Knowledge of the chemical composition, structure, and properties of substances and of the chemical processes and transformations that they undergo. This includes uses of chemicals, their danger signs, production techniques, and disposal methods.

WORK ENVIRONMENT—Using hands on objects, tools, or controls; hazardous equipment; standing; spend time kneeling, crouching, stooping, or crawling; indoors; sounds, noise levels are distracting or uncomfortable.

Legal Secretaries

- Growth: 18.8%
- Annual Job Openings: 39,000
- Annual Earnings: $35,660
- Percentage of Women: 96.5%

Related Apprenticeship	*Years*
Legal Secretary	1

Perform secretarial duties utilizing legal terminology, procedures, and documents. Prepare legal papers and correspondence, such as summonses, complaints, motions, and subpoenas. May also assist with legal research. Prepare and process legal documents and papers, such as summonses, subpoenas, complaints, appeals, motions, and pretrial agreements. Mail, fax, or arrange for delivery of legal correspondence to clients, witnesses, and court officials. Receive and place telephone calls. Schedule and make appointments. Make photocopies of correspondence, document, and other printed matter. Organize and maintain law libraries and document and case files. Assist attorneys in collecting information such as employment, medical, and other records. Attend legal meetings, such as client interviews, hearings, or depositions, and take notes. Draft and type office memos. Review legal publications and perform data base searches to identify laws and court decisions relevant to pending cases. Submit articles and information from searches to attorneys for review and approval for use. Complete various forms, such as accident reports, trial and courtroom requests, and applications for clients.

SKILLS—Time Management; Writing; Social Perceptiveness; Learning Strategies; Negotiation; Persuasion; Reading Comprehension; Active Listening; Instructing.

GOE—**Interest Area:** 09. Business Detail. **Work Group:** 09.02 Administrative Detail. **Other Apprenticeable Jobs in This Work Group:** Medical Secretaries; Secretaries, Except Legal, Medical, and Executive. **PERSONALITY TYPE:** Conventional. Conventional occupations frequently involve following set procedures and routines. These occupations can include working with data and details more than with ideas. Usually there is a clear line of authority to follow.

RELATED KNOWLEDGE/COURSES— **Clerical Practices:** Knowledge of administrative and clerical procedures and systems, such as word processing, managing files and records, stenography and transcription, designing forms, and other office procedures and terminology. **Law and Government:** Knowledge of laws, legal codes, court procedures, precedents, government regulations, executive orders, agency rules, and the democratic political process. **Customer and Personal Service:** Knowledge of principles and processes for providing customer and personal services. This includes customer needs assessment, meeting quality standards for services, and evaluation of customer satisfaction. **Economics and Accounting:** Knowledge of economic and accounting principles and practices, the financial markets, banking, and the analysis and reporting of financial data. **Computers and Electronics:** Knowledge of circuit boards, processors, chips, electronic equipment, and computer hardware and software, including applications and programming. **English Language:** Knowledge of the structure and content of the English language, including the meaning and spelling of words, rules of composition, and grammar.

WORK ENVIRONMENT—Sitting; physical proximity.

Letterpress Setters and Set-Up Operators

- Growth: 4.6%
- Annual Job Openings: 30,000
- Annual Earnings: $29,340
- Percentage of Women: 17.8%

Related Apprenticeship	Years
Cylinder-Press Operator	4
Platen-Press Operator	4
Web-Press Operator	4

Set up or set up and operate direct relief letterpresses, either sheet or roll (web) fed, to produce single or multicolor printed material, such as newspapers, books, and periodicals. Dismantles and reassembles printing unit or parts, using hand tools, to repair, clean, maintain, or adjust press. Operates specially-equipped presses and auxiliary equipment, such as cutting, folding, numbering, and pasting devices. Reads work orders and job specifications to select ink and paper stock. Record and maintain production logsheet. Directs and monitors activities of apprentices and feeding or stacking workers. Inspects printed materials for irregularities such as off-level areas, variations in ink volume, register slippage, and poor color register. Moves controls to set or adjust ink flow, tension rollers, paper guides, and feed controls. Positions and installs printing plates, cylinder packing, die, and type forms in press, according to specifications, using hand tools. Loads, positions, and adjusts unprinted materials on holding fixtures or in feeding mechanism of press. Pushes buttons or moves controls to start printing press and control operation. Mixes colors or inks and fills reservoirs. Monitors feeding and printing operations to maintain specified operating levels and detect malfunctions. **SKILLS**—Installation; Equipment Maintenance; Operation Monitoring; Operation and Control; Troubleshooting; Equipment Selection; Management of Personnel Resources; Quality Control Analysis.

GOE—**Interest Area:** 08. Industrial Production. **Work Group:** 08.03 Production Work. **Other Apprenticeable Jobs in This Work Group:** Bakers, Manufacturing; Bindery Machine Operators and Tenders; Chemical Equipment Controllers and Operators; Coating, Painting, and Spraying Machine Operators and Tenders; Cooling and Freezing Equipment Operators and Tenders; Crushing, Grinding, and Polishing Machine Setters, Operators, and Tenders; Cutters and Trimmers, Hand; Cutting and Slicing Machine Operators and Tenders; Design Printing Machine Setters and Set-Up Operators; Electrolytic Plating and Coating Machine Setters and Set-Up Operators, Metal and Plastic; Electrotypers and Stereotypers; Embossing Machine Set-Up Operators; Engraver Set-Up Operators; Extruding, Forming, Pressing, and Compacting Machine Operators and Tenders; Fabric and Apparel Patternmakers; Film Laboratory Technicians; Fitters, Structural Metal—Precision; Food Batchmakers; Furnace, Kiln, Oven, Drier, and Kettle Operators and Tenders; Hand Compositors and Typesetters; Job Printers; Metal Fabricators, Structural Metal Products; Metal-Refining Furnace Operators and Tenders; Mixing and Blending Machine Setters, Operators, and Tenders; Mold Makers, Hand; Molding and Casting Workers; Numerical Control Machine Tool Operators and Tenders, Metal and Plastic; Offset Lithographic Press Setters and Set-Up Operators; Painting, Coating, and Decorating Workers; Photographic Processing Machine Operators; Photographic Reproduction Technicians; Photographic Retouchers and Restorers; Plate Finishers; Platemakers; Precision Printing Workers; Printing Press Machine Operators and Tenders; Production Workers, All Other; Sawing Machine Operators and Tenders; Sawing Machine Setters and Set-Up Operators; Scanner Operators; Separating, Filtering, Clarifying, Precipitating, and Still Machine Setters, Operators, and Tenders; Sewing Machine Operators, Garment; Slaughterers and Meat Packers; Stone Sawyers; Strippers; Team Assemblers; Welder-Fitters; Welders and Cutters; Woodworking Machine Operators and Tenders, Except Sawing. **PERSONALITY TYPE:** Realistic. Realistic occupations frequently involve work activities that include practical, hands-on problems and solutions. They often deal with plants, animals, and real-world materials like wood, tools, and machinery. Many of the occupations require working outside and do not involve a lot of paperwork or working closely with others.

RELATED KNOWLEDGE/COURSES—**Production and Processing:** Knowledge of raw materials, production processes, quality control, costs, and other techniques for maximizing the effective manufacture and distribution of goods. **Economics and Accounting:** Knowledge of economic and accounting principles and practices, the financial markets, banking, and the analysis and reporting of financial data.

WORK ENVIRONMENT—Hazardous equipment; using hands on objects, tools, or controls; standing; indoors; common protective or safety equipment.

Licensed Practical and Licensed Vocational Nurses

- Growth: 20.2%
- Annual Job Openings: 105,000
- Annual Earnings: $32,390
- Percentage of Women: 93.0%

Related Apprenticeship	Years
Nurse, Licensed Practical	1

Care for ill, injured, convalescent, or disabled persons in hospitals, nursing homes, clinics, private homes, group homes, and similar institutions. May work under the supervision of a registered nurse. Licensing required. Observe patients, charting and reporting changes in patients' conditions, such as adverse reactions to medication or treatment, and taking any necessary action. Administer prescribed medications or start intravenous fluids, and note times and amounts on patients' charts. Answer patients' calls and determine how to assist them. Measure and record patients' vital signs, such as height, weight, temperature, blood pressure, pulse and respiration. Provide basic patient care and treatments, such as taking temperatures and blood pressure, dressing wounds, treating bedsores, giving enemas, douches, alcohol rubs, and massages, or performing catheterizations. Help patients with bathing, dressing, personal hygiene, moving in bed, and standing and walking. Supervise nurses' aides and assistants. Work as part of a health care team to assess patient needs, plan and modify care and implement interventions. Record food and fluid intake and output. Evaluate nursing intervention outcomes, conferring with other health-care team members as necessary. Assemble and use equipment such as catheters, tracheotomy tubes, and oxygen suppliers. Collect samples such as blood, urine and sputum from patients, and perform routine laboratory tests on samples. Prepare patients for examinations, tests and treatments and explain procedures. Prepare food trays and examine them for conformance to prescribed diet. Apply compresses, ice bags, and hot water bottles. Clean rooms and make beds. Inventory and requisition supplies and instruments. Provide medical treatment and personal care to patients in private home settings, such as cooking, keeping rooms orderly, seeing that patients are comfortable and in good spirits, and instructing family members in simple nursing tasks. Sterilize equipment and supplies, using germicides, sterilizer, or autoclave. Assist in delivery, care, and feeding of infants. Wash and dress bodies of deceased persons. Make appointments, keep records and perform other clerical duties in doctors' offices and clinics. Set up equipment and prepare medical treatment rooms. SKILLS—Service Orientation; Active Listening; Science; Time Management; Instructing; Judgment and Decision Making; Management of Personnel Resources; Learning Strategies.

GOE—**Interest Area:** 14. Medical and Health Services. **Work Group:** 14.07 Patient Care and Assistance. **Other Apprenticeable Jobs in This Work Group:** Nursing Aides, Orderlies, and Attendants. **PERSONALITY TYPE:** Social. Social occupations frequently involve working with, communicating with, and teaching people. These occupations often involve helping or providing service to others.

RELATED KNOWLEDGE/COURSES—Psychology: Knowledge of human behavior and performance; individual differences in ability, personality, and interests; learning and motivation; psychological research methods; and the assessment and treatment of behavioral and affective disorders. **Customer and Personal Service:** Knowledge of principles and processes for providing customer and personal services. This includes customer needs assessment, meeting quality standards for services, and evaluation of customer satisfaction. **Therapy and Counseling:** Knowledge of principles, methods, and procedures for diagnosis, treatment, and rehabilitation of physical and mental dysfunctions and for career counseling and guidance. **Medicine and Dentistry:** Knowledge of the information and techniques needed to diagnose and treat human injuries, diseases, and deformities. This includes symptoms, treatment alternatives, drug properties and interactions, and preventive health-care measures. **Education and Training:** Knowledge of principles and methods for curriculum and training design, teaching and instruction for individuals and groups, and the measurement of training effects. **Philosophy and Theology:** Knowledge of different philosophical systems and religions. This includes their basic principles, values, ethics, ways of thinking, customs, and practices and their impact on human culture.

WORK ENVIRONMENT—Physical proximity; disease or infections; sounds, noise levels are distracting or uncomfortable; walking and running; sitting.

Locksmiths and Safe Repairers

- Growth: 21.0%
- Annual Job Openings: 3,000
- Annual Earnings: $28,760
- Percentage of Women: 7.0%

Related Apprenticeship	Years
Locksmith	4
Safe-and-Vault Service Mechanic	4

Repair and open locks; make keys; change locks and safe combinations; and install and repair safes. Disassemble mechanical or electrical locking devices, and repair or replace worn tumblers, springs, and other parts, using hand tools. Insert new or repaired tumblers into locks in order to change combinations. Repair and adjust safes, vault doors, and vault components, using hand tools, lathes, drill presses, and welding and acetylene cutting apparatus. Cut new or duplicate keys, using keycutting machines. Install safes, vault doors, and deposit boxes according to blueprints, using equipment such as powered drills, taps, dies, truck cranes, and dollies. Open safe locks by drilling. Move picklocks in cylinders in order to open door locks without keys. Remove interior and exterior finishes on safes and vaults, and spray on new finishes. Keep records of company locks and keys. **SKILLS**—Installation; Repairing; Technology Design; Troubleshooting; Service Orientation; Equipment Maintenance.

GOE—Interest Area: 05. Mechanics, Installers, and Repairers. **Work Group:** 05.03 Mechanical Work. **Other Apprenticeable Jobs in This Work Group:** Aircraft Engine Specialists; Airframe-and-Power-Plant Mechanics; Automotive Body and Related Repairers; Automotive Glass Installers and Repairers; Automotive Master Mechanics; Automotive Specialty Technicians; Bus and Truck Mechanics and Diesel Engine Specialists; Camera and Photographic Equipment Repairers; Coin, Vending, and Amusement Machine Servicers and Repairers; Farm Equipment Mechanics; Gas Appliance Repairers; Hand and Portable Power Tool Repairers; Heating and Air Conditioning Mechanics; Helpers—Installation, Maintenance, and Repair Workers; Industrial Machinery Mechanics; Installation, Maintenance, and Repair Workers, All Other; Keyboard Instrument Repairers and Tuners; Maintenance and Repair Workers, General; Maintenance Workers, Machinery; Mechanical Door Repairers; Medical Appliance Technicians; Medical Equipment Repairers; Meter Mechanics; Millwrights; Mobile Heavy Equipment Mechanics, Except Engines; Motorboat Mechanics; Motorcycle Mechanics; Optical Instrument Assemblers; Outdoor Power Equipment and Other Small Engine Mechanics; Painters, Transportation Equipment; Rail Car Repairers; Recreational Vehicle Service Technicians; Reed or Wind Instrument Repairers and Tuners; Refrigeration Mechanics; Stringed Instrument Repairers and Tuners; Valve and Regulator Repairers; Watch Repairers. **PERSONALITY TYPE:** Realistic. Realistic occupations frequently involve work activities that include practical, hands-on problems and solutions. They often deal with plants, animals, and real-world materials like wood, tools, and machinery. Many of the occupations require working outside and do not involve a lot of paperwork or working closely with others.

RELATED KNOWLEDGE/COURSES— Mechanical Devices: Knowledge of machines and tools, including their designs, uses, repair, and maintenance. **Engineering and Technology:** Knowledge of the practical application of engineering science and technology. This includes applying principles, techniques, procedures, and equipment to the design and production of various goods and services. **Clerical Practices:** Knowledge of administrative and clerical procedures and systems, such as word processing, managing files and records, stenography and transcription, designing forms, and other office procedures and terminology. **Building and Construction:** Knowledge of the materials, methods, and tools involved in the construction or repair of houses, buildings, or other structures, such as highways and roads.

WORK ENVIRONMENT—Using hands on objects, tools, or controls; spend time kneeling, crouching, stooping, or crawling; minor burns, cuts, bites, or stings; standing; very hot or cold.

Locomotive Engineers

- Growth: −7.2%
- Annual Job Openings: 4,000
- Annual Earnings: $45,990
- Percentage of Women: 4.1%

Related Apprenticeship	*Years*
Locomotive Engineer	2

Drive electric, diesel-electric, steam, or gas-turbine-electric locomotives to transport passengers or freight. Interpret train orders, electronic or manual signals, and railroad rules and regulations. Confer with conductors or traffic control center personnel via radiophones to issue or receive information concerning stops, delays, or oncoming trains. Inspect locomotives to verify adequate fuel, sand, water, and other supplies before each run, and to check for mechanical problems. Interpret train orders, signals, and railroad rules and regulations that govern the operation of locomotives. Monitor gauges and meters that measure speed, amperage, battery charge, and air pressure in brake-lines and in main reservoirs. Observe tracks to detect obstructions. Operate locomotives to transport freight or passengers between stations, and to assemble and disassemble trains within rail yards. Receive starting signals from conductors, then move controls such as throttles and air brakes to drive electric, diesel-electric, steam, or gas-turbine-electric locomotives. Call out train signals to assistants in order to verify meanings. Check to ensure that brake examination tests are conducted at shunting stations. Check to ensure that documentation, including procedure manuals and logbooks, is in the driver's cab and available for staff use. Drive diesel-electric rail-detector cars to transport rail-flaw-detecting machines over tracks. Inspect locomotives after runs to detect damaged or defective equipment. Monitor train loading procedures to ensure that freight and rolling stock are loaded or unloaded without damage. Prepare reports regarding any problems encountered, such as accidents, signaling problems, unscheduled stops, or delays. Respond to emergency conditions or breakdowns, following applicable safety procedures and rules. **SKILLS—**Operation and Control; Operation Monitoring; Equipment Maintenance; Troubleshooting; Systems Analysis; Time Management; Reading Comprehension; Writing.

GOE—Interest Area: 07. Transportation. **Work Group:** 07.06 Rail Vehicle Operation. **Other Apprenticeable Jobs in This Work Group:** No other apprenticeable jobs in this group. **PERSONALITY TYPE:** Realistic. Realistic occupations frequently involve work activities that include practical, hands-on problems and solutions. They often deal with plants, animals, and real-world materials like wood, tools, and machinery. Many of the occupations require working outside and do not involve a lot of paperwork or working closely with others.

RELATED KNOWLEDGE/COURSES— Transportation: Knowledge of principles and methods for moving people or goods by air, rail, sea, or road, including the relative costs and benefits. **Geography:** Knowledge of principles and methods for describing the features of land, sea, and air masses, including their physical characteristics; locations; interrelationships; and distribution of plant, animal, and human life. **Public Safety and Security:** Knowledge of relevant equipment, policies, procedures, and strategies to promote effective local, state, or national security operations for the protection of people, data, property, and institutions. **Engineering and Technology:** Knowledge of the practical application of engineering science and technology. This includes applying principles, techniques, procedures, and equipment to the design and production of various goods and services. **Mechanical Devices:** Knowledge of machines and tools, including their designs, uses, repair, and maintenance. **Telecommunications:** Knowledge of transmission, broadcasting, switching, control, and operation of telecommunications systems.

WORK ENVIRONMENT—Hazardous equipment; hazardous conditions; sounds, noise levels are distracting or uncomfortable; contaminants; outdoors.

Machinists

- ◎ Growth: 8.2%
- ◎ Annual Job Openings: 30,000
- ◎ Annual Earnings: $33,090
- ◎ Percentage of Women: 5.3%

Related Apprenticeship	Years
Fixture Maker	2
Instrument Maker	4
Machinist	4
Machinist, Automotive	4
Machinist, Experimental	4
Machinist, Outside (Ship-Boat Manufacturing)	4
Maintenance Machinist	4
Rocket-Motor Mechanic	4
Instrument-Maker and Repairer	5
Test Technician	5

(This is one of the most popular apprenticeable jobs.)

Set up and operate a variety of machine tools to produce precision parts and instruments. Includes precision instrument makers who fabricate, modify, or repair mechanical instruments. May also fabricate and modify parts to make or repair machine tools or maintain industrial machines, applying knowledge of mechanics, shop mathematics, metal properties, layout, and machining procedures. Calculate dimensions and tolerances using knowledge of mathematics and instruments such as micrometers and vernier calipers. Machine parts to specifications using machine tools such as lathes, milling machines, shapers, or grinders. Measure, examine, and test completed units in order to detect defects and ensure conformance to specifications, using precision instruments such as micrometers. Set up, adjust, and operate all of the basic machine tools and many specialized or advanced variation tools in order to perform precision machining operations. Align and secure holding fixtures, cutting tools, attachments, accessories, and materials onto machines. Monitor the feed and speed of machines during the machining process. Study sample parts, blueprints, drawings, and engineering information in order to determine methods and sequences of operations needed to fabricate products, and determine product dimensions and tolerances. Select the appropriate tools, machines, and materials to be used in preparation of machinery work. Lay out, measure, and mark metal stock in order to display placement of cuts. Observe and listen to operating machines or equipment in order to diagnose machine malfunctions and to determine need for adjustments or repairs. Check workpieces to ensure that they are properly lubricated and cooled. Maintain industrial machines, applying knowledge of mechanics, shop mathematics, metal properties, layout, and machining procedures. Position and fasten workpieces. Operate equipment to verify operational efficiency. Install repaired parts into equipment, or install new equipment. Clean and lubricate machines, tools, and equipment in order to remove grease, rust, stains, and foreign matter. Advise clients about the materials being used for finished products. Program computers and electronic instruments such as numerically controlled machine tools. Set controls to regulate machining, or enter commands to retrieve, input, or edit computerized machine control media. Confer with engineering, supervisory, and manufacturing personnel in order to exchange technical information. **SKILLS**—Operation Monitoring; Operation and Control; Equipment Maintenance; Installation; Quality Control Analysis; Troubleshooting; Equipment Selection; Technology Design.

GOE—Interest Area: 08. Industrial Production. **Work Group:** 08.04 Metal and Plastics Machining Technology. **Other Apprenticeable Jobs in This Work Group:** Lay-Out Workers, Metal and Plastic; Metal Workers and Plastic Workers, All Other; Model Makers, Metal and Plastic; Patternmakers, Metal and Plastic; Tool and Die Makers; Tool Grinders, Filers, and Sharpeners. **PERSONALITY TYPE:** Realistic. Realistic occupations frequently involve work activities that include practical, hands-on problems and solutions. They often deal with plants, animals, and real-world materials like wood, tools, and machinery. Many of the occupations require working outside and do not involve a lot of paperwork or working closely with others.

RELATED KNOWLEDGE/COURSES—Mechanical Devices: Knowledge of machines and tools, including their designs, uses, repair, and maintenance. **Mathematics:** Knowledge of arithmetic, algebra, geometry, calculus, and statistics and their applications. **Engineering and Technology:** Knowledge of the practical application of engineering science and technology. This includes applying principles, techniques, procedures, and equipment to the design and production of various goods and services. **Design:** Knowledge of design techniques, tools, and principles involved in production of precision technical plans, blueprints, drawings, and models. **Production and Processing:** Knowledge of raw materials, production processes, quality control, costs, and other techniques for maximizing the effective manufacture and distribution of goods. **Computers and Electronics:** Knowledge of circuit boards, processors, chips, electronic equipment, and computer hardware and software, including applications and programming.

WORK ENVIRONMENT—Sounds, noise levels are distracting or uncomfortable; contaminants; hazardous equipment; indoors, not environmentally controlled; physical proximity.

Maids and Housekeeping Cleaners

- Growth: 9.2%
- Annual Job Openings: 352,000
- Annual Earnings: $16,600
- Percentage of Women: 87.6%

Related Apprenticeship	Years
Housekeeper, Commercial, Residential, or Industrial	1

Perform any combination of light cleaning duties to maintain private households or commercial establishments, such as hotels, restaurants, and hospitals, in a clean and orderly manner. Duties include making beds, replenishing linens, cleaning rooms and halls, and vacuuming. Clean rooms, hallways, lobbies, lounges, restrooms, corridors, elevators, stairways, locker rooms and other work areas so that health standards are met. Clean rugs, carpets, upholstered furniture, and/or draperies, using vacuum cleaners and/or shampooers. Empty wastebaskets, empty and clean ashtrays, and transport other trash and waste to disposal areas. Sweep, scrub, wax, and/or polish floors, using brooms, mops, and/or powered scrubbing and waxing machines. Dust and polish furniture and equipment. Keep storage areas and carts well-stocked, clean, and tidy. Polish silver accessories and metalwork such as fixtures and fittings. Remove debris from driveways, garages, and swimming pool areas. Replace light bulbs. Replenish supplies such as drinking glasses, linens, writing supplies, and bathroom items. Sort clothing and other articles, load washing machines, and iron and fold dried items. Sort, count, and mark clean linens, and store them in linen closets. Wash windows, walls, ceilings, and woodwork, waxing and polishing as necessary. Assign duties to other staff and give instructions regarding work methods and routines. Request repair services and wait for repair workers to arrive. Deliver television sets, ironing boards, baby cribs, and rollaway beds to guests' rooms. Disinfect equipment and supplies, using germicides or steam-operated sterilizers. Hang draperies, and dust window blinds. Move and arrange furniture, and turn mattresses. Observe precautions required to protect hotel and guest property, and report damage, theft, and found articles to supervisors. Plan menus, and cook and serve meals and refreshments following employer's instructions or own methods. Prepare rooms for meetings, and arrange decorations, media equipment, and furniture for social or business functions. Take care of pets by grooming, exercising, and/or feeding them. Wash dishes and clean kitchens, cooking utensils, and silverware. Answer telephones and doorbells. Care for children and/or elderly persons by overseeing their activities, providing companionship, and assisting them with dressing, bathing, eating, and other needs. **SKILLS**—None met the criteria.

GOE—Interest Area: 11. Recreation, Travel, and Other Personal Services. **Work Group:** 11.07 Cleaning and Building Services. **Other Apprenticeable Jobs in This Work Group:** Building Cleaning Workers, All Other; Janitors and Cleaners, Except Maids and Housekeeping Cleaners. **PERSONALITY TYPE:** Realistic. Realistic occupations frequently involve work activities that include practical, hands-on problems and solutions. They often deal with plants, animals, and real-world materials like wood, tools, and machinery. Many of the occupations require working outside and do not involve a lot of paperwork or working closely with others.

RELATED KNOWLEDGE/COURSES—Customer and Personal Service: Knowledge of principles and processes for providing customer and personal services. This includes customer needs assessment, meeting quality standards for services, and evaluation of customer satisfaction. **Chemistry:** Knowledge of the chemical composition, structure, and properties of substances and of the chemical processes and transformations that they undergo. This includes uses of chemicals, their danger signs, production techniques, and disposal methods.

WORK ENVIRONMENT—Standing; walking and running; spend time kneeling, crouching, stooping, or crawling; spend time making repetitive motions; spend time bending or twisting the body.

Maintenance and Repair Workers, General

- Growth: 16.3%
- Annual Job Openings: 155,000
- Annual Earnings: $29,800
- Percentage of Women: 4.1%

Related Apprenticeship	Years
Maintenance Repairer, Building	2
Marine-Services Technician	3
Maintenance Repairer, Industrial	4

Perform work involving the skills of two or more maintenance or craft occupations to keep machines, mechanical equipment, or the structure of an establishment in repair. Duties may involve pipe fitting; boiler making; insulating; welding; machining; carpentry; repairing electrical or mechanical equipment; installing, aligning, and balancing new equipment; and repairing buildings, floors, or stairs. Repair or replace defective equipment parts using hand tools and power tools, and reassemble equipment. Perform routine preventive maintenance to ensure that machines continue to run smoothly, building systems operate efficiently, and the physical condition of buildings does not deteriorate. Inspect drives, motors, and belts, check fluid levels, replace filters, and perform other maintenance actions, following checklists. Use tools ranging from common hand and power tools, such as hammers, hoists, saws, drills, and wrenches, to precision measuring instruments and electrical and electronic testing devices. Assemble, install and/or repair wiring, electrical and electronic components, pipe systems and plumbing, machinery, and equipment. Diagnose mechanical problems and determine how to correct them, checking blueprints, repair manuals, and parts catalogs as necessary. Inspect, operate, and test machinery and equipment in order to diagnose machine malfunctions. Record maintenance and repair work performed and the costs of the work. Clean and lubricate shafts, bearings, gears, and other parts of machinery. Dismantle devices to gain access to and remove defective parts, using hoists, cranes, hand tools, and power tools. Plan and lay out repair work using diagrams, drawings, blueprints, maintenance manuals, and schematic diagrams. Order parts, supplies, and equipment from catalogs and suppliers, or obtain them from storerooms. Adjust functional parts of devices and control instruments, using hand tools, levels, plumb bobs, and straightedges. Paint and repair roofs, windows, doors, floors, woodwork, plaster, drywall, and other parts of building structures. Operate cutting torches or welding equipment to cut or join metal parts. Align and balance new equipment after installation. Inspect used parts to determine changes in dimensional requirements, using rules, calipers, micrometers, and other measuring instruments. Set up and operate machine tools to repair or fabricate machine parts, jigs and fixtures, and tools. Maintain and repair specialized equipment and machinery found in cafeterias, laundries, hospitals, stores, offices, and factories. **SKILLS**—Equipment Maintenance; Installation; Repairing; Troubleshooting; Operation Monitoring; Equipment Selection; Operation and Control; Critical Thinking.

GOE—Interest Area: 05. Mechanics, Installers, and Repairers. **Work Group:** 05.03 Mechanical Work. **Other Apprenticeable Jobs in This Work Group:** Aircraft Engine Specialists; Airframe-and-Power-Plant Mechanics; Automotive Body and Related Repairers; Automotive Glass Installers and Repairers; Automotive Master Mechanics; Automotive Specialty Technicians; Bus and Truck Mechanics and Diesel Engine Specialists; Camera and Photographic Equipment Repairers; Coin, Vending, and Amusement Machine Servicers and Repairers; Farm Equipment Mechanics; Gas Appliance Repairers; Hand and Portable Power Tool Repairers; Heating and Air Conditioning Mechanics; Helpers—Installation, Maintenance, and Repair Workers; Industrial Machinery Mechanics; Installation, Maintenance, and Repair Workers, All Other; Keyboard Instrument Repairers and Tuners; Locksmiths and Safe Repairers; Maintenance Workers, Machinery; Mechanical Door Repairers; Medical Appliance Technicians; Medical Equipment Repairers; Meter Mechanics; Millwrights; Mobile Heavy Equipment Mechanics, Except Engines; Motorboat Mechanics; Motorcycle Mechanics; Optical Instrument Assemblers; Outdoor Power Equipment and Other Small Engine Mechanics; Painters, Transportation Equipment; Rail Car Repairers; Recreational Vehicle Service Technicians; Reed or Wind Instrument Repairers and Tuners; Refrigeration Mechanics;

Stringed Instrument Repairers and Tuners; Valve and Regulator Repairers; Watch Repairers. **PERSONALITY TYPE:** Realistic. Realistic occupations frequently involve work activities that include practical, hands-on problems and solutions. They often deal with plants, animals, and real-world materials like wood, tools, and machinery. Many of the occupations require working outside and do not involve a lot of paperwork or working closely with others.

RELATED KNOWLEDGE/COURSES— Mechanical Devices: Knowledge of machines and tools, including their designs, uses, repair, and maintenance. **Building and Construction:** Knowledge of the materials, methods, and tools involved in the construction or repair of houses, buildings, or other structures, such as highways and roads. **Design:** Knowledge of design techniques, tools, and principles involved in production of precision technical plans, blueprints, drawings, and models. **Public Safety and Security:** Knowledge of relevant equipment, policies, procedures, and strategies to promote effective local, state, or national security operations for the protection of people, data, property, and institutions. **Engineering and Technology:** Knowledge of the practical application of engineering science and technology. This includes applying principles, techniques, procedures, and equipment to the design and production of various goods and services. **Physics:** Knowledge and prediction of physical principles and laws and their interrelationships and applications to understanding fluid, material, and atmospheric dynamics and mechanical, electrical, atomic, and subatomic structures and processes.

WORK ENVIRONMENT—Very hot or cold; sounds, noise levels are distracting or uncomfortable; contaminants; minor burns, cuts, bites, or stings; extremely bright or inadequate lighting.

Maintenance Workers, Machinery

- Growth: 5.9%
- Annual Job Openings: 5,000
- Annual Earnings: $33,000
- Percentage of Women: 5.7%

Related Apprenticeship	Years
Pinsetter Mechanic, Automatic	2

Lubricate machinery, change parts, or perform other routine machinery maintenance. Sets up and operates machine and adjusts controls that regulate operational functions to ensure conformance to specifications. Lubricates, oils, or applies adhesive, or other material to machines, machine parts, or other equipment, according to specified procedures. Starts machine and observes mechanical operation to determine efficiency and to detect defects, malfunctions, or other machine damage. Installs, replaces, or changes machine parts and attachments, according to production specifications. Replaces or repairs metal, wood, leather, glass, or other lining in machine or equipment compartments or containers. Dismantles machine, removes machine parts, and reassembles machine, using hand tools, chain falls, jack, crane, or hoist. Cleans machine and machine parts, using cleaning solvent, cloth, air gun, hose, vacuum, or other equipment. Removes hardened material from machine or machine parts, using abrasives, power and hand tools, jackhammer, sledgehammer, or other equipment. Collects and discards worn machine parts and other garbage to maintain machinery and work areas. Transports machine parts, tools, equipment and other material between work areas and storage, using crane, hoist, or dolly. Inventories and requisitions machine parts, equipment, and other supplies to replenish and maintain stock. Records and maintains production, repair, and machine maintenance information. Marks, separates, ties, aligns, threads, attaches, or inserts material or product preparatory to machine operation or to identify machine process. Measures, mixes, prepares and tests chemical solutions used to clean or repair machinery and equipment, according to product specifications. Communicates with or assists other workers to repair or move machines, machine parts or equipment. Replaces, empties, or replenishes empty machine and equipment containers, such as gas tanks or boxes. Reads work orders and specifications to determine machines and equipment requiring repair or maintenance. Cuts, shapes, smoothes, attaches or assembles pieces of metal, wood, rubber, or other material repair and maintenance machines and equipment. **SKILLS**—Equipment Maintenance; Repairing; Installation; Operation Monitoring; Troubleshooting; Technology Design; Operation and Control; Quality Control Analysis.

GOE—Interest Area: 05. Mechanics, Installers, and Repairers. **Work Group:** 05.03 Mechanical Work. **Other Apprenticeable Jobs in This Work Group:** Aircraft Engine Specialists; Airframe-and-Power-Plant Mechanics; Automotive Body and Related Repairers; Automotive Glass

Installers and Repairers; Automotive Master Mechanics; Automotive Specialty Technicians; Bus and Truck Mechanics and Diesel Engine Specialists; Camera and Photographic Equipment Repairers; Coin, Vending, and Amusement Machine Servicers and Repairers; Farm Equipment Mechanics; Gas Appliance Repairers; Hand and Portable Power Tool Repairers; Heating and Air Conditioning Mechanics; Helpers—Installation, Maintenance, and Repair Workers; Industrial Machinery Mechanics; Installation, Maintenance, and Repair Workers, All Other; Keyboard Instrument Repairers and Tuners; Locksmiths and Safe Repairers; Maintenance and Repair Workers, General; Mechanical Door Repairers; Medical Appliance Technicians; Medical Equipment Repairers; Meter Mechanics; Millwrights; Mobile Heavy Equipment Mechanics, Except Engines; Motorboat Mechanics; Motorcycle Mechanics; Optical Instrument Assemblers; Outdoor Power Equipment and Other Small Engine Mechanics; Painters, Transportation Equipment; Rail Car Repairers; Recreational Vehicle Service Technicians; Reed or Wind Instrument Repairers and Tuners; Refrigeration Mechanics; Stringed Instrument Repairers and Tuners; Valve and Regulator Repairers; Watch Repairers. **PERSONALITY TYPE:** Realistic. Realistic occupations frequently involve work activities that include practical, hands-on problems and solutions. They often deal with plants, animals, and real-world materials like wood, tools, and machinery. Many of the occupations require working outside and do not involve a lot of paperwork or working closely with others.

RELATED KNOWLEDGE/COURSES—Mechanical Devices: Knowledge of machines and tools, including their designs, uses, repair, and maintenance. **Chemistry:** Knowledge of the chemical composition, structure, and properties of substances and of the chemical processes and transformations that they undergo. This includes uses of chemicals, their danger signs, production techniques, and disposal methods. **Production and Processing:** Knowledge of raw materials, production processes, quality control, costs, and other techniques for maximizing the effective manufacture and distribution of goods. **Engineering and Technology:** Knowledge of the practical application of engineering science and technology. This includes applying principles, techniques, procedures, and equipment to the design and production of various goods and services. **Physics:** Knowledge and prediction of physical principles and laws and their interrelationships and applications to understanding fluid, material, and atmospheric dynamics and mechanical, electrical, atomic, and subatomic structures and processes. **Transportation:** Knowledge of principles and methods for moving people or goods by air, rail, sea, or road, including the relative costs and benefits.

WORK ENVIRONMENT—Hazardous equipment; common protective or safety equipment; sounds, noise levels are distracting or uncomfortable; spend time kneeling, crouching, stooping, or crawling; spend time bending or twisting the body.

Mapping Technicians

- Growth: 23.1%
- Annual Job Openings: 10,000
- Annual Earnings: $29,520
- Percentage of Women: 8.9%

Related Apprenticeship	Years
Geodetic Computator	2
Photogrammetric Technician	3

Calculate mapmaking information from field notes, and draw and verify accuracy of topographical maps. Analyze aerial photographs in order to detect and interpret significant military, industrial, resource, or topographical data. Calculate latitudes, longitudes, angles, areas, and other information for mapmaking, using survey field notes and reference tables. Check all layers of maps in order to ensure accuracy, identifying and marking errors and making corrections. Compare topographical features and contour lines with images from aerial photographs, old maps, and other reference materials in order to verify the accuracy of their identification. Compute and measure scaled distances between reference points in order to establish relative positions of adjoining prints and enable the creation of photographic mosaics. Form three-dimensional images of aerial photographs taken from different locations, using mathematical techniques and plotting instruments. Lay out and match aerial photographs in sequences in which they were taken, and identify any areas missing from photographs. Monitor mapping work and the updating of maps in order to ensure accuracy, the inclusion of new and/or changed information, and compliance with rules and regulations. Produce and update overlay maps in order to show information boundaries, water locations, and topographic features on various base maps and at different scales. Redraw and correct maps, such as revising parcel maps to reflect tax code area changes, using information from official records and surveys. Trace contours and topographic details in order to generate maps that denote specific land and property locations and geographic attributes. Trim, align, and join prints in order to form photographic mosaics, maintaining scaled distances between reference points. Complete detailed source and method notes detailing the location of routine and complex land parcels. Create survey description pages and historical records related to the mapping activities and specifications of section plats. Determine scales, line sizes, and colors to be used for hard copies of computerized maps, using plotters. Enter GPS data, legal deeds, field notes, and land survey reports into GIS workstations so that information can be transformed into graphic land descriptions, such as maps and drawings. **SKILLS**—Mathematics; Technology Design; Management of Personnel Resources; Operations Analysis; Active Learning; Monitoring; Time Management.

GOE—Interest Area: 02. Science, Math, and Engineering. **Work Group:** 02.09 Engineering Technology. **Other Apprenticeable Jobs in This Work Group:** Aerospace Engineering and Operations Technicians; Architectural Drafters; Calibration and Instrumentation Technicians; Cartographers and Photogrammetrists; Civil Drafters; Construction and Building Inspectors; Electrical Drafters; Electrical Engineering Technicians; Electro-Mechanical Technicians; Electronic Drafters; Electronics Engineering Technicians; Engineering Technicians, Except Drafters, All Other; Industrial Engineering Technicians; Mechanical Drafters; Mechanical Engineering Technicians; Numerical Tool and Process Control Programmers; Surveying Technicians. **PERSONALITY TYPE:** Conventional. Conventional occupations frequently involve following set procedures and routines. These occupations can include working with data and details more than with ideas. Usually there is a clear line of authority to follow.

RELATED KNOWLEDGE/COURSES—
Geography: Knowledge of principles and methods for describing the features of land, sea, and air masses, including their physical characteristics; locations; interrelationships; and distribution of plant, animal, and human life. **Design:** Knowledge of design techniques, tools, and principles involved in production of precision technical plans, blueprints, drawings, and models. **Computers and Electronics:** Knowledge of circuit boards, processors, chips, electronic equipment, and computer hardware and software, including applications and programming. **Mathematics:** Knowledge of arithmetic, algebra, geometry, calculus, and statistics and their applications. **Administration and Management:** Knowledge of business and management principles involved in strategic planning, resource allocation, human resources modeling, leadership technique, production methods, and coordination of people and resources. **Engineering and Technology:** Knowledge of the practical application of engineering science and technology. This includes applying principles, techniques, procedures, and equipment to the design and production of various goods and services.

WORK ENVIRONMENT—Sitting; indoors; using hands on objects, tools, or controls; spend time making repetitive motions.

Materials Inspectors

- Growth: 4.7%
- Annual Job Openings: 87,000
- Annual Earnings: $27,750
- Percentage of Women: 45.7%

Related Apprenticeship	Years
Experimental Assembler	2
Quality-Control Inspector	2
Operational Test Mechanic	3
Inspector, Metal Fabricating	4
Inspector, Outside Production	4
Inspector, Set-Up and Lay-Out	4
Radiographer	4
Rubber Tester	4

Examine and inspect materials and finished parts and products for defects and wear and to ensure conformance with work orders, diagrams, blueprints, and template specifications. Usually specialize in a single phase of inspection. Operates or tends machinery and equipment, and uses hand tools. Fabricates, installs, positions, or connects components, parts, finished products, or instruments for testing or operational purposes. Inspects materials, products, and work in progress for conformance to specifications, and adjusts process or assembly equipment to meet standards. Collects samples for testing, and computes findings. Reads dials and meters to verify functioning of equipment according to specifications. Analyzes and interprets blueprints, sample data, and other materials to determine, change, or measure specifications or inspection and testing procedures. Tests and measures finished products, components, or assemblies for functioning, operation, accuracy, or assembly to verify adherence to functional specifications. Observes and monitors production operations and equipment to ensure proper assembly of parts, or assists in testing and monitoring activities. Marks items for acceptance or rejection, records test results and inspection data, and compares findings with specifications to ensure conformance to standards. Confers with vendors and others regarding inspection results, recommends corrective procedures, and compiles reports of results, recommendations, and needed repairs. Supervises testing or drilling activities, and adjusts equipment to obtain sample fluids or to direct drilling. **SKILLS**—Quality Control Analysis; Operation Monitoring; Troubleshooting; Technology Design; Installation; Operation and Control; Science; Mathematics; Operations Analysis.

GOE—Interest Area: 08. Industrial Production. **Work Group:** 08.02 Production Technology. **Other Apprenticeable Jobs in This Work Group:** Aircraft Structure Assemblers, Precision; Aircraft Systems Assemblers, Precision; Bench Workers, Jewelry; Bindery Machine Setters and Set-Up Operators; Bookbinders; Buffing and Polishing Set-Up Operators; Coating, Painting, and Spraying Machine Setters and Set-Up Operators; Combination Machine Tool Setters and Set-Up Operators, Metal and Plastic; Dental Laboratory Technicians; Electrical and Electronic Equipment Assemblers; Electrical and Electronic Inspectors and Testers; Electromechanical Equipment Assemblers; Engine and Other Machine Assemblers; Extruding and Drawing Machine Setters, Operators, and Tenders, Metal and Plastic; Extruding, Forming, Pressing, and Compacting Machine Setters and Set-Up Operators; Forging Machine Setters, Operators, and Tenders, Metal and Plastic; Foundry Mold and Coremakers; Gem and Diamond Workers; Grinding, Honing, Lapping, and Deburring Machine Set-Up Operators; Heat Treating, Annealing, and Tempering Machine Operators and Tenders, Metal and Plastic; Jewelers; Lathe and Turning Machine Tool Setters, Operators, and Tenders, Metal and Plastic; Mechanical Inspectors; Metal Molding, Coremaking, and Casting Machine Operators and Tenders; Milling and Planing Machine Setters, Operators, and Tenders, Metal and Plastic; Model and Mold Makers, Jewelry; Motor Vehicle Inspectors; Paper Goods Machine Setters, Operators, and Tenders; Pewter Casters and Finishers; Plastic Molding and Casting Machine Setters and Set-Up Operators; Precision Devices Inspectors and Testers; Precision Lens Grinders and Polishers; Precision Mold and Pattern Casters, except Nonferrous Metals; Precision Pattern and Die Casters, Nonferrous Metals; Press and Press Brake Machine Setters and Set-Up Operators, Metal and Plastic; Production Inspectors, Testers, Graders, Sorters, Samplers, Weighers; Production Workers, All Other; Rolling Machine Setters, Operators, and Tenders, Metal and Plastic; Silversmiths; Textile Knitting and Weaving Machine Setters, Operators, and Tenders; Textile Winding, Twisting, and Drawing Out Machine Setters, Operators, and Tenders; Welding Machine Setters and Set-Up Operators; Woodworking Machine Setters and Set-Up Operators, Except Sawing. **PERSONALITY TYPE:** Realistic. Realistic occupations frequently involve work activities that include practical, hands-on problems and solutions. They often deal with plants, animals, and real-world materials like wood, tools, and machinery. Many of the occupations require working outside and do not involve a lot of paperwork or working closely with others.

RELATED KNOWLEDGE/COURSES— Design: Knowledge of design techniques, tools, and principles involved in production of precision technical plans, blueprints, drawings, and models. **Mechanical Devices:** Knowledge of machines and tools, including their designs, uses, repair, and maintenance. **Production and Processing:** Knowledge of raw materials, production processes, quality control, costs, and other techniques for maximizing the effective manufacture and distribution of goods. **Engineering and Technology:** Knowledge of the practical application of engineering science and technology. This includes applying principles, techniques, procedures, and equipment to the design and production of various goods and services. **Physics:** Knowledge and prediction of physical principles and laws and their interrelationships and applications to understanding fluid, material, and atmospheric dynamics and mechanical, electrical, atomic, and subatomic structures and processes. **Public Safety and Security:** Knowledge of relevant equipment, policies, procedures, and strategies to promote effective local, state, or national security operations for the protection of people, data, property, and institutions.

WORK ENVIRONMENT—Hazardous equipment; common protective or safety equipment; standing; walking and running; very hot or cold; spend time making repetitive motions.

Mechanical Door Repairers

- ◎ Growth: 21.8%
- ◎ Annual Job Openings: 1,000
- ◎ Annual Earnings: $29,620
- ◎ Percentage of Women: 4.8%

Related Apprenticeship	Years
Door-Closer Mechanic	3

Install, service, or repair opening and closing mechanisms of automatic doors and hydraulic door closers. Includes garage door mechanics. Adjust doors to open or close with the correct amount of effort, and make simple adjustments to electric openers. Apply hardware to door sections, such as drilling holes to install locks. Assemble and fasten tracks to structures or bucks, using impact wrenches or welding equipment. Bore and cut holes in flooring as required for installation, using hand tools and power tools. Carry springs to tops of doors, using ladders or scaffolding, and attach springs to tracks in order to install spring systems. Clean door closer parts, using caustic soda, rotary brushes, and grinding wheels. Cover treadles with carpeting or other floor covering materials and test systems by operating treadles. Cut door stops and angle irons to fit openings. Fasten angle iron back-hangers to ceilings and tracks, using fasteners or welding equipment. Inspect job sites, assessing headroom, side room, and other conditions in order to determine appropriateness of door for a given location. Install dock seals, bumpers, and shelters. Install door frames, rails, steel rolling curtains, electronic-eye mechanisms, and electric door openers and closers, using power tools, hand tools, and electronic test equipment. Lubricate door closer oil chambers and pack spindles with leather washers. Remove or disassemble defective automatic mechanical door closers, using hand tools. Repair or replace worn or broken door parts, using hand tools. Run low voltage wiring on ceiling surfaces, using insulated staples. Set doors into place or stack hardware sections into openings after rail or track installation. Set in and secure floor treadles for door activating mechanisms; then connect power packs and electrical panelboards to treadles. Study blueprints and schematic diagrams in order to determine appropriate methods of installing and repairing automated door openers. Wind large springs with upward motion of arm. Collect payment upon job completion. Complete required paperwork, such as work orders, according to services performed or required. Fabricate replacements for worn or broken parts, using welders, lathes, drill presses, and shaping and milling machines. **SKILLS—**Installation; Repairing; Equipment Maintenance; Technology Design; Troubleshooting.

GOE—Interest Area: 05. Mechanics, Installers, and Repairers. **Work Group:** 05.03 Mechanical Work. **Other Apprenticeable Jobs in This Work Group:** Aircraft Engine Specialists; Airframe-and-Power-Plant Mechanics; Automotive Body and Related Repairers; Automotive Glass Installers and Repairers; Automotive Master Mechanics; Automotive Specialty Technicians; Bus and Truck Mechanics and Diesel Engine Specialists; Camera and Photographic Equipment Repairers; Coin, Vending, and Amusement Machine Servicers and Repairers; Farm Equipment Mechanics; Gas Appliance Repairers; Hand and Portable Power Tool Repairers; Heating and Air Conditioning Mechanics; Helpers—Installation, Maintenance, and Repair Workers; Industrial Machinery Mechanics; Installation, Maintenance, and Repair Workers, All Other; Keyboard Instrument Repairers and Tuners; Locksmiths and Safe Repairers; Maintenance and Repair Workers, General; Maintenance Workers, Machinery; Medical Appliance Technicians; Medical Equipment Repairers; Meter Mechanics; Millwrights; Mobile Heavy Equipment Mechanics, Except Engines; Motorboat Mechanics; Motorcycle Mechanics; Optical Instrument Assemblers; Outdoor Power Equipment and Other Small Engine Mechanics; Painters, Transportation Equipment; Rail Car Repairers; Recreational Vehicle Service Technicians; Reed or Wind Instrument Repairers and Tuners; Refrigeration Mechanics; Stringed Instrument Repairers and Tuners; Valve and Regulator Repairers; Watch Repairers. **PERSONALITY TYPE:** Realistic. Realistic occupations frequently involve work activities that include practical, hands-on problems and solutions. They often deal with plants, animals, and real-world materials like wood, tools, and machinery. Many of the occupations require working outside and do not involve a lot of paperwork or working closely with others.

RELATED KNOWLEDGE/COURSES—Mechanical Devices: Knowledge of machines and tools, including their designs, uses, repair, and maintenance. **Engineering and Technology:** Knowledge of the practical application of engineering science and technology. This includes applying principles, techniques, procedures, and equipment to the design and production of various goods and services. **Building and Construction:** Knowledge of the materials, methods, and tools involved in the construction or repair of houses, buildings, or other structures, such as highways and roads. **Physics:** Knowledge and prediction of physical principles and laws and their interrelationships and applications to understanding fluid, material, and atmospheric dynamics and mechanical, electrical, atomic, and subatomic structures and processes. **Design:** Knowledge of design techniques, tools, and principles involved in production of precision technical plans, blueprints, drawings, and models.

WORK ENVIRONMENT—Hazardous equipment; spend time kneeling, crouching, stooping, or crawling; standing; spend time bending or twisting the body; outdoors.

Mechanical Drafters

- Growth: 1.9%
- Annual Job Openings: 9,000
- Annual Earnings: $41,520
- Percentage of Women: 19.9%

Related Apprenticeship	Years
Mold Designer (Plastics Industry)	2
Detailer	4
Die Designer	4
Drafter, Automotive Design	4
Drafter, Automotive Design Layout	4
Drafter, Detail	4
Drafter, Mechanical	4

Prepare detailed working diagrams of machinery and mechanical devices, including dimensions, fastening methods, and other engineering information. Develop detailed design drawings and specifications for mechanical equipment, dies/tools, and controls, using computer-assisted drafting (CAD) equipment. Coordinate with and consult other workers to design, lay out, or detail components and systems and to resolve design or other problems. Review and analyze specifications, sketches, drawings, ideas, and related data to assess factors affecting component designs and the procedures and instructions to be followed. Compute mathematical formulas to develop and design detailed specifications for components or machinery, using computer-assisted equipment. Position instructions and comments onto drawings. Modify and revise designs to correct operating deficiencies or to reduce production problems. Design scale or full-size blueprints of specialty items, such as furniture and automobile body or chassis components. Check dimensions of materials to be used and assign numbers to the materials. Lay out and draw schematic, orthographic, or angle views to depict functional relationships of components, assemblies, systems, and machines. Confer with customer representatives to review schematics and answer questions pertaining to installation of systems. Draw freehand sketches of designs, trace finished drawings onto designated paper for the reproduction of blueprints, and reproduce working drawings on copy machines. Supervise and train other drafters, technologists, and technicians. Lay out, draw, and reproduce illustrations for reference manuals and technical publications to describe operation and maintenance of mechanical systems. **SKILLS—** Technology Design; Installation; Equipment Selection; Operations Analysis; Persuasion; Quality Control Analysis; Instructing; Mathematics.

GOE—Interest Area: 02. Science, Math, and Engineering. **Work Group:** 02.09 Engineering Technology. **Other Apprenticeable Jobs in This Work Group:** Aerospace Engineering and Operations Technicians; Architectural Drafters; Calibration and Instrumentation Technicians; Cartographers and Photogrammetrists; Civil

Drafters; Construction and Building Inspectors; Electrical Drafters; Electrical Engineering Technicians; Electro-Mechanical Technicians; Electronic Drafters; Electronics Engineering Technicians; Engineering Technicians, Except Drafters, All Other; Industrial Engineering Technicians; Mapping Technicians; Mechanical Engineering Technicians; Numerical Tool and Process Control Programmers; Surveying Technicians. **PERSONALITY TYPE:** Realistic. Realistic occupations frequently involve work activities that include practical, hands-on problems and solutions. They often deal with plants, animals, and real-world materials like wood, tools, and machinery. Many of the occupations require working outside and do not involve a lot of paperwork or working closely with others.

RELATED KNOWLEDGE/COURSES— **Design:** Knowledge of design techniques, tools, and principles involved in production of precision technical plans, blueprints, drawings, and models. **Engineering and Technology:** Knowledge of the practical application of engineering science and technology. This includes applying principles, techniques, procedures, and equipment to the design and production of various goods and services. **Building and Construction:** Knowledge of the materials, methods, and tools involved in the construction or repair of houses, buildings, or other structures, such as highways and roads. **Mathematics:** Knowledge of arithmetic, algebra, geometry, calculus, and statistics and their applications. **Physics:** Knowledge and prediction of physical principles and laws and their interrelationships and applications to understanding fluid, material, and atmospheric dynamics and mechanical, electrical, atomic, and subatomic structures and processes. **English Language:** Knowledge of the structure and content of the English language,

including the meaning and spelling of words, rules of composition, and grammar.

WORK ENVIRONMENT—Sitting; sounds, noise levels are distracting or uncomfortable; physical proximity; contaminants; very hot or cold.

Mechanical Inspectors

- Growth: 4.7%
- Annual Job Openings: 87,000
- Annual Earnings: $27,750
- Percentage of Women: 45.7%

Related Apprenticeship	Years
Airplane Inspector	3
Automobile Tester	4
Automobile-Repair-Service Estimator	4
Diesel-Engine Tester	4

Inspect and test mechanical assemblies and systems, such as motors, vehicles, and transportation equipment for defects and wear to ensure compliance with specifications. Tests and measures finished products, components, or assemblies for functioning, operation, accuracy, or assembly to verify adherence to functional specifications. Inspects materials, products, and work in progress for conformance to specifications, and adjusts process or assembly equipment to meet standards. Starts and operates finished products for testing or inspection.

Reads dials and meters to ensure that equipment is operating according to specifications. Collects samples for testing, and computes findings. Marks items for acceptance or rejection, records test results and inspection data, and compares findings with specifications to ensure conformance to standards. Discards or rejects products, materials, and equipment not meeting specifications. Reads and interprets materials, such as work orders, inspection manuals, and blueprints, to determine inspection and test procedures. Analyzes and interprets sample data. Installs and positions new or replacement parts, components, and instruments. Estimates and records operational data. Completes necessary procedures to satisfy licensing requirements, and indicates concurrence with acceptance or rejection decisions. Confers with vendors and others regarding inspection results, recommends corrective procedures, and compiles reports of results, recommendations, and needed repairs. Cleans and maintains test equipment and instruments to ensure proper functioning. **SKILLS**—Science; Quality Control Analysis; Installation; Operation Monitoring; Troubleshooting; Equipment Maintenance; Operation and Control; Writing; Repairing.

GOE—**Interest Area:** 08. Industrial Production. **Work Group:** 08.02 Production Technology. **Other Apprenticeable Jobs in This Work Group:** Aircraft Structure Assemblers, Precision; Aircraft Systems Assemblers, Precision; Bench Workers, Jewelry; Bindery Machine Setters and Set-Up Operators; Bookbinders; Buffing and Polishing Set-Up Operators; Coating, Painting, and Spraying Machine Setters and Set-Up Operators; Combination Machine Tool Setters and Set-Up Operators, Metal and Plastic; Dental Laboratory Technicians; Electrical and Electronic Equipment Assemblers; Electrical and Electronic Inspectors and Testers; Electromechanical Equipment Assemblers; Engine and Other Machine Assemblers; Extruding and Drawing Machine Setters, Operators, and Tenders, Metal and Plastic; Extruding, Forming, Pressing, and Compacting Machine Setters and Set-Up Operators; Forging Machine Setters, Operators, and Tenders, Metal and Plastic; Foundry Mold and Coremakers; Gem and Diamond Workers; Grinding, Honing, Lapping, and Deburring Machine Set-Up Operators; Heat Treating, Annealing, and Tempering Machine Operators and Tenders, Metal and Plastic; Jewelers; Lathe and Turning Machine Tool Setters, Operators, and Tenders, Metal and Plastic; Materials Inspectors; Metal Molding, Coremaking, and Casting Machine Operators and Tenders; Milling and Planing Machine Setters, Operators, and Tenders, Metal and Plastic; Model and Mold Makers, Jewelry; Motor Vehicle Inspectors; Paper Goods Machine Setters, Operators, and Tenders; Pewter Casters and Finishers; Plastic Molding and Casting Machine Setters and Set-Up Operators; Precision Devices Inspectors and Testers; Precision Lens Grinders and Polishers; Precision Mold and Pattern Casters, except Nonferrous Metals; Precision Pattern and Die Casters, Nonferrous Metals; Press and Press Brake Machine Setters and Set-Up Operators, Metal and Plastic; Production Inspectors, Testers, Graders, Sorters, Samplers, Weighers; Production Workers, All Other; Rolling Machine Setters, Operators, and Tenders, Metal and Plastic; Silversmiths; Textile Knitting and Weaving Machine Setters, Operators, and Tenders; Textile Winding, Twisting, and Drawing Out Machine Setters, Operators, and Tenders; Welding Machine Setters and Set-Up Operators; Woodworking Machine Setters and Set-Up Operators, Except Sawing. **PERSONALITY TYPE:** Realistic. Realistic occupations frequently involve work activities that include practical, hands-on problems and solutions. They often deal with plants, animals, and real-world materials like wood, tools, and machinery. Many of the occupations require working outside and do not involve a lot of paperwork or working closely with others.

RELATED KNOWLEDGE/COURSES—**Mechanical Devices:** Knowledge of machines and tools, including their designs, uses, repair, and maintenance. **Design:** Knowledge of design techniques, tools, and principles involved in production of precision technical plans, blueprints, drawings, and models. **Engineering and Technology:** Knowledge of the practical application of engineering science and technology. This includes applying principles, techniques, procedures, and equipment to the design and production of various goods and services. **Public Safety and Security:** Knowledge of relevant equipment, policies, procedures, and strategies to promote effective local, state, or national security operations for the protection of people, data, property, and institutions. **Production and Processing:** Knowledge of raw materials, production processes, quality control, costs, and other techniques for maximizing the effective manufacture and distribution of goods. **Physics:** Knowledge and prediction of physical principles and laws and their interrelationships and applications to understanding fluid, material, and atmospheric dynamics and mechanical, electrical, atomic, and subatomic structures and processes.

WORK ENVIRONMENT—Sounds, noise levels are distracting or uncomfortable; hazardous equipment; standing; walking and running; common protective or safety equipment.

Medical Appliance Technicians

- Growth: 16.1%
- Annual Job Openings: 1,000
- Annual Earnings: $27,890
- Percentage of Women: 47.2%

Related Apprenticeship	Years
Orthotics Technician	1
Prosthetics Technician	4
Artificial-Plastic-Eye Maker	5

Construct, fit, maintain, or repair medical supportive devices, such as braces, artificial limbs, joints, arch supports, and other surgical and medical appliances. Bend, form, and shape fabric or material so that it conforms to prescribed contours needed to fabricate structural components. Construct or receive casts or impressions of patients' torsos or limbs for use as cutting and fabrication patterns. Cover or pad metal or plastic structures and devices, using coverings such as rubber, leather, felt, plastic, or fiberglass. Drill and tap holes for rivets, and glue, weld, bolt, and rivet parts together in order to form prosthetic or orthotic devices. Fit appliances onto patients, and make any necessary adjustments. Instruct patients in use of prosthetic or orthotic devices. Lay out and mark dimensions of parts, using templates and precision measuring instruments. Make orthotic/prosthetic devices using materials such as thermoplastic and thermosetting materials, metal alloys and leather, and hand and power tools. Mix pigments to match patients' skin coloring, according to formulas, and apply mixtures to orthotic or prosthetic devices. Polish artificial limbs, braces, and supports, using grinding and buffing wheels. Read prescriptions or specifications in order to determine the type of product or device to be fabricated, and the materials and tools that will be required. Repair, modify, and maintain medical supportive devices, such as artificial limbs, braces, and surgical supports, according to specifications. Test medical supportive devices for proper alignment, movement, and biomechanical stability, using meters and alignment fixtures. Service and repair machinery used in the fabrication of appliances. Take patients' body or limb measurements for use in device construction. **SKILLS**—Technology Design; Operations Analysis; Repairing; Equipment Maintenance; Quality Control Analysis; Instructing; Equipment Selection; Science.

GOE—Interest Area: 05. Mechanics, Installers, and Repairers. **Work Group:** 05.03 Mechanical Work. **Other Apprenticeable Jobs in This Work Group:** Aircraft Engine Specialists; Airframe-and-Power-Plant Mechanics; Automotive Body and Related Repairers; Automotive Glass Installers and Repairers; Automotive Master Mechanics; Automotive Specialty Technicians; Bus and Truck Mechanics and Diesel Engine Specialists; Camera and Photographic Equipment Repairers; Coin, Vending, and Amusement Machine Servicers and Repairers; Farm Equipment Mechanics; Gas Appliance Repairers; Hand and Portable Power Tool Repairers; Heating and Air Conditioning Mechanics; Helpers—Installation, Maintenance, and Repair Workers; Industrial Machinery Mechanics; Installation, Maintenance, and Repair Workers, All Other; Keyboard Instrument Repairers and Tuners; Locksmiths and Safe Repairers; Maintenance and Repair Workers, General; Maintenance Workers, Machinery; Mechanical Door Repairers; Medical Equipment Repairers; Meter Mechanics; Millwrights; Mobile Heavy Equipment Mechanics, Except Engines; Motorboat Mechanics; Motorcycle Mechanics; Optical Instrument Assemblers; Outdoor Power Equipment and Other Small Engine Mechanics; Painters, Transportation Equipment; Rail Car Repairers; Recreational Vehicle Service Technicians; Reed or Wind Instrument Repairers and Tuners; Refrigeration Mechanics; Stringed Instrument Repairers and Tuners; Valve and Regulator Repairers; Watch Repairers. **PERSONALITY TYPE:** Realistic. Realistic occupations frequently involve work activities that include practical, hands-on problems and solutions. They often deal with plants, animals, and real-world materials like wood, tools, and machinery. Many of the occupations require working outside and do not involve a lot of paperwork or working closely with others.

RELATED KNOWLEDGE/COURSES— Design: Knowledge of design techniques, tools, and principles involved in production of precision technical plans, blueprints, drawings, and models. **Mechanical Devices:** Knowledge of machines and tools, including their designs, uses, repair, and maintenance. **Engineering and Technology:** Knowledge of the practical application of engineering science and technology. This includes applying principles, techniques, procedures, and equipment to the design and production of various goods and services. **Medicine and Dentistry:** Knowledge of the information and techniques needed to diagnose and treat human injuries, diseases, and deformities. This includes symptoms, treatment alternatives, drug properties and interactions, and preventive health-care measures. **Physics:** Knowledge and prediction of physical principles and laws and their interrelationships and applications to understanding fluid, material, and atmospheric dynamics and mechanical, electrical, atomic, and subatomic structures and processes. **Therapy and Counseling:** Knowledge of principles, methods, and procedures for diagnosis, treatment, and rehabilitation of physical and mental dysfunctions and for career counseling and guidance.

WORK ENVIRONMENT—Hazardous equipment; spend time making repetitive motions; minor burns, cuts, bites, or stings; common protective or safety equipment; spend time kneeling, crouching, stooping, or crawling; spend time bending or twisting the body.

Medical Assistants

◉ Growth: 58.9%

◉ Annual Job Openings: 78,000

◉ Annual Earnings: $24,170

◉ Percentage of Women: 88.0%

Related Apprenticeship	*Years*
Podiatric Assistant	2

Perform administrative and certain clinical duties under the direction of physician. Administrative duties may include scheduling appointments, maintaining medical records, billing, and coding for insurance purposes. Clinical duties may include taking and recording vital signs and medical histories, preparing patients for examination, drawing blood, and **administering medications as directed by physician.** Interview patients to obtain medical information and measure their vital signs, weight, and height. Show patients to examination rooms and prepare them for the physician. Record patients' medical history, vital statistics and information such as test results in medical records. Prepare and administer medications as directed by a physician. Collect blood, tissue or other laboratory specimens, log the specimens, and prepare them for testing. Explain treatment procedures, medications, diets and physicians' instructions to patients. Help physicians examine and treat patients, handing them instruments and materials or performing such tasks as giving injections and removing sutures. Authorize drug refills and provide prescription information to pharmacies. Prepare treatment rooms for patient examinations, keeping the rooms neat and clean. Clean and sterilize instruments and dispose of contaminated supplies. Schedule appointments for patients. Change dressings on wounds. Greet and log in patients arriving at office or clinic. Contact medical facilities or departments to schedule patients for tests and/or admission. Perform general office duties such as answering telephones, taking dictation and completing insurance forms. Inventory and order medical, lab, and office supplies and equipment. Perform routine laboratory tests and sample analyses. Set up medical laboratory equipment. Keep financial records and perform other bookkeeping duties, such as handling credit and collections and mailing monthly statements to patients. Operate x-ray, electrocardiogram (EKG), and other equipment to administer routine diagnostic tests. **SKILLS**—Social Perceptiveness; Service Orientation; Instructing; Active Listening; Learning Strategies; Negotiation; Time Management; Persuasion.

GOE—**Interest Area:** 14. Medical and Health Services. **Work Group:** 14.02 Medicine and Surgery. **Other Apprenticeable Jobs in This Work Group:** Pharmacy Technicians; Surgical Technologists. **PERSONALITY TYPE:** Social. Social occupations frequently involve working with, communicating with, and teaching people. These occupations often involve helping or providing service to others.

RELATED KNOWLEDGE/COURSES— **Customer and Personal Service:** Knowledge of principles and processes for providing customer and personal services. This includes customer needs assessment, meeting quality standards for services, and evaluation of customer satisfaction. **Medicine and Dentistry:** Knowledge of the information and techniques needed to diagnose and treat human injuries, diseases, and deformities. This includes symptoms, treatment alternatives, drug properties and interactions, and preventive health-care measures. **Clerical Practices:** Knowledge of administrative and clerical procedures and systems, such as word processing, managing files and records, stenography and transcription, designing forms, and other office procedures and terminology. **Psychology:** Knowledge of human behavior and performance; individual differences in ability, personality, and interests; learning and motivation; psychological research methods; and the assessment and treatment of behavioral and affective disorders. **Therapy and Counseling:** Knowledge of principles, methods, and procedures for diagnosis, treatment, and rehabilitation of physical and mental dysfunctions and for career counseling and guidance. **English Language:** Knowledge of the structure and content of the English language, including the meaning and spelling of words, rules of composition, and grammar.

WORK ENVIRONMENT—Physical proximity; disease or infections; indoors; sounds, noise levels are distracting or uncomfortable; walking and running.

Medical Equipment Repairers

- Growth: 14.8%
- Annual Job Openings: 4,000
- Annual Earnings: $37,960
- Percentage of Women: 12.1%

Related Apprenticeship	Years
Electromedical-Equipment Repairer	2
Dental-Equipment Installer and Servicer	3
Biomedical Equipment Technician	4

Test, adjust, or repair biomedical or electromedical equipment. Inspect and test malfunctioning medical and related equipment following manufacturers' specifications, using test and analysis instruments. Examine medical equipment and facility's structural environment and check for proper use of equipment, to protect patients and staff from electrical or mechanical hazards and to ensure compliance with safety regulations. Disassemble malfunctioning equipment and remove, repair and replace defective parts such as motors, clutches or transformers. Keep records of maintenance, repair, and required updates of equipment. Perform preventive maintenance or service such as cleaning, lubricating and adjusting equipment. Test and calibrate components and equipment following manufacturers' manuals and troubleshooting techniques, using hand tools, power tools and measuring devices. Explain and demonstrate correct operation and preventive maintenance of medical equipment to personnel. Study technical manuals and attend training sessions provided by equipment manufacturers to maintain current knowledge. Plan and carry out work assignments, using blueprints, schematic drawings, technical manuals, wiring diagrams, and liquid and air flow sheets, while following prescribed regulations, directives, and other instructions as required. Solder loose connections, using soldering iron. Test, evaluate, and classify excess or in-use medial equipment and determine serviceability, condition, and disposition in accordance with regulations. Research catalogs and repair part lists to locate sources for repair parts, requisitioning parts and recording their receipt. Evaluate technical specifications to identify equipment and systems best suited for intended use and possible purchase based on specifications, user needs and technical requirements. Contribute expertise to develop medical maintenance standard operating procedures. Compute power and space requirements for installing medical, dental or related equipment and install units to manufacturers' specifications. Supervise and advise subordinate personnel. **SKILLS—** Repairing; Installation; Equipment Maintenance; Troubleshooting; Service Orientation; Instructing; Operation Monitoring; Technology Design.

GOE—Interest Area: 05. Mechanics, Installers, and Repairers. **Work Group:** 05.03 Mechanical Work. **Other Apprenticeable Jobs in This Work Group:** Aircraft Engine Specialists; Airframe-and-Power-Plant Mechanics; Automotive Body and Related Repairers; Automotive Glass Installers and Repairers; Automotive Master Mechanics; Automotive Specialty Technicians; Bus and Truck Mechanics and Diesel Engine Specialists; Camera and Photographic Equipment Repairers; Coin, Vending, and Amusement Machine Servicers and Repairers; Farm Equipment Mechanics; Gas Appliance Repairers; Hand and Portable Power Tool Repairers; Heating and Air Conditioning Mechanics; Helpers—Installation, Maintenance, and Repair Workers; Industrial Machinery Mechanics; Installation, Maintenance, and Repair Workers, All Other; Keyboard Instrument Repairers and Tuners; Locksmiths and Safe Repairers; Maintenance and Repair Workers, General; Maintenance Workers, Machinery; Mechanical Door Repairers; Medical Appliance Technicians; Meter Mechanics; Millwrights; Mobile Heavy Equipment Mechanics, Except Engines; Motorboat Mechanics; Motorcycle Mechanics; Optical Instrument Assemblers; Outdoor Power Equipment and Other Small Engine Mechanics; Painters, Transportation Equipment; Rail Car Repairers; Recreational Vehicle Service Technicians; Reed or Wind Instrument Repairers and Tuners; Refrigeration Mechanics; Stringed Instrument Repairers and Tuners; Valve and Regulator Repairers; Watch Repairers. **PERSONALITY TYPE:** Realistic. Realistic occupations frequently involve work activities that include practical, hands-on problems and solutions. They often deal with plants, animals, and real-world materials like wood, tools, and machinery. Many of the occupations require working outside and do not involve a lot of paperwork or working closely with others.

RELATED KNOWLEDGE/COURSES—
Computers and Electronics: Knowledge of circuit boards, processors, chips, electronic equipment, and computer hardware and software, including applications and programming. **Mechanical Devices:** Knowledge of machines and tools, including their designs, uses, repair, and maintenance. **Customer and Personal Service:** Knowledge of principles and processes for providing customer and personal services. This includes customer needs assessment, meeting quality standards for services, and evaluation of customer satisfaction. **Engineering and Technology:** Knowledge of the practical application of engineering science and technology. This includes applying principles, techniques, procedures, and equipment to the design and production of various goods and services. **Public Safety and Security:** Knowledge of relevant equipment, policies, procedures, and strategies to promote effective local, state, or national security operations for the protection of people, data, property, and institutions. **Clerical Practices:** Knowledge of administrative and clerical procedures and systems, such as word processing, managing files and records, stenography and transcription, designing forms, and other office procedures and terminology.

WORK ENVIRONMENT—Physical proximity; contaminants; extremely bright or inadequate lighting; cramped work space, awkward positions; sounds, noise levels are distracting or uncomfortable; hazardous conditions.

Medical Secretaries

- Growth: 17.2%
- Annual Job Openings: 50,000
- Annual Earnings: $26,000
- Percentage of Women: 96.5%

Related Apprenticeship	*Years*
Medical Secretary	1

Perform secretarial duties utilizing specific knowledge of medical terminology and hospital, clinic, or laboratory procedures. Duties include scheduling appointments, billing patients, and compiling and recording medical charts, reports, and correspondence. Schedule and confirm patient diagnostic appointments, surgeries and medical consultations. Compile and record medical charts, reports, and correspondence, using typewriter or personal computer. Answer telephones, and direct calls to appropriate staff. Receive and route messages and documents such as laboratory results to appropriate staff. Greet visitors, ascertain purpose of visit, and direct them to appropriate staff. Interview patients in order to complete documents, case histories, and forms such as intake and insurance forms. Maintain medical records, technical library and correspondence files. Operate office equipment such as voice mail messaging systems, and use word processing, spreadsheet, and other software applications to prepare reports, invoices, financial statements, letters, case histories and medical records. Transmit correspondence and medical records by mail, e-mail, or fax. Perform various clerical and administrative functions, such as ordering and maintaining an inventory of supplies. Arrange hospital admissions for patients. Transcribe recorded messages and practitioners' diagnoses and recommendations into patients' medical records. Perform bookkeeping duties, such as credits and collections, preparing and sending financial statements and bills, and keeping financial records. Complete insurance and other claim forms. Prepare correspondence and assist physicians or medical scientists with preparation of reports, speeches, articles and conference proceedings. **SKILLS**—Social Perceptiveness; Instructing; Active Listening; Time Management; Writing; Management of Personnel Resources; Speaking; Service Orientation.

GOE—Interest Area: 09. Business Detail. **Work Group:** 09.02 Administrative Detail. **Other Apprenticeable Jobs in This Work Group:** Legal Secretaries; Secretaries, Except Legal, Medical, and Executive. **PERSONALITY TYPE:** Conventional. Conventional occupations frequently involve following set procedures and routines. These occupations can include working with data and details more than with ideas. Usually there is a clear line of authority to follow.

RELATED KNOWLEDGE/COURSES—**Customer and Personal Service:** Knowledge of principles and processes for providing customer and personal services. This includes customer needs assessment, meeting quality standards for services, and evaluation of customer satisfaction. **Clerical Practices:** Knowledge of administrative and clerical procedures and systems, such as word processing, managing files and records, stenography and transcription, designing forms, and other office procedures and terminology. **English Language:** Knowledge of the structure and content of the English language, including

the meaning and spelling of words, rules of composition, and grammar. **Telecommunications:** Knowledge of transmission, broadcasting, switching, control, and operation of telecommunications systems. **Computers and Electronics:** Knowledge of circuit boards, processors, chips, electronic equipment, and computer hardware and software, including applications and programming. **Communications and Media:** Knowledge of media production, communication, and dissemination techniques and methods. This includes alternative ways to inform and entertain via written, oral, and visual media.

WORK ENVIRONMENT—Sounds, noise levels are distracting or uncomfortable; physical proximity; sitting; disease or infections; cramped work space, awkward positions.

Merchandise Displayers and Window Trimmers

- Growth: 11.3%
- Annual Job Openings: 10,000
- Annual Earnings: $22,030
- Percentage of Women: 55.4%

Related Apprenticeship	Years
Displayer, Merchandise	1
Decorator	4

Plan and erect commercial displays, such as those in windows and interiors of retail stores and at trade exhibitions. Arrange properties, furniture, merchandise, backdrops, and other accessories, as shown in prepared sketches. Change or rotate window displays, interior display areas, and signage to reflect changes in inventory or promotion. Construct or assemble displays and display components from fabric, glass, paper, and plastic, using hand tools and woodworking power tools, according to specifications. Consult with advertising and sales staff to determine type of merchandise to be featured and time and place for each display. Cut out designs on cardboard, hardboard, and plywood, according to motif of event. Develop ideas or plans for merchandise displays or window decorations. Obtain plans from display designers or display managers, and discuss their implementation with clients or supervisors. Place prices and descriptive signs on backdrops, fixtures, merchandise, or floor. Plan and erect commercial displays to entice and appeal to customers. Prepare sketches, floor plans or models of proposed displays. Select themes, lighting, colors, and props to be used. Attend training sessions and corporate planning meetings to obtain new ideas for product launches. Collaborate with others to obtain products and other display items. Create and enhance mannequin faces by mixing and applying paint and attaching measured eyelash strips, using artist's brush, airbrush, pins, ruler, and scissors. Dress mannequins for displays. Install booths, exhibits, displays, carpets, and drapes, as guided by floor plan of building and specifications. Install decorations such as flags, banners, festive lights, and bunting on or in building, street, exhibit hall, or booth. Instruct sales staff in color-coordination of clothing racks and counter displays. Maintain props and mannequins, inspecting them for imperfections and applying preservative coatings as necessary. Store, pack, and maintain records of props and display items. Take photographs of displays and signage. Use computers to produce signage. **SKILLS**—Installation; Operations Analysis; Equipment Selection; Technology Design.

GOE—Interest Area: 01. Arts, Entertainment, and Media. **Work Group:** 01.04 Visual Arts. **Other Apprenticeable Jobs in This Work Group:** Cartoonists; Commercial and Industrial Designers; Exhibit Designers; Fashion Designers; Floral Designers; Graphic Designers; Interior Designers; Painters and Illustrators. **PERSONALITY TYPE:** Artistic. Artistic occupations frequently involve working with forms, designs, and patterns. They often require self-expression, and the work can be done without following a clear set of rules.

RELATED KNOWLEDGE/COURSES— **Sales and Marketing:** Knowledge of principles and methods for showing, promoting, and selling products or services. This includes marketing strategy and tactics, product demonstration, sales techniques, and sales control systems. **Fine Arts:** Knowledge of the theory and techniques required to compose, produce, and perform works of music, dance, visual arts, drama, and sculpture. **Design:** Knowledge of design techniques, tools, and principles involved in production of precision technical plans, blueprints, drawings, and models. **Sociology and Anthropology:** Knowledge of group behavior and dynamics, societal trends and influences, human migrations, ethnicity, and cultures and their history and origins. **Communications and Media:** Knowledge of media production, communication, and dissemination techniques and methods. This includes alternative ways to inform and entertain via written, oral, and visual media. **Building and Construction:** Knowledge of the materials, methods, and tools involved in the construction or repair of houses, buildings, or other structures, such as highways and roads.

WORK ENVIRONMENT—Climbing ladders, scaffolds, or poles; minor burns, cuts, bites, or stings; spend time bending or twisting the body; cramped work space, awkward positions; extremely bright or inadequate lighting.

Metal Fabricators, Structural Metal Products

- Growth: 6.2%
- Annual Job Openings: 14,000
- Annual Earnings: $28,990
- Percentage of Women: 4.7%

Related Apprenticeship	Years
Former, Hand (Any Industry)	2
Ship Propeller Finisher	3
Fabricator-Assembler, Metal Products	4
Metal Fabricator	4

Fabricate and assemble structural metal products, such as frameworks or shells for machinery, ovens, tanks, and stacks, and metal parts for buildings and bridges, according to job order or blueprints. Develops layout and plans sequence of operations for fabricating and assembling structural metal products, applying trigonometry and knowledge of metal. Locates and marks bending and cutting lines onto workpiece, allowing for stock thickness and machine and welding shrinkage. Hammers, chips, and grinds workpiece to cut, bend, and straighten metal. Verifies conformance of workpiece to specifications, using square, ruler, and measuring tape. Preheats workpieces to render them malleable, using hand torch or furnace. Positions, aligns, fits, and welds together parts, using jigs, welding torch, and hand tools. Sets up and operates fabricating machines, such as brakes, rolls, shears, flame cutters, and drill presses. Sets up and operates machine tools associated with fabricating shops, such as radial drill, end mill, and edge planer. Designs and constructs templates and fixtures, using hand tools. **SKILLS**—Operation and Control; Mathematics; Operations Analysis; Quality Control Analysis; Equipment Selection; Operation Monitoring; Technology Design; Science.

GOE—Interest Area: 08. Industrial Production. **Work Group:** 08.03 Production Work. **Other Apprenticeable Jobs in This Work Group:** Bakers, Manufacturing; Bindery Machine Operators and Tenders; Chemical Equipment Controllers and Operators; Coating, Painting, and Spraying Machine Operators and Tenders; Cooling and Freezing Equipment Operators and Tenders; Crushing, Grinding, and Polishing Machine Setters, Operators, and Tenders; Cutters and Trimmers, Hand; Cutting and Slicing Machine Operators and Tenders; Design Printing Machine Setters and Set-Up Operators; Electrolytic Plating and Coating Machine Setters and Set-Up Operators, Metal and Plastic; Electrotypers and Stereotypers; Embossing Machine Set-Up Operators; Engraver Set-Up Operators; Extruding, Forming, Pressing, and Compacting Machine Operators and Tenders; Fabric and Apparel Patternmakers; Film Laboratory Technicians; Fitters, Structural Metal—Precision; Food Batchmakers; Furnace, Kiln, Oven, Drier, and

Kettle Operators and Tenders; Hand Composi- tors and Typesetters; Job Printers; Letterpress Setters and Set-Up Operators; Metal-Refining Furnace Operators and Tenders; Mixing and Blending Machine Setters, Operators, and Ten- ders; Mold Makers, Hand; Molding and Cast- ing Workers; Numerical Control Machine Tool Operators and Tenders, Metal and Plastic; Off- set Lithographic Press Setters and Set-Up Oper- ators; Painting, Coating, and Decorating Workers; Photographic Processing Machine Operators; Photographic Reproduction Techni- cians; Photographic Retouchers and Restorers; Plate Finishers; Platemakers; Precision Printing Workers; Printing Press Machine Operators and Tenders; Production Workers, All Other; Saw- ing Machine Operators and Tenders; Sawing Machine Setters and Set-Up Operators; Scanner Operators; Separating, Filtering, Clarifying, Precipitating, and Still Machine Setters, Opera- tors, and Tenders; Sewing Machine Operators, Garment; Slaughterers and Meat Packers; Stone Sawyers; Strippers; Team Assemblers; Welder- Fitters; Welders and Cutters; Woodworking Machine Operators and Tenders, Except Saw- ing. **PERSONALITY TYPE:** Realistic. Realis- tic occupations frequently involve work activities that include practical, hands-on prob- lems and solutions. They often deal with plants, animals, and real-world materials like wood, tools, and machinery. Many of the occupations require working outside and do not involve a lot of paperwork or working closely with others.

RELATED KNOWLEDGE/COURSES— **Design:** Knowledge of design techniques, tools, and principles involved in production of preci- sion technical plans, blueprints, drawings, and models. **Building and Construction:** Knowl- edge of the materials, methods, and tools involved in the construction or repair of houses, buildings, or other structures, such as highways

and roads. **Production and Processing:** Knowl- edge of raw materials, production processes, quality control, costs, and other techniques for maximizing the effective manufacture and dis- tribution of goods. **Mechanical Devices:** Knowledge of machines and tools, including their designs, uses, repair, and maintenance. **Engineering and Technology:** Knowledge of the practical application of engineering science and technology. This includes applying princi- ples, techniques, procedures, and equipment to the design and production of various goods and services. **Mathematics:** Knowledge of arith- metic, algebra, geometry, calculus, and statistics and their applications. **Physics:** Knowledge and prediction of physical principles and laws and their interrelationships and applications to understanding fluid, material, and atmospheric dynamics and mechanical, electrical, atomic, and subatomic structures and processes.

WORK ENVIRONMENT—Hazardous equip- ment; common protective or safety equipment; standing; sounds, noise levels are distracting or uncomfortable; minor burns, cuts, bites, or stings; using hands on objects, tools, or controls.

Metal Molding, Coremaking, and Casting Machine Operators and Tenders

- Growth: 8.9%
- Annual Job Openings: 18,000
- Annual Earnings: $23,930
- Percentage of Women: 22.4%

Related Apprenticeship	Years
Caster	2

Operate or tend metal molding, casting, or coremaking machines to mold or cast metal products, such as pipes, brake drums, and rods, and metal parts, such as automobile trim, carburetor housings, and motor parts. Machines include centrifugal casting machines, vacuum casting machines, turnover draw-type coremaking machines, conveyor-screw coremaking machines, and die casting machines. Starts and operates furnace, oven, diecasting, coremaking, metal molding, or rotating machines to pour metal or create molds and casts. Removes casting from mold, mold from press, or core from core box, using tongs, pliers, hydraulic ram, or by inversion. Pours or loads metal or sand into melting pot, furnace, mold, core box or hopper, using shovel, ladle, or machine. Inspects metal casts, and molds for cracks, bubbles, or other defects and measures castings to ensure specifications met. Cleans, glues, and racks cores, ingots, or finished products for storage. Cuts spouts and pouring holes in molds and sizes hardened cores, using saws. Signals or directs other workers to load conveyor, spray molds, or remove ingots. Requisitions molds and supplies and inventories and records finished products. Weighs metals and powders and computes amounts of materials necessary to produce mixture of specified content. Smoothes and cleans inner surface of mold, using brush, scraper, airhose, or grinding wheel, and fills imperfections with refractory material. Sprays, smokes, or coats molds with compounds to lubricate or insulate mold, using acetylene torches or sprayers. Skims or pours dross, slag, or impurities from molten metal, using ladle, rake, hoe, spatula, or spoon. Assembles shell halves, patterns, and foundry flasks, and reinforces core boxes, using glue, clamps, wire, bolts, rams, or machines. Repairs or replaces damaged molds, pipes, belts, chains, or other equipment, using hand tools, hand-powered press, or jib crane. Fills core boxes and mold patterns with sand or powders, using ramming tools or pneumatic hammers, and removes excess. Observes and records data from pyrometers, lights, and gauges to monitor molding process and adjust furnace temperature. Positions, aligns, and secures molds or core boxes in holding devices or under pouring spouts and tubes, using hand tools. Positions ladles or pourers and adjusts controls to regulate the flow of metal, sand, or coolant into mold. SKILLS—Operation Monitoring; Equipment Maintenance; Repairing; Operation and Control; Quality Control Analysis; Installation; Technology Design; Troubleshooting.

GOE—Interest Area: 08. Industrial Production. Work Group: 08.02 Production Technology. Other Apprenticeable Jobs in This Work Group: Aircraft Structure Assemblers, Precision; Aircraft Systems Assemblers, Precision; Bench Workers, Jewelry; Bindery Machine Setters and Set-Up Operators; Bookbinders; Buffing and Polishing Set-Up Operators; Coating, Painting, and Spraying Machine Setters and Set-Up Operators; Combination Machine Tool Setters and Set-Up Operators, Metal and Plastic; Dental Laboratory Technicians; Electrical and Electronic Equipment Assemblers; Electrical and Electronic Inspectors and Testers; Electromechanical Equipment Assemblers; Engine and Other Machine Assemblers; Extruding and Drawing Machine Setters, Operators, and Tenders, Metal and Plastic; Extruding, Forming, Pressing, and Compacting Machine Setters and Set-Up Operators; Forging Machine Setters, Operators, and Tenders, Metal and Plastic; Foundry Mold and Coremakers; Gem and Diamond Workers; Grinding, Honing, Lapping, and Deburring Machine Set-Up Operators; Heat Treating, Annealing, and Tempering Machine Operators and Tenders, Metal and Plastic; Jewelers; Lathe and Turning Machine Tool Setters, Operators, and Tenders, Metal and Plastic; Materials Inspectors; Mechanical Inspectors; Milling and Planing Machine Setters, Operators, and Tenders, Metal and Plastic; Model and Mold Makers, Jewelry; Motor Vehicle Inspectors; Paper Goods Machine Setters, Operators, and Tenders; Pewter Casters and Finishers; Plastic Molding and Casting Machine Setters and Set-Up Operators; Precision Devices Inspectors and Testers; Precision Lens Grinders and Polishers; Precision Mold and Pattern Casters, except Nonferrous Metals; Precision Pattern and Die Casters, Nonferrous Metals; Press and Press Brake Machine Setters and Set-Up Operators, Metal and Plastic; Production Inspectors, Testers, Graders, Sorters, Samplers, Weighers; Production Workers, All Other; Rolling Machine Setters, Operators, and Tenders, Metal and Plastic; Silversmiths; Textile Knitting and Weaving Machine Setters, Operators, and Tenders; Textile Winding, Twisting, and Drawing Out Machine Setters, Operators, and Tenders; Welding Machine Setters and Set-Up Operators; Woodworking Machine Setters and Set-Up Operators, Except Sawing. **PERSONALITY TYPE:** Realistic. Realistic occupations frequently involve work activities that include practical, hands-on problems and solutions. They often deal with plants, animals, and real-world materials like wood, tools, and machinery. Many of the occupations require working outside and do not involve a lot of paperwork or working closely with others.

RELATED KNOWLEDGE/COURSES— Mechanical Devices: Knowledge of machines and tools, including their designs, uses, repair, and maintenance. **Production and Processing:** Knowledge of raw materials, production processes, quality control, costs, and other techniques for maximizing the effective manufacture and distribution of goods. **Building and Construction:** Knowledge of the materials, methods, and tools involved in the construction or repair of houses, buildings, or other structures, such as highways and roads. **Public Safety and Security:** Knowledge of relevant equipment, policies, procedures, and strategies to promote effective local, state, or national security operations for the protection of people, data, property, and institutions. **Foreign Language:** Knowledge of the structure and content of a foreign (non-English) language, including the meaning and spelling of words, rules of composition and grammar, and pronunciation. **Physics:** Knowledge and prediction of physical principles and laws and their interrelationships and applications to understanding fluid, material, and atmospheric dynamics and mechanical, electrical, atomic, and subatomic structures and processes. **Chemistry:** Knowledge of the chemical composition, structure, and properties of substances and of the chemical processes and transformations that they undergo. This includes uses of chemicals, their danger signs, production techniques, and disposal methods.

WORK ENVIRONMENT—Hazardous equipment; common protective or safety equipment; very hot or cold; hazardous conditions; minor burns, cuts, bites, or stings.

Metal Workers and Plastic Workers, All Other

- Growth: 6.6%
- Annual Job Openings: 11,000
- Annual Earnings: $28,400
- Percentage of Women: 28.5%

Related Apprenticeship	Years
Blacksmith	4
Multi-Operation-Forming-Machine Setter	4

All metalworkers and plastic workers not listed separately. **SKILLS**—No data available.

GOE—Interest Area: 08. Industrial Production. **Work Group:** 08.04 Metal and Plastics Machining Technology. **Other Apprenticeable Jobs in This Work Group:** Lay-Out Workers, Metal and Plastic; Machinists; Model Makers, Metal and Plastic; Patternmakers, Metal and Plastic; Tool and Die Makers; Tool Grinders, Filers, and Sharpeners. **PERSONALITY TYPE:** No data available.

RELATED KNOWLEDGE/COURSES—No data available.

WORK ENVIRONMENT—No data available.

Meter Mechanics

- Growth: 12.0%
- Annual Job Openings: 5,000
- Annual Earnings: $42,540
- Percentage of Women: 4.8%

Related Apprenticeship	Years
Gas-Meter Mechanic I	3
Meter Repairer	3

Test, adjust, and repair gas, water, and oil meters. Adjusts meter and repeats test until meter registration is within specified limits. Inspects, repairs and maintains gas meters at wells or processing plants. Dismantles meter and replaces defective parts, such as case, shafts, gears, disks, and recording mechanisms, using soldering iron and hand tools. Connects gas, oil, water, or air meter to test apparatus to detect leaks. Reassembles meter and meter parts, using soldering gun, power tools and hand tools. Lubricates moving meter parts, using oil gun. Records test results, materials used, and meters needing repair on log or card and segregates meters requiring repair. Caps meter housing and activates controls on paint booth to spray paint meter case. Cleans plant growth, scale, and rust from meter housing, using wire brush, buffer, sandblaster, or cleaning compounds. Analyzes test results to determine cause of persistent meter registration errors. **SKILLS**—Repairing; Equipment Maintenance; Installation; Quality Control Analysis; Troubleshooting; Operation Monitoring; Operation and Control.

GOE—**Interest Area:** 05. Mechanics, Installers, and Repairers. **Work Group:** 05.03 Mechanical Work. **Other Apprenticeable Jobs in This Work Group:** Aircraft Engine Specialists; Airframe-and-Power-Plant Mechanics; Automotive Body and Related Repairers; Automotive Glass Installers and Repairers; Automotive Master Mechanics; Automotive Specialty Technicians; Bus and Truck Mechanics and Diesel Engine Specialists; Camera and Photographic Equipment Repairers; Coin, Vending, and Amusement Machine Servicers and Repairers; Farm Equipment Mechanics; Gas Appliance Repairers; Hand and Portable Power Tool Repairers; Heating and Air Conditioning Mechanics; Helpers—Installation, Maintenance, and Repair Workers; Industrial Machinery Mechanics; Installation, Maintenance, and Repair Workers, All Other; Keyboard Instrument Repairers and Tuners; Locksmiths and Safe Repairers; Maintenance and Repair Workers, General; Maintenance Workers, Machinery; Mechanical Door Repairers; Medical Appliance Technicians; Medical Equipment Repairers; Millwrights; Mobile Heavy Equipment Mechanics, Except Engines; Motorboat Mechanics; Motorcycle Mechanics; Optical Instrument Assemblers; Outdoor Power Equipment and Other Small Engine Mechanics; Painters, Transportation Equipment; Rail Car Repairers; Recreational Vehicle Service Technicians; Reed or Wind Instrument Repairers and Tuners; Refrigeration Mechanics; Stringed Instrument Repairers and Tuners; Valve and Regulator Repairers; Watch Repairers. **PERSONALITY TYPE:** Realistic. Realistic occupations frequently involve work activities that include practical, hands-on problems and solutions. They often deal with plants, animals, and real-world materials like wood, tools, and machinery. Many of the occupations require working outside and do not involve a lot of paperwork or working closely with others.

RELATED KNOWLEDGE/COURSES—Mechanical Devices: Knowledge of machines and tools, including their designs, uses, repair, and maintenance. **Engineering and Technology:** Knowledge of the practical application of engineering science and technology. This includes applying principles, techniques, procedures, and equipment to the design and production of various goods and services. **Clerical Practices:** Knowledge of administrative and clerical procedures and systems, such as word processing, managing files and records, stenography and transcription, designing forms, and other office procedures and terminology.

WORK ENVIRONMENT—Outdoors; spend time kneeling, crouching, stooping, or crawling; minor burns, cuts, bites, or stings; walking and running; extremely bright or inadequate lighting.

Millwrights

- Growth: 5.3%
- Annual Job Openings: 7,000
- Annual Earnings: $42,390
- Percentage of Women: 2.2%

Related Apprenticeship	Years
Automated Equipment Engineer-Technician	4

| Machinery Erector | 4 |
| Millwright | 4 |

(This is one of the most popular apprenticeable jobs.)

Install, dismantle, or move machinery and heavy equipment according to layout plans, blueprints, or other drawings. Replace defective parts of machine or adjust clearances and alignment of moving parts. Align machines and equipment, using hoists, jacks, hand tools, squares, rules, micrometers, and plumb bobs. Connect power unit to machines or steam piping to equipment, and test unit to evaluate its mechanical operation. Repair and lubricate machines and equipment. Assemble and install equipment, using hand tools and power tools. Position steel beams to support bedplates of machines and equipment, using blueprints and schematic drawings, to determine work procedures. Signal crane operator to lower basic assembly units to bedplate, and align unit to centerline. Insert shims, adjust tension on nuts and bolts, or position parts, using hand tools and measuring instruments, to set specified clearances between moving and stationary parts. Move machinery and equipment, using hoists, dollies, rollers, and trucks. Attach moving parts and subassemblies to basic assembly unit, using hand tools and power tools. Assemble machines, and bolt, weld, rivet, or otherwise fasten them to foundation or other structures, using hand tools and power tools. Lay out mounting holes, using measuring instruments, and drill holes with power drill. Bolt parts, such as side and deck plates, jaw plates, and journals, to basic assembly unit. Level bedplate and establish centerline, using straightedge, levels,

and transit. Dismantle machines, using hammers, wrenches, crowbars, and other hand tools. Shrink-fit bushings, sleeves, rings, liners, gears, and wheels to specified items, using portable gas heating equipment. Dismantle machinery and equipment for shipment to installation site, usually performing installation and maintenance work as part of team. Construct foundation for machines, using hand tools and building materials such as wood, cement, and steel. **SKILLS**—Installation; Repairing; Troubleshooting; Equipment Maintenance; Equipment Selection; Mathematics; Coordination; Learning Strategies; Technology Design.

GOE—Interest Area: 05. Mechanics, Installers, and Repairers. **Work Group:** 05.03 Mechanical Work. **Other Apprenticeable Jobs in This Work Group:** Aircraft Engine Specialists; Airframe-and-Power-Plant Mechanics; Automotive Body and Related Repairers; Automotive Glass Installers and Repairers; Automotive Master Mechanics; Automotive Specialty Technicians; Bus and Truck Mechanics and Diesel Engine Specialists; Camera and Photographic Equipment Repairers; Coin, Vending, and Amusement Machine Servicers and Repairers; Farm Equipment Mechanics; Gas Appliance Repairers; Hand and Portable Power Tool Repairers; Heating and Air Conditioning Mechanics; Helpers—Installation, Maintenance, and Repair Workers; Industrial Machinery Mechanics; Installation, Maintenance, and Repair Workers, All Other; Keyboard Instrument Repairers and Tuners; Locksmiths and Safe Repairers; Maintenance and Repair Workers, General; Maintenance Workers, Machinery; Mechanical Door Repairers; Medical Appliance Technicians; Medical Equipment Repairers; Meter Mechanics; Mobile Heavy Equipment

Mechanics, Except Engines; Motorboat Mechanics; Motorcycle Mechanics; Optical Instrument Assemblers; Outdoor Power Equipment and Other Small Engine Mechanics; Painters, Transportation Equipment; Rail Car Repairers; Recreational Vehicle Service Technicians; Reed or Wind Instrument Repairers and Tuners; Refrigeration Mechanics; Stringed Instrument Repairers and Tuners; Valve and Regulator Repairers; Watch Repairers. **PERSONALITY TYPE:** Realistic. Realistic occupations frequently involve work activities that include practical, hands-on problems and solutions. They often deal with plants, animals, and real-world materials like wood, tools, and machinery. Many of the occupations require working outside and do not involve a lot of paperwork or working closely with others.

RELATED KNOWLEDGE/COURSES— Mechanical Devices: Knowledge of machines and tools, including their designs, uses, repair, and maintenance. **Building and Construction:** Knowledge of the materials, methods, and tools involved in the construction or repair of houses, buildings, or other structures, such as highways and roads. **Engineering and Technology:** Knowledge of the practical application of engineering science and technology. This includes applying principles, techniques, procedures, and equipment to the design and production of various goods and services. **Design:** Knowledge of design techniques, tools, and principles involved in production of precision technical plans, blueprints, drawings, and models. **Physics:** Knowledge and prediction of physical principles and laws and their interrelationships and applications to understanding fluid, material, and atmospheric dynamics and mechanical, electrical, atomic, and subatomic structures and processes. **Public Safety and Security:** Knowledge of relevant equipment, policies, procedures, and strategies to promote effective local, state, or national security operations for the protection of people, data, property, and institutions.

WORK ENVIRONMENT—Sounds, noise levels are distracting or uncomfortable; very hot or cold; extremely bright or inadequate lighting; contaminants; hazardous conditions.

FURTHER INFORMATION—Contact a local joint union-management apprenticeship committee or the nearest office of your state employment service or apprenticeship agency (see Appendix C). To identify the local union office, contact United Brotherhood of Carpenters and Joiners of America, 101 Constitution Ave. NW, Washington DC 20001. Internet: http://www.Carpenters.org.

Mixing and Blending Machine Setters, Operators, and Tenders

- Growth: –6.5%
- Annual Job Openings: 14,000
- Annual Earnings: $27,940
- Percentage of Women: 14.4%

Related Apprenticeship	Years
Tinter (Paint and Varnish)	2

Set up, operate, or tend machines to mix or blend materials, such as chemicals, tobacco, liquids, color pigments, or explosive ingredi-

ents. Add or mix chemicals and ingredients for processing, using hand tools or other devices. Compound and process ingredients or dyes according to formulas. Dislodge and clear jammed materials or other items from machinery and equipment, using hand tools. Dump or pour specified amounts of materials into machinery and equipment. Examine materials, ingredients, or products visually or with hands, in order to ensure conformance to established standards. Observe production and monitor equipment to ensure safe and efficient operation. Open valves to drain slurry from mixers into storage tanks. Operate or tend machines to mix or blend any of a wide variety of materials such as spices, dough batter, tobacco, fruit juices, chemicals, livestock feed, food products, color pigments, or explosive ingredients. Read work orders to determine production specifications and information. Start machines to mix or blend ingredients; then allow them to mix for specified times. Stop mixing or blending machines when specified product qualities are obtained, and open valves and start pumps to transfer mixtures. Tend accessory equipment such as pumps and conveyors to move materials or ingredients through production processes. Weigh or measure materials, ingredients, and products to ensure conformance to requirements. Clean and maintain equipment, using hand tools. Test samples of materials or products to ensure compliance with specifications, using test equipment. Transfer materials, supplies, and products between work areas, using moving equipment and hand tools. Unload mixtures into containers or onto conveyors for further processing. Collect samples of materials or products for laboratory testing. Record operational and production data on specified forms. **SKILLS**—Operation Monitoring; Operation and Control; Equipment Maintenance; Quality Control Analysis.

GOE—Interest Area: 08. Industrial Production. **Work Group:** 08.03 Production Work. **Other Apprenticeable Jobs in This Work Group:** Bakers, Manufacturing; Bindery Machine Operators and Tenders; Chemical Equipment Controllers and Operators; Coating, Painting, and Spraying Machine Operators and Tenders; Cooling and Freezing Equipment Operators and Tenders; Crushing, Grinding, and Polishing Machine Setters, Operators, and Tenders; Cutters and Trimmers, Hand; Cutting and Slicing Machine Operators and Tenders; Design Printing Machine Setters and Set-Up Operators; Electrolytic Plating and Coating Machine Setters and Set-Up Operators, Metal and Plastic; Electrotypers and Stereotypers; Embossing Machine Set-Up Operators; Engraver Set-Up Operators; Extruding, Forming, Pressing, and Compacting Machine Operators and Tenders; Fabric and Apparel Patternmakers; Film Laboratory Technicians; Fitters, Structural Metal—Precision; Food Batchmakers; Furnace, Kiln, Oven, Drier, and Kettle Operators and Tenders; Hand Compositors and Typesetters; Job Printers; Letterpress Setters and Set-Up Operators; Metal Fabricators, Structural Metal Products; Metal-Refining Furnace Operators and Tenders; Mold Makers, Hand; Molding and Casting Workers; Numerical Control Machine Tool Operators and Tenders, Metal and Plastic; Offset Lithographic Press Setters and Set-Up Operators; Painting, Coating, and Decorating Workers; Photographic Processing Machine Operators; Photographic Reproduction Technicians; Photographic Retouchers and Restorers; Plate Finishers; Platemakers; Precision Printing Workers; Printing Press Machine Operators and Tenders; Production Workers, All Other; Sawing Machine Operators and Tenders; Sawing Machine Setters and Set-Up Operators; Scanner Operators; Separating, Filtering, Clarifying, Precipitating, and

Still Machine Setters, Operators, and Tenders; Sewing Machine Operators, Garment; Slaughterers and Meat Packers; Stone Sawyers; Strippers; Team Assemblers; Welder-Fitters; Welders and Cutters; Woodworking Machine Operators and Tenders, Except Sawing. **PERSONALITY TYPE:** Realistic. Realistic occupations frequently involve work activities that include practical, hands-on problems and solutions. They often deal with plants, animals, and real-world materials like wood, tools, and machinery. Many of the occupations require working outside and do not involve a lot of paperwork or working closely with others.

RELATED KNOWLEDGE/COURSES—Production and Processing: Knowledge of raw materials, production processes, quality control, costs, and other techniques for maximizing the effective manufacture and distribution of goods. **Mechanical Devices:** Knowledge of machines and tools, including their designs, uses, repair, and maintenance. **Chemistry:** Knowledge of the chemical composition, structure, and properties of substances and of the chemical processes and transformations that they undergo. This includes uses of chemicals, their danger signs, production techniques, and disposal methods. **Physics:** Knowledge and prediction of physical principles and laws and their interrelationships and applications to understanding fluid, material, and atmospheric dynamics and mechanical, electrical, atomic, and subatomic structures and processes.

WORK ENVIRONMENT—Common protective or safety equipment; hazardous equipment; sounds, noise levels are distracting or uncomfortable; extremely bright or inadequate lighting; contaminants.

Mobile Heavy Equipment Mechanics, Except Engines

- Growth: 9.6%
- Annual Job Openings: 12,000
- Annual Earnings: $36,800
- Percentage of Women: 1.0%

Related Apprenticeship	Years
Construction-Equipment Mechanic	4
Logging-Equipment Mechanic	4
Mechanic, Endless Track Vehicle	4

Diagnose, adjust, repair, or overhaul mobile mechanical, hydraulic, and pneumatic equipment, such as cranes, bulldozers, graders, and conveyors, used in construction, logging, and surface mining. Test mechanical products and equipment after repair or assembly to ensure proper performance and compliance with manufacturers' specifications. Repair and replace damaged or worn parts. Operate and inspect machines or heavy equipment in order to diagnose defects. Diagnose faults or malfunctions to determine required repairs, using engine diagnostic equipment such as computerized test equipment and calibration devices. Dismantle and reassemble heavy equipment using hoists and hand tools. Clean, lubricate, and perform

M

other routine maintenance work on equipment and vehicles. Examine parts for damage or excessive wear, using micrometers and gauges. Schedule maintenance for industrial machines and equipment, and keep equipment service records. Read and understand operating manuals, blueprints, and technical drawings. Overhaul and test machines or equipment to ensure operating efficiency. Assemble gear systems, and align frames and gears. Fit bearings to adjust, repair, or overhaul mobile mechanical, hydraulic, and pneumatic equipment. Weld or solder broken parts and structural members, using electric or gas welders and soldering tools. Clean parts by spraying them with grease solvent or immersing them in tanks of solvent. Adjust, maintain, and repair or replace subassemblies, such as transmissions and crawler heads, using hand tools, jacks, and cranes. Adjust and maintain industrial machinery, using control and regulating devices. Fabricate needed parts or items from sheet metal. Direct workers who are assembling or disassembling equipment or cleaning parts. **SKILLS**—Installation; Equipment Maintenance; Repairing; Troubleshooting; Operation Monitoring; Equipment Selection; Persuasion; Operation and Control.

GOE—Interest Area: 05. Mechanics, Installers, and Repairers. **Work Group:** 05.03 Mechanical Work. **Other Apprenticeable Jobs in This Work Group:** Aircraft Engine Specialists; Airframe-and-Power-Plant Mechanics; Automotive Body and Related Repairers; Automotive Glass Installers and Repairers; Automotive Master Mechanics; Automotive Specialty Technicians; Bus and Truck Mechanics and Diesel Engine Specialists; Camera and Photographic Equipment Repairers; Coin, Vending, and Amusement Machine Servicers and Repairers; Farm Equipment Mechanics; Gas Appliance Repair-

ers; Hand and Portable Power Tool Repairers; Heating and Air Conditioning Mechanics; Helpers—Installation, Maintenance, and Repair Workers; Industrial Machinery Mechanics; Installation, Maintenance, and Repair Workers, All Other; Keyboard Instrument Repairers and Tuners; Locksmiths and Safe Repairers; Maintenance and Repair Workers, General; Maintenance Workers, Machinery; Mechanical Door Repairers; Medical Appliance Technicians; Medical Equipment Repairers; Meter Mechanics; Millwrights; Motorboat Mechanics; Motorcycle Mechanics; Optical Instrument Assemblers; Outdoor Power Equipment and Other Small Engine Mechanics; Painters, Transportation Equipment; Rail Car Repairers; Recreational Vehicle Service Technicians; Reed or Wind Instrument Repairers and Tuners; Refrigeration Mechanics; Stringed Instrument Repairers and Tuners; Valve and Regulator Repairers; Watch Repairers. **PERSONALITY TYPE:** Realistic. Realistic occupations frequently involve work activities that include practical, hands-on problems and solutions. They often deal with plants, animals, and real-world materials like wood, tools, and machinery. Many of the occupations require working outside and do not involve a lot of paperwork or working closely with others.

RELATED KNOWLEDGE/COURSES— Mechanical Devices: Knowledge of machines and tools, including their designs, uses, repair, and maintenance. **Engineering and Technology:** Knowledge of the practical application of engineering science and technology. This includes applying principles, techniques, procedures, and equipment to the design and production of various goods and services. **Customer and Personal Service:** Knowledge of principles and processes for providing customer and personal services. This includes customer needs assessment, meeting quality standards for services, and evaluation of customer satisfaction. **Physics:** Knowledge and prediction of physical principles and laws and their interrelationships and applications to understanding fluid, material, and atmospheric dynamics and mechanical, electrical, atomic, and subatomic structures and processes. **Chemistry:** Knowledge of the chemical composition, structure, and properties of substances and of the chemical processes and transformations that they undergo. This includes uses of chemicals, their danger signs, production techniques, and disposal methods. **Transportation:** Knowledge of principles and methods for moving people or goods by air, rail, sea, or road, including the relative costs and benefits.

WORK ENVIRONMENT—Sounds, noise levels are distracting or uncomfortable; contaminants; very hot or cold; hazardous conditions; indoors, not environmentally controlled; in an open vehicle or equipment.

Model Makers, Metal and Plastic

- ⊚ Growth: 14.6%
- ⊚ Annual Job Openings: 1,000
- ⊚ Annual Earnings: $43,470
- ⊚ Percentage of Women: 14.8%

Related Apprenticeship	Years
Model Builder (Furniture)	2
Engineering Model Maker	4

Experimental Mechanic	4
Mock-Up Builder	4
Model Maker (Automobile Manufacturing)	4
Model Maker (Clock and Watch)	4
Model Maker, Firearms	4
Prototype Model Maker	4
Sample Maker, Appliances	4
Tool Builder	4

Set up and operate machines, such as lathes, milling and engraving machines, and jig borers to make working models of metal or plastic objects. Sets up and operates machines, such as lathes, drill presses, punch presses, or bandsaw, to fabricate prototypes or models. Determines fixtures, machines, tooling, and sequence of operations to fabricate parts, dies, and tooling, according to drawings and sketches. Drills, countersinks, and reams holes in parts and assemblies for bolts, screws, and other fasteners, using power tools. Lays out and marks reference points and dimension on materials, using measuring instruments and drawing or scribing tools. Cuts, shapes, and forms metal parts, using lathe, power saw, snips, power brakes and shear, files, and mallets. Grinds, files, and sands parts to finished dimensions. Studies blueprint, drawings, or sketches, and computes dimensions for laying out materials and planning model production. Fabricates metal or plastic parts, using hand tools. Aligns, fits, and joins parts, using bolts or screws or by welding or gluing. Assembles mechanical, electrical, and electronic components into models or prototypes, using hand tools, power tools, and fabricating machines. Wires and solders electrical and electronic connections and components. Reworks or alters component model or parts as required to ensure performance of equipment or that parts meet standards. Inspects and tests model or other product to verify conformance to specifications, using precision measuring instruments or circuit tester. Devises and constructs own tools, dies, molds, jigs, and fixtures, or modifies existing tools and equipment. Makes bridges, plates, wheels, cutting teeth on wheels and pinions, and threaded screws. Consults and confers with engineering personnel to discuss developmental problems and recommend modifications to correct or improve performance of product. Records specifications, production operations, and final dimensions of model for use in establishing operating standards and machinery procedures. SKILLS—Technology Design; Quality Control Analysis; Operations Analysis; Equipment Selection; Troubleshooting; Operation Monitoring; Operation and Control; Systems Analysis.

GOE—Interest Area: 08. Industrial Production. Work Group: 08.04 Metal and Plastics Machining Technology. Other Apprenticeable Jobs in This Work Group: Lay-Out Workers, Metal and Plastic; Machinists; Metal Workers and Plastic Workers, All Other; Patternmakers, Metal and Plastic; Tool and Die Makers; Tool Grinders, Filers, and Sharpeners. PERSONALITY TYPE: Realistic. Realistic occupations frequently involve work activities that include practical, hands-on problems and solutions. They often deal with plants, animals, and real-world materials like wood, tools, and machinery. Many of the occupations require working outside and do not involve a lot of paperwork or working closely with others.

RELATED KNOWLEDGE/COURSES— Mechanical Devices: Knowledge of machines

and tools, including their designs, uses, repair, and maintenance. Design: Knowledge of design techniques, tools, and principles involved in production of precision technical plans, blueprints, drawings, and models. Building and Construction: Knowledge of the materials, methods, and tools involved in the construction or repair of houses, buildings, or other structures, such as highways and roads. Computers and Electronics: Knowledge of circuit boards, processors, chips, electronic equipment, and computer hardware and software, including applications and programming. Engineering and Technology: Knowledge of the practical application of engineering science and technology. This includes applying principles, techniques, procedures, and equipment to the design and production of various goods and services. Production and Processing: Knowledge of raw materials, production processes, quality control, costs, and other techniques for maximizing the effective manufacture and distribution of goods. Telecommunications: Knowledge of transmission, broadcasting, switching, control, and operation of telecommunications systems.

WORK ENVIRONMENT—Hazardous equipment; minor burns, cuts, bites, or stings; common protective or safety equipment; indoors; using hands on objects, tools, or controls.

Mold Makers, Hand

- ◎ Growth: 6.4%
- ◎ Annual Job Openings: 6,000
- ◎ Annual Earnings: $24,780
- ◎ Percentage of Women: 20.4%

Related Apprenticeship	*Years*
Mold Maker	
(Pottery and Porcelain)	3

Construct or form molds from existing forms for use in casting objects. Constructs molds used for casting metal, clay or plaster objects, using plaster, fiberglass, rubber, casting machine, patterns and flasks. Assembles hardened molds and seals joints. Places form around model and separately immerses each half portion of model in plaster, wax, or other mold-making material. Covers portions of model with layers of modeling or casting material treated to harden when allowed to set or dry. Removes excess modeling or mold material, such as plaster, wax, or rubber, using straightedge. Smoothes surfaces of mold, using scraping tool and sandpaper. Covers model or pattern of object from which mold is to be made with lubricant or parting agent to prevent mold from sticking to model. Bores holes or cuts grates and risers in mold, using power tools. Separates model or pattern from mold. Examines mold for accuracy. Allows mold to harden or dry in oven and repeats process until mold is complete. Repairs cracks and broken edges of mold, using hand tools. Mixes modeling material, such as plaster powder and water, or mud, sand, and loam, to specified formula. Melts metal pieces using torch and casts products, such as inlays and crowns, using centrifugal casting machine. **SKILLS**—Repairing; Science; Equipment Selection.

GOE—Interest Area: 08. Industrial Production. **Work Group:** 08.03 Production Work. **Other Apprenticeable Jobs in This Work Group:** Bakers, Manufacturing; Bindery Machine Operators and Tenders; Chemical Equipment Controllers and Operators; Coating, Painting, and Spraying Machine Operators and Tenders; Cooling and Freezing Equipment Operators and Tenders; Crushing, Grinding, and Polishing Machine Setters, Operators, and Tenders; Cutters and Trimmers, Hand; Cutting and Slicing Machine Operators and Tenders; Design Printing Machine Setters and Set-Up Operators; Electrolytic Plating and Coating Machine Setters and Set-Up Operators, Metal and Plastic; Electrotypers and Stereotypers; Embossing Machine Set-Up Operators; Engraver Set-Up Operators; Extruding, Forming, Pressing, and Compacting Machine Operators and Tenders; Fabric and Apparel Patternmakers; Film Laboratory Technicians; Fitters, Structural Metal—Precision; Food Batchmakers; Furnace, Kiln, Oven, Drier, and Kettle Operators and Tenders; Hand Compositors and Typesetters; Job Printers; Letterpress Setters and Set-Up Operators; Metal Fabricators, Structural Metal Products; Metal-Refining Furnace Operators and Tenders; Mixing and Blending Machine Setters, Operators, and Tenders; Molding and Casting Workers; Numerical Control Machine Tool Operators and Tenders, Metal and Plastic; Offset Lithographic Press Setters and Set-Up Operators; Painting, Coating, and Decorating Workers; Photographic Processing Machine Operators; Photographic Reproduction Technicians; Photographic Retouchers and Restorers; Plate Finishers; Platemakers; Precision Printing Workers; Printing Press Machine Operators and Tenders; Production Workers, All Other; Sawing Machine Operators and Tenders; Sawing Machine Setters and Set-Up Operators; Scanner Operators; Separating, Filtering, Clarifying, Precipitating, and

M

Still Machine Setters, Operators, and Tenders; Sewing Machine Operators, Garment; Slaughterers and Meat Packers; Stone Sawyers; Strippers; Team Assemblers; Welder-Fitters; Welders and Cutters; Woodworking Machine Operators and Tenders, Except Sawing. **PERSONALITY TYPE:** Realistic. Realistic occupations frequently involve work activities that include practical, hands-on problems and solutions. They often deal with plants, animals, and real-world materials like wood, tools, and machinery. Many of the occupations require working outside and do not involve a lot of paperwork or working closely with others.

RELATED KNOWLEDGE/COURSES— **Production and Processing:** Knowledge of raw materials, production processes, quality control, costs, and other techniques for maximizing the effective manufacture and distribution of goods. **Building and Construction:** Knowledge of the materials, methods, and tools involved in the construction or repair of houses, buildings, or other structures, such as highways and roads.

WORK ENVIRONMENT—Common protective or safety equipment; using hands on objects, tools, or controls; hazardous equipment; contaminants; indoors; spend time making repetitive motions.

Molding and Casting Workers

- Growth: 6.4%
- Annual Job Openings: 6,000
- Annual Earnings: $24,780
- Percentage of Women: 20.4%

Related Apprenticeship	*Years*
Cell Maker	1
Rubber-Stamp Maker	4

Perform a variety of duties such as mixing materials, assembling mold parts, filling molds, and stacking molds to mold and cast a wide range of products. Fills mold with mixed material or applies material to mold to specified thickness. Molds parts or products using vibrator, handpress, or casting equipment and taps or tilts mold to ensure uniformity. Operates and adjusts controls of heating equipment to melt material or to cure, dry or bake filled molds according to specifications. Opens mold and removes finished products. Measures ingredients and mixes molding or casting material or sealing compound, to prescribed consistency according to formula. Assembles, inserts and adjusts wires, tubes, cores, fittings, rods, or patterns into mold, using hand tools and depth gauge. Removes excess material and levels and smoothes wet mold mixture. Loads or stacks filled molds in oven, drier, or curing box, or on storage racks or carts. Reads work order or examines part to determine part or section of product to be produced. Selects size and type of mold according to instructions. Installs and secures mold or mold parts together. Brushes or sprays surface of mold with parting agent or inserts paper to ensure smoothness and prevent sticking or seepage. Measures and cuts product to specified dimensions, using measuring and cutting instruments. Aligns and assembles parts to produce completed product, using gauges and hand tools. Inspects and tests parts or products for defects and to verify accuracy and adherence to standards. Fastens metal inserts, such as drainage tubes, bolts, or electrical connections to product, using hand tools and power tools. Cleans, trims, smoothes, and polishes products or parts. Cleans and lubricates mold and mold parts. Engraves or stamps identifying symbols, letters or numbers on product. **SKILLS**—Operation Monitoring; Operation and Control; Quality Control Analysis; Installation; Equipment Maintenance; Repairing; Equipment Selection.

GOE—Interest Area: 08. Industrial Production. **Work Group:** 08.03 Production Work. **Other Apprenticeable Jobs in This Work Group:** Bakers, Manufacturing; Bindery Machine Operators and Tenders; Chemical Equipment Controllers and Operators; Coating, Painting, and Spraying Machine Operators and Tenders; Cooling and Freezing Equipment Operators and Tenders; Crushing, Grinding, and Polishing Machine Setters, Operators, and Tenders; Cutters and Trimmers, Hand; Cutting and Slicing Machine Operators and Tenders; Design Printing Machine Setters and Set-Up Operators; Electrolytic Plating and Coating Machine Setters and Set-Up Operators, Metal and Plastic; Electrotypers and Stereotypers; Embossing Machine Set-Up Operators; Engraver Set-Up Operators; Extruding, Forming, Pressing, and Compacting Machine Operators and Tenders; Fabric and Apparel Patternmakers; Film Laboratory Technicians; Fitters, Structural Metal—Precision; Food Batchmakers; Furnace, Kiln, Oven, Drier, and Kettle Operators and Tenders; Hand Compositors and Typesetters; Job Printers; Letterpress Setters and Set-Up Operators; Metal Fabricators, Structural Metal Products; Metal-Refining Furnace Operators and Tenders; Mixing and Blending Machine Setters, Operators, and Tenders; Mold Makers, Hand; Numerical Control Machine Tool Operators and Tenders, Metal and Plastic; Offset Lithographic Press Setters and Set-Up Operators; Painting, Coating, and Decorating Workers; Photographic Processing Machine Operators; Photographic Reproduction Technicians; Photographic Retouchers and Restorers; Plate Finishers; Platemakers; Precision Printing Workers; Printing Press Machine Operators and Tenders; Production Workers, All Other; Sawing Machine Operators and Tenders; Sawing Machine Setters and Set-Up Operators; Scanner Operators; Separating, Filtering, Clarifying, Precipitating, and Still Machine Setters, Operators, and Tenders; Sewing Machine Operators, Garment; Slaughterers and Meat Packers; Stone Sawyers; Strippers; Team Assemblers; Welder-Fitters; Welders and Cutters; Woodworking Machine Operators and Tenders, Except Sawing. **PERSONALITY TYPE:** Realistic. Realistic occupations frequently involve work activities that include practical, hands-on problems and solutions. They often deal with plants, animals, and real-world materials like wood, tools, and machinery. Many of the occupations require working outside and do not involve a lot of paperwork or working closely with others.

RELATED KNOWLEDGE/COURSES—**Production and Processing:** Knowledge of raw materials, production processes, quality control, costs, and other techniques for maximizing the effective manufacture and distribution of goods. **Building and Construction:** Knowledge of the materials, methods, and tools involved in the construction or repair of houses, buildings, or other structures, such as highways and roads.

WORK ENVIRONMENT—Using hands on objects, tools, or controls; spend time making repetitive motions; indoors; spend time bending or twisting the body; hazardous equipment; standing.

Motor Vehicle Inspectors

- Growth: 7.7%
- Annual Job Openings: 5,000
- Annual Earnings: $49,590
- Percentage of Women: 16.2%

Related Apprenticeship	Years
Inspector, Motor Vehicles	4

Inspect automotive vehicles to ensure compliance with governmental regulations and safety standards. Inspects truck accessories, air lines and electric circuits, and reports needed repairs. Examines vehicles for damage, and drives vehicle to detect malfunctions. Tests vehicle components for wear, damage, or improper adjustment, using mechanical or electrical devices. Applies inspection sticker to vehicles that pass inspection, and rejection sticker to vehicles that fail. Prepares report on each vehicle for follow-up action by owner or police. Prepares and keeps record of vehicles delivered. Positions trailer and drives car onto truck trailer. Notifies authorities of owners having illegal equipment installed on vehicle. Services vehicles with fuel and water. **SKILLS**—Troubleshooting; Science; Quality Control Analysis; Operation Monitoring; Technology Design; Equipment Maintenance; Systems Evaluation.

GOE—Interest Area: 08. Industrial Production. **Work Group:** 08.02 Production Technology. **Other Apprenticeable Jobs in This Work Group:** Aircraft Structure Assemblers, Precision; Aircraft Systems Assemblers, Precision; Bench Workers, Jewelry; Bindery Machine Setters and Set-Up Operators; Bookbinders; Buffing and Polishing Set-Up Operators; Coating, Painting, and Spraying Machine Setters and Set-Up Operators; Combination Machine Tool Setters and Set-Up Operators, Metal and Plastic; Dental Laboratory Technicians; Electrical and Electronic Equipment Assemblers; Electrical and Electronic Inspectors and Testers; Electromechanical Equipment Assemblers; Engine and Other Machine Assemblers; Extruding and Drawing Machine Setters, Operators, and Tenders, Metal and Plastic; Extruding, Forming, Pressing, and Compacting Machine Setters and Set-Up Operators; Forging Machine Setters, Operators, and Tenders, Metal and Plastic; Foundry Mold and Coremakers; Gem and Diamond Workers; Grinding, Honing, Lapping, and Deburring Machine Set-Up Operators; Heat Treating, Annealing, and Tempering Machine Operators and Tenders, Metal and Plastic; Jewelers; Lathe and Turning Machine Tool Setters, Operators, and Tenders, Metal and Plastic; Materials Inspectors; Mechanical Inspectors; Metal Molding, Coremaking, and Casting Machine Operators and Tenders; Milling and Planing Machine Setters, Operators, and Tenders, Metal and Plastic; Model and Mold Makers, Jewelry; Paper Goods Machine Setters, Operators, and Tenders; Pewter Casters and Finishers; Plastic Molding and Casting Machine Setters and Set-Up Operators; Precision Devices Inspectors and Testers; Precision Lens Grinders and Polishers; Precision Mold and Pattern Casters, except Nonferrous Metals; Precision Pattern and Die Casters, Nonferrous Metals; Press and Press Brake Machine Setters and Set-Up Operators, Metal and Plastic; Production Inspectors, Testers, Graders, Sorters, Samplers, Weighers; Production Workers, All Other; Rolling Machine Setters, Operators, and Tenders, Metal and Plastic; Silversmiths; Textile Knitting and Weaving Machine Setters, Operators, and Tenders; Textile Winding, Twisting, and Drawing Out Machine Setters, Operators, and Tenders; Welding Machine Setters and Set-Up Operators; Woodworking Machine Setters and Set-Up Operators, Except Sawing. **PERSONALITY TYPE:** Realistic. Realistic occupations frequently involve work activities that include practical, hands-on problems and solutions. They often deal with plants, animals, and real-world materials like wood, tools, and machinery. Many of the occupations require working outside and do not involve a lot of paperwork or working closely with others.

RELATED KNOWLEDGE/COURSES— Public Safety and Security: Knowledge of relevant equipment, policies, procedures, and strategies to promote effective local, state, or national security operations for the protection of people, data, property, and institutions. **Mechanical Devices:** Knowledge of machines and tools, including their designs, uses, repair, and maintenance. **Computers and Electronics:** Knowledge of circuit boards, processors, chips, electronic equipment, and computer hardware and software, including applications and programming. **Engineering and Technology:** Knowledge of the practical application of engineering science and technology. This includes applying principles, techniques, procedures, and equipment to the design and production of various goods and services. **Law and Government:** Knowledge of laws, legal codes, court procedures, precedents, government regulations, executive orders, agency rules, and the democratic political process. **Transportation:** Knowledge of principles and methods for moving people or goods by air, rail, sea, or road, including the relative costs and benefits.

WORK ENVIRONMENT—Outdoors; spend time kneeling, crouching, stooping, or crawling; spend time bending or twisting the body; cramped work space, awkward positions; hazardous equipment; minor burns, cuts, bites, or stings.

Motorboat Mechanics

- Growth: 18.3%
- Annual Job Openings: 2,000
- Annual Earnings: $29,170
- Percentage of Women: 1.7%

Related Apprenticeship	*Years*
Outboard-Motor Mechanic	2
Motorboat Mechanic	3

Repairs and adjusts electrical and mechanical equipment of gasoline or diesel powered inboard or inboard-outboard boat engines. Adjust carburetor mixtures, electrical point settings, and timing while motors are running in water-filled test tanks. Adjust generators and replace faulty wiring, using hand tools and soldering irons. Disassemble and inspect motors to locate defective parts, using mechanic's hand tools and gauges. Idle motors and observe thermometers to determine the effectiveness of cooling systems. Inspect and repair or adjust propellers and propeller shafts. Repair engine mechanical equipment such as power-tilts, bilge pumps, or power take-offs. Repair or rework parts, using machine tools such as lathes, mills, drills, and grinders. Replace parts such as gears, magneto points, piston rings, and spark plugs, and reassemble engines. Set starter locks, and align and repair steering or throttle controls, using gauges, screwdrivers, and wrenches. Start motors, and monitor performance for signs of malfunctioning such as smoke, excessive vibration, and misfiring. Document inspection and test results, and work performed or to be performed. Mount motors to boats and operate boats at various speeds on waterways to conduct operational tests. **SKILLS**—Repairing; Troubleshooting; Quality Control Analysis; Equipment Maintenance; Installation; Operation Monitoring; Operation and Control; Equipment Selection.

GOE—Interest Area: 05. Mechanics, Installers, and Repairers. **Work Group:** 05.03 Mechanical Work. **Other Apprenticeable Jobs in This Work Group:** Aircraft Engine Specialists; Airframe-and-Power-Plant Mechanics; Automotive Body and Related Repairers; Automotive Glass Installers and Repairers; Automotive Master Mechanics; Automotive Specialty Technicians; Bus and Truck Mechanics and Diesel Engine Specialists; Camera and Photographic Equipment Repairers; Coin, Vending, and Amusement Machine Servicers and Repairers; Farm Equipment Mechanics; Gas Appliance Repairers; Hand and Portable Power Tool Repairers; Heating and Air Conditioning Mechanics; Helpers—Installation, Maintenance, and Repair Workers; Industrial Machinery Mechanics; Installation, Maintenance, and Repair Workers, All Other; Keyboard Instrument Repairers and Tuners; Locksmiths and Safe Repairers; Maintenance and Repair Workers, General; Maintenance Workers, Machinery; Mechanical Door Repairers; Medical Appliance Technicians; Medical Equipment Repairers;

Meter Mechanics; Millwrights; Mobile Heavy Equipment Mechanics, Except Engines; Motorcycle Mechanics; Optical Instrument Assemblers; Outdoor Power Equipment and Other Small Engine Mechanics; Painters, Transportation Equipment; Rail Car Repairers; Recreational Vehicle Service Technicians; Reed or Wind Instrument Repairers and Tuners; Refrigeration Mechanics; Stringed Instrument Repairers and Tuners; Valve and Regulator Repairers; Watch Repairers. **PERSONALITY TYPE:** Realistic. Realistic occupations frequently involve work activities that include practical, hands-on problems and solutions. They often deal with plants, animals, and real-world materials like wood, tools, and machinery. Many of the occupations require working outside and do not involve a lot of paperwork or working closely with others.

RELATED KNOWLEDGE/COURSES—Mechanical Devices: Knowledge of machines and tools, including their designs, uses, repair, and maintenance. **Engineering and Technology:** Knowledge of the practical application of engineering science and technology. This includes applying principles, techniques, procedures, and equipment to the design and production of various goods and services. **Physics:** Knowledge and prediction of physical principles and laws and their interrelationships and applications to understanding fluid, material, and atmospheric dynamics and mechanical, electrical, atomic, and subatomic structures and processes.

WORK ENVIRONMENT—Outdoors; spend time kneeling, crouching, stooping, or crawling; hazardous conditions; very hot or cold; using hands on objects, tools, or controls; common protective or safety equipment.

Motorcycle Mechanics

- Growth: 18.7%
- Annual Job Openings: 1,000
- Annual Earnings: $27,630
- Percentage of Women: 1.7%

Related Apprenticeship	Years
Motorcycle Repairer	3

Diagnose, adjust, repair, or overhaul motorcycles, scooters, mopeds, dirt bikes, or similar motorized vehicles. Dismantle engines and repair or replace defective parts, such as magnetos, carburetors, and generators. Remove cylinder heads, grind valves, and scrape off carbon, and replace defective valves, pistons, cylinders and rings, using hand tools and power tools. Hammer out dents and bends in frames, weld tears and breaks; then reassemble frames and reinstall engines. Repair or replace other parts, such as headlights, horns, handlebar controls, gasoline and oil tanks, starters, and mufflers. Repair and adjust motorcycle subassemblies such as forks, transmissions, brakes, and drive chains, according to specifications. Replace defective parts, using hand tools, arbor presses, flexible power presses, or power tools. Reassemble and test subassembly units. Disassemble subassembly units and examine condition, movement or alignment of parts visually or using gauges. Listen to engines, examine vehicle frames, and confer with customers in order to determine nature and extent of malfunction or damage. Connect test panels to engines and measure generator output, ignition timing, and other engine performance indicators.

SKILLS—Repairing; Troubleshooting; Equipment Maintenance; Technology Design; Installation; Operation Monitoring; Operation and Control; Quality Control Analysis.

GOE—Interest Area: 05. Mechanics, Installers, and Repairers. **Work Group:** 05.03 Mechanical Work. **Other Apprenticeable Jobs in This Work Group:** Aircraft Engine Specialists; Airframe-and-Power-Plant Mechanics; Automotive Body and Related Repairers; Automotive Glass Installers and Repairers; Automotive Master Mechanics; Automotive Specialty Technicians; Bus and Truck Mechanics and Diesel Engine Specialists; Camera and Photographic Equipment Repairers; Coin, Vending, and Amusement Machine Servicers and Repairers; Farm Equipment Mechanics; Gas Appliance Repairers; Hand and Portable Power Tool Repairers; Heating and Air Conditioning Mechanics; Helpers—Installation, Maintenance, and Repair Workers; Industrial Machinery Mechanics; Installation, Maintenance, and Repair Workers, All Other; Keyboard Instrument Repairers and Tuners; Locksmiths and Safe Repairers; Maintenance and Repair Workers, General; Maintenance Workers, Machinery; Mechanical Door Repairers; Medical Appliance Technicians; Medical Equipment Repairers; Meter Mechanics; Millwrights; Mobile Heavy Equipment Mechanics, Except Engines; Motorboat Mechanics; Optical Instrument Assemblers; Outdoor Power Equipment and Other Small Engine Mechanics; Painters, Transportation Equipment; Rail Car Repairers; Recreational Vehicle Service Technicians; Reed or Wind Instrument Repairers and Tuners; Refrigeration Mechanics; Stringed Instrument Repairers and Tuners; Valve and Regulator Repairers; Watch Repairers. **PERSONALITY TYPE:** Realistic. Realistic occupations frequently involve work activities that include practical, hands-on problems and solutions. They often deal with plants, animals, and real-world materials like wood, tools, and machinery. Many of the occupations require working outside and do not involve a lot of paperwork or working closely with others.

RELATED KNOWLEDGE/COURSES—**Mechanical Devices:** Knowledge of machines and tools, including their designs, uses, repair, and maintenance. **Engineering and Technology:** Knowledge of the practical application of engineering science and technology. This includes applying principles, techniques, procedures, and equipment to the design and production of various goods and services. **Customer and Personal Service:** Knowledge of principles and processes for providing customer and personal services. This includes customer needs assessment, meeting quality standards for services, and evaluation of customer satisfaction. **Physics:** Knowledge and prediction of physical principles and laws and their interrelationships and applications to understanding fluid, material, and atmospheric dynamics and mechanical, electrical, atomic, and subatomic structures and processes.

WORK ENVIRONMENT—Spend time kneeling, crouching, stooping, or crawling; contaminants; cramped work space, awkward positions; minor burns, cuts, bites, or stings; using hands on objects, tools, or controls.

Municipal Fire Fighters

- ☺ Growth: 20.7%
- ☺ Annual Job Openings: 29,000
- ☺ Annual Earnings: $37,060
- ☺ Percentage of Women: 3.6%

Related Apprenticeship	Years
Fire Engineer	1
Fire Fighter, Crash, Fire, and Rescue	1
Fire Apparatus Engineer	3
Fire Fighter	3
Fire Medic	3

Control and extinguish municipal fires, protect life and property and conduct rescue efforts. Administer first aid and cardiopulmonary resuscitation to injured persons. Rescue victims from burning buildings and accident sites. Search burning buildings to locate fire victims. Drive and operate fire fighting vehicles and equipment. Dress with equipment such as fire resistant clothing and breathing apparatus. Move toward the source of a fire using knowledge of types of fires, construction design, building materials, and physical layout of properties. Position and climb ladders in order to gain access to upper levels of buildings, or to rescue individuals from burning structures. Take action to contain hazardous chemicals that might catch fire, leak, or spill. Assess fires and situations and report conditions to superiors in order to receive instructions, using two-way radios. Respond to fire alarms and other calls for assistance, such as automobile and industrial accidents. Operate pumps connected to high-pressure hoses. Select and attach hose nozzles, depending on fire type, and direct streams of water or chemicals onto fires. Create openings in buildings for ventilation or entrance, using axes, chisels, crowbars, electric saws, or core cutters. Inspect fire sites after flames have been extinguished in order to ensure that there is no further danger. Lay hose lines and connect them to water supplies. Protect property from water and smoke using water-proof salvage covers, smoke ejectors, and deodorants. Participate in physical training activities in order to maintain a high level of physical fitness. Salvage property by removing broken glass, pumping out water, and ventilating buildings to remove smoke. Participate in fire drills and demonstrations of fire fighting techniques. Clean and maintain fire stations and fire fighting equipment and apparatus. Collaborate with police to respond to accidents, disasters, and arson investigation calls. Establish firelines to prevent unauthorized persons from entering areas near fires. Inform and educate the public on fire prevention. Inspect buildings for fire hazards and compliance with fire prevention ordinances, testing and checking smoke alarms and fire suppression equipment as necessary. **SKILLS**—Service Orientation; Equipment Maintenance; Social Perceptiveness; Equipment Selection; Coordination; Learning Strategies; Critical Thinking; Complex Problem Solving; Operation Monitoring.

GOE—Interest Area: 04. Law, Law Enforcement, and Public Safety. **Work Group:** 04.04 Public Safety. **Other Apprenticeable Jobs in This Work Group:** Emergency Medical Technicians and Paramedics; Fire Inspectors; Forest Fire Fighters; Government Property Inspectors and Investigators; Nuclear Monitoring Technicians; Occupational Health and Safety Specialists. **PERSONALITY TYPE:** Realistic. Realistic occupations frequently involve work activities that include practical, hands-on problems and solutions. They often deal with plants, animals, and real-world materials like wood, tools, and machinery. Many of the occupations require working outside and do not involve a lot of paperwork or working closely with others.

RELATED KNOWLEDGE/COURSES— Customer and Personal Service: Knowledge of principles and processes for providing customer and personal services. This includes customer needs assessment, meeting quality standards for services, and evaluation of customer satisfaction. **Medicine and Dentistry:** Knowledge of the information and techniques needed to diagnose and treat human injuries, diseases, and deformities. This includes symptoms, treatment alternatives, drug properties and interactions, and preventive health-care measures. **Public Safety and Security:** Knowledge of relevant equipment, policies, procedures, and strategies to promote effective local, state, or national security operations for the protection of people, data, property, and institutions. **Physics:** Knowledge and prediction of physical principles and laws and their interrelationships and applications to understanding fluid, material, and atmospheric dynamics and mechanical, electrical, atomic, and subatomic structures and processes. **Psychology:** Knowledge of human behavior and performance; individual differences in ability, personality, and interests; learning and motivation; psychological research methods; and the assessment and treatment of behavioral and affective disorders. **Chemistry:** Knowledge of the chemical composition, structure, and properties of substances and of the chemical processes and transformations that they undergo. This includes uses of chemicals, their danger signs, production techniques, and disposal methods.

WORK ENVIRONMENT—Physical proximity; very hot or cold; contaminants; sounds, noise levels are distracting or uncomfortable; outdoors; hazardous conditions.

Municipal Fire Fighting and Prevention Supervisors

- Growth: 18.7%
- Annual Job Openings: 8,000
- Annual Earnings: $57,000
- Percentage of Women: 2.9%

Related Apprenticeship	Years
Fire Captain	3

Supervise fire fighters who control and extinguish municipal fires, protect life and property, and conduct rescue efforts. Assess nature and extent of fire, condition of building, danger to adjacent buildings, and water supply status in order to determine crew or company requirements. Assign firefighters to jobs at strategic locations in order to facilitate rescue of persons and maximize application of extinguishing agents. Attend in-service training classes to remain current in knowledge of codes, laws, ordinances, and regulations. Direct the training of firefighters, assigning of instructors to training classes, and providing of supervisors with reports on training progress and status. Evaluate fire station procedures in order to ensure efficiency and enforcement of departmental regulations. Evaluate the performance of assigned firefighting personnel. Inspect and test new and existing fire protection systems, fire detection systems, and fire safety equipment in order to ensure that they are operating properly. Instruct and drill fire department personnel in assigned duties, including firefighting, medical care, hazardous materials response, fire prevention, and related subjects. Participate in creating fire safety guidelines and evacuation schemes for nonresidential buildings. Prepare activity reports listing fire call locations, actions taken, fire types and probable causes, damage estimates, and situation dispositions. Provide emergency medical services as required, and perform light to heavy rescue functions at emergencies. Recommend personnel actions related to disciplinary procedures, performance, leaves of absence, and grievances. Supervise and participate in the inspection of properties in order to ensure that they are in compliance with applicable fire codes, ordinances, laws, regulations, and standards. Compile and maintain equipment and personnel records, including accident reports. Conduct fire drills for building occupants and report on the outcomes of such drills. Coordinate the distribution of fire prevention promotional materials. Develop or review building fire exit plans. Direct firefighters in station maintenance duties, and participate in these duties. Direct investigation of cases of suspected arson, hazards, and false alarms and submit reports outlining findings. **SKILLS**—Management of Personnel Resources; Service Orientation; Management of Material Resources; Coordination; Management of Financial Resources; Systems Evaluation; Systems Analysis; Instructing.

GOE—Interest Area: 04. Law, Law Enforcement, and Public Safety. **Work Group:** 04.01 Managerial Work in Law, Law Enforcement, and Public Safety. **Other Apprenticeable Jobs in This Work Group:** Emergency Management Specialists. **PERSONALITY TYPE:** Realistic. Realistic occupations frequently involve work activities that include practical, hands-on problems and solutions. They often deal with plants, animals, and real-world materials like wood, tools, and machinery. Many of the occupations require working outside and do not involve a lot of paperwork or working closely with others.

RELATED KNOWLEDGE/COURSES— **Public Safety and Security:** Knowledge of relevant equipment, policies, procedures, and strategies to promote effective local, state, or national security operations for the protection of people, data, property, and institutions. **Education and Training:** Knowledge of principles and methods for curriculum and training design, teaching and instruction for individuals and groups, and the measurement of training effects. **Personnel and Human Resources:** Knowledge of principles and procedures for personnel recruitment, selection, training, compensation and benefits, labor relations and negotiation, and personnel information systems. **Building and Construction:** Knowledge of the materials, methods, and tools involved in the construction or repair of houses, buildings, or other structures, such as highways and roads. **Administration and Management:** Knowledge of business and management principles involved in strategic planning, resource allocation, human resources modeling, leadership technique, production methods, and coordination of people and resources. **Medicine and Dentistry:** Knowledge of the information and techniques needed to diagnose and treat human injuries, diseases, and deformities. This includes symptoms, treatment alternatives, drug properties and interactions, and preventive health-care measures.

WORK ENVIRONMENT—Specialized protective or safety equipment; very hot or cold; extremely bright or inadequate lighting; outdoors; minor burns, cuts, bites, or stings.

Nonfarm Animal Caretakers

- Growth: 22.2%
- Annual Job Openings: 32,000
- Annual Earnings: $17,190
- Percentage of Women: 68.1%

Related Apprenticeship	Years
Horseshoer	2

Feed, water, groom, bathe, exercise, or otherwise care for pets and other nonfarm animals, such as dogs, cats, ornamental fish or birds, zoo animals, and mice. Work in settings such as kennels, animal shelters, zoos, circuses, and aquariums. May keep records of feedings, treatments, and animals received or discharged. May clean, disinfect, and repair cages, pens, or fish tanks. Adjust controls to regulate specified temperature and humidity of animal quarters, nurseries, or exhibit areas. Clean, organize, and disinfect animal quarters such as pens, stables, cages, and yards, and animal equipment such as saddles and bridles. Collect and record animal information such as weight, size, physical condition, treatments received, medications given, and food intake. Examine and observe animals in order to detect signs of illness, disease, or injury. Exercise animals in order to maintain their physical and mental health. Feed and water animals according to schedules and feeding instructions. Mix food, liquid formulas, medications, or food supplements according to instructions, prescriptions,

N

and knowledge of animal species. Perform animal grooming duties such as washing, brushing, clipping, and trimming coats, cutting nails, and cleaning ears. Provide treatment to sick or injured animals, or contact veterinarians in order to secure treatment. Administer laboratory tests to experimental animals, and keep records of responses. Anesthetize and inoculate animals, according to instructions. Answer telephones and schedule appointments. Clean and disinfect surgical equipment. Discuss with clients their pets' grooming needs. Install, maintain, and repair animal care facility equipment such as infrared lights, feeding devices, and cages. Observe and caution children petting and feeding animals in designated areas in order to ensure the safety of humans and animals. Order, unload, and store feed and supplies. Respond to questions from patrons, and provide information about animals, such as behavior, habitat, breeding habits, or facility activities. Saddle and shoe animals. Train animals to perform certain tasks. Transfer animals between enclosures in order to facilitate breeding, birthing, shipping, or rearrangement of exhibits. Find homes for stray or unwanted animals. Sell pet food and supplies. Teach obedience classes. **SKILLS—** Installation; Repairing; Service Orientation; Equipment Maintenance; Troubleshooting; Technology Design.

GOE—Interest Area: 03. Plants and Animals. **Work Group:** 03.02 Animal Care and Training. **Other Apprenticeable Jobs in This Work Group:** Animal Trainers. **PERSONALITY TYPE:** Realistic. Realistic occupations frequently involve work activities that include practical, hands-on problems and solutions. They often deal with plants, animals, and real-world materials like wood, tools, and machinery. Many of the occupations require working outside and do not involve a lot of paperwork or working closely with others.

RELATED KNOWLEDGE/COURSES— Medicine and Dentistry: Knowledge of the information and techniques needed to diagnose and treat human injuries, diseases, and deformities. This includes symptoms, treatment alternatives, drug properties and interactions, and preventive health-care measures. **Building and Construction:** Knowledge of the materials, methods, and tools involved in the construction or repair of houses, buildings, or other structures, such as highways and roads. **Biology:** Knowledge of plant and animal organisms and their tissues, cells, functions, interdependencies, and interactions with each other and the environment. **Chemistry:** Knowledge of the chemical composition, structure, and properties of substances and of the chemical processes and transformations that they undergo. This includes uses of chemicals, their danger signs, production techniques, and disposal methods. **Clerical Practices:** Knowledge of administrative and clerical procedures and systems, such as word processing, managing files and records, stenography and transcription, designing forms, and other office procedures and terminology.

WORK ENVIRONMENT—Outdoors; disease or infections; contaminants; minor burns, cuts, bites, or stings; spend time kneeling, crouching, stooping, or crawling.

Numerical Control Machine Tool Operators and Tenders, Metal and Plastic

- ◉ Growth: 9.3%
- ◉ Annual Job Openings: 11,000
- ◉ Annual Earnings: $29,420
- ◉ Percentage of Women: 12.1%

Related Apprenticeship	Years
Numerical Control Machine Operator	4

Set up and operate numerical control (magnetic- or punched-tape-controlled) machine tools that automatically mill, drill, broach, and ream metal and plastic parts. May adjust machine feed and speed, change cutting tools, or adjust machine controls when automatic programming is faulty or if machine malfunctions. Starts automatic operation of numerical control machine to machine parts or test setup, workpiece dimensions, or programming. Confers with supervisor or programmer to resolve machine malfunctions and production errors and obtains approval to continue production. Maintains machines and removes and replaces broken or worn machine tools, using hand tools. Examines electronic components for defects and completeness of laser-beam trimming, using microscope. Operates lathe, drill-press, jig-boring machine, or other machines manually or semiautomatically. Measures dimensions of finished workpiece to ensure conformance to specifications, using precision measuring instruments, templates, and fixtures. Lifts workpiece to machine manually, with hoist or crane, or with tweezers. Enters commands or manually adjusts machine controls to correct malfunctions or tolerances. Stops machine to remove finished workpiece or change tooling, setup, or workpiece placement, according to required machining sequence. Monitors machine operation and control panel displays to detect malfunctions and compare readings to specifications. Cleans machine, tooling, and parts, using solvent or solution and rag. Selects, measures, assembles, and sets machine tools, such as drill bits and milling or cutting tools, using precision gauges and instruments. Mounts, installs, aligns, and secures tools, attachments, fixtures, and workpiece on machine, using hand tools and precision measuring instruments. Determines specifications or procedures for tooling set-up, machine operation, workpiece dimensions, or numerical control sequences, using blueprints, instructions, and machine knowledge. Calculates and sets machine controls to position tools, synchronize tape and tool, or regulate cutting depth, speed, feed, or coolant flow. Lays out and marks areas of part to be shot-peened, and fills hopper with shot. Positions and secures workpiece on machine bed, indexing table, fixture, or dispensing or holding device. Loads control media, such as tape, card, or disk, in machine controller or enters commands to retrieve programmed instructions. SKILLS—Operation Monitoring; Equipment Maintenance; Operation and Control; Quality Control Analysis; Installation; Equipment Selection; Mathematics; Troubleshooting.

N

GOE—Interest Area: 08. Industrial Production. **Work Group:** 08.03 Production Work. **Other Apprenticeable Jobs in This Work Group:** Bakers, Manufacturing; Bindery Machine Operators and Tenders; Chemical Equipment Controllers and Operators; Coating, Painting, and Spraying Machine Operators and Tenders; Cooling and Freezing Equipment Operators and Tenders; Crushing, Grinding, and Polishing Machine Setters, Operators, and Tenders; Cutters and Trimmers, Hand; Cutting and Slicing Machine Operators and Tenders; Design Printing Machine Setters and Set-Up Operators; Electrolytic Plating and Coating Machine Setters and Set-Up Operators, Metal and Plastic; Electrotypers and Stereotypers; Embossing Machine Set-Up Operators; Engraver Set-Up Operators; Extruding, Forming, Pressing, and Compacting Machine Operators and Tenders; Fabric and Apparel Patternmakers; Film Laboratory Technicians; Fitters, Structural Metal—Precision; Food Batchmakers; Furnace, Kiln, Oven, Drier, and Kettle Operators and Tenders; Hand Compositors and Typesetters; Job Printers; Letterpress Setters and Set-Up Operators; Metal Fabricators, Structural Metal Products; Metal-Refining Furnace Operators and Tenders; Mixing and Blending Machine Setters, Operators, and Tenders; Mold Makers, Hand; Molding and Casting Workers; Offset Lithographic Press Setters and Set-Up Operators; Painting, Coating, and Decorating Workers; Photographic Processing Machine Operators; Photographic Reproduction Technicians; Photographic Retouchers and Restorers; Plate Finishers; Platemakers; Precision Printing Workers; Printing Press Machine Operators and Tenders; Production Workers, All Other; Sawing Machine Operators and Tenders; Sawing Machine Setters and Set-Up Operators; Scanner Operators; Separating, Filtering, Clarifying, Precipitating, and Still Machine Setters, Operators, and Tenders; Sewing Machine Operators, Garment; Slaughterers and Meat Packers; Stone Sawyers; Strippers; Team Assemblers; Welder-Fitters; Welders and Cutters; Woodworking Machine Operators and Tenders, Except Sawing. **PERSONALITY TYPE:** Realistic. Realistic occupations frequently involve work activities that include practical, hands-on problems and solutions. They often deal with plants, animals, and real-world materials like wood, tools, and machinery. Many of the occupations require working outside and do not involve a lot of paperwork or working closely with others.

RELATED KNOWLEDGE/COURSES— Production and Processing: Knowledge of raw materials, production processes, quality control, costs, and other techniques for maximizing the effective manufacture and distribution of goods. **Mechanical Devices:** Knowledge of machines and tools, including their designs, uses, repair, and maintenance. **Engineering and Technology:** Knowledge of the practical application of engineering science and technology. This includes applying principles, techniques, procedures, and equipment to the design and production of various goods and services. **Design:** Knowledge of design techniques, tools, and principles involved in production of precision technical plans, blueprints, drawings, and models. **Computers and Electronics:** Knowledge of circuit boards, processors, chips, electronic equipment, and computer hardware and software, including applications and programming. **Physics:** Knowledge and prediction of physical principles and laws and their interrelationships and applications to understanding fluid, material, and atmospheric dynamics and mechanical, electrical, atomic, and subatomic structures and processes.

WORK ENVIRONMENT—Hazardous equipment; standing; common protective or safety equipment; indoors; sounds, noise levels are distracting or uncomfortable; minor burns, cuts, bites, or stings.

Numerical Tool and Process Control Programmers

- Growth: 13.0%
- Annual Job Openings: 2,000
- Annual Earnings: $38,330
- Percentage of Women: 12.1%

Related Apprenticeship	Years
Tool Programmer, Numerical Control	3

Develop programs to control machining or processing of parts by automatic machine tools, equipment, or systems. Prepares geometric layout from graphic displays, using computer-assisted drafting software or drafting instruments and graph paper. Writes instruction sheets, cutter lists, and machine instructions programs to guide setup and encode numerical control tape. Analyzes drawings, specifications, printed circuit board pattern film, and design data to calculate dimensions, tool selection, machine speeds, and feed rates. Determines reference points, machine cutting paths, or hole locations and computes angular and linear dimensions, radii, and curvatures. Compares encoded tape or computer printout with original program sheet to verify accuracy of instructions. Draws machine tool paths on pattern film, using colored markers and following guidelines for tool speed and efficiency. Revises numerical control machine tape programs to eliminate instruction errors and omissions. Enters computer commands to store or retrieve parts patterns, graphic displays, or programs to transfer data to other media. Aligns and secures pattern film on reference table of optical programmer and observes enlarger scope view of printed circuit board. Moves reference table to align pattern film over circuit board holes with reference marks on enlarger scope. Depresses pedal or button of programmer to enter coordinates of each hole location into program memory. Loads and unloads disks or tapes and observes operation of machine on trial run to test taped or programmed instructions. Reviews shop orders to determine job specifications and requirements. Sorts shop orders into groups to maximize materials utilization and minimize machine setup. **SKILLS**—Programming; Troubleshooting; Operations Analysis; Technology Design; Operation Monitoring; Mathematics; Quality Control Analysis; Operation and Control.

GOE—Interest Area: 02. Science, Math, and Engineering. **Work Group:** 02.09 Engineering Technology. **Other Apprenticeable Jobs in This Work Group:** Aerospace Engineering and Operations Technicians; Architectural Drafters; Calibration and Instrumentation Technicians; Cartographers and Photogrammetrists; Civil Drafters; Construction and Building Inspectors; Electrical Drafters; Electrical Engineering Technicians; Electro-Mechanical Technicians; Electronic Drafters; Electronics Engineering Technicians; Engineering Technicians, Except Drafters, All Other; Industrial Engineering

Technicians; Mapping Technicians; Mechanical Drafters; Mechanical Engineering Technicians; Surveying Technicians. **PERSONALITY TYPE:** Realistic. Realistic occupations frequently involve work activities that include practical, hands-on problems and solutions. They often deal with plants, animals, and real-world materials like wood, tools, and machinery. Many of the occupations require working outside and do not involve a lot of paperwork or working closely with others.

RELATED KNOWLEDGE/COURSES— **Computers and Electronics:** Knowledge of circuit boards, processors, chips, electronic equipment, and computer hardware and software, including applications and programming. **Design:** Knowledge of design techniques, tools, and principles involved in production of precision technical plans, blueprints, drawings, and models. **Mathematics:** Knowledge of arithmetic, algebra, geometry, calculus, and statistics and their applications. **Production and Processing:** Knowledge of raw materials, production processes, quality control, costs, and other techniques for maximizing the effective manufacture and distribution of goods. **Engineering and Technology:** Knowledge of the practical application of engineering science and technology. This includes applying principles, techniques, procedures, and equipment to the design and production of various goods and services. **Foreign Language:** Knowledge of the structure and content of a foreign (non-English) language, including the meaning and spelling of words, rules of composition and grammar, and pronunciation.

WORK ENVIRONMENT—Sitting; indoors; using hands on objects, tools, or controls; walking and running; spend time bending or twisting the body.

Nursing Aides, Orderlies, and Attendants

- Growth: 24.9%
- Annual Job Openings: 302,000
- Annual Earnings: $20,490
- Percentage of Women: 87.8%

Related Apprenticeship	Years
Nurse Assistant	1

Provide basic patient care under direction of nursing staff. Perform duties, such as feed, bathe, dress, groom, or move patients, or change linens. Turn and re-position bedridden patients, alone or with assistance, to prevent bedsores. Answer patients' call signals. Feed patients who are unable to feed themselves. Observe patients' conditions, measuring and recording food and liquid intake and output and vital signs, and report changes to professional staff. Provide patient care by supplying and emptying bed pans, applying dressings and supervising exercise routines. Provide patients with help walking, exercising, and moving in and out of bed. Bathe, groom, shave, dress, and/or drape patients to prepare them for surgery, treatment, or examination. Collect specimens such as urine, feces, or sputum. Prepare, serve, and collect food trays. Clean rooms and change linens. Transport patients to treatment units, using a wheelchair or stretcher. Deliver messages, documents and specimens. Answer phones and direct visitors. Administer medications and treatments, such as catheterizations, suppositories, irrigations, enemas, massages, and douches, as directed by a physician or nurse. Restrain patients if necessary. Maintain inventory by storing, preparing, sterilizing, and issuing supplies such as dressing packs and treatment trays. Explain medical instructions to patients and family members. Perform clerical duties such as processing documents and scheduling appointments. Work as part of a medical team that examines and treats clinic outpatients. Set up equipment such as oxygen tents, portable X-ray machines, and overhead irrigation bottles. **SKILLS**—Social Perceptiveness; Time Management; Instructing; Service Orientation; Monitoring; Persuasion; Operation Monitoring; Coordination.

GOE—**Interest Area:** 14. Medical and Health Services. **Work Group:** 14.07 Patient Care and Assistance. **Other Apprenticeable Jobs in This Work Group:** Licensed Practical and Licensed Vocational Nurses. **PERSONALITY TYPE:** Social. Social occupations frequently involve working with, communicating with, and teaching people. These occupations often involve helping or providing service to others.

RELATED KNOWLEDGE/COURSES—**Customer and Personal Service:** Knowledge of principles and processes for providing customer and personal services. This includes customer needs assessment, meeting quality standards for services, and evaluation of customer satisfaction. **Psychology:** Knowledge of human behavior and performance; individual differences in ability, personality, and interests; learning and motivation; psychological research methods; and the assessment and treatment of behavioral and affective disorders. **Medicine and Dentistry:** Knowledge of the information and techniques needed to diagnose and treat human injuries, diseases, and deformities. This includes

symptoms, treatment alternatives, drug properties and interactions, and preventive health-care measures. **Education and Training:** Knowledge of principles and methods for curriculum and training design, teaching and instruction for individuals and groups, and the measurement of training effects. **English Language:** Knowledge of the structure and content of the English language, including the meaning and spelling of words, rules of composition, and grammar. **Foreign Language:** Knowledge of the structure and content of a foreign (non-English) language, including the meaning and spelling of words, rules of composition and grammar, and pronunciation.

WORK ENVIRONMENT—Physical proximity; walking and running; sounds, noise levels are distracting or uncomfortable; disease or infections; contaminants.

Office Machine and Cash Register Servicers

- Growth: 15.1%
- Annual Job Openings: 19,000
- Annual Earnings: $33,780
- Percentage of Women: 13.5%

Related Apprenticeship	Years
Assembly Technician	2
Cash-Register Servicer	3
Dictating-Transcribing-Machine Servicer	3
Office-Machine Servicer	3

Repair and service office machines, such as adding, accounting, calculating, duplicating, and typewriting machines. Includes the repair of manual, electrical, and electronic office machines. Tests machine to locate cause of electrical problems, using testing devices, such as voltmeter, ohmmeter, and circuit test equipment. Disassembles machine and examines parts, such as wires, gears, and bearings for wear and defects, using hand tools, power tools, and measuring devices. Operates machine, such as typewriter, cash-register, or adding machine to test functioning of parts and mechanisms. Assembles and installs machine according to specifications, using hand tools, power tools, and measuring devices. Cleans and oils mechanical parts to maintain machine. Reads specifications, such as blueprints, charts, and schematics to determine machine settings and adjustments. Repairs, adjusts, or replaces electrical and mechanical components and parts, using hand tools, power tools, and soldering or welding equipment. Instructs operators and servicers in operation, maintenance, and repair of machine. **SKILLS**—Installation; Equipment Maintenance; Instructing; Repairing; Technology Design; Troubleshooting; Quality Control Analysis; Science.

GOE—Interest Area: 05. Mechanics, Installers, and Repairers. **Work Group:** 05.02 Electrical and Electronic Systems. **Other Apprenticeable Jobs in This Work Group:** Avionics Technicians; Battery Repairers; Central Office and PBX Installers and Repairers; Communication Equipment Mechanics, Installers, and Repairers; Data Processing Equipment Repairers; Electric Home Appliance and Power Tool Repairers; Electric Meter Installers and Repairers; Electric Motor and Switch Assemblers and Repairers; Electrical and Electronics Installers and Repairers, Transportation Equipment; Electrical and Electronics Repairers, Commercial and Industrial Equipment; Electrical and Electronics Repairers, Powerhouse, Substation, and Relay; Electrical Power-Line Installers and Repairers; Electronic Equipment Installers and Repairers, Motor Vehicles; Electronic Home Entertainment Equipment Installers and Repairers; Elevator Installers and Repairers; Installation, Maintenance, and Repair Workers, All Other; Radio Mechanics; Signal and Track Switch Repairers; Station Installers and Repairers, Telephone; Telecommunications Line Installers and Repairers; Transformer Repairers. **PERSONALITY TYPE:** Realistic. Realistic occupations frequently involve work activities that include practical, hands-on problems and solutions. They often deal with plants, animals, and real-world materials like wood, tools, and machinery. Many of the occupations require working outside and do not involve a lot of paperwork or working closely with others.

RELATED KNOWLEDGE/COURSES— Computers and Electronics: Knowledge of circuit boards, processors, chips, electronic equipment, and computer hardware and software, including applications and programming. **Mechanical Devices:** Knowledge of machines and tools, including their designs, uses, repair, and maintenance. **Engineering and Technology:** Knowledge of the practical application of engineering science and technology. This includes applying principles, techniques, procedures, and equipment to the design and production of various goods and services. **Design:** Knowledge of design techniques, tools, and principles involved in production of precision technical plans, blueprints, drawings, and models. **Education and Training:** Knowledge of principles and methods for curriculum and training design, teaching and instruction for individuals and groups, and the measurement of training effects. **Telecommunications:** Knowledge of transmission, broadcasting, switching, control, and operation of telecommunications systems.

WORK ENVIRONMENT—Hazardous equipment; using hands on objects, tools, or controls; indoors; spend time bending or twisting the body; spend time making repetitive motions.

Offset Lithographic Press Setters and Set-Up Operators

- Growth: 4.6%
- Annual Job Openings: 30,000
- Annual Earnings: $29,340
- Percentage of Women: 17.8%

Related Apprenticeship	*Years*
Offset-Press Operator I	4

Set up or set up and operate offset printing press, either sheet or web fed, to print single and multicolor copy from lithographic plates. Examine job order to determine press operating time, quantity to be printed, and stock specifications. Examines job order to determine quantity to be printed, stock specifications, colors, and special printing instructions. Installs and locks plate into position, using hand tools, to achieve pressure required for printing. Measures plate thickness and inserts packing sheets on plate cylinder to build up plate to printing height. Fills ink and dampening solution fountains, and adjusts controls to regulate flow of ink and dampening solution to plate cylinder. Removes and cleans plate and cylinders. Loads paper into feeder or installs rolls of paper, adjusts feeder and delivery mechanisms, and unloads printed material from delivery mechanism. Applies packing sheets to blanket cylinder to build up blanket thickness to diameter of plate cylinder. Washes plate to remove protective gum coating. Measures paper thickness and adjusts space between blanket and impression cylinders according to thickness of paper stock. Makes adjustments to press throughout production run to maintain specific registration and color density. Starts press and examines printed copy for ink density, position on paper, and registration. **SKILLS**—Operation Monitoring; Operation and Control; Installation; Equipment Maintenance; Management of Personnel Resources; Equipment Selection; Technology Design; Troubleshooting.

GOE—Interest Area: 08. Industrial Production. **Work Group:** 08.03 Production Work. **Other Apprenticeable Jobs in This Work Group:** Bakers, Manufacturing; Bindery Machine Operators and Tenders; Chemical Equipment Controllers and Operators; Coating, Painting, and Spraying Machine Operators and Tenders; Cooling and Freezing Equipment Operators and Tenders; Crushing, Grinding, and Polishing Machine Setters, Operators, and Tenders; Cutters and Trimmers, Hand; Cutting and Slicing Machine Operators and Tenders; Design Printing Machine Setters and Set-Up Operators; Electrolytic Plating and Coating Machine Setters and Set-Up Operators, Metal and Plastic; Electrotypers and Stereotypers; Embossing Machine Set-Up Operators; Engraver Set-Up Operators; Extruding, Forming, Pressing, and Compacting Machine Operators and Tenders; Fabric and Apparel Pattern-makers; Film Laboratory Technicians; Fitters, Structural Metal—Precision; Food Batchmakers; Furnace, Kiln, Oven, Drier, and Kettle Operators and Tenders; Hand Compositors and Typesetters; Job Printers; Letterpress Setters and Set-Up Operators; Metal Fabricators, Structural Metal Products; Metal-Refining Furnace Operators and Tenders; Mixing and Blending Machine Setters, Operators, and Tenders; Mold Makers, Hand; Molding and Casting Workers; Numerical Control Machine Tool Operators and Tenders, Metal and Plastic; Painting, Coating, and Decorating Workers; Photographic Processing Machine Operators; Photographic Reproduction Technicians; Photographic Retouchers and Restorers; Plate Finishers; Platemakers; Precision Printing Workers; Printing Press Machine Operators and Tenders; Production Workers, All Other; Sawing Machine Operators and Tenders; Sawing Machine Setters and Set-Up Operators; Scanner Operators; Separating, Filtering, Clarifying, Precipitating, and Still Machine Setters, Operators, and Tenders; Sewing Machine Operators, Garment; Slaughterers and Meat Packers; Stone Sawyers; Strippers; Team Assemblers; Welder-Fitters; Welders and Cutters; Woodworking Machine Operators and Tenders, Except Sawing. **PERSONALITY TYPE:** Realistic. Realistic occupations frequently involve work activities that include practical, hands-on problems and solutions. They often deal with plants, animals, and real-world materials like wood, tools, and machinery. Many of the occupations require working outside and do not involve a lot of paperwork or working closely with others.

RELATED KNOWLEDGE/COURSES—Production and Processing: Knowledge of raw materials, production processes, quality control, costs, and other techniques for maximizing the effective manufacture and distribution of goods. **Mechanical Devices:** Knowledge of machines and tools, including their designs, uses, repair, and maintenance. **Communications and Media:** Knowledge of media production, communication, and dissemination techniques and methods. This includes alternative ways to inform and entertain via written, oral, and visual media.

WORK ENVIRONMENT—Standing; indoors; sounds, noise levels are distracting or uncomfortable; hazardous equipment; spend time making repetitive motions.

Operating Engineers

- Growth: 10.4%
- Annual Job Openings: 45,000
- Annual Earnings: $35,030
- Percentage of Women: 2.2%

Related Apprenticeship	Years
Operating Engineer	3

(This is one of the most popular apprenticeable jobs.)

Operate several types of power construction equipment, such as compressors, pumps, hoists, derricks, cranes, shovels, tractors, scrapers, or motor graders to excavate, move and grade earth, erect structures, or pour concrete or other hard surface pavement. May repair and maintain equipment in addition to other duties. Adjusts handwheels and depresses pedals to drive machines and control attachments, such as blades, buckets, scrapers, and swing booms. Turns valves to control air and water output of compressors and pumps. Repairs and maintains equipment. **SKILLS—** Repairing; Equipment Maintenance; Operation and Control; Operation Monitoring; Troubleshooting; Installation.

GOE—Interest Area: 06. Construction, Mining, and Drilling. **Work Group:** 06.02 Construction. **Other Apprenticeable Jobs in This Work Group:** Boat Builders and Shipwrights; Boilermakers; Brickmasons and Blockmasons; Carpet Installers; Ceiling Tile Installers; Cement Masons and Concrete Finishers; Construction and Related Workers, All Other; Construction Carpenters; Drywall Installers; Electricians; Fence Erectors; Floor Layers, Except Carpet, Wood, and Hard Tiles; Glaziers; Grader, Bulldozer, and Scraper Operators; Insulation Workers, Floor, Ceiling, and Wall; Insulation Workers, Mechanical; Painters, Construction and Maintenance; Paperhangers; Paving, Surfacing, and Tamping Equipment Operators; Pipe Fitters; Plasterers and Stucco Masons; Plumbers; Reinforcing Iron and Rebar Workers; Riggers; Roofers; Rough Carpenters; Sheet Metal Workers; Ship Carpenters and Joiners; Stone Cutters and Carvers; Stonemasons; Structural Iron and Steel Workers; Tapers; Terrazzo Workers and Finishers; Tile and Marble Setters. **PERSONALITY TYPE:** Realistic. Realistic occupations frequently involve work activities that include practical, hands-on problems and solutions. They often deal with plants, animals, and real-world materials like wood, tools, and machinery. Many of the occupations require working outside and do not involve a lot of paperwork or working closely with others.

RELATED KNOWLEDGE/COURSES— Mechanical Devices: Knowledge of machines and tools, including their designs, uses, repair, and maintenance. **Building and Construction:** Knowledge of the materials, methods, and tools involved in the construction or repair of houses, buildings, or other structures, such as highways and roads. **Sales and Marketing:** Knowledge of principles and methods for showing, promoting, and selling products or services. This includes marketing strategy and tactics, product demonstration, sales techniques, and sales control systems. **Engineering and Technology:** Knowledge of the practical application of engineering science and technology. This includes applying principles, techniques, procedures, and equipment to the design and production of various goods and services. **Physics:** Knowledge and prediction of physical principles and laws and their interrelationships and applications to understanding fluid, material, and atmospheric dynamics and mechanical, electrical, atomic, and subatomic structures and processes. **Public Safety and Security:** Knowledge of relevant equipment, policies, procedures, and strategies to promote effective local, state, or national security operations for the protection of people, data, property, and institutions.

WORK ENVIRONMENT—Hazardous equipment; exposed to whole-body vibration; outdoors; common protective or safety equipment; very hot or cold.

FURTHER INFORMATION—Contact a local joint union-management apprenticeship committee or the nearest office of your state employment service or apprenticeship agency (see Appendix C). To identify the local union office, contact International Union of Operating Engineers, 1125 17th St. NW, Washington, DC 20036. Internet: http://www.iuoe.org.

Opticians, Dispensing

- Growth: 18.2%
- Annual Job Openings: 10,000
- Annual Earnings: $26,350
- Percentage of Women: 65.6%

Related Apprenticeship	Years
Optician, Dispensing	2

Design, measure, fit, and adapt lenses and frames for client according to written optical prescription or specification. Assist client with selecting frames. Measure customer for size of eyeglasses and coordinate frames with facial and eye measurements and optical prescription. Prepare work order for optical laboratory containing instructions for grinding and mounting lenses in frames. Verify exactness of finished lens spectacles. Adjust frame and lens position to fit client. May shape or reshape frames. Measure clients' bridge and eye size, temple length, vertex distance, pupillary distance, and optical centers of eyes, using measuring devices. Prepare work orders and instructions for grinding lenses and fabricating eyeglasses. Verify that finished lenses are ground to specifications. Determine clients' current lens prescriptions, when necessary, using lensometers or lens analyzers and clients' eyeglasses. Recommend specific lenses, lens coatings, and frames to suit client needs. Assist clients in selecting frames according to style and color and ensure that frames are coordinated with facial and eye measurements and optical prescriptions. Heat, shape, or bend plastic or metal frames in order to adjust eyeglasses to fit clients, using pliers and hands. Evaluate prescriptions in conjunction with clients' vocational and avocational visual requirements. Repair damaged frames. Fabricate lenses to meet prescription specifications. Instruct clients in how to wear and care for eyeglasses. Grind lens edges or apply coatings to lenses. Arrange and maintain displays of optical merchandise. Assemble eyeglasses by cutting and edging lenses and then fitting the lenses into frames. Fit contact lenses by measuring the shape and size of the eye, using various measuring instruments. Maintain records of customer prescriptions, work orders, and payments. Obtain a customer's previous record or verify a prescription with the examining optometrist or ophthalmologist. Perform administrative duties such as tracking inventory and sales, submitting patient insurance information, and performing simple bookkeeping. Sell goods such as contact lenses, spectacles, sunglasses, and other goods related to eyes in general. Show customers how to insert, remove, and care for their contact lenses. Supervise the training of student opticians. **SKILLS**—Management of Financial Resources; Technology Design; Science; Management of Personnel Resources; Service Orientation; Time Management; Management of Material Resources; Critical Thinking.

GOE—Interest Area: 14. Medical and Health Services. **Work Group:** 14.04 Health Specialties. **Other Apprenticeable Jobs in This Work Group:** No other apprenticeable jobs in this group. **PERSONALITY TYPE:** Enterprising. Enterprising occupations frequently involve starting up and carrying out projects. These occupations can involve leading people and making many decisions. They sometimes require risk taking and often deal with business.

RELATED KNOWLEDGE/COURSES— **Administration and Management:** Knowledge of business and management principles involved in strategic planning, resource allocation, human resources modeling, leadership technique, production methods, and coordination of people and resources. **Sales and Marketing:** Knowledge of principles and methods for showing, promoting, and selling products or services. This includes marketing strategy and tactics, product demonstration, sales techniques, and sales control systems. **Customer and Personal Service:** Knowledge of principles and processes for providing customer and personal services. This includes customer needs assessment, meeting quality standards for services, and evaluation of customer satisfaction. **Economics and Accounting:** Knowledge of economic and accounting principles and practices, the financial markets, banking, and the analysis and reporting of financial data. **Personnel and Human Resources:** Knowledge of principles and procedures for personnel recruitment, selection, training, compensation and benefits, labor relations and negotiation, and personnel information systems. **Clerical Practices:** Knowledge of administrative and clerical procedures and systems, such as word processing, managing files and records, stenography and transcription, designing forms, and other office procedures and terminology.

WORK ENVIRONMENT—Sitting; indoors.

Outdoor Power Equipment and Other Small Engine Mechanics

- Growth: 18.9%
- Annual Job Openings: 3,000
- Annual Earnings: $24,820
- Percentage of Women: 1.7%

Related Apprenticeship	Years
Small-Engine Mechanic	2
Power-Saw Mechanic	3
Engine Repairer, Service	4
Gas-Engine Repairer	4

Diagnose, adjust, repair, or overhaul small engines used to power lawn mowers, chain saws, and related equipment. Repairs or replaces defective parts, such as water pump, carburetor, thermostat, gears, solenoid, pistons, valves, and crankshaft, using hand tools. Adjusts points, valves, carburetor, distributor, and spark plug gaps, using feeler gauges. Repairs fractional-horsepower gasoline engines used to power lawn mowers, garden tractors, and similar machines. Positions and bolts engine to engine stand. Grinds, reams, rebores, and retaps parts to obtain specified clearances, using grinders, lathes, taps, reamers, boring machines, and micrometer. Tests and inspects engine to determine malfunctions and locate missing and broken parts, using diagnostic instruments. Repairs and maintains gas internal-combustion engines that power electric generators, compressor, and similar equipment. Reassembles engines and listens to engines in action to detect operational difficulties. Tests and repairs turbo or superchargers. Dismantles engines, using hand tools; examines parts for defects; and cleans parts. Repairs and maintains portable saws powered by internal combustion engines, following manufacturer's repair manuals and using hand tools. Tests and repairs magnetos used in gasoline and diesel engines, using meters, gauges, and hand tools. Records repairs made, time spent, and parts used. **SKILLS—** Repairing; Equipment Maintenance; Troubleshooting; Installation; Quality Control Analysis; Operation Monitoring; Operation and Control; Systems Evaluation.

GOE—Interest Area: 05. Mechanics, Installers, and Repairers. **Work Group:** 05.03 Mechanical Work. **Other Apprenticeable Jobs in This Work Group:** Aircraft Engine Specialists; Airframe-and-Power-Plant Mechanics; Automotive Body and Related Repairers; Automotive Glass Installers and Repairers; Automotive Master Mechanics; Automotive Specialty Technicians; Bus and Truck Mechanics and Diesel Engine Specialists; Camera and Photographic Equipment Repairers; Coin, Vending, and Amusement Machine Servicers and Repairers; Farm Equipment Mechanics; Gas Appliance Repairers; Hand and Portable Power Tool Repairers; Heating and Air Conditioning Mechanics; Helpers—Installation, Maintenance, and Repair Workers; Industrial Machinery Mechanics; Installation, Maintenance, and Repair Workers, All Other; Keyboard Instrument Repairers and Tuners; Locksmiths and Safe Repairers; Maintenance and Repair Workers, General; Maintenance Workers, Machinery; Mechanical Door Repairers; Medical Appliance Technicians; Medical Equipment Repairers; Meter Mechanics; Millwrights; Mobile Heavy Equipment Mechanics, Except Engines; Motorboat Mechanics; Motorcycle Mechanics; Optical Instrument Assemblers; Painters, Transportation Equipment; Rail Car Repairers; Recreational Vehicle Service Technicians; Reed or Wind Instrument Repairers and Tuners; Refrigeration Mechanics; Stringed Instrument Repairers and Tuners; Valve and Regulator Repairers; Watch Repairers. **PERSONALITY TYPE:** Realistic. Realistic occupations frequently involve work activities that include practical, hands-on problems and solutions. They often deal with plants, animals, and real-world materials like wood, tools, and machinery. Many of the occupations require working outside and do not involve a lot of paperwork or working closely with others.

RELATED KNOWLEDGE/COURSES— Mechanical Devices: Knowledge of machines and tools, including their designs, uses, repair, and maintenance. **Engineering and Technology:** Knowledge of the practical application of engineering science and technology. This includes applying principles, techniques, procedures, and equipment to the design and production of various goods and services.

WORK ENVIRONMENT—Spend time kneeling, crouching, stooping, or crawling; hazardous equipment; contaminants; sounds, noise levels are distracting or uncomfortable; minor burns, cuts, bites, or stings.

Painters and Illustrators

- Growth: 16.5%
- Annual Job Openings: 4,000
- Annual Earnings: $35,420
- Percentage of Women: 47.1%

Related Apprenticeship	Years
Painter	1
Illustrator	4

Paint or draw subject material to produce original artwork or illustrations, using watercolors, oils, acrylics, tempera, or other paint mediums. Renders drawings, illustrations, and sketches of buildings, manufactured products, or models, working from sketches, blueprints, memory, or reference materials. Paints scenic backgrounds, murals, and portraiture for motion picture and television production sets, glass artworks, and exhibits. Etches, carves, paints, or draws artwork on material such as stone, glass, canvas, wood, and linoleum. Develops drawings, paintings, diagrams, and models of medical or biological subjects for use in publications, exhibits, consultations, research, and teaching. Studies style, techniques, colors, textures, and materials used by artist to maintain consistency in reconstruction or retouching procedures. Removes painting from frame or paint layer from canvas to restore artwork, following specified technique and equipment. Examines surfaces of paintings and proofs of artwork, using magnifying device, to determine method of restoration or needed corrections. Installs finished stained glass in window or door frame. Assembles, leads, and solders finished glass to fabricate stained glass article. Applies select solvents and cleaning agents to clean surface of painting and remove accretions, discolorations, and deteriorated varnish. Performs tests to determine factors such as age, structure, pigment stability, and probable reaction to various cleaning agents and solvents. Confers with professional personnel or client to discuss objectives of artwork and theme to be portrayed and to develop illustration ideas. Brushes or sprays protective or decorative finish on completed background panels, informational legends, exhibit accessories, or finished painting. Integrates and develops visual elements, such as line, space, mass, color, and perspective, to produce desired effect. **SKILLS**—Operations Analysis; Installation; Management of Material Resources; Active Listening; Quality Control Analysis; Repairing; Equipment Selection; Speaking.

GOE—Interest Area: 01. Arts, Entertainment, and Media. **Work Group:** 01.04 Visual Arts. **Other Apprenticeable Jobs in This Work Group:** Cartoonists; Commercial and Industrial Designers; Exhibit Designers; Fashion Designers; Floral Designers; Graphic Designers; Interior Designers; Merchandise Displayers and Window Trimmers. **PERSONALITY TYPE:** Artistic. Artistic occupations frequently involve working with forms, designs, and patterns. They often require self-expression, and the work can be done without following a clear set of rules.

RELATED KNOWLEDGE/COURSES— Fine Arts: Knowledge of the theory and techniques required to compose, produce, and perform works of music, dance, visual arts, drama, and sculpture. **Design:** Knowledge of design techniques, tools, and principles involved in production of precision technical plans, blueprints, drawings, and models. **Chemistry:** Knowledge of the chemical composition, structure, and properties of substances and of the chemical processes and transformations that they undergo. This includes uses of chemicals, their danger signs, production techniques, and disposal methods. **History and Archeology:** Knowledge of historical events and their causes, indicators, and effects on civilizations and cultures. **Communications and Media:** Knowledge of media production, communication, and dissemination techniques and methods. This includes alternative ways to inform and entertain via written, oral, and visual media. **Engineering and Technology:** Knowledge of the practical application of engineering science and technology. This includes applying principles, techniques, procedures, and equipment to the design and production of various goods and services.

WORK ENVIRONMENT—Spend time making repetitive motions; sitting; indoors; standing; using hands on objects, tools, or controls.

Painters, Construction and Maintenance

- Growth: 11.6%
- Annual Job Openings: 69,000
- Annual Earnings: $29,360
- Percentage of Women: 7.4%

Related Apprenticeship	Years
Painter	1
Pavement Striper	2
Architectural Coatings Finisher	3
Painter, Shipyard	3

(This is one of the most popular apprenticeable jobs.)

Paint walls, equipment, buildings, bridges, and other structural surfaces, using brushes, rollers, and spray guns. May remove old paint to prepare surface prior to painting. May mix colors or oils to obtain desired color or consistency. Covers surfaces with dropcloths or masking tape and paper to protect surface during painting. Burns off old paint, using blowtorch. Removes fixtures, such as pictures and electric switchcovers, from walls prior to painting. Sprays or brushes hot plastics or pitch onto surfaces. Smoothes surfaces, using sandpaper, scrapers, brushes, steel wool, or sanding machine. Paints surfaces, using brushes, spray gun, or rollers. Applies paint to simulate wood grain, marble, brick, or stonework. Cuts stencils and brushes and sprays lettering and decorations on surfaces. Sands surfaces between coats and polishes final coat to specified finish. Bakes finish on painted and enameled articles in baking oven. Washes and treats surfaces with oil, turpentine, mildew remover, or other preparations. Mixes and matches colors of paint, stain, or varnish. Fills cracks, holes, and joints with caulk, putty, plaster, or other filler, using caulking gun or putty knife. Reads work order or receives instructions from supervisor or homeowner. Erects scaffolding or sets up ladders to work above ground level. **SKILLS**—None met the criteria.

GOE—Interest Area: 06. Construction, Mining, and Drilling. **Work Group:** 06.02 Construction. **Other Apprenticeable Jobs in This Work Group:** Boat Builders and Shipwrights; Boilermakers; Brickmasons and Blockmasons; Carpet Installers; Ceiling Tile Installers; Cement Masons and Concrete Finishers; Construction and Related Workers, All Other; Construction Carpenters; Drywall Installers; Electricians; Fence Erectors; Floor Layers, Except Carpet, Wood, and Hard Tiles; Glaziers; Grader, Bulldozer, and Scraper Operators; Insulation Workers, Floor, Ceiling, and Wall; Insulation Workers, Mechanical; Operating Engineers; Paperhangers; Paving, Surfacing, and Tamping Equipment Operators; Pipe Fitters; Plasterers and Stucco Masons; Plumbers; Reinforcing Iron and Rebar Workers; Riggers; Roofers; Rough Carpenters; Sheet Metal Workers; Ship Carpenters and Joiners; Stone Cutters and Carvers; Stonemasons; Structural Iron and Steel Workers; Tapers; Terrazzo Workers and Finishers; Tile and Marble Setters. **PERSONALITY TYPE:** Realistic. Realistic occupations frequently involve work activities that include practical, hands-on problems and solutions. They often deal with plants, animals, and real-world materials like wood, tools, and machinery. Many of the occupations require working outside and do not involve a lot of paperwork or working closely with others.

RELATED KNOWLEDGE/COURSES—Building and Construction: Knowledge of the materials, methods, and tools involved in the construction or repair of houses, buildings, or other structures, such as highways and roads. **Chemistry:** Knowledge of the chemical composition, structure, and properties of substances and of the chemical processes and transformations that they undergo. This includes uses of chemicals, their danger signs, production techniques, and disposal methods.

WORK ENVIRONMENT—High places; climbing ladders, scaffolds, or poles; spend time making repetitive motions; standing; contaminants.

FURTHER INFORMATION—Contact a local joint union-management apprenticeship committee or the nearest office of your state employment service or apprenticeship agency (see Appendix C). To identify the local union office, contact International Union of Painters and Allied Trades, 1750 New York Ave. NW, Washington, DC 20006. Internet: http://www.iupat.org.

Painters, Transportation Equipment

- Growth: 17.5%
- Annual Job Openings: 9,000
- Annual Earnings: $34,100
- Percentage of Women: 16.8%

Related Apprenticeship	Years
Painter, Transportation Equipment	3

Operate or tend painting machines to paint surfaces of transportation equipment, such as automobiles, buses, trucks, trains, boats, and

airplanes. Adjust controls on infrared ovens, heat lamps, portable ventilators, and exhaust units in order to speed the drying of vehicles between coats. Allow the sprayed product to dry and then touch up any spots that may have been missed. Apply designs, lettering, or other identifying or decorative items to finished products, using paint brushes or paint sprayers. Apply primer over any repairs made to vehicle surfaces. Apply rust-resistant undercoats and caulk and seal seams. Buff and wax the finished paintwork. Fill small dents and scratches with body fillers and smooth surfaces in order to prepare vehicles for painting. Lay out logos, symbols, or designs on painted surfaces according to blueprint specifications, using measuring instruments, stencils, and patterns. Mix paints to match color specifications or vehicles' original colors and then stir and thin the paints, using spatulas or power mixing equipment. Monitor painting operations in order to identify flaws such as blisters and streaks so that their causes can be corrected. Operate lifting and moving devices in order to move equipment or materials so that areas to be painted are accessible. Paint by hand areas that cannot be reached with a spray gun or those that need retouching, using brushes. Pour paint into spray guns and adjust nozzles and paint mixes in order to get the proper paint flow and coating thickness. Remove accessories from vehicles, such as chrome or mirrors, and mask other surfaces with tape or paper in order to protect them from paint. Remove grease, dirt, paint, and rust from vehicle surfaces in preparation for paint application, using abrasives, solvents, brushes, blowtorches, washing tanks, or sandblasters. Sand the final finish and apply sealer once a vehicle has dried properly. Sand vehicle surfaces between coats of paint and/or primer in order to remove flaws and enhance adhesion for subsequent coats. Select paint according to company requirements and match colors of paint, following specified color charts. Select the correct spray gun system for the material being applied. Set up portable equipment such as ventilators, exhaust units, ladders, and scaffolding. **SKILLS**—Operation and Control; Equipment Maintenance.

GOE—Interest Area: 05. Mechanics, Installers, and Repairers. **Work Group:** 05.03 Mechanical Work. **Other Apprenticeable Jobs in This Work Group:** Aircraft Engine Specialists; Airframe-and-Power-Plant Mechanics; Automotive Body and Related Repairers; Automotive Glass Installers and Repairers; Automotive Master Mechanics; Automotive Specialty Technicians; Bus and Truck Mechanics and Diesel Engine Specialists; Camera and Photographic Equipment Repairers; Coin, Vending, and Amusement Machine Servicers and Repairers; Farm Equipment Mechanics; Gas Appliance Repairers; Hand and Portable Power Tool Repairers; Heating and Air Conditioning Mechanics; Helpers—Installation, Maintenance, and Repair Workers; Industrial Machinery Mechanics; Installation, Maintenance, and Repair Workers, All Other; Keyboard Instrument Repairers and Tuners; Locksmiths and Safe Repairers; Maintenance and Repair Workers, General; Maintenance Workers, Machinery; Mechanical Door Repairers; Medical Appliance Technicians; Medical Equipment Repairers; Meter Mechanics; Millwrights; Mobile Heavy Equipment Mechanics, Except Engines; Motorboat Mechanics; Motorcycle Mechanics; Optical Instrument Assemblers; Outdoor Power Equipment and Other Small Engine Mechanics; Rail Car Repairers; Recreational Vehicle Service Technicians; Reed or Wind Instrument Repairers and Tuners; Refrigeration Mechanics; Stringed Instrument Repairers and Tuners; Valve and Regulator Repairers; Watch Repairers. **PERSONALITY TYPE:** Realistic. Realistic occupations frequently involve work activities that include practical, hands-on problems and solutions. They often deal with plants, animals, and real-world materials like wood, tools, and machinery. Many of the occupations require working outside and do not involve a lot of paperwork or working closely with others.

RELATED KNOWLEDGE/COURSES— **Design:** Knowledge of design techniques, tools, and principles involved in production of precision technical plans, blueprints, drawings, and models. **Mechanical Devices:** Knowledge of machines and tools, including their designs, uses, repair, and maintenance. **Fine Arts:** Knowledge of the theory and techniques required to compose, produce, and perform works of music, dance, visual arts, drama, and sculpture. **Chemistry:** Knowledge of the chemical composition, structure, and properties of substances and of the chemical processes and transformations that they undergo. This includes uses of chemicals, their danger signs, production techniques, and disposal methods.

WORK ENVIRONMENT—Spend time making repetitive motions; climbing ladders, scaffolds, or poles; spend time bending or twisting the body; high places; contaminants.

Painting, Coating, and Decorating Workers

- Growth: 17.6%
- Annual Job Openings: 6,000
- Annual Earnings: $21,650
- Percentage of Women: 16.8%

Related Apprenticeship	Years
Screen Printer	2
Liner (Pottery and Porcelain)	3
Painter, Hand (Any Industry)	3
Decorator (Glass Manufacturing; Glass Products)	4

Paint, coat, or decorate articles such as furniture, glass, plateware, pottery, jewelry, cakes, toys, books, or leather. Cuts out sections in surface of material to be inlaid with decorative pieces, using pattern and knife or scissors. Places coated workpiece in oven or dryer for specified time to dry or harden finish. Melts or heats coating material to specified temperature. Selects and mixes ingredients to prepare coating substance according to specifications, using paddle or mechanical mixer. Cleans and maintains tools and equipment, using solvent, brushes, and rags. Applies coating, such as paint, ink, or lacquer, to protect or decorate workpiece surface, using spray gun, pen, or brush. Immerses workpiece into coating material for specified time. Positions and glues decorative pieces in cutout section, following pattern. Reads job order and inspects workpiece to determine work procedure and materials required. Conceals blemishes in workpiece, such as nicks and dents, using filler, such as putty. Rinses coated workpiece to remove excess coating material or to facilitate setting of finish coat on workpiece. Drains or wipes workpieces to remove excess coating material or to facilitate setting of finish coat on workpiece. Examines finished surface of workpiece to verify conformance to specifications and retouches defective areas of surface. Cleans surface of workpiece in preparation for coating, using cleaning fluid, solvent, brushes, scraper, steam, sandpaper, or cloth. **SKILLS—** None met the criteria.

GOE—Interest Area: 08. Industrial Production. **Work Group:** 08.03 Production Work. **Other Apprenticeable Jobs in This Work Group:** Bakers, Manufacturing; Bindery Machine Operators and Tenders; Chemical Equipment Controllers and Operators; Coating, Painting, and Spraying Machine Operators and Tenders; Cooling and Freezing Equipment Operators and Tenders; Crushing, Grinding, and Polishing Machine Setters, Operators, and Tenders; Cutters and Trimmers, Hand; Cutting and Slicing Machine Operators and Tenders; Design Printing Machine Setters and Set-Up Operators; Electrolytic Plating and Coating Machine Setters and Set-Up Operators, Metal and Plastic; Electrotypers and Stereotypers; Embossing Machine Set-Up Operators; Engraver Set-Up Operators; Extruding, Forming, Pressing, and Compacting Machine Operators and Tenders; Fabric and Apparel Patternmakers; Film Laboratory Technicians; Fitters, Structural Metal—Precision; Food Batchmakers; Furnace, Kiln, Oven, Drier, and Kettle Operators and Tenders; Hand Compositors and Typesetters; Job Printers; Letterpress Setters and Set-Up Operators; Metal Fabricators, Structural Metal Products; Metal-Refining Furnace Operators and Tenders; Mixing and Blending Machine Setters, Operators, and Tenders; Mold Makers, Hand; Molding and Casting Workers; Numerical Control Machine Tool Operators and Tenders, Metal and Plastic; Offset Lithographic Press Setters and Set-Up Operators; Photographic Processing Machine Operators; Photographic Reproduction Technicians; Photographic Retouchers and Restorers; Plate Finishers; Platemakers; Precision Printing Workers; Printing Press Machine Operators and Tenders; Production Workers, All Other; Sawing Machine Operators and Tenders; Sawing Machine Setters and Set-Up Operators; Scanner Operators; Separating, Filtering, Clarifying, Precipitating, and Still Machine Setters, Operators, and Tenders; Sewing Machine Operators, Garment; Slaughterers and Meat Packers; Stone Sawyers; Strippers; Team Assemblers; Welder-Fitters; Welders and Cutters; Woodworking Machine Operators and Tenders, Except Sawing. **PERSONALITY TYPE:** Realistic. Realistic occupations frequently involve work activities that include practical, hands-on problems and solutions. They often deal with plants, animals, and real-world materials like wood, tools, and machinery. Many of the occupations require working outside and do not involve a lot of paperwork or working closely with others.

RELATED KNOWLEDGE/COURSES— Production and Processing: Knowledge of raw materials, production processes, quality control, costs, and other techniques for maximizing the effective manufacture and distribution of goods. **Fine Arts:** Knowledge of the theory and techniques required to compose, produce, and perform works of music, dance, visual arts, drama, and sculpture. **Building and Construction:** Knowledge of the materials, methods, and tools involved in the construction or repair of houses, buildings, or other structures, such as highways and roads.

WORK ENVIRONMENT—Common protective or safety equipment; using hands on objects, tools, or controls; contaminants; indoors; spend time making repetitive motions.

Paper Goods Machine Setters, Operators, and Tenders

- Growth: −2.8%
- Annual Job Openings: 16,000
- Annual Earnings: $28,920
- Percentage of Women: 27.3%

Related Apprenticeship	Years
Envelope-Folding-Machine Adjuster	3
Machine Set-Up Operator, Paper Goods	4

Set up, operate, or tend paper goods machines that perform a variety of functions, such as converting, sawing, corrugating, banding, wrapping, boxing, stitching, forming, or sealing paper or paperboard sheets into products. Adjust guide assemblies, forming bars, and folding mechanisms according to specifications, using hand tools. Cut products to specified dimensions, using hand or power cutters. Examine completed work to detect defects and verify conformance to work orders; adjust machinery as necessary to correct production problems. Fill glue and paraffin reservoirs and position rollers to dispense glue onto paperboard. Install attachments to machines for gluing, folding, printing, or cutting. Load automatic stapling mechanisms. Measure, space, and set saw blades, cutters, and perforators, according to product specifications. Monitor finished cartons as they drop from forming machines into rotating hoppers and then into gravity feed chutes in order to prevent jamming. Observe operation of various machines to detect and correct machine malfunctions such as improper forming, glue flow, or pasteboard tension. Place rolls of paper or cardboard on machine feedtracks and thread paper through gluing, coating, and slitting rollers. Remove finished cores and stack or place them on conveyors for transfer to other work areas. Start machines and move controls to regulate tension on pressure rolls, to synchronize speed of machine components, and to adjust temperatures of glue or paraffin. Disassemble machines to maintain, repair, or replace broken or worn parts, using hand or power tools. Lift tote boxes of finished cartons and dump cartons into feed hoppers. Stamp products with information such as dates, using hand stamps or automatic stamping devices. **SKILLS**—Operation Monitoring; Equipment Maintenance; Installation; Operation and Control; Repairing; Troubleshooting; Quality Control Analysis; Technology Design.

GOE—Interest Area: 08. Industrial Production. **Work Group:** 08.02 Production Technology. **Other Apprenticeable Jobs in This Work Group:** Aircraft Structure Assemblers, Precision; Aircraft Systems Assemblers, Precision; Bench Workers, Jewelry; Bindery Machine Setters and Set-Up Operators; Bookbinders; Buffing and Polishing Set-Up Operators; Coating, Painting, and Spraying Machine Setters and Set-Up Operators; Combination Machine Tool Setters and Set-Up Operators, Metal and Plastic; Dental Laboratory Technicians; Electrical and Electronic Equipment Assemblers; Electrical and Electronic Inspectors and Testers; Electromechanical Equipment Assemblers;

P

Engine and Other Machine Assemblers; Extruding and Drawing Machine Setters, Operators, and Tenders, Metal and Plastic; Extruding, Forming, Pressing, and Compacting Machine Setters and Set-Up Operators; Forging Machine Setters, Operators, and Tenders, Metal and Plastic; Foundry Mold and Coremakers; Gem and Diamond Workers; Grinding, Honing, Lapping, and Deburring Machine Set-Up Operators; Heat Treating, Annealing, and Tempering Machine Operators and Tenders, Metal and Plastic; Jewelers; Lathe and Turning Machine Tool Setters, Operators, and Tenders, Metal and Plastic; Materials Inspectors; Mechanical Inspectors; Metal Molding, Coremaking, and Casting Machine Operators and Tenders; Milling and Planing Machine Setters, Operators, and Tenders, Metal and Plastic; Model and Mold Makers, Jewelry; Motor Vehicle Inspectors; Pewter Casters and Finishers; Plastic Molding and Casting Machine Setters and Set-Up Operators; Precision Devices Inspectors and Testers; Precision Lens Grinders and Polishers; Precision Mold and Pattern Casters, Except Nonferrous Metals; Precision Pattern and Die Casters, Nonferrous Metals; Press and Press Brake Machine Setters and Set-Up Operators, Metal and Plastic; Production Inspectors, Testers, Graders, Sorters, Samplers, Weighers; Production Workers, All Other; Rolling Machine Setters, Operators, and Tenders, Metal and Plastic; Silversmiths; Textile Knitting and Weaving Machine Setters, Operators, and Tenders; Textile Winding, Twisting, and Drawing Out Machine Setters, Operators, and Tenders; Welding Machine Setters and Set-Up Operators; Woodworking Machine Setters and Set-Up Operators, Except Sawing. **PERSONALITY TYPE:** Realistic. Realistic occupations frequently involve work activities that include practical, hands-on problems and solu-

tions. They often deal with plants, animals, and real-world materials like wood, tools, and machinery. Many of the occupations require working outside and do not involve a lot of paperwork or working closely with others.

RELATED KNOWLEDGE/COURSES— Production and Processing: Knowledge of raw materials, production processes, quality control, costs, and other techniques for maximizing the effective manufacture and distribution of goods. **Mechanical Devices:** Knowledge of machines and tools, including their designs, uses, repair, and maintenance.

WORK ENVIRONMENT—Hazardous equipment; sounds, noise levels are distracting or uncomfortable; common protective or safety equipment; indoors; standing.

Paperhangers

- Growth: 5.9%
- Annual Job Openings: 3,000
- Annual Earnings: $32,040
- Percentage of Women: 29.7%

Related Apprenticeship	Years
Paperhanger	2

Cover interior walls and ceilings of rooms with decorative wallpaper or fabric or attach advertising posters on surfaces such as walls and billboards. Duties include removing old materials from surface to be papered. Applies thinned glue to waterproof porous surfaces,

using brush, roller, or pasting machine. Measures and cuts strips from roll of wallpaper or fabric, using shears or razor. Trims rough edges from strips, using straightedge and trimming knife. Trims excess material at ceiling or baseboard, using knife. Smoothes strips or poster sections with brush or roller to remove wrinkles and bubbles and to smooth joints. Aligns and places strips or poster sections of billboard on surface to match adjacent edges. Mixes paste, using paste-powder and water, and brushes paste onto surface. Marks vertical guideline on wall to align first strip, using plumb bob and chalkline. Applies acetic acid to damp plaster to prevent lime from bleeding through paper. Staples or tacks advertising posters onto fences, walls, or poles. Measures walls and ceiling to compute number and length of strips required to cover surface. Fills holes and cracks with plaster, using trowel. Removes paint, varnish, and grease from surfaces, using paint remover and water soda solution. Erects and works from scaffold. Removes old paper, using water, steam machine, or chemical remover and scraper. Smoothes rough spots on walls and ceilings, using sandpaper. **SKILLS**—Mathematics.

GOE—**Interest Area:** 06. Construction, Mining, and Drilling. **Work Group:** 06.02 Construction. **Other Apprenticeable Jobs in This Work Group:** Boat Builders and Shipwrights; Boilermakers; Brickmasons and Blockmasons; Carpet Installers; Ceiling Tile Installers; Cement Masons and Concrete Finishers; Construction and Related Workers, All Other; Construction Carpenters; Drywall Installers; Electricians; Fence Erectors; Floor Layers, Except Carpet, Wood, and Hard Tiles; Glaziers; Grader, Bulldozer, and Scraper Operators; Insulation Workers, Floor, Ceiling, and Wall; Insulation Workers, Mechanical; Operating Engineers; Painters, Construction and Maintenance;

Paving, Surfacing, and Tamping Equipment Operators; Pipe Fitters; Plasterers and Stucco Masons; Plumbers; Reinforcing Iron and Rebar Workers; Riggers; Roofers; Rough Carpenters; Sheet Metal Workers; Ship Carpenters and Joiners; Stone Cutters and Carvers; Stonemasons; Structural Iron and Steel Workers; Tapers; Terrazzo Workers and Finishers; Tile and Marble Setters. **PERSONALITY TYPE:** Realistic. Realistic occupations frequently involve work activities that include practical, hands-on problems and solutions. They often deal with plants, animals, and real-world materials like wood, tools, and machinery. Many of the occupations require working outside and do not involve a lot of paperwork or working closely with others.

RELATED KNOWLEDGE/COURSES— **Building and Construction:** Knowledge of the materials, methods, and tools involved in the construction or repair of houses, buildings, or other structures, such as highways and roads. **Design:** Knowledge of design techniques, tools, and principles involved in production of precision technical plans, blueprints, drawings, and models.

WORK ENVIRONMENT—Climbing ladders, scaffolds, or poles; standing; spend time making repetitive motions; high places; keeping or regaining balance.

Parts Salespersons

- Growth: –2.0%
- Annual Job Openings: 37,000
- Annual Earnings: $24,510
- Percentage of Women: 10.4%

Related Apprenticeship	*Years*
Salesperson, Parts	2

Sell spare and replacement parts and equipment in repair shop or parts store. Read catalogs, microfiche viewers, or computer displays in order to determine replacement part stock numbers and prices. Determine replacement parts required, according to inspections of old parts, customer requests, or customers' descriptions of malfunctions. Receive and fill telephone orders for parts. Fill customer orders from stock. Prepare sales slips or sales contracts. Receive payment or obtain credit authorization. Take inventory of stock. Advise customers on substitution or modification of parts when identical replacements are not available. Examine returned parts for defects and exchange defective parts or refund money. Mark and store parts in stockrooms according to prearranged systems. Discuss use and features of various parts, based on knowledge of machines or equipment. Demonstrate equipment to customers and explain functioning of equipment. Place new merchandise on display. Measure parts, using precision measuring instruments, in order to determine whether similar parts may be machined to required sizes. **SKILLS**—Service Orientation; Negotiation; Management of Personnel Resources; Social Perceptiveness; Persuasion; Instructing; Time Management; Management of Financial Resources.

GOE—Interest Area: 10. Sales and Marketing. **Work Group:** 10.03 General Sales. **Other Apprenticeable Jobs in This Work Group:** No other apprenticeable jobs in this group. **PERSONALITY TYPE:** Enterprising. Enterprising occupations frequently involve starting up and carrying out projects. These occupations can involve leading people and making many decisions. They sometimes require risk taking and often deal with business.

RELATED KNOWLEDGE/COURSES— Customer and Personal Service: Knowledge of principles and processes for providing customer and personal services. This includes customer needs assessment, meeting quality standards for services, and evaluation of customer satisfaction. **Sales and Marketing:** Knowledge of principles and methods for showing, promoting, and selling products or services. This includes marketing strategy and tactics, product demonstration, sales techniques, and sales control systems. **Computers and Electronics:** Knowledge of circuit boards, processors, chips, electronic equipment, and computer hardware and software, including applications and programming. **Mechanical Devices:** Knowledge of machines and tools, including their designs, uses, repair, and maintenance. **Production and Processing:** Knowledge of raw materials, production processes, quality control, costs, and other techniques for maximizing the effective manufacture and distribution of goods. **Personnel and Human Resources:** Knowledge of principles and procedures for personnel recruitment, selection, training, compensation and benefits, labor relations and negotiation, and personnel information systems.

WORK ENVIRONMENT—Contaminants; sounds, noise levels are distracting or uncomfortable; physical proximity; very hot or cold; indoors, not environmentally controlled; hazardous conditions.

Paste-Up Workers

- Growth: –11.2%
- Annual Job Openings: 6,000
- Annual Earnings: $31,660
- Percentage of Women: 47.6%

Related Apprenticeship	Years
Paste-Up Artist	3

Arrange and mount typeset material and illustrations into pasteup for printing reproduction, based on artist's or editor's layout. Measures and marks board according to layout to indicate position of artwork, typeset copy, page edges, folds, and colors. Cuts typeset copy and artwork to size, applies adhesive, and aligns artwork and typeset copy on board, following position marks. Compares measurements, using ruler and proportion wheel, to determine proportions needed to make reduced or enlarged photographic prints for pasteup. Operates electronic plotter to draw artwork positions on pasteup. Applies masking film to artwork layout space on overlay to create clear space on negative for subsequent addition of artwork. Makes negatives or prints of artwork, using photographic equipment, to prepare artwork for pasteup. Covers photographs and artwork with tissue or tracing paper for protection. Writes specifications on tracing paper to provide information for other workers. Draws functional and decorative borders around layout, using marking and measuring instruments. Removes excess adhesive from board, using scissors, artist's knife, and drafting instruments. Indicates crop marks and enlargement or reduction measurements on photographs with grease pencil to facilitate processing. Operates phototypesetter to prepare typeset copy for pasteup. Tapes transparent plastic overlay to board and positions and applies copy to plastic. Measures artwork and layout space of artwork on pasteup. **SKILLS**—Operation Monitoring; Operation and Control.

GOE—Interest Area: 01. Arts, Entertainment, and Media. **Work Group:** 01.07 Graphic Arts. **Other Apprenticeable Jobs in This Work Group:** Camera Operators; Desktop Publishers; Dot Etchers; Engravers, Hand; Engravers/ Carvers; Pantograph Engravers; Photoengravers; Precision Etchers and Engravers, Hand or Machine. **PERSONALITY TYPE:** Realistic. Realistic occupations frequently involve work activities that include practical, hands-on problems and solutions. They often deal with plants, animals, and real-world materials like wood, tools, and machinery. Many of the occupations require working outside and do not involve a lot of paperwork or working closely with others.

RELATED KNOWLEDGE/COURSES— Communications and Media: Knowledge of media production, communication, and dissemination techniques and methods. This includes alternative ways to inform and entertain via written, oral, and visual media. **Design:** Knowledge of design techniques, tools, and principles involved in production of precision technical plans, blueprints, drawings, and models. **Clerical Practices:** Knowledge of administrative and clerical procedures and systems, such as word processing, managing files and records, stenography and transcription, designing forms, and other office procedures and terminology. **Fine Arts:** Knowledge of the theory and techniques required to compose, produce, and per-

P

form works of music, dance, visual arts, drama, and sculpture. **Production and Processing:** Knowledge of raw materials, production processes, quality control, costs, and other techniques for maximizing the effective manufacture and distribution of goods. **Computers and Electronics:** Knowledge of circuit boards, processors, chips, electronic equipment, and computer hardware and software, including applications and programming.

WORK ENVIRONMENT—Minor burns, cuts, bites, or stings; indoors; contaminants; sitting; using hands on objects, tools, or controls.

Patternmakers, Wood

- ◎ Growth: 11.8%
- ◎ Annual Job Openings: Fewer than 500
- ◎ Annual Earnings: $29,650
- ◎ Percentage of Women: 11.1%

Related Apprenticeship	Years
Patternmaker, Wood	5

Plan, lay out, and construct wooden unit or sectional patterns used in forming sand molds for castings. Plans, lays out, and draws outline of unit, sectional patterns, or full-scale mock-up of products. Sets up, operates, and adjusts variety of woodworking machines to cut and shape sections, parts, and patterns according to specifications. Constructs wooden models, templates, full scale mock-up, and molds for parts of products. Shellacs, lacquers, or waxes fin-

ished pattern or model. Issues patterns to designated machine operators and maintains pattern record for reference. Marks identifying information, such as colors or codes, on patterns, parts, and templates to indicate assembly method. Reads blueprints, drawing, or written specifications to determine size and shape of pattern and required machine setup. Fits, fastens, and assembles wood parts together to form pattern, model, or section, using glue, nails, dowels, bolts, and screws. Trims, smoothes, and shapes surfaces and planes, shaves, files, scrapes, and sands models to attain specified shapes, using hand tools. **SKILLS**—Operation and Control; Mathematics; Equipment Selection; Installation; Quality Control Analysis.

GOE—Interest Area: 08. Industrial Production. **Work Group:** 08.05 Woodworking Technology. **Other Apprenticeable Jobs in This Work Group:** Cabinetmakers and Bench Carpenters; Furniture Finishers; Model Makers, Wood. **PERSONALITY TYPE:** Realistic. Realistic occupations frequently involve work activities that include practical, hands-on problems and solutions. They often deal with plants, animals, and real-world materials like wood, tools, and machinery. Many of the occupations require working outside and do not involve a lot of paperwork or working closely with others.

RELATED KNOWLEDGE/COURSES—**Design:** Knowledge of design techniques, tools, and principles involved in production of precision technical plans, blueprints, drawings, and models. **Building and Construction:** Knowledge of the materials, methods, and tools involved in the construction or repair of houses, buildings, or other structures, such as highways and roads. **Engineering and Technology:** Knowledge of the practical application of engineering science and technology. This includes applying principles, techniques, procedures, and equipment to the design and production of various goods and services. **Mechanical Devices:** Knowledge of machines and tools, including their designs, uses, repair, and maintenance. **Production and Processing:** Knowledge of raw materials, production processes, quality control, costs, and other techniques for maximizing the effective manufacture and distribution of goods.

WORK ENVIRONMENT—Minor burns, cuts, bites, or stings; indoors; hazardous equipment; spend time making repetitive motions; using hands on objects, tools, or controls.

Paving, Surfacing, and Tamping Equipment Operators

- Growth: 12.6%
- Annual Job Openings: 8,000
- Annual Earnings: $29,240
- Percentage of Women: 4.6%

Related Apprenticeship	*Years*
Asphalt-Paving-Machine Operator	3

Operate equipment used for applying concrete, asphalt, or other materials to road beds, parking lots, or airport runways and taxiways or equipment used for tamping gravel, dirt, or other materials. Includes concrete and asphalt paving machine operators, form tampers, tamping machine operators, and stone spreader operators. Control paving machines to push dump trucks and to maintain a constant flow of asphalt or other material into hoppers or screeds. Drive and operate curbing machines to extrude concrete or asphalt curbing. Fill tanks, hoppers, or machines with paving materials. Install dies, cutters, and extensions to screeds onto machines, using hand tools. Light burners or start heating units of machines and regulate screed temperatures and asphalt flow rates. Observe distribution of paving material in order to adjust machine settings or material flow and indicate low spots for workers to add material. Operate machines that clean or cut expansion joints in concrete or asphalt and that rout out cracks in pavement. Operate tamping machines or manually roll surfaces to compact earth fills, foundation forms, and finished road materials according to grade specifications. Place strips of material such as cork, asphalt, or steel into joints or place rolls of expansion-joint material on machines that automatically insert material. Set up and tear down equipment. Start machine, engage clutch, and push and move levers to guide machine along forms or guidelines and to control the operation of machine attachments. Operate machines to spread, smooth, level, or steel-reinforce stone, concrete, or asphalt on road beds. Coordinate truck dumping. Cut or break up pavement and drive guardrail posts, using machines equipped with interchangeable hammers. Drive machines onto truck trailers and drive trucks to transport machines and material to and from job sites. Inspect, clean, maintain, and repair equipment, using mechanics' hand tools, or report malfunctions to supervisors. Operate oil distributors, loaders, chip spreaders, dump trucks, and snow plows. Set up forms and lay out guidelines for curbs, according to written specifications, using string, spray paint, and concrete/water mixes. Shovel blacktop. **SKILLS**—Equipment Maintenance; Operation and Control; Operation Monitoring; Installation; Equipment Selection; Repairing; Troubleshooting.

GOE—**Interest Area:** 06. Construction, Mining, and Drilling. **Work Group:** 06.02 Construction. **Other Apprenticeable Jobs in This Work Group:** Boat Builders and Shipwrights; Boilermakers; Brickmasons and Blockmasons; Carpet Installers; Ceiling Tile Installers; Cement Masons and Concrete Finishers; Construction and Related Workers, All Other; Construction Carpenters; Drywall Installers; Electricians; Fence Erectors; Floor Layers, Except Carpet, Wood, and Hard Tiles; Glaziers; Grader, Bulldozer, and Scraper Operators; Insulation Workers, Floor, Ceiling, and Wall; Insulation Workers, Mechanical; Operating Engineers; Painters, Construction and Maintenance; Paperhangers; Pipe Fitters; Plasterers and Stucco Masons; Plumbers; Reinforcing Iron and Rebar Workers; Riggers; Roofers; Rough Carpenters; Sheet Metal Workers; Ship Carpenters and Joiners; Stone Cutters and Carvers; Stonemasons; Structural Iron and Steel Workers; Tapers; Terrazzo Workers and Finishers; Tile and Marble Setters. **PERSONALITY TYPE:** Realistic. Realistic occupations frequently involve work activities that include practical, hands-on problems and solutions. They often deal with plants, animals, and real-world materials like wood, tools, and machinery. Many of the occupations require working outside and do not involve a lot of paperwork or working closely with others.

RELATED KNOWLEDGE/COURSES— **Transportation:** Knowledge of principles and methods for moving people or goods by air, rail, sea, or road, including the relative costs and benefits. **Mechanical Devices:** Knowledge of machines and tools, including their designs, uses, repair, and maintenance. **Production and Processing:** Knowledge of raw materials, production processes, quality control, costs, and other techniques for maximizing the effective manufacture and distribution of goods. **Physics:** Knowledge and prediction of physical principles and laws and their interrelationships and applications to understanding fluid, material, and atmospheric dynamics and mechanical, electrical, atomic, and subatomic structures and processes. **Building and Construction:** Knowledge of the materials, methods, and tools involved in the construction or repair of houses, buildings, or other structures, such as highways and roads. **Design:** Knowledge of design techniques, tools, and principles involved in production of precision technical plans, blueprints, drawings, and models.

WORK ENVIRONMENT—Outdoors; hazardous equipment; exposed to whole-body vibration; sounds, noise levels are distracting or uncomfortable; very hot or cold.

Pest Control Workers

- Growth: 17.0%
- Annual Job Openings: 11,000
- Annual Earnings: $24,990
- Percentage of Women: 6.3%

Related Apprenticeship	*Years*
Exterminator, Termite	2

Spray or release chemical solutions or toxic gases and set traps to kill pests and vermin, such as mice, termites, and roaches, that infest buildings and surrounding areas. Spray or dust chemical solutions, powders, or gases into rooms; onto clothing, furnishings or wood; and over marshlands, ditches, and catch-basins. Set mechanical traps and place poisonous paste or bait in sewers, burrows, and ditches. Inspect premises to identify infestation source and extent of damage to property, wall and roof porosity, and access to infested locations. Cut or bore openings in building or surrounding concrete, access infested areas, insert nozzle, and inject pesticide to impregnate ground. Study preliminary reports and diagrams of infested area and determine treatment type required to eliminate and prevent recurrence of infestation. Direct and/or assist other workers in treatment and extermination processes to eliminate and control rodents, insects, and weeds. Measure area dimensions requiring treatment, using rule; calculate fumigant requirements; and estimate cost for service. Clean and remove blockages from infested areas to facilitate spraying procedure and provide drainage, using broom, mop, shovel, and rake. Position and fasten edges of tarpaulins over building and tape vents to ensure airtight environment and check for leaks. Post warning signs and lock building doors to secure area to be fumigated. Drive truck equipped with power spraying equipment. Record work activities performed. Clean work site after completion of job. Dig up and burnweeds or spray them with herbicides. **SKILLS**—Mathematics; Operation and Control; Management of Personnel Resources; Judgment and Decision Making; Operation Monitoring; Equipment Selection; Operations Analysis.

GOE—**Interest Area:** 03. Plants and Animals. **Work Group:** 03.03 Hands-on Work in Plants and Animals. **Other Apprenticeable Jobs in This Work Group:** Agricultural Equipment Operators; Fallers; Farmworkers, Farm and Ranch Animals; Landscaping and Groundskeeping Workers; Pesticide Handlers, Sprayers, and Applicators, Vegetation; Tree Trimmers and Pruners. **PERSONALITY TYPE:** Realistic. Realistic occupations frequently involve work activities that include practical, hands-on problems and solutions. They often deal with plants, animals, and real-world materials like wood, tools, and machinery. Many of the occupations require working outside and do not involve a lot of paperwork or working closely with others.

RELATED KNOWLEDGE/COURSES—**Chemistry:** Knowledge of the chemical composition, structure, and properties of substances and of the chemical processes and transformations that they undergo. This includes uses of chemicals, their danger signs, production techniques, and disposal methods. **Mechanical Devices:** Knowledge of machines and tools, including their designs, uses, repair, and maintenance. **Biology:** Knowledge of plant and animal organisms and their tissues, cells, functions, interdependencies, and interactions with each other and the environment. **Customer and Personal Service:** Knowledge of principles and processes for providing customer and personal services. This includes customer needs assessment, meeting quality standards for services, and evaluation of customer satisfaction. **Public Safety and Security:** Knowledge of relevant equipment, policies, procedures, and strategies to promote effective local, state, or national security operations for the protection of people, data, property, and institutions.

P

WORK ENVIRONMENT—Specialized protective or safety equipment; hazardous conditions; contaminants; spend time kneeling, crouching, stooping, or crawling; minor burns, cuts, bites, or stings.

Pesticide Handlers, Sprayers, and Applicators, Vegetation

◉ Growth: 9.7%

◉ Annual Job Openings: 5,000

◉ Annual Earnings: $25,490

◉ Percentage of Women: 7.6%

Related Apprenticeship	Years
Agricultural Service Worker	2

Mix or apply pesticides, herbicides, fungicides, or insecticides through sprays, dusts, vapors, soil incorporation, or chemical application on trees, shrubs, lawns, or botanical crops. Usually requires specific training and state or federal certification. Lifts, pushes, and swings nozzle, hose, and tube to direct spray over designated area. Sprays livestock with pesticides. Plants grass with seed spreader and operates straw blower to cover seeded area with asphalt and straw mixture. Cleans and services machinery to ensure operating efficiency, using water, gasoline, lubricants, and hand tools. Fills sprayer tank with water and chemicals according to formula. Connects hoses and nozzles selected according to terrain, distribution pattern requirements, type of infestation, and velocity. Gives driving instructions to truck driver, using hand and horn signals, to ensure complete coverage of designated area. Starts motor and engages machinery, such as sprayer agitator and pump. Covers area to specified depth, applying knowledge of weather conditions, droplet size, elevation-to-distance ratio, and obstructions. SKILLS—Equipment Maintenance; Operation and Control; Repairing; Operation Monitoring; Troubleshooting.

GOE—Interest Area: 03. Plants and Animals. Work Group: 03.03 Hands-on Work in Plants and Animals. Other Apprenticeable Jobs in This Work Group: Agricultural Equipment Operators; Fallers; Farmworkers, Farm and Ranch Animals; Landscaping and Groundskeeping Workers; Pest Control Workers; Tree Trimmers and Pruners. PERSONALITY TYPE: Realistic. Realistic occupations frequently involve work activities that include practical, hands-on problems and solutions. They often deal with plants, animals, and real-world materials like wood, tools, and machinery. Many of the occupations require working outside and do not involve a lot of paperwork or working closely with others.

RELATED KNOWLEDGE/COURSES—Chemistry: Knowledge of the chemical composition, structure, and properties of substances and of the chemical processes and transformations that they undergo. This includes uses of chemicals, their danger signs, production techniques, and disposal methods. Mechanical Devices: Knowledge of machines and tools, including their designs, uses, repair, and maintenance. Engineering and Technology: Knowledge of the practical application of engineering science and technology. This includes applying principles, techniques, procedures, and equipment to the design and production of various goods and services. **Physics:** Knowledge and prediction of physical principles and laws and their interrelationships and applications to understanding fluid, material, and atmospheric dynamics and mechanical, electrical, atomic, and subatomic structures and processes. **Food Production:** Knowledge of techniques and equipment for planting, growing, and harvesting food products (both plant and animal) for consumption, including storage/handling techniques.

WORK ENVIRONMENT—Outdoors; hazardous conditions; contaminants; very hot or cold; standing.

Petroleum Refinery and Control Panel Operators

- Growth: –11.0%
- Annual Job Openings: 3,000
- Annual Earnings: $49,970
- Percentage of Women: 7.4%

Related Apprenticeship	Years
Refinery Operator	3

Analyze specifications and control continuous operation of petroleum refining and processing units. Operate control panel to regulate temperature, pressure, rate of flow, and tank level in petroleum refining unit according to process schedules. Reads and analyzes specifica-

tions, schedules, logs, and test results to determine changes to equipment controls required to produce specified product. Observes instruments, gauges, and meters to verify conformance to specified quality and quantity of product. Inspects equipment and listens for automated warning signals to determine location and nature of malfunction, such as leaks and breakage. Repairs, lubricates, and maintains equipment or reports malfunctioning equipment to supervisor to schedule needed repairs. Compiles and records operating data, instrument readings, documents, and results of laboratory analyses. Cleans interior of processing units by circulating chemicals and solvents within unit. Samples and tests liquids and gases for chemical characteristics and color of products or sends products to laboratory for analysis. Operates auxiliary equipment and controls multiple processing units during distilling or treating operations. Monitors and adjusts unit controls to ensure safe and efficient operating conditions. Operates control panel to coordinate and regulate process variables and to direct product flow rate according to prescribed schedules. **SKILLS**—Operation Monitoring; Operation and Control; Equipment Maintenance; Repairing; Troubleshooting; Science; Quality Control Analysis; Mathematics.

GOE—Interest Area: 08. Industrial Production. **Work Group:** 08.06 Systems Operation. **Other Apprenticeable Jobs in This Work Group:** Boiler Operators and Tenders, Low Pressure; Chemical Plant and System Operators; Gaugers; Power Distributors and Dispatchers; Power Generating Plant Operators, Except Auxiliary Equipment Operators; Stationary Engineers; Water and Liquid Waste Treatment Plant and System Operators. **PERSONALITY TYPE:** Realistic. Realistic occupations frequently involve work activities that include practical, hands-on problems and solutions. They often deal with plants, animals, and real-world materials like wood, tools, and machinery. Many of the occupations require working outside and do not involve a lot of paperwork or working closely with others.

RELATED KNOWLEDGE/COURSES— **Chemistry:** Knowledge of the chemical composition, structure, and properties of substances and of the chemical processes and transformations that they undergo. This includes uses of chemicals, their danger signs, production techniques, and disposal methods. **Mechanical Devices:** Knowledge of machines and tools, including their designs, uses, repair, and maintenance. **Physics:** Knowledge and prediction of physical principles and laws and their interrelationships and applications to understanding fluid, material, and atmospheric dynamics and mechanical, electrical, atomic, and subatomic structures and processes. **Production and Processing:** Knowledge of raw materials, production processes, quality control, costs, and other techniques for maximizing the effective manufacture and distribution of goods. **Public Safety and Security:** Knowledge of relevant equipment, policies, procedures, and strategies to promote effective local, state, or national security operations for the protection of people, data, property, and institutions. **Engineering and Technology:** Knowledge of the practical application of engineering science and technology. This includes applying principles, techniques, procedures, and equipment to the design and production of various goods and services.

WORK ENVIRONMENT—Hazardous conditions; walking and running; common protective or safety equipment; sounds, noise levels are distracting or uncomfortable; contaminants.

Pharmacy Technicians

- Growth: 28.8%
- Annual Job Openings: 39,000
- Annual Earnings: $22,760
- Percentage of Women: 80.7%

Related Apprenticeship	*Years*
Pharmacist Assistant	1

Prepare medications under the direction of a pharmacist. May measure, mix, count out, label, and record amounts and dosages of medications. Receive written prescription or refill requests and verify that information is complete and accurate. Maintain proper storage and security conditions for drugs. Answer telephones, responding to questions or requests. Fill bottles with prescribed medications and type and affix labels. Assist customers by answering simple questions, locating items, or referring them to the pharmacist for medication information. Price and file prescriptions that have been filled. Clean and help maintain equipment and work areas and sterilize glassware according to prescribed methods. Establish and maintain patient profiles, including lists of medications taken by individual patients. Order, label, and count stock of medications, chemicals, and supplies and enter inventory data into computer. Receive and store incoming supplies, verify quantities against invoices, and inform supervisors of stock needs and shortages. Transfer medication from vials to the appropriate number of sterile, disposable syringes, using aseptic techniques. Add measured drugs or nutrients to intravenous solutions under sterile conditions to prepare intravenous (IV) packs under pharmacist supervision. Supply and monitor robotic machines that dispense medicine into containers and label the containers. Prepare and process medical insurance claim forms and records. Mix pharmaceutical preparations according to written prescriptions. Operate cash registers to accept payment from customers. Compute charges for medication and equipment dispensed to hospital patients and enter data in computer. Deliver medications and pharmaceutical supplies to patients, nursing stations, or surgery. Price stock and mark items for sale. Maintain and merchandise home health-care products and services. **SKILLS**—Instructing; Service Orientation; Active Listening; Active Learning; Critical Thinking; Speaking; Learning Strategies; Troubleshooting.

GOE—**Interest Area:** 14. Medical and Health Services. **Work Group:** 14.02 Medicine and Surgery. **Other Apprenticeable Jobs in This Work Group:** Medical Assistants; Surgical Technologists. **PERSONALITY TYPE:** Conventional. Conventional occupations frequently involve following set procedures and routines. These occupations can include working with data and details more than with ideas. Usually there is a clear line of authority to follow.

RELATED KNOWLEDGE/COURSES— **Customer and Personal Service:** Knowledge of principles and processes for providing customer and personal services. This includes customer needs assessment, meeting quality standards for services, and evaluation of customer satisfaction. **Chemistry:** Knowledge of the chemical composition, structure, and properties of substances and of the chemical processes and transformations that they undergo. This includes uses of chemicals, their danger signs, produc-

tion techniques, and disposal methods. **Medicine and Dentistry:** Knowledge of the information and techniques needed to diagnose and treat human injuries, diseases, and deformities. This includes symptoms, treatment alternatives, drug properties and interactions, and preventive health-care measures. **Mathematics:** Knowledge of arithmetic, algebra, geometry, calculus, and statistics and their applications. **Clerical Practices:** Knowledge of administrative and clerical procedures and systems, such as word processing, managing files and records, stenography and transcription, designing forms, and other office procedures and terminology. **Education and Training:** Knowledge of principles and methods for curriculum and training design, teaching and instruction for individuals and groups, and the measurement of training effects.

WORK ENVIRONMENT—Physical proximity; sounds, noise levels are distracting or uncomfortable; standing; extremely bright or inadequate lighting; very hot or cold.

Photoengravers

- Growth: −11.2%
- Annual Job Openings: 6,000
- Annual Earnings: $31,660
- Percentage of Women: 47.6%

Related Apprenticeship	Years
Etcher, Photoengraving	4
Etcher, Hand	5

P

Photoengraver	5
Photoengraving Finisher	5
Photoengraving Printer	5
Photoengraving Proofer	5
Retoucher, Photoengraving	5
Photographer, Photoengraving	6

Photograph copy, develop negatives, and pre-pare photosensitized metal plates for use in letterpress and gravure printing. Computes camera machine settings for film exposure or reproduction, using equipment meter, computer, worksheets, and standard formulas and tables. Washes rollers and plates preparatory to etching or to remove resistant solution and photographic emulsion, using water, cleaning solution, and brush. Transfers images, designs, or patterns onto rollers, plates, or film, using photographic or pantographic equipment and techniques and hand tools. Develops and prints negatives, positives, film, or plates by controlled exposure to light, using exposure equipment, chemical baths, and vacuum. Positions, loads, or mounts copy, plates, film, or rollers and secures into place. Brushes protective solution and powder on plate and starts machine to distribute acid or photosensitizing solution over plate or rollers. Etches designs on metal rollers and plates, using etching machines, hand tools, and acidic chemicals, to produce printing plates and rollers. Modifies or repairs plates or film, using etching and artist's brush, acid, and hand tools. Matches colors with original to produce balanced color values or intensity design. Studies and compares film negatives or positives with originals or design to determine photographic requirements and verify reproduction. Examines developed film, proof, or engravings, using magnifier, chalk, or charcoal to evaluate quality and detect errors. Mixes caustic or acid solutions. **SKILLS**—Equipment Maintenance; Operation and Control; Repairing; Technology Design.

GOE—Interest Area: 01. Arts, Entertainment, and Media. **Work Group:** 01.07 Graphic Arts. **Other Apprenticeable Jobs in This Work Group:** Camera Operators; Desktop Publishers; Dot Etchers; Engravers, Hand; Engravers/Carvers; Pantograph Engravers; Paste-Up Workers; Precision Etchers and Engravers, Hand or Machine. **PERSONALITY TYPE:** Realistic. Realistic occupations frequently involve work activities that include practical, hands-on problems and solutions. They often deal with plants, animals, and real-world materials like wood, tools, and machinery. Many of the occupations require working outside and do not involve a lot of paperwork or working closely with others.

RELATED KNOWLEDGE/COURSES— Chemistry: Knowledge of the chemical composition, structure, and properties of substances and of the chemical processes and transformations that they undergo. This includes uses of chemicals, their danger signs, production techniques, and disposal methods. **Fine Arts:** Knowledge of the theory and techniques required to compose, produce, and perform works of music, dance, visual arts, drama, and sculpture. **Computers and Electronics:** Knowledge of circuit boards, processors, chips, electronic equipment, and computer hardware and software, including applications and programming. **Design:** Knowledge of design techniques, tools, and principles involved in production of precision technical plans, blueprints, drawings, and models. **Physics:** Knowledge and prediction of physical principles and laws and their interrelationships and applications to understanding fluid, material, and atmospheric dynamics and mechanical, electrical, atomic, and subatomic structures and processes.

WORK ENVIRONMENT—Contaminants; hazardous conditions; common protective or safety equipment; minor burns, cuts, bites, or stings; spend time making repetitive motions.

Pipe Fitters

- Growth: 18.7%
- Annual Job Openings: 56,000
- Annual Earnings: $40,950
- Percentage of Women: 1.7%

Related Apprenticeship	Years
Coppersmith	4
Gas-Main Fitter	4
Pipe Fitter—Sprinkler Fitter	4
Pipe Fitter, Construction	4
Pipe Fitter, Ship and Boat	4
Steam Service Inspector	4

(This is one of the most popular apprenticeable jobs.)

Lay out, assemble, install, and maintain pipe systems, pipe supports, and related hydraulic and pneumatic equipment for steam, hot water, heating, cooling, lubricating, sprinkling, and industrial production and processing systems. Assemble and secure pipes, tubes, fittings, and related equipment according to specifications by welding, brazing, cementing, soldering, and threading joints. Attach pipes to walls, structures, and fixtures such as radiators or tanks, using brackets, clamps, tools, or welding equipment. Cut and bore holes in structures such as bulkheads, decks, walls, and mains prior to pipe installation, using hand and power tools. Cut, thread, and hammer pipe to specifications, using tools such as saws, cutting torches, and pipe threaders and benders. Inspect, examine, and test installed systems and pipe lines, using pressure gauge, hydrostatic testing, observation, or other methods. Lay out full-scale drawings of pipe systems, supports, and related equipment, following blueprints. Measure and mark pipes for cutting and threading. Modify, clean, and maintain pipe systems, units, fittings, and related machines and equipment, following specifications and using hand and power tools. Plan pipe system layout, installation, or repair according to specifications. Select pipe sizes and types and related materials, such as supports, hangers, and hydraulic cylinders, according to specifications. Dip nonferrous piping materials in a mixture of molten tin and lead to obtain a coating that prevents erosion or galvanic and electrolytic action. Inspect work sites for obstructions and to ensure that holes will not cause structural weakness. Install automatic controls used to regulate pipe systems. Operate motorized pumps to remove water from flooded manholes, basements, or facility floors. Prepare cost estimates for clients. Remove and replace worn components. Turn valves to shut off steam, water, or other gases or liquids from pipe sections, using valve keys or wrenches. **SKILLS**—Installation; Equipment Maintenance; Repairing; Quality Control Analysis; Operation and Control; Technology Design; Troubleshooting; Equipment Selection.

P

GOE—**Interest Area:** 06. Construction, Mining, and Drilling. **Work Group:** 06.02 Construction. **Other Apprenticeable Jobs in This Work Group:** Boat Builders and Shipwrights; Boilermakers; Brickmasons and Blockmasons; Carpet Installers; Ceiling Tile Installers; Cement Masons and Concrete Finishers; Construction and Related Workers, All Other; Construction Carpenters; Drywall Installers; Electricians; Fence Erectors; Floor Layers, Except Carpet, Wood, and Hard Tiles; Glaziers; Grader, Bulldozer, and Scraper Operators; Insulation Workers, Floor, Ceiling, and Wall; Insulation Workers, Mechanical; Operating Engineers; Painters, Construction and Maintenance; Paperhangers; Paving, Surfacing, and Tamping Equipment Operators; Plasterers and Stucco Masons; Plumbers; Reinforcing Iron and Rebar Workers; Riggers; Roofers; Rough Carpenters; Sheet Metal Workers; Ship Carpenters and Joiners; Stone Cutters and Carvers; Stonemasons; Structural Iron and Steel Workers; Tapers; Terrazzo Workers and Finishers; Tile and Marble Setters. **PERSONALITY TYPE:** Realistic. Realistic occupations frequently involve work activities that include practical, hands-on problems and solutions. They often deal with plants, animals, and real-world materials like wood, tools, and machinery. Many of the occupations require working outside and do not involve a lot of paperwork or working closely with others.

RELATED KNOWLEDGE/COURSES— Building and Construction: Knowledge of the materials, methods, and tools involved in the construction or repair of houses, buildings, or other structures, such as highways and roads. **Mechanical Devices:** Knowledge of machines and tools, including their designs, uses, repair, and maintenance. **Design:** Knowledge of design techniques, tools, and principles involved in production of precision technical plans, blueprints, drawings, and models. **Physics:** Knowledge and prediction of physical principles and laws and their interrelationships and applications to understanding fluid, material, and atmospheric dynamics and mechanical, electrical, atomic, and subatomic structures and processes. **Production and Processing:** Knowledge of raw materials, production processes, quality control, costs, and other techniques for maximizing the effective manufacture and distribution of goods. **Engineering and Technology:** Knowledge of the practical application of engineering science and technology. This includes applying principles, techniques, procedures, and equipment to the design and production of various goods and services.

WORK ENVIRONMENT—Common protective or safety equipment; spend time kneeling, crouching, stooping, or crawling; using hands on objects, tools, or controls; spend time bending or twisting the body; very hot or cold.

FURTHER INFORMATION—Contact a local joint union-management apprenticeship committee or the nearest office of your state employment service or apprenticeship agency (see Appendix C). To identify the local union office, contact United Association of Journeymen and Apprentices of the Plumbing and Pipefitting Industry, 901 Massachusetts Ave. NW, Washington, DC 20001. Internet: http://www.ua.org.

Plasterers and Stucco Masons

- Growth: 13.5%
- Annual Job Openings: 8,000
- Annual Earnings: $33,060
- Percentage of Women: 1.3%

Related Apprenticeship	Years
Plasterer	2

Apply interior or exterior plaster, cement, stucco, or similar materials. May also set ornamental plaster. Apply coats of plaster or stucco to walls, ceilings, or partitions of buildings, using trowels, brushes, or spray guns. Apply weatherproof decorative coverings to exterior surfaces of buildings, such as troweling or spraying on coats of stucco. Clean and prepare surfaces for applications of plaster, cement, stucco, or similar materials, such as by drywall taping. Cure freshly plastered surfaces. Install guidewires on exterior surfaces of buildings to indicate thickness of plaster or stucco and nail wire mesh, lath, or similar materials to the outside surface to hold stucco in place. Mix mortar and plaster to desired consistency or direct workers who perform mixing. Mold and install ornamental plaster pieces, panels, and trim. Rough the undercoat surface with a scratcher so the finish coat will adhere. Spray acoustic materials or texture finish over walls and ceilings. Apply insulation to building exteriors by installing prefabricated insulation systems over existing walls or by covering the outer wall with insulation board, reinforcing mesh, and a base coat. Create decorative textures in finish coat, using brushes or trowels, sand, pebbles, or stones. **SKILLS**—Coordination; Installation; Management of Personnel Resources; Time Management.

GOE—Interest Area: 06. Construction, Mining, and Drilling. **Work Group:** 06.02 Construction. **Other Apprenticeable Jobs in This Work Group:** Boat Builders and Shipwrights; Boilermakers; Brickmasons and Blockmasons; Carpet Installers; Ceiling Tile Installers; Cement Masons and Concrete Finishers; Construction and Related Workers, All Other; Construction Carpenters; Drywall Installers; Electricians; Fence Erectors; Floor Layers, Except Carpet, Wood, and Hard Tiles; Glaziers; Grader, Bulldozer, and Scraper Operators; Insulation Workers, Floor, Ceiling, and Wall; Insulation Workers, Mechanical; Operating Engineers; Painters, Construction and Maintenance; Paperhangers; Paving, Surfacing, and Tamping Equipment Operators; Pipe Fitters; Plumbers; Reinforcing Iron and Rebar Workers; Riggers; Roofers; Rough Carpenters; Sheet Metal Workers; Ship Carpenters and Joiners; Stone Cutters and Carvers; Stonemasons; Structural Iron and Steel Workers; Tapers; Terrazzo Workers and Finishers; Tile and Marble Setters. **PERSONALITY TYPE:** Realistic. Realistic occupations frequently involve work activities that include practical, hands-on problems and solutions. They often deal with plants, animals, and real-world materials like wood, tools, and machinery. Many of the occupations require working outside and do not involve a lot of paperwork or working closely with others.

RELATED KNOWLEDGE/COURSES— Building and Construction: Knowledge of the materials, methods, and tools involved in the

P

construction or repair of houses, buildings, or other structures, such as highways and roads. **Design:** Knowledge of design techniques, tools, and principles involved in production of precision technical plans, blueprints, drawings, and models. **Engineering and Technology:** Knowledge of the practical application of engineering science and technology. This includes applying principles, techniques, procedures, and equipment to the design and production of various goods and services.

WORK ENVIRONMENT—Climbing ladders, scaffolds, or poles; high places; contaminants; common protective or safety equipment; spend time kneeling, crouching, stooping, or crawling; spend time bending or twisting the body.

Plastic Molding and Casting Machine Setters and Set-Up Operators

- Growth: 8.9%
- Annual Job Openings: 18,000
- Annual Earnings: $23,930
- Percentage of Women: 22.4%

Related Apprenticeship	*Years*
Injection-Molding-Machine Operator	1
Mold Setter	1
Plastic Process Technician	4

Set up or set up and operate plastic molding machines, such as compression or injection molding machines, to mold, form, or cast thermoplastic materials to specified shape. Positions, aligns, and secures assembled mold, mold components, and machine accessories onto machine press bed and attaches connecting lines. Installs dies onto machine or press and coats dies with parting agent according to work order specifications. Presses button or pulls lever to activate machine to inject dies and compress compounds to form and cure specified products. Observes and adjusts machine setup and operations to eliminate production of defective parts and products. Weighs premixed compounds and dumps compound into die well or fills hoppers of machines that automatically supply compound to die. Reads specifications to determine setup and prescribed temperature and time settings to mold, form, or cast plastic materials. Sets machine controls to regulate molding temperature, volume, pressure, and time according to knowledge of plastics and molding procedures. Mixes catalysts, thermoplastic materials, and coloring pigments according to formula, using paddle and mixing machine. Repairs and maintains machines and auxiliary equipment, using hand tools and power tools. Trims excess material from part, using knife, and grinds scrap plastic into powder for reuse. Removes finished or cured product from dies or mold, using hand tools and airhose. Measures and visually inspects products for surface and dimension defects, using precision measuring instruments, to ensure conformance to specifications. **SKILLS**—Equipment Maintenance; Operation Monitoring; Repairing; Operation and Control; Troubleshooting; Installation; Quality Control Analysis; Technology Design.

GOE—**Interest Area:** 08. Industrial Production. **Work Group:** 08.02 Production Technology. **Other Apprenticeable Jobs in This Work Group:** Aircraft Structure Assemblers, Precision; Aircraft Systems Assemblers, Precision; Bench Workers, Jewelry; Bindery Machine Setters and Set-Up Operators; Bookbinders; Buffing and Polishing Set-Up Operators; Coating, Painting, and Spraying Machine Setters and Set-Up Operators; Combination Machine Tool Setters and Set-Up Operators, Metal and Plastic; Dental Laboratory Technicians; Electrical and Electronic Equipment Assemblers; Electrical and Electronic Inspectors and Testers; Electromechanical Equipment Assemblers; Engine and Other Machine Assemblers; Extruding and Drawing Machine Setters, Operators, and Tenders, Metal and Plastic; Extruding, Forming, Pressing, and Compacting Machine Setters and Set-Up Operators; Forging Machine Setters, Operators, and Tenders, Metal and Plastic; Foundry Mold and Coremakers; Gem and Diamond Workers; Grinding, Honing, Lapping, and Deburring Machine Set-Up Operators; Heat Treating, Annealing, and Tempering Machine Operators and Tenders, Metal and Plastic; Jewelers; Lathe and Turning Machine Tool Setters, Operators, and Tenders, Metal and Plastic; Materials Inspectors; Mechanical Inspectors; Metal Molding, Coremaking, and Casting Machine Operators and Tenders; Milling and Planing Machine Setters, Operators, and Tenders, Metal and Plastic; Model and Mold Makers, Jewelry; Motor Vehicle Inspectors; Paper Goods Machine Setters, Operators, and Tenders; Pewter Casters and Finishers; Precision Devices Inspectors and Testers; Precision Lens Grinders and Polishers; Precision Mold and Pattern Casters, Except Nonferrous Metals; Precision Pattern and Die Casters, Nonferrous Metals; Press and Press Brake Machine Setters and Set-Up Operators, Metal and Plastic; Production Inspectors, Testers, Graders, Sorters, Samplers, Weighers; Production Workers, All Other; Rolling Machine Setters, Operators, and Tenders, Metal and Plastic; Silversmiths; Textile Knitting and Weaving Machine Setters, Operators, and Tenders; Textile Winding, Twisting, and Drawing Out Machine Setters, Operators, and Tenders; Welding Machine Setters and Set-Up Operators; Woodworking Machine Setters and Set-Up Operators, Except Sawing. **PERSONALITY TYPE:** Realistic. Realistic occupations frequently involve work activities that include practical, hands-on problems and solutions. They often deal with plants, animals, and real-world materials like wood, tools, and machinery. Many of the occupations require working outside and do not involve a lot of paperwork or working closely with others.

RELATED KNOWLEDGE/COURSES—Mechanical Devices: Knowledge of machines and tools, including their designs, uses, repair, and maintenance. **Production and Processing:** Knowledge of raw materials, production processes, quality control, costs, and other techniques for maximizing the effective manufacture and distribution of goods. **Chemistry:** Knowledge of the chemical composition, structure, and properties of substances and of the chemical processes and transformations that they undergo. This includes uses of chemicals, their danger signs, production techniques, and disposal methods.

WORK ENVIRONMENT—Hazardous equipment; contaminants; common protective or safety equipment; hazardous conditions; sounds, noise levels are distracting or uncomfortable.

Plate Finishers

⊚ Growth: –11.2%
⊚ Annual Job Openings: 6,000
⊚ Annual Earnings: $31,660
⊚ Percentage of Women: 47.6%

Related Apprenticeship	Years
Plate Finisher	6

Set up and operate equipment to trim and mount electrotype or stereotype plates. Selects cutting position and sets controls of saws, milling machines, and routers, following specifications. Operates plate curving machine to cut plates to fit printing press. Operates press to print proof of plate, observing printing quality. Taps plate with hammer and block to flatten until even. Examines plates with magnifier or microscope to detect flaws, using engraver's tools. Rubs surface with finishing material to reveal unevenness. Mounts finished plates on wood or metal blocks, using hammer and nails or thermoplastic adhesive and heat press. Operates cutting tools to shave and smooth plates to specified thickness. **SKILLS**—Operation and Control; Equipment Maintenance; Installation; Repairing; Quality Control Analysis.

GOE—Interest Area: 08. Industrial Production. **Work Group:** 08.03 Production Work. **Other Apprenticeable Jobs in This Work Group:** Bakers, Manufacturing; Bindery Machine Operators and Tenders; Chemical Equipment Controllers and Operators; Coating, Painting, and Spraying Machine Operators and Tenders; Cooling and Freezing Equipment Operators and Tenders; Crushing, Grinding, and Polishing Machine Setters, Operators, and Tenders; Cutters and Trimmers, Hand; Cutting and Slicing Machine Operators and Tenders; Design Printing Machine Setters and Set-Up Operators; Electrolytic Plating and Coating Machine Setters and Set-Up Operators, Metal and Plastic; Electrotypers and Stereotypers; Embossing Machine Set-Up Operators; Engraver Set-Up Operators; Extruding, Forming, Pressing, and Compacting Machine Operators and Tenders; Fabric and Apparel Patternmakers; Film Laboratory Technicians; Fitters, Structural Metal—Precision; Food Batchmakers; Furnace, Kiln, Oven, Drier, and Kettle Operators and Tenders; Hand Compositors and Typesetters; Job Printers; Letterpress Setters and Set-Up Operators; Metal Fabricators, Structural Metal Products; Metal-Refining Furnace Operators and Tenders; Mixing and Blending Machine Setters, Operators, and Tenders; Mold Makers, Hand; Molding and Casting Workers; Numerical Control Machine Tool Operators and Tenders, Metal and Plastic; Offset Lithographic Press Setters and Set-Up Operators; Painting, Coating, and Decorating Workers; Photographic Processing Machine Operators; Photographic Reproduction Technicians; Photographic Retouchers and Restorers; Platemakers; Precision Printing Workers; Printing Press Machine Operators and Tenders; Production Workers, All Other; Sawing Machine Operators and Tenders; Sawing Machine Setters and Set-Up Operators; Scanner Operators; Separating, Filtering, Clarifying, Precipitating, and Still Machine Setters, Operators, and Tenders; Sewing Machine Operators, Garment; Slaughterers and Meat Packers; Stone Sawyers; Strippers; Team Assemblers; Welder-Fitters; Welders and Cutters; Woodworking Machine Operators and Tenders, Except Sawing. **PERSONALITY**

TYPE: Realistic. Realistic occupations frequently involve work activities that include practical, hands-on problems and solutions. They often deal with plants, animals, and real-world materials like wood, tools, and machinery. Many of the occupations require working outside and do not involve a lot of paperwork or working closely with others.

RELATED KNOWLEDGE/COURSES—**Production and Processing:** Knowledge of raw materials, production processes, quality control, costs, and other techniques for maximizing the effective manufacture and distribution of goods. **Mechanical Devices:** Knowledge of machines and tools, including their designs, uses, repair, and maintenance.

WORK ENVIRONMENT—Hazardous equipment; using hands on objects, tools, or controls; spend time making repetitive motions; sounds, noise levels are distracting or uncomfortable; standing.

Platemakers

- Growth: –11.2%
- Annual Job Openings: 6,000
- Annual Earnings: $31,660
- Percentage of Women: 47.6%

Related Apprenticeship	Years
Lithographic Platemaker	4
Photographic-Plate Maker	4

Produce printing plates by exposing sensitized metal sheets to special light through a photographic negative. May operate machines that process plates automatically. Mounts negative and plate in camera that exposes exposed plate to artificial light through photographic negative, thus transferring image. Examines unexposed photographic plate to detect flaws or foreign particles prior to printing pattern of aperture masks on sensitized steel. Performs tests to determine time required for exposure by exposing plates and compares exposure to scale which measures tone ranges. Places plate in vacuum frame to align positives or negatives with each other and places masking paper over uncovered areas. Punches holes in light-sensitive plate and inserts pins in holes to prepare plate for contact with positive or negative film. Repairs defective plates with missing dots, using photographic touch-up tool and ink. Installs and aligns plates in printing case. Examines plate, using light-box and microscope to detect flaws, verify conformity with master plate, and measure dot size and center. Mixes and applies chemical-based developing solution to plates and replenishes solution in processor to maintain it in working order. Transfers image from master plate to unexposed plate and immerses plate in developing solution to develop image on plate. Transfers images by hand and covers surface of plates with photosensitive chemical, using brush, and allows plate to dry. Lowers vacuum frame onto plate-film assembly to establish contact between positive-negative film and plate and sets timer to expose plate. Removes plate-film assembly from vacuum frame and places exposed plate in automatic processor to develop image and dry plate. **SKILLS**—Quality Control Analysis; Installation; Operation Monitoring; Operation and Control; Repairing.

GOE—Interest Area: 08. Industrial Production. Work Group: 08.03 Production Work. Other Apprenticeable Jobs in This Work Group: Bakers, Manufacturing; Bindery Machine Operators and Tenders; Chemical Equipment Controllers and Operators; Coating, Painting, and Spraying Machine Operators and Tenders; Cooling and Freezing Equipment Operators and Tenders; Crushing, Grinding, and Polishing Machine Setters, Operators, and Tenders; Cutters and Trimmers, Hand; Cutting and Slicing Machine Operators and Tenders; Design Printing Machine Setters and Set-Up Operators; Electrolytic Plating and Coating Machine Setters and Set-Up Operators, Metal and Plastic; Electrotypers and Stereotypers; Embossing Machine Set-Up Operators; Engraver Set-Up Operators; Extruding, Forming, Pressing, and Compacting Machine Operators and Tenders; Fabric and Apparel Patternmakers; Film Laboratory Technicians; Fitters, Structural Metal—Precision; Food Batchmakers; Furnace, Kiln, Oven, Drier, and Kettle Operators and Tenders; Hand Compositors and Typesetters; Job Printers; Letterpress Setters and Set-Up Operators; Metal Fabricators, Structural Metal Products; Metal-Refining Furnace Operators and Tenders; Mixing and Blending Machine Setters, Operators, and Tenders; Mold Makers, Hand; Molding and Casting Workers; Numerical Control Machine Tool Operators and Tenders, Metal and Plastic; Offset Lithographic Press Setters and Set-Up Operators; Painting, Coating, and Decorating Workers; Photographic Processing Machine Operators; Photographic Reproduction Technicians; Photographic Retouchers and Restorers; Plate Finishers; Precision Printing Workers; Printing Press Machine Operators and Tenders; Production Workers, All Other; Sawing Machine Operators and Tenders; Sawing Machine Setters and Set-Up Operators; Scanner Operators; Separating, Filtering, Clarifying, Precipitating, and Still Machine Setters, Operators, and Tenders; Sewing Machine Operators, Garment; Slaughterers and Meat Packers; Stone Sawyers; Strippers; Team Assemblers; Welder-Fitters; Welders and Cutters; Woodworking Machine Operators and Tenders, Except Sawing. **PERSONALITY TYPE:** Realistic. Realistic occupations frequently involve work activities that include practical, hands-on problems and solutions. They often deal with plants, animals, and real-world materials like wood, tools, and machinery. Many of the occupations require working outside and do not involve a lot of paperwork or working closely with others.

RELATED KNOWLEDGE/COURSES— **Chemistry:** Knowledge of the chemical composition, structure, and properties of substances and of the chemical processes and transformations that they undergo. This includes uses of chemicals, their danger signs, production techniques, and disposal methods. **Production and Processing:** Knowledge of raw materials, production processes, quality control, costs, and other techniques for maximizing the effective manufacture and distribution of goods. **Fine Arts:** Knowledge of the theory and techniques required to compose, produce, and perform works of music, dance, visual arts, drama, and sculpture. **Physics:** Knowledge and prediction of physical principles and laws and their interrelationships and applications to understanding fluid, material, and atmospheric dynamics and mechanical, electrical, atomic, and subatomic structures and processes. **Engineering and Technology:** Knowledge of the practical application of engineering science and technology. This includes applying principles, techniques, procedures, and equipment to the design and production of various goods and services.

WORK ENVIRONMENT—Using hands on objects, tools, or controls; minor burns, cuts, bites, or stings; sitting; indoors; standing; spend time making repetitive motions.

Plumbers

- Growth: 18.7%
- Annual Job Openings: 56,000
- Annual Earnings: $40,950
- Percentage of Women: 1.7%

Related Apprenticeship	Years
Plumber	4

(This is one of the most popular apprenticeable jobs.)

Assemble, install, and repair pipes, fittings, and fixtures of heating, water, and drainage systems according to specifications and plumbing codes. Assemble pipe sections, tubing, and fittings, using couplings; clamps; screws; bolts; cement; plastic solvent; caulking; or soldering, brazing, and welding equipment. Fill pipes or plumbing fixtures with water or air and observe pressure gauges to detect and locate leaks. Review blueprints and building codes and specifications to determine work details and procedures. Prepare written work cost estimates and negotiate contracts. Study building plans and inspect structures to assess material and equipment needs, to establish the sequence of pipe installations, and to plan installation around obstructions such as electrical wiring. Keep records of assignments and produce detailed work reports. Perform complex calculations and planning for special or very large jobs. Locate and mark the position of pipe installations, connections, passage holes, and fixtures in structures, using measuring instruments such as rulers and levels. Measure, cut, thread, and bend pipe to required angle, using hand and power tools or machines such as pipe cutters, pipe-threading machines, and pipe-bending machines. Install pipe assemblies, fittings, valves, appliances such as dishwashers and water heaters, and fixtures such as sinks and toilets, using hand and power tools. Cut openings in structures to accommodate pipes and pipe fittings, using hand and power tools. Hang steel supports from ceiling joists to hold pipes in place. Repair and maintain plumbing, replacing defective washers, replacing or mending broken pipes, and opening clogged drains. Direct workers engaged in pipe-cutting and preassembly and installation of plumbing systems and components. Install underground storm, sanitary, and water piping systems and extend piping to connect fixtures and plumbing to these systems. Clear away debris in a renovation. Install oxygen and medical gas in hospitals. Use specialized techniques, equipment, or materials, such as performing computer-assisted welding of small pipes or working with the special piping used in microchip fabrication. **SKILLS**—Installation; Repairing; Troubleshooting; Management of Financial Resources; Coordination; Equipment Selection; Management of Material Resources; Management of Personnel Resources.

GOE—Interest Area: 06. Construction, Mining, and Drilling. **Work Group:** 06.02 Construction. **Other Apprenticeable Jobs in This Work Group:** Boat Builders and Shipwrights; Boilermakers; Brickmasons and Blockmasons;

Carpet Installers; Ceiling Tile Installers; Cement Masons and Concrete Finishers; Construction and Related Workers, All Other; Construction Carpenters; Drywall Installers; Electricians; Fence Erectors; Floor Layers, Except Carpet, Wood, and Hard Tiles; Glaziers; Grader, Bulldozer, and Scraper Operators; Insulation Workers, Floor, Ceiling, and Wall; Insulation Workers, Mechanical; Operating Engineers; Painters, Construction and Maintenance; Paperhangers; Paving, Surfacing, and Tamping Equipment Operators; Pipe Fitters; Plasterers and Stucco Masons; Reinforcing Iron and Rebar Workers; Riggers; Roofers; Rough Carpenters; Sheet Metal Workers; Ship Carpenters and Joiners; Stone Cutters and Carvers; Stonemasons; Structural Iron and Steel Workers; Tapers; Terrazzo Workers and Finishers; Tile and Marble Setters. **PERSONALITY TYPE:** Realistic. Realistic occupations frequently involve work activities that include practical, hands-on problems and solutions. They often deal with plants, animals, and real-world materials like wood, tools, and machinery. Many of the occupations require working outside and do not involve a lot of paperwork or working closely with others.

RELATED KNOWLEDGE/COURSES—Physics: Knowledge and prediction of physical principles and laws and their interrelationships and applications to understanding fluid, material, and atmospheric dynamics and mechanical, electrical, atomic, and subatomic structures and processes. **Building and Construction:** Knowledge of the materials, methods, and tools involved in the construction or repair of houses, buildings, or other structures, such as highways and roads. **Mechanical Devices:** Knowledge of machines and tools, including their designs, uses, repair, and maintenance. **Chemistry:** Knowledge of the chemical compo-

sition, structure, and properties of substances and of the chemical processes and transformations that they undergo. This includes uses of chemicals, their danger signs, production techniques, and disposal methods. **Sales and Marketing:** Knowledge of principles and methods for showing, promoting, and selling products or services. This includes marketing strategy and tactics, product demonstration, sales techniques, and sales control systems. **Customer and Personal Service:** Knowledge of principles and processes for providing customer and personal services. This includes customer needs assessment, meeting quality standards for services, and evaluation of customer satisfaction.

WORK ENVIRONMENT—Very hot or cold; contaminants; cramped work space, awkward positions; minor burns, cuts, bites, or stings; outdoors.

FURTHER INFORMATION—Contact a local joint union-management apprenticeship committee or the nearest office of your state employment service or apprenticeship agency (see Appendix C). To identify the local union office, contact United Association of Journeymen and Apprentices of the Plumbing and Pipefitting Industry, 901 Massachusetts Ave. NW, Washington, DC 20001. Internet: http://www.ua.org.

Police Patrol Officers

- Growth: 24.7%
- Annual Job Openings: 67,000
- Annual Earnings: $44,020
- Percentage of Women: 13.1%

Related Apprenticeship	Years
Police Officer I	2

Patrol assigned area to enforce laws and ordinances, regulate traffic, control crowds, prevent crime, and arrest violators. Provide for public safety by maintaining order, responding to emergencies, protecting people and property, enforcing motor vehicle and criminal laws, and promoting good community relations. Identify, pursue, and arrest suspects and perpetrators of criminal acts. Record facts to prepare reports that document incidents and activities. Review facts of incidents to determine if criminal act or statute violations were involved. Render aid to accident victims and other persons requiring first aid for physical injuries. Testify in court to present evidence or act as witness in traffic and criminal cases. Evaluate complaint and emergency-request information to determine response requirements. Patrol specific area on foot, horseback, or motorized conveyance, responding promptly to calls for assistance. Monitor, note, report, and investigate suspicious persons and situations, safety hazards, and unusual or illegal activity in patrol area. Investigate traffic accidents and other accidents to determine causes and to determine if a crime has been committed. Photograph or draw diagrams of crime or accident scenes and interview principals and eyewitnesses. Monitor traffic to ensure motorists observe traffic regulations and exhibit safe driving procedures. Relay complaint and emergency-request information to appropriate agency dispatchers. Issue citations or warnings to violators of motor vehicle ordinances. Direct traffic flow and reroute traffic in case of emergencies. Inform citizens of community services and recommend options to facilitate longer-term problem resolution. Provide road information to assist motorists. Process prisoners and prepare and maintain records of prisoner bookings and prisoner status during booking and pre-trial process. SKILLS—Persuasion; Negotiation; Social Perceptiveness; Service Orientation; Judgment and Decision Making; Active Listening; Critical Thinking; Coordination; Instructing.

GOE—Interest Area: 04. Law, Law Enforcement, and Public Safety. Work Group: 04.03 Law Enforcement. Other Apprenticeable Jobs in This Work Group: Correctional Officers and Jailers; Fire Investigators; Fish and Game Wardens; Private Detectives and Investigators; Security Guards. PERSONALITY TYPE: Social. Social occupations frequently involve working with, communicating with, and teaching people. These occupations often involve helping or providing service to others.

RELATED KNOWLEDGE/COURSES— Public Safety and Security: Knowledge of relevant equipment, policies, procedures, and strategies to promote effective local, state, or national security operations for the protection of people, data, property, and institutions. Law and Government: Knowledge of laws, legal codes, court procedures, precedents, government regulations, executive orders, agency rules, and the democratic political process. Customer and Personal Service: Knowledge of principles and processes for providing customer and personal services. This includes customer needs assessment, meeting quality standards for services, and evaluation of customer satisfaction. Psychology: Knowledge of human behavior and performance; individual differences in ability, personality, and interests; learning and motivation; psychological research methods; and the assessment and treatment of behavioral

P

and affective disorders. **Education and Training:** Knowledge of principles and methods for curriculum and training design, teaching and instruction for individuals and groups, and the measurement of training effects. **Sociology and Anthropology:** Knowledge of group behavior and dynamics, societal trends and influences, human migrations, ethnicity, and cultures and their history and origins. **Telecommunications:** Knowledge of transmission, broadcasting, switching, control, and operation of telecommunications systems.

WORK ENVIRONMENT—In an enclosed vehicle or equipment; contaminants; very hot or cold; sounds, noise levels are distracting or uncomfortable; outdoors.

Police, Fire, and Ambulance Dispatchers

- ◉ Growth: 12.7%
- ◉ Annual Job Openings: 15,000
- ◉ Annual Earnings: $28,290
- ◉ Percentage of Women: 53.1%

Related Apprenticeship	*Years*
Alarm Operator	1
Telecommunicator	4

Receive complaints from public concerning crimes and police emergencies. Broadcast orders to police patrol units in vicinity of complaint to investigate. Operate radio, telephone, or computer equipment to receive reports of fires and medical emergencies and relay information or orders to proper officials. Determine response requirements and relative priorities of situations and dispatch units in accordance with established procedures. Record details of calls, dispatches, and messages. Question callers to determine their locations and the nature of their problems in order to determine type of response needed. Enter, update, and retrieve information from teletype networks and computerized data systems regarding such things as wanted persons, stolen property, vehicle registration, and stolen vehicles. Scan status charts and computer screens and contact emergency response field units in order to determine emergency units available for dispatch. Relay information and messages to and from emergency sites, to law enforcement agencies, and to all other individuals or groups requiring notification. Receive incoming telephone or alarm system calls regarding emergency and non-emergency police and fire service, emergency ambulance service, information, and after-hours calls for departments within a city. Maintain access to, and security of, highly sensitive materials. Observe alarm registers and scan maps in order to determine whether a specific emergency is in the dispatch service area. Maintain files of information relating to emergency calls such as personnel rosters and emergency call-out and pager files. Monitor various radio frequencies such as those used by public works departments, school security, and civil defense in order to keep apprised of developing situations. Learn material and pass required tests for certification. Read and effectively interpret small-scale maps and information from a computer screen in order to determine locations and provide directions. Answer routine inquiries and refer calls not requiring dispatches to appropriate departments and agencies. Provide emergency medical instructions to callers. Monitor alarm systems to detect emergencies such as fires and illegal entry into establishments. Test and adjust communication and alarm systems and report malfunctions to maintenance units. Operate and maintain mobile dispatch vehicles and equipment. **SKILLS**—Active Listening; Social Perceptiveness; Speaking; Critical Thinking; Service Orientation; Judgment and Decision Making; Active Learning; Instructing.

GOE—**Interest Area:** 09. Business Detail. **Work Group:** 09.06 Communications. **Other Apprenticeable Jobs in This Work Group:** Dispatchers, Except Police, Fire, and Ambulance. **PERSONALITY TYPE:** Social. Social occupations frequently involve working with, communicating with, and teaching people. These occupations often involve helping or providing service to others.

RELATED KNOWLEDGE/COURSES—**Customer and Personal Service:** Knowledge of principles and processes for providing customer and personal services. This includes customer needs assessment, meeting quality standards for services, and evaluation of customer satisfaction. **Telecommunications:** Knowledge of transmission, broadcasting, switching, control, and operation of telecommunications systems. **Public Safety and Security:** Knowledge of relevant equipment, policies, procedures, and strategies to promote effective local, state, or national security operations for the protection of people, data, property, and institutions. **Clerical Practices:** Knowledge of administrative and clerical procedures and systems, such as word processing, managing files and records, stenography and transcription, designing forms, and other office procedures and terminology. **Law and Government:** Knowledge of laws, legal codes, court procedures, precedents, government regulations, executive orders, agency rules, and the democratic political process. **Computers and Electronics:** Knowledge of circuit boards, processors, chips, electronic equipment, and computer hardware and software, including applications and programming.

WORK ENVIRONMENT—Sitting; sounds, noise levels are distracting or uncomfortable; physical proximity; indoors; contaminants.

Postal Service Clerks

- Growth: –0.5%
- Annual Job Openings: 5,000
- Annual Earnings: $39,790
- Percentage of Women: 53.8%

Related Apprenticeship	*Years*
Post-Office Clerk	2

Perform any combination of tasks in a post office, such as receive letters and parcels; sell postage and revenue stamps, postal cards, and stamped envelopes; fill out and sell money orders; place mail in pigeon holes of mail rack or in bags according to state, address, or other scheme; and examine mail for correct postage. Answer questions regarding mail regulations and procedures, postage rates, and post office boxes. Check mail in order to ensure correct postage and ensure that packages and letters are in proper condition for mailing. Complete forms regarding changes of address or theft or

P

loss of mail or for special services such as registered or priority mail. Feed mail into postage canceling devices or hand-stamp mail to cancel postage. Keep money drawers in order and record and balance daily transactions. Obtain signatures from recipients of registered or special delivery mail. Provide customers with assistance in filing claims for mail theft or lost or damaged mail. Put undelivered parcels away, retrieve them when customers come to claim them, and complete any related documentation. Receive letters and parcels and place mail into bags. Register, certify, and insure letters and parcels. Rent post office boxes to customers. Respond to complaints regarding mail theft, delivery problems, and lost or damaged mail, filling out forms and making appropriate referrals for investigation. Sell and collect payment for products such as stamps, prepaid mail envelopes, and money orders. Set postage meters and calibrate them to ensure correct operation. Sort incoming and outgoing mail according to type and destination by hand or by operating electronic mail-sorting and scanning devices. Transport mail from one work station to another. Weigh letters and parcels; compute mailing costs based on type, weight, and destination; and affix correct postage. Cash money orders. Post announcements or government information on public bulletin boards. Provide assistance to the public in complying with federal regulations of Postal Service and other federal agencies. **SKILLS**—Service Orientation; Active Listening.

GOE—**Interest Area:** 09. Business Detail. **Work Group:** 09.09 Clerical Machine Operation. **Other Apprenticeable Jobs in This Work Group:** Computer Operators; Data Entry Keyers; Typesetting and Composing Machine Operators and Tenders; Word Processors and Typists. **PERSONALITY TYPE:** Conventional. Conventional occupations frequently involve following set procedures and routines. These occupations can include working with data and details more than with ideas. Usually there is a clear line of authority to follow.

RELATED KNOWLEDGE/COURSES—**Clerical Practices:** Knowledge of administrative and clerical procedures and systems, such as word processing, managing files and records, stenography and transcription, designing forms, and other office procedures and terminology. **Customer and Personal Service:** Knowledge of principles and processes for providing customer and personal services. This includes customer needs assessment, meeting quality standards for services, and evaluation of customer satisfaction. **Geography:** Knowledge of principles and methods for describing the features of land, sea, and air masses, including their physical characteristics; locations; interrelationships; and distribution of plant, animal, and human life. **Law and Government:** Knowledge of laws, legal codes, court procedures, precedents, government regulations, executive orders, agency rules, and the democratic political process. **Public Safety and Security:** Knowledge of relevant equipment, policies, procedures, and strategies to promote effective local, state, or national security operations for the protection of people, data, property, and institutions. **Sales and Marketing:** Knowledge of principles and methods for showing, promoting, and selling products or services. This includes marketing strategy and tactics, product demonstration, sales techniques, and sales control systems.

WORK ENVIRONMENT—Spend time making repetitive motions; standing; spend time bending or twisting the body; indoors; walking and running; spend time kneeling, crouching, stooping, or crawling.

Potters

- Growth: 6.4%
- Annual Job Openings: 6,000
- Annual Earnings: $24,780
- Percentage of Women: 20.4%

Related Apprenticeship	Years
Model Maker, Pottery and Porcelain	2
Pottery-Machine Operator	3

Mold clay into ware as clay revolves on potter's wheel. Raises and shapes clay into ware, such as vases, saggers, and pitchers, on revolving wheel, using hands, fingers, and thumbs. Smoothes surfaces of finished piece, using rubber scrapers and wet sponge. Adjusts speed of wheel according to feel of changing firmness of clay. Positions ball of clay in center of potter's wheel. Starts motor or pumps treadle with foot to revolve wheel. Pulls wire through base of article and wheel to separate finished piece. Verifies size and form, using calipers and templates. Moves piece from wheel to dry. **SKILLS—** Operation and Control.

GOE—Interest Area: 01. Arts, Entertainment, and Media. **Work Group:** 01.06 Craft Arts. **Other Apprenticeable Jobs in This Work Group:** Craft Artists; Glass Blowers, Molders, Benders, and Finishers. **PERSONALITY TYPE:** Realistic. Realistic occupations frequently involve work activities that include practical, hands-on problems and solutions. They often deal with plants, animals, and real-world materials like wood, tools, and machin-ery. Many of the occupations require working outside and do not involve a lot of paperwork or working closely with others.

RELATED KNOWLEDGE/COURSES— Fine Arts: Knowledge of the theory and techniques required to compose, produce, and perform works of music, dance, visual arts, drama, and sculpture. **Production and Processing:** Knowledge of raw materials, production processes, quality control, costs, and other techniques for maximizing the effective manufacture and distribution of goods.

WORK ENVIRONMENT—Spend time making repetitive motions; sitting; spend time bending or twisting the body; using hands on objects, tools, or controls; contaminants.

Power Distributors and Dispatchers

- Growth: –3.0%
- Annual Job Openings: 1,000
- Annual Earnings: $55,010
- Percentage of Women: 7.4%

Related Apprenticeship	Years
Switchboard Operator, Utilities	3
Load Dispatcher	4
Substation Operator	4

Coordinate, regulate, or distribute electricity or steam. Accept and implement energy schedules, including real-time transmission reservations and schedules. Calculate and determine load estimates or equipment requirements in order to determine required control settings. Control, monitor, or operate equipment that regulates or distributes electricity or steam, using data obtained from instruments or computers. Coordinate with engineers, planners, field personnel, and other utility workers to provide information such as clearances, switching orders, and distribution process changes. Distribute and regulate the flow of power between entities such as generating stations, substations, distribution lines, and users, keeping track of the status of circuits and connections. Inspect equipment to ensure that specifications are met and to detect any defects. Manipulate controls to adjust and activate power distribution equipment and machines. Monitor and record switchboard and control board readings to ensure that electrical or steam distribution equipment is operating properly. Record and compile operational data, such as chart and meter readings, power demands, and usage and operating times, using transmission system maps. Respond to emergencies, such as transformer or transmission line failures, and route current around affected areas. Tend auxiliary equipment used in the power distribution process. Track conditions that could affect power needs, such as changes in the weather, and adjust equipment to meet any anticipated changes. Direct personnel engaged in controlling and operating distribution equipment and machinery (for example, instructing control room operators to start boilers and generators). Prepare switching orders that will isolate work areas without causing power outages, referring to drawings of power systems. Repair, maintain, and clean equipment and machinery, using hand tools. **SKILLS**—Operation Monitoring; Equipment Maintenance; Repairing; Management of Personnel Resources; Operation and Control; Troubleshooting; Instructing; Installation.

GOE—Interest Area: 08. Industrial Production. **Work Group:** 08.06 Systems Operation. **Other Apprenticeable Jobs in This Work Group:** Boiler Operators and Tenders, Low Pressure; Chemical Plant and System Operators; Gaugers; Petroleum Refinery and Control Panel Operators; Power Generating Plant Operators, Except Auxiliary Equipment Operators; Stationary Engineers; Water and Liquid Waste Treatment Plant and System Operators. **PERSONALITY TYPE:** Realistic. Realistic occupations frequently involve work activities that include practical, hands-on problems and solutions. They often deal with plants, animals, and real-world materials like wood, tools, and machinery. Many of the occupations require working outside and do not involve a lot of paperwork or working closely with others.

RELATED KNOWLEDGE/COURSES— **Mechanical Devices:** Knowledge of machines and tools, including their designs, uses, repair, and maintenance. **Physics:** Knowledge and prediction of physical principles and laws and their interrelationships and applications to understanding fluid, material, and atmospheric dynamics and mechanical, electrical, atomic, and subatomic structures and processes. **Engineering and Technology:** Knowledge of the practical application of engineering science and technology. This includes applying principles, techniques, procedures, and equipment to the design and production of various goods and services. **Telecommunications:** Knowledge of transmission, broadcasting, switching, control, and operation of telecommunications systems. **Computers and Electronics:** Knowledge of circuit boards, processors, chips, electronic equipment, and computer hardware and software, including applications and programming.

Administration and Management: Knowledge of business and management principles involved in strategic planning, resource allocation, human resources modeling, leadership technique, production methods, and coordination of people and resources.

WORK ENVIRONMENT—Hazardous conditions; sitting; using hands on objects, tools, or controls; spend time bending or twisting the body; extremely bright or inadequate lighting.

Power Generating Plant Operators, Except Auxiliary Equipment Operators

- Growth: 0.3%
- Annual Job Openings: 3,000
- Annual Earnings: $50,860
- Percentage of Women: 7.4%

Related Apprenticeship	Years
Hydroelectric-Station Operator	3
Power-Plant Operator	4
Turbine Operator	4

(This is one of the most popular apprenticeable jobs.)

Control or operate machinery, such as steam-driven turbogenerators, to generate electric power, often through the use of panelboards, control boards, or semiautomatic equipment. Operates or controls machinery that generates electric power, using control boards or semiautomatic equipment. Compiles and records operational data on specified forms. Maintains and repairs electrical power distribution machinery and equipment, using hand tools. Examines and tests electrical power distribution machinery and equipment, using testing devices. Monitors control and switchboard gauges to determine whether electrical power distribution meets specifications. Adjusts controls on equipment to generate specified electrical power. SKILLS—Operation Monitoring; Operation and Control; Troubleshooting; Equipment Maintenance; Repairing; Science; Quality Control Analysis; Installation.

GOE—Interest Area: 08. Industrial Production. Work Group: 08.06 Systems Operation. Other Apprenticeable Jobs in This Work Group: Boiler Operators and Tenders, Low Pressure; Chemical Plant and System Operators; Gaugers; Petroleum Refinery and Control Panel Operators; Power Distributors and Dispatchers; Stationary Engineers; Water and Liquid Waste Treatment Plant and System Operators. PERSONALITY TYPE: Realistic. Realistic occupations frequently involve work activities that include practical, hands-on problems and solutions. They often deal with plants, animals, and real-world materials like wood, tools, and machinery. Many of the occupations require working outside and do not involve a lot of paperwork or working closely with others.

RELATED KNOWLEDGE/COURSES—Mechanical Devices: Knowledge of machines and tools, including their designs, uses, repair, and maintenance. Engineering and Technology: Knowledge of the practical application of engi-

P

neering science and technology. This includes applying principles, techniques, procedures, and equipment to the design and production of various goods and services. **Physics:** Knowledge and prediction of physical principles and laws and their interrelationships and applications to understanding fluid, material, and atmospheric dynamics and mechanical, electrical, atomic, and subatomic structures and processes. **Computers and Electronics:** Knowledge of circuit boards, processors, chips, electronic equipment, and computer hardware and software, including applications and programming.

WORK ENVIRONMENT—Common protective or safety equipment; hazardous equipment; hazardous conditions; specialized protective or safety equipment; climbing ladders, scaffolds, or poles.

FURTHER INFORMATION—Contact a local joint union-management apprenticeship committee or the nearest office of your state employment service or apprenticeship agency (see Appendix C). To identify the local union office, contact International Brotherhood of Electrical Workers, 1125 15th St. NW, Washington, DC 20005.

Precision Devices Inspectors and Testers

- ⊚ Growth: 4.7%
- ⊚ Annual Job Openings: 87,000
- ⊚ Annual Earnings: $27,750
- ⊚ Percentage of Women: 45.7%

Related Apprenticeship	Years
Calibrator, Military (Instruments and Apparatus)	2
Hydrometer Calibrator	2
Inspector, Precision	2
X-Ray-Equipment Tester	2
Electric-Meter Tester	4
Inspector, Electromechanical	4

Verify accuracy of and adjust precision devices, such as meters and gauges, testing instruments, and clock and watch mechanisms, to ensure that operation of device is in accordance with design specifications. Inspects materials, products, and work in progress for conformance to specifications and adjusts process or assembly equipment to meet standards. Reads dials and meters to verify functioning of equipment according to specifications. Tests and measures finished products, components, or assemblies for functioning, operation, accuracy, or assembly to verify adherence to functional specifications. Marks items for acceptance or rejection, records test results and inspection data, and compares findings with specifications to ensure conformance to standards. Completes necessary procedures to satisfy licensing requirements. Computes and/or calculates data and other information. Confers with vendors and others regarding inspection results and recommends corrective procedures. Disassembles defective parts and components. Estimates operational data to meet acceptable standards. Operates or tends machinery and equipment and uses hand tools. Discards or rejects products, materials, and equipment not meeting specifications.

Analyzes and interprets blueprints, sample data, and other materials to determine, change, or measure specifications or inspection and testing procedures. Fabricates, installs, positions, or connects components, parts, finished products, or instruments for testing or operational purposes. Cleans and maintains test equipment and instruments and certifies that precision instruments meet standards. **SKILLS**—Quality Control Analysis; Operation Monitoring; Technology Design; Installation; Science; Equipment Maintenance; Troubleshooting; Operation and Control.

GOE—**Interest Area:** 08. Industrial Production. **Work Group:** 08.02 Production Technology. **Other Apprenticeable Jobs in This Work Group:** Aircraft Structure Assemblers, Precision; Aircraft Systems Assemblers, Precision; Bench Workers, Jewelry; Bindery Machine Setters and Set-Up Operators; Bookbinders; Buffing and Polishing Set-Up Operators; Coating, Painting, and Spraying Machine Setters and Set-Up Operators; Combination Machine Tool Setters and Set-Up Operators, Metal and Plastic; Dental Laboratory Technicians; Electrical and Electronic Equipment Assemblers; Electrical and Electronic Inspectors and Testers; Electromechanical Equipment Assemblers; Engine and Other Machine Assemblers; Extruding and Drawing Machine Setters, Operators, and Tenders, Metal and Plastic; Extruding, Forming, Pressing, and Compacting Machine Setters and Set-Up Operators; Forging Machine Setters, Operators, and Tenders, Metal and Plastic; Foundry Mold and Coremakers; Gem and Diamond Workers; Grinding, Honing, Lapping, and Deburring Machine Set-Up Operators; Heat Treating, Annealing, and Tempering Machine Operators and Tenders, Metal and Plastic; Jewelers; Lathe and Turning Machine Tool Setters, Operators, and Tenders, Metal and Plastic; Materials Inspectors; Mechanical Inspectors; Metal Molding, Coremaking, and Casting Machine Operators and Tenders; Milling and Planing Machine Setters, Operators, and Tenders, Metal and Plastic; Model and Mold Makers, Jewelry; Motor Vehicle Inspectors; Paper Goods Machine Setters, Operators, and Tenders; Pewter Casters and Finishers; Plastic Molding and Casting Machine Setters and Set-Up Operators; Precision Lens Grinders and Polishers; Precision Mold and Pattern Casters, Except Nonferrous Metals; Precision Pattern and Die Casters, Nonferrous Metals; Press and Press Brake Machine Setters and Set-Up Operators, Metal and Plastic; Production Inspectors, Testers, Graders, Sorters, Samplers, Weighers; Production Workers, All Other; Rolling Machine Setters, Operators, and Tenders, Metal and Plastic; Silversmiths; Textile Knitting and Weaving Machine Setters, Operators, and Tenders; Textile Winding, Twisting, and Drawing Out Machine Setters, Operators, and Tenders; Welding Machine Setters and Set-Up Operators; Woodworking Machine Setters and Set-Up Operators, Except Sawing. **PERSONALITY TYPE:** Realistic. Realistic occupations frequently involve work activities that include practical, hands-on problems and solutions. They often deal with plants, animals, and real-world materials like wood, tools, and machinery. Many of the occupations require working outside and do not involve a lot of paperwork or working closely with others.

RELATED KNOWLEDGE/COURSES— **Design:** Knowledge of design techniques, tools, and principles involved in production of precision technical plans, blueprints, drawings, and models. **Mechanical Devices:** Knowledge of machines and tools, including their designs, uses, repair, and maintenance. **Production and**

Processing: Knowledge of raw materials, production processes, quality control, costs, and other techniques for maximizing the effective manufacture and distribution of goods. **Mathematics:** Knowledge of arithmetic, algebra, geometry, calculus, and statistics and their applications. **Engineering and Technology:** Knowledge of the practical application of engineering science and technology. This includes applying principles, techniques, procedures, and equipment to the design and production of various goods and services. **Physics:** Knowledge and prediction of physical principles and laws and their interrelationships and applications to understanding fluid, material, and atmospheric dynamics and mechanical, electrical, atomic, and subatomic structures and processes.

WORK ENVIRONMENT—Spend time making repetitive motions; common protective or safety equipment; sitting; indoors; walking and running; spend time kneeling, crouching, stooping, or crawling.

Precision Mold and Pattern Casters, Except Nonferrous Metals

- ☺ Growth: 6.4%
- ☺ Annual Job Openings: 6,000
- ☺ Annual Earnings: $24,780
- ☺ Percentage of Women: 20.4%

Related Apprenticeship	Years
Plaster-Pattern Caster	5

Cast molds and patterns from a variety of materials (except nonferrous metals) according to blueprints and specifications. Pours, packs, spreads, or presses plaster, concrete, liquid plastic, or other materials into or around model or mold. Applies reinforcing strips and additional layers of materials to form pattern of model. Reviews specifications, blueprint, or sketch to plan and lay out work. Applies lubricant or parting agent to mold or pattern. Constructs or assembles wooden mold, using clamps and bolts, hand tools, and power tools. Locates and scribes parting line on patterns, using measuring instruments such as calipers, square, and depth gauge. Positions and secures reinforcing structure or materials, flask, mold, model, or pattern. Combines or melts ingredients to attain specified viscosity and shape. Removes casting from mold after specified time, using tools and equipment such as hand tools, power tools, and crane. Verifies dimensions, using measuring instruments such as calipers, vernier gauge, and protractor. Mixes ingredients according to standard formula. Trims or removes excess material, using scraper, knife, or bandsaw. Patches broken edges and fractures, using clay or plaster and molder's hand tools. SKILLS—Installation.

GOE—**Interest Area:** 08. Industrial Production. **Work Group:** 08.02 Production Technology. **Other Apprenticeable Jobs in This Work Group:** Aircraft Structure Assemblers, Precision; Aircraft Systems Assemblers, Precision; Bench Workers, Jewelry; Bindery Machine Setters and Set-Up Operators; Bookbinders; Buffing and Polishing Set-Up Operators; Coating, Painting, and Spraying Machine Setters and Set-Up Operators; Combination Machine Tool Setters and Set-Up Operators, Metal and Plastic; Dental Laboratory Technicians; Electrical and Electronic Equipment Assemblers; Electrical and Electronic Inspectors and Testers; Electromechanical Equipment Assemblers; Engine and Other Machine Assemblers; Extruding and Drawing Machine Setters, Operators, and Tenders, Metal and Plastic; Extruding, Forming, Pressing, and Compacting Machine Setters and Set-Up Operators; Forging Machine Setters, Operators, and Tenders, Metal and Plastic; Foundry Mold and Coremakers; Gem and Diamond Workers; Grinding, Honing, Lapping, and Deburring Machine Set-Up Operators; Heat Treating, Annealing, and Tempering Machine Operators and Tenders, Metal and Plastic; Jewelers; Lathe and Turning Machine Tool Setters, Operators, and Tenders, Metal and Plastic; Materials Inspectors; Mechanical Inspectors; Metal Molding, Coremaking, and Casting Machine Operators and Tenders; Milling and Planing Machine Setters, Operators, and Tenders, Metal and Plastic; Model and Mold Makers, Jewelry; Motor Vehicle Inspectors; Paper Goods Machine Setters, Operators, and Tenders; Pewter Casters and Finishers; Plastic Molding and Casting Machine Setters and Set-Up Operators; Precision Devices Inspectors and Testers; Precision Lens Grinders and Polishers; Precision Pattern and Die Casters, Nonferrous Metals; Press and Press Brake Machine Setters and Set-Up Operators, Metal and Plastic; Production Inspectors, Testers, Graders, Sorters, Samplers, Weighers; Production Workers, All Other; Rolling Machine Setters, Operators, and Tenders, Metal and Plastic; Silversmiths; Textile Knitting and Weaving Machine Setters, Operators, and Tenders; Textile Winding, Twisting, and Drawing Out Machine Setters, Operators, and Tenders; Welding Machine Setters and Set-Up Operators; Woodworking Machine Setters and Set-Up Operators, Except Sawing. **PERSONALITY TYPE:** Realistic. Realistic occupations frequently involve work activities that include practical, hands-on

problems and solutions. They often deal with plants, animals, and real-world materials like wood, tools, and machinery. Many of the occupations require working outside and do not involve a lot of paperwork or working closely with others.

RELATED KNOWLEDGE/COURSES— Production and Processing: Knowledge of raw materials, production processes, quality control, costs, and other techniques for maximizing the effective manufacture and distribution of goods. **Design:** Knowledge of design techniques, tools, and principles involved in production of precision technical plans, blueprints, drawings, and models. **Building and Construction:** Knowledge of the materials, methods, and tools involved in the construction or repair of houses, buildings, or other structures, such as highways and roads. **Engineering and Technology:** Knowledge of the practical application of engineering science and technology. This includes applying principles, techniques, procedures, and equipment to the design and production of various goods and services. **Mechanical Devices:** Knowledge of machines and tools, including their designs, uses, repair, and maintenance. **Physics:** Knowledge and prediction of physical principles and laws and their interrelationships and applications to understanding fluid, material, and atmospheric dynamics and mechanical, electrical, atomic, and subatomic structures and processes. **Chemistry:** Knowledge of the chemical composition, structure, and properties of substances and of the chemical processes and transformations that they undergo. This includes uses of chemicals, their danger signs, production techniques, and disposal methods.

WORK ENVIRONMENT—Standing; indoors; sounds, noise levels are distracting or uncomfortable; hazardous equipment; common protective or safety equipment.

Precision Pattern and Die Casters, Nonferrous Metals

- Growth: 6.4%
- Annual Job Openings: 6,000
- Annual Earnings: $24,780
- Percentage of Women: 20.4%

Related Apprenticeship	Years
Molder, Pattern	4

Cast metal patterns and dies according to specifications from a variety of nonferrous metals, such as aluminum or bronze. Shapes mold to specified contours with sand, using trowel and related tools. Tilts melting pot or uses ladle to pour molten alloy, bronze, or other nonferrous metal into sand mold. Preheats dies or patterns, using blowtorch or other equipment, and applies parting compound. Lowers metal jig into molten metal in prescribed manner to attach anchor bolts to punch. Clamps metal and plywood strips around die or pattern to form mold. Operates foundry furnaces and ovens. Constructs wood patterns used to form sand molds for metal casts. Operates hoist to position dies or patterns on foundry floor. Machines metal patterns to exact dimensions. SKILLS—Operation and Control.

GOE—Interest Area: 08. Industrial Production. **Work Group:** 08.02 Production Technology. **Other Apprenticeable Jobs in This Work Group:** Aircraft Structure Assemblers, Precision; Aircraft Systems Assemblers, Precision; Bench Workers, Jewelry; Bindery Machine Setters and Set-Up Operators; Bookbinders; Buffing and Polishing Set-Up Operators; Coating, Painting, and Spraying Machine Setters and Set-Up Operators; Combination Machine Tool Setters and Set-Up Operators, Metal and Plastic; Dental Laboratory Technicians; Electrical and Electronic Equipment Assemblers; Electrical and Electronic Inspectors and Testers; Electromechanical Equipment Assemblers; Engine and Other Machine Assemblers; Extruding and Drawing Machine Setters, Operators, and Tenders, Metal and Plastic; Extruding, Forming, Pressing, and Compacting Machine Setters and Set-Up Operators; Forging Machine Setters, Operators, and Tenders, Metal and Plastic; Foundry Mold and Coremakers; Gem and Diamond Workers; Grinding, Honing, Lapping, and Deburring Machine Set-Up Operators; Heat Treating, Annealing, and Tempering Machine Operators and Tenders, Metal and Plastic; Jewelers; Lathe and Turning Machine Tool Setters, Operators, and Tenders, Metal and Plastic; Materials Inspectors; Mechanical Inspectors; Metal Molding, Coremaking, and Casting Machine Operators and Tenders; Milling and Planing Machine Setters, Operators, and Tenders, Metal and Plastic; Model and Mold Makers, Jewelry; Motor Vehicle Inspectors; Paper Goods Machine Setters, Operators, and Tenders; Pewter Casters and Finishers; Plastic Molding and Casting Machine Setters and Set-Up Operators; Precision Devices Inspectors and Testers; Precision Lens Grinders and Polishers; Precision Mold and Pattern Casters, Except Nonferrous Metals; Press and Press Brake Machine Setters and Set-Up Operators, Metal and Plastic; Production Inspectors, Testers, Graders, Sorters, Samplers, Weighers; Production Workers, All Other; Rolling Machine Setters, Operators, and Tenders, Metal and Plastic; Silversmiths; Textile Knitting and Weaving Machine Setters, Operators, and Tenders; Textile Winding, Twisting, and Drawing Out Machine Setters, Operators, and Tenders; Welding Machine Setters and Set-Up Operators; Woodworking Machine Setters and Set-Up Operators, Except Sawing. **PERSONALITY TYPE:** Realistic. Realistic occupations frequently involve work activities that include practical, hands-on problems and solutions. They often deal with plants, animals, and real-world materials like wood, tools, and machinery. Many of the occupations require working outside and do not involve a lot of paperwork or working closely with others.

RELATED KNOWLEDGE/COURSES— Production and Processing: Knowledge of raw materials, production processes, quality control, costs, and other techniques for maximizing the effective manufacture and distribution of goods. **Building and Construction:** Knowledge of materials, methods, and the tools involved in the construction or repair of houses, buildings, or other structures such as highways and roads. **Engineering and Technology:** Knowledge of the practical application of engineering science and technology. This includes applying principles, techniques, procedures, and equipment to the design and production of various goods and services. **Design:** Knowledge of design techniques, tools, and principles involved in production of precision technical plans, blueprints, drawings, and models. **Physics:** Knowledge and prediction of physical principles and laws and their interrelationships and applications to

understanding fluid, material, and atmospheric dynamics and mechanical, electrical, atomic, and subatomic structures and processes.

WORK ENVIRONMENT—Very hot or cold; common protective or safety equipment; hazardous conditions; contaminants; hazardous equipment.

Precision Printing Workers

- ◎ Growth: 4.6%
- ◎ Annual Job Openings: 30,000
- ◎ Annual Earnings: $29,340
- ◎ Percentage of Women: 17.8%

Related Apprenticeship	Years
Letterer (Professional and Kindred)	2
Sketch Maker I (Printing and Publishing)	5
Ben-Day Artist	6

Perform variety of precision printing activities, such as duplication of microfilm and reproduction of graphic arts materials. Operates automatic processor to develop photographs, plates, or base material used in single or multi-color proofs. Sets up and operates bindery equipment to cut, assemble, staple, or bind materials. Maintains printing machinery and equipment. Examines and inspects printed material for clarity of print and specified color.

Mixes powdered ink pigments, using matching book and measuring and mixing tools. Reviews layout and customer order to determine size and style of type. Measures density levels of colors or color guides on proofs, using densitometer, and compares readings to set standards. Prints paper or film copies of completed material from computer. Scans artwork, using optical scanner, which changes image into computer-readable form. Enters, positions, and alters size of text, using computer, to make up and arrange pages to produce printed materials. Hand-rubs paper against printing plate to transfer specified design onto paper for use in etching glassware. Operates offset-duplicating machine or small printing press to reproduce single or multicolor copies of line drawings, graphs, or similar materials. Prepares microfiche duplicates of microfilm, using contact printer and developing machine. Positions and aligns negatives to assemble flats for reproduction. Compares test exposures to quality control color guides or exposure guides to determine data for exposure settings. Puts flats into vacuum frame to produce aluminum plate, microfiche print, or single or multicolor proof. Immerses exposed materials into chemical solutions to hand-develop single or multicolor proofs or printing plates. Sets up and operates various types of cameras to produce negatives, photostats, or plastic or paper printing plates. **SKILLS**—Technology Design; Equipment Maintenance; Quality Control Analysis; Operation and Control; Equipment Selection; Operation Monitoring; Troubleshooting; Operations Analysis.

GOE—**Interest Area:** 08. Industrial Production. **Work Group:** 08.03 Production Work. **Other Apprenticeable Jobs in This Work Group:** Bakers, Manufacturing; Bindery Machine Operators and Tenders; Chemical Equipment Controllers and Operators; Coating, Painting, and Spraying Machine Operators and Tenders; Cooling and Freezing Equipment Operators and Tenders; Crushing, Grinding, and Polishing Machine Setters, Operators, and Tenders; Cutters and Trimmers, Hand; Cutting and Slicing Machine Operators and Tenders; Design Printing Machine Setters and Set-Up Operators; Electrolytic Plating and Coating Machine Setters and Set-Up Operators, Metal and Plastic; Electrotypers and Stereotypers; Embossing Machine Set-Up Operators; Engraver Set-Up Operators; Extruding, Forming, Pressing, and Compacting Machine Operators and Tenders; Fabric and Apparel Patternmakers; Film Laboratory Technicians; Fitters, Structural Metal—Precision; Food Batchmakers; Furnace, Kiln, Oven, Drier, and Kettle Operators and Tenders; Hand Compositors and Typesetters; Job Printers; Letterpress Setters and Set-Up Operators; Metal Fabricators, Structural Metal Products; Metal-Refining Furnace Operators and Tenders; Mixing and Blending Machine Setters, Operators, and Tenders; Mold Makers, Hand; Molding and Casting Workers; Numerical Control Machine Tool Operators and Tenders, Metal and Plastic; Offset Lithographic Press Setters and Set-Up Operators; Painting, Coating, and Decorating Workers; Photographic Processing Machine Operators; Photographic Reproduction Technicians; Photographic Retouchers and Restorers; Plate Finishers; Platemakers; Printing Press Machine Operators and Tenders; Production Workers, All Other; Sawing Machine Operators and Tenders; Sawing Machine Setters and Set-Up Operators; Scanner Operators; Separating, Filtering, Clarifying, Precipitating, and Still Machine Setters, Operators, and Tenders; Sewing Machine Operators, Garment; Slaughterers and Meat Packers; Stone Sawyers; Strippers; Team Assemblers; Welder-Fitters; Welders and Cutters; Woodworking Machine Operators and Tenders, Except Sawing. **PERSONALITY TYPE**: Realistic. Realistic occupations frequently involve work activities that include practical, hands-on problems and solutions. They often deal with plants, animals, and real-world materials like wood, tools, and machinery. Many of the occupations require working outside and do not involve a lot of paperwork or working closely with others.

RELATED KNOWLEDGE/COURSES—Computers and Electronics: Knowledge of circuit boards, processors, chips, electronic equipment, and computer hardware and software, including applications and programming. **Chemistry**: Knowledge of the chemical composition, structure, and properties of substances and of the chemical processes and transformations that they undergo. This includes uses of chemicals, their danger signs, production techniques, and disposal methods. **Communications and Media**: Knowledge of media production, communication, and dissemination techniques and methods. This includes alternative ways to inform and entertain via written, oral, and visual media. **Production and Processing**: Knowledge of raw materials, production processes, quality control, costs, and other techniques for maximizing the effective manufacture and distribution of goods. **Fine Arts**: Knowledge of the theory and techniques required to compose, produce, and perform works of music, dance, visual arts, drama, and sculpture.

WORK ENVIRONMENT—Spend time making repetitive motions; standing; spend time kneeling, crouching, stooping, or crawling; using hands on objects, tools, or controls; walking and running; common protective or safety equipment.

Press and Press Brake Machine Setters and Set-Up Operators, Metal and Plastic

- Growth: 6.8%
- Annual Job Openings: 37,000
- Annual Earnings: $25,210
- Percentage of Women: 28.1%

Related Apprenticeship	Years
Press Operator, Heavy Duty	4
Spring Coiling Machine Setter	4

Set up or set up and operate power-press machines or power-brake machines to bend, form, stretch, notch, punch, or straighten metal or plastic plate and structural shapes as specified by work order, blueprints, drawing, templates, or layout. Sets stops on machine bed, changes dies, and adjusts components such as ram or power press when making multiple or successive passes. Operates power press, power brake, apron brake, swaging machine, foot-powered press, hydraulic press, or arbor press according to specifications. Installs, aligns, and secures gears, holding fixtures, and dies to machine bed, using gauges, templates, feelers, shims, and hand tools. Plans sequence of operations, applying knowledge of physical properties of metal. Inspects workpiece for defects. Measures workpiece and verifies dimensions

P

and weight, using micrometer, template, straightedge, and scale. Selects and positions flat, block, radius, or special-purpose die sets into ram and bed of machine, using hoist, crane, measuring instruments, and hand tools. Preheats workpiece, using heating furnace or hand torch. Hand-forms, cuts, or finishes workpiece, using tools such as table saw, hand sledge and anvil, flaring tool, and gauge. Grinds out burrs and sharp edges, using portable grinder, speed lathe, and polishing jack. Lubricates workpiece with oil. Lifts, positions, and secures workpiece between dies of machine, using crane and sledge. **SKILLS**—Science; Installation; Operation Monitoring; Technology Design; Operation and Control; Equipment Maintenance; Quality Control Analysis; Operations Analysis; Repairing.

GOE—Interest Area: 08. Industrial Production. **Work Group:** 08.02 Production Technology. **Other Apprenticeable Jobs in This Work Group:** Aircraft Structure Assemblers, Precision; Aircraft Systems Assemblers, Precision; Bench Workers, Jewelry; Bindery Machine Setters and Set-Up Operators; Bookbinders; Buffing and Polishing Set-Up Operators; Coating, Painting, and Spraying Machine Setters and Set-Up Operators; Combination Machine Tool Setters and Set-Up Operators, Metal and Plastic; Dental Laboratory Technicians; Electrical and Electronic Equipment Assemblers; Electrical and Electronic Inspectors and Testers; Electromechanical Equipment Assemblers; Engine and Other Machine Assemblers; Extruding and Drawing Machine Setters, Operators, and Tenders, Metal and Plastic; Extruding, Forming, Pressing, and Compacting Machine Setters and Set-Up Operators; Forging Machine Setters, Operators, and Tenders, Metal and Plastic; Foundry Mold and Coremakers; Gem and Diamond Workers; Grinding, Honing, Lapping, and Deburring Machine Set-Up Operators; Heat Treating, Annealing, and Tempering Machine Operators and Tenders, Metal and Plastic; Jewelers; Lathe and Turning Machine Tool Setters, Operators, and Tenders, Metal and Plastic; Materials Inspectors; Mechanical Inspectors; Metal Molding, Coremaking, and Casting Machine Operators and Tenders; Milling and Planing Machine Setters, Operators, and Tenders, Metal and Plastic; Model and Mold Makers, Jewelry; Motor Vehicle Inspectors; Paper Goods Machine Setters, Operators, and Tenders; Pewter Casters and Finishers; Plastic Molding and Casting Machine Setters and Set-Up Operators; Precision Devices Inspectors and Testers; Precision Lens Grinders and Polishers; Precision Mold and Pattern Casters, Except Nonferrous Metals; Precision Pattern and Die Casters, Nonferrous Metals; Production Inspectors, Testers, Graders, Sorters, Samplers, Weighers; Production Workers, All Other; Rolling Machine Setters, Operators, and Tenders, Metal and Plastic; Silversmiths; Textile Knitting and Weaving Machine Setters, Operators, and Tenders; Textile Winding, Twisting, and Drawing Out Machine Setters, Operators, and Tenders; Welding Machine Setters and Set-Up Operators; Woodworking Machine Setters and Set-Up Operators, Except Sawing. **PERSONALITY TYPE:** Realistic. Realistic occupations frequently involve work activities that include practical, hands-on problems and solutions. They often deal with plants, animals, and real-world materials like wood, tools, and machinery. Many of the occupations require working outside and do not involve a lot of paperwork or working closely with others.

RELATED KNOWLEDGE/COURSES— Mechanical Devices: Knowledge of machines and tools, including their designs, uses, repair, and maintenance. **Building and Construction:** Knowledge of the materials, methods, and tools involved in the construction or repair of houses, buildings, or other structures, such as highways and roads. **Public Safety and Security:** Knowledge of relevant equipment, policies, procedures, and strategies to promote effective local, state, or national security operations for the protection of people, data, property, and institutions. **Production and Processing:** Knowledge of raw materials, production processes, quality control, costs, and other techniques for maximizing the effective manufacture and distribution of goods. **Design:** Knowledge of design techniques, tools, and principles involved in production of precision technical plans, blueprints, drawings, and models. **Physics:** Knowledge and prediction of physical principles and laws and their interrelationships and applications to understanding fluid, material, and atmospheric dynamics and mechanical, electrical, atomic, and subatomic structures and processes.

WORK ENVIRONMENT—Hazardous equipment; common protective or safety equipment; minor burns, cuts, bites, or stings; sounds, noise levels are distracting or uncomfortable; indoors; standing.

Printing Press Machine Operators and Tenders

- Growth: 4.6%
- Annual Job Openings: 30,000
- Annual Earnings: $29,340
- Percentage of Women: 17.8%

Related Apprenticeship	Years
Assistant Press Operator	2
Printer-Slotter Operator	4
Rotogravure-Press Operator	4
Proof-Press Operator	5

Operate or tend various types of printing machines, such as offset lithographic presses, letter or letterset presses, or flexographic or gravure presses, to produce print on paper or on other materials, such as plastic, cloth, or rubber. Pushes buttons, turns handles, or moves controls and levers to start printing machine or manually controls equipment operation. Turns, pushes, or moves controls to set and adjust speed, temperature, inkflow, and position and pressure tolerances of press. Selects and installs printing plates, rollers, screens, stencils, type, die, and cylinders in machine according to specifications, using hand tools. Loads, positions, and adjusts unprinted materials on holding fixture or in loading and feeding mechanisms of press. Reviews work order to determine ink, stock, and equipment needed for production. Accepts orders, calculates and quotes prices, and receives payments from customers. Discards or corrects misprinted materials, using ink eradicators or solvents. Dismantles and reassembles printing unit or parts, using hand and power tools, to repair, maintain, or adjust machine. Cleans and lubricates printing machine and components (e.g., rollers, screens, typesetting, reservoirs), using oil, solvents, brushes, rags, and hoses. Removes printed materials from press, using handtruck, electric lift, or hoist, and transports them to drying, storage, or finishing areas. Inspects and examines printed products for print clarity, color accuracy, conformance to specifications, and external defects. Pours or spreads paint, ink, color compounds, and other materials into reservoirs, troughs, hoppers, or color holders of printing unit. Blends and tests paint, inks, stains, and solvents according to type of material being printed and workorder specifications. Monitors and controls operation of auxiliary equipment such as cutters, folders, drying ovens, and sanders to assemble and finish product. Directs and monitors activities of workers feeding, inspecting, and tending printing machines and materials. Keeps daily time and materials usage reports and records identifying information printed on manufactured products and parts. Packs and labels cartons, boxes, or bins of finished products. Monitors feeding, printing, and racking processes of press to maintain specified operating levels and detect malfunctions. **SKILLS—** Operation Monitoring; Management of Personnel Resources; Equipment Maintenance; Operation and Control; Installation; Repairing; Quality Control Analysis; Troubleshooting.

GOE—Interest Area: 08. Industrial Production. **Work Group:** 08.03 Production Work. **Other Apprenticeable Jobs in This Work Group:** Bakers, Manufacturing; Bindery Machine Operators and Tenders; Chemical Equipment Controllers and Operators; Coating, Painting, and Spraying Machine Operators and Tenders; Cooling and Freezing Equipment Operators and Tenders; Crushing, Grinding, and Polishing Machine Setters, Operators, and Tenders; Cutters and Trimmers, Hand; Cutting and Slicing Machine Operators and Tenders; Design Printing Machine Setters and Set-Up Operators; Electrolytic Plating and Coating Machine Setters and Set-Up Operators, Metal and Plastic; Electrotypers and Stereotypers; Embossing Machine Set-Up Operators; Engraver Set-Up Operators; Extruding, Form-

ing, Pressing, and Compacting Machine Operators and Tenders; Fabric and Apparel Patternmakers; Film Laboratory Technicians; Fitters, Structural Metal—Precision; Food Batchmakers; Furnace, Kiln, Oven, Drier, and Kettle Operators and Tenders; Hand Compositors and Typesetters; Job Printers; Letterpress Setters and Set-Up Operators; Metal Fabricators, Structural Metal Products; Metal-Refining Furnace Operators and Tenders; Mixing and Blending Machine Setters, Operators, and Tenders; Mold Makers, Hand; Molding and Casting Workers; Numerical Control Machine Tool Operators and Tenders, Metal and Plastic; Offset Lithographic Press Setters and Set-Up Operators; Painting, Coating, and Decorating Workers; Photographic Processing Machine Operators; Photographic Reproduction Technicians; Photographic Retouchers and Restorers; Plate Finishers; Platemakers; Precision Printing Workers; Production Workers, All Other; Sawing Machine Operators and Tenders; Sawing Machine Setters and Set-Up Operators; Scanner Operators; Separating, Filtering, Clarifying, Precipitating, and Still Machine Setters, Operators, and Tenders; Sewing Machine Operators, Garment; Slaughterers and Meat Packers; Stone Sawyers; Strippers; Team Assemblers; Welder-Fitters; Welders and Cutters; Woodworking Machine Operators and Tenders, Except Sawing. **PERSONALITY TYPE:** Realistic. Realistic occupations frequently involve work activities that include practical, hands-on problems and solutions. They often deal with plants, animals, and real-world materials like wood, tools, and machinery. Many of the occupations require working outside and do not involve a lot of paperwork or working closely with others.

RELATED KNOWLEDGE/COURSES— **Production and Processing:** Knowledge of raw materials, production processes, quality control, costs, and other techniques for maximizing the effective manufacture and distribution of goods. **Mechanical Devices:** Knowledge of machines and tools, including their designs, uses, repair, and maintenance. **Chemistry:** Knowledge of the chemical composition, structure, and properties of substances and of the chemical processes and transformations that they undergo. This includes uses of chemicals, their danger signs, production techniques, and disposal methods.

WORK ENVIRONMENT—Common protective or safety equipment; indoors; hazardous equipment; spend time bending or twisting the body; sounds, noise levels are distracting or uncomfortable.

Private Detectives and Investigators

- Growth: 25.3%
- Annual Job Openings: 9,000
- Annual Earnings: $30,410
- Percentage of Women: 34.8%

Related Apprenticeship	Years
Investigator, Private	1

Detect occurrences of unlawful acts or infractions of rules in private establishment or seek, examine, and compile information for client. Write reports and case summaries to document investigations. Alert appropriate personnel to suspects' locations. Count cash and review transactions, sales checks, and register tapes in order to verify amounts and to identify shortages. Expose fraudulent insurance claims or stolen funds. Investigate companies' financial standings or locate funds stolen by embezzlers, using accounting skills. Testify at hearings and court trials to present evidence. Warn troublemakers causing problems on establishment premises and eject them from premises when necessary. Apprehend suspects and release them to law enforcement authorities or security personnel. Conduct background investigations of individuals, such as pre-employment checks, to obtain information about an individual's character, financial status, or personal history. Conduct private investigations on a paid basis. Confer with establishment officials, security departments, police, or postal officials to identify problems, provide information, and receive instructions. Monitor industrial or commercial properties to enforce conformance to establishment rules and to protect people or property. Observe and document activities of individuals in order to detect unlawful acts or to obtain evidence for cases, using binoculars and still or video cameras. Obtain and analyze information on suspects, crimes, and disturbances in order to solve cases, to identify criminal activity, and to gather information for court cases. Perform undercover operations such as evaluating the performance and honesty of employees by posing as customers or employees. Question persons to obtain evidence for cases of divorce, child custody, or missing persons or information about individuals' character or financial status. Search computer databases, credit reports, public records, tax and legal filings, and other resources in order to locate persons or to compile information for investigations. **SKILLS**—Persuasion; Critical Thinking; Systems Evaluation; Active Listening; Social Perceptiveness; Writing; Speaking; Service Orientation.

GOE—Interest Area: 04. Law, Law Enforcement, and Public Safety. **Work Group:** 04.03 Law Enforcement. **Other Apprenticeable Jobs in This Work Group:** Correctional Officers and Jailers; Fire Investigators; Fish and Game Wardens; Police Patrol Officers; Security Guards. **PERSONALITY TYPE:** Enterprising. Enterprising occupations frequently involve starting up and carrying out projects. These occupations can involve leading people and making many decisions. They sometimes require risk taking and often deal with business.

RELATED KNOWLEDGE/COURSES— **Public Safety and Security:** Knowledge of relevant equipment, policies, procedures, and strategies to promote effective local, state, or national security operations for the protection of people, data, property, and institutions. **Psychology:** Knowledge of human behavior and performance; individual differences in ability, personality, and interests; learning and motivation; psychological research methods; and the assessment and treatment of behavioral and affective disorders. **Law and Government:** Knowledge of laws, legal codes, court procedures, precedents, government regulations, executive orders, agency rules, and the democratic political process. **Telecommunications:** Knowledge of transmission, broadcasting, switching, control, and operation of telecommunications systems. **Medicine and Dentistry:** Knowledge of the information and techniques needed to diagnose and treat human injuries, diseases, and deformities. This includes symptoms, treatment alternatives, drug properties and interactions, and preventive health-care measures. **Therapy and Counseling:** Knowl-

edge of principles, methods, and procedures for diagnosis, treatment, and rehabilitation of physical and mental dysfunctions and for career counseling and guidance. **Communications and Media:** Knowledge of media production, communication, and dissemination techniques and methods. This includes alternative ways to inform and entertain via written, oral, and visual media.

WORK ENVIRONMENT—Outdoors; standing; walking and running; climbing ladders, scaffolds, or poles; keeping or regaining balance.

Production Inspectors, Testers, Graders, Sorters, Samplers, Weighers

- Growth: 4.7%
- Annual Job Openings: 87,000
- Annual Earnings: $27,750
- Percentage of Women: 45.7%

Related Apprenticeship	Years
Thermometer Tester	1
Grader	4

Inspect, test, grade, sort, sample, or weigh nonagricultural raw materials or processed, machined, fabricated, or assembled parts or products. Work may be performed before, dur-

ing, or after processing. Grades, classifies, and sorts products according to size, weight, color, or other specifications. Marks, affixes, or stamps product or container to identify defects or denote grade or size information. Records inspection or test data, such as weight, temperature, grade, or moisture content, and number inspected or graded. Collects or selects samples for testing or for use as model. Discards or routes defective products or contaminants for rework or reuse. Notifies supervisor or specified personnel of deviations from specifications, machine malfunctions, or need for equipment maintenance. Reads work order to determine inspection criteria and to verify identification numbers and product type. Uses or operates product to test functional performance. Computes percentages or averages, using formulas and calculator, and prepares reports of inspection or test findings. Sets controls, starts machine, and observes machine that automatically sorts or inspects products. Counts number of product tested or inspected and stacks or arranges for further processing, shipping, or packing. Cleans, trims, makes adjustments, or repairs product or processing equipment to correct defects found during inspection. Transports inspected or tested products to other work stations, using handtruck or lift truck. Wraps and packages product for shipment or delivery. Weighs materials, products, containers, or samples to verify packaging weight, to determine percentage of each ingredient, or to determine sorting. Compares color, shape, texture, or grade of product or material with color chart, template, or sample to verify conformance to standards. Tests samples, materials, or products, using test equipment such as thermometer, voltmeter, moisture meter, or tensiometer, for conformance to specifications. Measures dimensions of product, using measuring instruments such as rulers, calipers, gauges, or micrometers, to verify conformance to specifications. Examines product or monitors processing of product, using any or all of five senses, to determine defects or grade. **SKILLS**—Quality Control Analysis; Operation Monitoring; Operation and Control; Equipment Maintenance; Troubleshooting; Repairing; Management of Material Resources; Science.

GOE—Interest Area: 08. Industrial Production. **Work Group:** 08.02 Production Technology. **Other Apprenticeable Jobs in This Work Group:** Aircraft Structure Assemblers, Precision; Aircraft Systems Assemblers, Precision; Bench Workers, Jewelry; Bindery Machine Setters and Set-Up Operators; Bookbinders; Buffing and Polishing Set-Up Operators; Coating, Painting, and Spraying Machine Setters and Set-Up Operators; Combination Machine Tool Setters and Set-Up Operators, Metal and Plastic; Dental Laboratory Technicians; Electrical and Electronic Equipment Assemblers; Electrical and Electronic Inspectors and Testers; Electromechanical Equipment Assemblers; Engine and Other Machine Assemblers; Extruding and Drawing Machine Setters, Operators, and Tenders, Metal and Plastic; Extruding, Forming, Pressing, and Compacting Machine Setters and Set-Up Operators; Forging Machine Setters, Operators, and Tenders, Metal and Plastic; Foundry Mold and Coremakers; Gem and Diamond Workers; Grinding, Honing, Lapping, and Deburring Machine Set-Up Operators; Heat Treating, Annealing, and Tempering Machine Operators and Tenders, Metal and Plastic; Jewelers; Lathe and Turning Machine Tool Setters, Operators, and Tenders, Metal and Plastic; Materials Inspectors; Mechanical Inspectors; Metal Molding, Coremaking, and Casting Machine Operators and Tenders; Milling and Planing Machine Setters, Operators, and Tenders, Metal and Plastic; Model and Mold Makers, Jewelry; Motor Vehicle Inspectors; Paper Goods Machine Setters, Operators, and Tenders; Pewter Casters and Finishers; Plastic Molding and Casting Machine Setters and Set-Up Operators; Precision Devices Inspectors and Testers; Precision Lens Grinders and Polishers; Precision Mold and Pattern Casters, Except Nonferrous Metals; Precision Pattern and Die Casters, Nonferrous Metals; Press and Press Brake Machine Setters and Set-Up Operators, Metal and Plastic; Production Workers, All Other; Rolling Machine Setters, Operators, and Tenders, Metal and Plastic; Silversmiths; Textile Knitting and Weaving Machine Setters, Operators, and Tenders; Textile Winding, Twisting, and Drawing Out Machine Setters, Operators, and Tenders; Welding Machine Setters and Set-Up Operators; Woodworking Machine Setters and Set-Up Operators, Except Sawing. **PERSONALITY TYPE:** Realistic. Realistic occupations frequently involve work activities that include practical, hands-on problems and solutions. They often deal with plants, animals, and real-world materials like wood, tools, and machinery. Many of the occupations require working outside and do not involve a lot of paperwork or working closely with others.

RELATED KNOWLEDGE/COURSES— **Production and Processing:** Knowledge of raw materials, production processes, quality control, costs, and other techniques for maximizing the effective manufacture and distribution of goods. **Engineering and Technology:** Knowledge of the practical application of engineering science and technology. This includes applying principles, techniques, procedures, and equipment to the design and production of various goods and services. **Mechanical Devices:** Knowledge of machines and tools, including their designs, uses, repair, and maintenance.

WORK ENVIRONMENT—Indoors; walking and running; using hands on objects, tools, or controls; spend time bending or twisting the body; hazardous equipment; spend time making repetitive motions.

Production Workers, All Other

- Growth: 11.3%
- Annual Job Openings: 67,000
- Annual Earnings: $22,260
- Percentage of Women: 34.0%

Related Apprenticeship	Years
Sign Writer, Hand	1
Model-And-Mold Maker, Brick	2
Plastics Fabricator	2
Stencil Cutter	2
Canvas Worker	3
Patternmaker, Plaster	3
Airplane Coverer	4

All production workers not listed separately. **SKILLS**—No data available.

GOE—**Interest Area:** 08. Industrial Production. **Work Group:** 08.02 Production Technology; 08.03 Production Work. **Other Apprenticeable Jobs in This Work Group:** Aircraft Structure Assemblers, Precision; Aircraft Systems Assemblers, Precision; Bakers, Manufacturing; Bench Workers, Jewelry; Bindery Machine Operators and Tenders; Bindery Machine Setters and Set-Up Operators; Bookbinders; Buffing and Polishing Set-Up Operators; Chemical Equipment Controllers and Operators; Coating, Painting, and Spraying Machine Operators and Tenders; Coating, Painting, and Spraying Machine Setters and Set-Up Operators; Combination Machine Tool Setters and Set-Up Operators, Metal and Plastic; Cooling and Freezing Equipment Operators and Tenders; Crushing, Grinding, and Polishing Machine Setters, Operators, and Tenders; Cutters and Trimmers, Hand; Cutting and Slicing Machine Operators and Tenders; Dental Laboratory Technicians; Design Printing Machine Setters and Set-Up Operators; Electrical and Electronic Equipment Assemblers; Electrical and Electronic Inspectors and Testers; Electrolytic Plating and Coating Machine Setters and Set-Up Operators, Metal and Plastic; Electromechanical Equipment Assemblers; Electrotypers and Stereotypers; Embossing Machine Set-Up Operators; Engine and Other Machine Assemblers; Engraver Set-Up Operators; Extruding and Drawing Machine Setters, Operators, and Tenders, Metal and Plastic; Extruding, Forming, Pressing, and Compacting Machine Operators and Tenders; Extruding, Forming, Pressing, and Compacting Machine Setters and Set-Up Operators; Fabric and Apparel Patternmakers; Film Laboratory Technicians; Fitters, Structural Metal—Precision; Food Batchmakers; Forging Machine Setters, Operators, and Tenders, Metal and Plastic; Foundry Mold and Coremakers; Furnace, Kiln, Oven, Drier, and Kettle Operators and Tenders; Gem and Diamond Workers; Grinding, Honing, Lapping, and Deburring Machine Set-Up Operators; Hand Compositors and Typesetters; Heat Treating, Annealing, and Tempering

Machine Operators and Tenders, Metal and Plastic; Jewelers; Job Printers; Lathe and Turning Machine Tool Setters, Operators, and Tenders, Metal and Plastic; Letterpress Setters and Set-Up Operators; Materials Inspectors; Mechanical Inspectors; Metal Fabricators, Structural Metal Products; Metal Molding, Coremaking, and Casting Machine Operators and Tenders; Metal-Refining Furnace Operators and Tenders; Milling and Planing Machine Setters, Operators, and Tenders, Metal and Plastic; Mixing and Blending Machine Setters, Operators, and Tenders; Model and Mold Makers, Jewelry; Mold Makers, Hand; Molding and Casting Workers; Motor Vehicle Inspectors; Numerical Control Machine Tool Operators and Tenders, Metal and Plastic; Offset Lithographic Press Setters and Set-Up Operators; Painting, Coating, and Decorating Workers; Paper Goods Machine Setters, Operators, and Tenders; Pewter Casters and Finishers; Photographic Processing Machine Operators; Photographic Reproduction Technicians; Photographic Retouchers and Restorers; Plastic Molding and Casting Machine Setters and Set-Up Operators; Plate Finishers; Platemakers; Precision Devices Inspectors and Testers; Precision Lens Grinders and Polishers; Precision Mold and Pattern Casters, Except Nonferrous Metals; Precision Pattern and Die Casters, Nonferrous Metals; Precision Printing Workers; Press and Press Brake Machine Setters and Set-Up Operators, Metal and Plastic; Printing Press Machine Operators and Tenders; Production Inspectors, Testers, Graders, Sorters, Samplers, Weighers; Rolling Machine Setters, Operators, and Tenders, Metal and Plastic; Sawing Machine Operators and Tenders; Sawing Machine Setters and Set-Up Operators; Scanner Operators; Separating, Filtering, Clarifying, Precipitating, and Still Machine Setters, Operators, and Tenders; Sewing Machine Operators, Garment; Silversmiths; Slaughterers and Meat Packers; Stone Sawyers; Strippers; Team Assemblers; Textile Knitting and Weaving Machine Setters, Operators, and Tenders; Textile Winding, Twisting, and Drawing Out Machine Setters, Operators, and Tenders; Welder-Fitters; Welders and Cutters; Welding Machine Setters and Set-Up Operators; Woodworking Machine Operators and Tenders, Except Sawing; Woodworking Machine Setters and Set-Up Operators, Except Sawing. **PERSONALITY TYPE:** No data available.

RELATED KNOWLEDGE/COURSES—No data available.

WORK ENVIRONMENT—No data available.

Production, Planning, and Expediting Clerks

- ⊚ Growth: 14.1%
- ⊚ Annual Job Openings: 51,000
- ⊚ Annual Earnings: $34,820
- ⊚ Percentage of Women: 53.0%

Related Apprenticeship	Years
Material Coordinator	2
Supercargo	2

Coordinate and expedite the flow of work and materials within or between departments of an establishment according to production sched-ule. **Duties include reviewing and distributing production, work, and shipment schedules; conferring with department supervisors to determine progress of work and completion dates; and compiling reports on progress of work, inventory levels, costs, and production problems.** Reviews documents, such as production schedules, staffing tables, and specifications, to obtain information, such as materials, priorities, and personnel requirements. Compiles schedules and orders, such as personnel assignments, production, work flow, transportation, and maintenance and repair. Monitors work progress; provides services, such as furnishing permits, tickets, and union information; and directs workers to expedite work flow. Requisitions and maintains inventory of materials and supplies to meet production demands. Calculates figures, such as labor and materials amounts, manufacturing costs, and wages, using pricing schedules, adding machine, or calculator. Maintains files, such as maintenance records, bills of lading, and cost reports. Arranges for delivery and distributes supplies and parts to expedite flow of materials to meet production schedules. Examines documents, materials, and products and monitors work processes for completeness, accuracy, and conformance to standards and specifications. Completes status reports, such as production progress, customer information, and materials inventory. Confers with establishment personnel, vendors, and customers to coordinate processing and shipping and to resolve complaints. **SKILLS**—Management of Material Resources; Management of Personnel Resources; Management of Financial Resources; Time Management; Service Orientation; Systems Analysis; Negotiation; Systems Evaluation.

GOE—Interest Area: 09. Business Detail. Work Group: 09.04 Material Control. **Other Apprenticeable Jobs in This Work Group:** No other apprenticeable jobs in this group. **PERSONALITY TYPE:** Conventional. Conventional occupations frequently involve following set procedures and routines. These occupations can include working with data and details more than with ideas. Usually there is a clear line of authority to follow.

RELATED KNOWLEDGE/COURSES— **Clerical Practices:** Knowledge of administrative and clerical procedures and systems, such as word processing, managing files and records, stenography and transcription, designing forms, and other office procedures and terminology. **Production and Processing:** Knowledge of raw materials, production processes, quality control, costs, and other techniques for maximizing the effective manufacture and distribution of goods. **Economics and Accounting:** Knowledge of economic and accounting principles and practices, the financial markets, banking, and the analysis and reporting of financial data. **Mathematics:** Knowledge of arithmetic, algebra, geometry, calculus, and statistics and their applications. **Computers and Electronics:** Knowledge of circuit boards, processors, chips, electronic equipment, and computer hardware and software, including applications and programming. **Administration and Management:** Knowledge of business and management principles involved in strategic planning, resource allocation, human resources modeling, leadership technique, production methods, and coordination of people and resources.

WORK ENVIRONMENT—Sitting; indoors; walking and running; disease or infections; climbing ladders, scaffolds, or poles.

Professional Photographers

- Growth: 13.6%
- Annual Job Openings: 18,000
- Annual Earnings: $25,050
- Percentage of Women: 38.3%

Related Apprenticeship	*Years*
Photographer, Still	3

Photograph subjects or newsworthy events, using still cameras, color or black-and-white film, and variety of photographic accessories. Frames subject matter and background in lens to capture desired image. Focuses camera and adjusts settings based on lighting, subject material, distance, and film speed. Selects and assembles equipment and required background properties according to subject, materials, and conditions. Directs activities of workers assisting in setting up photographic equipment. Arranges subject material in desired position. Estimates or measures light level, distance, and number of exposures needed, using measuring devices and formulas. SKILLS—Equipment Selection; Management of Material Resources; Technology Design; Operation and Control; Social Perceptiveness; Management of Personnel Resources; Equipment Maintenance; Monitoring; Time Management.

GOE—**Interest Area:** 01. Arts, Entertainment, and Media. **Work Group:** 01.08 Media Technology. **Other Apprenticeable Jobs in This Work Group:** Audio and Video Equipment

Technicians; Broadcast Technicians; Camera Operators, Television, Video, and Motion Picture; Film and Video Editors; Radio Operators; Sound Engineering Technicians. **PERSONALITY TYPE:** Artistic. Artistic occupations frequently involve working with forms, designs, and patterns. They often require self-expression, and the work can be done without following a clear set of rules.

RELATED KNOWLEDGE/COURSES— Fine Arts: Knowledge of the theory and techniques required to compose, produce, and perform works of music, dance, visual arts, drama, and sculpture. **Communications and Media:** Knowledge of media production, communication, and dissemination techniques and methods. This includes alternative ways to inform and entertain via written, oral, and visual media. **Chemistry:** Knowledge of the chemical composition, structure, and properties of substances and of the chemical processes and transformations that they undergo. This includes uses of chemicals, their danger signs, production techniques, and disposal methods. **Geography:** Knowledge of principles and methods for describing the features of land, sea, and air masses, including their physical characteristics; locations; interrelationships; and distribution of plant, animal, and human life. **Physics:** Knowledge and prediction of physical principles and laws and their interrelationships and applications to understanding fluid, material, and atmospheric dynamics and mechanical, electrical, atomic, and subatomic structures and processes. **Transportation:** Knowledge of principles and methods for moving people or goods by air, rail, sea, or road, including the relative costs and benefits.

WORK ENVIRONMENT—Standing; extremely bright or inadequate lighting; outdoors; very hot or cold; hazardous conditions.

Rail Car Repairers

- Growth: 4.5%
- Annual Job Openings: 1,000
- Annual Earnings: $39,610
- Percentage of Women: 1.0%

Related Apprenticeship	Years
Mine-Car Repairer	2
Car Repairer	4
Mechanical-Unit Repairer	4

Diagnose, adjust, repair, or overhaul railroad rolling stock, mine cars, or mass transit rail cars. Adjust repaired or replaced units as needed to ensure proper operation. Disassemble units such as water pumps, control valves, and compressors so that repairs can be made. Examine car roofs for wear and damage and repair defective sections, using roofing material, cement, nails, and waterproof paint. Inspect components such as bearings, seals, gaskets, wheels, and coupler assemblies to determine if repairs are needed. Inspect the interior and exterior of rail cars coming into rail yards in order to identify defects and to determine the extent of wear and damage. Install and repair interior flooring, fixtures, walls, plumbing, steps, and platforms. Paint car exteriors, interiors, and fixtures. Perform scheduled maintenance and clean units and components. Repair and maintain electrical and electronic controls for propulsion and braking systems. Repair or replace defective or worn parts such as bearings, pistons, and gears, using hand tools, torque wrenches, power tools, and welding equipment.

Repair window sash frames, attach weather stripping and channels to frames, and replace window glass, using hand tools. Repair, fabricate, and install steel or wood fittings, using blueprints, shop sketches, and instruction manuals. Replace defective wiring and insulation and tighten electrical connections, using hand tools. Test electrical systems of cars by operating systems and using testing equipment such as ammeters. Test units for operability before and after repairs. Align car sides for installation of car ends and crossties, using width gauges, turnbuckles, and wrenches. Measure diameters of axle wheel seats, using micrometers, and mark dimensions on axles so that wheels can be bored to specified dimensions. Record conditions of cars and repair and maintenance work performed or to be performed. Remove locomotives, car mechanical units, or other components, using pneumatic hoists and jacks, pinch bars, hand tools, and cutting torches. Repair car upholstery. **SKILLS**—Repairing; Equipment Maintenance; Installation; Troubleshooting; Quality Control Analysis; Equipment Selection; Operation Monitoring.

GOE—**Interest Area:** 05. Mechanics, Installers, and Repairers. **Work Group:** 05.03 Mechanical Work. **Other Apprenticeable Jobs in This Work Group:** Aircraft Engine Specialists; Airframe-and-Power-Plant Mechanics; Automotive Body and Related Repairers; Automotive Glass Installers and Repairers; Automotive Master Mechanics; Automotive Specialty Technicians; Bus and Truck Mechanics and Diesel Engine Specialists; Camera and Photographic Equipment Repairers; Coin, Vending, and Amusement Machine Servicers and Repairers; Farm Equipment Mechanics; Gas Appliance Repairers; Hand and Portable Power Tool Repairers; Heating and Air Conditioning Mechanics; Helpers—Installation, Maintenance, and Repair Workers; Industrial Machinery Mechanics; Installation, Maintenance, and Repair Workers, All Other; Keyboard Instrument Repairers and Tuners; Locksmiths and Safe Repairers; Maintenance and Repair Workers, General; Maintenance Workers, Machinery; Mechanical Door Repairers; Medical Appliance Technicians; Medical Equipment Repairers; Meter Mechanics; Millwrights; Mobile Heavy Equipment Mechanics, Except Engines; Motorboat Mechanics; Motorcycle Mechanics; Optical Instrument Assemblers; Outdoor Power Equipment and Other Small Engine Mechanics; Painters, Transportation Equipment; Recreational Vehicle Service Technicians; Reed or Wind Instrument Repairers and Tuners; Refrigeration Mechanics; Stringed Instrument Repairers and Tuners; Valve and Regulator Repairers; Watch Repairers. **PERSONALITY TYPE:** Realistic. Realistic occupations frequently involve work activities that include practical, hands-on problems and solutions. They often deal with plants, animals, and real-world materials like wood, tools, and machinery. Many of the occupations require working outside and do not involve a lot of paperwork or working closely with others.

RELATED KNOWLEDGE/COURSES— **Mechanical Devices:** Knowledge of machines and tools, including their designs, uses, repair, and maintenance. **Building and Construction:** Knowledge of the materials, methods, and tools involved in the construction or repair of houses, buildings, or other structures, such as highways and roads. **Engineering and Technology:** Knowledge of the practical application of engineering science and technology. This includes applying principles, techniques, procedures, and equipment to the design and production of various goods and services. **Design:** Knowledge of design techniques, tools, and principles involved in production of precision technical plans, blueprints, drawings, and models. **Transportation:** Knowledge of principles and methods for moving people or goods by air, rail, sea, or road, including the relative costs and benefits. **Physics:** Knowledge and prediction of physical principles and laws and their interrelationships and applications to understanding fluid, material, and atmospheric dynamics and mechanical, electrical, atomic, and subatomic structures and processes.

WORK ENVIRONMENT—Outdoors; hazardous equipment; minor burns, cuts, bites, or stings; spend time kneeling, crouching, stooping, or crawling; sounds, noise levels are distracting or uncomfortable.

Recreational Vehicle Service Technicians

- Growth: 21.8%
- Annual Job Openings: 4,000
- Annual Earnings: $27,270
- Percentage of Women: 1.6%

Related Apprenticeship	Years
Repairer, Recreational Vehicle	4

Diagnose, inspect, adjust, repair, or overhaul recreational vehicles including travel trailers. May specialize in maintaining gas, electrical, hydraulic, plumbing, or chassis/towing systems as well as repairing generators, appliances, and interior components. Connects water hose to inlet pipe of plumbing system and tests operation of toilets and sinks. Repairs leaks with caulking compound or replaces pipes, using pipe wrench. Inspects, examines, and tests operation of parts or systems to be repaired and to verify completeness of work performed. Locates and repairs frayed wiring, broken connections, or incorrect wiring, using ohmmeter, soldering iron, tape, and hand tools. Repairs plumbing and propane gas lines, using caulking compounds and plastic or copper pipe. Removes damaged exterior panels, repairs and replaces structural frame members, and seals leaks, using hand tools. Connects electrical system to outside power source and activates switches to test operation of appliances and light fixtures. Confers with customer or reads work order to determine nature and extent of damage to unit. Seals open side of modular units to prepare them for shipment, using polyethylene sheets, nails, and hammer. Resets hardware, using chisel, mallet, and screwdriver. Refinishes wood surfaces on cabinets, doors, moldings, and floors, using power sander, putty, spray equipment, brush, paints, or varnishes. Opens and closes doors, windows, and drawers to test their operation and trims edges to fit, using jack-plane or drawknife. Lists parts needed, estimates costs, and plans work procedure, using parts list, technical manuals, and diagrams. **SKILLS**—Installation; Repairing; Troubleshooting; Equipment Maintenance; Equipment Selection; Quality Control Analysis; Technology Design; Systems Evaluation.

GOE—Interest Area: 05. Mechanics, Installers, and Repairers. **Work Group:** 05.03 Mechanical Work. **Other Apprenticeable Jobs in This Work Group:** Aircraft Engine Specialists; Airframe-and-Power-Plant Mechanics; Automotive Body and Related Repairers; Automotive Glass Installers and Repairers; Automotive Master Mechanics; Automotive Specialty Technicians; Bus and Truck Mechanics and Diesel Engine Specialists; Camera and Photographic Equipment Repairers; Coin, Vending, and Amusement Machine Servicers and Repairers; Farm Equipment Mechanics; Gas Appliance Repairers; Hand and Portable Power Tool Repairers; Heating and Air Conditioning Mechanics; Helpers—Installation, Maintenance, and Repair Workers; Industrial Machinery Mechanics; Installation, Maintenance, and Repair Workers, All Other; Keyboard Instrument Repairers and Tuners; Locksmiths and Safe Repairers; Maintenance and Repair Workers, General; Maintenance Workers, Machinery; Mechanical Door Repairers; Medical Appliance Technicians; Medical Equipment Repairers; Meter Mechanics; Millwrights; Mobile Heavy Equipment Mechanics, Except Engines; Motorboat Mechanics; Motorcycle Mechanics; Optical Instrument Assemblers; Outdoor Power Equipment and Other Small Engine Mechanics; Painters, Transportation Equipment; Rail Car Repairers; Reed or Wind Instrument Repairers and Tuners; Refrigeration Mechanics; Stringed Instrument Repairers and Tuners; Valve and Regulator Repairers; Watch Repairers. **PERSONALITY TYPE:** Realistic. Realistic occupations frequently involve work activities that include practical, hands-on problems and solutions. They often deal with plants, animals, and real-world materials like wood, tools, and machinery. Many of the occupations require working outside and do not involve a lot of paperwork or working closely with others.

RELATED KNOWLEDGE/COURSES— Building and Construction: Knowledge of the materials, methods, and tools involved in the construction or repair of houses, buildings, or other structures, such as highways and roads. **Mechanical Devices:** Knowledge of machines and tools, including their designs, uses, repair, and maintenance. **Design:** Knowledge of design techniques, tools, and principles involved in production of precision technical plans, blueprints, drawings, and models. **Engineering and Technology:** Knowledge of the practical application of engineering science and technology. This includes applying principles, techniques, procedures, and equipment to the design and production of various goods and services. **Physics:** Knowledge and prediction of physical principles and laws and their interrelationships and applications to understanding fluid, material, and atmospheric dynamics and mechanical, electrical, atomic, and subatomic structures and processes.

WORK ENVIRONMENT—Hazardous conditions; outdoors; standing; climbing ladders, scaffolds, or poles; spend time kneeling, crouching, stooping, or crawling.

Refrigeration Mechanics

- Growth: 31.8%
- Annual Job Openings: 35,000
- Annual Earnings: $35,160
- Percentage of Women: 1.8%

Related Apprenticeship	Years
Refrigeration Mechanic	3
Refrigeration Unit Repairer	3

Install and repair industrial and commercial refrigerating systems. Adjust or replace worn or defective mechanisms and parts, and reassemble repaired systems. Adjust valves according to specifications and charge system with proper type of refrigerant by pumping the specified gas or fluid into the system. Braze or solder parts to repair defective joints and leaks. Cut, bend, thread, and connect pipe to functional components and water, power, or refrigeration system. Dismantle malfunctioning systems and test components, using electrical, mechanical, and pneumatic testing equipment. Drill holes and install mounting brackets and hangers into floor and walls of building. Fabricate and assemble structural and functional components of refrigeration system, using hand tools, power tools, and welding equipment. Install expansion and control valves, using acetylene torches and wrenches. Install wiring to connect components to an electric power source. Lay out reference points for installation of structural and functional components, using measuring instruments. Lift and align components into position, using hoist or block and tackle. Mount compressor, condenser, and other components in specified locations on frames, using hand tools and acetylene welding equipment. Observe and test system operation, using gauges and instruments. Perform mechanical overhauls and refrigerant reclaiming. Read blueprints to determine location, size, capacity, and type of components needed to build refrigeration system. Test lines, components, and connections for leaks. Estimate, order, pick up, deliver, and install materials and supplies needed to maintain equipment in good working condition. Insulate shells and cabinets of systems. Keep records of repairs and replacements made and causes of malfunctions. Schedule work with customers and initiate work orders, house requisitions and orders from stock. Supervise and instruct assistants. **SKILLS**—Installation; Repairing; Troubleshooting; Equipment Maintenance; Quality Control Analysis; Operation Monitoring; Technology Design; Equipment Selection.

GOE—Interest Area: 05. Mechanics, Installers, and Repairers. **Work Group:** 05.03 Mechanical Work. **Other Apprenticeable Jobs in This Work Group:** Aircraft Engine Specialists; Airframe-and-Power-Plant Mechanics; Automotive Body and Related Repairers; Automotive Glass Installers and Repairers; Automotive Master Mechanics; Automotive Specialty Technicians; Bus and Truck Mechanics and Diesel Engine Specialists; Camera and Photographic Equipment Repairers; Coin, Vending, and Amusement Machine Servicers and Repairers; Farm Equipment Mechanics; Gas Appliance Repairers; Hand and Portable Power Tool Repairers; Heating and Air Conditioning Mechanics; Helpers—Installation, Maintenance, and Repair Workers; Industrial Machinery Mechanics; Installation, Maintenance, and Repair Workers, All Other; Keyboard Instrument Repairers and Tuners; Locksmiths and Safe Repairers; Maintenance and Repair Workers, General; Maintenance Workers, Machinery; Mechanical Door Repairers; Medical Appliance Technicians; Medical Equipment Repairers; Meter Mechanics; Millwrights; Mobile Heavy Equipment Mechanics, Except Engines; Motorboat Mechanics; Motorcycle Mechanics; Optical Instrument Assemblers; Outdoor Power Equipment and Other Small Engine Mechanics; Painters, Transportation Equipment; Rail Car Repairers; Recreational Vehicle Service Technicians; Reed or Wind Instrument Repairers and Tuners; Stringed Instrument Repairers and Tuners; Valve and Regulator Repairers; Watch Repairers. **PERSONALITY TYPE:**

Realistic. Realistic occupations frequently involve work activities that include practical, hands-on problems and solutions. They often deal with plants, animals, and real-world materials like wood, tools, and machinery. Many of the occupations require working outside and do not involve a lot of paperwork or working closely with others.

RELATED KNOWLEDGE/COURSES— **Mechanical Devices:** Knowledge of machines and tools, including their designs, uses, repair, and maintenance. **Engineering and Technology:** Knowledge of the practical application of engineering science and technology. This includes applying principles, techniques, procedures, and equipment to the design and production of various goods and services. **Building and Construction:** Knowledge of the materials, methods, and tools involved in the construction or repair of houses, buildings, or other structures, such as highways and roads. **Design:** Knowledge of design techniques, tools, and principles involved in production of precision technical plans, blueprints, drawings, and models. **Physics:** Knowledge and prediction of physical principles and laws and their interrelationships and applications to understanding fluid, material, and atmospheric dynamics and mechanical, electrical, atomic, and subatomic structures and processes. **Clerical Practices:** Knowledge of administrative and clerical procedures and systems, such as word processing, managing files and records, stenography and transcription, designing forms, and other office procedures and terminology. **Chemistry:** Knowledge of the chemical composition, structure, and properties of substances and of the chemical processes and transformations that they undergo. This includes uses of chemicals, their danger signs, production techniques, and disposal methods.

WORK ENVIRONMENT—Hazardous equipment; spend time kneeling, crouching, stooping, or crawling; hazardous conditions; using hands on objects, tools, or controls; spend time bending or twisting the body.

Reinforcing Iron and Rebar Workers

- Growth: 16.7%
- Annual Job Openings: 2,000
- Annual Earnings: $34,950
- Percentage of Women: 2.4%

Related Apprenticeship	*Years*
Reinforcing-Metal Worker	3

Position and secure steel bars or mesh in concrete forms in order to reinforce concrete. Use a variety of fasteners, rod-bending machines, blowtorches, and hand tools. Cut and fit wire mesh or fabric, using hooked rods, and position fabric or mesh in concrete to reinforce concrete. Cut rods to required lengths, using metal shears, hacksaws, bar cutters, or acetylene torches. Bend steel rods with hand tools and rod-bending machines, and weld them with arc-welding equipment. Determine quantities, sizes, shapes, and locations of reinforcing rods from blueprints, sketches, or oral instructions. Position and secure steel bars, rods, cables, or mesh in concrete forms, using fasteners, rod-bending machines, blowtorches, and hand tools. Space and fasten together rods in forms according to blueprints, using wire and pliers. Place blocks under rebar to hold the bars off the deck when reinforcing floors. **SKILLS**—None met the criteria.

GOE—Interest Area: 06. Construction, Mining, and Drilling. **Work Group:** 06.02 Construction. **Other Apprenticeable Jobs in This Work Group:** Boat Builders and Shipwrights; Boilermakers; Brickmasons and Blockmasons; Carpet Installers; Ceiling Tile Installers; Cement Masons and Concrete Finishers; Construction and Related Workers, All Other; Construction Carpenters; Drywall Installers; Electricians; Fence Erectors; Floor Layers, Except Carpet, Wood, and Hard Tiles; Glaziers; Grader, Bulldozer, and Scraper Operators; Insulation Workers, Floor, Ceiling, and Wall; Insulation Workers, Mechanical; Operating Engineers; Painters, Construction and Maintenance; Paperhangers; Paving, Surfacing, and Tamping Equipment Operators; Pipe Fitters; Plasterers and Stucco Masons; Plumbers; Riggers; Roofers; Rough Carpenters; Sheet Metal Workers; Ship Carpenters and Joiners; Stone Cutters and Carvers; Stonemasons; Structural Iron and Steel Workers; Tapers; Terrazzo Workers and Finishers; Tile and Marble Setters. **PERSONALITY TYPE:** Realistic. Realistic occupations frequently involve work activities that include practical, hands-on problems and solutions. They often deal with plants, animals, and real-world materials like wood, tools, and machinery. Many of the occupations require working outside and do not involve a lot of paperwork or working closely with others.

RELATED KNOWLEDGE/COURSES— Building and Construction: Knowledge of the materials, methods, and tools involved in the construction or repair of houses, buildings, or other structures, such as highways and roads. **Physics:** Knowledge and prediction of physical principles and laws and their interrelationships and applications to understanding fluid, material, and atmospheric dynamics and mechanical, electrical, atomic, and subatomic structures and processes. **Engineering and Technology:** Knowledge of the practical application of engineering science and technology. This includes applying principles, techniques, procedures, and equipment to the design and production of various goods and services. **Design:** Knowledge of design techniques, tools, and principles involved in production of precision technical plans, blueprints, drawings, and models. **Public Safety and Security:** Knowledge of relevant equipment, policies, procedures, and strategies to promote effective local, state, or national security operations for the protection of people, data, property, and institutions.

WORK ENVIRONMENT—Minor burns, cuts, bites, or stings; common protective or safety equipment; outdoors; hazardous equipment; spend time bending or twisting the body.

Riggers

- Growth: 14.3%
- Annual Job Openings: 3,000
- Annual Earnings: $33,800
- Percentage of Women: 1.7%

Related Apprenticeship	Years
Rigger (Ship-Boat Manufacturing)	2
Rigger (Any Industry)	3

Set up or repair rigging for construction projects, manufacturing plants, logging yards, ships and shipyards, or for the entertainment industry. Align, level, and anchor machinery. Attach loads to rigging to provide support or prepare them for moving, using hand and power tools. Attach pulleys and blocks to fixed overhead structures such as beams, ceilings, and gin pole booms, using bolts and clamps. Control movement of heavy equipment through narrow openings or confined spaces, using chainfalls, gin poles, gallows frames, and other equipment. Dismantle and store rigging equipment after use. Fabricate, set up, and repair rigging, supporting structures, hoists, and pulling gear, using hand and power tools. Manipulate rigging lines, hoists, and pulling gear to move or support materials such as heavy equipment, ships, or theatrical sets. Select gear such as cables, pulleys, and winches, according to load weights and sizes, facilities, and work schedules. Signal or verbally direct workers engaged in hoisting and moving loads, in order to ensure safety of workers and materials. Test rigging to ensure safety and reliability. Tilt, dip, and turn suspended loads to maneuver over, under, and/or around obstacles, using multi-point suspension techniques. Clean and dress machine surfaces and component parts. Install ground rigging for yarding lines, attaching chokers to logs and then to the lines. SKILLS—Technology Design; Repairing; Coordination; Science; Installation; Operation Monitoring; Operation and Control; Management of Personnel Resources.

GOE—Interest Area: 06. Construction, Mining, and Drilling. Work Group: 06.02 Construction. Other Apprenticeable Jobs in This Work Group: Boat Builders and Shipwrights; Boilermakers; Brickmasons and Blockmasons; Carpet Installers; Ceiling Tile Installers; Cement Masons and Concrete Finishers; Construction and Related Workers, All Other; Construction Carpenters; Drywall Installers; Electricians; Fence Erectors; Floor Layers, Except Carpet, Wood, and Hard Tiles; Glaziers; Grader, Bulldozer, and Scraper Operators; Insulation Workers, Floor, Ceiling, and Wall; Insulation Workers, Mechanical; Operating Engineers; Painters, Construction and Maintenance; Paperhangers; Paving, Surfacing, and Tamping Equipment Operators; Pipe Fitters; Plasterers and Stucco Masons; Plumbers; Reinforcing Iron and Rebar Workers; Roofers; Rough Carpenters; Sheet Metal Workers; Ship Carpenters and Joiners; Stone Cutters and Carvers; Stonemasons; Structural Iron and Steel Workers; Tapers; Terrazzo Workers and Finishers; Tile and Marble Setters. PERSONALITY TYPE: Realistic. Realistic occupations frequently involve work activities that include practical, hands-on problems and solutions. They often deal with plants, animals, and real-world materials like wood, tools, and machinery. Many of the occupations require working outside and do not involve a lot of paperwork or working closely with others.

RELATED KNOWLEDGE/COURSES— Public Safety and Security: Knowledge of relevant equipment, policies, procedures, and strategies to promote effective local, state, or national security operations for the protection of people, data, property, and institutions. Mechanical Devices: Knowledge of machines and tools, including their designs, uses, repair, and maintenance. Engineering and Technology: Knowledge of the practical application of engineering science and technology. This includes applying principles, techniques, procedures, and equipment to the design and production of various goods and services. Building and Construction: Knowledge of the materials, methods, and tools involved in the construction or repair of houses, buildings, or other structures, such as highways and roads. **Physics:** Knowledge and prediction of physical principles and laws and their interrelationships and applications to understanding fluid, material, and atmospheric dynamics and mechanical, electrical, atomic, and subatomic structures and processes.

WORK ENVIRONMENT—Climbing ladders, scaffolds, or poles; high places; outdoors; keeping or regaining balance; hazardous equipment.

Roofers

- Growth: 18.6%
- Annual Job Openings: 38,000
- Annual Earnings: $30,020
- Percentage of Women: 1.6%

Related Apprenticeship	*Years*
Roofer	2

(This is one of the most popular apprenticeable jobs.)

Cover roofs of structures with shingles, slate, asphalt, aluminum, wood, and related materials. May spray roofs, sidings, and walls with material to bind, seal, insulate, or soundproof sections of structures. Fastens composition shingles or sheets to roof with asphalt, cement, or nails. Cuts roofing paper to size and nails or staples paper to roof in overlapping strips to form base for roofing materials. Cleans and maintains equipment. Removes snow, water, or debris from roofs prior to applying roofing materials. Insulates, soundproofs, and seals buildings with foam, using spray gun, air compressor, and heater. Punches holes in slate, tile, terra cotta, or wooden shingles, using punch and hammer. Applies gravel or pebbles over top layer, using rake or stiff-bristled broom. Applies alternate layers of hot asphalt or tar and roofing paper until roof covering is completed as specified. Overlaps successive layers of roofing material, determining distance of overlap, using chalkline, gauge on shingling hatchet, or lines on shingles. Cuts strips of flashing and fits them into angles formed by walls, vents, and intersecting roof surfaces. Mops or pours hot asphalt or tar onto roof base when applying asphalt or tar and gravel to roof. Aligns roofing material with edge of roof. **SKILLS**—Repairing; Installation; Coordination; Equipment Selection; Operation and Control; Equipment Maintenance.

GOE—Interest Area: 06. Construction, Mining, and Drilling. **Work Group:** 06.02 Construction. **Other Apprenticeable Jobs in This Work Group:** Boat Builders and Shipwrights; Boilermakers; Brickmasons and Blockmasons; Carpet Installers; Ceiling Tile Installers; Cement Masons and Concrete Finishers; Construction and Related Workers, All Other; Construction Carpenters; Drywall Installers; Electricians; Fence Erectors; Floor Layers, Except Carpet, Wood, and Hard Tiles; Glaziers; Grader, Bulldozer, and Scraper Operators; Insulation Workers, Floor, Ceiling, and Wall; Insulation Workers, Mechanical; Operating Engineers; Painters, Construction and Maintenance; Paperhangers; Paving, Surfacing, and

Tamping Equipment Operators; Pipe Fitters; Plasterers and Stucco Masons; Plumbers; Reinforcing Iron and Rebar Workers; Riggers; Rough Carpenters; Sheet Metal Workers; Ship Carpenters and Joiners; Stone Cutters and Carvers; Stonemasons; Structural Iron and Steel Workers; Tapers; Terrazzo Workers and Finishers; Tile and Marble Setters. **PERSONALITY TYPE:** Realistic. Realistic occupations frequently involve work activities that include practical, hands-on problems and solutions. They often deal with plants, animals, and real-world materials like wood, tools, and machinery. Many of the occupations require working outside and do not involve a lot of paperwork or working closely with others.

RELATED KNOWLEDGE/COURSES— Building and Construction: Knowledge of the materials, methods, and tools involved in the construction or repair of houses, buildings, or other structures, such as highways and roads. **Mechanical Devices:** Knowledge of machines and tools, including their designs, uses, repair, and maintenance.

WORK ENVIRONMENT—High places; outdoors; climbing ladders, scaffolds, or poles; spend time kneeling, crouching, stooping, or crawling; keeping or regaining balance.

FURTHER INFORMATION—Contact a local joint union-management apprenticeship committee or the nearest office of your state employment service or apprenticeship agency (see Appendix C). To identify the local union office, contact United Union of Roofers, Waterproofers, and Allied Workers, 1660 L St. NW, Suite 800, Washington, DC 20036. Internet: http://www.unionroofers.org.

Rotary Drill Operators, Oil and Gas

- Growth: 1.5%
- Annual Job Openings: 2,000
- Annual Earnings: $34,910
- Percentage of Women: 1.3%

Related Apprenticeship	Years
Prospecting Driller	2

Set up or operate a variety of drills to remove petroleum products from the earth and to find and remove core samples for testing during oil and gas exploration. Bolt together pump and engine parts, and connect tanks and flow lines. Cap wells with packers, or turn valves, in order to regulate outflow of oil from wells. Clean and oil pulleys, blocks, and cables. Connect sections of drill pipe, using hand tools and powered wrenches and tongs. Count sections of drill rod in order to determine depths of boreholes. Dig holes, set forms, and mix and pour concrete, for foundations of steel or wooden derricks. Direct rig crews in drilling and other activities, such as setting up rigs and completing or servicing wells. Line drilled holes with pipes, and install all necessary hardware, in order to prepare new wells. Lower and explode charges in boreholes in order to start flow of oil from wells. Monitor progress of drilling operations, and select and change drill bits according to the nature of strata, using hand tools. Observe pressure gauge and move throttles and levers in order to control the speed of rotary tables, and to regulate pressure of tools at bottoms of boreholes. Position and prepare truck-mounted derricks at drilling areas that are specified on field maps. Push levers and brake pedals in order to control gasoline, diesel, electric, or steam draw works that lower and raise drill pipes and casings in and out of wells. Remove core samples during drilling in order to determine the nature of the strata being drilled. Start and examine operation of slush pumps in order to ensure circulation and consistency of drilling fluid or mud in well. Weigh clay, and mix with water and chemicals to make drilling mud. Locate and recover lost or broken bits, casings, and drill pipes from wells, using special tools. Maintain and adjust machinery in order to ensure proper performance. Maintain records of footage drilled, location and nature of strata penetrated, materials and tools used, services rendered, and time required. Plug observation wells, and restore sites. Repair or replace defective parts of machinery, such as rotary drill rigs, water trucks, air compressors, and pumps, using hand tools. Train crews, and introduce procedures to make drill work more safe and effective. **SKILLS**—Repairing; Operation Monitoring; Operation and Control; Equipment Maintenance; Equipment Selection.

GOE—**Interest Area:** 06. Construction, Mining, and Drilling. **Work Group:** 06.03 Mining and Drilling. **Other Apprenticeable Jobs in This Work Group:** Mine Cutting and Channeling Machine Operators; Well and Core Drill Operators. **PERSONALITY TYPE:** Realistic. Realistic occupations frequently involve work activities that include practical, hands-on problems and solutions. They often deal with plants, animals, and real-world materials like wood, tools, and machinery. Many of the occupations require working outside and do not involve a lot of paperwork or working closely with others.

RELATED KNOWLEDGE/COURSES—**Mechanical Devices:** Knowledge of machines and tools, including their designs, uses, repair, and maintenance. **Physics:** Knowledge and prediction of physical principles and laws and their interrelationships and applications to understanding fluid, material, and atmospheric dynamics and mechanical, electrical, atomic, and subatomic structures and processes. **Engineering and Technology:** Knowledge of the practical application of engineering science and technology. This includes applying principles, techniques, procedures, and equipment to the design and production of various goods and services. **Geography:** Knowledge of principles and methods for describing the features of land, sea, and air masses, including their physical characteristics; locations; interrelationships; and distribution of plant, animal, and human life. **Building and Construction:** Knowledge of the materials, methods, and tools involved in the construction or repair of houses, buildings, or other structures, such as highways and roads. **Transportation:** Knowledge of principles and methods for moving people or goods by air, rail, sea, or road, including the relative costs and benefits.

WORK ENVIRONMENT—Outdoors; hazardous equipment; minor burns, cuts, bites, or stings; hazardous conditions; exposed to whole-body vibration.

Rough Carpenters

- Growth: 10.1%
- Annual Job Openings: 193,000
- Annual Earnings: $34,250
- Percentage of Women: 1.9%

Related Apprenticeship	*Years*
Form Builder	2
Carpenter, Piledriver	4
Carpenter, Rough	4

Build rough wooden structures, such as concrete forms, scaffolds, tunnel, bridge, or sewer supports, billboard signs, and temporary frame shelters, according to sketches, blueprints, or oral instructions. Anchor and brace forms and other structures in place, using nails, bolts, anchor rods, steel cables, planks, wedges, and timbers. Assemble and fasten material together to construct wood or metal framework of structure, using bolts, nails, or screws. Bore boltholes in timber, masonry or concrete walls, using power drill. Cut or saw boards, timbers, or plywood to required size, using handsaw, power saw, or woodworking machine. Erect forms, framework, scaffolds, hoists, roof supports, or chutes, using hand tools, plumb rule, and level. Install rough door and window frames, subflooring, fixtures, or temporary supports in structures undergoing construction or repair. Mark cutting lines on materials, using pencil and scriber. Measure materials or distances, using square, measuring tape, or rule to lay out work. Study blueprints and diagrams to determine dimensions of structure or form to be constructed. Build chutes for pouring concrete. Dig or direct digging of post holes and set poles to support structures. Examine structural timbers and supports to detect decay, and replace timbers as required, using hand tools, nuts, and bolts. Fabricate parts, using woodworking and metalworking machines. Build sleds from logs and timbers for use in hauling camp buildings and machinery through wooded areas. **SKILLS**—Installation; Repairing; Operation and Control; Management of Material Resources.

GOE—Interest Area: 06. Construction, Mining, and Drilling. **Work Group:** 06.02 Construction. **Other Apprenticeable Jobs in This Work Group:** Boat Builders and Shipwrights; Boilermakers; Brickmasons and Blockmasons; Carpet Installers; Ceiling Tile Installers; Cement Masons and Concrete Finishers; Construction and Related Workers, All Other; Construction Carpenters; Drywall Installers; Electricians; Fence Erectors; Floor Layers, Except Carpet, Wood, and Hard Tiles; Glaziers; Grader, Bulldozer, and Scraper Operators; Insulation Workers, Floor, Ceiling, and Wall; Insulation Workers, Mechanical; Operating Engineers; Painters, Construction and Maintenance; Paperhangers; Paving, Surfacing, and Tamping Equipment Operators; Pipe Fitters; Plasterers and Stucco Masons; Plumbers; Reinforcing Iron and Rebar Workers; Riggers; Roofers; Sheet Metal Workers; Ship Carpenters and Joiners; Stone Cutters and Carvers; Stonemasons; Structural Iron and Steel Workers; Tapers; Terrazzo Workers and Finishers; Tile and Marble Setters. **PERSONALITY TYPE:** Realistic. Realistic occupations frequently involve work activities that include practical, hands-on problems and solutions. They often deal with plants, animals, and real-world materials like wood, tools, and machinery. Many of the occupations require working outside and do not involve a lot of paperwork or working closely with others.

RELATED KNOWLEDGE/COURSES—Building and Construction: Knowledge of the materials, methods, and tools involved in the construction or repair of houses, buildings, or other structures, such as highways and roads.

Design: Knowledge of design techniques, tools, and principles involved in production of precision technical plans, blueprints, drawings, and models. **Engineering and Technology:** Knowledge of the practical application of engineering science and technology. This includes applying principles, techniques, procedures, and equipment to the design and production of various goods and services. **Physics:** Knowledge and prediction of physical principles and laws and their interrelationships and applications to understanding fluid, material, and atmospheric dynamics and mechanical, electrical, atomic, and subatomic structures and processes. **Mechanical Devices:** Knowledge of machines and tools, including their designs, uses, repair, and maintenance.

WORK ENVIRONMENT—Outdoors; climbing ladders, scaffolds, or poles; high places; hazardous equipment; common protective or safety equipment.

Scanner Operators

◎ Growth: −11.2%

◎ Annual Job Openings: 6,000

◎ Annual Earnings: $31,660

◎ Percentage of Women: 47.6%

Related Apprenticeship	Years
Scanner Operator	2

Operate electronic or computerized scanning equipment to produce and screen film separations of photographs or art for use in producing lithographic printing plates. Evaluate and correct for deficiencies in the film. Activates scanner to produce positive or negative films for each primary color and black in original copy. Unloads exposed film from scanner and places film in automatic processor to develop image on film. Inspects developed film for specified results and quality and forwards acceptable negatives or positives to other workers or customer. Performs tests to determine exposure adjustments on scanner and adjusts scanner controls until specified results are obtained. Positions color transparency, negative, or reflection copy on scanning drum and mounts drum and head on scanner. Analyzes original to evaluate color density, gradation highlights, middle tones, and shadows, using densitometer and knowledge of light and color. Types on scanner keyboard or touches mouse to symbols on scanner video display unit to input software or moves controls to set scanner to specific color density, size, screen ruling, and exposure adjustments. Loads film into holder, places holder in exposing chamber, and starts mechanism that loads and secures film on scanner drum. SKILLS—Quality Control Analysis; Operation and Control; Monitoring; Operation Monitoring.

GOE—Interest Area: 08. Industrial Production. Work Group: 08.03 Production Work. Other Apprenticeable Jobs in This Work Group: Bakers, Manufacturing; Bindery Machine Operators and Tenders; Chemical Equipment Controllers and Operators; Coating, Painting, and Spraying Machine Operators and Tenders; Cooling and Freezing Equipment Operators and Tenders; Crushing, Grinding, and Polishing Machine Setters, Operators, and Tenders; Cutters and Trimmers, Hand; Cutting and Slicing Machine Operators and Tenders;

Design Printing Machine Setters and Set-Up Operators; Electrolytic Plating and Coating Machine Setters and Set-Up Operators, Metal and Plastic; Electrotypers and Stereotypers; Embossing Machine Set-Up Operators; Engraver Set-Up Operators; Extruding, Forming, Pressing, and Compacting Machine Operators and Tenders; Fabric and Apparel Patternmakers; Film Laboratory Technicians; Fitters, Structural Metal—Precision; Food Batchmakers; Furnace, Kiln, Oven, Drier, and Kettle Operators and Tenders; Hand Compositors and Typesetters; Job Printers; Letterpress Setters and Set-Up Operators; Metal Fabricators, Structural Metal Products; Metal-Refining Furnace Operators and Tenders; Mixing and Blending Machine Setters, Operators, and Tenders; Mold Makers, Hand; Molding and Casting Workers; Numerical Control Machine Tool Operators and Tenders, Metal and Plastic; Offset Lithographic Press Setters and Set-Up Operators; Painting, Coating, and Decorating Workers; Photographic Processing Machine Operators; Photographic Reproduction Technicians; Photographic Retouchers and Restorers; Plate Finishers; Platemakers; Precision Printing Workers; Printing Press Machine Operators and Tenders; Production Workers, All Other; Sawing Machine Operators and Tenders; Sawing Machine Setters and Set-Up Operators; Separating, Filtering, Clarifying, Precipitating, and Still Machine Setters, Operators, and Tenders; Sewing Machine Operators, Garment; Slaughterers and Meat Packers; Stone Sawyers; Strippers; Team Assemblers; Welder-Fitters; Welders and Cutters; Woodworking Machine Operators and Tenders, Except Sawing. **PERSONALITY TYPE:** Realistic. Realistic occupations frequently involve work activities that include practical, hands-on problems and solutions.

They often deal with plants, animals, and real-world materials like wood, tools, and machinery. Many of the occupations require working outside and do not involve a lot of paperwork or working closely with others.

RELATED KNOWLEDGE/COURSES— Production and Processing: Knowledge of raw materials, production processes, quality control, costs, and other techniques for maximizing the effective manufacture and distribution of goods. **Fine Arts:** Knowledge of the theory and techniques required to compose, produce, and perform works of music, dance, visual arts, drama, and sculpture. **Computers and Electronics:** Knowledge of circuit boards, processors, chips, electronic equipment, and computer hardware and software, including applications and programming. **Communications and Media:** Knowledge of media production, communication, and dissemination techniques and methods. This includes alternative ways to inform and entertain via written, oral, and visual media. **Physics:** Knowledge and prediction of physical principles and laws and their interrelationships and applications to understanding fluid, material, and atmospheric dynamics and mechanical, electrical, atomic, and subatomic structures and processes. **Chemistry:** Knowledge of the chemical composition, structure, and properties of substances and of the chemical processes and transformations that they undergo. This includes uses of chemicals, their danger signs, production techniques, and disposal methods.

WORK ENVIRONMENT—Sitting; using hands on objects, tools, or controls; extremely bright or inadequate lighting; spend time making repetitive motions.

Secretaries, Except Legal, Medical, and Executive

- Growth: −2.9%
- Annual Job Openings: 254,000
- Annual Earnings: $25,420
- Percentage of Women: 96.5%

Related Apprenticeship	Years
Script Supervisor	1

Perform routine clerical and administrative functions such as drafting correspondence, scheduling appointments, organizing and maintaining paper and electronic files, or providing information to callers. Operate office equipment such as fax machines, copiers, and phone systems, and use computers for spreadsheet, word processing, database management, and other applications. Answer telephones and give information to callers, take messages, or transfer calls to appropriate individuals. Greet visitors and callers, handle their inquiries, and direct them to the appropriate persons according to their needs. Set up and maintain paper and electronic filing systems for records, correspondence, and other material. Locate and attach appropriate files to incoming correspondence requiring replies. Open, read, route, and distribute incoming mail and other material, and prepare answers to routine letters. Complete forms in accordance with company procedures. Make copies of correspondence and other printed material. Review work done by others to check for correct spelling and grammar, ensure that company format policies are followed, and recommend revisions. Compose, type, and distribute meeting notes, routine correspondence, and reports. Learn to operate new office technologies as they are developed and implemented. Maintain scheduling and event calendars. Schedule and confirm appointments for clients, customers, or supervisors. Manage projects, and contribute to committee and team work. Mail newsletters, promotional material, and other information. Order and dispense supplies. Conduct searches to find needed information, using such sources as the Internet. Provide services to customers, such as order placement and account information. Collect and disburse funds from cash accounts, and keep records of collections and disbursements. Prepare and mail checks. Establish work procedures and schedules, and keep track of the daily work of clerical staff. Coordinate conferences and meetings. Take dictation in shorthand or by machine, and transcribe information. Arrange conferences, meetings, and travel reservations for office personnel. Operate electronic mail systems and coordinate the flow of information both internally and with other organizations. Supervise other clerical staff, and provide training and orientation to new staff. **SKILLS**—Social Perceptiveness; Instructing; Writing; Active Listening; Time Management; Learning Strategies; Persuasion; Speaking.

GOE—Interest Area: 09. Business Detail. **Work Group:** 09.02 Administrative Detail. **Other Apprenticeable Jobs in This Work Group:** Legal Secretaries; Medical Secretaries. **PERSONALITY TYPE:** Conventional. Conventional occupations frequently involve following set procedures and routines. These occupations can include working with data and details more than with ideas. Usually there is a clear line of authority to follow.

RELATED KNOWLEDGE/COURSES— Clerical Practices: Knowledge of administrative and clerical procedures and systems, such as word processing, managing files and records, stenography and transcription, designing forms, and other office procedures and terminology. **Customer and Personal Service:** Knowledge of principles and processes for providing customer and personal services. This includes customer needs assessment, meeting quality standards for services, and evaluation of customer satisfaction. **Computers and Electronics:** Knowledge of circuit boards, processors, chips, electronic equipment, and computer hardware and software, including applications and programming. **English Language:** Knowledge of the structure and content of the English language, including the meaning and spelling of words, rules of composition, and grammar. **Economics and Accounting:** Knowledge of economic and accounting principles and practices, the financial markets, banking, and the analysis and reporting of financial data. **Personnel and Human Resources:** Knowledge of principles and procedures for personnel recruitment, selection, training, compensation and benefits, labor relations and negotiation, and personnel information systems.

WORK ENVIRONMENT—Sitting; sounds, noise levels are distracting or uncomfortable; physical proximity; contaminants; indoors.

Security Guards

- Growth: 31.9%
- Annual Job Openings: 228,000
- Annual Earnings: $19,660
- Percentage of Women: 21.0%

Related Apprenticeship	Years
Guard, Security	1.5

Guard, patrol, or monitor premises to prevent theft, violence, or infractions of rules. Patrol industrial and commercial premises to prevent and detect signs of intrusion and ensure security of doors, windows, and gates. Answer alarms and investigate disturbances. Monitor and authorize entrance and departure of employees, visitors, and other persons to guard against theft and maintain security of premises. Write reports of daily activities and irregularities, such as equipment or property damage, theft, presence of unauthorized persons, or unusual occurrences. Call police or fire departments in cases of emergency, such as fire or presence of unauthorized persons. Circulate among visitors, patrons, and employees to preserve order and protect property. Answer telephone calls to take messages, answer questions, and provide information during non-business hours or when switchboard is closed. Warn persons of rule infractions or violations, and apprehend or evict violators from premises, using force when necessary. Operate detecting devices to screen individuals and prevent passage of prohibited articles into restricted areas. Escort or drive motor vehicle to transport individuals to specified locations and to provide personal protection. Inspect and adjust security systems, equipment, and machinery to ensure operational use and to detect evidence of tampering. Drive and guard armored vehicle to transport money and valuables to prevent theft and ensure safe delivery. **SKILLS**—Social Perceptiveness; Negotiation; Learning Strategies; Time Management; Speaking; Active Listening; Monitoring; Critical Thinking.

GOE—Interest Area: 04. Law, Law Enforcement, and Public Safety. **Work Group:** 04.03 Law Enforcement. **Other Apprenticeable Jobs in This Work Group:** Correctional Officers and Jailers; Fire Investigators; Fish and Game Wardens; Police Patrol Officers; Private Detectives and Investigators. **PERSONALITY TYPE:** Social. Social occupations frequently involve working with, communicating with, and teaching people. These occupations often involve helping or providing service to others.

RELATED KNOWLEDGE/COURSES— **Public Safety and Security:** Knowledge of relevant equipment, policies, procedures, and strategies to promote effective local, state, or national security operations for the protection of people, data, property, and institutions. **Customer and Personal Service:** Knowledge of principles and processes for providing customer and personal services. This includes customer needs assessment, meeting quality standards for services, and evaluation of customer satisfaction. **Law and Government:** Knowledge of laws, legal codes, court procedures, precedents, government regulations, executive orders, agency rules, and the democratic political process. **Clerical Practices:** Knowledge of administrative and clerical procedures and systems, such as word processing, managing files and records, stenography and transcription,

designing forms, and other office procedures and terminology. **English Language:** Knowledge of the structure and content of the English language, including the meaning and spelling of words, rules of composition, and grammar. **Telecommunications:** Knowledge of transmission, broadcasting, switching, control, and operation of telecommunications systems.

WORK ENVIRONMENT—Very hot or cold; physical proximity; sounds, noise levels are distracting or uncomfortable; extremely bright or inadequate lighting; sitting.

Separating, Filtering, Clarifying, Precipitating, and Still Machine Setters, Operators, and Tenders

- Growth: 0.8%
- Annual Job Openings: 5,000
- Annual Earnings: $31,720
- Percentage of Women: 14.1%

Related Apprenticeship	Years
Recovery Operator (Paper and Pulp)	1
Buttermaker	1.2
Fourdrinier-Machine Operator	3
Purification Operator II	4

Set up, operate, or tend continuous flow or vat-type equipment; filter presses; shaker screens; centrifuges; condenser tubes; precipitating, fermenting, or evaporating tanks; scrubbing towers; or batch stills. These machines extract, sort, or separate liquids, gases, or solids from other materials to recover a refined product. Includes dairy processing equipment operators. Connect pipes between vats and processing equipment. Inspect machines and equipment for hazards, operating efficiency, malfunctions, wear, and leaks. Install and maintain or repair hoses, pumps, filters, or screens in order to maintain processing equipment, using hand tools. Maintain logs of instrument readings, test results, and shift production, and send production information to computer databases. Pack bottles into cartons or crates, using machines. Remove full bags or containers from discharge outlets, and replace them with empty ones. Test samples to determine viscosity, acidity, specific gravity, or degree of concentration, using test equipment such as viscometers, pH meters, and hydrometers. Turn valves to pump sterilizing solutions and rinsewater through pipes and equipment, and to spray vats with atomizers. Clean and sterilize tanks, screens, inflow pipes, production areas, and equipment, using hoses, brushes, scrapers, or chemical solutions. Collect samples of materials or products for laboratory analysis. Dump, pour, or load specified amounts of refined or unrefined materials into equipment or containers for further processing or storage. Examine samples visually or by hand to verify qualities such as clarity, cleanliness, consistency, dryness, and texture. Measure or weigh materials to be refined, mixed, transferred, stored, or otherwise processed. Monitor material flow and instruments such as temperature and pressure gauges, indicators, and meters, in order to ensure optimal processing conditions. Remove clogs, defects, and impurities from machines, tanks, conveyors, screens, or other processing equipment. Set or adjust machine controls to regulate conditions such as material flow, temperature, and pressure. Start agitators, shakers, conveyors, pumps, or centrifuge machines, then turn valves or move controls to admit, drain, separate, filter, clarify, mix, or transfer materials. Assemble fittings, valves, bowls, plates, disks, impeller shafts, and other parts to equipment in order to prepare equipment for operation. Communicate processing instructions to other workers. **SKILLS**—Operation Monitoring; Equipment Maintenance; Repairing; Operation and Control; Installation; Quality Control Analysis; Troubleshooting; Science.

GOE—Interest Area: 08. Industrial Production. **Work Group:** 08.03 Production Work. **Other Apprenticeable Jobs in This Work Group:** Bakers, Manufacturing; Bindery Machine Operators and Tenders; Chemical Equipment Controllers and Operators; Coating, Painting, and Spraying Machine Operators and Tenders; Cooling and Freezing Equipment Operators and Tenders; Crushing, Grinding, and Polishing Machine Setters, Operators, and Tenders; Cutters and Trimmers, Hand; Cutting and Slicing Machine Operators and Tenders; Design Printing Machine Setters and Set-Up Operators; Electrolytic Plating and Coating Machine Setters and Set-Up Operators, Metal and Plastic; Electrotypers and Stereotypers; Embossing Machine Set-Up Operators; Engraver Set-Up Operators; Extruding, Forming, Pressing, and Compacting Machine Operators and Tenders; Fabric and Apparel Patternmakers; Film Laboratory Technicians; Fitters, Structural Metal—Precision; Food Batchmakers; Furnace, Kiln, Oven, Drier, and Kettle Operators and Tenders; Hand Compositors and Typesetters; Job Printers; Letterpress Setters and Set-Up Operators; Metal Fabricators, Structural Metal Products; Metal-Refining Furnace Operators and Tenders; Mixing and Blending Machine Setters, Operators, and Tenders; Mold Makers, Hand; Molding and Casting Workers; Numerical Control Machine Tool Operators and Tenders, Metal and Plastic; Offset Lithographic Press Setters and Set-Up Operators; Painting, Coating, and Decorating Workers; Photographic Processing Machine Operators; Photographic Reproduction Technicians; Photographic Retouchers and Restorers; Plate Finishers; Platemakers; Precision Printing Workers; Printing Press Machine Operators and Tenders; Production Workers, All Other; Sawing Machine Operators and Tenders; Sawing Machine Setters and Set-Up Operators; Scanner Operators; Sewing Machine Operators, Garment; Slaughterers and Meat Packers; Stone Sawyers; Strippers; Team Assemblers; Welder-Fitters; Welders and Cutters; Woodworking Machine Operators and Tenders, Except Sawing. **PERSONALITY TYPE:** Realistic. Realistic occupations frequently involve work activities that include practical, hands-on problems and solutions. They often deal with plants, animals, and real-world materials like wood, tools, and machinery. Many of the occupations require working outside and do not involve a lot of paperwork or working closely with others.

RELATED KNOWLEDGE/COURSES—Chemistry: Knowledge of the chemical composition, structure, and properties of substances and of the chemical processes and transformations that they undergo. This includes uses of chemicals, their danger signs, production techniques, and disposal methods. **Mechanical Devices:** Knowledge of machines and tools, including their designs, uses, repair, and maintenance. **Production and Processing:** Knowledge of raw materials, production processes, quality control, costs, and other techniques for maximizing the effective manufacture and distribution of goods. **Clerical Practices:** Knowledge of administrative and clerical procedures and systems, such as word processing, managing files and records, stenography and transcription, designing forms, and other office procedures and terminology.

WORK ENVIRONMENT—Common protective or safety equipment; contaminants; using hands on objects, tools, or controls; standing; spend time making repetitive motions.

Sheet Metal Workers

- Growth: 19.8%
- Annual Job Openings: 30,000
- Annual Earnings: $35,000
- Percentage of Women: 4.1%

Related Apprenticeship	Years
Sheet-Metal Worker	4

(This is one of the most popular apprenticeable jobs.)

Fabricate, assemble, install, and repair sheet metal products and equipment, such as ducts, control boxes, drainpipes, and furnace casings. Work may involve any of the following: setting up and operating fabricating machines to cut, bend, and straighten sheet metal; shaping

metal over anvils, blocks, or forms using hammer operating soldering and welding equipment to join sheet metal parts inspecting, assembling, and smoothing seams and joints of burred surfaces. Determine project requirements, including scope, assembly sequences, and required methods and materials, according to blueprints, drawings, and written or verbal instructions. Drill and punch holes in metal, for screws, bolts, and rivets. Fasten seams and joints together with welds, bolts, cement, rivets, solder, caulks, metal drive clips, and bonds in order to assemble components into products or to repair sheet metal items. Finish parts, using hacksaws, and hand, rotary, or squaring shears. Inspect individual parts, assemblies, and installations for conformance to specifications and building codes, using measuring instruments such as calipers, scales, and micrometers. Install assemblies, such as flashing, pipes, tubes, heating and air conditioning ducts, furnace casings, rain gutters, and down spouts, in supportive frameworks. Lay out, measure, and mark dimensions and reference lines on material, such as roofing panels, according to drawings or templates, using calculators, scribes, dividers, squares, and rulers. Select gauges and types of sheet metal or non-metallic material, according to product specifications. Shape metal material over anvils, blocks, or other forms, using hand tools. Trim, file, grind, deburr, buff, and smooth surfaces, seams, and joints of assembled parts, using hand tools and portable power tools. Convert blueprints into shop drawings to be followed in the construction and assembly of sheet metal products. Develop and lay out patterns that use materials most efficiently, using computerized metalworking equipment to experiment with different layouts. Fabricate or alter parts at construction sites, using shears, hammers, punches, and drills. Fasten roof panel edges and machine-made molding to structures, nailing or welding pieces into place. Maintain equipment, making repairs and modifications when necessary. Maneuver completed units into position for installation, and anchor the units. Secure metal roof panels in place, then interlock and fasten grooved panel edges. Transport prefabricated parts to construction sites for assembly and installation. **SKILLS**—Installation; Technology Design; Equipment Selection; Repairing; Operation and Control; Operations Analysis; Quality Control Analysis; Mathematics; Troubleshooting.

GOE—Interest Area: 06. Construction, Mining, and Drilling. **Work Group:** 06.02 Construction. **Other Apprenticeable Jobs in This Work Group:** Boat Builders and Shipwrights; Boilermakers; Brickmasons and Blockmasons; Carpet Installers; Ceiling Tile Installers; Cement Masons and Concrete Finishers; Construction and Related Workers, All Other; Construction Carpenters; Drywall Installers; Electricians; Fence Erectors; Floor Layers, Except Carpet, Wood, and Hard Tiles; Glaziers; Grader, Bulldozer, and Scraper Operators; Insulation Workers, Floor, Ceiling, and Wall; Insulation Workers, Mechanical; Operating Engineers; Painters, Construction and Maintenance; Paperhangers; Paving, Surfacing, and Tamping Equipment Operators; Pipe Fitters; Plasterers and Stucco Masons; Plumbers; Reinforcing Iron and Rebar Workers; Riggers; Roofers; Rough Carpenters; Ship Carpenters and Joiners; Stone Cutters and Carvers; Stonemasons; Structural Iron and Steel Workers; Tapers; Terrazzo Workers and Finishers; Tile and Marble Setters. **PERSONALITY TYPE:** Realistic. Realistic occupations frequently involve work activities that include practical, hands-on problems and solutions. They often deal with plants, animals, and real-world materials like wood, tools, and machinery. Many of the occupations require working outside and do not involve a lot of paperwork or working closely with others.

RELATED KNOWLEDGE/COURSES— **Production and Processing:** Knowledge of raw materials, production processes, quality control, costs, and other techniques for maximizing the effective manufacture and distribution of goods. **Mechanical Devices:** Knowledge of machines and tools, including their designs, uses, repair, and maintenance. **Building and Construction:** Knowledge of the materials, methods, and tools involved in the construction or repair of houses, buildings, or other structures, such as highways and roads. **Computers and Electronics:** Knowledge of circuit boards, processors, chips, electronic equipment, and computer hardware and software, including applications and programming. **Design:** Knowledge of design techniques, tools, and principles involved in production of precision technical plans, blueprints, drawings, and models. **Engineering and Technology:** Knowledge of the practical application of engineering science and technology. This includes applying principles, techniques, procedures, and equipment to the design and production of various goods and services.

WORK ENVIRONMENT—Hazardous equipment; common protective or safety equipment; sounds, noise levels are distracting or uncomfortable; indoors; standing.

FURTHER INFORMATION—Contact a local joint union-management apprenticeship committee or the nearest office of your state employment service or apprenticeship agency (see Appendix C). To identify a local union office, contact:

Sheet Metal and Air-Conditioning Contractors National Association, 4201 Lafayette Center Dr., Chantilly, VA 20151-1209. Internet: http://www.smacna.org.

Sheet Metal Workers International Association, 1750 New York Ave. NW, Washington, DC 20006. Internet: http://www.smwia.org.

Ship Carpenters and Joiners

- ◎ Growth: 10.1%
- ◎ Annual Job Openings: 193,000
- ◎ Annual Earnings: $34,250
- ◎ Percentage of Women: 1.9%

Related Apprenticeship	Years
Carpenter, Ship	4
Joiner	4

Fabricate, assemble, install, or repair wooden furnishings in ships or boats. Reads blueprints to determine dimensions of furnishings in ships or boats. Shapes and laminates wood to form parts of ship, using steam chambers, clamps, glue, and jigs. Repairs structural woodwork and replaces defective parts and equipment, using hand tools and power tools. Shapes irregular parts and trims excess material from bulkhead and furnishings to ensure fit meets specifications. Constructs floors, doors, and partitions, using woodworking machines, hand tools, and power tools. Cuts wood or glass to specified dimensions, using hand tools and power tools. Assembles and installs hardware, gaskets, floors, furnishings, or insulation, using adhesive, hand tools, and power tools. Transfers dimensions or measurements of wood parts or bulkhead on plywood, using measuring instruments and marking devices. Greases gears and other moving parts of machines on ship. **SKILLS—**Installation; Repairing; Equipment Maintenance; Operations Analysis; Technology Design.

GOE—Interest Area: 06. Construction, Mining, and Drilling. **Work Group:** 06.02 Construction. **Other Apprenticeable Jobs in This Work Group:** Boat Builders and Shipwrights; Boilermakers; Brickmasons and Blockmasons; Carpet Installers; Ceiling Tile Installers; Cement Masons and Concrete Finishers; Construction and Related Workers, All Other; Construction Carpenters; Drywall Installers; Electricians; Fence Erectors; Floor Layers, Except Carpet, Wood, and Hard Tiles; Glaziers; Grader, Bulldozer, and Scraper Operators; Insulation Workers, Floor, Ceiling, and Wall; Insulation Workers, Mechanical; Operating Engineers; Painters, Construction and Maintenance; Paperhangers; Paving, Surfacing, and Tamping Equipment Operators; Pipe Fitters; Plasterers and Stucco Masons; Plumbers; Reinforcing Iron and Rebar Workers; Riggers; Roofers; Rough Carpenters; Sheet Metal Workers; Stone Cutters and Carvers; Stonemasons; Structural Iron and Steel Workers; Tapers; Terrazzo Workers and Finishers; Tile and Marble Setters. **PERSONALITY TYPE:** Realistic. Realistic occupations frequently involve work activities that include practical, hands-on problems and solutions. They often deal with plants, animals, and real-world materials like wood, tools, and machinery. Many of the occupations require working outside and do not involve a lot of paperwork or working closely with others.

RELATED KNOWLEDGE/COURSES— Building and Construction: Knowledge of the materials, methods, and tools involved in the construction or repair of houses, buildings, or other structures, such as highways and roads. **Design:** Knowledge of design techniques, tools, and principles involved in production of precision technical plans, blueprints, drawings, and models. **Engineering and Technology:** Knowledge of the practical application of engineering science and technology. This includes applying principles, techniques, procedures, and equipment to the design and production of various goods and services. **Mechanical Devices:** Knowledge of machines and tools, including their designs, uses, repair, and maintenance.

WORK ENVIRONMENT—Hazardous equipment; climbing ladders, scaffolds, or poles; common protective or safety equipment; spend time kneeling, crouching, stooping, or crawling; using hands on objects, tools, or controls.

Signal and Track Switch Repairers

- Growth: –3.1%
- Annual Job Openings: 1,000
- Annual Earnings: $43,690
- Percentage of Women: 7.0%

Related Apprenticeship	Years
Electric-Track-Switch Maintainer	4
Signal Maintainer	4

Install, inspect, test, maintain, or repair electric gate crossings, signals, signal equipment, track switches, section lines, or intercommunications systems within a railroad system. Inspect and test operation, mechanical parts, and circuitry of gate crossings, signals, and signal equipment such as interlocks and hotbox detectors. Inspect, maintain, and replace batteries as needed. Inspect electrical units of railroad grade crossing gates and repair loose bolts and defective electrical connections and parts. Inspect switch-controlling mechanisms on trolley wires and in track beds, using hand tools and test equipment. Install, inspect, maintain, and repair various railroad service equipment on the road or in the shop, including railroad signal systems. Lubricate moving parts on gate-crossing mechanisms and swinging signals. Replace defective wiring, broken lenses, or burned-out light bulbs. Test air lines and air cylinders on pneumatically operated gates. Tighten loose bolts, using wrenches, and test circuits and connections by opening and closing gates. Clean lenses of lamps with cloths and solvents. Drive motor vehicles to job sites. Maintain high tension lines, de-energizing lines for power companies when repairs are requested. Record and report information about mileage or track inspected, repairs performed, and equipment requiring replacement. **SKILLS—** Installation; Equipment Maintenance; Repairing; Troubleshooting; Operation Monitoring; Quality Control Analysis; Science; Systems Evaluation.

GOE—Interest Area: 05. Mechanics, Installers, and Repairers. **Work Group:** 05.02 Electrical and Electronic Systems. **Other Apprenticeable Jobs in This Work Group:** Avionics Technicians; Battery Repairers; Central Office and PBX Installers and Repairers; Communication Equipment Mechanics, Installers, and Repair-ers; Data Processing Equipment Repairers; Electric Home Appliance and Power Tool Repairers; Electric Meter Installers and Repairers; Electric Motor and Switch Assemblers and Repairers; Electrical and Electronics Installers and Repairers, Transportation Equipment; Electrical and Electronics Repairers, Commercial and Industrial Equipment; Electrical and Electronics Repairers, Powerhouse, Substation, and Relay; Electrical Power-Line Installers and Repairers; Electronic Equipment Installers and Repairers, Motor Vehicles; Electronic Home Entertainment Equipment Installers and Repairers; Elevator Installers and Repairers; Installation, Maintenance, and Repair Workers, All Other; Office Machine and Cash Register Servicers; Radio Mechanics; Station Installers and Repairers, Telephone; Telecommunications Line Installers and Repairers; Transformer Repairers. **PERSONALITY TYPE:** Realistic. Realistic occupations frequently involve work activities that include practical, hands-on problems and solutions. They often deal with plants, animals, and real-world materials like wood, tools, and machinery. Many of the occupations require working outside and do not involve a lot of paperwork or working closely with others.

RELATED KNOWLEDGE/COURSES— Transportation: Knowledge of principles and methods for moving people or goods by air, rail, sea, or road, including the relative costs and benefits. **Mechanical Devices:** Knowledge of machines and tools, including their designs, uses, repair, and maintenance. **Telecommunications:** Knowledge of transmission, broadcasting, switching, control, and operation of telecommunications systems. **Engineering and Technology:** Knowledge of the practical application of engineering science and technology. This includes applying principles, techniques, procedures, and equipment to the design and production of various goods and services. **Public Safety and Security:** Knowledge of relevant equipment, policies, procedures, and strategies to promote effective local, state, or national security operations for the protection of people, data, property, and institutions. **Physics:** Knowledge and prediction of physical principles and laws and their interrelationships and applications to understanding fluid, material, and atmospheric dynamics and mechanical, electrical, atomic, and subatomic structures and processes.

WORK ENVIRONMENT—Outdoors; hazardous conditions; hazardous equipment; minor burns, cuts, bites, or stings; common protective or safety equipment.

Slaughterers and Meat Packers

⊚ Growth: 18.1%
⊚ Annual Job Openings: 23,000
⊚ Annual Earnings: $20,420
⊚ Percentage of Women: 23.7%

Related Apprenticeship	Years
Butcher, All-Round	3

Work in slaughtering, meat packing, or wholesale establishments performing precision functions involving the preparation of meat. Work may include specialized slaughtering tasks, cutting standard or premium cuts of meat for marketing, making sausage, or wrapping meats. Cut, trim, skin, sort, and wash viscera of slaughtered animals to separate edible portions from offal. Grind meat into hamburger and into trimmings used to prepare sausages, luncheon meats, and other meat products. Remove bones, and cut meat into standard cuts in preparation for marketing. Saw, split, or scribe carcasses into smaller portions to facilitate handling. Sever jugular veins to drain blood and facilitate slaughtering. Shackle hind legs of animals to raise them for slaughtering or skinning. Shave or singe and defeather carcasses, and wash them in preparation for further processing or packaging. Skin sections of animals or whole animals. Slit open, eviscerate, and trim carcasses of slaughtered animals. Stun animals prior to slaughtering. Trim head meat, and sever or remove parts of animals' heads or skulls. Trim, clean, and/or cure animal hides. Wrap dressed carcasses and/or meat cuts. Tend assembly lines, performing a few of the many cuts needed to process a carcass. Slaughter animals in accordance with religious law, and determine that carcasses meet specified religious standards. **SKILLS**—None met the criteria.

GOE—**Interest Area:** 08. Industrial Production. **Work Group:** 08.03 Production Work. **Other Apprenticeable Jobs in This Work Group:** Bakers, Manufacturing; Bindery Machine Operators and Tenders; Chemical Equipment Controllers and Operators; Coating, Painting, and Spraying Machine Operators and Tenders; Cooling and Freezing Equipment Operators and Tenders; Crushing, Grinding, and Polishing Machine Setters, Operators, and Tenders; Cutters and Trimmers, Hand; Cutting and Slicing Machine Operators and Tenders; Design Printing Machine Setters and Set-Up Operators; Electrolytic Plating and Coating Machine Setters and Set-Up Operators, Metal and Plastic; Electrotypers and Stereotypers;

Embossing Machine Set-Up Operators; Engraver Set-Up Operators; Extruding, Forming, Pressing, and Compacting Machine Operators and Tenders; Fabric and Apparel Patternmakers; Film Laboratory Technicians; Fitters, Structural Metal—Precision; Food Batchmakers; Furnace, Kiln, Oven, Drier, and Kettle Operators and Tenders; Hand Compositors and Typesetters; Job Printers; Letterpress Setters and Set-Up Operators; Metal Fabricators, Structural Metal Products; Metal-Refining Furnace Operators and Tenders; Mixing and Blending Machine Setters, Operators, and Tenders; Mold Makers, Hand; Molding and Casting Workers; Numerical Control Machine Tool Operators and Tenders, Metal and Plastic; Offset Lithographic Press Setters and Set-Up Operators; Painting, Coating, and Decorating Workers; Photographic Processing Machine Operators; Photographic Reproduction Technicians; Photographic Retouchers and Restorers; Plate Finishers; Platemakers; Precision Printing Workers; Printing Press Machine Operators and Tenders; Production Workers, All Other; Sawing Machine Operators and Tenders; Sawing Machine Setters and Set-Up Operators; Scanner Operators; Separating, Filtering, Clarifying, Precipitating, and Still Machine Setters, Operators, and Tenders; Sewing Machine Operators, Garment; Stone Sawyers; Strippers; Team Assemblers; Welder-Fitters; Welders and Cutters; Woodworking Machine Operators and Tenders, Except Sawing. **PERSONALITY TYPE:** Realistic. Realistic occupations frequently involve work activities that include practical, hands-on problems and solutions. They often deal with plants, animals, and real-world materials like wood, tools, and machinery. Many of the occupations require working outside and do not involve a lot of paperwork or working closely with others.

RELATED KNOWLEDGE/COURSES—Food Production: Knowledge of techniques and equipment for planting, growing, and harvesting food products (both plant and animal) for consumption, including storage/handling techniques. **Philosophy and Theology:** Knowledge of different philosophical systems and religions. This includes their basic principles, values, ethics, ways of thinking, customs, and practices and their impact on human culture. **Biology:** Knowledge of plant and animal organisms and their tissues, cells, functions, interdependencies, and interactions with each other and the environment. **Public Safety and Security:** Knowledge of relevant equipment, policies, procedures, and strategies to promote effective local, state, or national security operations for the protection of people, data, property, and institutions. **Production and Processing:** Knowledge of raw materials, production processes, quality control, costs, and other techniques for maximizing the effective manufacture and distribution of goods. **Law and Government:** Knowledge of laws, legal codes, court procedures, precedents, government regulations, executive orders, agency rules, and the democratic political process.

WORK ENVIRONMENT—Common protective or safety equipment; minor burns, cuts, bites, or stings; spend time making repetitive motions; sounds, noise levels are distracting or uncomfortable; contaminants; disease or infections.

Social and Human Service Assistants

- Growth: 48.7%
- Annual Job Openings: 63,000
- Annual Earnings: $23,860
- Percentage of Women: 64.2%

Related Apprenticeship	*Years*
Direct Support Specialist, Human Services	competency

Assist professionals from a wide variety of fields, such as psychology, rehabilitation, or social work, to provide client services, as well as support for families. May assist clients in identifying available benefits and social and community services and help clients obtain them. May assist social workers with developing, organizing, and conducting programs to prevent and resolve problems relevant to substance abuse, human relationships, rehabilitation, or adult daycare. Visit individuals in homes or attend group meetings to provide information on agency services, requirements and procedures. Advise clients regarding food stamps, child care, food, money management, sanitation, and housekeeping. Interview individuals and family members to compile information on social, educational, criminal, institutional, or drug history. Provide information on and refer individuals to public or private agencies and community services for assistance. Assist clients with preparation of forms, such as tax or rent forms. Assist in locating housing for displaced individuals. Assist in planning of food budget, utilizing charts and sample budgets. Monitor free, supplementary meal program to ensure cleanliness of facility and that eligibility guidelines are met for persons receiving meals. Meet with youth groups to acquaint them with consequences of delinquent acts. Observe clients' food selections and recommend alternate economical and nutritional food choices. Observe and discuss meal preparation and suggest alternate methods of food preparation. Consult with supervisor concerning programs for individual families. Oversee day-to-day group activities of residents in institution. Transport and accompany clients to shopping area and to appointments, using automobile. Explain rules established by owner or management, such as sanitation and maintenance requirements, and parking regulations. Demonstrate use and care of equipment for tenant use. Inform tenants of facilities, such as laundries and playgrounds. Submit to and review reports and problems with superior. Keep records and prepare reports for owner or management concerning visits with clients. Care for children in client's home during client's appointments. **SKILLS**—Service Orientation; Social Perceptiveness; Persuasion; Speaking; Learning Strategies; Negotiation; Active Listening; Critical Thinking; Systems Evaluation.

GOE—Interest Area: 12. Education and Social Service. **Work Group:** 12.02 Social Services. **Other Apprenticeable Jobs in This Work Group:** No other apprenticeable jobs in this group. **PERSONALITY TYPE:** Social. Social occupations frequently involve working with, communicating with, and teaching people. These occupations often involve helping or providing service to others.

RELATED KNOWLEDGE/COURSES—Therapy and Counseling: Knowledge of principles, methods, and procedures for diagnosis, treatment, and rehabilitation of physical and mental dysfunctions and for career counseling and guidance. **Customer and Personal Service:** Knowledge of principles and processes for providing customer and personal services. This includes customer needs assessment, meeting quality standards for services, and evaluation of customer satisfaction. **Psychology:** Knowledge of human behavior and performance; individual differences in ability, personality, and interests; learning and motivation; psychological research methods; and the assessment and treatment of behavioral and affective disorders. **Sociology and Anthropology:** Knowledge of group behavior and dynamics, societal trends and influences, human migrations, ethnicity, and cultures and their history and origins. **Clerical Practices:** Knowledge of administrative and clerical procedures and systems, such as word processing, managing files and records, stenography and transcription, designing forms, and other office procedures and terminology. **Transportation:** Knowledge of principles and methods for moving people or goods by air, rail, sea, or road, including the relative costs and benefits.

WORK ENVIRONMENT—Disease or infections; sitting; walking and running; outdoors; standing.

Sound Engineering Technicians

- Growth: 25.5%
- Annual Job Openings: 2,000
- Annual Earnings: $38,290
- Percentage of Women: 14.2%

Related Apprenticeship	*Years*
Recording Engineer	2
Sound Mixer	4

Operate machines and equipment to record, synchronize, mix, or reproduce music, voices, or sound effects in sporting arenas, theater productions, recording studios, or movie and video productions. Confer with producers, performers, and others in order to determine and achieve the desired sound for a production such as a musical recording or a film. Mix and edit voices, music, and taped sound effects for live performances and for prerecorded events, using sound mixing boards. Record speech, music, and other sounds on recording media, using recording equipment. Regulate volume level and sound quality during recording sessions, using control consoles. Reproduce and duplicate sound recordings from original recording media, using sound editing and duplication equipment. Separate instruments, vocals, and other sounds, then combine sounds later during the mixing or post-production stage. Set up, test, and adjust recording equipment for recording sessions and live performances; tear down equipment after event completion. Synchronize and equalize prerecorded dialogue, music, and sound effects with visual action of motion pictures or television productions, using control consoles. Create musical instrument digital interface programs for music projects, commercials or film post-production. Keep logs of recordings. Prepare for recording sessions by performing activities such as selecting and setting up microphones. Report equipment problems, and ensure that required repairs are made. **SKILLS**—Operation and Control; Operation Monitoring; Equipment Maintenance; Management of Personnel Resources; Equipment Selection; Troubleshooting; Management of Material Resources; Technology Design; Installation.

GOE—**Interest Area:** 01. Arts, Entertainment, and Media. **Work Group:** 01.08 Media Technology. **Other Apprenticeable Jobs in This Work Group:** Audio and Video Equipment Technicians; Broadcast Technicians; Camera Operators, Television, Video, and Motion Picture; Film and Video Editors; Professional Photographers; Radio Operators. **PERSONALITY TYPE:** Realistic. Realistic occupations frequently involve work activities that include practical, hands-on problems and solutions. They often deal with plants, animals, and real-world materials like wood, tools, and machinery. Many of the occupations require working outside and do not involve a lot of paperwork or working closely with others.

RELATED KNOWLEDGE/COURSES— **Computers and Electronics:** Knowledge of circuit boards, processors, chips, electronic equipment, and computer hardware and software, including applications and programming. **Engineering and Technology:** Knowledge of the practical application of engineering science and technology. This includes applying principles, techniques, procedures, and equipment to the design and production of various goods and services. **Telecommunications:** Knowledge of transmission, broadcasting, switching, control, and operation of telecommunications systems. **Communications and Media:** Knowledge of media production, communication, and dissemination techniques and methods. This includes alternative ways to inform and entertain via written, oral, and visual media. **Administration and Management:** Knowledge of business and management principles involved in strategic planning, resource allocation, human resources modeling, leadership technique, production methods, and coordination of people and resources. **Fine Arts:** Knowledge of the theory and techniques required to compose, produce, and perform works of music, dance, visual arts, drama, and sculpture.

WORK ENVIRONMENT—Sitting; using hands on objects, tools, or controls; indoors; spend time making repetitive motions; sounds, noise levels are distracting or uncomfortable.

Station Installers and Repairers, Telephone

- Growth: –0.6%
- Annual Job Openings: 23,000
- Annual Earnings: $48,230
- Percentage of Women: 13.0%

Related Apprenticeship	Years
Maintenance Mechanic, Telephone	3
Station Installer-and-Repairer	4

Install and repair telephone station equipment, such as telephones, coin collectors, telephone booths, and switching-key equipment. Installs communication equipment, such as intercommunication systems and related apparatus, using schematic diagrams, testing devices, and hand tools. Assembles telephone equipment, mounts brackets, and connects wire leads, using hand tools and following installation diagrams or work order. Analyzes equipment operation, using testing devices to locate and diagnose nature of malfunction and ascertain needed repairs. Operates and tests equipment to ensure elimination of malfunction. Climbs poles to install or repair outside service lines. Disassembles components and replaces, cleans, adjusts and repairs parts, wires, switches, relays, circuits, or signaling units, using hand tools. Repairs cables, lays out plans for new equipment, and estimates material required. **SKILLS**—Troubleshooting; Installation; Repairing; Equipment Maintenance; Quality Control Analysis; Operations Analysis; Technology Design; Operation Monitoring; Operation and Control.

GOE—Interest Area: 05. Mechanics, Installers, and Repairers. **Work Group:** 05.02 Electrical and Electronic Systems. **Other Apprenticeable Jobs in This Work Group:** Avionics Technicians; Battery Repairers; Central Office and PBX Installers and Repairers; Communication Equipment Mechanics, Installers, and Repairers; Data Processing Equipment Repairers; Electric Home Appliance and Power Tool Repairers; Electric Meter Installers and Repairers; Electric Motor and Switch Assemblers and Repairers; Electrical and Electronics Installers and Repairers, Transportation Equipment; Electrical and Electronics Repairers, Commercial and Industrial Equipment; Electrical and Electronics Repairers, Powerhouse, Substation, and Relay; Electrical Power-Line Installers and Repairers; Electronic Equipment Installers and Repairers, Motor Vehicles; Electronic Home Entertainment Equipment Installers and Repairers; Elevator Installers and Repairers; Installation, Maintenance, and Repair Workers, All Other; Office Machine and Cash Register

Servicers; Radio Mechanics; Signal and Track Switch Repairers; Telecommunications Line Installers and Repairers; Transformer Repairers. **PERSONALITY TYPE:** Realistic. Realistic occupations frequently involve work activities that include practical, hands-on problems and solutions. They often deal with plants, animals, and real-world materials like wood, tools, and machinery. Many of the occupations require working outside and do not involve a lot of paperwork or working closely with others.

RELATED KNOWLEDGE/COURSES— Telecommunications: Knowledge of transmission, broadcasting, switching, control, and operation of telecommunications systems. **Computers and Electronics:** Knowledge of circuit boards, processors, chips, electronic equipment, and computer hardware and software, including applications and programming. **Mechanical Devices:** Knowledge of machines and tools, including their designs, uses, repair, and maintenance. **Engineering and Technology:** Knowledge of the practical application of engineering science and technology. This includes applying principles, techniques, procedures, and equipment to the design and production of various goods and services. **Design:** Knowledge of design techniques, tools, and principles involved in production of precision technical plans, blueprints, drawings, and models. **Geography:** Knowledge of principles and methods for describing the features of land, sea, and air masses, including their physical characteristics; locations; interrelationships; and distribution of plant, animal, and human life.

WORK ENVIRONMENT—Climbing ladders, scaffolds, or poles; high places; common protective or safety equipment; keeping or regaining balance; standing.

Stationary Engineers

- Growth: 0.3%
- Annual Job Openings: 4,000
- Annual Earnings: $43,420
- Percentage of Women: 3.3%

Related Apprenticeship	Years
Boiler Operator	4
Stationary Engineer	4

Operate and maintain stationary engines and mechanical equipment to provide utilities for buildings or industrial processes. Operate equipment such as steam engines, generators, motors, turbines, and steam boilers. Adjusts controls and valves on equipment to provide power and regulate and set operations of system and industrial processes. Lubricates, maintains, and repairs equipment, using hand tools and power tools. Tests electrical system to determine voltage, using voltage meter. Cleans equipment, using airhose, brushes, and rags, and drains water from pipes and air reservoir. Records temperature, pressure, water levels, fuel consumption, and other data at specified intervals in logbook. Adds chemicals or tends equipment to maintain temperature of fluids or atmosphere or to prevent scale buildup. Reads dials of temperature, pressure, and ampere gauges and meters to detect malfunctions and ensure specified operation of equipment. Inspects equipment to determine need for repair, lubrication, or adjustment. Lights burners and opens valves on equipment, such as condensers, pumps, and compressors, to prepare system for operation.

SKILLS—Equipment Maintenance; Operation Monitoring; Repairing; Operation and Control; Troubleshooting; Quality Control Analysis; Technology Design; Systems Evaluation.

GOE—Interest Area: 08. Industrial Production. Work Group: 08.06 Systems Operation. Other Apprenticeable Jobs in This Work Group: Boiler Operators and Tenders, Low Pressure; Chemical Plant and System Operators; Gaugers; Petroleum Refinery and Control Panel Operators; Power Distributors and Dispatchers; Power Generating Plant Operators, Except Auxiliary Equipment Operators; Water and Liquid Waste Treatment Plant and System Operators. PERSONALITY TYPE: Realistic. Realistic occupations frequently involve work activities that include practical, hands-on problems and solutions. They often deal with plants, animals, and real-world materials like wood, tools, and machinery. Many of the occupations require working outside and do not involve a lot of paperwork or working closely with others.

RELATED KNOWLEDGE/COURSES—Mechanical Devices: Knowledge of machines and tools, including their designs, uses, repair, and maintenance. Engineering and Technology: Knowledge of the practical application of engineering science and technology. This includes applying principles, techniques, procedures, and equipment to the design and production of various goods and services. Physics: Knowledge and prediction of physical principles and laws and their interrelationships and applications to understanding fluid, material, and atmospheric dynamics and mechanical, electrical, atomic, and subatomic structures and processes. Computers and Electronics: Knowledge of circuit boards, processors, chips, electronic equipment, and computer hardware and software, including applications and programming. **Chemistry:** Knowledge of the chemical composition, structure, and properties of substances and of the chemical processes and transformations that they undergo. This includes uses of chemicals, their danger signs, production techniques, and disposal methods. **Production and Processing:** Knowledge of raw materials, production processes, quality control, costs, and other techniques for maximizing the effective manufacture and distribution of goods.

WORK ENVIRONMENT—Sounds, noise levels are distracting or uncomfortable; hazardous conditions; specialized protective or safety equipment; minor burns, cuts, bites, or stings; contaminants.

Stone Cutters and Carvers

- ⬡ Growth: 6.4%
- ⬡ Annual Job Openings: 6,000
- ⬡ Annual Earnings: $24,780
- ⬡ Percentage of Women: 20.4%

Related Apprenticeship	Years
Sandblaster, Stone	3
Stone Carver	3
Stonecutter, Hand	3

Cut or carve stone according to diagrams and patterns. Guides nozzle over stone, following stencil outline or chips along marks, to create design or work surface down to desired finish. Drills holes or cuts molding and grooves in stone. Studies artistic objects or graphic materials, such as models, sketches, or blueprints, and plans carving or cutting technique. Lays out designs or dimensions on stone surface, by freehand or transfer from tracing paper, using scribe or chalk and measuring instruments. Selects chisels, pneumatic or surfacing tools, or sandblasting nozzles and determines sequence of their use according to intricacy of design or figure. Removes or adds stencil during blasting to create differences in depth of cuts, intricate designs, or rough, pitted finish. Loads sandblasting equipment with abrasive, attaches nozzle to hose, and turns valves to admit compressed air and activate jet. Verifies depth and dimensions of cut or carving, using measuring instruments, to ensure adherence to specifications. Moves fingers over surface of carving to ensure smoothness of finish. **SKILLS**—Operation and Control; Equipment Selection.

GOE—Interest Area: 06. Construction, Mining, and Drilling. **Work Group:** 06.02 Construction. **Other Apprenticeable Jobs in This Work Group:** Boat Builders and Shipwrights; Boilermakers; Brickmasons and Blockmasons; Carpet Installers; Ceiling Tile Installers; Cement Masons and Concrete Finishers; Construction and Related Workers, All Other; Construction Carpenters; Drywall Installers; Electricians; Fence Erectors; Floor Layers, Except Carpet, Wood, and Hard Tiles; Glaziers; Grader, Bulldozer, and Scraper Operators; Insulation Workers, Floor, Ceiling, and Wall; Insulation Workers, Mechanical; Operating Engineers; Painters, Construction and Maintenance; Paperhangers; Paving, Surfacing, and Tamping Equipment Operators; Pipe Fitters; Plasterers and Stucco Masons; Plumbers; Reinforcing Iron and Rebar Workers; Riggers; Roofers; Rough Carpenters; Sheet Metal Workers; Ship Carpenters and Joiners; Stonemasons; Structural Iron and Steel Workers; Tapers; Terrazzo Workers and Finishers; Tile and Marble Setters. **PERSONALITY TYPE:** Realistic. Realistic occupations frequently involve work activities that include practical, hands-on problems and solutions. They often deal with plants, animals, and real-world materials like wood, tools, and machinery. Many of the occupations require working outside and do not involve a lot of paperwork or working closely with others.

RELATED KNOWLEDGE/COURSES— Fine Arts: Knowledge of the theory and techniques required to compose, produce, and perform works of music, dance, visual arts, drama, and sculpture. **Design:** Knowledge of design techniques, tools, and principles involved in production of precision technical plans, blueprints, drawings, and models. **Physics:** Knowledge and prediction of physical principles and laws and their interrelationships and applications to understanding fluid, material, and atmospheric dynamics and mechanical, electrical, atomic, and subatomic structures and processes. **Building and Construction:** Knowledge of materials, methods, and the tools involved in the construction or repair of houses, buildings, or other structures such as highways and roads. **Engineering and Technology:** Knowledge of the practical application of engineering science and technology. This includes applying principles, techniques, procedures, and equipment to the design and production of various goods and services. **Mechanical Devices:** Knowledge of machines and tools, including their designs, uses, repair, and maintenance.

WORK ENVIRONMENT—Common protective or safety equipment; contaminants; sounds, noise levels are distracting or uncomfortable; using hands on objects, tools, or controls; exposed to whole body vibration; standing.

Stone Sawyers

- Growth: 6.6%
- Annual Job Openings: 12,000
- Annual Earnings: $26,060
- Percentage of Women: 26.9%

Related Apprenticeship	*Years*
Gang Sawyer, Stone	2
Wire Sawyer	2

Set up and operate gang saws, reciprocating saws, circular saws, or wire saws to cut blocks of stone into specified dimensions. Starts saw and moves blade across surface of material, such as stone, concrete slabs, and asbestos-cement sheets and pipes, to saw. Adjusts blade pressure against stone, using ammeter, and lowers blade in stone as cut depth increases. Changes or replaces saw blades, cables, and grinding wheels, using wrench. Operates crane or signals crane operator to position or remove stone from car or saw bed. Washes stone, using water hose, and verifies width or thickness of cut stone, using rule. Builds bed of timbers on car, and aligns and levels stone on bed, using crowbar, sledgehammer, wedges, blocks, rule, and spirit level.

Marks dimensions or traces on stone according to diagram, using chisel and hammer, straightedge, rule, and chalked string. Observes operation to detect uneven sawing and exhausted abrasive supply and tightens pulleys or adds abrasive to maintain cutting speed. Aligns cable or blades with marks on stone, and presses button or turns lever to lower sawing cable or blades to stone. Turns crank or presses button to move car under sawing cable or saw frame. Starts pump to circulate water and abrasive onto blade or cable during cutting. **SKILLS—** Equipment Maintenance; Operation Monitoring; Operation and Control; Equipment Selection; Repairing; Technology Design; Installation.

GOE—Interest Area: 08. Industrial Production. **Work Group:** 08.03 Production Work. **Other Apprenticeable Jobs in This Work Group:** Bakers, Manufacturing; Bindery Machine Operators and Tenders; Chemical Equipment Controllers and Operators; Coating, Painting, and Spraying Machine Operators and Tenders; Cooling and Freezing Equipment Operators and Tenders; Crushing, Grinding, and Polishing Machine Setters, Operators, and Tenders; Cutters and Trimmers, Hand; Cutting and Slicing Machine Operators and Tenders; Design Printing Machine Setters and Set-Up Operators; Electrolytic Plating and Coating Machine Setters and Set-Up Operators, Metal and Plastic; Electrotypers and Stereotypers; Embossing Machine Set-Up Operators; Engraver Set-Up Operators; Extruding, Forming, Pressing, and Compacting Machine Operators and Tenders; Fabric and Apparel Patternmakers; Film Laboratory Technicians; Fitters, Structural Metal—Precision; Food Batchmakers; Furnace, Kiln, Oven, Drier, and Kettle Operators and Tenders; Hand Compositors and Typesetters; Job Printers; Letterpress Setters and Set-Up Operators; Metal Fabricators, Structural Metal Products; Metal-Refining Furnace Operators and Tenders; Mixing and Blending Machine Setters, Operators, and Tenders; Mold Makers, Hand; Molding and Casting Workers; Numerical Control Machine Tool Operators and Tenders, Metal and Plastic; Offset Lithographic Press Setters and Set-Up Operators; Painting, Coating, and Decorating Workers; Photographic Processing Machine Operators; Photographic Reproduction Technicians; Photographic Retouchers and Restorers; Plate Finishers; Platemakers; Precision Printing Workers; Printing Press Machine Operators and Tenders; Production Workers, All Other; Sawing Machine Operators and Tenders; Sawing Machine Setters and Set-Up Operators; Scanner Operators; Separating, Filtering, Clarifying, Precipitating, and Still Machine Setters, Operators, and Tenders; Sewing Machine Operators, Garment; Slaughterers and Meat Packers; Strippers; Team Assemblers; Welder-Fitters; Welders and Cutters; Woodworking Machine Operators and Tenders, Except Sawing. **PERSONALITY TYPE:** Realistic. Realistic occupations frequently involve work activities that include practical, hands-on problems and solutions. They often deal with plants, animals, and real-world materials like wood, tools, and machinery. Many of the occupations require working outside and do not involve a lot of paperwork or working closely with others.

RELATED KNOWLEDGE/COURSES— Mechanical Devices: Knowledge of machines and tools, including their designs, uses, repair, and maintenance. **Building and Construction:** Knowledge of the materials, methods, and tools involved in the construction or repair of houses, buildings, or other structures, such as highways and roads. **Production and Processing:** Knowledge of raw materials, production processes, quality control, costs, and other techniques for maximizing the effective manufacture and distribution of goods. **Physics:** Knowledge and prediction of physical principles and laws and their interrelationships and applications to understanding fluid, material, and atmospheric dynamics and mechanical, electrical, atomic, and subatomic structures and processes.

WORK ENVIRONMENT—Hazardous equipment; sounds, noise levels are distracting or uncomfortable; common protective or safety equipment; standing; minor burns, cuts, bites, or stings.

Stonemasons

- Growth: 14.1%
- Annual Job Openings: 2,000
- Annual Earnings: $34,000
- Percentage of Women: 1.1%

Related Apprenticeship	Years
Marble Setter	3
Stonemason	3
Monument Setter	4

Build stone structures, such as piers, walls, and abutments. Lay walks, curbstones, or special types of masonry for vats, tanks, and floors. Clean excess mortar or grout from surface of marble, stone, or monument, using sponge, brush, water, or acid. Drill holes in marble or ornamental stone and anchor brackets in holes.

Lay out wall patterns or foundations, using straight edge, rule, or staked lines. Mix mortar or grout and pour or spread mortar or grout on marble slabs, stone, or foundation. Remove wedges, fill joints between stones, finish joints between stones, using a trowel, and smooth the mortar to an attractive finish, using a tuck pointer. Set stone or marble in place, according to layout or pattern. Shape, trim, face and cut marble or stone preparatory to setting, using power saws, cutting equipment, and hand tools. Smooth, polish, and bevel surfaces, using hand tools and power tools. Dig trench for foundation of monument, using pick and shovel. Line interiors of molds with treated paper and fill molds with composition-stone mixture. Position mold along guidelines of wall, press mold in place, and remove mold and paper from wall. Remove sections of monument from truck bed, and guide stone onto foundation, using skids, hoist, or truck crane. Repair cracked or chipped areas of stone or marble, using blowtorch and mastic, and remove rough or defective spots from concrete, using power grinder or chisel and hammer. Set vertical and horizontal alignment of structures, using plumb bob, gauge line, and level. Construct and install prefabricated masonry units. Lay brick to build shells of chimneys and smokestacks or to line or reline industrial furnaces, kilns, boilers and similar installations. Replace broken or missing masonry units in walls or floors. **SKILLS**—Repairing; Technology Design; Operation and Control; Equipment Selection; Installation.

GOE—Interest Area: 06. Construction, Mining, and Drilling. **Work Group:** 06.02 Construction. **Other Apprenticeable Jobs in This Work Group:** Boat Builders and Shipwrights; Boilermakers; Brickmasons and Blockmasons; Carpet Installers; Ceiling Tile Installers; Cement Masons and Concrete Finishers; Construction and Related Workers, All Other; Construction Carpenters; Drywall Installers; Electricians; Fence Erectors; Floor Layers, Except Carpet, Wood, and Hard Tiles; Glaziers; Grader, Bulldozer, and Scraper Operators; Insulation Workers, Floor, Ceiling, and Wall; Insulation Workers, Mechanical; Operating Engineers; Painters, Construction and Maintenance; Paperhangers; Paving, Surfacing, and Tamping Equipment Operators; Pipe Fitters; Plasterers and Stucco Masons; Plumbers; Reinforcing Iron and Rebar Workers; Riggers; Roofers; Rough Carpenters; Sheet Metal Workers; Ship Carpenters and Joiners; Stone Cutters and Carvers; Structural Iron and Steel Workers; Tapers; Terrazzo Workers and Finishers; Tile and Marble Setters. **PERSONALITY TYPE:** Realistic. Realistic occupations frequently involve work activities that include practical, hands-on problems and solutions. They often deal with plants, animals, and real-world materials like wood, tools, and machinery. Many of the occupations require working outside and do not involve a lot of paperwork or working closely with others.

RELATED KNOWLEDGE/COURSES— Building and Construction: Knowledge of the materials, methods, and tools involved in the construction or repair of houses, buildings, or other structures, such as highways and roads. **Design:** Knowledge of design techniques, tools, and principles involved in production of precision technical plans, blueprints, drawings, and models. **Mechanical Devices:** Knowledge of machines and tools, including their designs, uses, repair, and maintenance.

WORK ENVIRONMENT—Outdoors; spend time kneeling, crouching, stooping, or crawling; spend time bending or twisting the body; common protective or safety equipment; spend time making repetitive motions.

Strippers

- ☺ Growth: –11.2%
- ☺ Annual Job Openings: 6,000
- ☺ Annual Earnings: $31,660
- ☺ Percentage of Women: 47.6%

Related Apprenticeship	Years
Stripper	2
Stripper, Lithographic II	4

Cut and arrange film into flats (layout sheets resembling a film negative of text in its final form), which are used to make plates. Prepare separate flat for each color. Cuts image window area to allow exposure to plate or film, using razor or artist's knife. Selects and inserts screen tints in film flat, using knowledge of dot percentages required to obtain specific colors. Cuts masks and arranges negatives to prepare for contact printing, plate exposure, or proof making. Assembles and aligns negatives or positives to assure register and fit with units of color. Examines pasteup, artwork, film, prints, and instructions to determine size and dimensions, number of job colors, and camera work needed. Determines proportions needed to reduce or enlarge photographs and graphics to fit in designated area, using calculator or proportion scale. Determines or approves plans and page sequences to lay out job for specific printing press. Examines proof returned by customer and makes corrections according to customer specifications. Draws ruled lines and borders around negatives or positives. Sends completed flat to proofing area or platemaking area for preparation of final proof or lithographic plate. Touches up imperfections, using opaque and brush on negatives and needle and crayon pencil on photographs. Examines negatives and photographs to detect defective areas, using lighted viewing table. Makes proof from film flat to determine accuracy of flat. Strips negative from base. Aligns negatives and masks over unexposed film in vacuum frame to make negatives or positives for final film of each color. Applies rubber solution and collodion to toughen negative, cuts to size, and immerses in acid bath to prepare negative for stripping. Positions film negatives or positives on light table according to art layout, blueprint, and color register to form film flat. **SKILLS**—Equipment Selection; Operation and Control; Operations Analysis; Critical Thinking; Science.

GOE—Interest Area: 08. Industrial Production. **Work Group:** 08.03 Production Work. **Other Apprenticeable Jobs in This Work Group:** Bakers, Manufacturing; Bindery Machine Operators and Tenders; Chemical Equipment Controllers and Operators; Coating, Painting, and Spraying Machine Operators and Tenders; Cooling and Freezing Equipment Operators and Tenders; Crushing, Grinding, and Polishing Machine Setters, Operators, and Tenders; Cutters and Trimmers, Hand; Cutting and Slicing Machine Operators and Tenders; Design Printing Machine Setters and Set-Up Operators; Electrolytic Plating and Coating Machine Setters and Set-Up Operators, Metal and Plastic; Electrotypers and Stereotypers; Embossing Machine Set-Up Operators; Engraver Set-Up Operators; Extruding, Forming, Pressing, and Compacting Machine Operators and Tenders; Fabric and Apparel Patternmakers; Film Laboratory Technicians; Fitters, Structural Metal—Precision; Food Batchmakers; Furnace, Kiln, Oven, Drier, and Kettle Operators and Tenders; Hand Compositors and Typesetters; Job Printers; Letterpress Setters and Set-Up Operators; Metal Fabricators, Structural Metal Products; Metal-Refining Furnace Operators and Tenders; Mixing and Blending Machine Setters, Operators, and Tenders; Mold Makers, Hand; Molding and Casting Workers; Numerical Control Machine Tool Operators and Tenders, Metal and Plastic; Offset Lithographic Press Setters and Set-Up Operators; Painting, Coating, and Decorating Workers; Photographic Processing Machine Operators; Photographic Reproduction Technicians; Photographic Retouchers and Restorers; Plate Finishers; Platemakers; Precision Printing Workers; Printing Press Machine Operators and Tenders; Production Workers, All Other; Sawing Machine Operators and Tenders; Sawing Machine Setters and Set-Up Operators; Scanner Operators; Separating, Filtering, Clarifying, Precipitating, and Still Machine Setters, Operators, and Tenders; Sewing Machine Operators, Garment; Slaughterers and Meat Packers; Stone Sawyers; Team Assemblers; Welder-Fitters; Welders and Cutters; Woodworking Machine Operators and Tenders, Except Sawing. **PERSONALITY TYPE:** Realistic. Realistic occupations frequently involve work activities that include practical, hands-on problems and solutions. They often deal with plants, animals, and real-world materials like wood, tools, and machinery. Many of the occupations require working outside and do not involve a lot of paperwork or working closely with others.

RELATED KNOWLEDGE/COURSES—Fine Arts: Knowledge of the theory and techniques required to compose, produce, and perform works of music, dance, visual arts, drama, and sculpture. **Chemistry:** Knowledge of the chemical composition, structure, and properties of substances and of the chemical processes and transformations that they undergo. This includes uses of chemicals, their danger signs, production techniques, and disposal methods. **Production and Processing:** Knowledge of raw materials, production processes, quality control, costs, and other techniques for maximizing the effective manufacture and distribution of goods. **Design:** Knowledge of design techniques, tools, and principles involved in production of precision technical plans, blueprints, drawings, and models.

WORK ENVIRONMENT—Indoors; sitting; extremely bright or inadequate lighting; spend time making repetitive motions; using hands on objects, tools, or controls.

Structural Iron and Steel Workers

- ☺ Growth: 15.9%
- ☺ Annual Job Openings: 9,000
- ☺ Annual Earnings: $40,730
- ☺ Percentage of Women: 2.4%

Related Apprenticeship	Years
Assembler, Metal Building	2
Tank Setter	2
Structural-Steel Worker	3

(This is one of the most popular apprenticeable jobs.)

Raise, place, and unite iron or steel girders, columns, and other structural members to form completed structures or structural frameworks. May erect metal storage tanks and assemble prefabricated metal buildings. Assemble hoisting equipment and rigging, such as cables, pulleys, and hooks, to move heavy equipment and materials. Bolt aligned structural-steel members in position for permanent riveting, bolting, or welding into place. Connect columns, beams, and girders with bolts, following blueprints and instructions from supervisors. Drive drift pins through rivet holes in order to align rivet holes in structural-steel members with corresponding holes in previously placed members. Erect metal and precast concrete components for structures such as buildings, bridges, dams, towers, storage tanks, fences, and highway guard rails. Fasten structural-steel members to hoist cables, using chains, cables, or rope. Force structural-steel members into final positions, using turnbuckles, crowbars, jacks, and hand tools. Hoist steel beams, girders, and columns into place, using cranes, or signal hoisting equipment operators to lift and position structural-steel members. Pull, push, or pry structural-steel members into approximate positions for bolting into place. Ride on girders or other structural-steel members to position them, or use rope to guide them into position. Unload and position prefabricated steel units for hoisting as needed. Verify vertical and horizontal alignment of structural-steel members, using plumb bobs, laser equipment, transits, and/or levels. Catch hot rivets in buckets, and insert rivets in holes, using tongs. Cut, bend, and weld steel pieces, using metal shears, torches, and welding equipment. Dismantle structures and equipment. Fabricate metal parts such as steel frames, columns, beams, and girders, according to blueprints or instructions from supervisors. Hold rivets while riveters use air-hammers to form heads on rivets. Insert sealing strips, wiring, insulating material, ladders, flanges, gauges, and valves, depending on types of structures being assembled. Place blocks under reinforcing bars used to reinforce floors. Read specifications and blueprints to determine the locations, quantities, and sizes of materials required. **SKILLS**—Installation; Coordination; Repairing; Equipment Selection; Management of Material Resources; Operation and Control; Technology Design; Equipment Maintenance.

GOE—**Interest Area:** 06. Construction, Mining, and Drilling. **Work Group:** 06.02 Construction. **Other Apprenticeable Jobs in This Work Group:** Boat Builders and Shipwrights; Boilermakers; Brickmasons and Blockmasons; Carpet Installers; Ceiling Tile Installers; Cement Masons and Concrete Finishers; Construction and Related Workers, All Other; Construction Carpenters; Drywall Installers; Electricians; Fence Erectors; Floor Layers, Except Carpet, Wood, and Hard Tiles; Glaziers; Grader, Bulldozer, and Scraper Operators; Insulation Workers, Floor, Ceiling, and Wall; Insulation Workers, Mechanical; Operating Engineers; Painters, Construction and Maintenance; Paperhangers; Paving, Surfacing, and Tamping Equipment Operators; Pipe Fitters; Plasterers and Stucco Masons; Plumbers; Reinforcing Iron and Rebar Workers; Riggers; Roofers; Rough Carpenters; Sheet Metal Workers; Ship Carpenters and Joiners; Stone Cutters and Carvers; Stonemasons; Tapers; Terrazzo Workers and Finishers; Tile and Marble Setters. **PERSONALITY TYPE:** Realistic. Realistic occupations frequently involve work activities that include practical, hands-on problems and solutions. They often deal with plants, animals, and real-world materials like wood, tools, and machinery. Many of the occupations require working outside and do not involve a lot of paperwork or working closely with others.

RELATED KNOWLEDGE/COURSES— **Building and Construction:** Knowledge of the materials, methods, and tools involved in the construction or repair of houses, buildings, or other structures, such as highways and roads. **Mechanical Devices:** Knowledge of machines and tools, including their designs, uses, repair, and maintenance. **Public Safety and Security:** Knowledge of relevant equipment, policies, procedures, and strategies to promote effective local, state, or national security operations for the protection of people, data, property, and institutions. **Engineering and Technology:** Knowledge of the practical application of engineering science and technology. This includes applying principles, techniques, procedures, and equipment to the design and production of various goods and services. **Physics:** Knowledge and prediction of physical principles and laws and their interrelationships and applications to understanding fluid, material, and atmospheric dynamics and mechanical, electrical, atomic, and subatomic structures and processes. **Design:** Knowledge of design techniques, tools, and principles involved in production of precision technical plans, blueprints, drawings, and models.

WORK ENVIRONMENT—Common protective or safety equipment; climbing ladders, scaffolds, or poles; outdoors; sounds, noise levels are distracting or uncomfortable; very hot or cold; high places.

FURTHER INFORMATION—Contact a local joint union-management apprenticeship committee or the nearest office of your state employment service or apprenticeship agency (see Appendix C). To identify the local union office, contact International Association of Bridge, Structural, Ornamental, and Reinforcing Iron Workers, Apprenticeship Department, 1750 New York Ave. NW, Suite 400, Washington, DC 20006.

Surgical Technologists

- ⊚ Growth: 27.9%
- ⊚ Annual Job Openings: 13,000
- ⊚ Annual Earnings: $32,130
- ⊚ Percentage of Women: 80.7%

Related Apprenticeship	*Years*
Surgical Technologist	competency

Assist in operations, under the supervision of surgeons, registered nurses, or other surgical personnel. May help set up operating room, prepare and transport patients for surgery, adjust lights and equipment, pass instruments and other supplies to surgeons and surgeon's assistants, hold retractors, cut sutures, and help count sponges, needles, supplies, and instruments. Count sponges, needles, and instruments before and after operation. Hand instruments and supplies to surgeons and surgeons' assistants, hold retractors and cut sutures, and perform other tasks as directed by surgeon during operation. Scrub arms and hands and assist the surgical team to scrub and put on gloves, masks, and surgical clothing. Position patients on the operating table and cover them with sterile surgical drapes to prevent exposure. Provide technical assistance to surgeons, surgical nurses and anesthesiologists. Wash and sterilize equipment using germicides and sterilizers. Prepare, care for and dispose of tissue specimens taken for laboratory analysis. Clean and restock the operating room, placing equipment and supplies and arranging instruments according to instruction. Prepare dressings or bandages and apply or assist with their application following surgery. Operate, assemble, adjust, or monitor sterilizers, lights, suction machines, and diagnostic equipment to ensure proper operation. Monitor and continually assess operating room conditions, including patient and surgical team needs. Observe patients' vital signs to assess physical condition. Maintain supply of fluids, such as plasma, saline, blood and glucose, for use during operations. Maintain files and records of surgical procedures. **SKILLS**—Instructing; Troubleshooting; Learning Strategies; Equipment Selection; Social Perceptiveness; Active Learning; Service Orientation; Reading Comprehension.

GOE—Interest Area: 14. Medical and Health Services. **Work Group:** 14.02 Medicine and Surgery. **Other Apprenticeable Jobs in This Work Group:** Medical Assistants; Pharmacy Technicians. **PERSONALITY TYPE:** Realistic. Realistic occupations frequently involve work activities that include practical, hands-on problems and solutions. They often deal with plants, animals, and real-world materials like wood, tools, and machinery. Many of the occupations require working outside and do not involve a lot of paperwork or working closely with others.

RELATED KNOWLEDGE/COURSES—Medicine and Dentistry: Knowledge of the information and techniques needed to diagnose and treat human injuries, diseases, and deformities. This includes symptoms, treatment alternatives, drug properties and interactions, and preventive health-care measures. **Customer and Personal Service:** Knowledge of principles and processes for providing customer and personal services. This includes customer needs assessment, meeting quality standards for services, and evaluation of customer satisfaction. **Psychology:** Knowledge of human behavior and performance; individual differences in ability, personality, and interests; learning and motivation; psychological research methods; and the assessment and treatment of behavioral and affective disorders. **Chemistry:** Knowledge of the chemical composition, structure, and properties of substances and of the chemical processes and transformations that they undergo. This includes uses of chemicals, their danger signs, production techniques, and disposal methods. **Education and Training:** Knowledge of principles and methods for curriculum and training design, teaching and instruction for individuals and groups, and the measurement of training effects. **Philosophy and Theology:** Knowledge of different philosophical systems and religions. This includes their basic principles, values, ethics, ways of thinking, customs, and practices and their impact on human culture.

WORK ENVIRONMENT—Physical proximity; contaminants; hazardous conditions; disease or infections; exposed to radiation.

Surveying Technicians

- Growth: 23.1%
- Annual Job Openings: 10,000
- Annual Earnings: $29,520
- Percentage of Women: 8.9%

Related Apprenticeship	Years
Surveyor Assistant, Instruments	2
Chief of Party	4

Adjust and operate surveying instruments, such as the theodolite and electronic distance-measuring equipment, and compile notes, make sketches and enter data into computers. Adjust and operate surveying instruments such as prisms, theodolites, and electronic distance-measuring equipment. Compile information necessary to stake projects for construction, using engineering plans. Conduct surveys to ascertain the locations of natural features and human-made structures on the Earth's surface, underground, and underwater, using electronic distance-measuring equipment and other surveying instruments. Lay out grids, and determine horizontal and vertical controls. Operate and manage land-information computer systems, performing tasks such as storing data, making inquiries, and producing plots and reports. Perform calculations to determine earth curvature corrections, atmospheric impacts on measurements, traverse closures and adjustments, azimuths, level runs, and placement of markers. Place and hold measuring tapes when electronic distance-measuring equipment is not used. Position and hold the vertical rods, or targets, that theodolite operators use for sighting in order to measure angles, distances, and elevations. Record survey measurements and descriptive data, using notes, drawings, sketches, and inked tracings. Run rods for benches and cross-section elevations. Search for section corners, property irons, and survey points. Set out and recover stakes, marks, and other monumentation. Collect information needed to carry out new surveys, using source maps, previous survey data, photographs, computer records, and other relevant information. Compare survey computations with applicable standards in order to determine adequacy of data. Direct and supervise work of subordinate members of surveying parties. Maintain equipment and vehicles used by surveying crews. Perform manual labor, such as cutting brush for lines, carrying stakes, rebar, and other heavy items, and stacking rods. Provide assistance in the development of methods and procedures for conducting field surveys. Prepare topographic and contour maps of land surveyed, including site features and other relevant information such as charts, drawings, and survey notes. **SKILLS**—Mathematics.

GOE—**Interest Area:** 02. Science, Math, and Engineering. **Work Group:** 02.09 Engineering Technology. **Other Apprenticeable Jobs in This Work Group:** Aerospace Engineering and Operations Technicians; Architectural Drafters; Calibration and Instrumentation Technicians; Cartographers and Photogrammetrists; Civil Drafters; Construction and Building Inspectors; Electrical Drafters; Electrical Engineering Technicians; Electro-Mechanical Technicians; Electronic Drafters; Electronics Engineering Technicians; Engineering Technicians, Except Drafters, All Other; Industrial Engineering Technicians; Mapping Technicians; Mechanical Drafters; Mechanical Engineering Technicians; Numerical Tool and Process Control Programmers. **PERSONALITY TYPE:** Realistic. Realistic occupations frequently involve work activities that include practical, hands-on problems and solutions. They often deal with plants, animals, and real-world materials like wood, tools, and machinery. Many of the occupations require working outside and do not involve a lot of paperwork or working closely with others.

RELATED KNOWLEDGE/COURSES—**Design:** Knowledge of design techniques, tools, and principles involved in production of precision technical plans, blueprints, drawings, and models. **Engineering and Technology:** Knowledge of the practical application of engineering science and technology. This includes applying principles, techniques, procedures, and equipment to the design and production of various goods and services. **Geography:** Knowledge of principles and methods for describing the features of land, sea, and air masses, including their physical characteristics; locations; interrelationships; and distribution of plant, animal, and human life. **Mathematics:** Knowledge of arithmetic, algebra, geometry, calculus, and statistics and their applications. **Computers and Electronics:** Knowledge of circuit boards, processors, chips, electronic equipment, and computer hardware and software, including applications and programming.

WORK ENVIRONMENT—Outdoors; very hot or cold; standing; extremely bright or inadequate lighting; walking and running; spend time kneeling, crouching, stooping, or crawling.

Tapers

- Growth: 20.8%
- Annual Job Openings: 5,000
- Annual Earnings: $39,130
- Percentage of Women: 2.7%

Related Apprenticeship	*Years*
Taper	2

Seal joints between plasterboard or other wallboard to prepare wall surface for painting or papering. Spreads sealing compound between boards, using trowel, broadknife or spatula. Tapes joint, using mechanical applicator that spreads compound and embeds tape in one operation. Sands rough spots after cement has dried. Installs metal molding at corners in lieu of sealant and tape. Applies texturizing compound and primer to walls and ceiling preparatory to final finishing, using brushes, roller, or spray gun. Countersinks nails or screws below surface of wall prior to applying sealing compound, using hammer or screwdriver. Mixes sealing compound by hand or with portable electric mixer. Fills cracks and holes in walls and ceiling with sealing compound. Spreads and smoothes cementing material over tape, using trowel or floating machine to blend joint with wall surface. Presses paper tape over joint to embed tape into sealing compound and seal joint. **SKILLS**—None met the criteria.

GOE—Interest Area: 06. Construction, Mining, and Drilling. **Work Group:** 06.02 Construction. **Other Apprenticeable Jobs in This Work Group:** Boat Builders and Shipwrights; Boilermakers; Brickmasons and Blockmasons; Carpet Installers; Ceiling Tile Installers; Cement Masons and Concrete Finishers; Construction and Related Workers, All Other; Construction Carpenters; Drywall Installers; Electricians; Fence Erectors; Floor Layers, Except Carpet, Wood, and Hard Tiles; Glaziers; Grader, Bulldozer, and Scraper Operators; Insulation Workers, Floor, Ceiling, and Wall; Insulation Workers, Mechanical; Operating Engineers; Painters, Construction and Maintenance; Paperhangers; Paving, Surfacing, and Tamping Equipment Operators; Pipe Fitters; Plasterers and Stucco Masons; Plumbers; Reinforcing Iron and Rebar Workers; Riggers; Roofers; Rough Carpenters; Sheet Metal Workers; Ship Carpenters and Joiners; Stone Cutters and Carvers; Stonemasons; Structural Iron and Steel Workers; Terrazzo Workers and Finishers; Tile and Marble Setters. **PERSONALITY TYPE:** Realistic. Realistic occupations frequently involve work activities that include practical, hands-on problems and solutions. They often deal with plants, animals, and real-world materials like wood, tools, and machinery. Many of the occupations require working outside and do not involve a lot of paperwork or working closely with others.

RELATED KNOWLEDGE/COURSES— Building and Construction: Knowledge of the materials, methods, and tools involved in the construction or repair of houses, buildings, or other structures, such as highways and roads. **Sales and Marketing:** Knowledge of principles and methods for showing, promoting, and selling products or services. This includes marketing strategy and tactics, product demonstration, sales techniques, and sales control systems.

WORK ENVIRONMENT—Climbing ladders, scaffolds, or poles; contaminants; common protective or safety equipment; minor burns, cuts, bites, or stings; hazardous conditions.

T

Teacher Assistants

- Growth: 23.0%
- Annual Job Openings: 259,000
- Annual Earnings: $19,000
- Percentage of Women: 91.6%

Related Apprenticeship	*Years*
Teacher Aide I	2

Perform duties that are instructional in nature or deliver direct services to students or parents. Serve in a position for which a teacher or another professional has ultimate responsibility for the design and implementation of educational programs and services. Discuss assigned duties with classroom teachers in order to coordinate instructional efforts. Prepare lesson materials, bulletin board displays, exhibits, equipment, and demonstrations. Present subject matter to students under the direction and guidance of teachers, using lectures, discussions, or supervised role-playing methods. Tutor and assist children individually or in small groups in order to help them master assignments and to reinforce learning concepts presented by teachers. Supervise students in classrooms, halls, cafeterias, school yards, and gymnasiums, or on field trips. Conduct demonstrations to teach such skills as sports, dancing, and handicrafts. Distribute teaching materials such as textbooks, workbooks, papers, and pencils to students. Distribute tests and homework assignments, and collect them when they are completed. Enforce administration policies and rules governing students. Grade homework and tests and compute and record results, using answer sheets or electronic marking devices. Instruct and monitor students in the use and care of equipment and materials, in order to prevent injuries and damage. Observe students' performance and record relevant data to assess progress. Organize and label materials, and display students' work in a manner appropriate for their eye levels and perceptual skills. Organize and supervise games and other recreational activities to promote physical, mental, and social development. Participate in teacher-parent conferences regarding students' progress or problems. Plan, prepare, and develop various teaching aids such as bibliographies, charts, and graphs. Prepare lesson outlines and plans in assigned subject areas, and submit outlines to teachers for review. Provide extra assistance to students with special needs, such as non-English-speaking students or those with physical and mental disabilities. Take class attendance, and maintain attendance records. Assist in bus loading and unloading. Assist librarians in school libraries. Attend staff meetings, and serve on committees as required. Carry out therapeutic regimens such as behavior modification and personal development programs, under the supervision of special education instructors, psychologists, or speech-language pathologists. **SKILLS**—Instructing; Learning Strategies; Service Orientation; Speaking; Active Listening; Social Perceptiveness; Writing; Reading Comprehension.

GOE—Interest Area: 12. Education and Social Service. **Work Group:** 12.03 Educational Services. **Other Apprenticeable Jobs in This Work Group:** Child Care Workers; Educational, Vocational, and School Counselors. **PERSONALITY TYPE:** Social. Social occupations frequently involve working with, communicating with, and teaching people. These occupations often involve helping or providing service to others.

RELATED KNOWLEDGE/COURSES— **Education and Training:** Knowledge of principles and methods for curriculum and training design, teaching and instruction for individuals and groups, and the measurement of training effects. **English Language:** Knowledge of the structure and content of the English language, including the meaning and spelling of words, rules of composition, and grammar. **History and Archeology:** Knowledge of historical events and their causes, indicators, and effects on civilizations and cultures. **Psychology:** Knowledge of human behavior and performance; individual differences in ability, personality, and interests; learning and motivation; psychological research methods; and the assessment and treatment of behavioral and affective disorders. **Sociology and Anthropology:** Knowledge of group behavior and dynamics, societal trends and influences, human migrations, ethnicity, and cultures and their history and origins. **Philosophy and Theology:** Knowledge of different philosophical systems and religions. This includes their basic principles, values, ethics, ways of thinking, customs, and practices and their impact on human culture.

WORK ENVIRONMENT—Indoors; sitting; walking and running; standing; disease or infections.

Team Assemblers

- ⚙ Growth: –1.6%
- ⚙ Annual Job Openings: 143,000
- ⚙ Annual Earnings: $23,180
- ⚙ Percentage of Women: 43.4%

Related Apprenticeship	*Years*
Production Technologist	competency

Work as part of a team having responsibility for assembling an entire product or component of a product. Team assemblers can perform all tasks conducted by the team in the assembly process and rotate through all or most of them rather than being assigned to a specific task on a permanent basis. May participate in making management decisions affecting the work. Team leaders who work as part of the team should be included. Rotate through all the tasks required in a particular production process. Determine work assignments and procedures. Operate heavy equipment such as forklifts. Provide assistance in the production of wiring assemblies. Shovel and sweep work areas. SKILLS—No data available.

GOE—Interest Area: 08. Industrial Production. **Work Group:** 08.03 Production Work. **Other Apprenticeable Jobs in This Work Group:** Bakers, Manufacturing; Bindery Machine Operators and Tenders; Chemical Equipment Controllers and Operators; Coating, Painting, and Spraying Machine Operators and Tenders; Cooling and Freezing Equipment Operators and Tenders; Crushing, Grinding, and Polishing Machine Setters, Operators, and Tenders; Cutters and Trimmers, Hand; Cutting and Slicing Machine Operators and Tenders; Design Printing Machine Setters and Set-Up Operators; Electrolytic Plating and Coating Machine Setters and Set-Up Operators, Metal and Plastic; Electrotypers and Stereotypers; Embossing Machine Set-Up Operators; Engraver Set-Up Operators; Extruding, Forming, Pressing, and Compacting Machine Oper-

T

ators and Tenders; Fabric and Apparel Pattern-makers; Film Laboratory Technicians; Fitters, Structural Metal—Precision; Food Batchmakers; Furnace, Kiln, Oven, Drier, and Kettle Operators and Tenders; Hand Compositors and Typesetters; Job Printers; Letterpress Setters and Set-Up Operators; Metal Fabricators, Structural Metal Products; Metal-Refining Furnace Operators and Tenders; Mixing and Blending Machine Setters, Operators, and Tenders; Mold Makers, Hand; Molding and Casting Workers; Numerical Control Machine Tool Operators and Tenders, Metal and Plastic; Offset Lithographic Press Setters and Set-Up Operators; Painting, Coating, and Decorating Workers; Photographic Processing Machine Operators; Photographic Reproduction Technicians; Photographic Retouchers and Restorers; Plate Finishers; Platemakers; Precision Printing Workers; Printing Press Machine Operators and Tenders; Production Workers, All Other; Sawing Machine Operators and Tenders; Sawing Machine Setters and Set-Up Operators; Scanner Operators; Separating, Filtering, Clarifying, Precipitating, and Still Machine Setters, Operators, and Tenders; Sewing Machine Operators, Garment; Slaughterers and Meat Packers; Stone Sawyers; Strippers; Welder-Fitters; Welders and Cutters; Woodworking Machine Operators and Tenders, Except Sawing. **PERSONALITY TYPE:** No data available.

RELATED KNOWLEDGE/COURSES—No data available.

WORK ENVIRONMENT—No data available.

Telecommunications Line Installers and Repairers

- Growth: 18.8%
- Annual Job Openings: 13,000
- Annual Earnings: $39,540
- Percentage of Women: 6.5%

Related Apprenticeship	*Years*
Cable Television Installer	1
Line Installer-Repairer	4

String and repair telephone and television cable, including fiber optics and other equipment for transmitting messages or television programming. Measure signal strength at utility poles, using electronic test equipment. Place insulation over conductors, and seal splices with moisture-proof covering. Pull up cable by hand from large reels mounted on trucks; then pull lines through ducts by hand or with winches. Set up service for customers, installing, connecting, testing, and adjusting equipment. Splice cables, using hand tools, epoxy, or mechanical equipment. String cables between structures and lines from poles, towers, or trenches and pull lines to proper tension. Travel to customers' premises to install, maintain, and repair audio and visual electronic reception equipment and accessories. Access specific areas to string lines and install terminal boxes, auxiliary equipment, and appliances, using bucket trucks, or by climbing poles and ladders or entering tunnels, trenches, or crawl spaces. Inspect and test lines and cables, recording and analyzing test results, to assess transmission characteristics and locate faults and malfunctions. Install equipment such as amplifiers and repeaters in order to maintain the strength of communications transmissions. Lay underground cable directly in trenches, or string it through conduits running through trenches. Use a variety of construction equipment to complete installations, including digger derricks, trenchers, and cable plows. Clean and maintain tools and test equipment. Compute impedance of wires from poles to houses in order to determine additional resistance needed for reducing signals to desired levels. Dig holes for power poles, using power augers or shovels, set poles in place with cranes, and hoist poles upright, using winches. Dig trenches for underground wires and cables. Explain cable service to subscribers after installation, and collect any installation fees that are due. Fill and tamp holes, using cement, earth, and tamping devices. Participate in the construction and removal of telecommunication towers and associated support structures. **SKILLS**—Installation; Repairing; Troubleshooting; Equipment Maintenance; Operation Monitoring; Operation and Control; Systems Evaluation; Mathematics.

GOE—**Interest Area:** 05. Mechanics, Installers, and Repairers. **Work Group:** 05.02 Electrical and Electronic Systems. **Other Apprenticeable Jobs in This Work Group:** Avionics Technicians; Battery Repairers; Central Office and PBX Installers and Repairers; Communication Equipment Mechanics, Installers, and Repairers; Data Processing Equipment Repairers; Electric Home Appliance and Power Tool Repairers; Electric Meter Installers and Repairers; Electric Motor and Switch Assemblers and

Repairers; Electrical and Electronics Installers and Repairers, Transportation Equipment; Electrical and Electronics Repairers, Commercial and Industrial Equipment; Electrical and Electronics Repairers, Powerhouse, Substation, and Relay; Electrical Power-Line Installers and Repairers; Electronic Equipment Installers and Repairers, Motor Vehicles; Electronic Home Entertainment Equipment Installers and Repairers; Elevator Installers and Repairers; Installation, Maintenance, and Repair Workers, All Other; Office Machine and Cash Register Servicers; Radio Mechanics; Signal and Track Switch Repairers; Station Installers and Repairers, Telephone; Transformer Repairers. **PERSONALITY TYPE:** Realistic. Realistic occupations frequently involve work activities that include practical, hands-on problems and solutions. They often deal with plants, animals, and real-world materials like wood, tools, and machinery. Many of the occupations require working outside and do not involve a lot of paperwork or working closely with others.

RELATED KNOWLEDGE/COURSES—**Telecommunications:** Knowledge of transmission, broadcasting, switching, control, and operation of telecommunications systems. **Computers and Electronics:** Knowledge of circuit boards, processors, chips, electronic equipment, and computer hardware and software, including applications and programming. **Mechanical Devices:** Knowledge of machines and tools, including their designs, uses, repair, and maintenance. **Sales and Marketing:** Knowledge of principles and methods for showing, promoting, and selling products or services. This includes marketing strategy and tactics, product demonstration, sales techniques, and sales control systems. **Physics:** Knowledge and prediction of physical principles and laws and their interrelationships and applications to understanding fluid, material, and atmospheric dynamics and mechanical, electrical, atomic, and subatomic structures and processes. **Engineering and Technology:** Knowledge of the practical application of engineering science and technology. This includes applying principles, techniques, procedures, and equipment to the design and production of various goods and services.

WORK ENVIRONMENT—Outdoors; high places; very hot or cold; climbing ladders, scaffolds, or poles; spend time kneeling, crouching, stooping, or crawling.

Tellers

- Growth: 9.4%
- Annual Job Openings: 127,000
- Annual Earnings: $20,670
- Percentage of Women: 89.7%

Related Apprenticeship	*Years*
Teller (Financial)	1

Receive and pay out money. Keep records of money and negotiable instruments involved in a financial institution's various transactions. Balance currency, coin, and checks in cash drawers at ends of shifts, and calculate daily transactions using computers, calculators, or adding machines. Cash checks and pay out money after verifying that signatures are correct, that written and numerical amounts agree, and that accounts have sufficient funds. Receive checks and cash for deposit, verify amounts, and check accuracy of deposit slips. Examine checks for endorsements and to verify other information such as dates, bank names, identification of the persons receiving payments and the legality of the documents. Enter customers' transactions into computers in order to record transactions and issue computer-generated receipts. Count currency, coins, and checks received, by hand or using currency-counting machine, in order to prepare them for deposit or shipment to branch banks or the Federal Reserve Bank. Identify transaction mistakes when debits and credits do not balance. Prepare and verify cashier's checks. Arrange monies received in cash boxes and coin dispensers according to denomination. Process transactions such as term deposits, retirement savings plan contributions, automated teller transactions, night deposits, and mail deposits. Receive mortgage, loan, or public utility bill payments, verifying payment dates and amounts due. Resolve problems or discrepancies concerning customers' accounts. Explain, promote, or sell products or services such as travelers' checks, savings bonds, money orders, and cashier's checks, using computerized information about customers to tailor recommendations. Perform clerical tasks such as typing, filing, and microfilm photography. Monitor bank vaults to ensure cash balances are correct. Order a supply of cash to meet daily needs. Sort and file deposit slips and checks. Receive and count daily inventories of cash, drafts, and travelers' checks. Process and maintain records of customer loans. Count, verify, and post armored car deposits. Carry out special services for customers, such as ordering bank cards and checks. Compute financial fees, interest, and service charges. Obtain and process information required for the provision of services, such as opening accounts, savings plans, and purchasing bonds.

SKILLS—Service Orientation; Active Learning; Active Listening; Social Perceptiveness; Instructing; Time Management; Learning Strategies; Mathematics.

GOE—Interest Area: 09. Business Detail. **Work Group:** 09.05 Customer Service. **Other Apprenticeable Jobs in This Work Group:** No other apprenticeable jobs in this group. **PERSONALITY TYPE:** Conventional. Conventional occupations frequently involve following set procedures and routines. These occupations can include working with data and details more than with ideas. Usually there is a clear line of authority to follow.

RELATED KNOWLEDGE/COURSES— **Customer and Personal Service:** Knowledge of principles and processes for providing customer and personal services. This includes customer needs assessment, meeting quality standards for services, and evaluation of customer satisfaction. **English Language:** Knowledge of the structure and content of the English language, including the meaning and spelling of words, rules of composition, and grammar. **Sales and Marketing:** Knowledge of principles and methods for showing, promoting, and selling products or services. This includes marketing strategy and tactics, product demonstration, sales techniques, and sales control systems. **Clerical Practices:** Knowledge of administrative and clerical procedures and systems, such as word processing, managing files and records, stenography and transcription, designing forms, and other office procedures and terminology. **Public Safety and Security:** Knowledge of relevant equipment, policies, procedures, and strategies to promote effective local, state, or national security operations for the protection of people, data, property, and institutions. **Law and Government:** Knowledge of laws, legal codes, court procedures, precedents, government regulations, executive orders, agency rules, and the democratic political process.

WORK ENVIRONMENT—Physical proximity; sitting; keeping or regaining balance; contaminants; sounds, noise levels are distracting or uncomfortable; minor burns, cuts, bites, or stings.

Terrazzo Workers and Finishers

- Growth: 15.2%
- Annual Job Openings: 1,000
- Annual Earnings: $27,710
- Percentage of Women: 1.4%

Related Apprenticeship	Years
Terrazzo Finisher	2
Terrazzo Worker	3

Apply a mixture of cement, sand, pigment, or marble chips to floors, stairways, and cabinet fixtures to fashion durable and decorative surfaces. Blend marble chip mixtures and place into panels, then push a roller over the surface to embed the chips. Cut metal division strips and press them into the terrazzo base wherever there is to be a joint or change of color, to form desired designs or patterns, and to help prevent cracks. Grind curved surfaces and areas inaccessible to surfacing machine, such as stairways and cabinet tops, with portable hand grinder.

Grind surfaces with a power grinder and polish surfaces with polishing or surfacing machines. Measure designated amounts of ingredients for terrazzo or grout according to standard formulas and specifications, using graduated containers and scale, and load ingredients into portable mixer. Mix cement, sand, and water to produce concrete, grout, or slurry, using hoe, trowel, tamper, scraper, or concrete-mixing machine. Modify mixing, grouting, grinding, and cleaning procedures according to type of installation or material used. Mold expansion joints and edges, using edging tools, jointers, and straightedges. Position and secure moisture membrane and wire mesh prior to pouring base materials for terrazzo installation. Spread roofing paper on surface of foundation, and spread concrete onto roofing paper with trowel to form terrazzo base. Spread, level, and smooth concrete and terrazzo mixtures to form bases and finished surfaces, using rakes, shovels, hand or power trowels, hand or power screeds, and floats. Sprinkle colored marble or stone chips, powdered steel, or coloring powder over surface to produce prescribed finish. Wash polished terrazzo surface, using cleaner and water, and apply sealer and curing agent according to manufacturer's specifications, using brush or sprayer. Wet surface to prepare for bonding, fill holes and cracks with grout or slurry, and smooth, using trowel. Build wooden molds, clamping molds around areas to be repaired, and setting up frames to the proper depth and alignment. Chip, scrape, and grind high spots, ridges, and rough projections to finish concrete, using pneumatic chisel, hand chisel, or other hand tools. Clean chipped area, using wire brush, and feel and observe surface to determine if it is rough or uneven. **SKILLS**—Technology Design; Repairing; Operations Analysis; Installation; Science; Equipment Maintenance.

GOE—Interest Area: 06. Construction, Mining, and Drilling. **Work Group:** 06.02 Construction. **Other Apprenticeable Jobs in This Work Group:** Boat Builders and Shipwrights; Boilermakers; Brickmasons and Blockmasons; Carpet Installers; Ceiling Tile Installers; Cement Masons and Concrete Finishers; Construction and Related Workers, All Other; Construction Carpenters; Drywall Installers; Electricians; Fence Erectors; Floor Layers, Except Carpet, Wood, and Hard Tiles; Glaziers; Grader, Bulldozer, and Scraper Operators; Insulation Workers, Floor, Ceiling, and Wall; Insulation Workers, Mechanical; Operating Engineers; Painters, Construction and Maintenance; Paperhangers; Paving, Surfacing, and Tamping Equipment Operators; Pipe Fitters; Plasterers and Stucco Masons; Plumbers; Reinforcing Iron and Rebar Workers; Riggers; Roofers; Rough Carpenters; Sheet Metal Workers; Ship Carpenters and Joiners; Stone Cutters and Carvers; Stonemasons; Structural Iron and Steel Workers; Tapers; Tile and Marble Setters. **PERSONALITY TYPE:** Realistic. Realistic occupations frequently involve work activities that include practical, hands-on problems and solutions. They often deal with plants, animals, and real-world materials like wood, tools, and machinery. Many of the occupations require working outside and do not involve a lot of paperwork or working closely with others.

RELATED KNOWLEDGE/COURSES— Building and Construction: Knowledge of the materials, methods, and tools involved in the construction or repair of houses, buildings, or other structures, such as highways and roads. **Engineering and Technology:** Knowledge of the practical application of engineering science and technology. This includes applying principles, techniques, procedures, and equipment to the design and production of various goods and services. **Design:** Knowledge of design techniques, tools, and principles involved in production of precision technical plans, blueprints, drawings, and models. **Mechanical Devices:** Knowledge of machines and tools, including their designs, uses, repair, and maintenance. **Geography:** Knowledge of principles and methods for describing the features of land, sea, and air masses, including their physical characteristics; locations; interrelationships; and distribution of plant, animal, and human life. **Fine Arts:** Knowledge of the theory and techniques required to compose, produce, and perform works of music, dance, visual arts, drama, and sculpture.

WORK ENVIRONMENT—Outdoors; spend time kneeling, crouching, stooping, or crawling; spend time bending or twisting the body; very hot or cold; climbing ladders, scaffolds, or poles; keeping or regaining balance.

Tile and Marble Setters

- ◉ Growth: 26.5%
- ◉ Annual Job Openings: 4,000
- ◉ Annual Earnings: $35,610
- ◉ Percentage of Women: 2.5%

Related Apprenticeship	Years
Mosaic Worker	3
Tile Setter	3

Apply hard tile, marble, and wood tile to walls, floors, ceilings, and roof decks. Align and straighten tile using levels, squares and straightedges. Determine and implement the best layout to achieve a desired pattern. Cut and shape tile to fit around obstacles and into odd spaces and corners, using hand and power cutting tools. Finish and dress the joints and wipe excess grout from between tiles, using damp sponge. Apply mortar to tile back, position the tile and press or tap with trowel handle to affix tile to base. Mix, apply, and spread plaster, concrete, mortar, cement, mastic, glue or other adhesives to form a bed for the tiles, using brush, trowel and screed. Prepare cost and labor estimates based on calculations of time and materials needed for project. Measure and mark surfaces to be tiled, following blueprints. Level concrete and allow to dry. Build underbeds and install anchor bolts, wires and brackets. Prepare surfaces for tiling by attaching lath or waterproof paper, or by applying a cement mortar coat onto a metal screen. Study blueprints and examine surface to be covered to determine amount of material needed. Cut, surface, polish and install marble and granite and/or install pre-cast terrazzo, granite or marble units. Install and anchor fixtures in designated positions, using hand tools. Cut tile backing to required size, using shears. Remove any old tile, grout and adhesive using chisels and scrapers and clean the surface carefully. Lay and set mosaic tiles to create decorative wall, mural and floor designs. Assist customers in selection of tile and grout. Remove and replace cracked or damaged tile. Measure and cut metal lath to size for walls and ceilings, using tin snips. Select and order tile and other items to be installed, such as bathroom accessories, walls, panels, and cabinets, according to specifications. Mix and apply mortar or cement to edges and ends of drain tiles to seal halves and joints. Spread mastic or other adhesive base on roof deck to form base for promenade tile, using serrated spreader. **SKILLS**—Installation; Social Perceptiveness; Management of Financial Resources; Instructing; Coordination; Mathematics; Critical Thinking; Negotiation.

GOE—**Interest Area:** 06. Construction, Mining, and Drilling. **Work Group:** 06.02 Construction. **Other Apprenticeable Jobs in This Work Group:** Boat Builders and Shipwrights; Boilermakers; Brickmasons and Blockmasons; Carpet Installers; Ceiling Tile Installers; Cement Masons and Concrete Finishers; Construction and Related Workers, All Other; Construction Carpenters; Drywall Installers; Electricians; Fence Erectors; Floor Layers, Except Carpet, Wood, and Hard Tiles; Glaziers; Grader, Bulldozer, and Scraper Operators; Insulation Workers, Floor, Ceiling, and Wall; Insulation Workers, Mechanical; Operating Engineers; Painters, Construction and Maintenance; Paperhangers; Paving, Surfacing, and Tamping Equipment Operators; Pipe Fitters; Plasterers and Stucco Masons; Plumbers; Reinforcing Iron and Rebar Workers; Riggers; Roofers; Rough Carpenters; Sheet Metal Workers; Ship Carpenters and Joiners; Stone Cutters and Carvers; Stonemasons; Structural Iron and Steel Workers; Tapers; Terrazzo Workers and Finishers. **PERSONALITY TYPE:** Realistic. Realistic occupations frequently involve work activities that include practical, hands-on problems and solutions. They often deal with plants, animals, and real-world materials like wood, tools, and machinery. Many of the occupations require working outside and do not involve a lot of paperwork or working closely with others.

RELATED KNOWLEDGE/COURSES— **Building and Construction:** Knowledge of the materials, methods, and tools involved in the construction or repair of houses, buildings, or other structures, such as highways and roads. **Administration and Management:** Knowledge of business and management principles involved in strategic planning, resource allocation, human resources modeling, leadership technique, production methods, and coordination of people and resources. **Production and Processing:** Knowledge of raw materials, production processes, quality control, costs, and other techniques for maximizing the effective manufacture and distribution of goods. **Design:** Knowledge of design techniques, tools, and principles involved in production of precision technical plans, blueprints, drawings, and models. **Economics and Accounting:** Knowledge of economic and accounting principles and practices, the financial markets, banking, and the analysis and reporting of financial data. **Public Safety and Security:** Knowledge of relevant equipment, policies, procedures, and strategies to promote effective local, state, or national security operations for the protection of people, data, property, and institutions.

WORK ENVIRONMENT—Sounds, noise levels are distracting or uncomfortable; contaminants; cramped work space, awkward positions; physical proximity; spend time kneeling, crouching, stooping, or crawling.

Tool and Die Makers

- Growth: 0.4%
- Annual Job Openings: 3,000
- Annual Earnings: $42,990
- Percentage of Women: 3.1%

Related Apprenticeship	*Years*
Die Maker, Stamping	3
Die Maker, Wire Drawing	3
Saw Maker	3
Die Finisher	4
Die Maker, Bench, Stamping	4
Die Maker, Jewelry and Silver	4
Die Maker, Paper Goods	4

(This is one of the most popular apprenticeable jobs.)

Analyze specifications, lay out metal stock, set up and operate machine tools, and fit and assemble parts to make and repair dies, cutting tools, jigs, fixtures, gauges, and machinists' hand tools. Conduct test runs with completed tools or dies to ensure that parts meet specifications; make adjustments as necessary. Cut, shape, and trim blanks or blocks to specified lengths or shapes, using power saws, power shears, rules, and hand tools. File, grind, shim, and adjust different parts to properly fit them together. Fit and assemble parts to make, repair, or modify dies, jigs, gauges, and tools, using machine tools and hand tools. Inspect finished dies for smoothness, contour conformity, and defects. Lift, position, and secure machined parts on surface plates or worktables, using hoists, vises, v-blocks, or angle plates. Measure, mark, and scribe metal or plastic stock to lay out machining, using instruments such as protractors, micrometers, scribes, and rulers. Select metals to be used from a range of metals and alloys, based on properties such as hardness and heat tolerance. Set up and operate conventional or computer numerically controlled machine tools such as lathes, milling machines, and grinders to cut, bore, grind, or otherwise shape parts to prescribed dimensions and finishes. Set up and operate drill presses to drill and tap holes in parts for assembly. Smooth and polish flat and contoured surfaces of parts or tools, using scrapers, abrasive stones, files, emery cloths, or power grinders. Study blueprints, sketches, models, or specifications to plan sequences of operations for fabricating tools, dies, or assemblies. Verify dimensions, alignments, and clearances of finished parts for conformance to specifications, using measuring instruments such as calipers, gauge blocks, micrometers, and dial indicators. Visualize and compute dimensions, sizes, shapes, and tolerances of assemblies, based on specifications. Cast plastic tools or parts, or tungsten-carbide cutting tips, using pre-made molds. Design jigs, fixtures, and templates for use as work aids in the fabrication of parts or products. Develop and design new tools and dies, using computer-aided design software. Set pyrometer controls of heat-treating furnaces, and feed or place parts, tools, or assemblies into furnaces to harden. **SKILLS**—Installation; Operation and Control; Repairing; Technology Design; Equipment Maintenance; Equipment Selection; Operations Analysis; Quality Control Analysis.

GOE—Interest Area: 08. Industrial Production. **Work Group:** 08.04 Metal and Plastics Machining Technology. **Other Apprenticeable Jobs in This Work Group:** Lay-Out Workers, Metal and Plastic; Machinists; Metal Workers and Plastic Workers, All Other; Model Makers, Metal and Plastic; Patternmakers, Metal and Plastic; Tool Grinders, Filers, and Sharpeners. **PERSONALITY TYPE:** Realistic. Realistic occupations frequently involve work activities that include practical, hands-on problems and solutions. They often deal with plants, animals, and real-world materials like wood, tools, and machinery. Many of the occupations require working outside and do not involve a lot of paperwork or working closely with others.

RELATED KNOWLEDGE/COURSES—
Mechanical Devices: Knowledge of machines and tools, including their designs, uses, repair, and maintenance. **Production and Processing:** Knowledge of raw materials, production processes, quality control, costs, and other techniques for maximizing the effective manufacture and distribution of goods. **Building and Construction:** Knowledge of the materials, methods, and tools involved in the construction or repair of houses, buildings, or other structures, such as highways and roads. **Design:** Knowledge of design techniques, tools, and principles involved in production of precision technical plans, blueprints, drawings, and models. **Engineering and Technology:** Knowledge of the practical application of engineering science and technology. This includes applying principles, techniques, procedures, and equipment to the design and production of various goods and services. **Mathematics:** Knowledge of arithmetic, algebra, geometry, calculus, and statistics and their applications.

WORK ENVIRONMENT—Hazardous equipment; using hands on objects, tools, or controls; common protective or safety equipment; indoors; spend time making repetitive motions.

FURTHER INFORMATION—Contact a local joint union-management apprenticeship committee or the nearest office of your state employment service or apprenticeship agency (see Appendix C). Or contact the following:

National Tooling and Machining Association, 9300 Livingston Rd., Ft. Washington, MD 20744. Internet: http://www.ntma.org.

Precision Metalforming Association Educational Foundation, 6363 Oak Tree Blvd., Independence, OH 44131-2500. Internet: http://www.pmaef.org.

Transformer Repairers

- Growth: 5.3%
- Annual Job Openings: 3,000
- Annual Earnings: $32,310
- Percentage of Women: 4.5%

Related Apprenticeship	*Years*
Power-Transformer Repairer	4
Transformer Repairer	4

Clean and repair electrical transformers. Cleans transformer case, using scrapers and solvent. Fills reassembled transformer with oil until coils are submerged. Reassembles transformer. Drains and filters transformer oil. Disassembles distribution, streetlight, or instrument transformers. Replaces worn or defective parts, using hand tools. Winds replacement coils, using coil-winding machine. Signals crane operator to raise heavy transformer component subassemblies. Secures input and output wires in position. Inspects transformer for defects, such as cracked weldments. Dismantles lamination assembly, preparatory to cleaning and inspection. **SKILLS**—Repairing;

Installation; Troubleshooting; Equipment Maintenance.

GOE—Interest Area: 05. Mechanics, Installers, and Repairers. **Work Group:** 05.02 Electrical and Electronic Systems. **Other Apprenticeable Jobs in This Work Group:** Avionics Technicians; Battery Repairers; Central Office and PBX Installers and Repairers; Communication Equipment Mechanics, Installers, and Repairers; Data Processing Equipment Repairers; Electric Home Appliance and Power Tool Repairers; Electric Meter Installers and Repairers; Electric Motor and Switch Assemblers and Repairers; Electrical and Electronics Installers and Repairers, Transportation Equipment; Electrical and Electronics Repairers, Commercial and Industrial Equipment; Electrical and Electronics Repairers, Powerhouse, Substation, and Relay; Electrical Power-Line Installers and Repairers; Electronic Equipment Installers and Repairers, Motor Vehicles; Electronic Home Entertainment Equipment Installers and Repairers; Elevator Installers and Repairers; Installation, Maintenance, and Repair Workers, All Other; Office Machine and Cash Register Servicers; Radio Mechanics; Signal and Track Switch Repairers; Station Installers and Repairers, Telephone; Telecommunications Line Installers and Repairers. **PERSONALITY TYPE:** Realistic. Realistic occupations frequently involve work activities that include practical, hands-on problems and solutions. They often deal with plants, animals, and real-world materials like wood, tools, and machinery. Many of the occupations require working outside and do not involve a lot of paperwork or working closely with others.

RELATED KNOWLEDGE/COURSES— Mechanical Devices: Knowledge of machines and tools, including their designs, uses, repair, and maintenance. **Engineering and Technology:** Knowledge of the practical application of engineering science and technology. This includes applying principles, techniques, procedures, and equipment to the design and production of various goods and services. **Telecommunications:** Knowledge of transmission, broadcasting, switching, control, and operation of telecommunications systems. **Computers and Electronics:** Knowledge of circuit boards, processors, chips, electronic equipment, and computer hardware and software, including applications and programming.

WORK ENVIRONMENT—Outdoors; hazardous conditions; climbing ladders, scaffolds, or poles; common protective or safety equipment; high places.

Tree Trimmers and Pruners

- Growth: 18.6%
- Annual Job Openings: 11,000
- Annual Earnings: $25,630
- Percentage of Women: 7.6%

Related Apprenticeship	Years
Tree Trimmer (Line Clear)	2
Tree Surgeon	3

Cut away dead or excess branches from trees or shrubs to maintain right-of-way for roads, sidewalks, or utilities, or to improve appear-

ance, health, and value of tree. **Prune or treat trees or shrubs using handsaws, pruning hooks, sheers, and clippers. May use truck-mounted lifts and power pruners. May fill cavities in trees to promote healing and prevent deterioration.** Scrapes decayed matter from cavities in trees and fills holes with cement to promote healing and to prevent further deterioration. Applies tar or other protective substances to cut surfaces to seal surfaces against insects. Cuts away dead and excess branches from trees, using handsaws, pruning hooks, sheers, and clippers. Climbs trees, using climbing hooks and belts, or climbs ladders to gain access to work area. Prunes, cuts down, fertilizes, and sprays trees as directed by tree surgeon. Uses truck-mounted hydraulic lifts and pruners and power pruners. **SKILLS**—Operation and Control.

GOE—Interest Area: 03. Plants and Animals. **Work Group:** 03.03 Hands-on Work in Plants and Animals. **Other Apprenticeable Jobs in This Work Group:** Agricultural Equipment Operators; Fallers; Farmworkers, Farm and Ranch Animals; Landscaping and Groundskeeping Workers; Pest Control Workers; Pesticide Handlers, Sprayers, and Applicators, Vegetation. **PERSONALITY TYPE:** Realistic. Realistic occupations frequently involve work activities that include practical, hands-on problems and solutions. They often deal with plants, animals, and real-world materials like wood, tools, and machinery. Many of the occupations require working outside and do not involve a lot of paperwork or working closely with others.

RELATED KNOWLEDGE/COURSES—Chemistry: Knowledge of the chemical composition, structure, and properties of substances and of the chemical processes and transforma-

tions that they undergo. This includes uses of chemicals, their danger signs, production techniques, and disposal methods. **Biology:** Knowledge of plant and animal organisms and their tissues, cells, functions, interdependencies, and interactions with each other and the environment. **Mechanical Devices:** Knowledge of machines and tools, including their designs, uses, repair, and maintenance.

WORK ENVIRONMENT—Outdoors; high places; minor burns, cuts, bites, or stings; specialized protective or safety equipment; climbing ladders, scaffolds, or poles.

Truck Drivers, Heavy

- Growth: 19.0%
- Annual Job Openings: 299,000
- Annual Earnings: $33,310
- Percentage of Women: 5.9%

Related Apprenticeship	Years
Truck Driver, Heavy	3
Construction Driver	4

Drive truck with capacity of more than three tons to transport materials to specified destinations. Drives truck with capacity of more than 3 tons to transport and deliver cargo, materials, or damaged vehicle. Maintains radio or telephone contact with base or supervisor to receive instructions or be dispatched to new location. Maintains truck log according to state and federal regulations. Keeps record of materials and products transported. Position blocks and ties rope around items to secure cargo for transport. Cleans, inspects, and services vehicle. Operates equipment on vehicle to load, unload, or disperse cargo or materials. Obtains customer signature or collects payment for goods delivered and delivery charges. Assists in loading and unloading truck manually. **SKILLS—** Equipment Maintenance; Repairing; Operation Monitoring; Operation and Control; Management of Financial Resources; Troubleshooting.

GOE—Interest Area: 07. Transportation. **Work Group:** 07.05 Truck Driving. **Other Apprenticeable Jobs in This Work Group:** No other apprenticeable jobs in this group. **PERSONALITY TYPE:** Realistic. Realistic occupations frequently involve work activities that include practical, hands-on problems and solutions. They often deal with plants, animals, and real-world materials like wood, tools, and machinery. Many of the occupations require working outside and do not involve a lot of paperwork or working closely with others.

RELATED KNOWLEDGE/COURSES— Transportation: Knowledge of principles and methods for moving people or goods by air, rail, sea, or road, including the relative costs and benefits. **Geography:** Knowledge of principles and methods for describing the features of land, sea, and air masses, including their physical characteristics; locations; interrelationships; and distribution of plant, animal, and human life. **Telecommunications:** Knowledge of transmission, broadcasting, switching, control, and operation of telecommunications systems. **Mechanical Devices:** Knowledge of machines and tools, including their designs, uses, repair, and maintenance. **Public Safety and Security:** Knowledge of relevant equipment, policies, procedures, and strategies to promote effective

local, state, or national security operations for the protection of people, data, property, and institutions. **Law and Government:** Knowledge of laws, legal codes, court procedures, precedents, government regulations, executive orders, agency rules, and the democratic political process.

WORK ENVIRONMENT—Outdoors; sitting; extremely bright or inadequate lighting; very hot or cold; hazardous equipment.

Typesetting and Composing Machine Operators and Tenders

- Growth: −11.2%
- Annual Job Openings: 6,000
- Annual Earnings: $31,660
- Percentage of Women: 47.6%

Related Apprenticeship	Years
Linotype Operator	5
Monotype-Keyboard Operator	3

Operate or tend typesetting and composing equipment, such as phototypesetters, linotype or monotype keyboard machines, photocomposers, linocasters, and photoletterers. Selects printing plates, dies, or type according to work order. Mixes colors of paint according to formulas. Repairs or replaces worn or broken parts, using hand tools. Cleans and lubricates equipment. Measures and records amount of product produced. Inspects product to detect defects. Adjusts and changes gears, using hand tools. Fills reservoirs with paint or ink. Adjusts feed guides, gauges, and rollers, using hand tools. Mounts materials to be printed onto feed mechanisms and threads materials through guides on machine. Monitors machines and gauges to ensure and maintain standards. Installs printing plates, cylinders, or rollers on machine, using hand tools and gauges. **SKILLS**—Operation Monitoring; Operation and Control; Equipment Maintenance; Troubleshooting.

GOE—**Interest Area:** 09. Business Detail. **Work Group:** 09.09 Clerical Machine Operation. **Other Apprenticeable Jobs in This Work Group:** Computer Operators; Data Entry Keyers; Postal Service Clerks; Word Processors and Typists. **PERSONALITY TYPE:** Realistic. Realistic occupations frequently involve work activities that include practical, hands-on problems and solutions. They often deal with plants, animals, and real-world materials like wood, tools, and machinery. Many of the occupations require working outside and do not involve a lot of paperwork or working closely with others.

RELATED KNOWLEDGE/COURSES— **Computers and Electronics:** Knowledge of circuit boards, processors, chips, electronic equipment, and computer hardware and software, including applications and programming. **Economics and Accounting:** Knowledge of economic and accounting principles and practices, the financial markets, banking, and the analysis and reporting of financial data.

WORK ENVIRONMENT—Hazardous equipment; using hands on objects, tools, or controls; indoors; hazardous conditions; minor burns, cuts, bites, or stings.

Valve and Regulator Repairers

- Growth: 12.0%
- Annual Job Openings: 5,000
- Annual Earnings: $42,540
- Percentage of Women: 4.8%

Related Apprenticeship	*Years*
Gas Utility Worker	2
Gas-Regulator Repairer	3

Test, repair, and adjust mechanical regulators and valves. Replaces, repairs or adjusts defective valve or regulator parts and tightens attachments, using hand tools, power tools, and welder. Tests valves and regulators for leaks, temperature and pressure settings, using precision testing equipment. Examines valves or mechanical control device parts for defects, dents, or loose attachments. Measures salvageable parts removed from mechanical control devices for conformance to standards or specifications, using gauges, micrometers, and calipers. Dips valves and regulators in molten lead to prevent leakage and paints valves, fittings, and other devices, using spray gun. Advises customers on proper installation of valves or regulators and related equipment. Records repair work, inventories parts, and orders new parts. Correlates testing data, performs technical calculations, and writes test reports to record data. Cleans corrosives and other deposits from serviceable parts, using solvents, wire brushes, or sandblaster. Lubricates wearing surfaces of mechanical parts, using oils or other lubricants. Disassembles mechanical control devices or valves, such as regulators, thermostats, or hydrants, using power tools, hand tools, and cutting torch. **SKILLS**—Repairing; Equipment Maintenance; Installation; Troubleshooting; Quality Control Analysis; Writing; Mathematics; Science.

GOE—Interest Area: 05. Mechanics, Installers, and Repairers. **Work Group:** 05.03 Mechanical Work. **Other Apprenticeable Jobs in This Work Group:** Aircraft Engine Specialists; Airframe-and-Power-Plant Mechanics; Automotive Body and Related Repairers; Automotive Glass Installers and Repairers; Automotive Master Mechanics; Automotive Specialty Technicians; Bus and Truck Mechanics and Diesel Engine Specialists; Camera and Photographic Equipment Repairers; Coin, Vending, and Amusement Machine Servicers and Repairers; Farm Equipment Mechanics; Gas Appliance Repairers; Hand and Portable Power Tool Repairers; Heating and Air Conditioning Mechanics; Helpers—Installation, Maintenance, and Repair Workers; Industrial Machinery Mechanics; Installation, Maintenance, and Repair Workers, All Other; Keyboard Instrument Repairers and Tuners; Locksmiths and Safe Repairers; Maintenance and Repair Workers, General; Maintenance Workers, Machinery; Mechanical Door Repairers; Medical Appliance Technicians; Medical Equipment Repairers; Meter Mechanics; Millwrights; Mobile Heavy Equipment Mechanics, Except Engines; Motorboat Mechanics; Motorcycle Mechanics; Optical Instrument Assemblers; Outdoor Power Equipment and Other Small Engine Mechanics; Painters, Transportation Equipment; Rail Car Repairers; Recreational Vehicle Service Technicians; Reed or Wind Instrument Repairers and Tuners; Refrigeration Mechanics; Stringed Instrument Repairers and Tuners; Watch Repairers. **PERSONALITY TYPE:** Realistic. Realistic occupations frequently involve work activities that include practical, hands-on problems and solutions. They often deal with plants, animals, and real-world materials like wood, tools, and machinery. Many of the occupations require working outside and do not involve a lot of paperwork or working closely with others.

RELATED KNOWLEDGE/COURSES— Mechanical Devices: Knowledge of machines and tools, including their designs, uses, repair, and maintenance. **Physics:** Knowledge and prediction of physical principles and laws and their interrelationships and applications to understanding fluid, material, and atmospheric dynamics and mechanical, electrical, atomic, and subatomic structures and processes. **Engineering and Technology:** Knowledge of the practical application of engineering science and technology. This includes applying principles, techniques, procedures, and equipment to the design and production of various goods and services. **Mathematics:** Knowledge of arithmetic, algebra, geometry, calculus, and statistics and their applications. **Chemistry:** Knowledge of the chemical composition, structure, and properties of substances and of the chemical processes and transformations that they undergo. This includes uses of chemicals, their danger signs, production techniques, and disposal methods. **Clerical Practices:** Knowledge of administrative and clerical procedures and systems, such as word processing, managing files and records, stenography and transcription, designing forms, and other office procedures and terminology.

WORK ENVIRONMENT—Hazardous equipment; hazardous conditions; climbing ladders, scaffolds, or poles; spend time bending or twisting the body; using hands on objects, tools, or controls.

Water and Liquid Waste Treatment Plant and System Operators

- Growth: 16.0%
- Annual Job Openings: 9,000
- Annual Earnings: $33,910
- Percentage of Women: 5.4%

Related Apprenticeship	Years
Clarifying-Plant Operator	1
Waste-Treatment Operator	2
Wastewater-Treatment-Plant Operator	2
Water-Treatment-Plant Operator	3

Operate or control an entire process or system of machines, often through the use of control boards, to transfer or treat water or liquid waste. Add chemicals, such as ammonia, chlorine, and lime, to disinfect and deodorize water and other liquids. Operate and adjust controls on equipment to purify and clarify water, process or dispose of sewage, and generate power. Inspect equipment and monitor operating conditions, meters, and gauges to determine load requirements and detect malfunctions. Collect and test water and sewage samples, using test equipment and color analysis standards. Record operational data, personnel attendance, and meter and gauge readings on specified forms. Maintain, repair, and lubricate equipment, using hand tools and power tools. Clean and maintain tanks and filter beds, using hand tools and power tools. Direct and coordinate plant workers engaged in routine operations and maintenance activities. SKILLS—Operation Monitoring; Installation; Operation and Control; Troubleshooting; Equipment Maintenance; Operations Analysis; Management of Material Resources; Management of Personnel Resources.

GOE—Interest Area: 08. Industrial Production. Work Group: 08.06 Systems Operation. Other Apprenticeable Jobs in This Work Group: Boiler Operators and Tenders, Low Pressure; Chemical Plant and System Operators; Gaugers; Petroleum Refinery and Control Panel Operators; Power Distributors and Dispatchers; Power Generating Plant Operators, Except Auxiliary Equipment Operators; Stationary Engineers. PERSONALITY TYPE: Realistic. Realistic occupations frequently involve work activities that include practical, hands-on problems and solutions. They often deal with plants, animals, and real-world materials like wood, tools, and machinery. Many of the occupations require working outside and do not involve a lot of paperwork or working closely with others.

RELATED KNOWLEDGE/COURSES—Biology: Knowledge of plant and animal organisms and their tissues, cells, functions, interdependencies, and interactions with each other and the environment. Chemistry: Knowledge of the chemical composition, structure, and properties of substances and of the chemical processes and transformations that they undergo. This includes uses of chemicals, their danger signs, production techniques, and disposal methods. **Public Safety and Security:** Knowledge of relevant equipment, policies, procedures, and strategies to promote effective local, state, or national security operations for the protection of people, data, property, and institutions. **Physics:** Knowledge and prediction of physical principles and laws and their interrelationships and applications to understanding fluid, material, and atmospheric dynamics and mechanical, electrical, atomic, and subatomic structures and processes. **Law and Government:** Knowledge of laws, legal codes, court procedures, precedents, government regulations, executive orders, agency rules, and the democratic political process. **Mathematics:** Knowledge of arithmetic, algebra, geometry, calculus, and statistics and their applications.

WORK ENVIRONMENT—Contaminants; outdoors; in an enclosed vehicle or equipment; sounds, noise levels are distracting or uncomfortable; very hot or cold.

Welder-Fitters

- Growth: 17.0%
- Annual Job Openings: 71,000
- Annual Earnings: $29,640
- Percentage of Women: 7.4%

Related Apprenticeship	Years
Lead Burner	4
Welder-Fitter	4

Lay out, fit, and fabricate metal components to assemble structural forms, such as machinery frames, bridge parts, and pressure vessels, using knowledge of welding techniques, metallurgy, and engineering requirements. Includes experimental welders who analyze engineering drawings and specifications to plan welding operations where procedural information is unavailable. Lays out, positions, and secures parts and assemblies according to specifications, using straightedge, combination square, calipers, and ruler. Tack-welds or welds components and assemblies, using electric, gas, arc, or other welding equipment. Cuts workpiece, using powered saws, hand shears, or chipping knife. Melts lead bar, wire, or scrap to add lead to joint or to extrude melted scrap into reusable form. Installs or repairs equipment, such as lead pipes, valves, floors, and tank linings. Observes tests on welded surfaces, such as hydrostatic, X-ray, and dimension tolerance to evaluate weld quality and conformance to specifications. Inspects grooves, angles, or gap allowances, using micrometer, caliper, and precision measuring instruments. Removes rough spots from workpiece, using portable grinder, hand file, or scraper. Welds components in flat, vertical, or overhead positions. Heats, forms, and dresses metal parts, using hand tools, torch, or arc welding equipment. Ignites torch and adjusts valves, amperage, or voltage to obtain desired flame or arc. Analyzes engineering drawings and specifications to plan layout, assembly, and welding operations. Develops templates and other work aids to hold and align parts. Determines required equipment and welding method, applying knowledge of metallurgy, geometry, and welding techniques. **SKILLS**—Repairing; Installation; Equipment Maintenance; Equipment Selection; Quality Control Analysis; Mathematics; Operation Monitoring; Science.

GOE—**Interest Area:** 08. Industrial Production. **Work Group:** 08.03 Production Work. **Other Apprenticeable Jobs in This Work Group:** Bakers, Manufacturing; Bindery Machine Operators and Tenders; Chemical Equipment Controllers and Operators; Coating, Painting, and Spraying Machine Operators and Tenders; Cooling and Freezing Equipment Operators and Tenders; Crushing, Grinding, and Polishing Machine Setters, Operators, and Tenders; Cutters and Trimmers, Hand; Cutting and Slicing Machine Operators and Tenders; Design Printing Machine Setters and Set-Up Operators; Electrolytic Plating and Coating Machine Setters and Set-Up Operators, Metal and Plastic; Electrotypers and Stereotypers; Embossing Machine Set-Up Operators; Engraver Set-Up Operators; Extruding, Forming, Pressing, and Compacting Machine Operators and Tenders; Fabric and Apparel Patternmakers; Film Laboratory Technicians; Fitters, Structural Metal—Precision; Food Batchmakers; Furnace, Kiln, Oven, Drier, and Kettle Operators and Tenders; Hand Compositors and Typesetters; Job Printers; Letterpress Setters and Set-Up Operators; Metal Fabricators, Structural Metal Products; Metal-Refining Furnace Operators and Tenders; Mixing and Blending Machine Setters, Operators, and Tenders; Mold Makers, Hand; Molding and Casting Workers; Numerical Control Machine Tool Operators and Tenders, Metal and Plastic; Offset Lithographic Press Setters and Set-Up Operators; Painting, Coating, and Decorating Workers; Photographic Processing Machine Operators; Photographic Reproduction Technicians; Photographic Retouchers and Restorers; Plate Finishers; Platemakers; Precision Printing Workers; Printing Press Machine Operators and Tenders; Production Workers, All Other; Sawing Machine Operators and Tenders; Sawing Machine Setters and Set-Up Operators; Scanner Operators; Separating, Filtering, Clarifying, Precipitating, and Still Machine Setters, Operators, and Tenders; Sewing Machine Operators, Garment; Slaughterers and Meat Packers; Stone Sawyers; Strippers; Team Assemblers; Welders and Cutters; Woodworking Machine Operators and Tenders, Except Sawing. **PERSONALITY TYPE:** Realistic. Realistic occupations frequently involve work activities that include practical, hands-on problems and solutions. They often deal with plants, animals, and real-world materials like wood, tools, and machinery. Many of the occupations require working outside and do not involve a lot of paperwork or working closely with others.

RELATED KNOWLEDGE/COURSES—**Design:** Knowledge of design techniques, tools, and principles involved in production of precision technical plans, blueprints, drawings, and models. **Building and Construction:** Knowledge of the materials, methods, and tools involved in the construction or repair of houses, buildings, or other structures, such as highways and roads. **Mechanical Devices:** Knowledge of machines and tools, including their designs, uses, repair, and maintenance. **Production and Processing:** Knowledge of raw materials, production processes, quality control, costs, and other techniques for maximizing the effective manufacture and distribution of goods. **Engineering and Technology:** Knowledge of the practical application of engineering science and technology. This includes applying principles, techniques, procedures, and equipment to the design and production of various goods and services. **Physics:** Knowledge and prediction of physical principles and laws and their interrelationships and applications to understanding fluid, material, and atmospheric dynamics and mechanical, electrical, atomic, and subatomic structures and processes. **Public Safety and Security:** Knowledge of relevant equipment, policies, procedures, and strategies to promote effective local, state, or national security operations for the protection of people, data, property, and institutions.

WORK ENVIRONMENT—Hazardous equipment; minor burns, cuts, bites, or stings; common protective or safety equipment; hazardous conditions; very hot or cold.

Welders and Cutters

- Growth: 17.0%
- Annual Job Openings: 71,000
- Annual Earnings: $29,640
- Percentage of Women: 7.4%

Related Apprenticeship	Years
Welder, Combination	3
Welder, Arc	4

Use hand welding and flame-cutting equipment to weld together metal components and parts or to cut, trim, or scarf metal objects to dimensions, as specified by layouts, work orders, or blueprints. Welds metal parts or components together, using brazing, gas, or arc welding equipment. Repairs broken or cracked parts, fills holes and increases size of metal parts, using welding equipment. Welds in flat, horizontal, vertical, or overhead position. Cleans or degreases parts, using wire brush, portable grinder, or chemical bath. Inspects finished workpiece for conformance to specifications. Chips or grinds off excess weld, slag, or spatter, using hand scraper or power chipper, portable grinder, or arc-cutting equipment. Positions workpieces and clamps together or assembles in jigs or fixtures. Preheats workpiece, using hand torch or heating furnace. Ignites torch or starts power supply and strikes arc. Reviews layouts, blueprints, diagrams, or work orders in preparation for welding or cutting metal components. Selects and inserts electrode or gas nozzle into holder and connects hoses and cables to obtain gas or specified amperage, voltage, or polarity. Connects and turns regulator valves to activate and adjust gas flow and pressure to obtain desired flame. Selects and installs torch, torch tip, filler rod, and flux, according to welding chart specifications or type and thickness of metal. Guides electrodes or torch along weld line at specified speed and angle to weld, melt, cut, or trim metal. **SKILLS**—Operation Monitoring; Equipment Maintenance; Repairing; Operation and Control; Installation; Quality Control Analysis; Equipment Selection; Mathematics.

GOE—Interest Area: 08. Industrial Production. **Work Group:** 08.03 Production Work. **Other Apprenticeable Jobs in This Work Group:** Bakers, Manufacturing; Bindery Machine Operators and Tenders; Chemical Equipment Controllers and Operators; Coating, Painting, and Spraying Machine Operators and Tenders; Cooling and Freezing Equipment

W

Operators and Tenders; Crushing, Grinding, and Polishing Machine Setters, Operators, and Tenders; Cutters and Trimmers, Hand; Cutting and Slicing Machine Operators and Tenders; Design Printing Machine Setters and Set-Up Operators; Electrolytic Plating and Coating Machine Setters and Set-Up Operators, Metal and Plastic; Electrotypers and Stereotypers; Embossing Machine Set-Up Operators; Engraver Set-Up Operators; Extruding, Forming, Pressing, and Compacting Machine Operators and Tenders; Fabric and Apparel Patternmakers; Film Laboratory Technicians; Fitters, Structural Metal—Precision; Food Batchmakers; Furnace, Kiln, Oven, Drier, and Kettle Operators and Tenders; Hand Compositors and Typesetters; Job Printers; Letterpress Setters and Set-Up Operators; Metal Fabricators, Structural Metal Products; Metal-Refining Furnace Operators and Tenders; Mixing and Blending Machine Setters, Operators, and Tenders; Mold Makers, Hand; Molding and Casting Workers; Numerical Control Machine Tool Operators and Tenders, Metal and Plastic; Offset Lithographic Press Setters and Set-Up Operators; Painting, Coating, and Decorating Workers; Photographic Processing Machine Operators; Photographic Reproduction Technicians; Photographic Retouchers and Restorers; Plate Finishers; Platemakers; Precision Printing Workers; Printing Press Machine Operators and Tenders; Production Workers, All Other; Sawing Machine Operators and Tenders; Sawing Machine Setters and Set-Up Operators; Scanner Operators; Separating, Filtering, Clarifying, Precipitating, and Still Machine Setters, Operators, and Tenders; Sewing Machine Operators, Garment; Slaughterers and Meat Packers; Stone Sawyers; Strippers; Team Assemblers; Welder-Fitters; Woodworking Machine Operators and Tenders, Except Sawing. **PERSONALITY**

TYPE: Realistic. Realistic occupations frequently involve work activities that include practical, hands-on problems and solutions. They often deal with plants, animals, and real-world materials like wood, tools, and machinery. Many of the occupations require working outside and do not involve a lot of paperwork or working closely with others.

RELATED KNOWLEDGE/COURSES— Building and Construction: Knowledge of the materials, methods, and tools involved in the construction or repair of houses, buildings, or other structures, such as highways and roads. **Mechanical Devices:** Knowledge of machines and tools, including their designs, uses, repair, and maintenance. **Design:** Knowledge of design techniques, tools, and principles involved in production of precision technical plans, blueprints, drawings, and models. **Production and Processing:** Knowledge of raw materials, production processes, quality control, costs, and other techniques for maximizing the effective manufacture and distribution of goods. **Physics:** Knowledge and prediction of physical principles and laws and their interrelationships and applications to understanding fluid, material, and atmospheric dynamics and mechanical, electrical, atomic, and subatomic structures and processes. **Chemistry:** Knowledge of the chemical composition, structure, and properties of substances and of the chemical processes and transformations that they undergo. This includes uses of chemicals, their danger signs, production techniques, and disposal methods.

WORK ENVIRONMENT—Hazardous equipment; minor burns, cuts, bites, or stings; common protective or safety equipment; hazardous conditions; using hands on objects, tools, or controls.

Welding Machine Setters and Set-Up Operators

- ◉ Growth: 0.9%
- ◉ Annual Job Openings: 10,000
- ◉ Annual Earnings: $29,110
- ◉ Percentage of Women: 7.4%

Related Apprenticeship	Years
Welding-Machine Operator, Arc	3

Set up or set up and operate welding machines that join or bond together components to fabricate metal products or assemblies, according to specifications and blueprints. Sets up and operates welding machines that join or bond components to fabricate metal products or assemblies. Feeds workpiece into welding machine to join or bond components. Observes and listens to welding machine and its gauges to ensure welding process meets specifications. Turns and presses controls, such as cranks, knobs, and buttons to adjust and activate welding process. Operates welding machine to produce trial workpieces, used to examine and test. Lays out, fits, or tacks workpieces together, using hand tools. Examines metal product or assemblies to ensure specifications are met. Tends auxiliary equipment used in welding process. Tests products and records test results and operational data on specified forms. Devises and builds fixtures used to bond components, during the welding process. Cleans and maintains workpieces and welding machine parts, using hand tools and equipment. Adds components, chemicals, and solutions to welding machine, using hand tools. Stops and opens holding device on welding machine, using hand tools. Positions and adjusts fixtures, attachments, or workpieces on machine, using hand tools. **SKILLS**—Operation Monitoring; Equipment Selection; Equipment Maintenance; Quality Control Analysis; Operation and Control; Installation; Repairing; Mathematics; Troubleshooting.

GOE—Interest Area: 08. Industrial Production. **Work Group:** 08.02 Production Technology. **Other Apprenticeable Jobs in This Work Group:** Aircraft Structure Assemblers, Precision; Aircraft Systems Assemblers, Precision; Bench Workers, Jewelry; Bindery Machine Setters and Set-Up Operators; Bookbinders; Buffing and Polishing Set-Up Operators; Coating, Painting, and Spraying Machine Setters and Set-Up Operators; Combination Machine Tool Setters and Set-Up Operators, Metal and Plastic; Dental Laboratory Technicians; Electrical and Electronic Equipment Assemblers; Electrical and Electronic Inspectors and Testers; Electromechanical Equipment Assemblers; Engine and Other Machine Assemblers; Extruding and Drawing Machine Setters, Operators, and Tenders, Metal and Plastic; Extruding, Forming, Pressing, and Compacting Machine Setters and Set-Up Operators; Forging Machine Setters, Operators, and Tenders, Metal and Plastic; Foundry Mold and Coremakers; Gem and Diamond Workers; Grinding, Honing, Lapping, and Deburring Machine Set-Up Operators; Heat Treating, Annealing, and Tempering Machine Operators and Tenders, Metal and Plastic; Jewelers; Lathe and Turning Machine Tool Setters, Operators, and Tenders, Metal and Plastic; Materials Inspectors;

W

Mechanical Inspectors; Metal Molding, Core-making, and Casting Machine Operators and Tenders; Milling and Planing Machine Setters, Operators, and Tenders, Metal and Plastic; Model and Mold Makers, Jewelry; Motor Vehicle Inspectors; Paper Goods Machine Setters, Operators, and Tenders; Pewter Casters and Finishers; Plastic Molding and Casting Machine Setters and Set-Up Operators; Precision Devices Inspectors and Testers; Precision Lens Grinders and Polishers; Precision Mold and Pattern Casters, Except Nonferrous Metals; Precision Pattern and Die Casters, Nonferrous Metals; Press and Press Brake Machine Setters and Set-Up Operators, Metal and Plastic; Production Inspectors, Testers, Graders, Sorters, Samplers, Weighers; Production Workers, All Other; Rolling Machine Setters, Operators, and Tenders, Metal and Plastic; Silversmiths; Textile Knitting and Weaving Machine Setters, Operators, and Tenders; Textile Winding, Twisting, and Drawing Out Machine Setters, Operators, and Tenders; Woodworking Machine Setters and Set-Up Operators, Except Sawing. **PERSONALITY TYPE:** Realistic. Realistic occupations frequently involve work activities that include practical, hands-on problems and solutions. They often deal with plants, animals, and real-world materials like wood, tools, and machinery. Many of the occupations require working outside and do not involve a lot of paperwork or working closely with others.

RELATED KNOWLEDGE/COURSES—Mechanical Devices: Knowledge of machines and tools, including their designs, uses, repair, and maintenance. **Production and Processing:** Knowledge of raw materials, production processes, quality control, costs, and other techniques for maximizing the effective manufacture and distribution of goods. **Chemistry:** Knowledge of the chemical composition, structure, and properties of substances and of the chemical processes and transformations that they undergo. This includes uses of chemicals, their danger signs, production techniques, and disposal methods. **Design:** Knowledge of design techniques, tools, and principles involved in production of precision technical plans, blueprints, drawings, and models. **Building and Construction:** Knowledge of the materials, methods, and tools involved in the construction or repair of houses, buildings, or other structures, such as highways and roads. **Physics:** Knowledge and prediction of physical principles and laws and their interrelationships and applications to understanding fluid, material, and atmospheric dynamics and mechanical, electrical, atomic, and subatomic structures and processes.

WORK ENVIRONMENT—Hazardous equipment; sounds, noise levels are distracting or uncomfortable; common protective or safety equipment; standing; hazardous conditions.

Well and Core Drill Operators

- Growth: 7.7%
- Annual Job Openings: 3,000
- Annual Earnings: $32,540
- Percentage of Women: 1.5%

Related Apprenticeship	Years
Well-Drill Operator	4

Operate machine to drill wells and take samples or cores for analysis of strata. Starts and controls drilling action and lowering of well casing into well bore. Withdraws drill rod from hole and extracts core sample. Couples additional lengths of drill rod as bit advances. Changes drill bits as needed. Pours water into well or pumps water or slush into well to cool drill bit and remove drillings. Retrieves lost equipment from bore holes, using retrieval tools and equipment. Records drilling progress and geological data. Fabricates well casings. Lubricates machine, splices worn or broken cables, replaces parts, and builds up and repairs drill bits. Drives or guides truck-mounted equipment into position, levels and stabilizes rig, and extends telescoping derrick. Inspects core samples to determine nature of strata, or takes samples to laboratory for analysis. Assembles non-truck-mounted drilling equipment, using hand tools and power tools. Monitors operation of drilling equipment to determine changes in strata or variations in drilling. SKILLS—Operation Monitoring; Equipment Maintenance; Repairing; Operation and Control; Science; Equipment Selection; Installation; Troubleshooting; Management of Material Resources.

GOE—Interest Area: 06. Construction, Mining, and Drilling. Work Group: 06.03 Mining and Drilling. Other Apprenticeable Jobs in This Work Group: Mine Cutting and Channeling Machine Operators; Rotary Drill Operators, Oil and Gas. PERSONALITY TYPE: Realistic. Realistic occupations frequently involve work activities that include practical, hands-on problems and solutions. They often deal with plants, animals, and real-world materials like wood, tools, and machinery. Many of the occupations require working outside and do not involve a lot of paperwork or working closely with others.

RELATED KNOWLEDGE/COURSES—Mechanical Devices: Knowledge of machines and tools, including their designs, uses, repair, and maintenance. Physics: Knowledge and prediction of physical principles and laws and their interrelationships and applications to understanding fluid, material, and atmospheric dynamics and mechanical, electrical, atomic, and subatomic structures and processes. Transportation: Knowledge of principles and methods for moving people or goods by air, rail, sea, or road, including the relative costs and benefits. Engineering and Technology: Knowledge of the practical application of engineering science and technology. This includes applying principles, techniques, procedures, and equipment to the design and production of various goods and services. Geography: Knowledge of principles and methods for describing the features of land, sea, and air masses, including their physical characteristics; locations; interrelationships; and distribution of plant, animal, and human life. Public Safety and Security: Knowledge of relevant equipment, policies, procedures, and strategies to promote effective local, state, or national security operations for the protection of people, data, property, and institutions.

WORK ENVIRONMENT—Outdoors; sounds, noise levels are distracting or uncomfortable; hazardous equipment; common protective or safety equipment; very hot or cold.

Word Processors and Typists

- ◉ Growth: –38.6%
- ◉ Annual Job Openings: 45,000
- ◉ Annual Earnings: $27,150
- ◉ Percentage of Women: 93.0%

Related Apprenticeship	Years
Telegraphic-Typewriter Operator	3

Use word processor/computer or typewriter to type letters, reports, forms, or other material from rough draft, corrected copy, or voice recording. May perform other clerical duties as assigned. Check completed work for spelling, grammar, punctuation, and format. Perform other clerical duties such as answering telephone, sorting and distributing mail, running errands or sending faxes. Gather, register, and arrange the material to be typed, following instructions. Type correspondence, reports, text and other written material from rough drafts, corrected copies, voice recordings, dictation or previous versions, using a computer, word processor, or typewriter. File and store completed documents on computer hard drive or disk, and/or maintain a computer filing system to store, retrieve, update and delete documents. Print and makes copies of work. Keep records of work performed. Compute and verify totals on report forms, requisitions, or bills, using adding machine or calculator. Collate pages of reports and other documents prepared. Electronically sort and compile text and numerical data, retrieving, updating, and merging documents as required. Reformat documents, moving paragraphs and/or columns. Search for specific sets of stored, typed characters in order to make changes. Adjust settings for format, page layout, line spacing, and other style requirements. Address envelopes or prepare envelope labels, using typewriter or computer. Operate and resupply printers and computers, changing print wheels or fluid cartridges, adding paper, and loading blank tapes, cards, or disks into equipment. Transmit work electronically to other locations. Work with technical material, preparing statistical reports, planning and typing statistical tables, and combining and rearranging material from different sources. Use data entry devices, such as optical scanners, to input data into computers for revision or editing. Transcribe stenotyped notes of court proceedings. **SKILLS**—Persuasion; Social Perceptiveness; Learning Strategies; Instructing; Coordination; Service Orientation; Time Management; Negotiation.

GOE—Interest Area: 09. Business Detail. **Work Group:** 09.09 Clerical Machine Operation. **Other Apprenticeable Jobs in This Work Group:** Computer Operators; Data Entry Keyers; Postal Service Clerks; Typesetting and Composing Machine Operators and Tenders. **PERSONALITY TYPE:** Conventional. Conventional occupations frequently involve following set procedures and routines. These occupations can include working with data and details more than with ideas. Usually there is a clear line of authority to follow.

RELATED KNOWLEDGE/COURSES— Clerical Practices: Knowledge of administrative and clerical procedures and systems, such as word processing, managing files and records, stenography and transcription, designing forms, and other office procedures and terminology. **Customer and Personal Service:** Knowledge of principles and processes for providing customer and personal services. This includes customer needs assessment, meeting quality standards for services, and evaluation of customer satisfaction. **Computers and Electronics:** Knowledge of circuit boards, processors, chips, electronic equipment, and computer hardware and software, including applications and programming. **English Language:** Knowledge of the structure and content of the English language, including the meaning and spelling of words, rules of composition, and grammar. **Sales and Marketing:** Knowledge of principles and methods for showing, promoting, and selling products or services. This includes marketing strategy and tactics, product demonstration, sales techniques, and sales control systems. **Economics and Accounting:** Knowledge of economic and accounting principles and practices, the financial markets, banking, and the analysis and reporting of financial data. **Psychology:** Knowledge of human behavior and performance; individual differences in ability, personality, and interests; learning and motivation; psychological research methods; and the assessment and treatment of behavioral and affective disorders. **Law and Government:** Knowledge of laws, legal codes, court procedures, precedents, government regulations, executive orders, agency rules, and the democratic political process.

WORK ENVIRONMENT—Sitting; sounds, noise levels are distracting or uncomfortable; physical proximity.

PART V

Appendixes

Appendix A:
How to Read an Apprenticeship Standards Document

Appendix B:
Excerpts from Standards Documents

Appendix C:
State Apprenticeship Offices

Appendix D:
Explanation of Skills

Appendix A: How to Read an Apprenticeship Standards Document

In order to be registered, an apprenticeship must be governed by a standards agreement that meets certain requirements of the responsible state and/or federal agency. A typical apprenticeship standards document registered with the U.S. Department of Labor's Office of Apprenticeship Training, Employment and Labor Services (OATELS) contains the headings listed below. Under each heading you'll find some commentary about what the text of the standards document may specify.

Part I. Definition

Apprenticeship standards usually begin with definitions of key terms, especially "employer" and "apprentice," since these are the parties whose agreement is governed by these standards.

Part II. The Apprenticeship Committee

This section defines the membership of the apprenticeship committee (for example, it may consist of equal numbers of representatives of management and labor) and the committee's responsibilities: for example, establishing the standards for the apprenticeship program, screening and selecting apprentices, determining their progress, communicating with them about their progress or their complaints, maintaining records, monitoring the school where related classroom instruction is given, and issuing certificates to apprentices who have completed the program. The employer for whom an apprentice is working may also be required to appoint someone to act as a liaison with the committee.

Part III. Equal Opportunity in Apprenticeship

Usually there is a statement that the apprentices will be recruited, selected, employed, and trained without discrimination on the basis of race, color, religion, national origin, gender, sexual orientation, marital or familial status, disability, lawful political affiliation, or other factors unrelated to ability to do the job. There may also be a statement about affirmative action goals and/or a commitment to provide reasonable accommodation for apprentices with disabilities, although the particulars about these topics are often put into an appendix.

Part IV. Qualifications and Selection of Apprentices

This section defines the minimum requirements for people applying to become apprentices—for example, a minimum age, amount of education, measure of physical fitness, and access to transportation. It may also specify additional measures that are used to differentiate between the minimally qualified applicants and those who are highly qualified: for example, an aptitude test, a selection of relevant courses, and an interview. It may describe a point system by which you receive a certain number of points depending on how well you meet those requirements. Sometimes the specifics of the selection process are covered in an appendix rather than here.

Part V. Apprenticeship Agreement

This section mentions that the apprentice and the sponsor must sign an agreement—which in turn references this standards document.

Part VI. Obligations of the Employer and Apprentice

This is a general statement of the employer's agreement to provide employment and training (to the extent possible) to the apprentice and the apprentice's agreement to make satisfactory progress toward completion of the training. More specific commitments are to be found in the following sections.

Part VII. Ratio of Apprentices to Journey Workers

Here you can see the maximum number of apprentices who can be assigned to any one journey worker. Obviously a low number is better. (The national average is probably about eight.)

Part VIII. Term of Apprenticeship

This section specifies exactly how many hours of on-the-job training are included in the apprenticeship (for example, 8,000 hours, which is equivalent to four years). It may specify a certain number of calendar years in which these hours must be completed. It may state how many hours of prior experience (for example, in military training) can be counted toward your training commitment. Usually the work processes that are to be learned are specified in a separate document or an appendix rather than here.

Part IX. Probationary Period

Here you can see the length of the period in which the committee can terminate your apprenticeship without having to show cause. These hours, although probationary, typically do count toward your total training period.

Part X. Related Instruction

This section specifies the number of hours of related instruction that you must complete, but the actual subjects that must be studied are often listed on a separate document or in an appendix. The standards for passing course work (for example, achieving the 80 percent level) may also be specified elsewhere.

Part XI. Hours of Work

This statement usually says that you will work the same hours as a journey worker. This protects you from being assigned to a shift that might be atypical of the trade and on which you might not get enough supervision from journey workers. It also protects you from being required to work an abnormally long work week, which would cut into the time available for your night classes.

Part XII. Continuity of Employment

Here the employer promises to provide you with continuous employment during your apprenticeship. Although an escape clause is usually included that allows the employer to lay you off in the event of a lockout, loss of business, and so forth, the employer should state that you will be able to resume your apprenticeship as soon as work can be found.

Part XIII. Wages of Apprentices

This section states the arrangement by which you will be awarded steady increases in your pay as you accumulate hours of experience. Usually wages are expressed in terms of certain percentages of a journey worker's wages, and there is a commitment by the employer to determine the average journey worker's wages on a periodic basis. Sometimes the specific pay levels are itemized in the apprenticeship agreement or in an appendix rather than here. In some programs apprentices who make exceptional progress may be promoted to the next-higher wage level before the number of hours normally required.

Part XIV. Complaint Procedures

This section spells out the procedures for resolving disagreements between the apprentice and the employer. Usually the procedure is designed to avoid a lawsuit to the extent possible. Typically there are separate procedures for complaints regarding discrimination or sexual harassment.

Part XV. Registration

Here the committee states that it will register this standards document with a state and/or federal agency and is aware that this registration may be lost if the committee fails to uphold the standards. Registration is good for you, the apprentice, because it requires the committee to include specific standards in this document that protect you, and it also means that your journey worker status will be recognized everywhere. Usually the committee maintains the ability to withdraw from registration voluntarily, but doing so is likely to make their program much less attractive to would-be apprentices.

Part XVI. Amendments or Modifications

In this section the committee promises not to change the terms of the apprenticeship without notifying the state and/or federal agency with which the apprenticeship is registered. For your protection, there should also be a statement that the committee cannot change the terms of their agreement with you, the apprentice, without your approval.

Part XVII. Compliance Assurance

Here, as in many contracts, is a statement that nothing in the agreement should be construed as permitting violation of the law.

Part XVIII. Signature Page

Here you will find the signatures of the apprenticeship committee's officials and of the state and/or federal administrators with whom the apprenticeship is registered.

Part XIX. Appendix/Attachments

The appendix or attachments section is usually reserved for specifics that may need to be changed at a future date, such as the following:

- Work processes (all the phases of the job that you will learn through on-the-job training)
- Wage structure (the level of pay you will earn at each phase of the apprenticeship)
- Subjects covered in related instruction (together with the number of hours devoted to each subject)
- Examinations that must be passed
- The apprenticeship agreement form
- The employer's affirmative action plan

Appendix B: Excerpts from Standards Documents

Part I. National Standards for the Electrician Apprenticeship (RAIS Code 0159)

On-the-Job Training

UNIT	APPROXIMATE HOURS
1. Preliminary Work	600

A. Learning the names and uses of the equipment used in the trade, such as kind, size, and use of cable, wire, boxes, conduits, and fittings, switches, receptacles, service switches, cutouts, etc.

B. Learning names and uses of the various tools used in assembling this material, care of these tools, and other instructions necessary to familiarize the apprentice with the material and tools of the trade.

C. Safety

UNIT	APPROXIMATE HOURS
2. Residential and Commercial Rough Wiring	2,500

A. Assisting in getting the material from stockroom.

B. Loading truck and unloading material and equipment on the job.

C. Laying out the various outlets, switches, receptacles, and other details of the job from blueprints or by direction of the Superintendent of construction.

D. Laying out the system with materials to be used, where they are to be placed, and other details as to how they shall be run.

E. Cutting wires, cables, conduit and raceway; threading and reaming conduit, boring and cutting chases under the direction of the journeyperson.

(continued)

(continued)

On-the-Job Training

UNIT	APPROXIMATE HOURS

    F. Installing various kinds of wires, cables and conduits in accordance with requirements.

    G. Assisting journeyperson in pulling wires, attaching wires to fishtape, and keeping wires from kinds of abrasions.

    H. Connecting conductors to switches, receptacles, or appliances with proper methods of splicing, soldering and typing.

    I. Installing service switches or load center and subfeeders and fastening up these parts, running raceways and pulling in conductors under the direction of journeyperson electricians.

    J. Assisting in preparing lists of materials used, including names, number of pieces, or number of feet, etc., for office records.

    K. Loading unused material and cleaning up job area.

3. Residential and Commercial Finish Work 1,500

    A. Connecting and setting switches, receptacles, plates, etc.

    B. Installing proper size and types of fuses for each circuit.

    C. Installing and connecting various kinds of fixtures.

    D. Tracing and polarity of conductors and devices.

    E. Testing the circuit for grounds and shorts and locating and correcting job defects.

    F. Assisting journeyperson in installing and completion of the National Board of Fire Underwriters and special local regulations—proper sizes of wires, services, conduits, etc.

4. Industrial Lighting and Service Installation 2,000

    A. Installing rigid conduit, electric metallic tubing BX armored cable wiremolds on all types of heavy electrical equipment and major-size service entrance installation.

    B. Wiring all types (gas, oil, stoker, etc.) of heating equipment.

    C. Installing wiring and controls for air conditioning.

5. Troubleshooting 1,000

    A. Repairing all kinds of electrical work.

    B. Checking out trouble and making repairs under supervision of electrician.

    C. Checking out trouble and making repairs without supervision.

UNIT	APPROXIMATE HOURS

6. Motor Installation and Control...400
     A. Installing overcurrent devices.
     B. Checking for proper installation and rotation.
     C. Installing replacement motors.
     D. Analyzing motor circuits and troubleshooting.
     E. Installing emergency generators and controls.
     F. Installing pushbuttons, pilot lights, relays, timing devices, and interlocking controls.
TOTAL 8,000

Related Instruction

The apprentice shall receive theoretical related instruction for a minimum of 144 hours per year, for each year of their apprenticeship, in all aspects of the trade listed below:

FIRST YEAR

Safety instruction
History
Present and future of the trade
Trade jargon
Tools and equipment
Mathematics
Applied science
Introduction to electricity and electronics
Blueprint reading and specifications

SECOND YEAR

Mathematics for electricians
Electrical wiring, residential
Residential blueprint reading
D.C. fundamentals and circuits
Technical communications

THIRD YEAR

Geometry and trigonometry
Applied physics
Mathematics for electricians II
Motors and generators
Commercial and industrial blueprint reading
Electrical wiring, commercial

FOURTH YEAR

Electrical wiring, industrial
Transformers
Electrical drafting
Applied electronics for industry
Electrical machinery
Analysis and repair
Social economics
Advanced blueprint reading and layout

Part II. National Standards for the Dental Assistant Apprenticeship (RAIS Code 0101)

On-the-Job Training	
UNIT	**APPROXIMATE HOURS**

1. Ethics and Personal Appearance (proper vocabulary, grammar) 50
2. Care of Dental Equipment and Office (ordering supplies, cleaning, lubricating, maintenance, sterilization of fixed equipment) 50
3. Chair-side Assisting (adopting routine of dentist check list)...............800
   a. Seat and prepare patients
   b. Arrange instruments
   c. Dental charting
   d. Dental history
   e. Instrument passing
   f. Assist with high velocity suction
   g. Passing medication prior to filling
   h. Mixing filling material
   i. Releasing patient
   j. Clean-up after patient leaves
   k. Set up for new patient
   l. Greeting new patient

4. Dental Office Management 100
   a. Good organization
   b. Orderliness
   c. No idle gossip or distracting talk—must include patient in conversation
   d. Making appointments over telephone
   e. Use of pegboard bookkeeping
   f. Operation of telephone recorder
   g. Maintain professional dignity

On-the-Job Training

UNIT	APPROXIMATE HOURS

5. Dental Anatomy 50
   a. Tooth eruption
   b. Proper identification
   c. Know abbreviations for charting
   d. Know dental anatomy pathology

6. Dental Pathology..200
   a. Includes all soft tissue, intra- and extra-oral
   b. Observe all external face features
   c. Note swellings
   d. Note scars
   e. Note pupils of eyes
   f. Note fingernail beds
   g. Note distended vessels
   h. Note blood pressure
   i. Note texture and color of skin

7. Bacteriology and Sterilization 100
   a. Autoclave procedure
   b. Cold sterilization
   c. Cleaning of instruments
   d. Use of special chemicals

8. Anesthesia 50
   a. Preparation of syringe-local
   b. Correct temperature
   c. Advice to patient to prevent self injury
   d. Observe for any hyper-reactions

9. Dental Roentgenology 100
   a. Periapical film procedure
   b. Panolipse film procedure
   c. Developing film procedure
   d. Proper mounting of film
   e. Basic X-ray interpretation—able to recognize and correct mistakes

(continued)

(continued)

On-the-Job Training

UNIT	APPROXIMATE HOURS
10. Oral Hygiene of Pedondontra	100
a. Toothbrush instructions	
b. Communications and psychological entertainment of patient	
c. Demonstration of instruments	
11. Diet and Nutrition	50
a. Be able to supply patients with diet information	
b. Know carbohydrate chemistry and explain	
12. Orthodontra	50
a. Recognize predisposing factors	
b. Suggest corrections	
c. Inform and illustrate	
13. Pharmacology	50
a. Recognize basic dental drugs	
b. Know side effects	
14. Treatment of Emergencies	100
a. Acquire professional assistance	
b. Know basic life support systems	
c. Know CPR basics	
15. Impression Material and Models	150
a. Assist in impression taking	
b. Mix all impression material	
c. Pour models	
TOTAL	2,000

Related Instruction

UNIT	HOURS
1. Sterilization Procedures, Sanitation, and Personal Hygiene	24
2. Care of Dental Equipment	24
Recordkeeping and Charting	
X-Ray Technique and Safety	
Dental Prophylaxis and Oral Health	
Periodontics	
3. Care of Dental Equipment and Supplies	24
Use of Equipment	
4. Operative Dentistry	24
5. Diagnosis and Armamentarium	24
6. Dental Specialties and Instruments	24
TOTAL	144

Part III. From National Standards for Pipe Fitter—Sprinkler Fitter (RAIS Code 0414A)

Apprentice Wage Structure

1st 6 months	50 percent of journey worker's rate
2nd 6 months	55 percent of journey worker's rate
3rd 6 months	60 percent of journey worker's rate
4th 6 months	70 percent of journey worker's rate
5th 6 months	75 percent of journey worker's rate
6th 6 months	80 percent of journey worker's rate
7th 6 months	85 percent of journey worker's rate
8th 6 months	90 percent of journey worker's rate

Appendix C: State Apprenticeship Offices

The offices listed below are, for the most part, offices of the Bureau of Apprenticeship and Training. ("USDOL/ETA/OATELS-BAT" stands for "United States Department of Labor; Employment and Training Administration; Office of Apprenticeship Training, Employer and Labor Services, Bureau of Apprenticeship and Training.") For states and territories that lack a BAT office, the office listed is that of the State Apprenticeship Council. The Web site listed is not necessarily maintained by the office listed.

Alabama

USDOL/ETA/OATELS-BAT
Medical Forum Bldg. - Room 648
950 22nd Street North
Birmingham, Alabama 35203
(205) 731-1308
http://dir.alabama.gov/

Alaska

USDOL/ETA/OATELS-BAT
Room G-30
605 W. 4th Avenue
Anchorage, Alaska 99501
(907) 271-5035
http://www.ajcn.state.ak.us/apprentice/

Arizona

USDOL/ETA/OATELS-BAT
Suite 105
3221 North 16th Street
Phoenix, Arizona 85016
(602) 640-2964
http://www.commerce.state.az.us/
Workforce/cover.html

Arkansas

USDOL/ETA/OATELS-BAT
Federal Building - Room 3507
700 West Capitol Street
Little Rock, Arkansas 72201
(501) 324-5415
http://www.state.ar.us/directory/
detail2.cgi?ID=1859

California

USDOL/ETA/OATELS-BAT
Suite 1090-N
1301 Clay Street
Oakland, California 94612-5217
(510) 637-2951
http://www.dir.ca.gov/
apprenticeship.html

Colorado

USDOL/ETA/OATELS-BAT
U.S. Custom House
721 19th Street - Room 465
Denver, Colorado 80202
(303) 844-4794
http://www.coworkforce.com/lmi/
lmidir/eta.htm

Connecticut

USDOL/ETA/OATELS-BAT
Federal Building
135 High Street - Room 367
Hartford, Connecticut 06103
(860) 240-4311
http://www.ctdol.state.ct.us/progsupt/
appren/appren.htm

Delaware

Mr. Kevin Calio
State Administrator
Apprenticeship and Training Section
Division of Employment and Training
Delaware Department of Labor
4425 N. Market Street, Station 313
P.O. Box 9828
Wilmington, Delaware 19809
(302) 761-8118
http://www.delawareworks.com/
emptrain/welcome.cfm

District of Columbia

Mr. Lewis Brown, Director
DC Apprenticeship Council
609 H Street NE
Washington, DC 20001
(202) 698-3528
http://does.ci.washington.dc.us/
services/appren.shtm

Florida

USDOL/ETA/OATELS-BAT
550 Water Street, Room 1228
Federal Building
P.O. Box 14
Jacksonville, Florida 32202
(850) 245-0454
http://www.firn.edu/doe/
apprenticeship/index.html

Georgia

USDOL/ETA/OATELS-BAT
Room 6T80
61 Forsyth Street, SW
Atlanta, Georgia 30303
(404) 562-2323
http://www.dol.state.ga.us/

Guam

Ms. Terry L. Barnhart
Program Specialist
Apprenticeship and Training Division
Guam Community College
P.O. Box 23069, GMF
Guam, M.I. 96921
(671) 735-5571
http://www.guamcc.net/admissions/
4_Cert_Degree2002.pdf

Hawaii

USDOL/ETA/OATELS-BAT
Room 5-117
300 Ala Moana Boulevard
Honolulu, Hawaii 96850
(808) 541-2519
http://www.dlir.state.hi.us/

Idaho

USDOL/ETA/OATELS-BAT
Suite 204
1150 North Curtis Road
Boise, Idaho 83706-1234
(208) 321-2973
http://www.idahoworks.org/

Illinois

USDOL/ETA/OATELS-BAT
Room 656
230 South Dearborn Street
Chicago, Illinois 60604
(312) 596-5508
http://www.ides.state.il.us/individual/
special/apprentc.htm

Indiana

USDOL/ETA/OATELS-BAT
Federal Building and U.S. Courthouse
46 East Ohio Street - Room 414
Indianapolis, Indiana 46204
(317) 226-7592
http://www.in.gov/dwd/employer/
advanceindiana/program/sta_info.html

Iowa

USDOL/ETA/OATELS-BAT
210 Walnut Street - Room 715
Des Moines, Iowa 50309
(208) 321-2972
http://www.iowaworkforce.org/
region9/apprenticeship.htm

Kansas

USDOL/ETA/OATELS-BAT
444 SE Quincy Street - Room 247
Topeka, Kansas 66683-3571
(785) 295-2624
http://entkdhr.state.ks.us/
Apprenticeship.htm

Kentucky

USDOL/ETA/OATELS-BAT
Federal Building - Room 168
600 Martin Luther King Place
Louisville, Kentucky 40202
(502) 582-5223
http://www.labor.ky.gov/esat/
appren.htm

Louisiana

Mr. Percy Rodriguez, Director
(Member at Large)
Louisiana Department of Labor
Apprenticeship Division
P.O. Box 94094
Baton Rouge, Louisiana 70804-9094
(225) 342-7820
http://www.ldol.state.la.us/job_
websponsorsearch.asp?Portal=JOB

Maine

Mr. Kenneth "Skip" Hardt (Treasurer)
Director of Apprenticeship Standards
Department of Labor
Bureau of Employment & Training
Programs
55 State House Station
Augusta, Maine 04333-0055
(207) 624-6431
http://www.mainecareercenter.com/

Maryland

USDOL/ETA/OATELS-BAT
Federal Building - Room 430-B
31 Hopkins Plaza
Baltimore, Maryland 21201
(410) 962-2676
http://www.dllr.state.md.us/labor/
appr.html

Massachusetts

USDOL/ETA/OATELS-BAT
Room E-370
JFK Federal Building
Boston, Massachusetts 02203
(617) 788-0177
http://www.state.ma.us/dat/Pages/
WhoWeAre.htm

Michigan

USDOL/ETA/OATELS-BAT
Room 304
801 South Waverly
Lansing, Michigan 48917
(517) 377-1746
http://www.michigan.gov/mdcd/
0,1607,7-122-1680_2788_2792---
,00.html

Minnesota

USDOL/ETA/OATELS-BAT
316 N. Robert Street - Room 144
St. Paul, Minnesota 55101
(651) 290-3951
http://www.doli.state.mn.us/appr.html

Mississippi

USDOL/ETA/OATELS-BAT
Federal Building - Suite 321
100 West Capitol Street
Jackson, Mississippi 39269
(601) 965-4346

Missouri

USDOL/ETA/OATELS-BAT
1222 Spruce Street - Room 9.102E
Robert A. Young Federal Building
St. Louis, Missouri 63103
(314) 539-2522
http://www.dolir.state.mo.us/ls/
prevailingwage/employees.htm

Montana

USDOL/ETA/OATELS-BAT
Federal Building
10 West 15th Street
Suite 1300
Helena, Montana 59626
(406) 441-1076
http://jsd.dli.state.mt.us/service/
apprentice.asp

Nebraska

USDOL/ETA/OATELS-BAT
Suite C-49
111 South 18th Plaza
Omaha, Nebraska 68102-1322
(402) 221-3281
http://www.workforce.state.ne.us/bat/
default.htm

Nevada

USDOL/ETA/OATELS-BAT
600 S.Las Vegas Boulevard, Suite 520
Las Vegas, Nevada 89101
(702) 388-6396

New Hampshire

USDOL/ETA/OATELS-BAT
143 North Main Street - Room 205
Concord, New Hampshire 03301
(603) 225-1444
http://www.labor.state.nh.us/
apprenticeships.asp

New Jersey

USDOL/ETA/OATELS-BAT
485 Route 1 South
Building E, 3rd Floor
Iselin, New Jersey 08830
(732) 750-9191
http://wnjpin.state.nj.us/stc/
apprentice1.html

New Mexico

USDOL/ETA/OATELS-BAT
500 4th Street NW, Suite 401
Albuquerque, New Mexico 87102
(505) 245-2155
http://www.dol.state.nm.us/
WIA_PartnerA3.html

New York

USDOL/ETA/OATELS-BAT
Leo O'Brien Federal Building
Room 809
North Pearl & Clinton Avenue
Albany, New York 12207
(518) 431-4008
http://www.labor.state.ny.us/
business_ny/
apprenticeship_training/
apprenticeship_training.html

North Carolina

USDOL/ETA/OATELS-BAT
Terry Sanford Federal Building
310 New Bern Avenue, Suite 260
Raleigh, North Carolina 27601
(919) 856-4062
http://www.dol.state.nc.us/appren/
appindex.htm

North Dakota

USDOL/ETA/OATELS-BAT
Room 332
304 East Broadway
Bismarck, North Dakota 58501
(701) 250-4700
http://www.jobsnd.com/seekers/
train_wia_ojt.html

Ohio

USDOL/ETA/OATELS-BAT
200 North High Street, Room 605
Columbus, Ohio 43215
(614) 469-7375
http://www.state.oh.us/odjfs/
apprenticeship/index.stm

Oklahoma

USDOL/ETA/OATELS-BAT
1500 South Midwest Boulevard
Suite 202
Midwest City, Oklahoma 73110
(405) 732-4338
http://www.oesc.state.ok.us/

Oregon

USDOL/ETA/OATELS-BAT
256 Warner-Milne Road, Room 3
Oregon City, Oregon 97045
(503) 557-8257
http://www.boli.state.or.us/
apprenticeship/index.html

Pennsylvania

USDOL/ETA/OATELS-BAT
Federal Building
228 Walnut Street - Room 356
Harrisburg, Pennsylvania 17108
(717) 221-3496
http://www.apprentice.org/

Puerto Rico

Ms. Eva Cordero Cruz
Assistant Administrator
Employment, Training & Services to
Participants Area
Right to Employment Administration
P.O. Box 364452
San Juan, Puerto Rico 00936-4452
(787) 754-5151

Rhode Island

USDOL/ETA/OATELS-BAT
Federal Building
100 Hartford Avenue
Providence, Rhode Island 02909
(401) 528-5198
http://www.det.state.ri.us/webdev/
appren/appren.htm

South Carolina

USDOL/ETA/OATELS-BAT
Strom Thurmond Federal Building
1835 Assembly Street - Room 838
Columbia, South Carolina 29201
(803) 765-5547

South Dakota

USDOL/ETA/OATELS-BAT
Room 205
320 E. Capitol
Pierre, South Dakota 57501
(605) 224-6693

Tennessee

USDOL/ETA/OATELS-BAT
Airport Executive Plaza
1321 Murfreesboro Road, Suite 541
Nashville, Tennessee 37210
(615) 781-5318

Texas

USDOL/ETA/OATELS-BAT
300 East 8th Street
Suite 914
Austin, Texas 78701
(512) 916-5435
http://www.twc.state.tx.us/svcs/
apprentice.html

Utah

USDOL/ETA/OATELS-BAT
Suite 101
1600 West 2200 South
Salt Lake City, Utah 84119
(801) 975-3650

Vermont

Ms. Pat Nagy, Director
Apprenticeship and Training
Department of Employment &
Training
5 Green Mountain Drive
P.O. Box 488
Montpelier, Vermont 05601-0488
(802) 828-5082
http://www.det.state.vt.us/jt/
apprentice.cfm

Virgin Islands

Mrs. Harriett Tull-George
Director, Training Division
Virgin Islands Department of Labor
2162 King Cross Street
Christiansted, Saint Croix
U.S. Virgin Islands 00820-4958
(809) 773-1440 Ext. 244

Virginia

USDOL/ETA/OATELS-BAT
400 North 8th Street
Federal Building - Suite 404
Richmond, Virginia 23219-23240
(804) 771-2488
http://www.dli.state.va.us/whatwedo/
apprenticeship/apprenticeship_p1.html

Washington

USDOL/ETA/OATELS-BAT
1111 Third Avenue, Suite 815
Seattle, WA 98101-3212
(206) 553-0076
http://www.lni.wa.gov/scs/
apprenticeship/

West Virginia

USDOL/ETA/OATELS-BAT
One Bridge Place - 2nd Floor
No. 10 Hale Street
Charleston, West Virginia 25301
(304) 347-5794

Wisconsin

USDOL/ETA/OATELS-BAT
Suite 104
740 Regent Street
Madison, Wisconsin 53715-1233
(608) 441-5377
http://www.dwd.state.wi.us/dws/appr/
default.htm

Wyoming

USDOL/ETA/OATELS-BAT
American National Bank Building
1912 Capitol Avenue - Room 508
Cheyenne, Wyoming 82001-3661
(307) 772-2448

Appendix D: Explanation of Skills

In each of the descriptions of the best apprenticeable jobs found in Part IV, we've included a listing of skills required for each job. This table contains specific definitions of each skill. Use it as a key to gathering more information about the jobs that interest you.

Explanation of Skills

Skill	Definition
Basic Skills	**Developed capacities that facilitate learning or the more rapid acquisition of knowledge.**
Active Learning	Understanding the implications of new information for both current and future problem-solving and decision-making.
Active Listening	Giving full attention to what other people are saying, taking time to understand the points being made, asking questions as appropriate, and not interrupting at inappropriate times.
Critical Thinking	Using logic and reasoning to identify the strengths and weaknesses of alternative solutions, conclusions or approaches to problems.
Learning Strategies	Selecting and using training/instructional methods and procedures appropriate for the situation when learning or teaching new things.
Mathematics	Using mathematics to solve problems.
Monitoring	Monitoring/assessing performance of yourself, other individuals, or organizations to make improvements or take corrective action.
Reading Comprehension	Understanding written sentences and paragraphs in work related documents.
Science	Using scientific rules and methods to solve problems.
Speaking	Talking to others to convey information effectively.
Writing	Communicating effectively in writing as appropriate for the needs of the audience.
Resource Management Skills	**Developed capacities used to allocate resources efficiently**
Management of Financial Resources	Determining how money will be spent to get the work done, and accounting for these expenditures.
Management of Material Resources	Obtaining and seeing to the appropriate use of equipment, facilities, and materials needed to do certain work.
Management of Personnel Resources	Motivating, developing, and directing people as they work, identifying the best people for the job.

(continued)

(continued)

Explanation of Skills

Skill	Definition
Social Skills	**Developed capacities used to work with people to achieve goals**
Coordination	Adjusting actions in relation to others' actions.
Instructing	Teaching others how to do something.
Negotiation	Bringing others together and trying to reconcile differences.
Persuasion	Persuading others to change their minds or behavior.
Service Orientation	Actively looking for ways to help people.
Social Perceptiveness	Being aware of others' reactions and understanding why they react as they do.
Systems Skills	**Developed capacities used to understand, monitor, and improve socio-technical systems**
Judgment and Decision Making	Considering the relative costs and benefits of potential actions to choose the most appropriate one.
Systems Analysis	Determining how a system should work and how changes in conditions, operations, and the environment will affect outcomes.
Systems Evaluation	Identifying measures or indicators of system performance and the actions needed to improve or correct performance, relative to the goals of the system.
Technical Skills	**Developed capacities used to design, set-up, operate, and correct malfunctions involving application of machines or technological systems**
Operations Analysis	Analyzing needs and product requirements to create a design.
Technology Design	Generating or adapting equipment and technology to serve user needs.
Equipment Selection	Determining the kind of tools and equipment needed to do a job.
Installation	Installing equipment, machines, wiring, or programs to meet specifications.
Programming	Writing computer programs for various purposes.
Operation Monitoring	Watching gauges, dials, or other indicators to make sure a machine is working properly.
Operation and Control	Controlling operations of equipment or systems.
Equipment Maintenance	Performing routine maintenance on equipment and determining when and what kind of maintenance is needed.
Troubleshooting	Determining causes of operating errors and deciding what to do about it.
Repairing	Repairing machines or systems using the needed tools.
Quality Control Analysis	Conducting tests and inspections of products, services, or processes to evaluate quality or performance.

Index

C

D

E

F

G

H

M

N

O

P

U–V

W–Z